Stalking, Threatening, and Attacking Public Figures

Stalking, Threatening, and Attacking Public Figures

A Psychological and Behavioral Analysis

Edited by

J. Reid Meloy

Lorraine Sheridan

Jens Hoffmann

OXFORD
UNIVERSITY PRESS

2008

OXFORD
UNIVERSITY PRESS

Oxford University Press, Inc., publishes works that further
Oxford University's objective of excellence
in research, scholarship, and education.

Oxford New York
Auckland Cape Town Dar es Salaam Hong Kong Karachi
Kuala Lumpur Madrid Melbourne Mexico City Nairobi
New Delhi Shanghai Taipei Toronto

With offices in
Argentina Austria Brazil Chile Czech Republic France Greece
Guatemala Hungary Italy Japan Poland Portugal Singapore
South Korea Switzerland Thailand Turkey Ukraine Vietnam

Published by Oxford University Press, Inc.
198 Madison Avenue, New York, New York 10016

www.oup.com

Oxford is a registered trademark of Oxford University Press

Library of Congress Cataloging-in-Publication Data

Stalking, threatening, and attacking public figures : a psychological
and behavioral analysis / edited by J. Reid Meloy, Lorraine Sheridan,
and Jens Hoffmann.
p. ; cm.
Includes bibliographical references and index.
ISBN 978-0-19-532638-3 (cloth : alk. paper)
1. Stalking.   2. Celebrities.   3. Fans (Persons) I. Meloy, J. Reid.
II. Sheridan, Lorraine. III. Hoffmann, Jens, 1968-
[DNLM: 1. Crime Victims.   2. Famous Persons.   3. Crime—prevention &
control.   4. Criminal Psychology.   5. Forensic Psychiatry.   6. Mental
Disorders. WM 165 S782 2008]
HV6594.S742 2008
364.15—dc22   2008011577

9 8 7 6 5 4 3 2 1

Printed in the United States of America
on acid-free paper

To Janet Reid Meloy,
  Mary Jane Perez Meloy,
   Olivia Lindley Meloy,
  Generations

To my husband, Adrian

To Monika,
  my love,
   my joy,
    and my safe haven

Longing on a large scale is what makes history.

Don DeLillo, *Underworld*

Foreword

An epidemic of anorexia, insomnia and acute bodily discomfort
swept this nation late in 1963. One-half of its victims could not eat
or sleep. If the illness from which they were suffering had been
diagnosed as influenza, infectious mononucleosis or an unnamed
virus, the relevance of the syndrome to an audience of conscientious
physicians would be obvious. You might wonder why this syndrome
of epidemiologic proportion has not found its way into the medical
literature. When I add to this symptom complex the finding that
more than two-thirds of those affected also were nervous, tense,
and depressed, you may shift conceptually from physical pathology to psychopathology. When I tell you that this epidemic lasted
about one week and began on the afternoon of November 22, 1963,
you may be tempted to abandon the model of either pathology or
psychopathology and, recalling that it followed immediately the
assassination of President John F. Kennedy, see it instead as a widespread but normal reaction to a terrible political event.

> Freedman, L. Z. (1965). Assassination: Psychopathology and social
> pathology. *Postgraduate Medicine, 37* (June), 650–658

Assassinations of political leaders and public figures are, fortunately, rare
events. When they occur, the magnitude of harm they cause is great.

Attacks on Presidents and other high-profile leaders in the last half of
the 20th century stimulated waves of articles and books on assassination. The

assassinations of President John Kennedy, the Reverend Dr. Martin Luther King, and presidential candidate Robert Kennedy in the 1960s; attacks on presidential candidate George Wallace and President Gerald Ford in the 1970s; the attacks on President Ronald Reagan and Pope John Paul II; and the assassination of John Lennon in the early 1980s resulted in reams of speculation and analysis. Many efforts were historical in nature. Others focused on presumed psychopathologies of assassins and attackers and/or tried to develop typologies of persons who attack public figures. One writer even proposed retrospective psychiatric diagnoses of every American presidential assassin and attacker in the 19th and 20th centuries. But with few exceptions, until the 1990s, there was little systematic, let alone scientific, research on assassination, especially research that might inform protectors.

On July 18, 1989, Robert John Bardo assassinated actress Rebecca Schaeffer. Bardo's crime and the resulting publicity helped spark a legal reform movement that resulted in all 50 states and the Federal Government passing legislation that defined and outlawed the crime of stalking. These laws spoke to growing public, national concern about prevalence of domestic stalking (often by former intimates) and stalking by strangers.

It may fairly be said that "stalking" became the crime "celeb" of the early 1990s. The popular press literally printed thousands of articles about stalking, stalkers, and victims. Professional associations such as the Association of Threat Assessment Professionals drew hundreds to meetings and presentations about stalking. The Federal Government funded training seminars for law enforcement on how to intervene with stalking situations and large-scale studies about the prevalence of stalking. Individual researchers began systematic inquiries about stalkers and their victims.

In *Stalking, Threatening, and Attacking Public Figures,* Drs. J. Reid Meloy, Lorraine Sheridan, and Jens Hoffmann attempt to bring research about stalking, threats, and attacks on public figures into the 21st century. Meloy, Sheridan, and Hoffmann have invited and collected the work of some of the most well-known clinicians, scholars, and practitioners in the fields of stalking and public figure protection (and others who are less well known).

This ambitious book covers a wide range of thinking, scholarship, and practice. The book begins with a comprehensive and thought-provoking review of what is known scientifically about public figure stalking, threatening, and attacking. It then includes contributions from professionals who have evaluated persons charged with crimes against public figures: clinicians, researchers, and current and former law enforcement professionals who have worked with organizations with investigative and protective responsibilities; and attorneys who have prosecuted these cases.

Chapters include detailed case studies, analyses of quantitative data, reflections from attachment theory and psychoanalytic thought, descriptions of law enforcement and protective organization activities, mental health and psychiatric categorizations and understandings, consideration of risk assessment models and variables, victim perspectives, and others. Particularly welcome are contributions from European colleagues who work in these areas.

From the perspective of those trying to prevent harassment of and attacks on public officials and public figures, the identification, assessment, and management of persons who may pose risk will always be a combination of science and "art." Better information and clearer analysis may guide and supplement the experience, intuition, and thinking of those with protective responsibilities. *Stalking, Threatening, and Attacking Public Figures* is therefore a welcome and substantial, if inevitably incomplete, step in the right direction.

All in all, this book is a major contribution to a youthful and potentially significant field of research. Hopefully, it will stimulate more and better data collection, new and useful conceptualizations, and further careful study that will help keep public figures (and the rest of us) safe from unwanted contacts and potentially lethal attacks.

Robert Fein, PhD
Bryan Vossekuil

Contents

Contributors

JAMES BIESTERFELD
Special Agent (Retd)
U.S. Army Intelligence
Temecula, California

FREDERICK S. CALHOUN, PhD
Threat Management Consultant
Arlington, Virginia

WILLIAM R. CUPACH, PhD
Professor of Communication
Illinois State University
Normal, Illinois

BRIAN DARNLEY, MRCPSYCH
North London Forensic Service
The Ridgeway, Enfield
London, United Kingdom

JEFF DUNN
Detective III, Officer-in-Charge
Threat Management Unit, Los Angeles
  Police Department
Los Angeles, California

FRANK R. FARNHAM, BSc, MBBS,
MRCPSYCH
Consultant Forensic Psychiatrist
North London Forensic Service and
  Fixated Threat Assessment Centre
London, United Kingdom

DAVID GILES, PhD
Lecturer in Research Methods
University of Lancaster
Lancaster, United Kingdom

MILA GREEN, PhD
Program Analyst
California Department of Health and
  Human Services
Sacramento, CA

ROBERT D. HARE, PhD
Emeritus Professor of
  Psychology
University of British Columbia
Vancouver, British Columbia
Canada

STEPHEN D. HART, PhD
Professor of Psychology
Simon Fraser University
Burnaby, British Columbia
Canada

JENS HOFFMANN, PhD
Psychologist and Director
Team Psychologie & Sicherheit
Darmstadt, Germany

DAVID V. JAMES, MA, MBBS,
FRCPSYCH
Consultant Forensic Psychiatrist
North London Forensic Service and
*   Fixated Threat Assessment Centre*
London, England

P. RANDALL KROPP, PhD
Clinical and Forensic Psychologist
British Columbia Forensic Psychiatric
*   Services Commission*
Vancouver, British Columbia
Canada

DAVID R. LYON, LLB, PhD
Department of Criminology
Kwantlen University College
Surrey, British Columbia
Canada

JOHN MALTBY, PhD
Lecturer in Psychology
University of Leicester
Leicester, United Kingdom

J. REID MELOY, PhD, ABPP
Clinical Professor of Psychiatry
University of California
San Diego, California

V. BLAIR MESA, MA
Doctoral Student in Clinical Forensic
*   Psychology*
John Jay College of Criminal Justice
New York, New York

KRIS MOHANDIE, PhD
Operational Consulting
*   International, Inc.*
Pasadena, California

PAUL E. MULLEN, MBBS, DSc,
FRANZCP, FRCPSYCH
Professor of Forensic Psychiatry
Monash University
Melbourne, Victoria
Australia

MARY ELLEN O'TOOLE, PhD
Supervisory Special Agent
Behavioral Analysis Unit, Federal
*   Bureau of Investigation*
Quantico, Virginia

MICHELE T. PATHÉ, MBBS (HONS),
MD, FRANZCP
Forensic Psychiatrist
Victoria Institute of Forensic Mental
*   Health*
Melbourne, Victoria
Australia

ROBERT T. M. PHILLIPS, MD, PhD,
DFAPA
Senior Consultant Psychiatrist
United States Secret Service, Mental
*   Health Liaison Program*
Washington, DC

LULU PRESTON, MA, D CLIN PSY
North London Forensic Service and
*   Fixated Threat Assessment Centre*
London, United Kingdom

KARL ROBERTS, PhD
Head of Psychology
University of Sunderland
Sunderland, United Kingdom

RHONDA SAUNDERS, JD
Los Angeles, California

MARIO J. SCALORA, PhD
Associate Professor of Psychology
University of Nebraska-Lincoln
Lincoln, Nebraska

LOUIS B. SCHLESINGER, PhD
Professor of Forensic Psychology
John Jay College of Criminal Justice
New York, New York

LORRAINE SHERIDAN, PhD
Senior Research Fellow
Heriot Watt University
Edinburgh, United Kingdom

SHARON S. SMITH, PhD (FBI, RETD)
President
Forensic Psycholinguistics, L.L.C.
Fredericksburg, Virginia

BRIAN H. SPITZBERG, PhD
Professor
School of Communication
San Diego State University
San Diego, California

SEAN L. WAINWRIGHT, JD
Associate of Kaye Scholer L.L.P.
Los Angeles, California

DAVID G. WELLS
Supervisory Special Agent
Threat Assessment Section
United States Capitol Police
Washington, DC

STEPHEN W. WESTON
Attorney at Law
Lt. (Retd)
and
Commander
Threat Assessment Unit
California Highway Patrol
Sacramento, CA

WILLIAM J. ZIMMERMAN
Detective
Threat Assessment Section
United States Capitol Police
Washington, DC

Stalking, Threatening, and Attacking Public Figures

1

Public Figure Stalking, Threats, and Attacks: The State of the Science

J. Reid Meloy, Lorraine Sheridan, and Jens Hoffmann

Public figures are always at risk—whether it is a constituency that votes them in or out of office, shareholders who decide their economic benefit to the corporation, or fans who judge whether their performances merit continued and rapturous attention. On the periphery, however, resides a much smaller group of individuals who lack the ability to discriminate between their own private fantasies and the figure's public behavior, believe they are entitled to pursue the figure, and may present a risk of violence. They may feel personally insulted by perceived betrayal, be fanatically in love because of a perceived affectionate or sexual invitation, or simply be preoccupied with the daily life of the public figure. Such individuals may fixate on the public figure and do nothing more. Others communicate or approach in a disturbing way. A few will threaten. And on rare occasions, one will breach the public figure's security perimeter and attack.

Although protection of public figures has been recognized as a necessary adjunct to their daily lives for centuries, clinical and forensic research of threats and attacks against public figures is just beginning. Patterns of unwanted pursuit that threaten any individual—the crime of stalking—have received serious research attention for less than 20 years (Boon & Sheridan, 2002; Meloy, 1998; Mullen, Pathé, & Purcell, 2000), and a specific focus upon public figures as the targets of such pursuits is even more nascent. Published work on threatening and otherwise inappropriate letters toward politicians and celebrities appeared for the first time in 1991 (Dietz, Matthews, Martell, et al., 1991; Dietz, Matthews, Van Duyne, et al., 1991), and an analysis of threats and attacks toward public figures did not appear until later that decade (Calhoun, 1998; Fein & Vossekuil,

1997, 1998, 1999; Fein, Vossekuil, & Holden, 1995). Work has rapidly evolved in this area over the past few years, but empirical studies are still scant, and the theory that guides data collection is quite limited (Borum, Fein, Vossekuil, & Berglund, 1999; McCutcheon, Lange, & Houran, 2002; Meloy et al., 2004). Virtually all the existing work has been done in the United States, although the Home Office in Britain commissioned an exhaustive study of approaches, threats, and attacks toward members of the British Royal Family, which was completed in 2006, along with a comprehensive analysis of attacks toward Western European politicians (Fixated Research Group, 2006; James et al., 2007, in press) (Chapter 3).

Theoretical questions that beg for empirical answers abound: How do we discriminate between those who are simply fixated on a public figure and those who will inappropriately communicate and approach? Can we identify the factors that predict an attack upon a public figure? To what degree are these individuals severely mentally ill, and what is the role, if any, of the mental health professional in such cases? What is the nexus between pathological fixations and mental illness? What is the nexus between political motivation to attack and mental illness? What role does personality disorder play in the aggression exhibited by those who intently seek contact with the public figure? Does the media and culture influence the pursuit of celebrities? Can we identify the pathway to violence of these individuals? Can we identify markers along such a pathway and estimate the speed with which the subject is moving? And how best can we assess and manage the threat such persons pose toward public figures? Such empirical questions are ripe for investigation, but also need theories and operational experience to guide their formulation. Without theory, data collection is just counting; and without data, theory is just speculation. As the great psychologist and psychiatrist Martin Orne once said, "In God we trust. All others must have data."

The purpose of this book is to advance our understanding of stalking, violence risk, and threat management toward public figures, whether they be politicians, executives, judicial officers, or a wide array of celebrities. The book is divided into three sections, which focus upon defining, explaining, and risk-managing this increasingly complex global reality. Truly public figures are few and far between, and anathema to some, but they shape and lead culture and history as they walk through time—or time walks through them. Through our invitations to the most notable researchers and operators in this specialty area, of whom virtually all accepted our offer, we have assembled a book that is the first of its kind, international in scope, and rich in both depth and complexity.

Empirical Knowns and Contemporary Theory

The boundaries of science are known, and gradually expanded, through the construction and empirical testing of hypotheses, which are based upon current theory—what is commonly understood as the scientific method. We begin with some facts and theories concerning the state of the science in public figure stalking, threats, and attacks.

Normal and Pathological Fixations

The term fixation is from the Latin word *figo*, to be bound fast, and describes an intense preoccupation with an individual, activity, or idea. Normal fixations are readily apparent in the early stages of romantic love (Person, 1988); certain hobbies; intensely held political, social, or religious beliefs; and loyalty toward certain celebrity or other public figures (Mullen et al., in press). The basis for a fixation may be a "narcissistic linking fantasy," a conscious belief that one has a special and idealized relationship with another person or object (Meloy, 1989, 1998). Such fantasies, in turn, may compensate for an actual life that is blighted and forlorn, and the feelings that adhere to it.

Pathological fixations, moreover, are preoccupations that are more frequent, emotionally intense, and may be incessantly pursued. They are distinguished in this context from normal fixations by two characteristics: First, the belief places upon the public figure an obligation, and the believer demands acknowledgment, what we call *entitled reciprocity*; second, a behavioral progression begins, during which the fixation alienates others, undermines social networks, and erodes finances, leaving the person often isolated and destitute (Leets, de Becker, & Giles, 1995; Mullen et al., in press; Schlesinger, 2006). Pathological fixations may not lead to communication or approach behavior, and may be known only to a few friends and family members. However, those who pathologically fixate have established a debt, and believe that payment is due.

Public Figure Stalking

Pathological fixations do not necessarily lead to stalking, which is a criminal behavior in the United States, Canada, Australia, New Zealand, Great Britain, Germany, and several other European countries. The exact legal description of stalking varies among jurisdictions, but typically involves three elements: a pattern of unwanted pursuit, a credible threat, and the induction of fear in the victim. Most jurisdictions must prove each of these elements to attain a criminal conviction for stalking, and hence the necessity of victim testimony at trial to prove the third element. One of the paradoxes of the crime of stalking is that the victim must be aware of the behavior, and therefore fearful, for there to be a crime.

Public figures, however, may be stalked for months before they are aware of the behavior. Access is usually exceedingly difficult for the stalker; even if the stalker succeeds in raising concern among the public figure's security personnel, the latter may not inform the public figure of the ongoing threat. This has posed problems in the prosecution of certain public figure stalking cases, and has required that security apprise their protectee of all the details of the pursuit to establish the requisite personal fear for prosecution.[1] In other cases, the magnitude of potential threats to the public figure, such as the President of the United States, is so enormous that it would preclude any personal knowledge unless an attack was imminent. The crime of stalking would be subsumed by both statutory and case laws.[2]

In this book, we have modified the third element of the crime of stalking public figures to include *concern* on the part of those responsible for their safety that a pattern of behaviors poses a credible threat. This necessarily broadens our use of the term stalking, but unhinges it from the requisite induction of personal fear in the victim.[3]

Threats

The role of communicated threats in public figure cases remains ambiguous in large group studies (Meloy et al., 2004), but the operational position is clear: All communicated threats should be initially taken seriously because any particular individual may act subsequent to his threat. We define a threat as "a written or oral communication that implicitly or explicitly states a wish or intent to damage, injure, or kill the target" (Meloy, 1999a, p. 90).

A few empirical studies have noted the following trends when threats toward public figures are considered:

1. In public figure studies, there is a weak correlation, if any, between communicated threats and subsequent violence.
2. Unlike prior sexually intimate stalkers who commonly threaten and physically attack their victims, most individuals who inappropriately communicate with, approach, breach, or attack a public figure do not directly communicate a threat beforehand to their target.
3. Those who breach security and do launch an attack often engage in *warning behaviors* beforehand, and will communicate their intent to third parties.
4. The published scientific study of various aspects of the form and content of threatening communications, primarily in letters, has yielded some useful predictive data concerning who will and will not approach and attack.
5. Threatening communications, moreover, may be the only source of data upon which to plan a protective response, even in the absence of the identity of the threatener (see Chapters 10 and 17).
6. Those convicted of threatening to kill anyone are at significantly greater risk of killing another or themselves, or being killed by another, especially if they are young, mentally disordered, and abusing substances (MacDonald, 1968; Warren, Mullen, Thomas, Ogloff, & Burgess, in press).

We offer the following schematic for the descriptive analysis of threats, which at present has no proven predictive value, but helps with clarity of thought, and may guide further research. Communicated threats have a motivation, a means, a manner, and a material content.

Motivation   Communicated threats are either *expressive* or *instrumental*. An expressive threat is used to regulate affect in the threatener. For example, an individual telephones his local political representative and yells at his assistant for the chronic delays in garbage collection in the neighborhood. He threatens to come down to the representative's office and dump his garbage on the property if nothing is done. He does not identify himself, and slams the phone down. He immediately feels better because he has ventilated his emotion, but then feels guilty and anxious that he might get into trouble for his outburst.

An instrumental threat is intended to control or influence the behavior of the target through an aversive consequence. For example, a man with erotomanic delusions sends a letter to a local television news anchor, telling her she better wear her blue dress on his birthday when she appears on television, or he is going to kill himself.

Means   Communicated threats are conveyed through a *variety* of means, including verbalized statements, letters, e-mail, telephone, text messaging, facsimile transmission, nonverbal behavior that implies a threat, and any other vehicle that conveys to the target the intent of the message. Means are only limited by available technology, and will likely expand in concert with developments in the information technology field.

Manner   Threats are communicated either *directly* or *indirectly*. A direct threat is conveyed from the threatener to the target using a variety of means. An indirect threat is usually communicated to a third person, typically someone who knows the target, or is assumed to have access to the target, with the intent that the target will be told about the threat. Any other indirect means could be utilized, including the publication of a threat in code that is disseminated to many individuals but understood only by the target's representative, or the use of a "cutout," a term borrowed from intelligence, in which a third person acts as a conduit (in this case, communicating a threat) but may not know the specific identity of the threatener or the target, and may not even understand what he or she is communicating.

Material Content   Unlike the motivation (why) and the means and manner (how), material content refers to *what* was conveyed. The threat itself can have infinite variety and is usually analyzed according to form or content. Analysis at this level may range from forensic linguistics (the study of the language)[4] to scrutiny of the threat for fingerprints, DNA, or other transfer evidence from the threatener. Two computer-based software programs include Profiler +, which purports to measure personality characteristics from language use (Herman, 2003), and PCAD 2000, which uses content analysis to identify psychological states (Gottschalk & Bechtel, 2001). Whether a threat is conditional or unconditional would also be an aspect of material content.

The International Perspective

Most stalking research has been done in Westernized developed countries, including the United States, Canada, Europe, and Australia. The majority of contemporary work on threats toward public figures has also derived from studies in the United States, particularly the U.S. Secret Service and the U.S. Capitol Police (see Chapters 16 and 19). Both organizations have been world leaders in both tactical and strategic approaches to threats toward public figures. This book also introduces contributions from authors based in Germany, Canada, and the United Kingdom. The Fixated Research Group commissioned by the United Kingdom's Home Office in 2002 was composed of American, Australian, and British researchers, and has resulted in the establishment of the Fixated Threat Assessment Centre in London.

There is evidence from various international sources that stalking is a part of the human condition. Studies conducted in Japan (Chapman & Spitzberg, 2003), Trinidad (Jagessar & Sheridan, 2004), and Iran (Kordvani, 2000) have made clear that cultural variations exist, but there are core stalking behaviors regardless of culture or nationality. There is also a very small amount of research that suggests that immigration may be a risk factor for stalking because of cultural disparities in the perception of social behavior (Meyers, 1998; Meyers & Meloy, 1994). This research has focused upon immigration from traditional Arabic culture to more open Westernized culture. It is unclear if comparable intercultural patterns will become apparent when the target is a public figure and the relationship is solely a product of fantasy or delusion. One of the editors of this book (LS) is currently involved in a research program that is examining perceptions and experiences of stalking in several countries, including Armenia, Indonesia, and Japan. Early analyses indicate high levels of agreement concerning what constitutes stalking, as well as similar incident rates of stalking behavior across these disparate countries and cultures.

There is anecdotal evidence that public figure stalking is becoming more international in character. Schlesinger (2006) vividly described the case of an American Hispanic man who mailed an acid bomb from the United States to the Icelandic pop singer Björk living in Britain, and then committed suicide (see also Chapter 4). A Japanese entrepreneur stalked Britney Spears and was eventually deported from the United States. The founder of the ecumenical Taize Community Frere Roger was stabbed by a woman in Romania. The tennis star Martina Hingis was stalked by an eastern European male who was eventually tried in Florida. And in a study of erotomanic patients in a Thailand hospital (Kasantikul, 1998), the stalking of Thai celebrities was mentioned, and 1 of 20 patients had the delusional belief that he was romantically connected to a prominent Thai singer.

There is, however, simply not enough research. One study from Iran (Kordvani, 2000) asserted that local media culture is an extremely relevant factor influencing the rate of public figure stalking. Kordvani also noted that stalking of celebrities in Iran is virtually unknown because of the fact that "the media, the television in particular, do not tend to broadcast so much news or propaganda about celebrities" (p. 6). This observation is consistent with the findings reported in this book (Chapter 6) that the frequency of appearance of the celebrity in the media is a significant correlate of stalking behavior toward that celebrity. The Fixated Research Group (2006) found a similar dynamic in their study of inappropriate communications and approaches to members of the British Royal Family, and Meloy et al. (Chapter 2) report that frequently appearing female television actors are at high risk for multiple stalkers. A media culture that idealizes being famous—and then aggressively probes for vulnerabilities in the famous—appears to be a sociocultural risk factor for public figure stalking.

The nascent quality of the research, however, should not distort the fact that operational approaches to the protection of public figures have been developing over centuries, and continue to spawn networks of private and public practitioners such as the Association of Threat Assessment Professionals in the United States and Canada (www.atapworldwide.org).

In a world of increasing global connectivity, integration, interdependence, and almost instant media saturation (see, e.g., www.tmz.com), it is inevitable that those involved in the management of public figures will need to share information across traditional boundaries of nationality, language, culture, economic, and political persuasions. Those who target public figures are not only geographically mobile, but can easily tap into the virtual world of knowledge concerning their public target of pursuit, and utilize this knowledge in the planning of their stalking and attacking. Dietz, Matthews, Van Duyne et al. (1991) first noted that a proportion of inappropriate letters sent to Hollywood celebrities were posted from countries other than the United States; current research (Fixated Research Group, 2006) has found that 10% of those who fixated on a member of the British Royal Family, and 1.8% of those who successfully breached their security, had home addresses other than the United Kingdom.

It is paramount that practitioners and researchers alike share information and expertise concerning stalking, threats, and attacks against public figures. One of the aims of this book is to facilitate and extend such cooperation internationally by defining the nature of this problem, explaining it within our current limits of understanding, and offering risk management solutions.

The Pathway to Violence and Markers Along the Route

An attack on a public figure is a low-frequency but high-intensity event. Risk assessment and risk management of such cases render traditional methods of violence prediction—the use of base rates and actuarial estimates derived from large group data—not very useful because of the high number of false positives that would be generated.

The recognition of this problem and the development of an alternative, idiographic approach to assessing risk of violence toward identifiable targets has been a major breakthrough in this field. Dietz and Martell (1989) suggested this approach when they discerned the first warning signals that may precede an attack on a public figure. Through their anecdotal research, they suggested that emulating famous assassins, constructing a "hit list," creating a diary documenting the stalking of a famous target, and making efforts to acquire a weapon were regular features in such cases. Fein et al. (1995) and Fein and Vossekuil (1997, 1998, 1999) systematized this approach, which has been labeled "threat assessment of targeted violence," through their U.S. Secret Service Exceptional Case Study. They noted that the first marker is the point at which the offender decides that an attack on a public figure is the solution to his problems. Subsequent steps include the selection of a suitable target, and planning and preparation for the assault.

Borum et al. (1999) theoretically elaborated upon this functional model, stressing the dynamic, fact-based, and behavioral aspects of this approach, where the task is to identify individuals of concern who may be moving down a pathway of violence toward an identifiable target. In this approach, static factors such as demographics, and criminal, psychiatric, and drug abuse histories are minimized, while current behaviors are the focus of attention. Calhoun and Weston (2003) further advanced this work by describing in detail six markers along this pathway to violence: grievance, ideation, research and planning, preparation, breach, and attack.

Pathways to violence can be analyzed according to behavioral, cognitive, and emotional evidence. Behavioral aspects are often the most overt and address concrete actions of the subject of concern, such as researching a suitable attack location and procuring a weapon. The cognitive aspect of the pathway includes the formulation of a grievance and the use of various psychological defenses such as denial and projection to blame the target, obsessional patterns of thinking that may contain unrealistic or delusional beliefs and expectations concerning the target (Chapter 4), and certain other cognitive conditions that must be in place to warrant an attack: justification, a perceived lack of alternatives, and acceptance of the consequences of the attack (De Becker, 1997). The emotional aspect of such an attack can vary tremendously, and change over time, including states of dysphoria, anger, hatred, fear, anxiety, shame, excitement, and complete emotional detachment.

This mode of threat assessment is illustrated by a case. After the breakup of her marriage, Ms. S was diagnosed with paranoid schizophrenia (Hoffmann & Sheridan, 2005). She believed that underground flesh factories existed in Germany in which humans were killed and manufactured. Jesus appeared to her in a vision, telling her that she had to stop the slaughtering (grievance). She tried to draw public attention to these outrageous events, putting up posters in the street and placing advertisements in newspapers. This strategy failed, and Jesus appeared again, cajoling her to use violence (ideation). She then developed the idea to attack a national politician in order to warn the public of the flesh factories. She phoned different party headquarters for dates and locations of the upcoming election campaign (research/planning). She applied to authorities for a gun license and tried to buy a gun in a local Italian restaurant (preparation). Finally, she took a knife, and concealed it in a bouquet of flowers. Pretending to be a fan of a well-known political leader, she bypassed his security at a campaign rally (breach). She gained close proximity to him, and stabbed him in the neck (attack).

An idiographic approach, however, requires a sophisticated and often expensive intelligence network to be operationally successful because there are essentially no large group preventive measures—such as better mental health care for the pathologically fixated—that are advanced. Implicit in this approach is that an individual of concern can be identified in a timely manner to successfully interdict his movement along the pathway toward violence. In the case of Ms. S, she was not.

Epidemiologists note that there are two general approaches to reducing risk in a population: Identify those at highest risk and take actions to reduce their risk, or act on the population as a whole, targeting a known risk factor that will reduce the risk level in the entire population. We think these approaches complement each other, and in the specific domain of public figure threats, stalking, and attacks, they are represented by the idiographic (case study) model to identify individuals of concern and by a nomothetic (large group) model that *recognizes the high frequency of major mental illness and pathological fixation in those who pose a risk to public figures.* Our position strongly supports the value of better treatment and management of all severely mentally ill individuals in a population, even though very few will actually pose a risk to a public figure. We advocate the integration of these approaches throughout this book.

The Mode of Violence

Converging research over the past half century has continued to validate the theory that there are two psychobiologically distinctive modes of violence: affective and predatory (Meloy, 2006). *Affective violence* is characterized by autonomic arousal, anger or fear, a reaction to a perceived threat, a brevity of action due to the high state of physiological arousal, and the simple goal of reducing the threat. It is the consummate defensive violence and is also labeled reactive and impulsive by various researchers (Cornell et al., 1996; Tweed & Dutton, 1998). *Predatory violence* is characterized by the absence of autonomic arousal, the absence of emotion, and the absence of an imminent threat, and is planned and purposeful. It is the consummate offensive violence, and is also labeled instrumental and premeditated by various researchers (Barratt, Stanford, Dowdy, Liebman, & Kent, 1999; Cornell et al., 1996). The evolutionary basis of the former is self-protection. The evolutionary basis of the latter is hunting.

Stalking research has repeatedly found that violence between prior sexual intimates is typically affective; for example, an ex-husband who is stalking his former partner will likely assault her when threatened by abandonment, and will punch, choke, or slap her without the use of a weapon (Meloy, 2002; Mullen et al., 2000).

Violence toward public figures who are stalked, however, appears to be typically predatory, and a weapon, often a firearm, is utilized. This pattern was first documented by Fein and Vossekuil (1998, 1999), and the contrast between public and private stalkers was noted by Meloy (2001). It was further supported by the striking contrast—and logic—when comparing the frequency of threats between those who stalk prior sexual intimates and those who stalk public figures: The majority of prior sexual intimate stalkers directly communicate a threat before they attack, while very few public figure stalkers do so before they attack (Fein & Vossekuil, 1999; Mohandie, Meloy, McGowan, & Williams, 2006) (Chapter 2).

This demarcation, however, turns out to be too simple. Empirical testing of these hypotheses suggests that the *relationship* between the stalker and his victim is the determining factor in the mode of violence (Chapter 2). When there has been a prior relationship, affective violence is significantly more likely, but predatory violence does occur. When there has been no prior relationship (this, of course, would include most public figure cases[5]), predatory violence is significantly more likely, but affective violence does occur. The following photograph illustrates an affectively violent, although ultimately futile, attempt to assault Pope Benedict XVI on June 6, 2007, by a 27-year-old German in St. Peter's Square, Rome. The Pope's spokesman, Dr. Federico Lombardi, offered both a diagnosis and a motivation at the scene: "He was clearly deranged but did not want to kill or harm the pope. He only wanted to draw attention to himself" (*New York Times*, June 7, 2007, p. A10).

© 2007 Romano Gambineri/European Pressphoto Agency. Reprinted with permission.

Typologies

Psychologists and psychiatrists, in the tradition of most scientific endeavors, rely on typologies or classification systems to define and explain phenomena that they observe. They organize and structure complex realities, hope to reflect real differences among groups, and in case management they serve as a starting point for investigations. Typologies, however, are not *sui generis* but are dependent on the interests of the researchers, such as clinical versus operational endeavors. Stalking is no exception. There are presently at least a dozen typologies of stalkers (Spitzberg, 2007) based upon a variety of factors, including motivation, diagnosis, previous relationship with the victim, level of risk, private versus public context, or a combination of such variables (Mohandie et al., 2006). There is no "gold standard" typology at present, and professionals tend to select those that best suit their own clinical, research, or operational needs. The danger of typologies in risk assessment and case management is that a particular case may be adapted and deformed to fit a particular typological category. *The map is never the territory.* Public figure stalking typologies are beginning to be developed.

One of the most important discoveries in stalking, threats, and attacks against public figures came about through the U.S. Secret Service Exceptional Case Study (Fein & Vossekuil, 1997, 1998, 1999; Fein et al., 1995). The Exceptional Case Study documented that less than 10% of those who attacked, assassinated, or near lethally approached a U.S. public figure in the latter half of the 20th century communicated a direct threat to the target or law enforcement beforehand; and *none* who successfully attacked or assassinated did so. For the first time it was empirically documented—although it was theoretically suggested by Freedman (1971) 25 years earlier—that there may be an *inverse relationship* between those who threatened and those who attacked public figures. Fein and Vossekuil (1998, 1999) memorialized this finding with their assertion that those *who pose a threat may not make a threat, and those who make threats may not pose them*, implying the existence of two rather disparate groups.

Although reality turns out to be more complicated—those who threaten can also attack (Scalora, Baumgartner, & Plank, 2003), and in one study those who successfully breached security were more likely to threaten than those who just approached (Fixated Research Group, 2006)—this distinction paralleled an important conceptual leap by Calhoun (1998) and Calhoun and Weston (2003), who also posited two groups of individuals, *hunters* and *howlers*, representing a gross typology of those who pathologically fixate on public figures for a variety of reasons. Howlers were often disinterested in hunting; hunters purposefully did not howl. The howlers became a group worth studying on their own (Chapter 5).

The hunters and howlers, however, may both pose a tactical risk, and there are a few typologies that have been developed to begin to understand the motivations of these individuals (see Table 1.1).

Table 1.1. Typologies and various motivations of those who approach, threaten, attack, and/or assassinate public figures

Clarke (1982, 1990): $n = 17$ assassins or near assassins of U.S. Presidents

 Type I—Self sacrifice for a political ideal

 Type II—Egocentric need for recognition and status

 Type III—Psychopathic

 Type IV—Delusional

De Becker (1994): $n =$ unknown number of public figure and celebrity stalkers

 1. Attachment seeking

 2. Identity seeking

 3. Rejection based

 4. Delusion based

Fein and Vossekuil (1997, 1998, 1999): $n = 83$ near-lethal approachers, attackers, and assassins of U.S. public figures (1949–1996)

 1. Notoriety or fame

 2. Bring attention to a personal or public problem

 3. Avenge a perceived wrong

 4. End personal pain

 5. Save country or world

 6. Develop a special relationship with the target

 7. Make money

 8. Bring about political change

Phillips (2006): $n =$ unknown number of those who stalk and attack the U.S. President; and proposed celebrity stalking typology (2007)

1. Resentful	1. Intimacy
2. Pathologically obsessed	2. Rejected
3. Infamy seeking	3. Predatory (sexual)
4. Intimacy seeking	
5. Nuisance or attention seeking	

James et al. (in press): $n = 23$ attackers of the British monarch or immediate family members (1778–1994)

 1. Extremely politically motivated

 2. Petitioners—delusional

 3. Pretenders—delusional

 4. Persecuted—delusional

 5. Adolescent anomie

 6. Chaotically psychotic

(Continued)

Table 1.1. (Continued)

James et al. (2007): $n = 24$ nonterrorist attackers of western European politicians (1990–2004)

1. Extremely politically motivated

2. Intoxicated

3. Pathological fixation—delusion

4. Nonclassifiable—unknown

Fixated Research Group (2006): $n = 275$ cases randomly drawn from 5,685 files stratified according to behavior (preapproach, approach, breach) of those who pathologically fixated on members of the British Royal Family over the past 20 years, Axis III: motivation.

1. Pursuing an agenda

2. Delusions of kinship

3. Delusions of kingship

4. Chaotic

5. Amity seekers

6. Counselors

7. Erotomanics

8. Suitors

9. Entreaty for help

10. Royally persecuted

Perusal of this table indicates a number of commonalities among the research endeavors: (a) all have focused on motivation, although a few have made the distinction between psychosis and nonpsychosis as an element of their types; (b) all typologies have been published in the past 20 years, although the majority have appeared within the past 5 years; (c) all the typologies are empirically based and rationally derived—in other words, they are based upon actual cases, ranging from 17 American assassins to 275 randomly selected approachers of the British Royal Family, and the actual type is formulated by the researchers' inferences rather than statistical analysis; (d) there is no interrater reliability data for any of the typologies; (e) many of the groups within each type strongly suggest a major mental disorder, a personality disorder, or both, which is consistent with clinical findings in the general stalking research (Meloy, 1998; Mullen et al., 2000); (f) the typologies and motivational schemes cover a wide spectrum of behaviors (approaching, threatening, stalking, attacking, and assassinating) and targets (U.S. celebrities, political figures in the United States and Europe, and the British Royal Family), therefore making it difficult to generalize across research efforts.

The most rigorous and complex of the types is the one generated by the Fixated Research Group (2006) because of the stratified random sampling that was utilized and the development of a multiple-axis approach. The ten types represent the motivational axis of the typology. The other two axes include the nature of the fixation (person or cause) and reality testing (psychotic or nonpsychotic). The limitation of this typology is the idiosyncratic nature of the target group—the British Royal Family—which combines their celebrity and their legal-political authority and yields a very mixed group of mad, bad, desperate, and chaotic individuals.

Typologies must be cross-validated by other independent research groups. They advance research, but most importantly, they facilitate rapid communication concerning risk prediction and risk management among those whose task it is to prevent violence toward public figures. We believe it is worth continuing to develop broad-based typologies of those who stalk, threaten, and attack public figures, with an eye toward identifying variables that discriminate among groups that most powerfully predict violence risk. Such typologies should be rationally derived, empirically tested, and dynamically open to change as data accumulate.

Political Motivation and Psychiatric Disorder

The typology table also underscores a reality often obscured by operational approaches to the protection of public figures: What appears at first to be an issue-driven and politically motivated pursuit of a public figure can hide a severe psychiatric disturbance. Both may coexist. Mullen and Lester (2006) made this point in their excellent discussion of querulous paranoia and the vexatious litigant, and in the realm of public figure stalking, politics and psychiatric disorder may compel the need for both law enforcement and mental health intervention in any one particular case.

The case of Sirhan Sirhan illustrates this point. From a political perspective, he consciously assassinated Robert F. Kennedy in 1968 because he was furious at him for voting to sell 50 Phantom Jet fighter bombers to Israel and believed he had betrayed the Palestinian cause. From a psychiatric perspective, defense experts at his trial all agreed that he was either paranoid schizophrenic, or had pseudoneurotic schizophrenia. The prosecution expert, Seymour Pollack, M.D. (Pollack, 1969a) diagnosed him with borderline schizophrenia (what is now referred to as borderline personality disorder). He wrote, "Sirhan's motivation in killing Senator Kennedy was entirely political, and was not related to bizarre or psychotic motivation or accompanied by peculiar and highly idiosyncratic reasoning" (p. 3). In a supplemental report, he considered Sirhan a "developing paranoid personality whose assassination of Senator Robert Kennedy was motivated by political reasons which were highly emotionally charged" (1969b, p. 1). An interpretation of Sirhan's Rorschach test employing technology unavailable in 1969 suggested a borderline personality organization with hysterical, paranoid, and dependent features, consistent with the Pollack's findings (Meloy,

1992) (see also Chapter 7). The news media at the time worked hard to avoid characterizing this as a political assassination, which it was.

We would suggest that personality and psychopathology not be ignored, or even minimized, in the risk management of the most obviously issue-driven, political, religious, or romantically motivated case. There is a tendency for even the most seasoned professionals to normalize the most bizarre behavior— for instance, believing that "cultural differences" somehow account for severe psychopathology—especially when their exposure to such cases is the norm.

The Role of Mental Illness

Although most individuals with mental disorder are not violent, and do not attack public figures, there is substantial evidence that the majority of stalkers, attackers, and assassins are likely to have a major mental disorder, either historically or activated at the time of their attack (see Chapter 3). Media reports, however, overemphasize the importance of mental illness as the primary cause of the violent behavior, reinforcing the populist notion that, "he must have been crazy to have done that." For instance, Link and Stueve's (1994) large-scale representative study demonstrated that the presence of psychotic symptoms was a weaker predictor of violence than other variables including age, gender, and education.

Mental disorders differ in nature and intensity, and different mental disorders will have various relationships with violence. Some individuals are most violent when their mental disorder is untreated, while others will be sufficiently organized to commit offences only when adhering to a course of medication. The relationship between violence and mental disorder may be mediated by a variety of factors, including drug use, psychopathy, and specific symptoms such as delusions that provide a conscious rationale for acting violently.

The general literature on stalking would indicate that the question of whether individuals with particular mental health diagnoses are more likely to be violent is unclear. A recent review notes that the disorders associated with stalking occur over a wide range of diagnostic categories (McEwan, Mullen, & Purcell, 2007). It is not known how important mental disorder is as a predictor of stalking, let alone violence-related stalking activity. Taken together, the previous research findings would indicate that, en masse, those stalkers most likely to act out violently are nonpsychotic ex-partners (Farnham, James, & Cantrell, 2000). Public figure stalking data, however, indicate that despite the much lower frequencies of violence, mental illness is prominent in the history and behavior of the violent stalkers and attackers (Fein & Vossekuil, 1999; James et al., 2007, in press; Megargee, 1986; Mohandie et al., 2006; Mullen et al., in press). For instance, Calhoun's (1998) examination of threats and violence toward members of the judiciary noted that many inappropriate communicators were irrational; Fein and Vossekuil (1998, 1999) found a large proportion of their sample to evidence symptoms of major mental disorder despite their operational focus; Silva and Leong (1993) discussed cases of delusional misidentification where sufferers have threatened the life of public figures; and

Hoffman (1943) assessed the histories of 53 psychotic visitors to government offices in Washington. *It appears from the extant stalking research that the likelihood of severe mental illness is greatest when there has been no previous relationship between the stalker and his or her object of pursuit.* Findings from the general stalking arena, however, will not always be applicable to public figure stalking, and this fact further underlines the need for a dedicated, cohesive literature.

Most of the general literature on stalking has so far found a negative relationship between psychosis and stalker violence. This does not, however, rule out the prospect that a positive association exists in some cases. Stalkers are a heterogeneous group that includes children, the elderly, males, females, professionals, the unemployed, the gifted, the mentally disabled, the sane, and the insane. Although stalkers will engage in similar behaviors to achieve their goals (see Spitzberg's 2002 and 2007 meta-analyses), individual motivations will differ, as will the contingent success of various interventions (Sheridan & Boon, 2000). Therefore, stalker violence will share a complex and multidimensional relationship with many variables that cannot be charted via studies that feed lists of potential correlates into basic statistical models. Indeed, when Rosenfeld and Lewis (2005) utilized a regression tree approach to assess factors associated with stalker violence, they found psychosis to be positively or negatively related to stalking violence, depending on its interaction with additional risk factors. The regression tree approach is nonlinear and is able to identify *subgroups* of individuals with varying probabilities of violent behavior.

The obvious operational difficulty is translating large group research data that relies on correlational and predictive statistics into meaningful tools that can be applied to the individual case. We stress the importance of using large group data to anchor one's assessment, but then looking at the specific relationship in the individual case between active symptoms of mental disorder that may motivate stalking, threatening, and attacking; personality disorder (especially psychopathy); contextual and situational factors (Borum et al., 1999); and violence. The theoretical stance is a recognition that both nomothetic and idiographic approaches help understand and risk manage a particular case (Chapters 3, 5, 10, 15, 17, 19, and 20). Recent research, however, has arguably shown the severe limitations of actuarial predictions in violence risk due to the extraordinarily large confidence intervals when a probability estimate of a particular group's violence is applied to an individual within that group (Hart, Michie, & Cooke, 2007).

Psychopathy

Although there continues to be controversy about whether severe mental illness increases the risk of criminal violence (Wallace, Mullen, & Burgess, 2004), there is a growing body of research that suggests that psychopathy in the mentally ill may account for these differences of opinion. When psychopathy has been deliberately measured in research concerning criminal violence and the mentally ill, it has consistently emerged as the most significant predictor (Abushua'leh & Abu-Akel, 2006; Blum, 2004; Dolan & Davies, 2006; Fullam & Dolan, 2006; Monahan et al., 2001; Nolan, Volavka, Mohr, & Cxobor, 1999; Rice & Harris, 1995; Tengstrom, Grann, Langstrom, & Killgren, 2000). However, when psychopathy is controlled, a severe psychotic symptom complex (threat-control-override) significantly increases the risk of aggressive behavior (Hodgins, Hiscoke, & Freese, 2003). The most useful current formulation appears to be that *psychopathy may account for the largest proportion of explainable variance for the prediction of violence among the mentally ill, but active mental illness, especially certain psychotic symptoms associated with persecution, may also contribute to violence risk.*

Psychopathy among those who stalk, threaten, and attack public figures has yet to be systematically measured in any study. However, the construct, particularly when measured with tools such as the P-SCAN (Chapter 10), is being noted and recommended for inclusion in law enforcement and security operations. It is also implicit in several of the motivational typologies (see Table 1.1).

Reality Testing and Psychosis

Reality testing is the ability to differentiate between internal and external stimuli. When grossly impaired, the individual is considered psychotic: He or she is divorced from consensual reality, and has created a private, idiosyncratic, and often bizarre internal world. Psychosis, of course, can be caused by a variety of factors, including major mental disorder, drug abuse, and various medical conditions. Its common clinical manifestations are hallucinations (false sensations), delusions (fixed and false beliefs), and formal thought disorder (illogic or paralogic).

Reality testing impairments appear to be quite common among public figure stalkers and attackers (Fein & Vossekuil, 1999; Fixated Research Group, 2006; James et al., 2007; Meloy et al., 2004), although the causes of such impairments likely vary widely and have received little research attention. It appears from the research that a large proportion of public figure stalkers and attackers are psychotic at the time, but the majority are not (Fein & Vossekuil, 1999; Meloy et al., 2004; Mohandie et al., 2006). There is no demarcation between internal and external for a psychotic individual. Fantasy is reality. The personality organization from a psychoanalytic perspective would be considered psychotic (Kernberg, 1984).

Borderline Personality Organization

On the other hand, most nonpsychotic individuals who pursue, and occasionally attack, public figures may be organized at a *borderline* level of personality (Kernberg, 1984; Meloy, 1989) (see Chapters 8, 12, and 13). This is not synonymous with the diagnosis of borderline personality disorder, yet personality disorders of various permutations will be evident—often the cluster B variety (antisocial, histrionic, narcissistic, and borderline), but occasionally cluster A (paranoid) or cluster C (obsessive-compulsive, dependent) (American Psychiatric Association, 2000). Such individuals have four domains of psychological impairment.

First, although they can differentiate between internal fantasy and external reality, they are confused about the origin of perceptual stimuli. For example, the subject may become increasingly angry at the celebrity figure for not responding to his letters, yet sense that the celebrity figure is angry at him. He then initiates ways of reconciling with, or protecting himself from, the celebrity figure.

Second, psychological defenses tend to be more primitive and immature. The celebrity may be initially idealized, and then angrily devalued when he or she does not meet the subject's expectations. Denial that there is, in fact, a growing preoccupation may be utilized to fend off confrontations by family and friends. Projection—the attribution of one's own thoughts, feelings, and perceptions to others—may provide the lens through which the stalker perceives the motivations of the celebrity and is personally disturbed by them. And projective identification, composed of both attribution and control, leaves the stalker feeling threatened by his or her own anger that he or she has attributed to the celebrity, which may motivate a first approach to quash the threat. Sometimes this anger will be displaced and projected onto a third party (a celebrity's current lover or security detail), and the stalker comes to believe that he or she must rescue the celebrity from the nefarious activities of these other individuals (Meloy, 1999b).

Third, internal representations of self and others are simplified and polarized. The celebrity is a beauty without blemish, and the stalker is his or her perfect mate. Once rejected, the celebrity is an object of derision and disgust, unworthy of any respect. These part object, or self-object (Kohut, 1971) (Chapter 8), representations usually mean that feelings will also be intense, coarse, and rapidly changing, much as one observes in a young child. The advent of whole object representations wherein others are perceived as separate, real, and meaningful individuals has not been developmentally achieved. Such mature representations are anchored in the various shades of reality, supporting the toleration of ambiguity and the experience of mixed and modulated feelings. Such is not the case with most public figure stalkers.

Fourth, attachments are insecure. There is a growing body of research that most stalkers have histories of insecure attachments, and more specifically, preoccupied ones (Meloy, 2007). Attachments are biologically based, species-specific behavioral systems that ensure proximity to the caretaker for a child, and predict repetitive attempts to form sexual and affectional relationships as an adult (Bowlby, 1979). Most human beings form attachments. The great paradox among stalkers, whether pursuing prior sexual intimates or public figures, is that they are seeking proximity to an object that continues to actively reject them, whether personally or by proxy (attorneys, law enforcement officers, private security agents).

Copycat Effects

Imitation is a cornerstone of developmental psychology. Internalizations and identifications are important concepts in psychoanalytic theory. In 1911, MacDonald wrote in his study of attacks on public figures: "One means of protection is for newspapers, magazines and authors of books to cease publishing the names of the criminals... this would lessen the hope for glory, renown, or notoriety, which is a great incentive to such crimes" (p. 519). His early study raised two issues that are critical to understanding the power of copycat effects on attacks and assassinations of public figures. First, there is a longing to be someone special, a clinical dynamic that is a facet of pathological narcissism (Chapter 8). Second, there is the anticipation that the mass media will widely publicize the assault, transforming the attacker into a famous person. This is another aspect of pathological narcissism referred to as "grandiosity." Although empirical study of the general mechanisms of copycat crimes is very weak (Surette, 2002), anecdotal examples are legion. It would appear that relatively unusual crimes, including attacks on public figures, are particularly prone to copycat effects (Wilson & Hunter, 1983) because they accomplished in reality for the previous assassin what the aspiring assassin covets.

Dietz and Martell (1989) first noted in contemporary literature that efforts to study or emulate famous assassins as predecessors or role models may be one of several factors that predict such behavior. Fein and Vossekuil (1998, 1999) found that 44% of their sample of those who near lethally approached, attacked, or assassinated a public figure in the United States had demonstrated an intense interest in assassination, and in some cases had even corresponded with previous assassins.

John Wilkes Booth was an actor who coveted celebrity. On the night he shot President Abraham Lincoln in the Ford Theater in Washington, he gave tickets to his friends, saying that "there would be great acting" (MacDonald, 1911, p. 510). Sometimes attacks that initially appear to be motivated by political reasons are, instead, a product of media reports of another crime. Josef Bachmann fired three rounds at the leader of the left wing student movement Rudi Dutschke in Germany. This was labeled as a right wing extremist attack, but closer inspection indicated that Bachmann was inspired by the assassination of the American civil rights leader Martin Luther King (Doubek, 2003) in April, 1968. Before driving to the location of the assault, he told his colleagues, "you will hear from me; on TV, on radio and in the press" (Kellerhof, 2003, p. 73).

Modus operandi can also be heavily influenced by a previous assassin's behaviors. Robert Bardo read in a magazine that Arthur Jackson, the British man who almost murdered the American actor Theresa Saldana, had discovered her private address by hiring a detective agency (Saunders, 1998). Bardo did the same and murdered Rebecca Schaeffer on the doorstep of her apartment, in 1989.

Screenwriters and films often unwittingly engage in this public dance of death. Paul Shafer, a Hollywood screenwriter, based his screenplay for the movie *Taxi Driver*, on the real life diaries of Arthur Bremer who had attempted to assassinate, and only crippled, Governor George Wallace of Alabama a few years earlier. John Hinckley Jr., was influenced by, and identified with, the character Travis Bickle in the movie *Taxi Driver* when he attempted to assassinate President Ronald Reagan in 1981. Deadly fiction imitated deadly fact, which imitated deadly fiction over the course of one decade.

And then there is the influence of literature and various internalizations, the most striking example being the intense interest in, and identification with, Holden Caulfield, the angst-ridden adolescent in the book, *Catcher in the Rye*, written by J.D. Salinger and first published in 1945. Mark Chapman was 25 years old when he killed John Lennon in December, 1980, and then sat down on the curb and was reading the book when the police arrived. Three months later, John Hinckley Jr., was 25 when he attempted to assassinate President Ronald Reagan. The book was found in his hotel room. Robert Bardo was 19 when he killed Rebecca Schaeffer 8 years later. He had the book in his possession at the time. These young men not only identified with the Caulfield character—his loneliness, sadness, alienation, hatred, and occasional fantasies of violence—but they also *identified with each other*, as they, in turn, sought the limelight. As Arthur Bremer had written in his diaries a decade earlier: "to do SOMETHING BOLD AND DRAMATIC, FORCEFULL (*sic*) & DYNAMIC, A STATEMENT of my manhood for the world to see" (www.pbs.org/wgbh/amex/wallace/sfeature/assassin.html).

Mental Illness and Lapse of Care

A consistent finding throughout the public figure stalking, threatening, and attacking research is that mental illness, if present, has gone untreated for a period. This has been described as part of the downward spiral of these individuals' lives as they formulate an often grandiose plan to bring a notoriety to their sad existence through an attack on a public figure. This absence of mental health care is often a combination of individual noncompliance and limited public resources. Such an outcome is not the least bit surprising when it is consistently reported that half of normal individuals do not take their medications as prescribed by their physicians.

Limited public resources for mental health care have been a chronic problem for decades, and anything associated with "mental health" remains the stigmatized stepchild of modern medicine. Given the severe cognitive, perceptual, and emotional impairments that accompany mental illness, it is a wonder that individuals form a stable treatment alliance with their mental health care provider.

Noncompliance, however, does not predict an attack on a public figure, and only very few will vere in this dangerous direction. Improved public mental health care in general, moreover, would likely cast a wide enough net that a few individuals who were inclined toward a preoccupation with public figures would be dissuaded from acting out through a stable and reality-based relationship with a mental health professional.

Involuntary outpatient treatment (Meloy, Haroun, & Schiller, 1992) also offers a more specific and coercive treatment environment, while preserving most individual freedoms, for those mentally ill individuals who are less inclined to voluntarily seek treatment. Such programs target the more grossly psychotic and paranoid individuals who do not pose an imminent danger to others, but may be taking the first few steps down a pathway toward violence. Involuntary outpatient treatment has been enormously successful in the stabilization of patients in the community following a verdict of not guilty by reason of insanity (see, e.g., the Conditional Release Program in California). This model, however, is based upon tertiary care—after the fact of the felony—often a violent one. We are proposing such a model of treatment as preventive care (Mullen et al., in press), which would be the place of diversion for those individuals who raise concern in others because of their pathological fixations upon public figures. Such a program has been implemented in Britain (Fixated Research Group, 2006) and is called the Fixated Threat Assessment Centre.

A landmark psycholegal development 200 years ago in England was due in part to an attack on a public figure, namely his Majesty King George III. Before this case, the law did not properly distinguish "criminal lunatics" from more general "lunatics." James Hadfield, a 29-year-old man, was found not guilty of attempting to shoot and kill the king because of his delusional state of mind when he committed the crime. His acquittal was followed by a public outcry because until this time the fate of those acquitted by reason of insanity was not prescribed and such individuals were often released into the charge of their relatives. The result of this outcry was the Criminal Lunatics Act of 1800, drawn up to provide for the indefinite detention of insane defendants. Hadfield was held in the Bethlem Royal Hospital in London until he died of tuberculosis (James et al., 2007; Moran, 1985).

Criminal Histories

Within the general stalking literature some authors have found the stalker's criminal history to be a good predictor of violence (Mullen, Pathé, Purcell, & Stuart, 1999), although others have found it to be a weak predictor (Brewster, 2002) or a nonpredictor (Meloy, Davis, & Lovette, 2001; Palarea, Zona, Lane, & Langhinrichsen-Rohling, 1999; Rosenfeld & Lewis, 2005). This inconsistency is not surprising, given the wide-ranging methodological differences across studies, and it may be that certain types or combinations of prior criminal behavior may to some degree predict certain types of obsessional contact. The current state of knowledge is of value but is not sufficiently sophisticated to suggest marked criminal pathways or predictors.

In the more specific evidence relating to inappropriate contact with public figures, there is some indication that violent criminal history is a reasonable predictor or correlate of approach behavior. For instance, those who sought physical proximity to federal judicial officials were more likely to have previous histories of violence than those who maintained a distance (Calhoun, 1998). Similarly, Scalora et al.'s (2002) examination of U.S. Capitol Police Threat Assessment Section files revealed that approachers had significantly more prior convictions than did nonapproachers. This was particularly marked in terms of property offences, violent offenses, and drug and alcohol charges. Even so, the majority of members of both groups did not have any known criminal history. Neither did previous convictions for harassment and making threats differentiate the groups. Vossekuil, Fein, Borum, and Reddy (2001) noted that of those who had attacked and sought to attack judicial officials, few had histories of arrest for violent crimes or for crimes that involved weapons. In their study of 83 public figure assassins, attackers, and near-lethal approachers, few had histories of arrests for violent crimes or weapons crimes, and had ever been incarcerated (Fein & Vossekuil, 1998). Mohandie et al. (2006) found that only 8% of their sample of 271 celebrity stalkers had a violent criminal history, significantly less than their other groups combined (43%).

Among 24 individuals who attacked western European politicians between 1990 and 2004, 38% had a previous conviction for a violent crime, and two additional subjects were known for their violent activities. Moreover, for six subjects their conviction history was unknown (James et al., 2007). In another study of attacks against the British monarch or immediate members of the Royal Family, 23 cases were identified between 1778 and 1994. Data were insufficient to determine histories of violent criminal behavior (James et al., in press), although there was clear evidence of psychosis in half the cases. And in the study of contemporary approaches to the British Royal Family (see Table 1.1 for typology), 24% had a criminal record and 10% had a previous conviction for violence. Moreover, of those who *successfully breached* a security perimeter, they were significantly more likely to be male (92%), to have a criminal record (37%), to be intoxicated (37%), and to not be mentally ill (74%) (Fixated Research Group, 2006).

Schlesinger and Mesa (Chapter 4) report that at least one third of their sample of violent stalkers (homicide or attempted homicide) of nonpolitical celebrity figures ($n = 16$) had criminal histories, although some data were unavailable. The operational hypothesis at this point appears to be that *violent criminal histories are present in a significant minority of public figure stalking, threat, and attack cases, but should not be assumed. However, such histories, when present, may correlate with an increased risk of a breach or attack.* Further research is needed.

Violence and Weapons

It is clear that firearms are the weapons of choice for those who assassinate public figures in the United States. In Fein and Vossekuil's (1998, 1999) study of assassins, attackers, and near-lethal approachers, 81% employed firearms and 15% used knives. Given that many public figure attacks will be predatory rather than affective in nature, it would follow that the majority of cases involve use of a firearm to increase tactical advantage (see Meloy, 2001). Dietz, Matthews, Van Duyne, et al. (1991) noted that only about 6% of those who wrote inappropriate letters to Hollywood celebrities mentioned weapons, and the majority of these never went on to approach the target. Conversely, in Dietz, Matthews, Martell, et al.'s (1991) related study of written communications received by members of the U.S. Congress, 30% of writers mentioned weapons in their missives. Mention of weapons was not, however, significantly associated with approaching the target.

In contemporary approaches to the British Royal Family, 5% carried a weapon: firearms, swords, knives, a baseball bat, a screw driver, and a razor blade (Fixated Research Group, 2006). One third of these individuals had a criminal record, and were significantly more likely to be hostile or aggressive and have homicidal ideation, but less likely to be fixated on a particular person than those who did not carry a weapon. They were also significantly more likely to be both pursuing an agenda and chaotically psychotic (see Table 1.1). They were also more likely to be assaultive, intimidating, threatening, abusive, and angry when approached by a proxy (usually security or law enforcement) than those who did not carry a weapon.

Among the 23 individuals who had attacked members of the British Royal Family between 1778 and 1994, 57% used a firearm (usually a handgun), but half ($n = 6$) were not loaded. Other weapons included knives, stones, and a brass-headed walking cane (James et al., in press). In contemporary attacks on western European politicians, 83% used a weapon, including firearms, a letter bomb, a Molotov cocktail, and a samurai sword, knives, a cosh, a photographic tripod, a liquid-filled balloon, and a powder bomb. Fatalities were caused by the firearms and knives (James et al., 2007). Of the 16 homicidal stalker attackers of nonpolitical celebrity figures in North America and Europe, 71% used a firearm and 18% used a knife. Two others used a bomb and set a fire (Chapter 4).

New research into sensational interests (i.e., interest in weapons, the occult, martial arts, the paranormal, and militaristic topics) could prove fruitful in identifying an important potential risk factor. Interest in sensational topics has been found to be related to Eysenck's psychoticism (very similar to modern descriptions of psychopathy), low agreeableness, low conscientiousness, sensation seeking, and delinquency (see Egan et al., 2005). Indeed, a number of "gun-obsessed fanatics" have attacked high-profile celebrities (e.g., Barry George, who was convicted for killing BBC presenter Jill Dando), and most of the assassins in the Fein and Vossekuil (1999) work had a history of weapons

Table 1.2. Comparison of violent behavior between public figure stalkers and prior sexually intimate stalkers: Hypotheses based on empirical evidence

Public figure stalkers	Prior sexually intimate stalkers
Violence frequency very low (2%)	Violence frequency very high (>50%)
Usually predatory mode	Usually affective mode
Major mental disorder likely	No major mental disorder likely
Weapons use, a firearm	Weapons use unlikely
No direct threat communicated to target or police beforehand	Direct threats common

use and militaristic and other sensational interests. There is a parallel finding in the adolescent and adult mass murder research (Meloy et al., 2004).

When considering likely or actual weapons usage in relation to attacks on public figures, it must be borne in mind that observable temporal trends in weapons usage exist (see e.g., Fox & Zawitz, 2003), and that people in different countries and regions will have differing access to and preference for particular weapons. *The operational hypothesis appears to be that weapons will be used in attacks on public figures, and fatalities are associated with firearms and cutting instruments.*

Table 1.2 provides a summary that compares certain aspects of violence between public figure stalkers and prior sexually intimate stalkers. Although it is simplistic, and will not apply in all cases, we hope it emphasizes the striking differences between these two groups of stalkers when they are violent.

Violence Risk Management

A principle aim of the embryonic literature on stalking, threatening, and attacking public figures is the management of risk, but the problem itself must first be identified and accepted. The literature on stalking, which has now amassed over 300 articles in the social sciences alone, reliably demonstrates that stalking is a difficult concept to define. Stalking may often consist of the targeted repetition of behaviors that are, when considered in isolation, ostensibly routine and harmless. It is the chronic and frequently unpredictable nature of stalking that instills so much fear in its victims. But how do victims decide that a stalker or otherwise inappropriate communicator is targeting them? Victim's gender may influence such decisions (e.g., Sheridan, Gillett, & Davies, 2002), as may personal knowledge of stalking (e.g., Yanowitz, 2006) and individual attitudes and occupation (Kamphuis et al., 2005). Of course, in the case of public figures, it will often not be the targets themselves who decide whether stalking is occurring. We have been involved in cases, particularly outside the United States, where security and other personnel were insufficiently informed of the threat posed by individuals with pathological fixations and decided to ignore the problem or deal with it in-house. Such solutions may involve visiting the communicator and attempting to warn him or her off, or even allowing the communicator access to the public figure. Fortunately, teachings from the science of threat management are extending, and the need for a coordinated and consistent approach is becoming more apparent. This book provides a window into this theoretical and practical knowledge.

Traditional methods of predicting violence are being superseded by methods for managing the risk of violence. This is especially true when the targets are public figures because of the relatively low frequency of actual violence, yet the high social intensity of such a violent act. These traditional methods, which are all considered nomothetic (based upon large group data), can be divided into three groups:

1. Actuarial instruments that are based upon probability estimates of a future behavior within a group (e.g., VRAG, COVR, STATIC 99)
2. Structured professional judgment instruments that do not provide a quantitative prediction of risk, but organize data on a case according to known risk factors for violence (e.g., HCR-20, SAM, WAVR-21)
3. Other clinical instruments that happen to predict violence (e.g., PCL-R, LSI-R)

The fourth approach is idiographic (based upon individual case data) and eliminates the low base rate problem of the nomothetic instruments by focusing upon dynamic and behavioral aspects of an individual of concern (e.g., threat assessment model).

Violence is usually a choice or a decision, not an inevitable consequence of having a number of features (e.g., being young, male, unemployed, and a regular drug user). It is particularly so among public figure stalkers who are violent because of the planned and purposeful nature of most of their attacks. The risk of violence, however, is always uncertain: Even the most violent offenders choose not to be violent most of the time. We have to think about managing someone's behavior and implementing systems or interventions to address specific scenarios. If seeing the targeted celebrity out with her husband makes a particular individual engage in risky behavior, then during all public appearances of the couple, security personnel need to watch out for the particular individual. If the person is known to prefer arson as a method of getting the public figure's attention, then taking additional fire safety precautions is in order. Sometimes the best course is planning for all possible scenarios and defending against them. Human behavior is far too individualized and dynamic to just depend upon large group data; but humans also share many characteristics, some of which place them in subject pools of greater risk for certain behaviors, such as violence. The most advanced threat assessment programs are able to continuously input static and dynamic variables that emerge in new cases into their databases and therefore update their risk assessment algorithms and risk management approaches (Chapter 19).

The data in this book also make clear that every violence risk management of a threat toward a public figure must seriously consider the role of mental disorder. When assessing delusional individuals, the principle of rationality-within-irrationality (Link & Stueve, 1994) proves to be helpful for operations. This is the concept that psychotic persons behave rationally in the context of their delusional system. It is based upon the psychological premise that an individual's perception of his social world guides his or her action. For example, if a person believes that he or she is gravely threatened by a public figure because of a persecutory delusion, then violence is more likely because he or she will view it as justified self-defense (Link & Stueve, 1994). It is crucial in the process of threat assessment and risk management to understand the nature and content of the subject's internal experience, especially if there is evidence that he or she is psychotic. We can then individualize the risk management process and still apply nomothetic instruments such as the Stalking Assessment and Management (SAM), the only structured professional judgment instrument for stalking and violence yet developed (Chapter 15). Functional and behavioral approaches can then also be utilized during the real-time management of the case, applying the work of Fein and Vossekuil (1999), Borum et al. (1999), Scalora et al. (2002, 2003) (Chapter 19), Calhoun and Weston (2003), and Mullen et al. (2006) (Chapter 5).

The state of the science of public figure stalking, threats, and attacks provides a growing body of research for forensic scientists and security specialists in both the public and private sectors. It is with optimism and energy that we offer this book, and hope that it will contribute to better understanding of this global problem. Such problems, however, are ultimately always personal, and sometimes very painful, for the public figure. Katarina Witt, the two-time Olympic figure skating gold medalist, had such an experience when she was cross-examined by her erotomanic stalker who represented himself at his trial. He had written to her, "Don't be afraid when God allows me to pull you out of your body to hold you tight. Then you'll know that there is life beyond the flesh." (*Los Angeles Times*, March 12, 1992, p. A3, as referenced in Orion, 1997).

Notes

1. The timing of this varies, but often coincides with private security deciding to involve law enforcement in the case for potential criminal prosecution.
2. The California Supreme Court opined in 1976, "We would hesitate to hold that the therapist who is aware that his patient expects to attempt to assassinate the President of the United States would not be obligated to warn the authorities because the therapist cannot predict with accuracy that his patient will commit the crime....The protective privilege ends where the public peril begins" (*Tarasoff v. Regents of the University of California*, 17 Cal 3d 425, at 346–347).
3. The California Court of Appeal recently found in a public figure case that the victim's awareness does not have to be contemporaneous with the stalking behavior (*People v. Norman*, 75 Cal. App. 4th, 1234 [1999]).

4. SSA James Fitzgerald of the FBI Behavioral Analysis Unit 1, created in 2002, communicated threat assessment database, which currently holds over 3,000 criminally oriented communications for use in the linguistic and behavioral investigation of threats. He is currently with the Academy Group, Inc.
5. One exception are attacks on judicial officials which are predatory, but are typically perpetrated by someone who has appeared before the judicial official in a legal context, establishing a relationship which is typically quite antagonistic (Calhoun, 1998).

References

Abushua'leh, K., & Abu-Akel, A. (2006). Association of psychopathic traits and symptomatology with violence in patients with schizophrenia. *Psychiatry Research*, *143*, 205–211.

American Psychiatric Association (2000). *Diagnostic and statistical manual of mental disorders* (4th ed., text revision). Washington, DC: Author.

Barratt, E., Stanford, M., Dowdy, L., Liebman, M., & Kent, T. (1999). Impulsive and premeditated aggression: A factor analysis of self-reported acts. *Psychiatry Research*, *86*, 163–173.

Blum, F. (2004). Psychopathy, psychosis, drug abuse, and reoffense among conditionally released offenders (Doctoral dissertation, University of Southern California, Los Angeles, CA, 2004). *Dissertation Abstracts International Section B*, *64*(12-B), 6008.

Boon, J., & Sheridan, L. (2002). *Stalking and psychosexual obsession*. London: Wiley.

Borum, R., Fein, R., Vossekuil, B., & Berglund, J. (1999). Threat assessment: Defining an approach for evaluating risk of targeted violence. *Behavioral Sciences and the Law*, *17*, 323–337.

Bowlby, J. (1979). *The making and breaking of affectional bonds*. London: Tavistock.

Brewster, M. (2002). Stalking by former intimates: Verbal threats and other predictors of physical violence. In K. Davis, I. Frieze, & R. Maiuro (Eds.), *Stalking: Perspectives on victims and perpetrators* (pp. 292–311). New York: Springer.

Calhoun, F. (1998). *Hunters and howlers: Threats and violence against federal judicial officials in the United States, 1789–1993*. Arlington, VA: U.S. Marshals Service.

Calhoun, F., & Weston, S. (2003). *Contemporary threat management: A practical guide for identifying, assessing, and managing individuals of violent intent*. San Diego: Specialized Training Services.

Chapman, D., & Spitzberg, B. (2003). Are you following me? A study of unwanted relationship and pursuit in Japan: What behaviors are prevalent? *Bulletin of Hijiyama University*, *10*, 89–138.

Clarke, J. W. (1982). *American assassins: The darker side of politics*. Princeton: Princeton University Press.

Clarke, J. W. (1990). *On being mad or merely angry: John W. Hinckley, Jr. and other dangerous people*. Princeton: Princeton University Press.

Cornell, D., Warren, J., Hawk, G., Stafford, E., Oram, G., & Pine, D. (1996). Psychopathy in instrumental and reactive violent offenders. *Journal of Consulting Clinical Psychology*, *64*, 783–790.

De Becker, G. (1994). Intervention decisions: The value of flexibility. Unpublished white paper report.

De Becker, G. (1997). *The gift of fear.* Boston: Little, Brown.

Dietz, P., & Martell, D. (1989). *Mentally disordered offenders in pursuit of celebrities and politicians.* Washington, DC: National Institute of Justice.

Dietz, P., Matthews, D., Martell, D., Stewart, T., Hrouda, D., & Warren, J. (1991). Threatening and otherwise inappropriate letters to members of the United States Congress. *Journal of Forensic Sciences, 36,* 1445–1468.

Dietz, P., Matthews, D., Van Duyne, C., Martell, D., Parry, C., Stewart, T., et al. (1991). Threatening and otherwise inappropriate letters to Hollywood celebrities. *Journal of Forensic Sciences, 36,* 185–209.

Dolan, M., & Davies, G. (2006). Psychopathy and institutional outcome in patients with schizophrenia in forensic settings in the UK. *Schizophrenia Research, 81,* 277–281.

Doubek, K. (2003). *Lexikon der Attentate.* Munchen: Piper.

Egan, V., Figueredo, A. J., Wolf, P., McBride, K., Sefcek, J., Vasquez, G., et al. (2005). Sensational interests, mating effort, and personality: Evidence for cross-cultural validity. *Journal of Individual Differences, 26,* 11–19.

Farnham, F., James, D., & Cantrell, P. (2000). Association between violence, psychosis, and relationship to victim in stalkers. *The Lancet, 355,* 199.

Fein, R., & Vossekuil, B. (1997). *Preventing assassination: A monograph.* Washington, DC: U.S. Department of Justice.

Fein, R., & Vossekuil, B. (1998). Preventing attacks on public officials and public figures: A Secret Service perspective. In J. R. Meloy (Ed.), *The psychology of stalking: Clinical and forensic perspectives* (pp. 176–194). San Diego: Academic Press.

Fein, R., & Vossekuil, B. (1999). Assassination in the United States: An operational study of recent assassins, attackers, and near-lethal approachers. *Journal of Forensic Sciences, 44,* 321–333.

Fein, R., Vossekuil, B., & Holden, G. (1995). *Threat assessment: An approach to prevent targeted violence* (Publication NCJ 155000). Washington, DC: U.S. Department of Justice, Office of Justice Programs, National Institute of Justice.

Fixated Research Group (2006). *Inappropriate communications, approaches, and attacks on the British Royal Family.* London: The Home Office.

Fox, J. A., & Zawitz, M. W. (1998, updated 2000, 2001, 2002, 2003). *Homicide trends in the United States.* Washington, DC: Bureau of Justice Statistics. http://www.ojp.usdoj.gov/bjs/homicide/homtrnd.htm

Freedman, L. Z. (1971). Psychopathology of assassination. In W. J. Crotty (Ed.), *Assassination and the political order* (pp. 143–160). New York: Harper & Row.

Fullam, R., & Dolan, M. (2006). The criminal and personality profile of patients with schizophrenia and comorbid psychopathic traits. *Personality and Individual Differences, 40,* 1591–1602.

Gottschalk, L., & Bechtel, R. (2001). Computerized content analysis of speech plus speech recognition in the measurement of neuropsychiatric dimensions. *Computer Methods and Programs in Biomedicine, 77,* 81–86.

Hart, S., Michie, C., & Cooke, D. (2007). Precision of actuarial risk assessment instruments. *British Journal of Psychiatry, 190*(Suppl. 49), s60–s65.

Herman, M. (2003). Assessing leadership style: Trait analysis. In J. Post (Ed.), *The psychological assessment of political leaders*. Ann Arbor: University of Michigan Press.

Hodgins, S., Hiscoke, U., & Freese, R. (2003). The antecedents of aggressive behavior among men with schizophrenia: A prospective investigation of patients in community treatment. *Behavioral Sciences and the Law, 21,* 523–546.

Hoffman, J. L. (1943). Psychotic visitors to government offices in the national capital. *American Journal of Psychiatry, 99,* 571–575.

Hoffmann, J., & Sheridan, L. (2005). The stalking of public figures: Management and intervention. *Journal of Forensic Sciences, 6,* 1459–1465.

Jagessar, J., & Sheridan, L. (2004). Stalking: Perceptions and experiences across two cultures. *Criminal Justice and Behavior, 31,* 97–117.

James, D., Mullen, P., Meloy, J. R., Pathé, M., Farnham, F., & Preston, L. (2007). The role of mental disorder in attacks on European politicians 1990–2004. *Acta Psychiatrica Scandinavica, 116,* 334–344.

James, D., Mullen, P., Pathé, M., Meloy, J. R., Farnham, F., Preston, L., et al. (in press). Attacks on the British Royal Family: The role of psychotic illness. *Journal of the American Academy of Psychiatry and the Law.*

Kamphuis, J. H., Fazio, L. D., Emmelkamp, P. M., Farnham, F., Groenen, A., James, D., et al. (2005). Stalking: Perceptions and attitudes amongst helping professions. An EU cross-national comparison. *Clinical Psychology and Psychotherapy, 12,* 215–225.

Kasantikul, D. (1998). Erotomania in Thai patients: A study of 20 cases. *Journal of the Medical Association of Thailand, 81,* 852–856.

Kellerhof, S. F. (2003). *Attentater.* Koln: Bohlau Verlag.

Kernberg, O. (1984). *Severe personality disorders.* New Haven: Yale University Press.

Kohut, H. (1971). *The analysis of the self.* New York: International Universities Press.

Kordvani, A. (2000). *Women stalking in Iran.* Paper presented by proxy to the Criminal Justice Responses to Stalking Conference, Australian Institute of Criminology, Sydney, Australia.

Leets, L., de Becker, G., & Giles, H. (1995). Fans: Exploring expressed motivations for contacting celebrities. *Journal of Language and Social Psychology, 14,* 102–123.

Link, B., & Stueve, A. (1994). Psychotic symptoms and the violent/illegal behavior of mental patients compared to community controls. In J. Monahan, & H. Steadman (Eds.), *Violence and mental disorder: Developments in risk assessment* (pp. 137–159). Chicago: University of Chicago Press.

MacDonald, A. (1911). Assassins of rulers. *Journal of the American Institute of Criminal Law and Criminology, 2,* 505–520.

MacDonald, J. M. (1968). *Homicidal threats.* Springfield, IL: Charles C. Thomas.

McCutcheon, L., Lange, R., & Houran, J. (2002). Conceptualization and measurement of celebrity worship. *British Journal of Psychology, 93,* 67–87.

McEwan, T., Mullen, P. E., & Purcell, R. (2007). Identifying risk factors in stalking: A review of current research. *International Journal of Law and Psychiatry, 30,* 1–9.

Megargee, E. (1986). A psychometric study of incarcerated presidential threateners. *Criminal Justice and Behavior, 13,* 243–260.

Meloy, J. R. (1989). Unrequited love and the wish to kill: Diagnosis and treatment of borderline erotomania. *Bulletin of the Menninger Clinic, 53,* 477–492.

Meloy, J. R. (1992). Revisiting the Rorschach of Sirhan Sirhan. *Journal of Personality Assessment, 58,* 548–570.

Meloy, J. R. (1998). *The psychology of stalking: Clinical and forensic perspectives.* San Diego: Academic Press.

Meloy, J. R. (1999a). Stalking: An old behavior, a new crime. *Psychiatric Clinics of North America, 22,* 85–99.

Meloy, J. R. (1999b). Erotomania, triangulation, and homicide. *Journal of Forensic Sciences, 44,* 421–424.

Meloy, J. R. (2001). Communicated threats and violence toward public and private figures: Discerning differences among those who stalk and attack. *Journal of Forensic Sciences, 46,* 1211–1213.

Meloy, J. R. (2002). Stalking and violence. In J. Boon, & L. Sheridan (Eds.), *Stalking and psychosexual obsession* (pp. 105–125). London: Wiley.

Meloy, J. R. (2006). Empirical basis and forensic application of affective and predatory violence. *Australian and New Zealand Journal of Psychiatry, 40,* 539–547.

Meloy, J. R. (2007). Stalking: The state of the science. *Criminal Behaviour and Mental Health, 17,* 1–7.

Meloy, J. R., Davis, B., & Lovette, J. (2001). Risk factors for violence among stalkers. *Journal of Threat Assessment, 1,* 3–16.

Meloy, J. R., Haroun, A., & Schiller, E. (1992). *Clinical guidelines for involuntary outpatient treatment.* Odessa, FL: Professional Resource Exchange.

Meloy, J. R., Hempel, A., Mohandie, K., Shiva, A., Gray, T., & Richards, T. (2004). A comparative analysis of adolescent and adult mass murderers. *Behavioral Sciences and the Law, 22,* 291–309.

Meloy, J. R., James, D., Mullen, P., Pathé, M., Farnham, F., Preston, L., et al. (2004). A research review of public figure threats, approaches, attacks, and assassinations in the United States. *Journal of Forensic Sciences, 49,* 1086–1093.

Meyers, J. (1998). Cultural factors in erotomania. In J. R. Meloy (Ed.), The *psychology of stalking: Clinical and forensic perspectives* (pp. 213–224). San Diego: Academic Press.

Meyers, J., & Meloy, J. R. (1994). Discussion of "a comparative study of erotomanic and obsessional subjects in a forensic sample." *Journal of Forensic Sciences, 39,* 906–907.

Mohandie, K., Meloy, J. R., McGowan, M., & Williams, J. (2006). The RECON typology of stalking: Reliability and validity based upon a large sample of North American stalkers. *Journal of Forensic Sciences, 51,* 147–155.

Monahan, J., Steadman, H., Silver, E., Appelbaum, P., Robbins, P., Mulvey E., et al. (2001). *Rethinking risk assessment.* New York: Oxford University Press.

Moran, R. (1985). The origin of insanity as a special verdict: The trial for treason of James Hadfield, 1800. *Law and Society Review, 19,* 487–519.

Mullen, P., James, D., Meloy, J. R., Pathé, M., Farnham, F., Preston, L., et al. (in press). The fixated and the pursuit of public figures. *Journal of Forensic Psychiatry and Psychology.*

Mullen, P., & Lester, G. (2006). Vexatious litigants and unusually persistent complainants and petitioners: From querulous paranoia to querulous behavior. *Behavioral Sciences and the Law, 24,* 333–349.

Mullen, P., Mackenzie, R., Ogloff, J., Pathé, M., McEwan, T., & Purcell, R. (2006). Assessing and managing the risks in the stalking situation. *Journal of the American Academy of Psychiatry and the Law, 34*, 439–450.

Mullen, P., Pathé, M., & Purcell, R. (2000). *Stalkers and their victims.* Cambridge: Cambridge University Press.

Mullen, P., Pathé, M., Purcell, R., & Stuart, G. (1999). Study of stalkers. *American Journal of Psychiatry, 156*, 1244–1249.

Nolan, K., Volavka, J., Mohr, P., & Czobor, P. (1999). Psychopathy and violent behavior among patients with schizophrenia or schizoaffective disorder. *Psychiatric Services*, 50, 787–792.

Orion, D. (1997). *I know you really love me.* New York: Macmillan.

Palarea, R., Zona, M., Lane, J., & Langhinrichsen-Rohling, J. (1999). The dangerous nature of intimate relationship stalking: Threats, violence, and associated risk factors. *Behavioral Sciences and the Law, 17*, 269–283.

Person, E. (1988). *Dreams of love and fateful encounters.* New York: Penguin.

Phillips, R. T. (2006). Assessing presidential stalkers and assassins. *Journal of the American Academy of Psychiatry and the Law, 34*, 154–164.

Pollack, S. (1969a). Psychiatric report to the Honorable Evelle J. Younger, District Attorney, People v. Sirhan, February 5, 1969, People's Exhibit 111.

Pollack, S. (1969b). Supplemental psychiatric report to the Honorable Evelle J. Younger, District Attorney, People v. Sirhan, March 21, 1969.

Rice, M., & Harris, G. (1995). Psychopathy, schizophrenia, alcohol abuse, and violent recidivism. *International Journal of Law and Psychiatry, 18*, 333–342.

Rosenfeld, B., & Lewis, C. (2005). Assessing violence risk in stalking cases: A regression tree approach. *Law and Human Behavior, 29*, 343–357.

Saunders, R. (1998). The legal perspective on stalking. In J. R. Meloy (Ed.), *The psychology of stalking: Clinical and forensic perspectives* (pp. 28–49). San Diego: Academic Press.

Scalora, M., Baumgartner, J., & Plank, G. (2003). The relationship of mental illness to targeted contact behavior toward state government agencies and officials. *Behavioral Sciences and the Law, 21*, 239–249.

Scalora, M., Baumgartner, J., Zimmerman, W., Callaway, D., Mailletteer M., Covell, C., et al. (2002). Risk factors for approach behavior toward the U.S. Congress. *Journal of Threat Assessment, 2*, 35–55.

Schlesinger, L. (2006). Celebrity stalking, homicide, and suicide: A psychological autopsy. *International Journal of Offender Therapy and Comparative Criminology, 50*, 39–46.

Sheridan, L., & Boon, J. C. W. (2002). Stalker typologies: Implications for law enforcement. In J. C. W. Boon, & L. Sheridan (Eds.), *Stalking and psychosexual obsession: Psychological perspectives for prevention, policing and treatment* (pp. 63–82). Chichester: Wiley.

Sheridan, L., Gillett, R., & Davies, G. M. (2002). Perceptions and prevalence of stalking in a male sample. *Psychology, Crime and Law, 8*, 289–310.

Silva, J. A., & Leong, G. B. (1993). Delusional misidentification syndromes and prominent figures. *American Journal of Forensic Psychiatry, 14*, 39–44.

Spitzberg, B. H. (2002). The tactical topography of stalking victimization and management. *Trauma, Violence & Abuse, 3*, 261–288.

Spitzberg, B. H. (2007). The state of the art of stalking: Taking stock of the emerging literature. *Aggression and Violent Behavior, 12*, 64–86.

Surette, R. (2002). Self-reported copycat crime among a population of serious and violent juvenile offenders. *Crime and Delinquency, 48*, 46–69.

Tengstrom, A., Grann, M., Langstrom, N., & Kullgren, G. (2000). Psychopathy as a predictor of violent recidivism among criminal offenders with schizophrenia. *Law and Human Behavior, 24*, 45–58.

Tweed, R., & Dutton, D. (1998). A comparison of impulsive and instrumental subgroups of batterers. *Violence and Victims, 13*, 217–230.

Vossekuil, B., Fein, R., Borum, R., & Reddy, M. (2001). Preventing targeted violence against judicial officials and courts. *Annals of the American Academy of Political and Social Science, 576*, 78–90.

Wallace, C., Mullen, P., & Burgess, P. (2004). Criminal offending in schizophrenia over a 25-year period marked by deinstitutionalization and increasing prevalence of comorbid substance use disorders. *American Journal of Psychiatry, 161*, 716–727.

Warren, L., Mullen, P., Thomas, S., Ogloff, J., & Burgess, P. (in press). Threats to kill: A follow-up study. *Psychological Medicine.*

Wilson, W., & Hunter, R. (1983). Movie-inspired violence. *Psychological Reports, 53*, 435–441.

Yanowitz, K. L. (2006). Influence of gender and experience on college students' *stalking* schemas. *Violence and Victims, 21*, 91–99.

Section I

Defining the Risk

2

A Forensic Investigation of Those Who Stalk Celebrities

J. Reid Meloy, Kris Mohandie, and Mila Green

Violent attacks against celebrities by a few stalkers—most notably Arthur Jackson and Robert Bardo[1]—ushered in the criminalization of stalking in California almost 20 years ago. Despite the growing body of stalking research during the past decade (Meloy, 1998, 2006a; Mullen, Pathé, & Purcell, 2008), there remain very few published scientific efforts to discern the behavior of celebrity approachers (Dietz et al., 1991), those who worship celebrities (McCutcheon, Lange, & Houran, 2002), and those who otherwise contact celebrities (Leets, de Becker, & Giles, 1995). There is one published psychological autopsy of a celebrity stalker who committed suicide after he mailed a bomb to an Islandic female pop singer living in Britain (Schlesinger, 2006). Mohandie, Meloy, McGowan, and Williams (2006) published preliminary data on a non-random sample of celebrity stalkers within a larger North American sample of stalkers ($n = 1,005$) to validate a new stalking typology, RECON, defined by the relationship between the stalker and the victim and the context within which the stalking occurred. The typology yielded four groups—intimate, acquaintance, public figure, and private stranger—with both acceptable inter-rater reliability and extensive discriminant validity. The public figure group was the least violent and most frequently mentally ill of the four groups. This was a study of a sample of stalkers of celebrities, because virtually all the "public figure" group was drawn from a Los Angeles entertainment corporate security database.

Our intent in this study is to explore this sample of celebrity stalkers in detail, focusing upon demographic characteristics, pursuit motivations and patterns, clinical indicators, victim characteristics, threats, the nature and frequency of their violence, predictors of approach, and recidivism. Inferential comparisons will be made to a group ($n = 103$) of private stranger stalkers from the same study (Mohandie et al., 2006) on select variables.

Methods

Between March 2003 and June 2004, two trained researchers reviewed over 2,300 files dealing with instances of stalking, criminal harassment, menacing, terrorist threats, or domestic violence behaviors. The cases represented non-random samples of convenience and were gathered from six sources: three prosecutorial agencies in California, one police department in Canada, a security department for a large entertainment corporation in Los Angeles, and the first two authors' case files. All data were archival, and therefore the subjects' permission for inclusion in the study was not required. Forty-four percent of the overall reviewed cases ($n = 1,005$) met our operational definition of stalking behavior: two or more unwanted contacts by a subject toward a target that created a reasonable fear in that target. Twenty-three percent of the entertainment security department cases met our definition of stalking, yielding 248 cases. These cases were defined as celebrity cases because the victims were closely associated with the entertainment corporation and were targeted because of their prominence in the popular media (television, newsprint, and/or cinema). Eleven additional celebrity cases were drawn from the authors' consultation files, six celebrity cases were from two district attorneys' offices, and six from a law enforcement agency ($n = 271$). Four of these cases—a well-known police sergeant, an investigative reporter, a columnist for a large East Coast metropolitan newspaper, and an entertainment corporate executive—were included in this celebrity sample because they were widely known for what they did for a living but were not involved in entertainment as performers. Each case represented a closed, in-process, or open but dormant case of a stalker. Each file was originally created for threat assessment/management purposes, law enforcement investigation, or prosecution. Sampling was not done through a mental health or forensic mental health database. Intraclass correlation coefficient for assignment to one of the four RECON types, including the celebrity group, was .95. Dependent variables were recorded in a 50-variable codebook. Further details concerning methodology can be found in Mohandie et al. (2006).

Results

Demographic Characteristics

Seventy-four percent ($n = 200$) of the celebrity stalkers were male, and 26% ($n = 71$) were female. Their average age was 39 years (range, 12–81). Forty-nine percent ($n = 133$) were Caucasian, 15% ($n = 43$) were African American, 7% ($n = 18$) were Hispanic, 2% ($n = 7$) were Asian, 1% ($n = 2$) were Native

American, 2% ($n = 4$) were Middle Eastern, and 25% ($n = 64$) were unknown by ethnicity.

Forty-six percent were single ($n = 124$), 8% ($n = 21$) were separated or divorced, 9% ($n = 24$) were married, 3% ($n = 7$) were cohabitating, and the relationship status of 34% ($n = 95$) was unknown. Fifty-eight percent ($n = 158$) were identified as heterosexual, 6% ($n = 16$) as homosexual, 1% ($n = 1$) as bisexual, and 35% ($n = 96$) were of unknown sexual orientation.

Twenty-nine percent ($n = 79$) of the celebrity stalkers were unemployed; 7% ($n = 18$) were part-time, contract, or self-employed; 13% ($n = 34$) were full-time employed; 2% ($n = 5$) were underemployed; and the employment status of 40% ($n = 135$) was unknown. Ten percent ($n = 27$) were high school graduates, 8% ($n = 22$) were college graduates, 6% ($n = 15$) did not complete high school, 1% ($n = 3$) received a graduate equivalency degree, 1% ($n = 2$) graduated from a technology school, and the education of 73% ($n = 202$) was unknown.

The criminal history of 39% ($n = 108$) was unknown, whereas 8% ($n = 21$) had a violent criminal history, 21% ($n = 56$) had a nonviolent criminal history, and 32% ($n = 86$) had no criminal history. Seven percent ($n = 18$) had previously been arrested for stalking or harassment, and 51% ($n = 137$) had had no such previous arrests. When a celebrity stalker did harass another target (30%, $n = 80$), it was another celebrity, public figure, or stranger 84% of the time ($n = 67$). Twenty-four percent ($n = 66$) had not harassed anyone else, but whether or not there was harassment of another was unknown in 46% ($n = 125$) of the cases. At the time of the stalking event, 43% ($n = 117$) had no legal status, 8% ($n = 22$) were in custody, 4% ($n = 11$) were in a hospital, 3% ($n = 9$) were in community supervision, 2% ($n = 5$) were legally restrained, and there was no information about 40% ($n = 107$).

Clinical Indicators

Although a psychodiagnostic evaluation was completed in only 10% ($n = 27$) of the sample and was generally not archived, sufficient data were available in the files to suggest the mental status of the majority of subjects. Twenty-seven percent ($n = 73$) were psychotic at the time of the stalking, indicated by documentation of hallucinations, delusions, or both in the case record. Sixty-seven percent ($n = 182$) were not psychotic at the time of the stalking, and in the remaining 6% ($n = 16$), there were insufficient data to determine presence or absence of psychosis. Consistent with these findings, 17% ($n = 46$) had a psychiatric medication history. At least 7% ($n = 20$) of the subjects had attempted suicide, but suicidality (ideation, intent, or attempt) was unknown for 92% ($n = 251$) of the sample.

In 16% ($n = 43$) there was suggestion of a thought-perceptual disorder diagnosis, such as schizophrenia; 5% ($n = 13$) suggested a mood disorder diagnosis, such as major depression; and there was a suspected major mental disorder diagnosis in 31% ($n = 84$) additional cases. Documented evidence precluded a major mental disorder in 41% ($n = 111$) of the cases. Drug use—most often alcohol or stimulants, or both—was evident in 77% ($n = 208$) of the cases, absent in 11% ($n = 30$), and unknown in 12% ($n = 33$) of the cases.

Pursuit Characteristics and Motivations

The stalking began following a precipitating event—the ending of a relationship or rejection—in 14% ($n = 38$) of the cases. There was no such known event in 86% ($n = 231$) of the cases. The duration of the stalking of the celebrity averaged 16 months, with a range of 1 week to 180 months. The modal duration was 1 month. Contact frequency was daily in 15% of the cases ($n = 40$), weekly in 34% ($n = 93$), monthly in 26% ($n = 70$), every 2 to 3 months in 17% ($n = 45$), twice yearly in 5% ($n = 14$), annually in 2% ($n = 5$), and no pattern in 1% ($n = 4$). Seventy-one percent of the stalkers ($n = 192$) used indirect means of contact, such as writing to the celebrity figure or sending him or her a gift. Twenty-three percent ($n = 62$) were proximity based and made a direct approach, and 86% of these approachers ($n = 51$) also used other direct or indirect means of contact. Six percent ($n = 17$) communicated to others at the same time, usually the President, FBI, or another governmental agency. There was escalation in 29% ($n = 77$) of the cases, meaning that the frequency or intensity of the stalking behavior noticeably increased. Frequency was defined as the amount of contact or attempted contact with the celebrity figure over time. Intensity was defined as the level of intrusiveness or disruption the contact behavior could cause; for example, an increase of intensity would be the stalker's change from sending just e-mails to sending both e-mails and telephone calling.

The majority of the stalkers (52%, $n = 141$) sought a relationship (affectional or sexual, or both), and 20% ($n = 53$) sought help from the celebrity victims. Thirteen percent ($n = 36$) wanted to only communicate, whereas 8% ($n = 21$) insulted and 6% ($n = 16$) offered help.

Predicting an Approach

Based upon previous stalking research, 15 variables were selected to attempt to predict a physical approach to the celebrity: police intervention, gender, threats, quality of communication, recidivism, criminal history, mental health diagnosis other than thought disorder, presence of psychosis, age, pursuit patterns, escalation, duration, drug use, target gender, and whether the target was stalked previously. The 62 approach cases and 62 randomly selected nonapproach cases were initially selected for the analysis.

Only 10 of the 15 variables had sufficient data to be included as predictors in a logistic regression. The other five—recidivism, criminal history, age, drug use, and target stalked previously—were individually tested for significant difference between the two groups, and none was found. Because of missing variables within each case, 53 approachers and 57 nonapproachers were finally considered in the logistic regression. A significant result was found (-2 log likelihood, 84.941; df = 22; χ^2 = 67.402; p < .001). The 10 variables entered into the logistic regression were able to correctly classify 83% of the 110 cases as approach or nonapproach, an improvement of 31% over the base classification rate. They accounted for 40% to 60% of the variance in the approach/nonapproach variable:

- Police intervention
- Male gender
- Presence of threats
- Quality of communication
- Mental health diagnosis other than thought disorder
- Psychosis
- Pursuit patterns
- Escalation
- Duration
- Female target

However, only two of these variables, escalation and police intervention, were significant predictors of an approach: (a) if the stalking escalated (frequency, intensity, threatening, or violent), there was a ninefold increase in likelihood of an approach; and (b) if the subject was not reported to the criminal justice system, or there was nothing more than a police report taken and no other police response, the likelihood of an approach decreased by almost half (44%). A priori comparison utilizing χ^2 or ANOVA before entry into the logistic regression indicated that another 3 of the 10 variables were significantly more frequent ($p \leq$ .01) among the approachers—threatening, having a mental health diagnosis other than thought disorder, and a longer duration of stalking—but were not significant *predictors* of an approach.

Victims

One hundred and fifty nine celebrity victims were pursued by 271 stalkers: 93 (58%) women, 49 (31%) men, and 17 (11%) unknown by gender. Forty-one victims (26%) had more than one stalker, ranging from 2 to 20 stalkers. The mode was 2 stalkers and the mean was 3.66 stalkers. Further analysis indicated that most of the multiple stalking cases focused upon female newscasters or female television show actors. Those with more air play, such as television show main characters, were targeted more often. Sympathetic characters or emotionally "softer," more vulnerable characters were also targeted more often, especially by subjects who identified with or wanted to bond with them. When aggressive or strong women were targeted, the themes were more sexual. The two female victims with by far the most stalkers—10 pursuers and 20 pursuers, respectively—were television series main characters who portrayed professional women who were sexually attractive, not in a sexual pair bond, and at times, emotionally vulnerable. The one male victim with the most stalkers, 14, was the CEO of the entertainment corporation.

Threats

Threats were defined as "a written or oral communication that implicitly or explicitly states a wish or intent to damage, injure, or kill the target" (Meloy, 1999, p. 90). Threats were categorized according to manner (direct, indirect, implied, and conditional) and target (property, others, self, loved ones of victim, and victim). An example of a *direct threat* from the study: "I'm going to kill you and your new husband," was sent in a letter after the celebrity victim publicly announced that she had married another public figure. An example of an *indirect threat* from the study: A letter was sent to a television show's producer threatening the show's star that he would "come and find her because she has not returned my calls." An example of a *conditional threat* from the study: An inmate sent a letter to a newscaster telling her that "you need to keep wearing that pink suit and not the red one, it makes you look slutty, or else." An example of an *implied threat* from the study: A stalker sent roses to the home address of a celebrity after only contacting her at work and subsequent to a cease-and-desist letter sent to him. Eighteen percent of the stalkers ($n = 48$) threatened and made a total of 61 threats. There were no threats in 82% ($n = 223$) of the cases. If a threat was made, it was a direct threat half the time (9%). Four percent were indirect, 4% were implied, and 1% was conditional. Among the 61 threats, 30 targeted the celebrity, 11 targeted loved ones of the celebrity, 14 targeted others, 1 targeted property, and 5 targeted the stalker himself. Of the 48 subjects who threatened in any manner, four were violent, with a true-positive rate of 8% and a false-positive rate of 92%. Of the 23 subjects who directly threatened the target, four were violent, with a true-positive rate of 17% and a false-positive rate of 83%. One person was violent who did not threaten, with a false-negative rate of 0.4% and a true-negative rate of 99.6%.

Nature and Frequency of Violence

Violence was defined as an act of intentional physical aggression toward a person (personal violence) or object (property violence). In this sample, there were five *acts* of violence toward persons and one *act* of violence toward property, with an overall frequency of 2%. Four out of five (80%) personally violent stalkers communicated a threat before they attacked. Two of the violent stalkers were female and three were male. The average age was 37.6 years with a range of 31 to 46 years. Four had a psychiatric history with a psychotic diagnosis. Four of the celebrity victims were female and all were arguably younger than the attacker. One of the stalkers had a weapon, a knife, in his possession at the time of arrest. In three of the cases, the attack resulted from a successful breach of the celebrity's security. In no case was there physical injury to the victim requiring medical care.

Case 1 A 40-year-old male stalked a celebrity actress. His criminal history was replete with bizarre public behavior and a prior arrest for criminal threats. He was diagnosed with delusional disorder, erotomanic subtype, by a forensic psychiatrist. He believed the target was in love with him, knew how to reach him, had called him numerous times, and had agreed to marry him. The harassment was on a daily basis for 3 months. He started with letters and then traveled to Los Angeles. He threatened three times, both direct and conditional. He threatened to kidnap her, and then escalated at a local gym, saying he would hurt someone there if they did not get him the actress. He assaulted security when confronted at the entertainment corporation gate while attempting to find her. A large knife and survival equipment were found in his truck. He was eventually released into the custody of Canadian probation and hospitalized. There has been no recidivism to date.

Case 2   A 38-year-old male stalked a female television news reporter. His criminal history indicated both violent and nonviolent crimes, and he was diagnosed with schizophrenia, paranoid type. He delusionally believed that people were cutting out his eyes at night while he slept, poisoning him, and putting listening devices in his head. He pursued the victim for 3 years with telephone calls, then e-mails, then surveillance of her work site, and finally an approach at the television station. He never threatened, and only appeared to be seeking help. The violence occurred when he grabbed her arm while she was leaving work and she escaped his grasp. The subject's mother intervened and he was briefly hospitalized. Following his inpatient stay, he harassed another on-air talent for a few months and then ceased.

Case 3   A 33-year-old male stalked a female investigative television reporter who was frequently on air. The harassment was of a short-term with telephone calls and on-location approaches. He was angry with her, and accused her of scheming and not reporting the truth. There were no formal psychiatric diagnoses. He directly threatened her once during an on-air call, and also implied other threats. The violence occurred when he showed up on location to confront her and she tried to walk away. He grabbed her, and was charged with aggravated assault. The case was dismissed and a restraining order was put in place. There has been no recidivism to date.

Case 4   A 31-year-old female stalked a well-known male police sergeant. She was diagnosed with a major affective disorder and alcohol abuse/dependence. The harassment continued for 2 years for no apparent reason; he had never had contact with the subject through a case or an incident as an officer. The stalking began with third-party contacts and telephone calls, and escalated to following the police officer and appearing at the police station. She made four direct death threats toward the target, and carried out two planned assaults on him and the police station property. She was always intoxicated during the threats and violence. She was eventually charged with criminal threat, criminal harassment, and violation of a restraining order. She was convicted and placed on probation. Four months later, she appeared at the police station on three occasions to ostensibly collect her belongings while the sergeant was working.

Case 5   A 46-year-old female stalked a female celebrity. She was diagnosed with a "thought disorder" but no specific mental disorder. She previously targeted another celebrity she believed was "part of the conspiracy," suggesting some type of paranoid disorder. She had no prior criminal history. She harassed the victim for 5 months with telephone calls, third party contacts, letters, e-mails, and surveillance, and by showing up at the female celebrity's home. She issued at least 10 written or oral threats to the target. The violence occurred when she assaulted a member of the celebrity's family who came out of the house to confront her. She was convicted of criminal threats and stalking following a hospitalization to restore her to competency to stand trial. There has been no recidivism to date.

Meloy (2001, p. 1211) hypothesized, "Private targets appear to be most likely victimized by affective violence. Public targets are most likely to be victimized by predatory violence," following a comparison of violent stalkers across several studies who attacked victims with whom they had a previous relationship, usually a sexually intimate one, and those who near-lethally approached, attacked, or assassinated a public figure (Fein & Vossekuil, 1999). The former violence appeared to be unplanned, emotional, impulsive, and a reaction to a perceived threat; the latter violence appeared to be planned, purposeful, and emotionless, usually carried out over a period of days, weeks, or months. The distinction between affective and predatory violence has a lengthy and substantial scientific basis (Meloy, 2006b).

The violence in this celebrity sample, although quite small, raises questions about the validity of this hypothesis because the majority of the acts of personal violence were affective. The RECON study (Mohandie et al., 2006) in which this sample is embedded, moreover, allows for empirical testing of this hypothesis. Four hundred and sixty-seven acts of personal and property violence occurred in the overall sample of 1,005 cases of stalking. Among the total acts, 337 involved personal violence toward another individual, usually the object of pursuit (Mohandie et al., 2006). The violent acts were classified as either affective (unplanned, emotional, reactive, and impulsive) or predatory (planned, purposeful, emotionless). Table 2.1 illustrates the findings. Type I

Table 2.1. Comparison of affective and predatory violent acts ($n = 337$) among stalkers

Mode of violence	Type I[a]	Type II[b]
Affective*	172 (54%)	4 (19%)
Predatory*	110 (35%)	16 (76%)
Both	26 (8%)	1 (5%)
Unknown	8 (3%)	0 (0%)
Total	316 (100%)	21 (100%)

[a] Violent acts of stalkers who had a previous relationship with the victim.
[b] Violent acts of stalkers who did not.
* $\chi^2 = 13.376, p < .001$.

stalkers are individuals who had a prior relationship with the victim before stalking, either as an intimate or an acquaintance, and represent the first two RECON types. Type II stalkers are individuals who had no prior relationship with the victim before stalking, either a public figure (celebrity) or a private stranger, and represent the second two RECON types. Three hundred and two of the personally violent acts were able to be classified as either affective or predatory (89.6%). The remaining acts of violence contained elements of both ($n = 27$) or there were insufficient data to determine mode of violence ($n = 8$). Comparison across Type I and Type II stalkers who were violent indicates a significantly higher frequency of affective violence among those stalkers who had a prior relationship with the victim than those who did not ($\chi^2 = 13.376, p < .001$).

Recidivism

The criminal justice system (law enforcement and/or prosecution) was involved in 58 cases (21%). Criminal charges were filed in 23 cases (9%), usually crimes of stalking or assault. The most common sanction following the criminal litigation was hospitalization ($n = 8$, 35%). The reoffense rate among those stalkers of celebrities when there was criminal justice involvement was 50%. The mean time to reoffense was 7.9 months, with a range of 1 day to 6 years.

Comparison to Stalkers of Private Strangers

Mohandie et al. (2006) identified a fourth group of stalkers who pursued strangers not in the public eye ($n = 103$). This group provides a comparative context for the stalkers of celebrities because the absence of a prior relationship with the victim between the groups does not differ, yet the degree to which the victim became known to the stalker through the public media does. Table 2.2 lists selective variables that significantly differ between these two groups of stalkers.

Discussion

Stalkers of celebrity figures are the sensation of the popular media, particularly if they have threatened or been violent toward the object of their pursuit. Such anecdotal cases, however, often skew the perspective of the lay person and the professional because a few cases are generalized to all stalkers of celebrities, and scientific research has lagged far behind the conveyed "wisdom" of television experts. Ironically, there appears to be a strong negative correlation between an expert's energy invested in seeking the television limelight as an "entertainment profiler" and the number of scientific publications in the purported area of special knowledge claimed by the same expert.

This study of those who stalk celebrities both confirms and disconfirms certain areas of conventional beliefs. The vast majority of the offenders are

Table 2.2. Significant differences between stalkers of public figures (celebrities) (n = 271) and stalkers of private strangers (n = 103) (Mohandie et al., 2006)

Variable	Public figure (celebrity) (%)	Private stranger (%)
Gender*		
Male	74	85
Female	26	15
Any drug use**	77	38
Any mental disorder*	52	38
Daily contact**	15	44
Proximity-based contact**	23	80
Precipitating event**	14	43
Threats**	18	53
Violence**	2	38
Weapons possession/use**	3	12
Criminal justice involvement**	22	78

* $p < .01$, ** $p < .001$; all comparisons by either χ^2 or ANOVA.

men, although one in four are women, a higher proportion than is seen in most stalking samples (Spitzberg, 2007). Although the average age is comparable to other stalkers—most pursuits occur in the fourth decade of life—it is notable that those who homicidally attack celebrities in the United States, although few and far between, are often males in their early twenties. Robert Bardo, Mark Chapman, John Hinckley Jr., Sirhan Sirhan, and Lee Harvey Oswald were all young men when they lethally or near-lethally approached their targets.[2] The testosterone of the young male should be seriously taken into account when considering the likelihood of an extremely aggressive act toward a celebrity target (Fixated Research Group, 2006; Meloy et al., 2004). However, contemporary attacks on western European politicians (James et al., 2007) and historical attacks on the British Royal Family (James et al., in press) evidence a greater variability in the age of the attackers.

The inability of those who stalk celebrities to establish a stable history of both work and love is also apparent in the data. The absence of a history of stable attachments to other objects such as a sexual intimate or even a career is common among stalkers (Mullen, Pathé, & Purcell, 2000; Mullen et al., 2008), and suggests that a fantasized relationship with the celebrity figure—what Meloy (1999) termed a "narcissistic linking fantasy" in which one consciously imagines a special and idealized relationship with another—compensates for the actuality of a rather blighted personal life. "Dreams of love and fateful encounters" (Person, 1988) may come to preoccupy the stalker, negatively impacting his ability and desire to improve his lot in life and furthering his retreat into fantasy.

Although stalkers of celebrities have less frequent criminal histories than other groups of stalkers (Mohandie et al., 2006), almost 1 out of 10 had a violent criminal history, and twice this number had a nonviolent criminal history. It was also common for these men to stalk or harass another target, either historically or contemporaneously, and one out of five of the subjects were legally constrained in some fashion before or during their stalking. The obvious motivation of such stalkers, even if judged to be benign at the time, should not dissuade the threat assessor from a thorough investigation of the criminal background of the subject of concern. A propensity for habitual aggression may be masked by an initially loving and idealizing approach to the celebrity.

Major mental disorder emerged in our study as a clinical problem for the majority of the subjects, a finding which is similar to the presence of mental disorder in other public figure studies (Meloy et al., 2004), and most recently, in a large study of those who fixate on the British Royal Family (Fixated Research Group, 2006), wherein more than 80% of the subjects showed evidence of serious mental illness. One out of four of our subjects were psychotic at the time of their stalking. Although major mental disorder may reduce the risk of violence among stalkers as a whole (Mohandie et al., 2006)—parenthetically, this general finding may not be true when psychiatric disorder interacts with other violence risk variables (Rosenfeld & Lewis, 2005)—the threat assessment task is to determine the exact relationship between the symptoms of major mental disorder and the celebrity stalking behavior in any one particular case. For example, delusional beliefs concerning the relationship between the stalker and his celebrity object may bring a determination and resolve to his pursuit that defeats any intervention other than arrest and eventual forensic hospitalization. On the other hand, belief that one is being persecuted by the celebrity—fortunately, an unusual motivation (see also Dietz et al., 1991; Fixated Research Group, 2006)—may compel an act of paranoid violence that is not suggested at all by the subject's nonviolent history.

The pervasiveness of mental disorder in this sample, as well as other public figure samples that involve pursuit of politicians, celebrities, and royalty, bodes well for treatment interventions that address the needs of the mentally ill in the larger community, and the symptoms of those charged with the stalking of a celebrity. Most major mental disorders are currently treatable with medications if diagnosis is accurate and compliance can be monitored, the latter ensured through various forms of involuntary outpatient treatment.

A most unusual finding in this study is the absence of a precipitating event in the life of the subject in the months preceding the onset of stalking. Even when compared to stalkers of strangers who are not public figures (see Table 2.2), the ending of a relationship or rejection did not play a large role in precipitating these pursuits. Such an acute disruption, identified in other stalking research (Kienlen, Birmingham, Solberg, O'Regan, & Meloy, 1997), may be supplanted by a more chronic deterioration in social and emotional functioning among stalkers of public figures, including celebrities:

> Many subjects evidenced a downward spiral in their lives in the months or year before their approach or attack, usually a combination of social failure and personal vulnerability to chronic anger, depression, or psychosis. These failures and the subject's poor adaptation to them often marked a decision point wherein the public figure was identified as an object of salvation or persecution, and a plan was born to contact, approach, or attack the public figure.
>
> Meloy et al., 2004, p. 1092

Drug abuse is endemic in this sample and should be treated as a dynamic risk factor for violence when coupled with the presence of a major mental disorder (Monahan et al., 2001; see Table 2.2). The typical drugs of concern are alcohol and stimulants, which may physiologically fuel stalking behavior given their serotonergic antagonism and their dopaminergic agonism, respectively (Meloy & Fisher, 2005).

The pursuit characteristics of this sample are similar to those of other stalking studies. A recent meta-analysis found the duration of stalking to average 22 months (Spitzberg, 2007), compared with 16 months among the stalkers of celebrities. Contact is frequent, but notable is the modal duration of stalking, which was 1 month. Teasing out the mean from the mode in stalking duration has never been done in other studies, and it underscores the degree to which extraordinarily long stalking cases can skew the data if only the average is computed. Long-duration stalking cases may also be an artifact of a sample, reflecting data gathered immediately subsequent to the criminalization of stalking (Zona, Sharma, & Lane, 1993). The Zona sample likely had a heavy loading of cases that predated antistalking legislation and specialized techniques for intervention, thus artificially inflating the apparent duration of obsessions and pursuit behavior. Our data suggest that most celebrity cases will begin with a high frequency of indirect approaches, and then will be done within a month for a variety of reasons not fully understood.

The data further confirm that the motivation for stalkers of celebrities is usually sexual, affectional, or help seeking. Dietz et al. (1991) had similar findings in their 20-year-old data set of 214 subjects who wrote letters to celebrities: Most were motivated by a desire for face-to-face contact, and not violence. Among those who approach members of the British Royal Family, the most prominent members being celebrities in their own right, such as Queen Elizabeth and Prince William, one third of the approachers were motivated by a desire for friendship (Fixated Research Group, 2006). These findings, however, do not preclude the fact that motivations can suddenly change, particularly when faced with rejection by the celebrity or his or her representative, often security personnel. In such cases, rejection can suddenly usher in feelings of humiliation, which in turn can quickly become rage toward the object of desire or displaced onto his or her protector (Meloy, 1998).

Although most stalkers in our sample did not attempt to approach the celebrity, one out of four did. We were able to correctly classify 83% of the subjects who approached and did not approach. Two variables significantly predicted an approach in the logistic regression—police intervention and escalation—and the most important was the escalation of the stalking over time, which increased the risk of an approach ninefold. Physical approach is commonly used as an analog for risk of violence, because the latter is rare in public figure stalking, and physical proximity is usually necessary for a violent act toward a public figure.

Victims of these stalkers were usually women, consonant with a meta-analysis across 58 studies of stalking victims that indicated that 60% to 80% of victims are females (Spitzberg, 2007). Celebrity status does not appear to influence the fact that stalking is largely a crime against women perpetrated by men. Multiple stalkers hounded one out of four victims, and this study gives for the first time a glimpse of some of the quantitative and qualitative characteristics among female celebrity victims that may increase the risk of stalking:

a. The more frequent the appearance in the media, the greater the likelihood of stalking. This was most pronounced among female newscasters or female television show actors. This finding was also recently reported in the study of contemporary approachers of the British Royal Family (Fixated Research Group, 2006): the more frequent the public appearance, or the more publicized the event, the greater the likelihood of a subsequent pursuit.

b. A quartet of personality characteristics or fictional fact patterns that may almost guarantee celebrity stalking is a television series female actor who portrays a professional woman who is sexually attractive, not in a sexual pair bond, and at times, emotionally vulnerable. Portrayed aggressiveness by a female actor seems to correlate with increased sexual interest by a male stalker.

Although female television and film actors fictionally portray such personal characteristics in contrast to female newscasters, the latter exercise behaviors in their daily appearances that may uniquely increase the risk of stalking: They have direct eye contact with the viewer; they want to establish a one-on-one relationship with the viewer and stimulate pleasant feelings so that he or she watches the next night; they *are not* portraying a fictional character; and they are increasingly encouraged to use their personalities and reveal bits of personal data to stimulate an affectional connection with the audience and build market share. All these behaviors are quite benign when experienced by the mentally healthy viewer. However, for the lone (and likely lonely) male viewer with a history of failed relationships, a strong sense of entitlement, and difficulty discriminating between reality and fantasy, such an invitation, although communicated electronically *and not meant specifically for him*, can become a compulsion to pursue, as both erotic feelings and affectional longings are stirred amidst ideas of reference and delusions of grandeur.

The threat data in this study confirm general findings from other threat studies (Meloy, 1998, 2001) and specific findings from threats toward public figures: most stalkers who threaten do not act on their threats; and most threats, if made, are direct threats toward the object of pursuit. The public figure threat data, of which there is very little (Dietz et al., 1991; Fein & Vossekuil, 1999; Fixated Research Group, 2006; James et al., 2007; Meloy et al., 2004; Scalora et al., 2002), also indicate that the vast majority of public figure approachers and stalkers *do not directly threaten their target*. This finding is in striking contrast to those of studies of prior sexually intimate and acquaintance stalkers that indicate that the vast majority of subjects *do directly threaten their target* (Mohandie et al., 2006; Meloy, 2001). In this celebrity study, there were no threats in 82% of the cases. However, if a direct threat was made to the target, the true positive rate doubled, from 8% to 17%. Another surprising finding, particularly when compared to the Fein and Vossekuil (1999) data, was that four out of the five violent stalkers in this study did communicate a direct threat before they attacked the object of pursuit. We are, however, comparing apples and oranges when we consider mode of violence. The Fein and Vossekuil (1999) data, which found that less than 10% of their sample of attackers and assassins of public figures communicated a threat to the target or law enforcement beforehand, were acts of predatory violence: planned, purposeful, and carried out over days, weeks, or months. Most of the acts of violence toward our celebrity figures were affective: emotional, reactive, unplanned, and impulsive. This contrasting pattern of association in two public figure data sets—acts of predatory violence correlate with no direct threats and acts of affective violence correlate with direct threats—lends further empirical support to one aspect of Meloy's (2001) hypothesis but challenges another one: acts of violence toward public figures are all predatory rather than affective.

The findings concerning mode of violence question Meloy's (2001) assertion that "public figure" stalkers engage in predatory violence, while "private figure" stalkers engage in affective violence. Table 2.1 indicates that this formulation was both too simplistic and based upon an incorrect categorization. The reality, as usual, is much more complex. If stalkers are classified as pursuing someone with whom they had a prior relationship (sexual intimate or acquaintance) or someone they did not (public figure or private stranger) (Mohandie et al., 2006), then the data suggest a refinement in formulation: affective violence toward person and property is significantly more likely if there has been a prior relationship between the stalker and his victim, while predatory violence is significantly more likely if there has been no prior relationship between the stalker and his victim, *whether a public figure or not*. We would also be remiss to not underscore the remarkable disparity between frequency of violence toward these celebrity figures (2%) and frequency of violence toward prior sexual intimates (>50%) in a number of published studies (Mohandie et al., 2006). This is likely a result of both heightened security on the part of celebrities and the intensified emotion that will fuel affective violence toward a person who was once intimately known to the stalker, and now has rejected him.

Affective violence toward public figures who are *celebrities* may also be more likely when compared to public figures who are *politicians* because of the greater likelihood of a fantasized sexual or affectional relationship with the former type of target: perceived rejection by celebrity figures may carry a more intense emotional charge when an ideal relationship has been nurtured in fantasy, whereas perceived rejection by political figures who are being pursued for other reasons, such as beneficence, does not carry the risk of such an intense emotional reactivity.

The violence in our study was rare (2%), and when it occurred, was likely to be an affective attack without a weapon by a psychotic male stalker in his fourth decade of life targeting a younger female celebrity whose personal security had been breached. There was no physical injury requiring medical care; however, the psychological or emotional trauma was unknown. Anecdotal data from the authors' files suggest that celebrity victims of stalking will suffer the same degree of depression, anxiety, and traumatic symptoms that other members of the public do when stalked (Spitzberg, 2007), especially if they are fully apprised of the stalking events by their security personnel or are personally attacked. The violence typically followed a pattern of multiple and various means of contact and escalation, and the most likely victims of attack if the celebrity could not be accessed were members of his or her private security detail.

Half of this large sample of stalkers of celebrities went on to stalk again. The latency period was 8 months. This finding is virtually identical to the recidivism rate (49%) of a sample of stalkers in New York City (Rosenfeld, 2003), and underscores the chronicity of this behavior. The substrate of severe mental disorder in these celebrity stalkers may be the same pathology of "preoccupied" attachment found in other stalking studies (Meloy, 2007) wherein an intense, yet tumultuous bond is quickly formed with an initially idealized object. Among celebrity stalkers, this pathology of attachment, which is biologically rooted (Bowlby, 1958), is all the more remarkable *because it is solely based in fantasy* and there is no actual relationship with the object of desire, nor will there ever be. One stalker of a well-known female celebrity was asked at the end of his day-long forensic evaluation if he had any questions for the examiner. He politely requested that the examiner go visit the celebrity after he finished, administer the same psychological tests, and see if they matched as a couple. This same individual, living alone in his Midwestern apartment and severely mentally ill, would receive an occasional phone call late at night and be greeted with silence on the other end of the line. He was convinced that his celebrity love, the object of his heart's desire, was communicating with him in silence because her mother did not want them to actually speak. He eventually pursued her to Los Angeles after sending a slew of gifts, including sexual paraphernalia, and was arrested for stalking on his second approach to her property. He was diagnosed with delusional disorder, with both erotomanic and grandiose features, and personality disorder not otherwise specified with narcissistic, histrionic, compulsive, schizotypal, and dependent features. He was found legally insane, and committed to a forensic hospital until he was released in February 2008.

Limitations and Conclusions

This is an archival study subject to several limitations. Selection bias is present in the nonrandom sample of convenience utilized, and limits the generalizability of our findings because virtually all the subjects were drawn from the security department of one large entertainment corporation. Observation bias may be present in the differential recall and data-gathering strategies among investigators in the security department over time. Nonresponse bias is evident in the relatively large proportion of unknown data, such as relationship status, employment status, and education. Inferential statistics were kept to a minimum to reduce the influence of confounding variables unknown to the researchers.

This is the second study of those who stalk celebrities to be published in the scientific literature (Dietz et al., 1991, being the first). The independent variable in the Dietz study was threatening or otherwise inappropriate communications. The independent variable in our study was stalking. Although other databases of stalkers of celebrities exist, they are considered proprietary information by those who own them, and therefore have not yet contributed to, or been scrutinized by, the scientific community. Perhaps this will change and a fuller understanding of those who stalk celebrities will be known. As the great 19th century American novelist Nathanial Hawthorne wrote in *Fanshawe*, "If his inmost heart could have been laid open, there would have been discovered that dream of undying fame; which, dream as it is, is more powerful than a thousand realities" (Hawthorne, 1983).

Notes

1. Jackson stabbed Teresa Saldana multiple times in 1982 and was convicted of attempted murder. Bardo shot and killed Rebecca Shaeffer in 1989 and was convicted of murder. Both men used a private detective agency to locate their victims and attacked them at home. In subsequent forensic examinations, both men were found to have paranoid schizophrenia (Saunders, 1998).
2. Although both John and Robert Kennedy were politicians, we believe that both men had achieved celebrity status at the time of their assassinations.

References

Bowlby, J. (1958). The nature of the child's tie to his mother. *International Journal of Psychoanalysis, 39*, 350–373.

Dietz, P. E., Matthews, D., Van Duyne, C., Martell, D., Parry, C., Stewart, T., et al. (1991). Threatening and otherwise inappropriate letters to Hollywood celebrities. *Journal of Forensic Sciences, 36*, 185–209.

Fein, R., & Vossekuil, B. (1999). Assassination in the United States: An operational study of recent assassins, attackers, and near-lethal approaches. *Journal of Forensic Sciences, 44*, 321–333.

Fixated Research Group (2006). *Inappropriate communications, approaches, and attacks on the British Royal Family.* London: The Home Office.

Hawthorne, N. (1983). *Collected works.* New York: Penguin Putnam.

James, D., Mullen, P., Meloy, J. R., Pathé, M., Farnham, F., Preston, L., et al. (2007). The role of mental disorder in attacks on European politicians 1990–2004. *Acta Psychiatrica Scandinavica, 116,* 334–344.

James, D., Mullen, P., Pathé, M., Meloy, J. R., Farnham, F., Preston, L., et al. (in press). Attacks on the British Royal Family: The role of psychotic illness. *Journal of the American Academy of Psychiatry and the Law.*

Kienlen, K., Birmingham, D., Solberg, K., O'Regan, J., & Meloy, J. R. (1997). A comparative study of psychotic and nonpsychotic stalking. *Journal of the American Academy of Psychiatry and the Law, 25,* 317–334.

Leets, L., de Becker, G., & Giles, H. (1995). Fans: Exploring expressed motivations for contacting celebrities. *Journal of Language and Social Psychology, 14,* 102–123.

McCutcheon, L., Lange, R., & Houran, J. (2002). Conceptualization and measurement of celebrity worship. *British Journal of Psychology, 93,* 67–87.

Meloy, J. R. (Ed.) (1998). *The psychology of stalking: Clinical and forensic perspectives.* San Diego: Academic Press.

Meloy, J. R. (1999). Stalking: An old behavior, a new crime. *Psychiatric Clinics of North America, 22,* 85–99.

Meloy, J. R. (2001). Communicated threats and violence toward public and private targets: Discerning differences among those who stalk and attack. *Journal of Forensic Sciences, 46,* 1211–1213.

Meloy, J. R. (2006a). *The scientific pursuit of stalking.* San Diego: Specialized Training Services.

Meloy, J. R. (2006b). The empirical basis and forensic application of affective and predatory violence. *Australian and New Zealand Journal of Psychiatry, 40,* 539–547.

Meloy, J. R. (2007). Stalking: The state of the science. *Criminal Behavior and Mental Health, 17,* 1–7.

Meloy, J. R., & Fisher, H. (2005). Some thoughts on the neurobiology of stalking. *Journal of Forensic Sciences, 50,* 1472–1480.

Meloy, J. R., James, D., Farnham, F., Mullen, P., Pathé, M., Darnley, B., et al. (2004). A research review of public figure threats, approaches, attacks, and assassinations in the United States. *Journal of Forensic Sciences, 49,* 1086–1093.

Mohandie, K., Meloy, J. R., McGowan, M., & Williams, J. (2006). The RECON typology of stalking: Reliability and validity based upon a large sample of North American stalkers. *Journal of Forensic Sciences, 51,* 147–155.

Monahan, J., Steadman, H., Silver, E., Appelbaum, P., Robbins, P., Mulvey, E., et al. (2001). *Rethinking risk assessment: The MacArthur study of mental disorder and violence.* New York: Oxford University Press.

Mullen, P., Pathé, M., & Purcell, R. (2000). *Stalkers and their victims.* London: Cambridge University Press.

Mullen, P., Pathé, M., & Purcell, R. (2008). *Stalkers and their victims* (2nd ed.). London: Cambridge University Press.

Person, E. (1988). *Dreams of love and fateful encounters: The power of romantic passion.* New York: Norton.

Rosenfeld, B. (2003). Recidivisim in stalking and obsessional harassment. *Law and Human Behavior, 27,* 251–265.

Rosenfeld, B., & Lewis, C. (2005). Assessing violence risk in stalking cases: A regression tree approach. *Law and Human Behavior, 29,* 343–357.

Saunders, R. (1998). The legal perspective on stalking. In J. R. Meloy (Ed.), *The psychology of stalking: Clinical and forensic perspectives* (pp. 25–49). San Diego: Academic Press.

Scalora, M., Baumgartner, J., Callaway, D., Zimmerman, W., Hatch-Maillette, M. A., Covell, C. N., et al. (2002). An epidemiological assessment of problematic contacts to members of Congress. *Journal of Forensic Sciences, 47,* 1360–1364.

Schlesinger, L. B. (2006). Celebrity stalking, homicide, and suicide: A psychological autopsy. *International Journal of Offender Therapy and Comparative Criminology, 50,* 39–46.

Spitzberg, B. (2007). The state of the art of stalking: Taking stock of the emerging literature. *Aggression and Violent Behavior, 12,* 64–86.

Zona, M., Sharma, K., & Lane, J. (1993). A comparative study of erotomanic and obsessional subjects in a forensic sample. *Journal of Forensic Sciences, 38,* 894–903.

3

The Role of Psychotic Illnesses in Attacks on Public Figures

Paul E. Mullen, David V. James, J. Reid Meloy,
Michele T. Pathé, Frank R. Farnham,
Lulu Preston, and Brian Darnley

Maclean must be a madman,
Which is obvious to be seen,
Or else he wouldn't have tried to shoot
Our most beloved Queen
> *From William McGonagall's poem "Attempted*
> *Assassination of the Queen"*

It is worth being shot at—to see how much one is loved
> *Queen Victoria in a letter to her oldest daughter*
> *Kronberg letters, March 6, 1882*

The importance accorded to the role of mental illness as a factor in those who attack politicians and heads of state has varied widely over time. In the 19th century, at least in the English-speaking world, there was what amounted to a presumption that those who attacked heads of state, or other political leaders, were insane. William Gladstone (1809–1898), the British prime minister, reassured Queen Victoria, after yet another attack on her person, that whereas foreign assassins had political motives, in England, those who attempted such assassinations were all madmen (Longford, 1987, p. 446). Behind Gladstone's assurance to his Queen is not just an opinion about the state of mind of would-be assassins, but political hubris. Implicit in Gladstone's dictum is a boast about the perfection of British democracy and the nature of the constitutional monarchy. Gladstone, like most of his contemporaries in England, saw in Britain's political system the rational expression of the interests of the nation and people, with elections providing sufficient checks and balances for any reasonable citizen. Assassinations could make political sense only in countries where power was concentrated in the hands of single individuals who were not made subject to the constraints of a property-owning democracy. Thus, in Britain, only the mad could find reason, or the lack of reason, to enter on a project of political change through the mechanism of assassination. Naturally, the rest of the world, including Russia, the Austro-Hungarian Empire, and above all France, not being blessed with the English language and British institutions, was plagued by political assassinations.

The view that those who attempted to assassinate leaders were probably insane should not be confused with a liberal or forgiving attitude to those who committed such acts. The public furor around the acquittal on the grounds of insanity of Daniel McNaughton, who, in failing to assassinate British Prime Minister Robert Peel killed his private secretary, was not about whether McNaughton was mad, but about what should happen to the "merciless mad," to use the words of the *London Times* (West & Walk, 1977). The so-called McNaughton rules governing legal insanity were intended to limit the exculpatory effects of having a mental illness. The McNaughton rules began the separation of the legal discourse around responsibility and punishability from the psychiatric discourse around psychosis and competencies, a separation that plagues forensic mental health to this day, and as will be noted later in this chapter, a separation that continues to confound and confuse even the interpretation of contemporary data about what characterizes those who attack public figures, and how best to reduce the risks of such attacks.

A not dissimilar view about the relationship between assassination and mental illness appeared to hold sway early in the 19th century in Washington, where *The Intelligencer* of April 21, 1835, noted, "it is an obvious fact that this city being the centre of government, is liable to be visited by more than its proportion of insane persons" (quoted in Hoffman, 1943). In the United States, such confidence would have been dented if not shattered by the assassination of President Lincoln, which was politically motivated, and accomplished by a man who, whatever he might have been, was no lunatic, though perhaps in this instance Gladstone might have defended his thesis by pointing out that the Civil War had reflected a temporary breakdown in the broad consensus necessary for the functioning of a democracy and had *de facto* created in the figure of Lincoln an apparent source of power and influence unresponsive at least to a significant section of the body politic.

The 19th century and early 20th century commentators could point the finger at the mad, not just as would-be assassins, but as the pests and intruders who plagued the powerful, in part because it was generally accepted that psychotic people were not just troublesome and ungovernable, but violent. From the 1970s until relatively recently, such assumptions about the behavior of the seriously mentally ill were replaced, at least in professional circles, by an insistence that there was no substantial connection between having a mental illness and behaving in a criminal, let alone seriously violent, manner (Cohen, 1980; Hafner & Böker, 1982; Monahan, 1981; Rappeport & Lassen, 1965). Over the same period in the democracies of the West, the Panglossian confidence that all was for the best in the best of all possible worlds was challenged by the increasing alienation and restiveness of minority groups within the wider community. The paradigm for the would-be assassin shifted from the psychotic pursuing his delusional agenda to the angry social misfit hunting both those he held responsible for his plight, and for personal fame (Clarke, 1982). Today, the model projecting the alienated predator as archetypal assassin may in its turn be replaced by new models. The emerging constructions of the assassin incorporate both the current preoccupations with the terrorist threat and the emerging knowledge both about stalking behaviors and about predatory violence (Meloy, James, et al., 2004; Phillips, 2006). A reassessment of the role of severe psychopathology in driving attacks on prominent people may foster a second model to understand the potential assassin. Any new conceptualizations will need to be informed by recent systematic research, but equally importantly also by a fresh reading of existing data.

The cultural context has also shifted over recent years. The understandable preoccupation with the terrorist threat has redrawn the maps that guide not just the personal protection of prominent people, but security and protection at every level. In this chapter, we will not be concerned directly with this aspect of the emerging constructions of the assassin. We will focus on what we believe should be a reemergence of an interest in the role of mental disorder as a key both to understanding and potentially to preventing attacks on political leaders and other prominent people.

The association between violent behavior and psychotic disorders, particularly those in the schizophrenic spectrum, is now well established by systematic studies (e.g., Eronen, Tiihonen, & Hakola, 1996; Hodgins, Mednick, Brennar, Schulsinger, & Engberg, 1996; Mullen, 2006; Schanda et al., 2004; Swanson, Holzer, Ganju, & Jono, 1990; Taylor & Gunn, 1984a, 1984b; Tiihonen, Isohanni, Rasanen, Koiranen, & Moring, 1997; Wallace, Mullen, & Burgess, 2004). Whether we like it or not, 5% to 10% of homicides and serious crimes of violence are committed by the 0.4% to 0.7% of the population with a schizophrenic syndrome. There is no prior reason why they should not also contribute disproportionately to attacks on heads of state and political leaders. In our view, there are good reasons to believe that their contribution to this area of violence may be particularly marked.

This chapter will consider from an historical and empirical perspective attacks on British Royalty and U.S. Presidents, augmented with information from attacks on European politicians. The implications of the role of psychotic illnesses will be discussed not just for protecting potential victims, but equally importantly for assisting those driven by their psychopathology toward acts that, whatever else they may accomplish, will ruin their own lives and devastate those who care about them.

Attacks on the British Royal Family

Attacks on members of the British Royal Family are, fortunately, rare events. When such attacks occur, they occasion intense public interest and are often the subject not just of careful forensic scrutiny but of subsequent academic study. Given, however, the low frequency of attacks on members of the Royal Family, it is necessary to sample from a lengthy period to collect a sufficiently large number of cases for meaningful study. The potential disadvantages of doing so are the possibilities that the different circumstances of different ages may have produced different phenomena in terms of attack, or that the information available on attacks at different times may be distorted by the lens of contemporary understanding (or incomplete understanding) of psychological processes. It is therefore advisable to consider aspects of the period in which each attack occurred, as well as the details of the attacks themselves.

Between 1778 and 1994, 23 attacks on the life or safety of the monarch are known (James et al., in press).

Details of all known incidents before the reign of Queen Elizabeth II have been explored in a number of studies employing primary materials, including court records, government papers, the archives of lunatic asylums, newspapers of the day, and the published and unpublished letters of politicians and Royal Family members from various libraries and archives (Eigen, 1995; Keeton, 1961; Macalpine & Hunter, 1969; Poole, 2000; Walker, 1968; West & Walk, 1977; and various editions of the Newgate Calendar). Records of attacks and assaults on the current Queen and members of her family were studied by James and colleagues (Fixated Research Group, 2006) by examining over 8,000 files held by the Royalty Protection Police, which cover the period from the early 1970s until July 2003.

Attack ($n = 23$) was taken as meaning any hostile act against the person of a Royal Family member involving a weapon or the making of physical contact. Alarming intrusions, such as Michael Fagan's appearance in the Queen's bedroom in 1982 and Darryl Marcus's intrusion on the Queen's floor of Buckingham Palace in 1992, do not qualify as attacks. Not included are group events, such as the stoning of George III's coach in London in 1795, the attempted storming of the Princess of Wales' convoy by antinuclear protesters in Barrow-in-Furness in 1992, or the rushing of the royal coach at the inauguration of the Scottish Parliament and during the Chinese state visit, both in 1999. Events that involved unwelcome, but nonhostile physical contact, such as model Jane Priest's encounter with Prince Charles in the Australian surf in 1979, were also excluded. Attack is not synonymous with homicidal intent, and indeed the exact nature of the intent was often difficult to infer from the events.

It is unlikely that all relevant incidents were captured, although all major incidents in the public domain were included. Six of the attacks were against

George III, one against William IV, eight against Queen Victoria, one against her son Prince Alfred, one against Edward VIII, three against Elizabeth II, one against Prince Charles, one against Princess Anne, and one against Princess Diana. In other words, 83% involved the reigning monarch, 13% the monarch's children, and the remaining case the spouse of the heir to the throne. No attacks occurred in royal residences. Thirteen cases (57%) occurred while the victims were in transit; riding in, or alighting from, carriages or cars; or as in one case (Edward VIII), riding through a royal park on horseback. Six cases (26%) occurred at public royal events (including those abroad), two others occurred at the theater, and one at the races. The location of one attack is not recorded. Fifteen attacks occurred in London, three elsewhere in the United Kingdom, and the remainder in the Antipodes (three in New Zealand and two in Australia).

Thirteen cases (57%) involved firearms, all except one being a handgun. Of the 12 handguns, six (50%) were not loaded with live ammunition. Three cases involved knives, three involved stones, and one a brass-headed walking cane. The remaining three cases involved no potential for serious injury. These concerned the wet T-shirt thrown at the Queen by a female Maori demonstrator in New Zealand in 1990, the aerosol sprayed on Prince Charles's face by a 58-year-old antimonarchist Croatian in Auckland in 1994, and the indecent assault on Princess Diana by a 57-year-old schizophrenic man in the United Kingdom in 1989 who grabbed for her breasts.

Only two attacks resulted in serious injury, in one case to a Royal family member and, in the other, to those trying to protect them. Prince Alfred was shot in the side at a Grand Charity Picnic in the Sydney suburb of Clontarf in 1864, but survived. In Ian Ball's attempted kidnap of Princess Anne in the Mall in 1974, four people were shot and seriously injured: Princess Anne's personal protection officer, her chauffeur, a taxi passenger, and a policeman on protection duty nearby. Minor injuries were sustained by King William IV when he was hit full on the forehead by a large flint thrown by Dennis Collins, a destitute, one-legged, septuagenarian ex-sailor, at Ascot Races in 1832. Queen Victoria received a black eye and bruise to the head when hit with a brass-headed walking cane by Robert Pate, a former cavalry officer, while riding in her carriage in 1850. The remaining 19 attacks did not lead to any form of physical injury.

Eighty-three percent of the attackers were men. Seven cases (30%) involved teenaged boys. Only two attackers were known to be married.

The six cases with handguns that did not contain live ammunition originated from the Victorian era and the last part of the 20th century, and they all involved young men. Sergeant, before firing blanks at the Queen during the Trooping of the Colour in 1981, had tried to get hold of real bullets. At his trial, it was said that he conducted a fantasy assassination only because he did not have the means to conduct a real one. The other cases are unlikely to have involved any desire to kill. Francis loaded his gun only with powder when he shot at Queen Victoria in her carriage in 1842. He made two attempts on consecutive days, the gun not firing on the first occasion. It seems likely that he would have had the means to load his gun with substances in addition to powder, had he chosen to do so. Bean, in imitating Francis on the day after he was reprieved, knew that the old flintlock that he had filled with powder, wadding, and a piece of clay pipe would not go off because the flint was covered with paper. Hamilton, the Irish youth who fired his landlady's pistol at the Queen's carriage on Constitution Hill in 1849, seems only to have wanted to create a stir. O'Connor's intention outside Buckingham Palace in 1872 was said to be to frighten the Queen into signing a petition, rather than harm her. David Kang's rushing at Prince Charles while firing a starter pistol in Sydney in January 1994 appears to have been done for publicity for the cause of Cambodian refugees and in the belief that he would be shot.

In summary, most attackers cannot be considered to have had murderous motives, based on their stated intentions and nonlethal weapons choices.

It is probable from the available evidence that 15 (65%) of the attackers suffered from mental disorders. Seven out of the 23 attackers were not subject to any form of psychiatric assessment that might have provided such evidence, and little information is known about several of the cases. Sufficient information is available to divide the cases as follows.

1. Psychotic illness

Eleven of the 23 cases (48%) were clearly suffering from psychotic illnesses. There is ample evidence in the public record of their delusional beliefs. The obviously deluded include six attackers of George III, three attackers of Queen Victoria, and two of the recent attackers, Ian Ball and Alfred Adcock, both of whom suffered from schizophrenia.

The young man who shot at Queen Elizabeth II at the Trooping the Colour in 1981 was admitted to a psychiatric hospital with a psychotic illness several years after the incident, which must raise some question over his state of mind when he launched the attack. Similarly, the transfer of the adolescent who attacked the Queen in New Zealand in 1986 to a secure psychiatric hospital some months after his initial imprisonment may also raise a question over his mental state at the time of the attack. Neither of these two young men, however, has been counted among the 11 clearly suffering from a psychotic illness.

Although Oxford was found insane after his attack on Queen Victoria in 1840, review of the evidence presented at court, together with that of his progress at Broadmoor Hospital and his eventual successful career in Melbourne, casts doubt on the diagnosis of a psychotic illness and the court's finding of insanity. He has also not been counted among the 11 psychotic cases.

2. Depressive illness

Two of the attackers are known to have been severely depressed when they launched their attacks. The exact nature of the depression and the appropriate diagnosis among a number of depressive disorders is unknown.

3. Possible mental illness

O'Farrell, who shot Queen Victoria's son Alfred in 1868, had a history suggestive of mental illness, but no adequate records of his evaluation, if any were attempted, survived. The possibility of mental illness in two of the adolescent attackers has already been noted.

4. Psychopathy and predatory violence

The histories of most of the would-be assassins are not sufficiently detailed or appropriately focused to clearly identify psychopathic traits. Oxford certainly showed features before and after his attack on Queen Victoria to suggest the manipulative propensities, pathological lying, and more than his fair share of callousness. Similarly, the other members of the adolescent group of would-be regicides can be regarded as having marked psychopathic traits. Without more details, particularly of the earlier cases, it is difficult to separate predatory from affective violence. Given that 13 cases involved firearms, which would have not been easy to obtain, there can be assumed a degree of prior planning. Similarly, in a number of other deluded attackers who employed knives or clubs, there is evidence of prior stalking behaviors and planning to bring themselves to within striking distance of their royal target.

5. No mental disorder

There is no evidence available that six of the attackers suffered from mental illness, although none underwent any form of psychiatric examination.

The motivations of the attackers appear to fall into the following categories:

1. Delusions of kingship

Rebecca O'Hara, who attacked George III, believed that she was the true monarch.

2. Pursuing an agenda

a. *Petitioners* Five of the attackers had petitioned the King and/ or Parliament repeatedly before the attack. Margaret Nicholson, for example, was pursuing her entitlements under the 1686 Bill of Rights, though she interpreted this as involving the King having an obligation to find her a suitable husband. All the petitioners could be regarded as chronic querulants and several, like Margaret Nicholson, were obviously deluded.

b. *Religious delusions* James Hadfield, who shot at George III in 1799, believed that he had to engineer his own death to ensure the Second Coming.

c. *Politically motivated psychotic* Only one attacker clearly fell into this category.

3. Chaotic psychotics

Ian Ball's kidnap plot of Princess Anne was confused in aims and in general reasoning, and Alfred Adcock, who assaulted Princess Diana, appeared beset by psychotically driven sexual obsessions.

4. Psychotic: Insufficient information to group

Urban Metcalf (an attacker of George III) and Robert Pate (an attacker of Queen Victoria) were probably deluded, but insufficient evidence remains in the public record to classify their disorders. The motives of these two attackers remain completely unknown.

5. Probably mentally ill: Insufficient information

Henry James O'Farrell, who shot Prince Alfred, refused to explain himself, and his motives remain obscure as a result of the unseemly haste with which he was hanged, and the attempts of the New South Wales government to use the incident for its own political purposes.

6. Political

Four assailants were clearly attempting to advance political agendas. Although they may have been extreme, and in one case eccentric, in their political commitments, none had a major mental disorder.

7. Adolescent anomie

Six cases involved adolescent men who used firearms, four without live ammunition, in what appear to be expressions of frustration and personal rebellion against the status quo.

The Consideration of Political Motivation

Purely political motivations seem to have been unusual. They can be clearly adduced in very few of the attackers. Motivation is complicated, and political positions are part of the psychological makeup of most people, including those who became involved in attacks on the Royal Family. However, this does not mean that they were the predominant factor in the mix. Both Oxford, who fired blanks at Queen Victoria, and Lewis, who shot at Queen Elizabeth in 1981, each described a fantasized private army. Two of the adolescent offenders harbored resentments about the contrast between their own situations and the privilege and wealth of the monarch. Another was angry about his unemployment, but also obsessed with the notion of achieving fame by killing the Queen. Only four cases stand out clearly as acts of political protest.

Personal Crisis

A number of the attackers can be described as having come to the "end of their tethers." They subsequently claimed they were forced into a position of "last resort." Sergeant, the Trooping of the Colour shooter, for example, had failed in his introductory course in the Royal Marines and had been rejected by both the police and the fire brigade. He described himself as desperate, with nowhere to turn.

Terrorism and Extremist Organizations

During the last 200 years, Lord Mountbatten, uncle to the Duke of Edinburgh, was the only victim of an organized militant group. He was assassinated by an Irish nationalist splinter group at the height of the republican military campaign in 1979. Only two other cases belonged to extremist organizations, but both were of their own invention. Oxford was probably the only member of his "Young England" group. Lewis had two friends in his "National Imperial Guerrilla Army."

Warning Behaviors

Eight of these attackers are known to have evidenced warning behaviors before the attacks. Given the gaps in the records, it is probable that others also gave notice of their intent to attack the royal personage.

Suicidal Intent

Only two cases intended to die as part of their attack. Hadfield had religious delusions about the meaning of his death, and Kang who fired a starting pistol at Prince Charles in Sydney in 1994 was suffering from depression.

Remand

Ten of the 23 cases (43%) were committed to psychiatric hospitals, and two more were transferred to a psychiatric hospital from prison. Seven cases (30%) were imprisoned, four cases underwent transportation (17%), and one was executed despite almost certainly having been insane. One received 500 hours of community service. One person who was probably not mentally ill was sent to hospital; one who probably was mentally ill was transported; and another who was mentally ill agreed to voluntary exile with remission of his prison sentence. He was later committed to a lunatic asylum when he returned to Buckingham Palace.

The Context of the Relationship Between Subject and Monarch

In the earlier period of this study, the relationship between the monarch and their subjects reflected, at least in part, the provisions of the Bill of Rights. This bill assigned the monarch the role of mediating for the benefit of the ordinary citizen between the power of the House of Commons, representing property owners largely from trade and industry, and the House of Lords, representing the aristocracy whose power was based in landed wealth. The monarch was allotted the role of a prototypical ombudsman for the common people—a role not always embraced with enthusiasm by the reigning monarch. At the beginning of the period, there was a more or less formalized process with the monarch regularly receiving petitions in person, both at his levee and in public places. There was still faith among ordinary people in royal intercession. And, indeed, the Sovereign did on occasion intercede. With ex-servicemen, such as two of the attackers Frith and Collins, the Sovereign was also the head of the armed forces and therefore had a particular responsibility in their eyes for the welfare of those who had fought in their army. This degree of belief in a close and reciprocal relationship between monarch and subject, a form of contractualism, may have been stronger at the end of the 18th century, and it lingers on in modern times. The Queen is still the Head of State and the ultimate authority for appeal. What Frith, Nicholson, Collins, and others in this series share with many of those who engage in inappropriate demands and intrusions on the current Royal family is an apparent inability to understand the limits of that relationship and a presumption that it incorporates a form of mutuality, with allegiance requiring a response in kind.

Adolescent Attackers

A singular element both in the 19th century attacks and in those of the late 20th century is the cases of adolescents who make largely unannounced attacks upon the monarch. The elements that appear to be present in the adolescent cases include a failure to achieve a sense of any personal success and a need to bolster self-esteem; a difficulty in accomplishing the material success that society sanctioned; and an accompanying sense of rejection, sometimes accompanied by wishing to gain revenge on the world. They all shared a feeling of not belonging, a sense of hopelessness, a wish to bring matters to a head, a desire to become notorious through a violent act, and an ennui with life that was expressed in a preoccupation with suicide.

The U.S. studies of attackers have remarked on similar factors in a subsample of those who have attacked prominent people in the last 60 years. In the U.S. literature, there is an attempt to separate out the desire to die, the wish to become famous through a destructive act, and the fascination with arms or assassination. It is far from clear in the sample of royal attacks that these various elements of the adolescent psyche can be split from each other. It is interesting that some of the characteristics of this adolescent group are shared with those who have engaged in high school shootings in the United States. Of the latter, the majority had experienced some loss, including loss of status or perceived failure; many felt bullied persecuted or injured, and suicidal ideas were common (Meloy, Hempel, Mohandie, Shiva, & Gray, 2001; Vossekuil, Fein, Reddy, Borum, & Modzeleski, 2002).

Pragmatic Considerations Regarding Prosecution

It is notable that there are occasions on which governments have decided not to bring attacks on the Royal Family into the public domain through prosecution. This was the case in two attacks, neither of which was noticed until after the event. Not long before the little known attack on Queen Elizabeth in 1981, there had been a potentially lethal attack on the British Prime Minister by a politically motivated adolescent, which had also been effectively kept out of the media for fear of triggering copycat attacks. There are arguments against popularizing the idea that people make casual attacks on the monarch or on prominent politicians. In part, this reflects concern lest anyone doing so should have been deemed *not* to be mad—a powerful consideration in the early 19th century when the idea of a rational attack on the monarch could scarcely be permitted. It also concerns the fear of copycat attacks. Oxford is recorded as having said while in Bedlam about the attacks that followed his: "If only they had hanged me, the dear Queen would not have had all this bother." The authors of *The Court Journal* of June 4, 1842, did not agree. In the context of Peel's Royal Protection Bill, they wrote: "It has been found that the more exemplary and excruciating the punishment, the more numerous the appearance of assassins of kings; ridicule, silence or the charge of lunacy being more effective than the severest retribution." This is a message that might bear repeating in the context of those who indulge in mass homicides today, be it in schools or other public places (Meloy, Hempel, et al., 2004; Mullen, 2004).

The following are the common behavioral and psychopathological elements of attackers of the British Royalty across the 2 centuries.

- The cases fall roughly into three groups, the mentally ill, the straightforwardly political, and the adolescents. The largest group is the mentally ill.
- All the attackers are pursuing their own causes, issues, and quests, most of which appear idiosyncratic and several obviously delusional.
- It is clear that very few attacks, even those involving firearms, are carried out with a firm commitment to kill. Their manifest purpose would appear often to have been to commit an outrageous act to draw attention to their grievances.

The relationship, if any, between attacks on Royalty over the last couple of centuries and attacks on today's political leaders is unlikely to be simple. Throughout the period discussed, the British Royal Family were more symbols of national identity than sources of real political power. This is not to say the Sovereign lacked influence, but that influence was exerted either at the specific level of individual cases or at the general level of embodying a particular form of authority deriving from tradition and position. One might think that those wishing to change the political structure, to remove particularly powerful individuals, or to express rage against the system would be more likely to have targeted the real embodiments of political power: politicians and corporations.

A case could be made that the reason so many of those who in the last 200 years attacked the British Royal Family were mad is that only the mad would be likely to make the error of thinking that was where the real power lay. An alternative proposition is that it was exactly the Sovereign's role as the ultimate source of intervention for the common man enshrined in the Bill of Rights that made them the national target for those on a quest for personal assistance or individual vindication.

Presidents and Other Public Figures in the United States

Moving across the Atlantic, a similar set of assumptions about those who attack the President and other prominent political figures usually being mad appears to have held sway in the 19th century. The importance assigned to mental disorder in attacks on public figures has, however, gradually waned over the last 50 years to a point where it is almost totally discounted by some authorities.

Early research on attacks and assassinations of public figures in the United States focused on the small number of assassins of the President, subjects who had only threatened the President, or subjects who had visited the White House, behaved peculiarly, and insisted on seeing the President (Hoffman, 1943; Megargee, 1986; Rothstein, 1964; Sebastiani & Foy, 1965; Shore et al., 1985). The latter two groups resembled each other in many ways. They were predominantly unmarried, unemployed Caucasian men in their mid-30s, with a common diagnosis of schizophrenia, histories of suicidal behavior, and previous hospitalizations. Rothstein (1964, 1966, 1971) hypothesized a "presidential assassination syndrome" on the basis of such studies. Subsequent writers however found no evidence for such a discrete syndrome (Freedman, 1971; Megargee, 1986).

Clarke (1982, 1990, 1992) analyzed 17 case studies of presidential assassins and others who had attacked prominent political figures in the United States. Seven of the victims died of their wounds, a 44% mortality rate. Clarke (1982) proposed four types of assassins. *Type I assassins* viewed their acts as a "sacrifice of self for a political ideal" and personal interest or evident psychopathology was secondary to a primary political motivation. John Wilkes Booth, the assassin of Abraham Lincoln in 1865, was an example of this type (Swanson, 2007). *Type II assassins* were persons with "overwhelming and aggressive egocentric needs for acceptance, recognition, and status." They were highly anxious and dysphoric individuals who had experienced much emotional deprivation in their personal lives. The assassination was a rage-fueled seeking of attention that was politically rationalized. Lee Harvey Oswald, the assassin of John F. Kennedy in 1963, was given as an example of this type. *Type III assassins* were psychopathic individuals who experienced life as meaningless, and the motivation was an emotionless display of contempt toward a society from which they felt completely alienated. John Hinckley Jr., the man who attempted to assassinate President Ronald Reagan in 1981, was given as an example of this type. *Type IV assassins* were those with a diagnosable major mental disorder, and who experienced both persecutory and grandiose delusions. Charles Guiteau, the assassin of President James Garfield in 1881, was given as an example of this type. Clarke's work is informative, but suffers from a necessarily small sample size, and his typology is limited by the absence of any direct investigative or interview data on the subjects, and by his negative attitude toward medical explanations for assassination behavior, which he sought to supplant. For example, he dismisses the arguable psychotic disorder in John Hinkley Jr. at the time of his attack.

The study of the assassination of public figures was taken in a different direction by the work of Robert Fein and Bryan Vossekuil of the U.S. Secret Service. Fein, Vossekuil, and Holden (1995) and Fein and Vossekuil (1998, 1999) recognized the shortcomings of previous studies that had focused only upon threateners and approachers, and redefined the task as "threat assessment of targeted violence." Their methodology eschewed the traditional violence risk approach, which emphasized more static factors, such as demographics or mental illness. Instead, they took a more functional-behavioral approach, which emphasized the identification of a pathway toward violence that a certain high-risk individual could take, and ways in which law enforcement interventions could successfully interrupt such movement toward assassination. Their research approach was designed primarily to aid law enforcement, and their subjects of interest were individuals who had acted in lethal or near-lethal ways toward a prominent person of public status. The time frame selected was 1949 to 1996, and their Exceptional Case Study (ECS) project captured the universe of individuals who had assassinated, attacked, or "near-lethally" approached a protectee of the U.S. Secret Service (President, Vice President, their families, former Presidents, candidates for President, and visiting heads of state); other major federal officials and office holders; governors and large city mayors; celebrities; and the chief executives of major corporations. They identified 83 subjects involved in 74 incidents. Forty-six percent were attacks or assassinations and 54% were "near-lethal approaches," by which was meant those who had been apprehended in the vicinity of possible victims with a weapon. The primary target was the President of the United States (34%) and other Secret Service protectees (19%). Another one third, however, comprised other national figures, business executives, and film, sports, or media celebrities. Twenty of the subjects were interviewed by the principal investigators, a forensic psychologist and a senior secret service agent.

In contrast to attacks on British Royalty, most attacks, assassinations, or near-lethal approaches occurred in the target's home, office, hotel, campaign rally, or temporary work-site. The most common weapon was a handgun (51%) or a rifle/shotgun (30%). Knives were used in 15% of the cases. The primary goal in most of the incidents was to kill or harm the target (68%). Again, this is somewhat at variance with those attacking British Royalty. A wide range of motivations from avenging perceived wrongs to saving the country or even the world was noted. Presidential targeting was most often motivated by a desire to achieve notoriety or to be killed by law enforcement.

Fein and Vossekuil (1998) considered that the "pathway to attack or assassination" was marked by two important features. The first was that in virtually all cases the attacks were planned over the course of weeks, months, or even years. As Fein and Vossekuil wrote, "in every case, assassination was the end result of an understandable process, involving the attacker's pattern of thoughts, decisions, behaviors, and actions that preceded the attack" (p. 185). Subjects ruminated about assassination, they read about it, they sometimes kept journals and talked to others, they chose a target, they planned carefully, they engaged in approach behavior and surveillance, they considered whether to escape, and they chose the moment and the weapon for the attack. They were also capable of postponing an attack if plans did not unfold as antici- pated. It was concluded that attacks and assassinations of U.S. public figures were not impulsive, emotionally laden, sudden, or spontaneous acts. They were acts of predatory violence: planned, purposeful, and emotionless (Meloy, 1988, 2006). This contrasts in some measure with the picture that emerges from the review of attacks on British Royalty. Next, the pathway to attack or assassina- tion was marked by the absence of any directly communicated threat to the target or law enforcement agencies beforehand. In fact, none of the 43 assas- sins or attackers communicated a direct threat to the target before their attack. On the other hand, two thirds of the subjects did communicate their intent to mount an attack to a third party or in a written diary or journal before the incident. They told family members, friends, workers, colleagues, and associ- ates about their thoughts and plans.

Fein and Vossekuil (1998), differing from prior writers on the subject, emphasized that there is no profile of an American assassin. What they identified was a range of factors that tended to be found relatively frequently, but from which no single type, or even series of types, could usefully be extracted. Historical and personal characteristics indicated that the age range was 16 to 73; almost half had attended some college or graduate school; they often had histories of mobility and transience; they were often social isolates; few had histories or arrests for violent crimes; few had ever been incarcerated in state or federal prison; most had a history of weapons interest and use, but few had formal weapons training; many had histories of harassing other persons; most had histories of explosive and angry behavior, but only half had known histories of violent behavior; many had histories of interest in militant or radical ideas and groups, but were not members of such groups; many had histories of serious depression or despair; many had histories of attempted suicide; and almost all had histories of grievances and resentments, usually against a public official or public figure. In the year before the incident, almost half of the subjects experienced a major loss or life change, including marital problems and break-ups, personal illness, death of a family member, failure at school or work, and personal setbacks that stimulated feelings of despair or depression.

Two thirds of the subjects had histories of contact with mental health services, and 23% had been evaluated or treated in the year before the attack.

In Fein and Vossekuil's opinion, 43% of the subjects were deluded at the time of their attacks.

The conspicuous presence in Fein and Vossekuil's sample of prior psychiatric histories and delusional states might have led to the expectation that this aspect would receive particular attention in the discussion of their findings. This is not the case. The ECS project places no particular emphasis on the possible role of psychotic illnesses; it is instead de-emphasized. This becomes understandable when placed in the context of the agenda behind the ECS. One of the study's objectives was to identify risk factors that would assist in evaluating the threat that particular individuals might present to U.S. politicians. Mental illness is common in the general community, with somewhere in the region of 1% of the population likely to be psychotic at any given moment. Mental illness is so common as to verge on the usual among those who attempt to approach, repeatedly communicate with, or threaten the President and other senior politicians (see Chapter 19) (see Scalora, Baumgartner, Callaway, et al., 2002; Scalora, Baumgartner, & Plank, 2003; Scalora, Baumgartner, Zimmerman, et al., 2002). And the attackers rarely come from the ranks of these harassers. As a marker or predictor of the potential for attacking a prominent person, mental illness is therefore useless. The ECS study may also have underestimated the potential role of mental illness because they equated psychosis with legal insanity. Most of those they studied planned and executed their attack in a manner that left little doubt about their intentions and their knowledge that their actions were wrong. This might well have excluded an insanity defense in many U.S. jurisdictions, but it says little about whether these individuals were psychotic. In short, Fein and Vossekuil effectively applied the legal criteria deriving from the McNaughton rules rather than a contemporary psychiatric classification.

General Findings Across the Public Figure Studies From the United States

A review of threats, approaches, and attacks on all public figures in the United States yields a number of consistent findings (Meloy, James, et al., 2004):

- A significant proportion of subjects who threaten, approach, or attack public figures are mentally ill.
- In many subjects with mental illness, there has been a lapse of recent mental health care, often a result of noncompliance with medication by the subject, inadequate community resources, or a combination of both.
- Many subjects evidenced a downward spiral in their lives in the months or year before their approach or attack, usually a combination of social failure and personal vulnerability to chronic anger, depression, or psychosis. These failures and the subject's poor adaptation to them often marked a decision point wherein the public figure(s) was

identified as an object of salvation or persecution, and a plan was born to contact, approach, or attack the public figure.

- The motivations and goals of subjects who contact, approach, and in a few cases attack public figures vary considerably, and determine the selection of the target. A target may be a specific individual or a member of an identified group (legislator, judicial officer, celebrity, executive) but in most cases is a means to an end that has a strong personal and emotional value for the subject.
- Even where the subject is deluded, the concerns are still likely to be of a very personal and emotional nature.
- The intensity of preapproach behavior (contact behavior not involving a physical approach) may signal the presence of mental illness in the subject.
- Subjects will often contact and approach multiple targets within their domain of interest (legislators, celebrities, judicial figures, etc.). This behavioral pattern necessitates strong linkages among jurisdictions to see if subjects have approached other targets.
- Many subjects who approach are not initially motivated by aggression, but instead are seeking help, beneficence, or a personal meeting. The inherent risk with such a motivation, however, is perceived rejection by the public figure, and the consequent stimulation of angry and aggressive feelings.
- Directly communicated threats appear to have no statistically significant relationship with an approach.
- Indirect threats, or declarations of intention to others, are, by contrast to direct threats, commonly encountered in subjects who attack.
- Analyses of various detailed aspects (form and content) of threatening communications, primarily letters, have yielded some predictive data (see Chapters 1 and 20) (Schoeneman-Morris, Scalora, Chang, Zimmerman, & Garner, 2007).
- The central question concerning threat assessment and threat management is whether or not the subject *poses* a threat toward the public figure(s), rather than just making a threat. Posing a threat means that the individual is engaging in behavior to plan, prepare, and implement an attack; such behavior is often viewed as suspicious by threat assessment professionals. Often those who pose a threat do not make a direct threat for tactical reasons.
- A significant proportion of subjects who threaten, approach, or attack public figures also have criminal histories, indicating the importance of criminal background checks of subjects of concern and cross-jurisdictional cooperation among various law enforcement agencies when there is no unified national system of criminal history data collection.
- If a serious attack occurred, it tended to be a predatory (instrumental, premeditated) mode of violence, rather than an affective (emotional,

reactive) mode of violence (Meloy, 2006). Such violence was planned over the course of weeks or months, and involved careful preparation and implementation. Most attackers of public figures do not "snap" and are not engaging in spur of the moment, impulsive behaviors. Even if the attacker is psychotic and severely mentally ill, he demonstrates a capacity and ability to organize his behavior to accomplish his goal.

- If a public figure is attacked, the weapon of choice in a majority of the cases is a firearm, usually a handgun.
- Those who attack may intend to kill the target and also commit suicide at the hands of law enforcement officers (Mohandie & Meloy, 2000).
- Threats are much more common than approaches, and approaches are much more common than attacks. Most predictions of escalation from threat to approach to attack will therefore be false positives.
- Preventive efforts should focus on false negatives: subjects who do not directly threaten, but instead are planning and preparing to attack, are evident in their suspicious approach or "warning" behavior toward the target or targets of interest.

An important attempt is made in the work of Phillips (2006, 2007) to bring together knowledge from the stalking literature and the work stemming from the ECS studies. Five descriptive categories developed on the basis of Mullen and coworkers' (1999, 2000) typology are proposed:

1. The resentful stalker or assassin who is driven by a quest for retribution; the example provided is John Wilkes Booth.
2. The pathologically obsessed, characterized by the presence of a severe psychosis of a persecutory or grandiose nature. Charles Guiteau, the assassin of President Garfield, is said to be of this type (Rosenberg, 1968).
3. The presidential infamy seeker who is intending to make a grand political statement. Typically, these are antisocial individuals with fanatical political commitments who are attempting to publicize their views and themselves. Francisco Duran, who fired repeatedly into the White House grounds in 1994, was suggested to be of this type.
4. Presidential intimacy seekers who are seeking a close relationship, usually romantic in nature. Most have erotomanic delusions.
5. Presidential nuisance or attention seekers are those who typically attempt to approach the president not to do harm but simply to associate themselves with power and celebrity. Many but not all are delusional. The indefatigable Richard Weaver is given as an example.

The research from the United States is important in indicating factors that should be considered in research upon threats to prominent people elsewhere in the world. It is, however, necessary to recognize the different foci of the U.S. research. The earlier period of the research was concerned with assassination or with descriptions of those who approach government buildings inappropriately. This was written predominantly by psychiatrists and tends to have mental illness as a focus. The later period of research is the product of behavioral scientists or policing personnel. Its focus is upon identifying individuals who are likely to attack, and it is less concerned with those who may cause a nuisance, alarm, embarrassment, or cost.

It may well prove to be the case that some of the later U.S. findings apply equally in other jurisdictions, but this needs to be tested. Although it is a prominent finding in the United States that many of those involved in inappropriate communications and approaches to public figures are mentally ill, this is not accorded central importance, either in the conceptualization of the problem or in its management. This is probably for two reasons, both of which differentiate the United States from Europe and the United Kingdom. In the United States, civil mental health laws are such that it is difficult to intervene in mentally ill cases through compulsory treatment, and there is no hospital disposal directly from the courts for the mentally ill, unless they are unfit to plead or satisfy strict insanity criteria. Most mentally ill people who are convicted of criminal offences therefore receive penal disposals. In the United Kingdom and Europe, the underlying principle is that mental illness per se is an exculpatory factor in offending, and on a pragmatic level, it is accepted that mentally ill offenders are better dealt with by the healthcare system than the penal system. In the United States, mental illness per se is not seen as offering any formal diminution of culpability. Curiously, the United States remains more firmly wedded to the House of Lords' rules formulated following the McNaughton case than do the British. This means that mental health solutions are eschewed, attempts to understand attackers are colored by issues of criminal responsibility, and the main interventional focus is a behavioral one, concentrating on law enforcement and criminal justice interventions.

Attacks on Western European Politicians

James and colleagues (Fixated Research Group, 2006; James et al., 2007) carried out a survey of attacks on elected politicians in the United Kingdom and western Europe covering the period 1990 to 2004. They excluded attacks by the well-organized national liberation groups in Ireland and the Basque region of Spain. This left 24 nonterrorist attacks over the 14 years, which had occurred in eight of the European nations.

Twenty of the cases involved national politicians, and comprised attacks on the German President, the French President, the Italian Prime Minister, the German Chancellor, the British Prime Minister, the German Interior Minister, the German Foreign Minister, the French Minister of Culture, the Swedish Foreign Minister, three leaders of German political parties, one leader of a Dutch political party, the Hamburg Minister of Justice, the Saxony-Anhalt Interior Minister, the Defence Spokesman for the German Green Party, the leader of the U.K. Liberal Democrat Party, a junior U.K. minister, and one further member each of the British and German Parliaments. Of the local politicians, one case involved a local council in France and one a regional assembly in Switzerland. The remaining two cases concerned attacks on the mayors of Vienna and Paris.

In the attack on the U.K. M.P. Nigel Jones, the victim was a third party who came to the politician's aid. In one mass shooting, the apparent target escaped injury, while others died. The target in the second mass shooting appears to have been a group of politicians rather than a single figure. In these two episodes, a total of 22 people were killed and 34 injured. In the remaining 22 cases, three attacks resulted in deaths, two being of the politicians attacked and one of a third party who intervened. Three attacks resulted in serious injury—paraplegia, a severed carotid artery, and a serious knife wound to the abdomen. Lesser injuries comprised the loss of two fingers, a stab wound to the thigh, concussion, cuts to the arm, a broken nose and a ruptured eardrum. Three attacks resulted in light bruising. In the remaining five cases, no injury was sustained. These included a rifle shot off target, an exploding parcel bomb, a Molotov cocktail that was poorly aimed, two knife attacks that were warded off, a blow to the head with a hand, and a flour bomb attack.

Weapons were used in 20 of the 24 cases (83%), whereas in the remaining four cases, fists alone were used. Five cases involved the use of firearms, one a letter bomb, one a Molotov cocktail, one a samurai sword, eight involved knives, one a cosh, one a photographic tripod, one a balloon full of paint, and one a flour bomb. Of the five fatal cases, two involved handguns alone, one a handgun, assault rifle, and a shotgun, one a samurai sword, and one a knife.

Seven attacks (29%) occurred at campaign rallies and one at a political parade. Nine further cases were in public places (two as part of election campaigning and one further case in the context of a referendum campaign), three were in the chambers of elected assemblies, one in a constituency surgery, one in a car, one in a private office, and one at an official party to which the public were invited. In all, 22 of the 24 cases concerned public functions or public places.

There appears to be evidence in three cases (Lafontaine, Schäuble, Kusch) that the choice of victim was chance and that another politician of similar status would have been equally acceptable. In two other cases (Delanoë and Lindh), there is some indication that the attack was impulsive and that the choice of victim was more or less accidental. In the remainder of the cases (79%), the attack was either clearly planned or the presence of specific weapons enabled planning to be inferred—predatory rather than affective violence, consistent with the U.S. data (Meloy, 2006). The planning in each case was a matter of only days before the attack, although one assailant had suffered hallucinations for many years telling her to kill a politician.

Five assailants were women and the remaining 19 attacks were carried out by men. The age range was 25 to 57 with a mean age of 38.7 (SD 8.8). In all except one case, the attacker acted alone. In 10 cases (42%), there was evidence that the assailant was a loner or social isolate. In 6 cases (25%), there was evidence of profound social alienation. Five assailants were known to be members of militant or radical organizations. In 11 cases (46%), there was evidence of intent to kill or recklessness as to whether death resulted. In three cases (12.5%), the assailant intended to die as part of the incident.

Attempts were made to fit the assailants into the motivational groups suggested by Fein and Vossekuil (1999). Two cases (8%) wished to achieve notoriety or fame, both wishing to die in the attempt. Three (12.5%) wished to avenge a perceived wrong. Eight (33%) wished to bring national attention to a perceived problem. Four (17%) wished to save the country. These categories were not mutually exclusive. It was difficult to assess which cases wished "to bring about political change," a concept that remains ill defined in Fein and Vossekuil's account. The remaining seven cases (29%) seemed to be motivated simply by varying degrees of political hatred.

In one case, the assailant was unknown. Evidence as to abnormalities in mental state was available in 13 of the remaining 23 cases (57%). In 10 further cases, the issue of mental health was not raised by the police or at court, other than four cases being drunk. This is taken to indicate the likelihood that no serious form of mental illness was present. This is a conservative assumption in that mental disorders (and, in particular in this context, delusional disorders) may be present and unsuspected where no psychiatric examination is undertaken. Of the 13 cases with a probable mental health diagnosis, schizophrenia occurred in 8 cases (33% of the whole sample), paranoid disorders of uncertain etiology in 2 cases, personality disorder in 2 cases (1 obsessive and 1 borderline), and a presumed depressive disorder in 1 case.

In 11 of the 24 cases (46%), there had been some form of warning behavior shown by the attacker. These involved posters, newspaper advertisements, attempted law suits against the government, chaotic deluded letters to politicians and police, threatening letters to politicians, leafleting the public, and telling friends. In some cases, these behaviors had gone on for some years.

Of the 23 cases for which the perpetrator was known, 8 (33%) resulted in the admission of the attacker to psychiatric hospital for treatment. Six (25%) attackers were given a prison sentence. Three were given a fine, and three a suspended sentence. One committed suicide at the scene and one a day after the attack. One avoided any judicial sanction.

This study provides a general picture of nonterrorist attacks on western European politicians. Some of the most senior politicians in western Europe have been subject to attack during the 14 years in question, including five government leaders or heads of state. Fifty-seven percent of the known attackers were suffering from a mental disorder. This was psychotic in nature in 42% of the whole sample. Death or serious injury was more likely when the perpetrator had a mental disorder. More than half of the attackers fell into the definition of the group we term the fixated (Mullen et al., in press). The second largest group (38% of cases) had a purely political motivation. The fixated cases were significantly more likely to be mentally disordered and to be suffering from a psychotic illness. Among the fixated, there were no cases of people seeking a relationship and no cases of erotomanic illness. This would appear to be a major difference between attacks on elected politicians and attacks on celebrities (see Chapters 2 and 4). Those who were fixated were focused on a cause rather than an individual. This was associated with paranoid delusions in the majority of fixated cases.

In 46% of cases, there had been some form of warning behavior. Most warning behaviors were in the form of communications rather than approaches. An important feature about such warning behaviors was that, for the most part, they did not constitute direct threats to an individual, but rather evidence of gross disturbance and psychopathology, which failed to illicit any systematic risk assessment or management response. This finding is consistent with the U.S. data.

Two of the fatal cases involved mass killings, which are highly unusual in Europe. In one of these, the perpetrator was a fixated querulant, and in the other, a man with a history of rejection and resentment. In a continent where the possession of firearms is not widespread, both had licenses for the weapons with which they carried out their attacks; in one case, despite having previously pulled out a firearm in front of a mental health worker, he had retained his license. Of the three remaining firearms cases, one weapon was legally held by the father of the attacker, one purchased legally, and one acquired from illegal sources.

Comparison With the Exceptional Case Study

The authors of the ECS in the United States (Fein & Vossekuil, 1998, 1999) pointed out that previous studies of assassinations had generally seen assassins and attackers of political leaders as either possessing political motives or as being deranged, a view of assassination that they found narrow and inaccurate. Only one of their assassination cases was seen as possibly having had a primary political motive. Sixty-one percent of their cases had had previous contact with a mental health professional and 43% had a history of delusional ideas. Motivation was often confused and the presence of mental health issues was nonspecific. They noted that from an operational perspective, focus on mental illness may not be useful in preventing assassination. A linked observation was that in only 7% of cases had the subject communicated a direct threat about the target to the target or to law enforcement. In none of the 34 cases of assassins or attackers was such a direct threat communicated: Thus, in their view, attention to the making of threats was not a sufficient strategy in the prevention of attacks. The authors place emphasis on identifying people who "pose" a threat, rather than concentrating on people who "make" threats. They state that only one of their 34 attackers was known not to have planned the attack. Planning was often a lengthy process, going on over weeks and months or even years. The attacker was following a "path" to attack, and attackers often engaged in "attack-related" behaviors, that is, discernible activities that precede an attack. These might include scouting out the sites of attack, practicing with their chosen weapon, and learning about security arrangements. Emphasis in their study was on an operational perspective, with the object being to identify those who were on the path to attack and intercepting them before they reached its end. The authors concluded that many, if not most, attacks on public officials and public figures were potentially preventable.

Comparing this with the Fixated Research Group's (2006) study of European cases, differences and similarities emerge. The ECS conflates attacks, assassinations, and approaches with weapons, and assumes that they are part of the same phenomenon. The European sample includes cases where the attacker clearly had no desire to kill a politician, as well as cases where assassination was a clear aim. Some of the attacks were clearly political in motive, whereas others clearly arose out of delusional beliefs unrelated to any obvious political agenda.

Fein and Vossekuil (1998, p. 183) stated, "Many persons who demonstrate unusual or inappropriate interests in, or make threats against, public officials and figures are mentally ill. But...the great majority of attackers and assassins are *not* mentally ill"—a statement contradicted by their data. In the European sample, excluding one case where the identity of the attacker was unknown, there was sufficient evidence in 33% of cases to establish the presence of psychotic illness, and in a further 17% there was serious mental disorder that may have been psychotic in character. Two further cases (9%) suffered from personality disorders. In the ten cases in the sample that resulted in death or serious injury, six attackers appear to have been psychotic at the time of the attack, with some information to suggest that two more may also have been psychotic (80%). Direct comparison with the U.S. cases is limited by the lack of information as to what proportion of the ECS incidents concerned politicians rather than celebrities. It can be presumed that nine of the individuals and eight of the attacks concerned the President, given that this was the relevant number in the period studied. The nature of the remaining 24 cases is unclear. However, looking at the ECS results as a whole, there is in fact a degree of similarity with the findings from the European cases in that 43% of the 73 subjects were deluded at the time of the principal incident. This would appear to be clearly at odds with the authors' statement that "the great majority of attackers and assassins are *not* mentally ill" (p. 183). Where there is a major difference between this survey and the ECS is the divergent interpretations of the importance of the presence of mental illness among attackers and assassins.

Fein and Vossekuil (1999) also wrote, "No attacker or near-lethal approacher has ever been a model of emotional well-being. Almost all had psychological problems. However, relatively few suffered from mental illnesses that caused their attack behaviors" (p. 331). They argue that even for those attackers who were mentally ill, in almost every case an attack was a means to achieve some ends, such as calling attention to a perceived problem. Doubt is also cast upon whether the attackers had severe and untreated mental illness, arguing that such illnesses disable the person's usual problem-solving abilities and render them incapable of mounting an attack. This is clearly a legal rather than a psychiatric construction of mental illness.

Conclusions

From the late 18th century until relatively recently, harassers and attackers of prominent public figures, in particular royalty, were assumed to contain a high proportion of insane offenders. In fact, the insanity laws that still exist in many parts of the English-speaking world, including the United States, derive directly from cases involving attacks on public figures. The case of McNaughton who attempted to assassinate Peel, the British Prime Minister, became the impetus for the rules to be laid down defining legal insanity, rules that still echo through the courts of the English-speaking world.

The attempted assassination of President Reagan by John Hinkley Jr. initiated a similar process of reassessing the nature and place of the insanity defense in the criminal justice system 150 years later. As in the case of McNaughton, this was driven by public outrage and press campaigns directed at the insanity defense as an escape—not just from responsibility, but also from punishment.

In part, the view that assassins were insane embodied the age-old belief that the mad were more likely to act in a violent manner; in part, it reflected the actual observations of those who launched attacks on public figures; in part, it reflected the self-satisfaction of the age that assumed only the mad would attempt to lay violent hands upon their leaders.

The view that psychotics played the major role in attacks on the prominent waned in the later part of the 20th century. The increasing resistance to accepting a connection between psychotic disorders and either harassment or attempted assassination was fed by the following viewpoints and developments.

1. The labeling of those who plagued or attacked politicians and heads of state as psychotic was a politically motivated ploy to delegitimize and dismiss their acts of dissent and opposition.
2. The consensus among mental health professionals that emerged in the 1960s and 1970s that there was absolutely no connection between psychotic disorders and violent and antisocial behavior made it politically incorrect even to raise the question of a relationship with assassination.
3. The rise of systematic and data-based approaches to the protection of the senior politicians in the United States, particularly following the assassination of President Kennedy. The Secret Service and other agencies became understandably concerned to identify robust predictors of the risk of such attacks. Psychotic disorders were in and of themselves so common, and attacks so rare, that even if an association existed, its predictive value was nil. Political extremists and publicity-seeking predators seemed far more threatening than common or garden-variety psychotics. The security agencies were not concerned with theory, but simply with the pragmatics of protection.

> Mental illness of whatever variety simply did not assist in the attempt
> to decide which particular individuals among all those who came
> to the attention of protective services were likely to progress to an
> attack.

The time may have come to reassess the role of psychotic illnesses in attacks on public figures. There is no reason to return to the simplistic notion that you must be mad to attack a political leader in a democratic nation. A place must, however, be found in our thinking for what appears to be a robust association between having a psychotic disorder, characterized by the presence of delusional beliefs, and launching attacks on public figures. Over 50% of those who have attacked British Royalty over the last 200 years have been mentally disordered and most of this group were actively deluded when they launched their assaults. Fein and Vossekuil's (1998, 1999) ECS in the United States suggests even higher rates of mental disorder, almost certainly because of better methods of ascertainment, with mental disorder present in over 60% of cases and 43% having delusional beliefs. The Fixated Research Group's (2006) study of attacks on European politicians found remarkably similar rates of mental disorder. This needs to be compared with somewhere between 0.4% and 0.7% of the general population likely to be suffering from a psychotic disorder characterized by delusions at any one time.

If the association is accepted, how might it alter the approach of services charged with protecting a nation's leaders? The presence of a mental disorder associated with delusional thinking will have little value in identifying which individuals, if any, of those who repeatedly write to, threaten, or otherwise harass public figures will attack. The frequency of such a progression from nuisance to danger is just too low, and the presence of delusional individuals too high in this population. Psychotic disorders are even less useful as a marker for potential assassins in the wider community, where such illnesses afflict only 1%, but potential assassins are as rare as hen's teeth. To make any use of the knowledge that psychotic disorders are common among those who attack public figures, it is necessary to move from a prevention model based on spotting the dangerous individual to a model based on reducing risk by reducing the level of a risk factor in a population. Such intervention may be more easily accomplished in countries with comprehensive systems of care for the mentally ill, as well as mental health legislation, which incorporates broad powers of detention (Mullen et al., in press).

The section of the population that is brought to the attention of protective services as a result of its behavior, through unauthorized approaches, making threats, or showing a concerning interest in a public figure, contains a high proportion of mentally ill people. A significant proportion have delusional fixations on a public figure, which have come to dominate their lives and totally disrupt their functioning (Mullen et al., in press). These people need psychiatric help. Providing that help will not only reduce whatever residual risk they might present to a public figure, but also reduce the number of people on whom the protection services need to maintain surveillance, and against whom they must provide personal protection. Most importantly, it will bring into mental health care, or in most cases bring back into care, a disordered and distressed group acutely in need of psychiatric treatment (Mullen et al., in press).

This strategy of intervening to provide mental health care to all those obviously psychotic who bring themselves to notice by harassing or threatening public figures can only be one part of a comprehensive program of protection of public figures. The struggle to find more robust risk factors to identify those at high probability of progressing to violence needs to continue. Personal protection for high-profile political leaders is one of the realities of our age. Surveillance of those who create concern will continue to have its place. We are suggesting that the data on those who attack public figures indicate a further, and relatively low cost, addendum to current approaches to protecting the nations' leaders. Ensuring appropriate and continuing mental health care of psychotic individuals, whose behavior makes them a matter of concern to protective services, will benefit the mentally disordered people, and make the task of those charged with protecting public figures easier.

References

Clarke, J. W. (1982). *American assassins: The darker side of politics*. Princeton, NJ: Princeton University Press.

Clarke, J. W. (1990). *On being mad or merely angry*. Princeton, NJ: Princeton University Press.

Clarke, J. W. (1992). *American assassins: The darker side of politics* (2nd ed.). Princeton: Princeton University Press.

Cohen, C. I. (1980). Crime among mental patients—A critical analysis. *Psychiatric Quarterly, 52*, 100–107.

Eigen, J. P. (1995). *Witnessing insanity: Madness and mad-doctors in the English court*. New Haven: Yale University Press.

Eronen, M., Tiihonen, J., & Hakola, P. (1996). Schizophrenia and homicidal behaviour. *Schizophrenia Bulletin, 22*, 83–89.

Fein, R. A., & Vossekuil, B. (1998). Preventing attacks on public officials and public figures: A Secret Service perspective. In J. R. Meloy (Ed.), *The psychology of stalking* (pp. 176–191). San Diego: Academic Press.

Fein, R. A., & Vossekuil, B. (1999). Assassination in the United States: An operational study of recent assassins, attackers and near-lethal approachers. *Journal of Forensic Sciences, 44*(2), 321–333.

Fein, R., Vossekuil, B., & Holden, G. (1995). *Threat assessment: An approach to prevent targeted violence* (NCJ 155000). Washington, DC: U.S. Department of Justice.

Fixated Research Group (2006). *Inappropriate communications, approaches, and attacks on the British Royal Family with additional consideration of attacks on politicians*. London: The Home Office.

Freedman, L. Z. (1971). Psychopathology of assassination. In W. J. Crotty (Ed.), *Assassination and the political order* (pp. 143–160). New York: Harper & Row.

Hafner, H., & Böker, W. (1982). *Crimes of violence by mentally abnormal offenders.* London: Cambridge University Press.

Hodgins, S., Mednick, S., Brennar, P. A., Schulsinger, F., & Engberg, M. (1996). Mental disorder and crime: Evidence from a Danish birth cohort. *Archives of General Psychiatry, 53,* 489–496.

Hoffman, J. L. (1943). Psychotic visitors to government offices in the national capital. *American Journal of Psychiatry, 99,* 571–575.

James, D., Mullen, P., Meloy, J. R., Pathe, M., Farnham, F., Preston, L., et al. (2007). The role of mental disorder in attacks on European politicians 1990–2004. *Acta Psychiatrica Scandinavica, 116,* 334–344.

James, D., Mullen, P., Pathe, M., Meloy, J. R., Farnham, F., Preston, L., et al. (in press). Attacks on the British Royal Family: The role of psychotic illness. *Journal of the American Academy of Psychiatry and the Law.*

Keeton, G. W. (1961). *Guilty but insane.* London: MacDonald.

Longford, E. (1987). *Victoria R.I.* (2nd ed.). London: Weidenfeld & Nicolson.

Macalpine, I., & Hunter, R. (1969). *George III and the mad-business.* London: Allen Lane.

Megargee, E. (1986). A psychometric study of incarcerated Presidential threateners. *Criminal Justice and Behavior, 13,* 243–260.

Meloy, J. R. (1988). *The psychopathic mind: Origins, dynamics, and treatment.* Northvale, NJ: Aronson.

Meloy, J. R. (2006). The empirical basis and forensic application of affective and predatory violence. *Australian and New Zealand Journal of Psychiatry, 40,* 539–547.

Meloy, J. R., Hempel, A., Mohandie, K., Shiva, A., & Gray, T. (2001). Offender and offense characteristics of a non-random sample of adolescent mass murderers. *Journal of the American Academy of Child and Adolescent Psychiatry, 40,* 719–728.

Meloy, J. R., Hempel, A., Mohandie, K., Shiva, A., Gray, T., & Richards, T. (2004). A comparative analysis of North American adolescent and adult mass murderers. *Behavioral Sciences and the Law, 22,* 291–309.

Meloy, J. R., James, D. V., Farnham, F. R., Mullen, P. E., Pathé, M., Darnley, B., et al. (2004). A research review of public figure threats, approaches, attacks, and assassinations in the United States. *Journal of Forensic Sciences, 49*(5), 1086–1093.

Mohandie, K., & Meloy, J. R. (2000). Clinical and forensic indicators of "suicide by cop." *Journal of Forensic Sciences, 45,* 384–389.

Monahan, J. (1981). *The clinical prediction of violent behaviour.* Rockville, MD: United States Department of Health and Human Services.

Mullen, P. E. (2004). The autogenic (self generated) massacre. *Behavioral Sciences and the Law, 22,* 311–323. Special issue.

Mullen, P. E. (2006). Schizophrenia and violence: From correlations to preventive strategies. *Advances in Psychiatric Treatment, 2,* 239–248.

Mullen, P., James, D., Meloy, J. R., Pathe, M., Farnham, F., Preston, L., et al. (in press). The fixated and the pursuit of public figures. *Journal of Forensic Psychiatry and Psychology.*

Mullen, P. E., Pathé, M., & Purcell, R. (2000). *Stalkers and their victims.* Cambridge: Cambridge University Press.

Mullen, P. E., Pathé, M., Purcell, R., & Stuart, G. W. (1999). Study of stalkers. *American Journal of Psychiatry, 156,* 1244–1249.

Phillips, R. T. M. (2006). Assessing presidential stalkers and assassins. *Journal of the American Academy of Psychiatry and the Law, 34,* 154–164.

Phillips, R. T. M. (2007). Celebrity and presidential targets. In D. Pinels (Ed.), *Stalking: Psychiatric perspectives and practical approaches* (pp. 227–250). Washington, DC: APA Press.

Poole, S. (2000). *The politics of regicide in England, 1760–1850: Troublesome subjects.* New York: Manchester University Press.

Rappeport, J. R., & Lassen, G. (1965). Dangerousness—Arrest rate comparison of discharged patients and the general population. *American Journal of Psychiatry, 121,* 776–783.

Rosenberg, C. E. (1968). *The trial of the assassin Guiteau.* Chicago: University of Chicago Press.

Rothstein, D. A. (1964). Presidential assassination syndrome. *Archives of General Psychiatry, 11,* 245–254.

Rothstein, D. A. (1966). Presidential assassination syndrome II: Application to Lee Harvey Oswald. *Archives of General Psychiatry, 15,* 260–266.

Rothstein, D. A. (1971). Presidential assassination syndrome: A psychiatric study of the threat, the deed, and the message. In W. J. Crotty (Ed.), *Assassination and the political order* (pp. 161–222). New York: Harper & Row.

Scalora, M. J., Baumgartner, J. V., Callaway, D., Zimmerman, W., Hatch-Maillette, M. A., Covell, C. N., et al. (2002). An epidemiological assessment of problematic contacts to members of Congress. *Journal of Forensic Sciences, 47,* 1360–1364.

Scalora, M. J., Baumgartner, J., & Plank, G. (2003). The relationship of mental illness to targeted contact behavior toward state government agencies and officials. *Behavioral Sciences and the Law, 21,* 239–249.

Scalora, M. J., Baumgartner, J. V., Zimmerman, W., Callaway, D., Hatch-Maillette, M. A., Covell, C. N., et al. (2002). Risk factors for approach behavior toward the U.S. Congress. *Journal of Threat Assessment, 2,* 35–55.

Schanda, H., Knecht, G., Schreinzer, D., Stompe, T., Ortwein-Swoboda, G., & Waldhör, T. (2004). Homicide and major mental disorders: A 25 year study. *Acta Psychiatrica Scandinavica, 110,* 98–107.

Schoeneman-Morris, K., Scalora, M., Chang, G., Zimmerman, W., & Garner, Y. (2007). A comparison of email versus letter threat contacts toward Members of the United States Congress. *Journal of Forensic Sciences, 52,* 1142–1147.

Sebastiani, J. A., & Foy, J. L. (1965). Psychotic visitors to the White House. *American Journal of Psychiatry, 122,* 679–686.

Shore, D., Filson, C. R., Davis, T. S., Olivos, G., DeLisi, L., & Wyatt, R. J. (1985). White House cases: Psychiatric patients and the Secret Service. *American Journal of Psychiatry, 142,* 308–312.

Swanson, J. (2007). *Manhunt.* New York: Harper.

Swanson, J. W., Holzer, C., Ganju, V. K., & Jono, R. T. (1990). Violence and psychiatric disorder in the community. Evidence from the Epidemiologic Catchment Area Surveys. *Hospital and Community Psychiatry, 41,* 761–770.

Taylor, P. J., & Gunn, J. (1984a). Violence and psychosis, I: The risk of violence among psychotic men. *British Medical Journal, 288,* 1945–1949.

Taylor, P. J., & Gunn, J. (1984b). Violence and psychosis, II: Effect of psychiatric diagnosis on conviction and sentencing of offenders. *British Medical Journal*, *289*, 9–12.

Tiihonen, J., Isohanni, M., Rasanen, P., Koiranen, M., & Moring, J. (1997). Specific major mental disorders and criminality: A 26-year prospective study of the 1966 Northern Finland birth cohort. *American Journal of Psychiatry*, *154*, 840–845.

Vossekuil, B., Fein, R. A., Reddy, M., Borum, R., & Modzeleski, W. (2002). *The final report and findings of the safe school initiative: Implications for the prevention of school attacks in the United States*. Washington, DC: United States Secret Service and United States Department of Education.

Walker, N. (1968). *Crime and insanity in England, Vol. 1: The Historical perspective*. Edinburgh: Edinburgh University Press.

Wallace, C., Mullen, P. E., & Burgess, P. (2004). Criminal offending in schizophrenia over a 25-year period marked by deinstitutionalization and increasing prevalence of comorbid substance use disorders. *American Journal of Psychiatry*, *161*, 716–727.

West, D. J., & Walk, A. (1977). *Daniel McNaughton*. London: Gaskell.

4

Homicidal Celebrity Stalkers: Dangerous Obsessions With Nonpolitical Public Figures

Louis B. Schlesinger and V. Blair Mesa

Since the mid-1990s, stalking has received an enormous amount of attention in the scientific, legal, and public press. Although most stalkers do not become violent, an estimated 3% to 36% of them do engage in various aggressive acts (Mullen, Pathé, & Purcell, 2000), including fondling, grabbing, and punching, as well as using a weapon (Meloy & Gothard, 1995). Among those stalkers who do become violent, most target former intimate partners rather than strangers (Harmon, Rosner, & Owens, 1995; Meloy, Davis, & Lovette, 2001; Palarea, Zona, Lane, & Langhinrichsen-Rohling, 1999).

Although few women get killed by their abusive partners or former partners, cases of intimate partner violence that end in homicide are well known (American Psychological Association, 1996; Browne, 1993). However, it is difficult to accurately determine how many of the victims who were killed were also stalked before the homicide. According to Meloy (1998), the stalker most likely to become violent is a simple obsessional (Zona, Sharma, & Lane, 1993)—one who has been unable to let go of a prior intimate relationship. Research by Moracco, Runyaan, and Butts (1998), as well as by McFarlane et al. (1999), has revealed that anywhere from 23% to 76% of women who were killed by a partner or former partner were stalked before their deaths, but most of these women had not reported the stalking to the police. Walker and Meloy (1998) also found that in these circumstances, it is extremely difficult to stop a man who is intent on "using surveillance and eventually finding [the victim]" (p. 142). Meloy (1996) has reported a number of such cases and has concluded that "a man who is obsessed with a woman and stalks may kill her to possess her" (Walker & Meloy, 1998, p. 142).

Although information about stalkers who kill former intimate partners is increasing, considerably less is known about stalkers who attempt to kill and actually kill strangers (Meloy, 1998; Schlesinger, 2002). Individuals who are particularly vulnerable to being stalked by strangers are public figures such as film, television, musical, and sports celebrities. Hoffmann and Sheridan (2005) describe the relatively high risk such public figures are at from obsessed individuals, many of whom are current or former fans. These authors report that direct threats rarely precede attacks on this group of victims, notwithstanding evidence of preplanning and some type of communication by the offender with the future victim before the actual assault.

One of the cases that brought national attention to the problem of celebrity stalking and was an impetus for enactment of the first antistalking law in California was the murder of actor Rebecca Schaeffer by an obsessed fan who had a long history of disturbed interpersonal attachments. The offender was 19-year-old Robert Bardo, whose early life was marked by generalized violent threats, suicide attempts, a psychiatric hospitalization, school failure, and few friendships, either male or female. Bardo first became obsessed with a teenage celebrity, then switched obsessions to Schaeffer, whom he described to an evaluating psychiatrist as a "goddess...too sweet, clean, and pure for [sexual] fantasies." However, after Schaeffer appeared in a movie that included a bedroom scene, Bardo became incensed, and his attitude toward Schaeffer shifted dramatically from adulation to intense anger. He eventually located her residence, and on his second visit shot and killed her. This case highlights not only the problem of celebrity stalking but also the potential for extreme violence among this small subgroup of offenders.

Celebrity stalkers are similar to noncelebrity stalkers in an important way—few become very violent and even fewer kill (Schlesinger, 2006). Because the number of celebrity stalkers who do act out in an aggressive way is so small, little research has been carried out on this subgroup of individuals. However, in an unpublished paper, de Becker (1990) addressed the problem of fans who stalk and also attack celebrities. He found his sample of violent celebrity stalkers to be quite homogenous.

> Public figure attackers and stalkers are not a type unto themselves with necessarily common features. Efforts to categorize them as loners, frustrated about their lack of impact on the world, striving for greatness by destroying greatness, may be wrong as often as right. There certainly are commonalities, but there are just as many differences, and defining the "typical" assassin is not more practical than defining the "typical" murderer. They are as complex and as various as people in general. They can be motivated by jealousy, fear, anger, revenge, frustration, just as any other person....They can be as different as the spouse killer and the hired killer. (p. 7)

In the first empirical study of celebrity stalkers, Dietz et al. (1991) reviewed threatening and inappropriate letters sent to Hollywood celebrities.

These researchers studied approximately 1,800 such letters from 214 subjects. Results indicated that the 107 subjects who pursued encounters with celebrities were different in a number of ways from those letter writers who did not pursue encounters. And, contrary to expectation, the making of threats or the absence of threats was not associated with pursuit behavior. In addition, none of the subjects studied who pursued celebrities actually assaulted, attempted to assault, or killed their celebrity targets.

In an attempt to build upon Dietz et al.'s (1991) findings, Leets, de Becker, and Giles (1995) carried out a study comparing the letters of normal (college student) fans with inappropriate letters received by Hollywood celebrities. They found that while "normal" fans were the same as fans who wrote inappropriate letters in that both groups had a desire for contact with the celebrity, the two groups differed in that "the inappropriate pursuers [had] unreasonable and bizarre expectations. In particular, the fringe desires from the inappropriate sample, such as requests for marriage, sexual contact, valuable gifts, and having children with the celebrities, are not seen among the desires of the normal sample" (p. 116). Thus, Leets et al. (1995) found the reasonableness of expectations to be the most significant difference between the two groups. But even the inappropriate letter writers with unreasonable expectations did not perpetrate violence—and certainly not homicidal violence—against any of the celebrities to whom letters were sent.

In an attempt to determine whether an obsession with a celebrity is predictive of subsequent aggressive behavior against the celebrity, McCutcheon, Lange, and Houran (2002) developed a psychometric scale to assess the degree of obsession (or "celebrity worship") a fan might have. The authors contend that their "celebrity worship scale" is helpful in determining which individuals might be predisposed to act out. The results are complex but seem to indicate that "overidentification" with a celebrity may lead to a form of dissociation, which could be connected to violent encounters. In a follow-up study, McCutcheon, Ashe, Houran, and Maltby (2003) found a cognitive profile that predisposes an individual to develop celebrity worship behavior similar to thinking patterns found in cases of erotomania.

Homicidal Celebrity Stalker Cases

Although numerous celebrities have been stalked over the years, relatively few have been victims of severe violence or, more specifically, homicidal violence. To gain an understanding of this small, but potentially lethal, subgroup of celebrity stalkers, a descriptive study was conducted. Political public figures were not included because the underlying motivation and type of obsession of those who stalk politicians are different from the motivation and obsessional type of those who stalk celebrity actors, musicians, or athletes. For example, political figures are usually followed and assassinated for a variety of motives (Fein & Vossekuil, 1999), but not involving sexual-affectional expectations. Sometimes the motivation grows out of a psychosis (Harris, 1978; Kalian,

Zabow, & Witztum, 2003), but rarely, if ever, is the motive a result of an obsessive interpersonal attachment.

Accordingly, through a comprehensive archival search, we identified cases of (nonpolitical) celebrities who had been stalked and killed—or who had a serious homicidal attempt made on their life (or the life of another individual) by a fan. Our research—the sources for which included the Internet, personal interviews, and several books on the topic (Mair, 1995; Sauerwein, 2006)— identified 16 celebrities (from 1949 through 2004) who had been victimized in this manner. Although we found a lot of information on the celebrities, unfortunately, we uncovered less information on the offenders. But, based on the evidence available, some interesting findings emerged.

The following are brief summaries of each case of homicidal celebrity stalking, grouped according to the connection between the stalker and victim: cases where the stalker killed or attempted to kill the celebrity with whom he or she was obsessed (11 cases); cases where the violence was displaced to a person directly connected to the celebrity (3 cases); and cases where the violence was displaced to an individual completely independent of the celebrity (3 cases). Four cases of celebrity stalkers who threatened, attempted, or committed suicide are also included as a separate group because their behavior was not homicidal but rather involved harming themselves.

Stalker Killed or Attempted to Kill the Celebrity

1. Eddie Waitkus (1949)

Ruth Anne Steinhagen had been following Waitkus through his professional baseball career from its beginning in 1941, when she was 11 years old. She collected clippings and pictures of the first baseman, wrote him letters, and would sometimes set a place for him at the family table. Despite this, her parents believed her interest in Waitkus was harmless. Steinhagen was upset after Waitkus was traded to a rival team in December 1948. She found out when Waitkus was scheduled to play his old team in her hometown of Chicago and booked a room at the hotel where he would be staying. She used a false name and paid the bellhop to leave Waitkus a cryptic note to lure him to her room. When he arrived, Steinhagen shot him in the chest. She called for help when she realized Waitkus was still alive. He survived, and Steinhagen was found legally insane and hospitalized.

2. John Lennon (1980)

Mark David Chapman had been a fan of the iconic musician and founder of the Beatles. In fact, Chapman reportedly married a Japanese American woman because she reminded him of Lennon's wife, Yoko Ono. He had a history of drug addiction and mental illness and had been hospitalized for suicide attempts in the past. He also claimed to have had thoughts of killing other celebrities but fixated on Lennon after he perceived the former Beatle to be "selling out." He considered Lennon to be a phony in that Lennon called for love and peace while enjoying a privileged lifestyle. Chapman had gone to New York City once before to find Lennon but had not followed through with his plan. But this time was different. Chapman brought a gun and spent hours outside Lennon's apartment building. When Lennon autographed an album for Chapman one afternoon, he could not have known that several hours later Chapman would fatally shoot him. After the shooting, Chapman waited patiently for authorities to arrive. He pled guilty to murdering Lennon and received a sentence of 20 years to life.

3. Theresa Saldana (1982)

The precipitating factor in Arthur Jackson's obsession with Theresa Saldana is not known, but it is commonly thought to have been her performance in the movie *Raging Bull*. Jackson believed that his love for Saldana would prevent him from having a relationship with any other woman. He was a paranoid schizophrenic and thought that he could be with Saldana in the afterlife if he murdered her and then killed himself. The future offender sent letters to the actor and called her agent and her mother to find out personal information about her. He also hired a private investigator to learn her address. Saldana, informed she might be in danger, called the police, who did not take the threats seriously. Jackson traveled to Los Angeles from Scotland, found Saldana's apartment, and stabbed her 10 times before being subdued by a water deliveryman who witnessed the attack. Saldana survived, and Jackson went to prison for the crime. While incarcerated, he continued to send Saldana death threats, thereby lengthening his sentence. He died in prison in 2004.

4. Rebecca Schaeffer (1989)

Rebecca Schaeffer was beginning a promising acting career in the 1980s, her popularity growing because of her role in the sitcom *My Sister Sam*. Robert Bardo, a disturbed paranoid schizophrenic young man, fell in love with Schaeffer after seeing her in the television show. However, Bardo became angry when he saw a movie in which Schaeffer was in a bedroom scene, which ruined Bardo's perception of Schaeffer as his perfect woman. He decided she had become another "Hollywood tramp" and had to be punished. He hired a detective who got her address from California motor vehicle records. Bardo then went to Schaeffer's apartment, rang the bell, and fatally shot her when she came to the door. Following the shooting, he fled and subsequently went to Arizona, where police apprehended him as he was running in freeway traffic. He confessed to Schaeffer's murder and received a sentence of life in prison without the possibility of parole. As recently as 2005, Bardo said he continued to think of the actress daily.

5. Sharon Gless (1990)

Sharon Gless acquired a number of female fans while starring in the 1970s television show Cagney and Lacey. Joani Leigh Penn was one of these fans. At first, her fan mail seemed harmless, but her letters became increasingly bizarre and threatening; some included pictures of Penn holding guns to her own head. Gless obtained a restraining order against Penn in 1988, but it did not deter this stalker. Penn said she was in love with Gless and had decided that she would break into her home, sexually assault the actress, and then commit suicide in front of her. Her decision to take action may have been prompted by Gless's testimony before the California legislature about the need to increase the privacy of actors' records. Penn broke into Gless's house with a rifle and over 500 rounds of ammunition. Gless was not at home at the time, and Penn became involved in a 7-hour standoff with police before finally surrendering. The offender was sent to prison but was paroled in 1992.

6. Jerry Lewis (1994)

Actor and comedian Jerry Lewis probably had no idea that doing a favor for a long-time employee would result in years of threats and harassment. A woman who worked for Lewis had been dating Gary Randolph Benson and asked Lewis to obtain a background check on her new beau. Later, the woman told Benson what had been done, prompting him to begin calling and threatening Lewis. Benson eventually arrived at Lewis's home with a gun and threatened to kill him. Benson pled guilty to charges filed against him and received probation. However, his obsession with Lewis did not end, and he continued to threaten him; Benson was finally sent to prison, where he died in August 2001.

7. Björk Gudmonsdottir (1996)

Björk had a difficult year in 1996. Personal matters and an assault on a member of the press were creating problems for the singer. She was also being fixated upon by Ricardo Lopez, a disturbed young fan who kept a lengthy diary in which he often wrote about Björk. He became enraged after she became involved in an interracial relationship, and he made up his mind to kill her. After discarding a few ideas as unworkable, he decided to assemble an acid bomb and place it in a hollowed-out book. He videotaped his preparations, mailed the bomb, and then committed suicide while still on video, surrounded by pictures of Björk and listening to her music. Neighbors alerted the police, who, on finding Lopez deceased and the video camera nearby, were able to have the bomb intercepted before anyone could be injured by it.

8. Jill Dando (1999)

Jill Dando was a popular television personality in England, who had recently been engaged. Dando became concerned about threatening phone calls and letters she was receiving. In addition, someone had tried to get some of her utility bills switched to a different name. Barry Michael George, who had assumed false identities and had long been obsessed with celebrities—Princess Diana before her death—as well as the BBC, shot Dando execution style on her doorstep with a small caliber handgun. Dando bore a striking resemblance to Diana. The case was not immediately solved, and in the interim George was vocal about the need to erect a memorial for Dando. After several months, George was charged with the murder. He was convicted and received a life sentence.

9. George Harrison (1999)

Michael Abram believed he was possessed by George Harrison and that he was apparently on a mission from God to kill the former Beatle. To do so, he broke into the musician's home and stabbed him multiple times. Harrison's injuries were not fatal; Abram was found insane.

10. Ken Dodd (2001)

It is not unusual for stalking victims to be older than victims of other types of crimes. Still, British comedian Ken Dodd was likely surprised to learn that he was being stalked at age 73. Thirty-four-year-old Ruth Tagg had spent months weaving a tapestry of Dodd, as well as sending him letters and nude photos of herself. After her attempts to begin a relationship with Dodd were unsuccessful, Tagg felt insulted and rejected. She viewed Dodd's live-in girlfriend as her rival and began to send sinister items—threatening letters, offensive T-shirts, and a perfumed dead rat. Ultimately, Tagg pled guilty to harassment and arson and was hospitalized after she pushed burning rags through the mail slot of Dodd's home.

11. "Dimebag" Darrell Abbott (2004)

"Dimebag" Darrell was one of the founding members of the heavy metal band Pantera. Nathan Gale had long been a fan of Pantera, having listened to their music to energize himself before his high school football games. However, over time, Gale's increasingly erratic and disturbing behavior prompted many of his friends to distance themselves from him. For instance, Gale had accused Pantera of stealing his lyrics and said that he was going to sue the band. Gale spent a short time in the Marines, but was discharged, evidently because of mental illness. In the meantime, Pantera had broken up, and Abbott was now the guitarist for a new band, Damageplan. Gale brought a gun and sneaked into the show when Damageplan played near his hometown in Ohio. He stormed the stage and began shooting, killing four people, including Abbott, and injuring three others. Gale was fatally shot by police during this attack. Some witnesses stated that they might have heard Gale make a comment about the break-up of Pantera before he began shooting.

Displaced Violence Toward Individuals Directly Connected to the Celebrity

1. Peggy Lennon (1969)

Peggy Lennon, a member of the 1950s singing group the Lennon Sisters, was pursued for several years by an obsessed fan, Chester W. H. Young. He wrote strange and intimate letters to the singer and would often show up at various places to be near her, including lunches and church services. The offender believed that he and Lennon were married and had a child together. A judge ordered Young to stay away from the singer, but to no avail. For a time, he also wrote letters to Lyndon Johnson, threatening to harm the president if he did not help Young "reunite" with Peggy Lennon. Young also blamed Peggy's father and manager, Bill Lennon, for keeping the couple apart. He went to the golf course where Bill Lennon worked as a pro and shot him to death. Young then committed suicide with the same gun.

2. Steffi Graf (1993)

Steffi Graf and Monica Seles were two women with many things in common: Both were young professional tennis players, among the best in the world, and both were being stalked by a German man named Gunter Parche. Parche was obsessed with Graf and had a collection of posters and videos of the athlete. He was upset by the thought that Seles had cost Graf her number one world ranking, especially after Seles had beaten Graf in a controversial match. Parche attacked Seles during a break in one of her matches in Germany, stabbing her in the back. Seles recovered, and Parche was deemed to be "psychologically abnormal" and received probation and treatment for his crime.

3. Michael Landon (1988)

Michael Landon was a popular television actor, known mostly for playing wholesome, family-oriented characters. His stalker, Nathan Trupp, had different ideas. He believed Landon was a Nazi and that God had given Trupp a divine mission—to kill Landon. Trupp bought a ticket to tour Universal studios and asked where Landon could be found. He approached a guard shack and asked to use the phone to call his victim but was refused. He then shot and killed two security guards before being shot by police. He was later found to be insane and was sent to a forensic hospital in California.

Displaced Violence Toward Individuals Totally Unconnected to the Celebrity

1. Jodie Foster (1981)

After seeing Jodie Foster in Taxi Driver, John Hinckley Jr. became enamored of the young actress. He wrote Foster letters and called her, managing to speak with her twice. Hinckley even moved to Connecticut to be near her when he found out that she was enrolled at Yale. The offender believed that he needed to impress Foster to have a relationship with her. He eventually made an attempt on Ronald Reagan's life; he shot the president outside a Washington, DC, hotel, injuring Reagan and three others. Hinckley was found insane and remains (partially) hospitalized. It has been reported that for many years, he continued his obsession with Foster, and he also developed an obsession with a female pharmacist at St. Elizabeths Hospital, who looked like Jodi Foster.

2. Olivia Newton-John (1983)

Michael Perry had been obsessed with Newton-John since 1980, when he saw her in the movie *Xanadu*. He had escaped from a mental hospital, and believed that Newton-John was a muse who had been locked beneath the earth and needed to be rescued by him. Perry spent hours listening to Newton-John's music, wrote her letters, and believed that the singer communicated with him through her eyes. He camped in the hills behind her property to watch her. After Perry was returned to the care of his family, he murdered five of his relatives by shooting them through the eyes.

3. Olivia Newton-John (1984)

Ralph Nau had stalked the singer-actor for 10 years. During this time, he had obsessions with several other celebrities, including Sheena Easton. He believed that he and Newton-John were involved in a romantic relationship and were being kept apart by someone named Maria. Nau wrote Newton-John hundreds of letters, some threatening, and collected pictures and posters of her. He even traveled to Australia to find the singer. He returned to the United States and moved in with his family on their farm. While he was there, his family noticed that Nau displayed some bizarre behaviors: he would often scream for no reason, he mentioned thoughts of suicide, and, at one point, he even cut open a cow that had died on the farm and slept inside the cow's body for a night. Subsequently, Nau beat his younger brother to death, apparently delusional at the time.

Stalker Threatened, Attempted, or Committed Suicide

1. Justine Bateman (1989)

John Thomas Smetek had stalked actress Justine Bateman for 7 months, convinced that he had had an affair with her 7 years before in his home state of Texas. He showed up at one of Bateman's rehearsals in California, threatening to shoot himself in front of her unless she agreed to return "home" with him. It took the police 3 hours to get him to surrender.

2. Andrea Evans (1990)

The soap opera actor Andrea Evans discovered she was being stalked in 1987 while talking with her friend Regis Philbin. Philbin mentioned a letter that he had received from Evans regarding a dog. Evans denied having mailed such a letter and soon realized that someone was impersonating her, sending letters in her name. She also began to receive fake legal documents. The Russian immigrant stalker came to Evans's studio, grabbed her, and began yelling at her about legal documents and dogs, until he was removed by security. He returned to her studio on another occasion and, frustrated at not being able to locate Evans, slashed his own wrists. He was admitted to a psychiatric hospital, where he listed Evans as his next of kin. The actress left her role in *One Life to Live* and essentially went into hiding for nearly a decade following this incident.

3. David Letterman (1998)

Margaret Ray stalked the late night television host for years, breaking into one of his homes and even going for a drive in his car. She believed she was Letterman's wife. After going through many court proceedings and interventions by the authorities, Ray (who was also schizophrenic) committed suicide by kneeling in front of an oncoming train.

4. Michael Douglas (2004)

Dawnette Knight was obsessed with actor Michael Douglas and viewed his wife, Catherine Zeta-Jones, as a threat to their relationship. Knight believed she and Douglas had had an affair years before she began her pursuit of him, and she claimed she was still in love with him. As a result, she began to send threatening letters to Zeta-Jones, describing in detail how she would kill and dismember her. Knight's stalking behavior persisted when Zeta-Jones was staying in hotels or filming on various locations. She even sent letters to actor Kirk Douglas, inviting him to his daughter-in-law's funeral. After being arrested and charged with stalking and several counts of making criminal threats, Knight pled not guilty, then allegedly tried to kill herself with an overdose of barbiturates while incarcerated. She recovered, changed her plea to no contest, and received a 3-year sentence.

Demographic and Behavioral Patterns

The frequency of homicidal celebrity stalking has increased significantly since 1980. As shown in Figure 4.1, there were only 2 cases (one in 1949 and one in 1969) before 1980, and there have been 19 cases since that time. Because suicide often follows homicide as well as homicidal threats, and homicide sometimes follows suicide threats (Harrer & Kofler-Westergren, 1986; MacDonald, 1963, 1967), we analyzed most of our data using all 21 offenders, including the

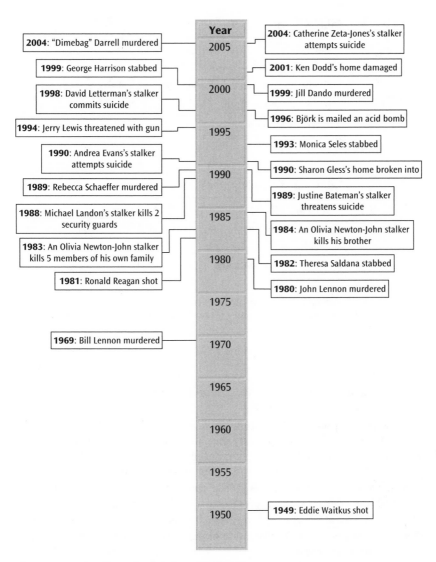

Figure 4.1. Timeline of celebrity stalking cases.

4 suicide cases. Tables 4.1 and 4.2 show that the majority of offenders were not only homicidal but suicidal as well. Even most of those who committed or attempted to commit homicide following the stalking had suicidal threats or attempts in their backgrounds.

Table 4.3 shows that 76% of offenders were male and Caucasian, and that the overall age of the offenders ranged from 19 to 55 years. Their level of education, housing situation, and employment status, however, remain unclear as complete and reliable information in these areas was not always available.

Table 4.1. Homicide/suicide target type

Single celebrity	11 (53%)
Individual connected to celebrity	3 (14%)
Individual not connected to celebrity	3 (14%)
Self (suicide or attempt)	8 (38%)

Note. Total number of offenders = 21. Numbers exceed 21 and percentages exceed 100% because more than one variable was measured at times.

Table 4.2. Offender intent

Homicidal with any target	17 (81%)
Homicidal with celebrity target	14 (67%)
Suicidal	12 (57%)
Suicidal without homicidal intent	4 (19%)
Committed suicide	3 (14%)

Note. Total number of offenders = 21. Numbers exceed 21 and percentages exceed 100% because more than one variable was measured at times.

As shown in Table 4.4, many had prior psychiatric diagnoses, treatment, and hospitalizations; at least seven had committed prior criminal offenses, and three were previously incarcerated.

The predominant method of attack of the 17 homicidal offenders was the use of a firearm (71%), followed by the use of a knife (18%), with one individual using a bomb and another committing arson. As shown in Table 4.5, the majority of offenders called or wrote letters to the celebrities and/or showed up at their workplaces or residences. Many threatened their targets, and several collected items related to the targets (such as photos, magazine articles, albums, movies); 13 individuals engaged in various forms of bizarre behavior related to their celebrity obsession. The duration of the stalking behavior varied greatly, as displayed in Table 4.6.

A direct homicidal attempt was made on 14 celebrity victims: 5 died, 5 were injured, and 4 managed to escape the attack without injury, for a lethality rate of 36% and a casualty rate of 71%. Table 4.7 shows the celebrity victim data. Eight (57%) were male celebrities, and six (43%) were females. The ages of the victims ranged from 19 to over 70; most victims were Caucasian (93%), and their celebrity occupations varied widely with no single pattern standing out.

Other individuals connected to 12 of the offenders (57%), such as family members or friends, knew that the subject was more than just an enthusiastic fan and was, in fact, obsessed with the celebrity. Almost all offenders (18, or 86%) had either unrealistic expectations or delusional expectations of

Table 4.3. Offender demographics

Gender		Age[a]		Ethnicity		Employment		Education		Housing	
Male	16	19–29	7	Caucasian	16	Employed	6	HS dropout	1	Alone	4
Female	5	30–39	8	Hispanic	1	Unemployed	4	HS grad	2	With spouse	1
		40–49	2	African American	1	Unknown	11	College dropout	3	With family	3
		50–55	2	Unknown	3			College grad	1	Other	2
		60 and above	0					Unknown	14	Unknown	11

Note. Total number of offenders = 21.
[a] Age unknown for two offenders.

Table 4.4. Offender psychiatric treatment and offense history[a]

Prior offenses	7 (33%)
Incarceration	3 (14%)
Psychiatric diagnosis	11 (52%)
Psychiatric treatment	12 (57%)
Psychiatric hospitalization	8 (38%)

Note. Total number of offenders = 21. Numbers exceed 21 and percentages exceed 100% because more than one variable was measured at times.
[a] Includes only offenders for whom this information is known.

Table 4.5. Offender stalking behaviors[a]

Letters/calls	14 (67%)
Threats	8 (38%)
Showing up	13 (62%)
Collections	6 (29%)
Bizarre behaviors	13 (62%)

Note. Total number of offenders = 21. Numbers exceed 21 and percentages exceed 100% because more than one variable was measured at times.
[a] Includes only offenders for whom information is known.

Table 4.6. Duration of stalking

<1 year	3
1–2 years	4
3–5 years	9
>5 years	3
Unknown	2

Note. Total number of offenders = 21.

Table 4.7. Celebrity victim data

Gender		Age[a]		Ethnicity		Career type		Attack severity	
Male	8	19–29	4	Caucasian	13	Actor/actress	3	Deceased	5
Female	6	30–39	3	Hispanic	1	Singer/musician	4	Injured	5
		40–49	2	Other	0	Athlete	2	Neither	4
		50–55	1			Comedian	2		
		60–73	3			Other	3		

Note. Total number of celebrity victims on whom an attempt was made = 14.
[a] Age unknown for one victim.

Table 4.8. Sample content of the delusions of celebrity stalkers

Type of delusion	Sample content
Having a relationship with the celebrity	I'm married to him and the mother of his child.
	Your father is keeping us from getting back together.
The celebrity is a threat	That band is stealing my lyrics.
	This actor is a Nazi and must be eliminated.
	I'm possessed by this singer.
Divine missions	God told me to kill him.
	She was just like all the others and had to be stopped.
Need to impress or protect celebrity	She will only want to be with me if I kill someone famous.
	I'll help her by getting rid of her top rival.
"If I can't have you..." delusions	Killing you and then myself is the only way for us to be together.
	When I kill her, I'll be the most important person in her life.
Bizarre ideas	This singer has an evil double who teases me and leads me on.
	She is a muse who is being held captive until I rescue her.
	She causes dead bodies to haunt me.
	She communicates to me with her eyes.
Eliminating perceived love rivals	I'll kill you so I can be with your husband.
	I'll kill you unless you get rid of your girlfriend.

the celebrity. Samples of the content of the disturbed thinking of the stalkers are provided in Table 4.8. With six (possibly nine) offenders, something the celebrity did in his or her personal life offended or angered the stalker and seems to have precipitated the attack.

Case Study

The following case provides a unique opportunity to gain additional insight into the motivational dynamics and behavioral patterns of a homicidal celebrity stalker. An obsessed fan—who made a serious homicidal attempt on a rock star and then committed suicide—kept a detailed, 803-page diary that was begun 2 years before the crime. In addition, the offender left a 20-hour videotape of his planning the murder and the completed suicide.

The subject was unable to be directly evaluated because of his death, but the information that he left—particularly the diary—provides a fascinating glimpse into the psychology of this type of stalker. Although it is most desirable to personally evaluate a subject before drawing definitive conclusions, a form of indirect personality assessment—which has been utilized for decades (Ault & Hazelwood, 1991; Meloy, 2004)—is frequently "conducted without benefit of direct observation but often with greater access to behavioral data about a person than a [direct] evaluation [alone] would provide" (Ebert, 1987, p. 52). There is no standard procedure for conducting a psychological autopsy of this type (Litman, Curphey, Shneidman, Farberow, & Tabachnick, 1963; Selkin, 1994; Shneidman & Farberow, 1961), but guidelines suggest analyzing aspects of the deceased's background such as family and interpersonal relationships, psychiatric and substance abuse treatment, employment, education, and, most pertinent for this case, suicide notes, writings, and diaries.

Background

Ricardo Lopez emigrated to the United States from Uruguay as a young child and was raised in a middle class family in a suburban area of the Southeast. In many ways, his life could be considered rather ordinary in that he had no criminal record and only a few brief outpatient psychiatric contacts just before the offense. At the time of the incident, Ricardo lived by himself in a garden apartment in Hollywood, Florida, working sporadically as an exterminator at his brother's pest control company. He was introverted, but he did have a few male friends and a good relationship with his family.

The future offender had fantasized for years about being a famous artist and dreamed about going to art school. He never had a girlfriend and never even had a friendship with a member of the opposite sex. Those who knew Ricardo described him as easygoing and shy; they had no inkling of the content of his internal life, which was dominated by violent fantasies along with pronounced feelings of inadequacy extending into the sexual area. Family members and friends—and even the psychiatrist who treated him briefly, for anxiety, just before the offense—had no idea that Ricardo was capable of such violent conduct.

The Obsession

Approximately 2 years before the attempted homicide and completed suicide, Ricardo began keeping a diary. On the first page, he made a reference to suicide ("a few years from now... if I'm still here"), and on the next few pages, he wrote about his obsession with a well-known U.S. female film star. However, his adulation of her shifted to anger after he read press reports that described the celebrity's abrupt termination of a long-term relationship and quick and intense involvement with another man. Ricardo severely disapproved of her conduct; however, his anger diminished when he switched obsessions from the movie star to 30-year-old Icelandic pop star Björk Gudmonsdottir. Björk's music has been characterized as somewhat offbeat and rebellious with an erotic dark side involving, for example, images of animals in a gothic forest attacking hunters.

Soon after his interest with Björk began, Ricardo researched all aspects of the celebrity's life. He sent her many fan letters and closely followed her career in an obsessive way. In his diary, he described his fantasy of using a time machine to travel back to the mid-1970s to become friends with Björk's family and become involved in her upbringing. He did not describe his fixation with Björk in sexual—or even romantic—terms; instead, he wanted to be "accepted" by her and become an important part of her life. He wanted to "have an effect on her life." In his diary, he also referred to the Madonna-prostitute syndrome in describing his obsession ("I couldn't have sex with Björk because I love her"). Ricardo did not keep his fascination with Björk completely private; he told his friends and his brother, who told him to "get a real woman, you're obsessed."

Throughout his writings about Björk, the future offender described strong and disturbing feelings of inadequacy that extended into the sexual area. His feelings of inadequacy were much greater than just low self-esteem, as he referred to himself as "a loser who never even learned to drive...I don't respect myself...I never had a girl in my arms [and have never been] loved or even liked by a girl...[I feel] completely alone...Someone said I smell like a dog...You can't begin to realize how weird I feel." Adding to his strong feelings of inadequacy was gynecomastia (the development of breasts in a male), which led him to feel repulsed by his own body.

The diary indicates a clear split between his fantasy life and reality. For example, he wrote that he wanted to become a famous artist but also knew that doing so was unrealistic: "I wouldn't take it seriously, no formal training... What if I'm rejected by art school? They are not used to seeing someone so deformed and young...I am terribly deformed." He also fantasized about being a presenter at the MTV video awards, but he then immediately wrote about his severe financial problems, such as his inability to pay the rent and what he considered to be his menial work as a bug exterminator.

An empirical analysis of the journal (Schlesinger, 2006) revealed an interesting pattern in Ricardo's preoccupations. In the 803 pages, he made 14 direct and indirect references to homicide and 34 references to suicide. He referred to various other celebrities 52 times and described deep feelings of inadequacy and low self-esteem 168 times. But by far the most frequent reference (408 times) was to Björk.

Homicidal Plan

Ricardo's positive obsession with Björk went on for almost 2 years, but switched suddenly to extreme hostility when he learned that Björk had left her long-time boyfriend and had quickly become romantically involved in an interracial relationship with another musician, a relationship Ricardo considered "unacceptable." The exact course of the obsession, specifically, intense anger after disappointment in the celebrity's behavior, was repeated with Björk as it had been approximately 18 months earlier with the first celebrity with whom he was obsessed. However, the obsession with Björk was lengthier and was described by Ricardo as stronger and more fixed. Ricardo angrily wrote, "I wasted eight months and she has a f...king lover." Day after day, he described his anger and feelings of betrayal over Björk's conduct. He slowly developed the idea to punish her. Fifteen months lapsed from the time Ricardo first became angry with the singer to the time he mailed the bomb. However, once he decided to kill the victim, he pursued it relatively quickly, taking less than 3 months to formulate his homicidal plan and carry it out.

When Ricardo became determined to kill Björk, he stopped writing in his diary and began videotaping himself. He first thought of sending the rock star a hollowed-out book containing a device that, when the book was opened, would release several needles designed to pop out and inject her with AIDS-tainted blood he had hoped to obtain from a prostitute. In this way, Björk would not die but would have a fatal disease, and Ricardo would be a part of the rest of her life. He abandoned this plan because he concluded that it was not possible to create a contraption that would work. Instead, he decided to assemble a bomb—which also contained sulfuric acid—and place it in a hollowed-out book. He hoped that when the book opened, the bomb would explode and spray acid on Björk's face. If she did not die, Björk would be disfigured by the acid, and Ricardo would be a part of the rest of her life.

Homicidal Action

It is unknown where Ricardo learned to make a bomb, but, while assembling it, he played the singer's music and referred to himself as her "angel of death." He degraded himself in a bizarre way by shaving his head and painting his face and body half black and half red. Toward the end of the videotaping, Ricardo placed the explosive device in an envelope and held it to the camera, displaying the victim's London address; he said, "I'm going to mail this." A short time later, he returned to his apartment and stated on tape, "I mailed it." He labeled his final videotape "last day, Ricardo Lopez." On the wall behind him he had written, "The 8 mm videos documentation of a crime, terrorist matter, and for the FBI." He evidently thought the FBI would find the case interesting and perhaps use it as a basis for learning about offenders such as himself. Then, while listening to Björk's music, Ricardo put a .38-caliber revolver in his mouth and shot himself.

Posthomicidal Events

Several days after his death, neighbors noticed a foul odor coming from Ricardo's apartment and called the police. The authorities discovered that his assembling, packaging, and mailing the bomb, along with his suicide, were memorialized in the 22 hours of videotape. After watching some of the video, the police contacted Scotland Yard, which intercepted the bomb before it arrived at Björk's London home. The police considered the bomb to be viable; fortunately, no one other than Ricardo was killed or injured.

Discussion

The homicidal risk for noncelebrity stalking has been considered to be quite low (Rosenfeld, 2004), and it seems that the homicidal risk for celebrity stalking may even be lower. In the past 50 years, for example, there have been many thousands of potential celebrity targets, but only 17 cases where a homicide was carried out or a serious homicidal attempt was made. Accordingly, from a purely statistical probability perspective, the chances of a celebrity being seriously attacked or killed by an obsessed fan are extremely remote. Nevertheless, there has been a clear increase in such cases over the past 25 years. Perhaps, cultural changes, such as the introduction of the Internet, cable, and reality television, allow potential offenders to learn intimate information about celebrities, and access to that information fuels the formation of such dangerous obsessions. Extreme caution is always necessary in drawing a profile of a typical offender because there is wide variation in the demographic and behavioral patterns of such individuals. And, especially because the number of homicidal celebrity stalkers is so small, broad conclusions are tenuous. Nevertheless, most of the individuals who engaged in such stalking behavior were Caucasian men, below the age of 40, who had serious psychiatric histories (which often included delusional symptomatology) and used a firearm in the attack. The Björk case, however, is a good illustration of the need for caution in profiling, as this homicidal celebrity stalker had only a few of the typical demographics; he was not Caucasian, but Hispanic; he used a bomb rather than a gun, and he had only two brief outpatient mental health contacts for symptoms of anxiety.

We believe a dynamic approach to risk assessment in cases of potential homicidal celebrity stalking is more useful than reliance on a static profile based on demographics (Wong & Gordon, 2006). For instance, a review of our cases supports Schlesinger's (2006) contention that three red flags are useful indicators of a dangerously obsessed person: (1) all the celebrity stalkers seemed to have crossed the line from being loyal fans to being obsessed with their celebrity victims, and the level of obsession was apparent to others in at least half the cases; (2) almost every offender had unrealistic or delusional expectations of the celebrity; and (3) where information was available, almost half the offenders were angry about some personal behavior of the celebrity, which seemed to have served as a trigger for the violent acting out. Accordingly, our findings strongly suggest that mental health practitioners, law enforcement officers, physicians, and others who may have contact with such potentially dangerous individuals ask a few brief questions of the (possibly) obsessed fan to try to uncover the aforementioned ideation.

Clearly, not all individuals who have the three risk factors will act out in a violent manner. Identifying those individuals who are at risk of actually acting out is aided by an understanding of the catathymic process (Meloy, 1992; Schlesinger, 2002, 2004, 2006). The concept of catathymia was first used by Wertham (1937) to explain homicides that result from strong, underlying, emotionally charged conflicts that produce a change in thinking so that the future offender acquires a fixed idea that he must carry out a violent act as a solution to his internal conflicts. Revitch and Schlesinger (1981, 1989) and Schlesinger (2004) described two types of catathymic homicides, the acute and the chronic. Acute cases involve sudden violence, while chronic cases involve violence following a period of obsessive rumination.

The chronic form of the catathymic process—most relevant to understanding the motivational dynamics of homicidal stalking (Meloy, 1992)—encompasses three stages: incubation, violent act, and a subsequent feeling of relief. During the incubation period, which may last from several days to over a year, the future offender becomes obsessively preoccupied with the future victim. This obsession develops into an idea that he or she must carry out a violent act against someone he or she professes to love or whom he or she previously loved, such as a current or former intimate partner or, in the case of public figures, a celebrity who has become an intimate part of his fantasy life. Initially, the idea to kill is ego-dystonic and resisted, but subsequently, the thought evolves and takes on a root-like fixation; the individual cannot shake the thought, and he develops a tremendous urge to act out. Virtually all of the cases of homicidal celebrity stalking studied involved violence that was planned (during the incubation phase), demonstrating the predatory nature (Meloy, 2006) of these attacks and killings.

Following the violence in a catathymic attack, the perpetrator frequently feels a distinct sense of relief, accompanied by a change in attitude toward the victim, who is often remembered with sympathy rather than with anger. "Thus, catathymic homicides are a way to secure liberation from deep seated conflicts—such as fear of control, intimacy, and sexual inadequacy—that the offender is otherwise unable to resolve" (Schlesinger, 2006, p. 44). If the catathymic tension is not released through the homicidal act, suicide often follows, as was also found in our study.

In many cases of celebrity stalking, the catathymic process is applicable and helps explain why a particular offender acts out violently while others who have similar obsessive ideas manage to contain their behavior. Homicidal celebrity stalkers not only place at risk the celebrity but also those closely connected to the celebrity, individuals totally unconnected to the celebrity, as well as themselves. Because so many homicidal celebrity stalkers have had prior contact with a mental health professional, an understanding of the catathymic process—specifically the future offender's idea that violent behavior is a solution to an internal conflict—as well as questioning of potential offenders for the presence of the three red flags noted seems to be a good practical prevention strategy.

References

American Psychological Association (1996). *APA presidential task force on violence and the family report*. Washington, DC: Author.

Ault, R. L., & Hazelwood, R. R. (1991). Indirect personality assessment. In R. R. Hazelwood, & A. W. Burgess (Eds.), *Practical aspects of rape investigation* (2nd ed.) (pp. 205–218). Boca Raton, FL: CRC.

Browne, A. C. (1993). Violence against women by male partners. *American Psychologist, 48,* 1077–1087.

de Becker, G. (1990). *Better to be wanted by the police than not to be wanted at all.* Studio City, CA: Gavin de Becker.

Dietz, P. E., Matthews, D. B., Van Duyne, C., Martell, D. A., Parry, C. D. H., Stewart, T., et al. (1991). Threatening and otherwise inappropriate letters sent to Hollywood celebrities. *Journal of Forensic Sciences, 36,* 185–209.

Ebert, B. W. (1987). Guide to conducting a psychological autopsy. *Professional Psychology: Research and Practice, 18,* 52–56.

Fein, R., & Vossekuil, B. (1999). Assassination in the United States: An operational study of recent assassins, attackers, and near-lethal approachers. *Journal of Forensic Sciences, 44,* 321–333.

Harmon, R., Rosner, R., & Owens, H. (1995). Obsessional harassment and erotomania in a criminal court population. *Journal of Forensic Sciences, 40,* 188–196.

Harrer, G., & Kofler-Westergren, B. (1986). Depression and criminality. *Psychopathology, 19,* 215–219.

Harris, I. D. (1978). Assassins. In I. L. Kutash, S. B. Kutash, & L. B. Schlesinger (Eds.), *Violence: Perspectives on murder and aggression* (pp. 198–218). San Francisco: Jossey-Bass.

Hoffmann, J. M., & Sheridan, L. P. (2005). The stalking of public figures: Management and intervention. *Journal of Forensic Sciences, 50,* 1–7.

Kalian, M., Zabow, A., & Witztum, E. (2003). Political assassins: The psychiatric perspective and beyond. *Medicine and Law, 22,* 113–130.

Leets, L., de Becker, G., & Giles, H. (1995). Fans: Exploring expressed motivations for contacting celebrities. *Journal of Language and Social Psychology, 14,* 102–123.

Litman, R. E., Curphey, T. J., Shneidman, E. S., Farberow, N. L., & Tabachnick, N. O. (1963). Investigation of equivocal suicides. *Journal of the American Medical Association, 184,* 924–930.

MacDonald, J. M. (1963). The threat to kill. *American Journal of Psychiatry, 120,* 125–130.

MacDonald, J. M. (1967). Homicidal threats. *American Journal of Psychiatry, 124,* 475–482.

Mair, G. (1995). *Star stalkers.* New York: Kensington Publicity.

McCutcheon, L. E., Ashe, D. D., Houran, J., & Maltby, J. (2003). A cognitive profile of individuals who tend to worship celebrities. *Journal of Psychology, 137,* 309–322.

McCutcheon, L. E., Lange, R., & Houran, J. (2002). Conceptualization and measurement of celebrity worship. *British Journal of Psychology, 93,* 67–87.

McFarlane, J. M., Campbell, J. C., Wilt, S., Sachs, C. J., Ulrich, Y., & Xu, X. (1999). Stalking and intimate partner femicide. *Homicide Studies, 3,* 300–316.

Meloy, J. R. (1992). *Violent attachments.* Northvale, NJ: Aronson.

Meloy, J. R. (1996). Stalking (obsessional following): A review of some preliminary studies. *Aggression and Violent Behavior, 1,* 147–162.

Meloy, J. R. (Ed.). (1998). *The psychology of stalking: Clinical and forensic perspectives.* New York: Academic Press.

Meloy, J. R. (2004). Indirect personality assessment of the violent true believer. *Journal of Personality Assessment, 82,* 138–146.

Meloy, J. R. (2006). The empirical basis and forensic application of affective and predatory violence. *Australian and New Zealand Journal of Psychiatry, 40,* 539–547.

Meloy, J. R., Davis, B., & Lovette, J. (2001). Risk factors for violence among stalkers. *Journal of Threat Assessment, 1,* 3–16.

Meloy, J. R., & Gothard, S. (1995). Demographic and clinical comparisons of obsessional followers and offenders with mental disorders. *American Journal of Psychiatry, 152,* 258–263.

Moracco, K. E., Runyan, C. W., & Butts, J. D. (1998). Femicide in North Carolina, 1991–1993. *Homicide Studies, 2,* 422–446.

Mullen, P. E., Pathè, M., & Purcell, R. (2000). *Stalkers and their victims.* Cambridge, UK: Cambridge University Press.

Palarea, R. E., Zona, M. A., Lane, J. L., & Langhinrichsen-Rohling, J. (1999). The dangerous nature of intimate relationship stalking: Threats, violence, and associated risk factors. *Behavioral Science and Law, 17,* 269–283.

Revitch, E., & Schlesinger, L. B. (1981). *Psychopathology of homicide.* Springfield, IL: Thomas.

Revitch, E., & Schlesinger, L. B. (1989). *Sex murder and sex aggression.* Springfield, IL: Thomas.

Rosenfeld, B. (2004). Violence risk factors in stalking and obsessional harassment: A review and preliminary meta-analysis. *Criminal Justice and Behavior, 31,* 9–36.

Sauerwein, S. (2006). *Celebrity stalkers.* Canmore, Alberta: Altitude Publishing.

Schlesinger, L. B. (2002). Stalking, homicide, and catathymic process: A case study. *International Journal of Offender Therapy and Comparative Criminology, 46,* 64–74.

Schlesinger, L. B. (2004). *Sexual murder: Catathymic and compulsive homicides.* Boca Raton, FL: CRC.

Schlesinger, L. B. (2006). Celebrity stalking, homicide, and suicide: A psychological autopsy. *International Journal of Offender Therapy and Comparative Criminology, 50,* 39–46.

Selkin, J. (1994). Psychological autopsy: Scientific psychohistory or clinical intuition? *American Psychologist, 49,* 74–75.

Shneidman, E. S., & Farberow, N. L. (1961). Sample investigations of equivocal deaths. In N. L. Farberow, & E. S. Shneidman (Eds.), *The cry for help* (pp. 118–129). New York: McGraw-Hill.

Walker, L. E., & Meloy, J. R. (1998). Stalking and domestic violence. In J. R. Meloy (Ed.), *The psychology of stalking* (pp. 140–161). New York: Academic Press.

Wertham, F. (1937). The catathymic crisis: A clinical entity. *Archives of Neurology and Psychiatry, 37,* 974–977.

Wong, S. L. P., & Gordon, A. (2006). The validity and reliability of the Violence Risk Scale: A treatment-friendly violence risk assessment tool. *Psychology, Public Policy, and Law, 12,* 279–309.

Zona, M., Sharma, K., & Lane, J. (1993). A comparative study of erotomania and obsessional subjects in a forensic sample. *Journal of Forensic Sciences, 38,* 894–903.

5

On Public Figure Howlers

Frederick S. Calhoun and
Stephen W. Weston

Public figures risk becoming prey to two distinct and entirely different types of problem individuals. One group consists of *hunters*. Fortunately, they compose a very small percentage of the problem individuals. Hunters truly act on their intent to use lethal violence to avenge some perceived injustice. They target the public figure in the belief (however mythical or irrational) that attacking that public figure will achieve their purpose. Mark Chapman killed John Lennon because Chapman considered Lennon a "phony" who did not deserve his worldwide fame. John Hinckley Jr. tried to assassinate President Ronald Reagan to link his name to the actress Jodie Foster (Clarke, 1990) forever. Although he failed to kill the president, he succeeded in forging that link. Robert Bardo initially stalked the actress Rebecca Schaeffer out of an obsessive infatuation with the innocent character she played in a television series. He killed her when her career turned to more mature, sexy roles. Hunters like these focus on public figures as the escape route from the banality of their own lives.

In doing so, hunters of every stripe follow a particular process for culminating the violence they intend (Fein & Vossekuil, 1995, 2000). The path to intended violence requires hunters to

- develop a grievance toward a particular target;
- come up with the idea that violence is the best, perhaps only, relief to that grievance;
- research and plan their attack;
- prepare for it;

- breach their target's security; and
- actually attack (Calhoun & Weston, 2003).

These behaviors are graphically illustrated in Figure 5.1. As the figure illustrates, the path from grievance to attack is a linear progression, but hunters can falter and go back and forth along the way. Most importantly, anyone who intends to act violently *must* traverse the path to intended violence.

We call the second group of problem individuals who focus on public figures *howlers*. They like to threaten and frighten with words, or to express some unrequited emotional attachment, but they never follow through with any actions. In effect, howlers intend to cause fear or gain attention to themselves through threats, alarming statements, or some expression of a need to be recognized by the targeted public figure. Many howlers communicate with their target repeatedly, thus proving themselves to be more an annoyance than a true or credible threat to the public figure. In effect, howlers do not try to follow the path to intended violence. Instead, they satisfy themselves communicating inappropriately.

In almost all cases involving public figure howlers, the howler does not have a personal relationship with the target. Impersonal howlers usually seek to gain some kind of attention for themselves or they seek a reaction from their target. They almost always communicate from a distance, that is, howlers who focus on celebrities or public figures rarely confront their targets up close and in person. They prefer to keep their distance writing letters, sending e-mails, making telephone calls, or using some other method that maintains a safe distance between the howler and the target. Because their purpose is to frighten, disturb, or get attention, they have no need to be in close proximity to their target. Impersonal howlers *make* threats or other inappropriate communications, but they never actually *pose* a threat.

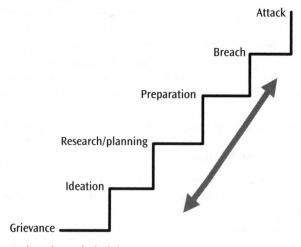

Figure 5.1. Path to intended violence.

Obviously, we use the terms hunters and howlers as shorthand for much more complex concepts. The concept of hunter actually refers to individuals who engage in *attack-related* behaviors. The concept of howler refers to individuals who engage in behaviors designed to unnerve or prompt emotional reactions or gain attention for themselves, but which do not culminate in violence. Fortunately, a simple rule distinguishes hunters from howlers: Hunters hunt and rarely howl; howlers howl and rarely hunt (Calhoun, 1998). This simple analogy expresses a fundamental maxim of threat management. Simply put, hunters and howlers behave differently. What individuals do provides the best indicators for determining if the individual plans to resort to violence or to inappropriate communications. Actions distinguish hunters from howlers. Focusing on that distinction promises the best way for identifying, assessing, and managing those who hunt and those who howl.

Not surprisingly, those who hunt public figures have received far more attention from researchers than those who howl at public figures. Because hunters kill or maim, their focus on public figures is significantly more costly and disruptive than the problems howlers cause. Hence, hunters draw far more attention from scholars. A succession of studies from the Secret Service's National Threat Assessment Center focused exclusively on public figure attackers or suburban school shooters (Borum, Fein, Vossekuil, & Berglund, 1999; Fein & Vossekuil, 1995, 1999, 2000; Fein, Vossekuil, Pollack, & Boram, 2002; Reddy et al., 2001; Vossekuil, Borum, Fein, & Reddy, 2001; Vossekuil, Fein, Reddy, & Borum, 2002; Vossekuil, Reddy, & Fein, 2000). Interestingly, the Secret Service studies admitted from the start that the research targeted a small minority of problem individuals. The studies were clumped under the general title Exceptional Cases Study. Other researchers also restricted their sight exclusively to hunters (e.g., Clarke, 1982, 1989; Friedman, 1983; Laucella, 1998; Restak, 1981; Slomich & Kantor, 1969).

Howlers thus far have received short shrift. Dietz et al. (Dietz, Matthews, Martell, et al., 1991; Dietz, Matthews, Van Duyne, et al., 1991) distinguished those who approached members of Congress and Hollywood celebrities (whom we call hunters) from those who communicated inappropriately but made no effort to approach (whom we call howlers). The two studies published a decade and a half ago, were among the first to distinguish between those who hunt and those who howl (Dietz, Matthews, Martell, et al., 1991; Dietz, Matthews, Van Duyne, et al., 1991). Calhoun, who coined the terms hunter and howler, also compared attackers to nonattackers within the realm of the federal judiciary (Calhoun, 1998). He and Weston eventually expanded the concepts to all venues of intended violence (Calhoun & Weston, 2003). These studies essentially conclude that hunters differ from howlers through their behaviors. Hunters engage in attack-related behaviors; howlers do not. Howlers communicate inappropriately, even threateningly; public figure hunters tend not to do so.

In one fascinating study, Leets et al. studied sinister and innocent celebrity fans. They then compared their findings to those of Dietz et al. (Dietz, Matthews,

Martell, et al., 1991; Dietz, Matthews, Van Duyne, et al., 1991). Leets et al. found that both innocent and sinister fans behaved in similar ways. Both the innocent and the sinister, for example, willingly traveled cross-country to see their celebrity. Both wrote letters to the celebrity, often repeatedly. The differences between them grew out of their expectations. Innocent fans expected "reasonable" outcomes from their fan letters, perhaps a form letter, autograph, small memento, or, most of the time, nothing in return. Sinister fans had "unreasonable and bizarre expectations." They expected marriage, sexual contact, valuable gifts, or children from the celebrity. The sinister fans who approached the celebrity were hunters; those who communicated inappropriately from a distance were howlers (Leets, de Becker, & Giles, 1995).

Both hunters and howlers present problems for public figures, although in very different ways. Hunters represent a serious physical risk; howlers cause mental and emotional distress. Although howlers should never be ignored, the problems they cause are frustrating and disruptive, not menacing. *Sinister howlers*, who threaten public figures, intend to instill fear in their targets. Too often, they succeed. *Binder howlers* communicate their feelings or improbable demands, sometimes romantic, toward their targets. The problem they pose grows out of the feeling of unease and distress they cause the public figure.

Because hunters have received far more scrutiny than howlers, we propose in this chapter to offset some of that imbalance by describing various types of public figure howlers. The typology is derived from a judicious mix of research, practical experience, and stimulating discussions with such nationally recognized experts as Gavin de Becker, James Cawood, John Lane, and others. We offer these views in the hope that they will stimulate much needed additional research on public figure howlers. Because howlers may well outnumber hunters on a magnitude of as much as nine to one (Calhoun, 1998), they compose an overwhelming majority of the problem individuals who prey on public figures.

Figure 5.2 shows an organizational diagram summarizing the several types of impersonal howlers.[1] It divides them into two large groups based on their purpose in making the inappropriate communication or contact. Sinister howlers seek to frighten or disturb; binder howlers look for some emotional attachment from the target.

Impersonally Sinister Howlers

Howlers who do not know their targets but who communicate with them in sinister or ominous ways can be grouped into six categories:

- *Self-defender howlers* feel that the target or an organization has attacked them and they need to defend themselves
- *Celebrity-seeking howlers* direct their threats and inappropriate communications to public figures or other celebrities precisely because of the target's public status

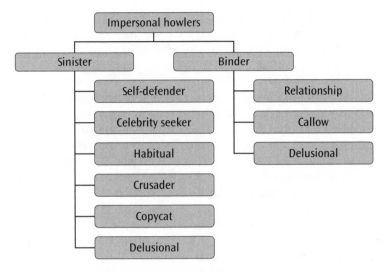

Figure 5.2. Typology of impersonal howlers.

- *Habitual howlers* like to make threats as a way to meet their own needs, almost as a hobby
- *Crusader howlers* use threats to advance some personal cause
- *Copycat howlers* are inspired to make threats and inappropriate communications by news reports of an act of violence or threatened acts of violence
- *Delusional howlers* suffer a mental delusion compelling them to threaten their target

What marks impersonal sinister howlers is their lack of information about the target that is not publicly available. The U.S. Secret Service once had a case of an individual who clearly demonstrated his complete lack of personal knowledge about his target. This subject threatened to kill presidential candidate George H. W. Bush. The howler addressed his threatening letters to President Ronald Reagan at the White House, not the Naval Observatory, where the Vice President lived. When Secret Service agents tracked down the threatener, they asked why he addressed the letters to President Reagan when his actual target was the Vice President. The howler explained that he knew the White House address was 1600 Pennsylvania Avenue, but he did not know the Vice President's address. Thus, it was easier for him to send the threats to the President, presumably hoping the President would be kind enough to forward them along (Vossekuil & Fein, 2000).

In many cases, the sinister howler feels under attack and is lashing back in anger or despair. These *self-defenders* feel imposed upon by something they believe the target has done or is about to do to them. More precisely, the self-defender perceives that he or she has suffered some injury or indignity through some action by the target. In fact, self-defenders may risk losing their job or face prison or be embroiled in a divorce or child custody dispute. They feel, and often with good reason, that the target has power and control over them and is using that power and control adversely against the self-defending howler. Whatever the insult or injury, they feel it very personally. The wound goes deep into their egos.

Self-defenders seek to solve their problem through instilling fear in the target. If they can scare the target away or scare the target into doing what the self-defender wants, then the self-defender's problem will go away. His or her ego will be repaired. Consequently, communications from self-defenders tend to make a complaint or reference an issue or dispute. They talk about their particular problem, usually in great detail. They are desperate to be heard; their efforts to defend themselves justify making the threat. Self-defenders are specific in what they want and how they want it done. They rarely accept any responsibility for their personal situation or problems. They blame their targets entirely, which serves to increase their wrath. Self-defenders reason that if the target caused the problem, then the target must fix it. They seek both justice and restitution, but it is a justice and restitution on their terms only.

Because self-defenders express a specific complaint, they tend to be the howlers most likely to communicate only once. Many of them make their complaint inappropriately, but feel better for having gotten it off their chest. They then get on with their lives. Given the American emphasis on freedom of expression, many self-defenders may not even realize they have communicated inappropriately.

For example, Jonathan W. ran his own business, had a wife and three children, and played a prominent role in his church and community. One day, a customer slipped and broke his arm at Jonathan's business establishment. The customer sued, claiming negligence on Jonathan's part. The costs of the lawsuit escalated enough that Jonathan finally had to dismiss his attorney and begin representing himself. When he failed to follow court procedures and decorum, the judge personally rebuked him. The next day, Jonathan called the judge's chambers and asked to speak to the judge. When told the judge was unavailable, Jonathan replied, "Tell the judge to show me some respect. This is my life we're talking about and if he takes mine, I'll take his." Jonathan then hung up the telephone. Having expressed his anger at the judge, Jonathan calmed down. He returned to court and successfully avoided any additional admonishments from the judge. He also won the lawsuit. Jonathan never tried to contact the judge again.

Thus, self-defender howlers can be recognized by their

- focus on a specific issue, complaint or dispute affecting them;
- desire for the target to rectify the situation;
- use of threats or ominous references to frighten the target into acting;
- refusal to take personal responsibility for their conduct as it relates to the dispute; and
- insistence on a resolution according to their terms.

Because self-defenders are issue specific, they direct their inappropriate communications to those whom they hold responsible for their situation. If they send inappropriate communications to other public figures, it is for the purpose of enlisting those figures' support against the injustice or to oppose the original target. They feel empowered by their threats even though their situation reveals their impotence. If they had the power to effect the change, they would not need to threaten or communicate inappropriately.

Celebrity-seeking sinister howlers focus on public figures or celebrities precisely because the target is famous. The threat or inappropriate communication may have been inspired by something the celebrity did or it could be directed at the celebrity simply because he or she is well known. Hundreds of celebrity howlers threaten the President of the United States every year, sometimes because they disagree with his policies, but more often just because he is the President. Other politicians, such as governors, mayors, and members of Congress, also receive inappropriate communications both because of their public stance on issues and because of the position they hold. Similarly, actors and other public figures often become the target of celebrity howlers. They, too, are targeted both for what they do or say and for the persona they project in the media.

Celebrity-seeking howlers obviously focus on their chosen public figure. Their communications may contain explicit threats, but they may also make ominous comments, suggestions, or proposals. Also, generally celebrity-seeking howlers evince little knowledge of the celebrity beyond what is popularly available. Some action by the public figure may attract the howler's attention. Typically, however, the celebrity-seeking howler addresses the celebrity because the celebrity is famous. The howler envies that fame and tries to steal some of it by communicating with the public figure. It is not the celebrity's stance on the issues of the day or how they behave or what they do that enrages the celebrity-seeking howler. Rather, the howler objects to the fact that the *celebrity* is famous, not the howler.

For example, Tom Q. became obsessed with a male movie star after the star appeared in an action film in which he was portrayed as having near superhuman strength and stamina. Tom completely bought into the movie's premise and the star's feats and did not seem to understand the power of special effects. Instead, he repeatedly wrote the star claiming that he, Tom, could do everything the star had done in the movie. He challenged the star to fight him, then explained in great detail how he would overpower the star and show the world how much stronger he was. The letters never showed any evidence of detailed knowledge about the star. Quite the opposite, the letters all indicated that Tom thought the star was, in reality, the character he had played in the action movie.

Thus, celebrity-seeking sinister howlers can be recognized by their

- focus on the celebrity as a celebrity or on individuals portrayed in the media, or on fictional characters in a movie or on television;
- lack of personal knowledge or information not reported in the media about the public figure;

- expressions of animosity due to the celebrity's fame, fortune, popularity, or position of power and influence; and
- perception that the howler is equal to or better than the howler's opinion of the public figure.

Because celebrity-seeking howlers are attracted to fame and power, they may focus on one particular public figure or more than one. Their interest may shift from target to target, either because the public figure's public position shifts or simply because a different celebrity attracts the howler's attention. For example, former presidents receive far fewer inappropriate communications than they did while in office or their successors receive.

A profound indignation over the celebrity's fame or power undergirds the celebrity-seeking sinister howler's inappropriate communications. They do not profess their love for the celebrity nor their delusions of sharing their lives together. Sinister celebrity-seeking howlers are envious. By threatening the public figure, or communicating in disturbing, ominous ways, the howler imagines bringing the celebrity down a few notches by the fear and trembling the communication causes. In essence, the communications somehow validate the celebrity-seeking howler's sense of self-worth.

Some sinister howlers simply enjoy the act of making explicit threats. They have no ulterior motive other than scaring their targets or, more precisely, imagining the fear their communications cause. These *habitual howlers* howl repeatedly and frequently to multiple targets who have no connection among themselves other than being targets of these communications. For habitual howlers, the act of communicating is just as important as the message they are trying to get across. Most of the time, they do not know their targets personally. Instead, they find them in business directories, by reading news stories, or by sending to-whom-it-may-concern type messages to particular organizations, businesses, or government agencies. For example, doctors obviously work at Veterans Administration hospitals, so it is easy for howlers to address their communications to Head of Surgery or Chief Oncologist or some other title typically associated with a Veterans Administration hospital. Large corporations have chairs and presidents. Reproductive health care facilities have doctors, nurses, and patients. Courts have judges, prosecutors, and clerks. Cities have mayors, states have governors, and the United States has a president. All of them are easy targets for letter writing. For habitual howlers, the self-satisfaction comes in composing the threatening communications, then imagining the reactions they will cause.

Many habitual howlers are inmates confined to either prisons or mental health facilities, or even prison psychiatric wards. Inmate howlers, whether incarcerated or institutionalized, make threats as a way of bringing attention to themselves. Bored or frustrated with their incarceration or institutionalization, and with plenty of time on their hands, they direct their communications generally at public officials or individuals featured recently in the news. By threatening a government official, they invite an investigation. The investigation usually includes law enforcement officers interviewing the inmate. That interview breaks the monotony of life in a prison or mental health facility. It gets the inmate attention, thus confirming that he or she is important and cannot be ignored.

For example, in December 2002, Rodney Yoder, an inmate at a maximum security mental hospital in Illinois, admitted sending over 100 threatening letters to judges, a staff assistant to a U.S. Senator, and other public figures in 1995 and 1996. Yoder hoped the letters would get him reassigned from the hospital to a federal prison, which would give him a fixed release date. At his recommitment hearing in 2002, Yoder assured the jury that he never carried out the threats he mailed. He promised the court he would not do so if he was released from the hospital. The jury voted to recommit him for at least another 6 months (*Associated Press*, December 5, 2002).

Thus, habitual howlers can be recognized by their

- focus on making voluminous communications, frequently to multiple, unrelated targets or to public figures or individuals recently featured in the media;
- lack of expressed personal motive or complaint for making threats to the particular target;
- emphasis on threatening or violent references;
- markings that the communication was sent from a prison or institution, such as envelope stamped "legal mail" or an institution's return address;
- indications of mental illness in the writing; and
- insistence on making multiple threats as a means of getting attention.

Simply put, habitual howlers like to make threats. They send their communications to multiple targets over long periods of time. They have no personal complaint or issue, find their targets in public directories or by good guessing, and make no effort to draw any connection between them. They communicate inappropriately solely for the purpose of communicating inappropriately.

In one bizarre case beginning in the early 1990s, C. D. was incarcerated in a state penitentiary. One afternoon, U.S. marshals held some federal prisoners in the state facility overnight while en route to the federal penitentiary to which the prisoners had been sentenced. That night, C. D. fell in love with one of the federal prisoners, but the next morning, the marshals took their prisoners away. C. D. determined that committing a federal crime was his ticket to get into the federal prison system and reunite with the object of his affection. Because he was already in state prison, his ability to commit such a crime was severely limited in almost every act, except writing threatening letters to federal officials. He began a long campaign of mailing threatening letters to federal judges, prosecutors, and individual marshals.

Crusaders howl as a way of advancing some cause they perceive as larger than themselves. They threaten political or social opponents in the hope of disrupting the target's operations, business, or social activities. They use threats to persuade their opponents to adopt their views or at least abandon the target's.

Crusader howlers are specific in their choice of targets. They go after individuals who represent some political or social cause opposed by the crusader. Religious, moral, or political beliefs motivate them, which allows them to justify the threats as a necessary evil in a larger war. In their minds, the purity of their motives justifies the filth of their tactics.

For example, Clayton Waagner virulently opposed abortions and those who performed them. He expressed his opposition in religious and moral terms. At one point, he toyed with the idea of killing abortion providers, but he could never quite work up the courage to attack. Instead, he settled on a unique way of howling. Inspired by the anthrax letters addressed to two U.S. senators and several newscasters in the fall of 2001 that resulted in the deaths of five people, Waagner tried a howler-style variation of the tactic. "In October of 2001," he explained, "I mailed fake anthrax to 500 abortion clinics. In November of 2001, I Federal Expressed another 300 fake anthrax letters. The white powder I used was harmless, but tested positive for anthrax." Inside each envelope, he also included a brief letter explaining that whoever opened the letter had just been exposed to anthrax. Waagner calculated that his letters resulted in "3,940 clinic closure days, and the disruption of nearly 20,000 scheduled abortions. According to abortion clinic numbers, 5,000 or more babies are alive today because of my act of 'Domestic Terrorism'" (Waagner, undated). Waagner now crusades from a prison cell.

Thus, crusading howlers can be recognized by their

- focus on political, moral, or social issues;
- presenting their issue as larger than themselves;
- portraying themselves as part of a larger group or collective (which usually does not exist); and
- insistence on justifying their behavior because of the way they perceive the importance of their particular issue.

Crusaders have causes. They use threats and inappropriate communications to advance those causes. In effect, they believe that the importance of their issue outweighs everything else. It also excuses their behavior.

A portion of sinister impersonal howlers are *copycats*. They hear or read about some incident, usually an instance of violence, and use that as the inspiration for their threats. This usually happens in the immediate aftermath of some well-publicized tragedy. The copycat then refers to the event as part of the threat or ominous communication. In early March 2001, Charles "Andy" Williams killed 2 and wounded 13 at his high school in Santee, California (*Washington Post*, March 6, 2001). Over a month later, 18-year-old Patrick A. Smith of Maryland e-mailed two high school girls in California. One of the girls attended Williams's high school. Smith wrote, "I'm finishing what Andy started and this time its going to work." Police arrested Smith for making the threat (*Washington Post*, April 25, 2001). Copycat howlers follow the news.

In the week or two after Timothy McVeigh bombed the Murrah Federal Building in Oklahoma City in 1995, law enforcement agencies throughout the country received reports on threats against government buildings. Some were straightforward bomb threats. Others specifically referenced the Oklahoma bombing, saying that the same thing should happen to the building targeted by the threatener. Law enforcement had to take each threat seriously because hunters can be copycats too.

Thus, copycat sinister howlers can be recognized by their

- focus on recent well-publicized acts or threats of violence;
- nonviolent use of past well-publicized tactics that resulted in violence or threat of violence; and
- attempt to replicate the fear caused by someone else's act of violence or threat of violence.

Copycats get their inspiration from the news. They want to wrap themselves in the aura of an actual hunter without going through the necessary steps of taking up the hunt. By referring to someone else's violence, these howlers try to piggyback on the fear the previous violence caused. They ride into infamy on the coattails of the actual hunter.

Finally, some impersonal sinister howlers suffer from some mental disorder that compels them to threaten or harass their target. They may perceive the public figure as the devil or some evil force. Many *delusional impersonal sinister howlers* feel threatened by the public figure or, at a more grandiose level, these howlers may feel that the public figure poses some danger to the community at large, perhaps even the entire world.

One delusional impersonal howler believed that he and a female gospel singer loved each other even though they had never met. He knew of her feelings toward him through the messages she sent him in her song lyrics and by the way she looked at him from the pictures on her album covers. He sent her an average of five letters and packages a day, plus scores of e-mails. When the singer's management staff began returning the letters and packages unopened and then blocked his e-mails, he convinced himself that she had been corrupted and had become the devil's consort. His love turned to hate. His e-mails took on an ominous tone. He made references to an ending, as though the singer would bring on the end of the world. He expressed a desire to stop her, to make a last good-bye, and to be present at the end. Throughout, however, the writer maintained his distance and continued to communicate only through e-mails.

Thus, delusional sinister howlers can be recognized by their

- focus on some imaginary or unreal perception of the public figure;
- belief that the public figure represents a threat to the howler or to others; and
- insistence that the public figure is something other than who the public figure really is.

Impersonally sinister howlers vary in their motives and purposes. Some believe they are defending themselves, others try to bask in a celebrity's glow.

Habitual howlers make threats almost as a hobby. Crusader howlers promote some cause. Copycat howlers use references to the acts of hunters to cloak themselves in the hunter's act. Delusional sinister howlers view the public figure through the distorted prism of their delusions.

Just because howlers do not escalate to violence does not mean that their inappropriate communications do not have to be assessed. Sinister howlers create fear and disrupt the lives of their targets. They must be managed in order to mitigate or offset that fear and disruption.

Impersonally Binding Howlers

Many impersonal howlers try to bind themselves to strangers, almost always public figures or celebrities. These types of binders use the target and their perceived or desired relationship with that target to escape the banality of their own lives by essentially stealing or borrowing the more exciting life of the target. Failures on their own, they lust after the public figure's success. We classify these impersonal binders into three types:

- *Relationship binders* look to the public figure for a relationship. They seek to be a lover, relative, employee, or friend to the target, even if at a distance, and feel somehow incomplete if that relationship does not materialize. Relationship binders frequently see themselves through their pretended relationship with the target. They have little sense of self-worth beyond that relationship.
- *Delusional binders* suffer a mental illness that results in their convincing themselves that they have a binding relationship with their target. They may believe that the public figure sends them messages through the public figure's activities or they believe destiny will bring them and the public figure together;
- *Callow binders* simply do not realize how inappropriate their communications with the target are. They convince themselves that they have a binding relationship with the target and, therefore, this is the way people in a binding relationship act.

Impersonal binders look beyond the dreariness or boredom of their own lives to find fulfillment in someone else's life. Seeking that fulfillment explains why so many impersonal binders focus on public figures or celebrities. People in positions of power or glamour give the appearance of transcending mundane existences.

Relationship binders draw great satisfaction simply from communicating with the target. The communications forge the relationship. They are happy with the long-distance communications because it gives them a connection to their target. Receiving a response from the target does not matter much to relationship binders because they still have the relationship through their communications.

For example, a state senator began receiving numerous overfamiliar letters and cards. All were signed the "U.S. Ambassador to Singapore." The alleged ambassador also sent a package containing a plaque and a written commendation. Through liaison with other agencies, the sender was identified as a 60-year-old woman who has used other titles in the past to communicate with public figures and send them bogus awards. Her pattern was to begin numerous and intense communications with a target, then lose interest, presumably to move on to another target. Her communications, though they were clearly efforts at personal relationships, had never escalated or turned sinister.

Thus, relationship impersonal binders can be recognized by their

- focus on a public figure, especially the powerful, exciting, or glamorous aspects of the public figure's activities;
- expressed desire to continue communicating with the public figure as though those communications formed a bond between them;
- claims to be the best or closest or top supporter or defender of the target; and
- insistence on believing that the binder and the target have a true connection.

Relationship binders want a friend, someone in whom they can confide or share. They find that relationship among the famous and the well known.

Delusional binders step beyond reality in believing that they have a personal, even intimate relationship with the target. They believe that their target responds to the delusional binder's communications by sending coded messages in speeches, songs, performances, even by secret looks in photographs or film footage. The delusion is usually tenacious and the delusional binder refuses to accept any reality that challenges the delusion.

For example, when the local city police department, in an effort to recruit more female officers, posted the photographs and biographies of its highest ranking female officers, Kathy J. took notice. One of them was a deputy chief. Kathy began sending the deputy chief e-mails to her work account and leaving voice mails on the chief's office telephone. All of the phone messages were left late at night when Kathy had some assurance no one would actually answer the phone. In the e-mails and phone messages, Kathy talked about how she had seen the chief's photograph on the police web site. Kathy immediately felt a special kinship with the chief. She knew they were destined to have a love affair. Over time, the e-mails became more sexually explicit, including fantasies involving the chief's law enforcement equipment, especially her handcuffs. When the local newspaper did a story on the deputy chief that mentioned her children, Kathy began talking about her plans to form a family with the chief and the children.

Thus, delusional binders can be recognized by their

- focus on a nonexistent reciprocal relationship between the binder and the target;
- claims that the target is sending messages or signals through the target's work, appearances, or other improbable means;

- insistence that the target feels toward the binder as the binder feels toward the target; and
- evincing possible mental illness in their behavior.

Delusional impersonal binders usually enjoy their delusions without trying to actually live them. They communicate from a distance and rarely engage in approach behavior.

Callow binders are generally too unsophisticated to realize the inappropriateness of their communications. They have a naïve and innocent approach to the world. Infatuated with the target, they express themselves in ways they think lovers always do. They cannot fathom that their communications might be misunderstood and their intentions misinterpreted. If confronted, they frequently act shocked or horrified that anyone would take offense at what they did or how they communicated.

For example, on one occasion, an entire group of individuals banded together by a common hobby became callow impersonal binders. Shortly after Arnold Schwarzenegger took office as the governor of California, the value of his autograph skyrocketed among autograph seekers. One autograph club came up with the idea of making a contest out of it. Through their web site, they offered bragging rights to the first member who could get Governor Schwarzenegger's signature.

The members took the game seriously. Since being governor included having a law enforcement security detail, getting physically close to Schwarzenegger meant getting past the security. Club members began crashing events, sneaking into places the governor was scheduled to appear, and lining the route through which Schwarzenegger would have to walk to get to his next location. Although all the members wanted was his autograph, their efforts to get it disrupted the security.

Thus, callow impersonal binders can be recognized by their

- focus on presuming the target will accept or respond to their communication;
- nonviolent motivations or intentions; and
- insistence on acting on their presumptions.

Frequently, the callow binder can be quite stubborn in contacting the target, but with the right persuasion and approach, they can be convinced of the error of their ways.

Impersonal binding howlers try to fill some gap in their lives. They believe that their binding with someone else, whether stranger or acquaintance, will fill that void. The emptiness can be oppressive enough to compel the impersonal binding howler to turn sinister or, worse, take up the hunt. Consequently, how the threat manager manages these individuals is crucial. Making them feel rejected or ignored compounds the problem that drove them toward seeking a relationship in the first place.

What Howlers Want

Howlers want something very different from what hunters want. Howlers use their communications to cause a reaction, to frighten or enamor, to upset or provoke. They have no need to do anything beyond speaking, writing, or calling, even if they speak, write, or call repeatedly. They never intend to take any action in furtherance of their inappropriate communications. For the howler, communicating is action aplenty. It results in the end they seek. Hunters, by comparison, want a more tangible result. They intend to take violent action to rectify their issues. For them, justice is expressed in force, vengeance in blood, affection in approaching.

Sinister howlers seek fearful reactions from their targets. They communicate to frighten or disturb. As a result, and as odd as it sounds, the target actually invests the threat with whatever value it ultimately has. For the howler, how the target reacts to his or her threat, or, just as importantly, how the howler imagines the target to react is the primary goal. Making the threat is sufficient unto itself.

Sometimes, sinister howlers strike gold. On December 2, 2005, Javier Rodriquez of Connecticut had a court date over driving violations. Because the court had suspended his driver's license, he decided not to drive himself. Unfortunately, he could not find anyone to take him. To get out of this pickle, Rodriquez walked to a telephone booth near his home and placed five telephone calls to various locations across the state. During each call, Rodriquez claimed that bombs had been placed in courthouses and judicial buildings all over the state. In response, all 45 state court buildings were evacuated and searched, including the one at which Rodriquez was scheduled to appear. After police traced the bomb threat calls to the pay phone, they compared the names of nearby residents to the names of people who were scheduled to appear in court, but who did not show up. That led them to Rodriquez (*Associated Press*, December 3 and 6, 2005). He caused plenty of panic, which was the purpose of his phone calls. Unfortunately for him, it did not keep him out of court.

In sum, what howlers want is achieved through the act of communicating inappropriately. Impersonal howlers, both sinister and binder, serve their purposes through their communications. What they want is the reaction, real or, better yet, imagined from the target. Sinister howlers of every stripe seek to cause fear or disquiet in their targets. Binder howlers hope their communications will spawn a relationship with the target. For all howlers, the act of communicating suffices.

Impersonal howlers, whether sinister or binder, generally prefer to keep their distance from their targets. They rely on distance communications to get their inappropriate communications across. They let these communications do all the work. They design their letters, phone calls, faxes, e-mails, or whatever to cause the desired reaction from the target. Even better, once an impersonal howler launches a communication, he or she is then free to imagine that reaction. Thus, no matter what really happens, the howler always believes that he or she succeeded in getting the result he or she sought. Doing anything more risks letting reality intrude.

Distinguishing Hunters From Howlers

Identifying hunters requires focusing on the types of behaviors in which they engage as they traverse the path to intended violence. Traversing the path requires engaging in noticeable activities called attack-related behaviors. Individuals who intend to engage in violence against a target need to research how best to launch the attack, make preparations based on that research, and then actually initiate the violence. Because of that emphasis on behavior, our description of hunters zeroed in on the actions they take rather than discerning the reasons prompting those behaviors. This approach mirrored the reality that threat managers confront. Frequently, the threat manager will receive reports describing suspicious behaviors without any clue concerning the subject's motive. Although the threat manager knows with certainty that the hunter has a grievance, the hunter may not choose to reveal exactly what that grievance is. As a result, threat managers often must manage the hunter without knowing what prompted the hunt.

For howlers, we described various categories in which howlers seem to fall. We could have as easily categorized hunters; indeed, they too fall into most of the same categories as howlers. James Kopp, for example, killed Dr. Bernard Slepian because Slepian conducted abortions. Kopp was a crusading hunter. Similarly, Mark Chapman, who assassinated John Lennon, was a celebrity-seeking hunter. Jack McKnight, who killed one and wounded two during his assault on the Topeka Federal Court, Kansas, acted out of revenge for his arrest and imminent imprisonment for growing marijuana. He was a *self-defending hunter.* Dennis Rader, the notorious "BTK"[2] serial killer from Wichita, Kansas, killed 10 people between 1974 and 1991. He was an *habitual hunter.* Thus, the categories clearly apply to both howlers and hunters.

But while such categorizations work well for understanding howlers, they can be distracting when dealing with hunters. First, determining to which category a hunter belongs may not be so clear until the latter stages of the case. Howlers tend to self-identify their categories up front through their communications. Because hunters may not communicate anything, their motives may take the threat manager longer to discern. In the meantime, the hunter continues to engage in attack-related behaviors to which the threat manager has to respond. Although the threat manager knows with certainty that the hunter has a grievance, because grievances come first on the path to intended violence, the particulars of that individual grievance may not be so clear or certain until fully investigated.

Next, the category into which the hunter falls is less important than identifying which stage along the path to intended violence the hunter has reached. Whether self-defender, crusader, or copycat, those who hunt ultimately have to engage in attack-related behaviors. Hunters in different categories do not necessarily behave or communicate differently. When Chapman shot Lennon, the act differed very little from Kopp's shooting Slepian 20 years later. Both hunters aimed and fired. Ultimately, acts of violence and their outcomes resemble other acts and outcomes. Thus, we did not categorize hunters even though we recognize that many of the howler categories easily apply to them.

Also, at this point the categories are largely hypothetical. Too little research has been done on howlers, on those individuals who focus their unwanted attentions on public figures not to physically harm them, but to frighten them or form some unfounded attachment with them. Ironically, howlers compose the majority of the individuals who communicate inappropriately with public figures. Although their behavior does not have the same impact as hunters, howlers nevertheless distract the public figure and compel security and law enforcement officials to spend time assessing and managing them.

More research may well identify facile ways to identify them, thus separating the larger number of howlers from the much smaller number of actual hunters. Just as importantly, since how one manages howlers differs entirely from how one manages hunters, early identification of them is crucial. Certainly, no one wants to accidentally manage them into becoming a hunter. Only more detailed research on the habits and activities of howlers promises a way to distinguish them from hunters and devise better strategies for managing them.

Notes

1. We have also identified another category of howlers who focus on people they know. Personal howlers differ from impersonal howlers precisely because of the nature of their relationship with their targets.
2. "BTK" stood for "Bind, Torture, Kill" and was Rader's pseudonym for himself.

References

Borum, R., Fein, R., Vossekuil, B., & Berglund, J. (1999). Threat assessment: Defining an approach for evaluating risk of targeted violence. *Behavioral Sciences and the Law, 17*, 327–337.

Calhoun, F. S. (1998). *Hunters and howlers: Threats against federal judicial officials in the United States, 1789–1993*. Arlington, VA: Department of Justice, U.S. Marshals Service.

Calhoun, F. S., & Weston, S. W. (2003). *Contemporary threat management: A practical guide for identifying, assessing, and managing individuals of violent intent*. San Diego, CA: Specialized Training Services.

Clarke, J. W. (1982). *American assassins*. Princeton, NJ: Princeton University Press.

Clarke, J. W. (1989). Identifying potential assassins: Some situational correlates of dangerousness. In T. R. Gurr (Ed.), *Violence in America* (Vol. 1) (pp. 178–196). Newbury Park, CA: Sage.

Clarke, J. W. (1990). *On being mad or merely angry: John W. Hinckley, Jr., and other dangerous people*. Princeton, NJ: Princeton University Press.

Dietz, P. E., Matthews, D. B., Van Duyne, C., Martell, D. A., Parry, C. D. H., Stewart, T., et al. (1991). Threatening and otherwise inappropriate letters to Hollywood celebrities. *Journal of Forensic Sciences, 36*(1), 185–209.

Dietz, P. E., Matthews, D. B., Martell, D. A., Stewart, T., Hrouda, D. R., & Warren, J. (1991). Threatening and otherwise inappropriate letters to members of the United States Congress. *Journal of Forensic Sciences, 36*(5), 1445–1468.

Fein, R., & Vossekuil, B. (1995). *Threat assessment: An approach to prevent targeted violence.* Washington, DC: National Institute of Justice, Department of Justice.

Fein, R., & Vossekuil, B. (1999). Assassination in the United States: An operational study of recent assassins, attackers, and near-lethal approachers. *Journal of Forensic Sciences, 44*, 321–333.

Fein, R., & Vossekuil, B. (2000). *Protective intelligence and threat assessment investigations: A guide for state and local law enforcement officials.* Washington, DC: U.S. Department of Justice, Office of Justice Programs.

Fein, R., Vossekuill, B., Pollack, W., & Borum, R. (2002). *Threat assessment in schools: A guide to managing threatening situations and to creating safe school climates.* Washington, DC: U.S. Secret Service and U.S. Department of Education.

Friedman, L. (Ed.) (1983). *Final report of the National Commission on the Causes and Prevention of Violence* (16 vols.). New York: Praeger.

Laucella, L. (1998). *Assassination: The politics of murder.* Los Angeles, CA: RGA Publishing.

Leets, L., de Becker, G., & Giles, H. (1995). Fans: Explaining expressed motivations for contacting celebrities. *Journal of Language and Social Psychology, 14*, 102–123.

Reddy, M., Borum, R., Berglund, J., Vossekuil, B., Fein, R., & Modzeleski, W. (2001). Evaluating risk for targeted violence in schools: Comparing risk assessment, threat assessment, and other approaches. *Psychology in the Schools, 38*, 157–172.

Restak, R. (1981, December). Assassin. *Science Digest, 81.*

Slomich, S., & Kantor, R. (1969, March). Social psychopathology of political assassination. *Bulletin of the Atomic Scientists, 9.*

Vossekuil, B., Borum, R., Fein, R., & Reddy, M. (2001). Preventing targeted violence against judicial officials and courts. *The Annals of the American Academy of Political and Social Science, 576*, 78–90.

Vossekuil, B., & Fein, R. (2000). Seminar presentation at National Sheriff's Association training, Newark, NJ.

Vossekuil, B., Fein, R., Reddy, M., & Borum, R. (2002). *The final report and the findings of the Safe School Initiative: Implications for the prevention of school attacks in the United States.* Washington, DC: U.S. Secret Service and U.S. Department of Education.

Vossekuil, B., Reddy, M., & Fein, R. (2000). *Safe School Initiative: An interim report on the prevention of targeted violence in schools.* Washington, DC: U.S. Secret Service; U.S. Department of Education; National Institute of Justice.

6

Stalking, Threatening, and Attacking Corporate Figures

Jens Hoffmann and Lorraine Sheridan

Fixations on business representatives have rarely been a focus of interest for behavioral scientists. In their Exceptional Case Study, the United States Secret Service analyzed details of all persons known to have attacked or approached to attack a prominent public official or public figure in the United States between 1949 and 1996 (Fein & Vossekuil, 1997a, 1999). Business executives were explicitly included in this work, but they numbered just 3 out of a total sample of 74 cases. Despite the small sample size, different dynamics could be detected when the motives underlying assaults were examined. In one of the three cases, a deluded woman killed her victim in an attempt to avenge a perceived wrong:

> NN developed the idea that she owned a world-famous commodities trading company. Over a period of years, while mentally ill and living a nomadic life, NN called, wrote, and visited the president of the company. She was dismissed as a crank. Apparently concerned about an alleged scandal regarding the firm's activities, and its loss of reputation and money she believed to be hers, NN visited the company's headquarters. She entered the president's office suite and demanded to see him. When he came to the reception area to find out what the commotion was about, she took a gun and shot him.
>
> Fein and Vossekuil, 1997a, p. 57

In another case, a business leader died because a criminal intended to profit by exploiting his status:

> Joseph Corbett spent several years in the late 1950s planning the kidnapping of Adolph Coors III, the chief executive of the Coors brewing company. In February 1960, Corbett attempted to kidnap Coors, hoping to receive a large ransom. Corbett botched the kidnapping and shot Coors dead.

Fein and Vossekuil, 1997a, p. 59

In the Exceptional Case Study, most of the incidents examined affected the President of the United States (34%) and other U.S. Secret Service protectees (19%), due to the statutory mission of the U.S. Secret Service, now a part of the Department of Homeland Security. However, film, sport, and media celebrities did comprise 19% of the cases, with federal judges (5%) and business executives (4%) representing the smallest proportion of the sample.

Looking generally at different studies of violent attacks toward public figures (for reviews see Fein & Vossekuil, 1997b; Meloy et al., 2004), it would seem that well-known business executives are seldom the victim of violent attacks from fixated persons. This is especially true if we exclude politically and criminally motivated assaults. As an example of the former, during the 1970s and 1980s a German left-wing group known as the Red Army Faction, murdered several representatives of the biggest enterprises in the country (Kellen, 1998). Chapter 10 details further instances of cases where business leaders died in the context of criminal activities.

Even less is known about the experiences of renowned business people becoming the victim of stalking or threats. Although research has been conducted on threats and unusual contact behavior directed toward politicians (Dietz et al., 1991b; Scalora, Baumgartner, & Plank, 2003; Scalora et al., 2002) (Chapter 19) and celebrities (Dietz et al., 1991a) (Chapter 2), to our knowledge no equivalent data exist for corporate executives. To a lesser extent this is also true for stalking. The majority of studies focus on stalking in the general population (Spitzberg & Cupach, 2007) and of those few that focus on public figures, most examined celebrities (Malsch, Visscher, & Blaauw, 2002) (Chapters 2, 4, and 9). One exception is a study conducted by Meloy and Mohandie (Chapter 11), where two cases of corporate celebrity stalking have been analyzed. From a clinical point of view, both offenders shared characteristics of antisocial or psychopathic personality disorder, and in both cases, a major mental disorder and drug abuse were diagnosed.

We might therefore assume that prominent corporate leaders are less likely than politicians and celebrities to be the victim of violent attacks. This is unlikely to be a safe assumption, however. We simply do not know how often business leaders are the target of stalking and threatening behavior, based on their public personas or on their representative status. Generalizable research studies do not exist. Furthermore, corporations may seek to keep stalking, threats, and attacks secret out of fear of negative business impact, or it may be the case that well-known corporate leaders are better protected than many other types of public figures. For now, when examining the dynamics of cases where well-known business people have been the object of unusual attention, we must rely not only on the limited research but also our own and our colleagues' case experiences. It may be that when the stalker or threatener is a stranger, mental illness regularly plays an important role—at least when the target is nationally or internationally well known. This would be in accordance with studies of individuals who stalk, threaten, or attack public figures, where psychiatric illness has been reported in more than 50% of sample cases (Dietz & Martell, 1989; Fein & Vossekuil, 1999) (Chapters 1 and 3). Exceptions may arise if the harassing person is a former or current employee of the company or has an extreme political or criminal intent. In these cases, a more rational aim is often evident, such as financial gain or a change in corporate procedures.

Relevance of the Problem

During the 1990s, the international economy began to be of greater interest to a broader segment of the general public. With the boom of the "New Economy" in many Western countries, more and more people started to invest their money in stocks and bonds. The mass media followed this trend, and enterprises and their leaders became an inherent part of daily news coverage. The names of company figureheads suddenly were known not only to financial experts but also to the general populace. Therefore, it may be more than coincidence that security officers and other representatives of major companies have in recent years reported increasing numbers of unusual letters, e-mails, and physical approaches. Anecdotal evidence must always be interpreted with caution, as there exists a general tendency to assume that any form of criminal behavior is on the rise (e.g., Warr, 1995). Still, we are personally aware of many cases of corporate security professionals presenting huge files full of disturbing material sent to corporate leaders, along with comments that these types of communications appear to be increasing exponentially. This presumably mirrors a trend that arose a few decades before, when specialized police units and private security reported rising numbers of stalking incidents concerning politicians and celebrities (Dietz & Martell, 1989).

Quite obviously, there exists a clear connection between the number of media appearances and the chance of becoming a victim of stalking. To put it into a simple formula, the more a public figure is present in the media the more viewers and readers have virtual contact with her or him, which includes a small percentage of disturbed people capable of developing pathological fixations. But another dynamic may play an even bigger role. In recent years, greater numbers of business representatives have been encouraged to reveal their private personas. For example, in business magazines, readers can regularly find portraits of a CEO in which his or her personal history is revealed, along with "lifestyle" photographs. It is also more normal for business executives to display a human touch and to speak in talk shows about topics that are out of their area of business interest. As research in the field of celebrity stalking suggests, this amplification of personal characteristics may be a crucial factor for a higher risk of stalking victimization (Chapter 9).

This dynamic seems to be part of a general change in the perception of public figures following the introduction of television as mass media entertainment and the source of most news coverage. The borderline between real interpersonal experiences and media "relationships" has blurred, and the frontier between real life and fiction is more permeable. Schickel (2000) argued that the increasing distribution of gossip, even in the so-called serious media, contributes to a false perception of closeness with celebrities; he introduced the term "intimate strangers" to describe this phenomenon. It is evident that the cult of celebrity has the potential to attract emotionally unbalanced and mentally disturbed people. "When the Bible was the principal medium of communication with greatness and the only medium in most homes, the mentally ill most often had religious delusions. In a secular age in which television, radio, and the movies have replaced the role of the Bible in most lives, it should not surprise us that the mentally ill have delusions about the new secular 'gods,' particularly the gods of love and power" (Dietz & Martell, 1989, pp. 16-2–16-3).

Dimensions of Fixations on Business Leaders

Fixations on business representatives take many forms, ranging from those rooted in the private realm, such as ex-partner and familial stalking, to stalking by delusional individuals who incorporate the public image of a company figurehead into their fantasies. Because of the variety of personal and psychological characteristics and motivations of those who stalk, threaten, and attack corporate leaders, we need to identify some fundamental dimensions to help us discriminate different subgroups. Every individual can be evaluated on each of these dimensions, a procedure that we have found to be helpful in understanding the dynamics of a case. In the following paragraphs, the different dimensions will be briefly discussed and their connections to research in the field of stalking and unusual contacts with public figures will be examined.

The Dimension of Endurance

Some fixations on public figures are more transitory than others. Our rather subjective impressions, rooted in individual case experience, suggest that those who initiate unusual contacts with business representatives fixate for shorter periods than do individuals who target celebrities. One reason for this may be that celebrity stalkers—more often than harassers of other types of public figures—have a personal relationship fantasy fueling their approach behavior (Dietz et al., 1991a, 1991b; Malsch et al., 2002) (Chapter 13). It seems that individuals who harass company figureheads have more in common from a motivational viewpoint with those who fixate on politicians, focusing on an issue or a grievance rather than an individual person. Intervention in these cases may be more often successful than when the fixation is on a person (de Becker, 1994). Malsch et al. (2002) report that politicians are frequently stalked for reasons relating to their work, and their stalkers' motives tend to center around contemporary topics being dealt with by the government in question. We have obtained the same impressions when examining cases where business representatives are targeted. For instance, when a CEO receives repeated and unwanted communications, in many cases, the fixated person focuses on events involving him or his company that have been recently reported by the mass media. Although we can provide no empirical support for this other than anecdotal data, we also assume that those who harass corporate leaders are more likely to have a history also of stalking politicians rather than entertainment celebrities. One of the authors conducted a workshop for a police unit that has responsibility for the protection of well-known politicians. While discussing cases, both sides were surprised to learn that they had experienced contact with the same stalkers who, it transpired, were fixated on political as well as corporate leaders.

A concept in threat assessment that at least indirectly addresses the aspect of endurance is the distinction between hunters and howlers (Calhoun, 1998) (Chapter 5). Hunters are a rare species. They target the public figure in order to prepare for an attack with perhaps the ultimate aim of addressing a perceived injustice. Howlers, in contrast, satisfy their needs by simply communicating inappropriately with others. There exist subtypes of howlers who differ in how long they tend to fixate on a single target. Some, like the celebrity-seeking howler, communicate with multiple targets, of whom many would have been recently featured in the media (Chapter 5). Chairpersons or presidents of large corporations may become the victims of this subtype. The threatening or annoying behavior of the celebrity-seeking howler often rather quickly shifts to another target, once the next public figure attracts the howler's attention. Thus, their harassment is frequently short lived.

From a threat assessment perspective, it is important to identify communications indicative of more lasting and obsessive fixations. An example from a case file of one of the authors may illustrate this. The complaints office of a well-known international corporation typically receives dozens of angry and threatening calls every day. A woman working in the complaints office who never had received any security training contacted corporate security for the first time in her career. She said that she had taken a call that worried her deeply. The caller introduced himself as a businessman claiming to have been a client of the company for decades. Because of financial problems, he was unable to keep paying his bills, and as a result, the corporation stopped delivering goods that endangered the business of the caller. He requested that the company immediately resume deliveries. He explained that if this did not happen, he would clear his debt and then set fire to the office of the executive board. Interestingly, it was not just the content of the threat that so alarmed the assistant in the complaints office, but also the cool tone of voice employed by the threatener. Subsequent investigations revealed that the man had already conducted internet research on how to fabricate a Molotov cocktail.

Obviously, the woman working in the complaints office instinctively perceived the danger of an act of predatory violence (see Chapter 1, 2, and 20). Being one of the two inherent modes of violence in mammals, the evolutionary genesis of predatory violence was to facilitate hunting and therefore survival; in the current age, it more often serves other goals such as obtaining power or revenge (Meloy, 2006). The behavioral and physical pattern of this form of aggression comprises minimal autonomic arousal, a paucity of emotion, the absence of an acute threatening situation, and planning. Therefore, such enduring fixations, which may reflect an intention of predatory violence, must be seen as a highly alarming sign, activating an immediate threat assessment process.

The Dimension of Relationship

Following Mohandie, Meloy, McGowan, and Williams's (2006) argument that prior stalker-victim relationship is a central factor in the classification of different types of harassment, we have also found this dimension to be helpful when examining cases where a business representative is the target of stalking or threats. We have chosen three broad categories that are not mutually exclusive. We nevertheless believe that each of them reflects one or more prototypical dynamics that can usually be observed in such cases. From a methodological point of view, overlapping categories are sometimes considered a disadvantage because one problem individual can fall into more than one category. For example, the stalker of a company figurehead could be a former secretary to whom the victim was personally close. This stalker would fall into the personal relationship category as well as into the company relationship category described subsequently. So in a case like this, we would look to see whether one of the two relationship dynamics was more dominant than the other, or whether both dynamics played an equally crucial role.

Personal Relationship

Research on general stalking consistently shows that former intimate partners represent the largest group of all stalkers (e.g., Mohandie et al., 2006; Spitzberg & Cupach, 2007). It is no surprise that ex-lovers or former spouses sometimes harass company figureheads. Being in the public eye, they share a special vulnerability common to all public figures, namely that intimate or compromising information may be released to the media by a stalker who has knowledge about personal details (de Becker, 1997). On a more positive note, if business representatives occupy a leading position in a large enough company, they often have access to better security services and protection than the average stalking victim. But in general, the pattern of harassment is typical of ex-partner stalking cases, where one frequently finds a mixture of hope, desperation, and anger evident in the communication of the obsessive follower.

To be sure, not all fixated individuals in this category are former intimate partners. Every other significant and close personal relationship that was terminated by one party against the will of the other party may be found here (e.g., friends, relatives, or long-time working partnerships). The operationally useful subtype of "rejected stalking" was coined by Mullen, Pathé, and Purcell (2000) and covers all such cases. In other cases, the personal relationship is only a product of the fantasy of the stalker living or working in proximity to the public figure.

> The personal assistant of a best-selling author was fired from her job after making inappropriate advances toward the author. She had accomplished her duties well and the author was aware that she had been diagnosed some years ago with erotomania (the delusional belief that another person, usually of elevated status, returns intense feelings of romantic love). However, when her erotomanic delusions switched to him, the working relationship was severely disrupted. Upon being fired, the woman was distraught and repeatedly tried to gain access to the author, believing that if they could only meet, then the "misunderstanding" would be cleared up and they would live happily together as man and wife. She blamed other employees of the author for keeping them apart and was ultimately judged to present a danger to these other employees—but not to the author. A mental health intervention was deemed most appropriate.

Company Relationship

In this group, the link between the fixated person and the business leader is primarily based on the fact that they are or were both employed by the same organization. Sometimes it is simply the aspect of spatial or social proximity that is most relevant. For instance, an employee may observe a business leader during her daily work routines without knowing her personally, and come to develop an erotomanic or paranoid fixation on her. But more often, it is a functional characteristic of the target, or what the target represents, that determines her or his victimization. In such a context, the perpetrator can still be working for the company or be a former employee. In cases of the former, anonymous threats or defamation can often take place. It is only on rare occasions that harassers from within the company reveal their identity from the beginning, because they will fear negative employment consequences. If they do reveal their identity early on, then we are most likely to see enraged or self-confident employees who sometimes display narcissistic or paranoid personality traits. In our experience, former staff members who stalk or threaten are often not concerned about disclosing their identity. They tend to feel entitled from their point of view and consider that the damage has already been done, and that ultimately they stand to lose little by harassing a manager of their former company.

> A narcissistic individual was fired from his role as a senior executive within a large retail organization. He believed himself

to be superior to all other employees and had consistently inflated his personal accomplishments while harshly devaluing the contributions of others. He believed that he had generated billions of dollars for the company and that he had not been rewarded for this. He conducted lengthy legal campaigns and was determined to reveal what he saw as profound ignorance and corruption within the organization. Because of his former status, it was relatively easy for him to make public accusations within the financial and retail worlds. His own personal and financial life was damaged irreparably because of the extensive time and effort he devoted to his campaign. He eventually focused on one of the owners of the company, an individual well known for his past sporting achievements. Following public accusations and counteraccusations, the organization paid the former employee an undisclosed sum on the proviso that he keep quiet. He saw this as an admission of guilt, however, and continues to try and raise the profile of his "anticorruption campaign" to this day.

Outside Company Relationship

A tragic example of a fixated individual coming from an external source was presented in the beginning of this chapter, where a delusional woman who shot the president of a company was described. Although the mentally ill form a large proportion of this category, more rational motivations can also be present when an individual believes that a business leader is responsible for a significant (usually financial) loss affecting him or her. This may be due to the actions of a large company—for example, a factory is built close to the home of a person, who in response starts a harassing campaign. Another example is when an individual has invested money that is subsequently lost, and he or she holds the management responsible.

> A married couple in their 20s came to the attention of one of the authors when they claimed that they were the victims of a lengthy harassment campaign by a major British banking corporation. The husband had run up debts, which ultimately led to the repossession of his plumbing business, and he claimed that this was the result of a conspiracy by banking executives. The couple believed that, amongst other things, the bank had paid external individuals to pose as customers of the husband's business and make spurious complaints, and that board members of the bank vandalized his tools late at night. At first, a local news reporter believed the couple. Once he realized that they were delusional and refused to give them further publicity, they then moved on to picketing various branches of the bank on a daily basis. When this action failed to produce the desired effect of a public apology from the bank and financial compensation, the couple targeted a well-known board member of the bank and began a campaign of harassment against

him that culminated in their driving an SUV into a front window of his London residence, many miles from their own home.

Another possible motivation is seen when a fixated individual wants to highlight an issue that is important to him or her, and tries to attract the attention of a business leader whom he or she believes can help. Quite often, the important issue is centered on the individual himself, and getting in contact with a well-known person serves to raise his own feeling of prominence, a narcissistic configuration that is known as a mirror transference (Kohut, 1971) (Chapter 8). However, a perceived wrong with more general implications (e.g., economic, political, or ecological issues) can drive the fixated person either to ask for support from the company figurehead or to challenge him or her to take rectifying measures. Others have noted that pathological fixations are quite different than commitment to a cause: the former typically erode the individual's personal social and emotional network, whereas the latter may enhance them (see Chapter 1).

The Dimension of Psychopathology

As we have mentioned, psychotic illness frequently plays an important role in the stalking of public figures, and business representatives are not exempt from the attentions of the psychotic. In our casework, we regularly see signs of the following disorders, sometimes with more than one psychopathology being present in the same individual.

1. **Psychotic disorders**

   Persons who are obviously schizophrenic are often responsible for the most disorganized communications and intensive approach attempts. Typically in these cases, the well-known business leader is integrated into an idiosyncratic and bizarre universe of meanings that frequently is populated by other public figures. Fixated persons with more clear-cut delusions, such as the paranoid type, normally have a more organized behavioral pattern and therefore more often pose a problem for corporate security.

2. **Personality disorders**

   Personality disorders are distinctive and often rigid character traits that are evident in a person's interactions with others and have negative consequences for the individual himself and/or for those around him. Narcissistic traits and disorders are ubiquitous in persons who are fixated on public figures. Their unstable feelings of self-worth drive them to seek compensation in order to override their deeply rooted self-doubts. They want to be someone special, and this may be achieved via a connection with an extraordinary person, such as a business leader. More dangerous individuals show signs of antisocial personality disorder, or its more extreme and biologically rooted variant, psychopathy, and indeed these have been identified as one the most problematic and dangerous groups among both general stalkers (Sheridan & Boon, 2002) and those who target public figures (Chapters 10 and 11).

3. Depressive disorders

Not surprisingly, some former employees who have not only lost their jobs but also their family, friends, and social support systems view themselves as occupying a position of hopelessness and helplessness, and show clinical signs of depression. As stalking may be predisposed by both early loss as a child and recent loss as an adult (Chapter 8) (Kienlen, 1998), a proportion of fixated persons will be particularly vulnerable to depressive episodes and other affective disorders, such as dysthymia, cyclothymia, or bipolar disorder. Depression significantly increases the risk of suicide—up to 15% of individuals who are severely depressed will kill themselves—which then may become an element of the public figure pursuit as a threat or a homicide-suicide dynamic.

The Dimension of Motivation

In accordance with other authors in the field (e.g., de Becker, 1994; Mohandie et al., 2006), we often consider motivation as a fluctuating aspect covering the surface of an underlying attachment pathology (Chapter 8) (Meloy, 2007), rather than a stable category by which we can distinguish different groups of individuals who stalk, threaten, or attack public figures. *Motivation may change or more than one motivation can be present in a given case.* However, insight into the current motivational makeup of a fixated person regularly proves to be helpful in understanding his ongoing psychological dynamics. Some primary motivations we have seen when working on corporate figure cases are:

1. Attachment-seeking

An attachment-seeking fixated person is trying to develop a relationship that will bear a positive yield for him or her, such as a friendship or a business partnership. As in general stalking of this type, the perception of the business representative is often idealistic and nonsexual in nature (see Mullen et al., 2000; Sheridan & Boon, 2002). Comparable with fixations on politicians, it is seldom the case that romantic feelings or sexual impulses are predominant, in contrast to individuals who are seeking a close relationship with an entertainment celebrity (Chapter 2).

2. Attention-seeking

Pathologically narcissistic stalkers desire attention from the company figurehead in order to elevate their own feelings of self-worth and importance. These individuals may seek to point out a problem or raise an issue that they believe will surely attract the attention of the business representative. Their commitment to the issue is secondary to their self-aggrandizement and hunger for notoriety.

3. Revenge-seeking

The revenge-seeking stalker aims to terrorize his or her target because of a perceived sense of injustice (Kropp, Hart, & Lyon, 2002; Mullen et al., 2000). Sometimes the instillation of fear in the victim is sufficient gratification and allows the stalker to transform his feelings of powerlessness into power, suggesting a sadistic motivation. In a few instances, however, the drive for revenge also leads to violent incidents. The disgruntled current or former employee can typically be found in this motivational group.

4. Profit-seeking

The primary motivation here is criminal: to obtain money or other goods by stalking, threatening, or attacking a business leader. Regularly the personality of these individuals will display some psychopathic features (Chapters 10 and 11).

5. Other or unclear motivations

In cases where the fixated person is highly psychotic, it is often difficult to detect any of the above motivations for the harassing behavior, which often appears chaotic (see Chapter 3). We provide this category to address those individuals for whom motivational background is difficult to reconstruct from an external viewpoint.

Motivations are dynamic, not static. Sometimes, the reaction of the target or his environment will influence the choice of whether the harassment will stop or continue interminably. Motivations may shift, such as an attachment-seeking individual nursing a wish for revenge because he feels that he has not been treated with respect. Without proposing that these various dimensions—endurance, relationship, psychopathology, and motivation—have specific protective remedies, we find them helpful in obtaining a grasp of the dynamics of the case. One example from our files may help illustrate this point.

A man living in the same village as a CEO sent regular letters to him for several years. Sometimes he was also seen loitering around the business leader's home. In his writings, he praised the competence of the CEO and was full of admiration for him, but at the same time he stressed that he likewise had extraordinary economic competence, and proposed that they meet personally as entrepreneur to entrepreneur. In this case, the dimension of endurance was *long-term*, the relationship *personal*, and on a psychopathological level, a clear *narcissistic* profile seemed to be present. The motivation was *attachment seeking*. From a threat assessment perspective, none of the dimensions revealed any problematic indicators, and therefore a low level of case management was proposed. However, ongoing monitoring of the case was necessary because of the changeable nature of his motivations.

Prevention

Business leaders know the impact that imprudent statements may have on stock prices (Gerald Ratner effectively killed his jewelry company in 1991 when he joked that one of his firm's products was "total crap," wiping around $1 billion from the value of the company). Business leaders may also attract the attention of stalkers and other fixated individuals by candidly releasing too much private information, a lesson that many celebrities already have had to learn (de Becker, 1997) (Chapter 9). Obviously there is a Janus-faced media effect, which holds true for all public figures: presenting one's home, family life, and personal habits makes a company figurehead appear more human and may raise the popularity of him and his product, but such an accessible and attractive appearance heightens the risk of a long-term stalking problem. That such complications may arise from talking to the media should be explained to high-profile business representatives, and they, like entertainment celebrities, should also learn some general dos and don'ts to avoid becoming an easy target for fixated persons. Needless to say, public relations and other corporate departments that regularly communicate with the outside world likewise should engage in awareness-raising exercises.

When examining the evolution of pathological fixations on public figures, one can frequently see that the reaction of the business executive or his professional environment to an unusual communication has played a crucial role. Being provided with special attention from a prominent figure or his or her agents often influences the decision of an unbalanced person to maintain and intensify his or her approach behavior, or to include more targets in the campaign. Therefore, well-known business leaders and their office staff need to be trained in how to react to unusual contacts. One case example may illustrate how an innocent and injudicious response contributed to a fixation on a business leader.

> An obviously mentally disturbed man managed to telephone his way through the headquarters of an international company until he was finally connected with the secretary of the CEO. He explained that the entire country was in great danger because of a secret army being formed by an Eastern European state. The man asked to speak urgently with the CEO because in his opinion the business leader needed to warn high-ranking colleagues from other companies and also politicians. The secretary did not know what to do and replied that the CEO was out of office. She added that she would forward the message on to him. Believing that the CEO would take care of the problem from then on, the delusional man began a campaign of letters and phone calls in which he gave further advice and asked for reports on the progress the CEO had made in fighting off the danger of the secret army.

Coaching office staff on the nature of mental illness and how to respond to such calls can have a great impact on the management of situations such as these. Furthermore, simple warning signs concerning the recognition of unusual behavior can be taught, and security personnel can be alerted. Untrained persons may often believe that obviously "loony" letters, faxes, or e-mails are not of any importance and can be safely ignored. Those in the frontline for receiving communications may also be coached on how to recognize when someone is trying to obtain sensitive information by employing clever ruses. The following case example describes such an attempt that failed because of the fact that the office staff were adequately trained and prepared.

> A phone call came in to the office of a member of the board of directors of an international company. The caller introduced himself as a colleague of the director, and told the secretary that he was at the airport and desperately needed to speak with her boss. Having forgotten his electronic address list, he asked her for the number of the cellular phone of the director. Despite hearing background noises that seemed to come from an airport hall, and also recognizing the accent of a foreign-born colleague she personally knew, the secretary still hesitated. She remembered that if there should be any doubt about the identity of a caller, no information should leave the office. Therefore, she refused to give out the requested number in spite of sharp protests from the other end of the line. Investigations by corporate security quickly revealed that the caller was not the person he pretended to be and his true identity was never discovered.

Former or current employees can stalk, harass, or attempt to blackmail a business representative. Therefore, preemployment screening should also consider this possibility. It is clear that past stalking behavior is a reliable risk factor for future harassment, but in most cases, such information concerning job applicants is not readily available. Even so, there do exist some psychological factors that could help indicate the risk of a future pathological fixation on a company figurehead. Research and clinical wisdom suggest exercising caution if possessiveness, hypersensitivity, dependence, jealousy, and moods that oscillate between extremes of undying devotion and angry rejection are present (Mullen et al., 2000). From our experience with corporate stalking cases, pathological narcissism can play a particularly important role, as well as the expectation or hope of having a special relationship with the business leader and his or her family, or an identification with the role of rescuer or guardian (Chapter 8). The latter point can be exemplified regularly among personal security professionals, and it may be no coincidence that many people working in that field state that their favorite movie is *The Bodyguard*, the story of a romance between a pop singer and her security expert. One must always ensure, however, that equal opportunity practices relating to recruitment and selection are adhered to.

Threat Assessment and Case Management

A systematic threat assessment approach is essential for the effective management of persons who fixate on business representatives. Such an approach must be implemented across different internal departments of the organization, including security, corporate communications, the legal department, human resources, medical and psychological services, offices of board members, the post-room, and the switchboard. This is imperative because to secure management of the case, these internal departments must share information and work cohesively. Every relevant office should contain employees who are trained in at least some of the basic ideas of threat assessment, and who are also familiar with their counterparts in other departments. Put simply, if an employee has sight of a strange or disturbing letter, then he or she should know whom to contact. A clear and simple procedure needs to be installed that details a hierarchy of response and reaction. Often, a professional exchange of information, good case documentation, and deliberate coordination between the involved parties make the difference between a successful intervention and offender escalation (White & Meloy, 2007). If things go wrong, then it is typically the case that important information has gone astray, that decisions about risk assessment and intervention strategies are made arbitrarily, and that there is an inconsistent response from the offices concerned to the fixated person.

Raising an employer's awareness of the possibility of stalking and attacks is another central task. Members of the company who may be contacted by fixated persons because of their work position should be informed about different types of problematic behavior and some general risk factors. Relevant personnel include but are not limited to janitors, guards, switchboard operators, personal assistants and—frequently overlooked—high status business representatives themselves. The latter point may be illustrated by a case example.

> A CEO was irritated because a woman followed him almost every morning as he moved from the car park to his office. She would walk nearby and enter the elevator with him but showed no reaction when he greeted her. The CEO informed security. It was quickly ascertained that the woman was an assistant working in a remote part of the building and there was no obvious explanation as to why she should share the same morning routine as the CEO. To discover more about the background of this potentially stalking-like behavior, an external psychologist was engaged. Corporate security was particularly anxious to find out whether the women may be mentally ill. The psychologist interviewed her in order to learn more about her motivation and mental state, and also to make clear that her behavior was worrying other people and should be curtailed. The interview did not reveal any evidence of mental disorder and after this session, the CEO never saw the woman again.

The most obvious goal of threat assessment is to identify as early as possible psychological and social dynamics that may contribute to violent acts and then defuse any possible risk. When adopting a threat management approach, the prevention of physical violence is not the sole aim. The psychological well-being of the targeted person is also of vital interest for companies. Therefore, an oft-formulated ambition is to protect the managing board from the harassment of fixated persons in order to avoid unnecessary psychological damage that could impact their profit-making capacity.

In some corporations, a structured threat assessment and case management approach is already in use, and an example of such a model appears in the following text. For a more detailed description of the scheme, see Hoffmann and Sheridan (2005).

Screening

All incoming communications to relevant departments should be at least briefly checked to determine whether any content indicative of a problem might be identified. Appropriately training employees and providing them with a checklist to aid the filtering of problematic letters, faxes, calls, and e-mails are therefore essential. Also, first-line staff such as doorpersons, assistants, or drivers, who may have face-to-face contact with fixated persons, need to be vigilant. These persons are able to act as the eyes and ears of corporate security, and should be particularly attentive to individuals loitering in places where the corporate leader appears, when an unknown person asks unusual questions about him or her, or if other signs indicate that someone may be pathologically fixated on the company figurehead. These employees should be alert to hunting behavior (Chapter 5), a precursor of predatory violence, which finds its expression in acts of researching, planning, or preparation for an attack. Conspicuous behaviors from fellow employees should also be carefully observed, as illustrated by the following case example.

> A female assistant appeared on the floor occupied by the CEO of an international company and explained to a bewildered secretary that she would be taking over the office of CEO. A threat manager, after making discreet enquiries, discovered that the employee was laboring under acute delusions of grandeur. Psychiatric treatment involving the family of the woman was arranged. This proved successful and the employee was able to return to her workplace within a short period of time.

It is, of course, beneficial to recognize problematic contact behavior as early as possible. In a majority of cases, it is easier to stop or manage a stalking case in its initial stages because the emotional investment of the fixated person will not be as intensive as later on. The surmounting of obstacles over time often increases commitment to a task or a belief. It is advisable to transmit all communications and recordable behavior that are defined as potentially problematic to the lead person responsible for threat assessment within the corporation.

First Analysis

At this stage, the first professional assessment takes place. A simple examination by a threat assessment professional of the content of an unusual contact can inform the decision to take no further action at that time. In some cases, however, a deeper analysis, which considers more detailed data, such as background information on the harasser and an overview of all of his or her unusual behavior, will prove fruitful. The psychological and behavioral dimensions of fixations on business leaders such as those described earlier can help structure these cases. First assessment reveals on many occasions that there is no identifiable current risk of escalation, and therefore the only necessary strategy is the monitoring of additional unusual communications or behavior. If there is any doubt regarding the nonhazardous nature of the case, or if there is evidence of ill intent, then it is recommended that operatives progress to the next stage of the threat assessment process. There is one exception: If an immediate danger is deemed present, then intervention and protection of the company figurehead must have the highest priority before a more detailed research process is initiated (Meloy, 2003).

Research and Further Analysis

Reliable information is one of the most valuable tools available to threat assessors. There are two basic strategies to obtain the information that is crucial for further analysis. *Passive research* avoids communicating to the harassing individual that any assessment or intervention is taking place. Examples of techniques employed under this heading include using the internet to research the individual, checking police files if accessible, or interviewing any personnel from the organization known to have had contact with the harasser. The latter point may be beneficial when trying to establish the individual's mental state, the nature of their fixation, possible triggers, and likely intent. Implementing passive research reduces the risk of causing an escalation, because the investigated individual does not usually know that any investigation is taking place. Engaging in *active research* does not normally yield the same result because it involves direct contact with the harasser and/or those close to him or her, such as friends or relatives. When the threat assessment expert talks openly to the fixated person or his or her associates, thereby revealing the true nature of the interview, this action inevitably forms part of the management strategy. One should carefully consider taking this step, bearing in mind the risk that the behavior of the harasser will be reinforced (Hoffmann & Sheridan, 2005). For instance, the fixated individual may interpret the attention as an indication of their importance to the business leader, or may perceive that they have had an impact on the life of a well-known person. Naturally, the information obtained by passive or active research, once collected, has to be the subject of further analysis. It still may be the case that no active intervention is required. The research stage may suggest that the case is not as problematic as first assumed, or that overt intervention may prove counterproductive or could even heighten future risk.

Management Strategies

When involved in cases where corporate leaders are being targeted, it often becomes evident that direct advice to the target may be a crucial aspect of intervention. Because of their professional experience and their personality characteristics (which likely contributed to their occupational success), business leaders frequently believe themselves able to achieve a solution by either ignoring the problematic individual or having a brief conversation with him or her. Unfortunately, in most cases, this does not work and there is a high risk of exacerbating the situation. Attempts to verbally placate a disgruntled former employee, for example, or hearing out a narcissist will more often than not backfire. Thus, the corporate leader should be instructed on how to react if the fixated person makes a physical appearance. If the corporate leader has little option but to respond, as a general strategy, it is advisable to create as much physical and emotional distance as possible between himself or herself and the harasser. If the fixated person wishes to report a perceived injustice or asks for some form of compensation, it is vital that an executive board member does not respond, and that the names of high-ranking and well-known company officials are not mentioned in any communications with the harasser. The general rule is that any conflict has to be distanced from the corporate leader and should be transferred to another office or contact person from within (or preferably outside of) the company. This also dilutes any transference feelings that may be part of the case. The following list offers some examples of management strategies that have previously been employed to positive effect. Of course, as every case and its circumstances are singular, there exists no one-size-fits-it-all strategy. Often, several different approaches have to be adopted before a viable solution is found, and because of the dynamic nature of stalking and harassment incidents, management strategies need to be adjusted to fit new conditions.

- **Legal interventions:** Typically, criminal law, antistalking legislation, or civil law measures, such as restraining orders, may be applied (see also Chapter 18).
- **Police intervention:** Police may be able to investigate additional angles or enforce limitations against unwanted behavior (see also Chapter 14).
- **Target hardening:** Measures under this heading include increasing security or screening all individuals who have access to the corporate leader or his or her premises because it is anticipated that the fixated person may use a proximity-seeking ruse.
- **Psychiatric experts or social support:** As problematic behavior frequently occurs within a context of mental illness or personal crises, offering professional help often has the potential to defuse the risk.

- **External agencies:** Sometimes private security experts or threat managers can be helpful if resources within the company are not sufficient.
- **Talking with the fixated person:** Conversations with fixated individuals usually have multiple goals. They can, for example, identify ways out of the conflict or highlight the negative consequences of a continuation of the problematic contact. Meetings must always be approached with extreme caution as personal exchanges can aggravate the situation.
- **Monitoring the fixated person:** Sometimes colleagues (if the harasser is a company employee) or family members of the harasser can be used as valuable listening posts who can alarm security if they observe negative behavioral developments. Such a strategy is not without danger because involving close persons may enrage the fixated person, increase his vigilance and suspicions, or provide hints about the threat management strategies in place.

Conclusions

Although little literature exists concerning fixations on well-known corporate figures, we can learn valuable lessons from the more general literature on stalking and threat assessment. It is evident that business leaders are the target of individuals with the potential to cause harm, although we do not yet possess any reliable incidence or prevalence data. We also know that fixated individuals will have a variety of reasons for their behavior. Some are driven by delusion or fantasy, others seek revenge for wrongs that may or may not exist, others will have shared an intimate relationship with the target, and still others desire attention or financial or emotional profit. There are various dimensions along which we can plot individual cases to enable our understanding of endurance, relationship, motivation, and psychopathology. The delineation of these dimensions can, in turn, aid threat assessment professionals in their decisions concerning whether to take action and, if so, of what type. To this end, we have offered a simple model of threat assessment and case management for use in corporate cases. Investigators should feel free to use all or parts of this where appropriate, and to adapt the model as best suits their needs. It is imperative that we continue to share our professional experience and expertise to enable the development of adaptable tools that provide real world results.

References

Calhoun, F. S. (1998). *Hunters and howlers: Threats and violence against Federal Judicial Officials in the United States, 1789–1993*. Arlington: U.S. Marshals Service.

de Becker, G. (1994). *Intervention decisions: The value of flexibility*. White paper report prepared for the 1994 CIA Threat Management Conference.

de Becker, G. (1997). *The gift of fear*. Boston: Little, Brown.

Dietz, P. E., & Martell, D. A. (1989). *Mentally disordered offenders in pursuit of celebrities and politicians.* Washington, DC: National Institute of Justice.

Dietz, P. E., Matthews, D. B., Van Duyne, C., Martell, D. A., Parry, C. D. H., Stewart, T., et al. (1991a). Threatening and otherwise inappropriate letters to Hollywood celebrities. *Journal of Forensic Sciences, 36,* 185–209.

Dietz, P. E., Matthews, D. B., Van Duyne, C., Martell, D. A., Parry, C. D. H., Stewart, T., et al. (1991b). Threatening and otherwise inappropriate letters to members of the United States Congress. *Journal of Forensic Sciences, 36,* 1445–1468.

Fein, R. A., & Vossekuil, B. (1997a). *Preventing assassination: A monograph.* Washington, DC: U.S. Department of Justice.

Fein, R. A., & Vossekuil, B. (1997b). *Preventing assassination: A literature review.* Washington, DC: U.S. Department of Justice.

Fein, R. A., & Vossekuil, B. (1999). Assassination in the United States. An operational study of recent assassins, attackers, and near lethal approachers. *Journal of Forensic Sciences, 44,* 321–333.

Hoffmann, J., & Sheridan, L. (2005). The stalking of public figures: Management and intervention. *Journal of Forensic Sciences, 6,* 1459–1465.

Kellen, K. (1998). Ideology and rebellion: Terrorism in West Germany. In W. Reich (Ed.), *Origins of terrorism.* (pp. 43–58). Washington, DC: Woodrow Wilson Center Press.

Kienlen, K. (1998). Development and social antecedents of stalking. In J. R. Meloy (Ed.), *The psychology of stalking: Clinical and forensic perspectives* (pp. 52–67). San Diego: Academic Press.

Kohut, H. (1971). *The analysis of the self. A systematic approach to the psychoanalytic treatment of narcissistic personality disorders.* New York: International Universities Press. Reprinted 1977.

Kropp, R. P., Hart, S. D., & Lyon, D. R. (2002). Risk assessment of stalkers: Some problems and possible solutions. *Criminal Justice and Behavior, 29,* 590–616.

Malsch, M., Visscher M., & Blaauw E. (2002). *Stalking van bekende personen* [Stalking of celebrities]. Den Haag, The Netherlands: Boom.

Meloy, J. R. (2003). When stalkers become violent: The threat to public figures and private lives. *Psychiatric Annals, 33,* 658–665.

Meloy, J. R. (2006). The empirical basis and forensic application of affective and predatory violence. *Australian and New Zealand Journal of Psychiatry, 40,* 539–547.

Meloy, J. R. (2007). Stalking: The state of the science. *Criminal Behaviour and Mental Health, 17*(1), 1–7.

Meloy J. R., James, D. V., Farnham, F. R., Mullen, P. E., Pathé, M., Darnley, B., et al. (2004). A research review of public figure threats, approaches, attacks, and assassinations in the United States. *Journal of Forensic Sciences, 5,* 1–8.

Mohandie, K., Meloy, J. R., McGowan, M. G., & Williams, J. (2006). The RECON typology of stalking: Reliability and validity based upon a large sample of North American stalkers. *Journal of Forensic Sciences, 51,* 147–155.

Mullen, P. E., Pathé, M., & Purcell, R. (2000). *Stalkers and their victims.* Cambridge: Cambridge University Press.

Scalora, M. J., Baumgartner, J. V., & Plank, G. L. (2003). The relationship of mental illness to targeted contact behavior toward state government agencies and officials. *Behavioral Sciences and the Law, 21,* 239–249.

Scalora, M. J., Baumgartner, J. V., Zimmerman, W., Callaway, D., Hatch Maillette, M. A., Covell, C. N., et al. (2002). An epidemiological assessment of problematic contacts to members of Congress. *Journal of Forensic Sciences, 47,* 1360–1364.

Schickel, R. (2000). *Intimate strangers. The culture of celebrity in America.* Chicago: Ivan R. Dee.

Sheridan, L., & Boon, J. C. W. (2002). Stalker typologies: Implications for law enforcement. In J. C. W. Boon, & L. Sheridan (Eds.), *Stalking and psychosexual obsession* (pp. 63–82). Chichester: Wiley.

Spitzberg, B. H., & Cupach, W. R. (2007). The state of the art of stalking: Taking stock of the emerging literature. *Aggression and Violent Behavior, 12,* 64–86.

Warr, M. (1995). Public opinion on crime and punishment. *Public Opinion Quarterly, 59,* 296–310.

White, S., & Meloy, J. R. (2007). *Workplace assessment of violence risk-21.* San Diego: Specialized Training Services.

7

The Public Figure Assassin as Terrorist

James Biesterfeld and J. Reid Meloy

According to the United States Federal Bureau of Investigation, terrorism is defined as "The unlawful use of force or violence committed by a group or individual against persons or property to intimidate or coerce a government, the civilian population, or any segment thereof, in furtherance of political or social objectives" (Federal Bureau of Investigation, 1996). Although the history of public figure stalking, attacks, and assassinations is largely a product of a behavior that would not fit this definition, there is a subgroup of individuals who carry out stalking and attacks that would specifically meet this definition of terrorism. We offer this chapter as a counterpoint to the emphasis on other motivations and the predominance of mentally ill individuals that character-izes much of the contemporary research in this area. Our interest is the subject who stalks and attempts to kill a public figure to explicitly further a political, social, or in some cases, religious objective.

The Assassins—12th Century Murder, Incorporated

One of the earliest examples of terrorism in this context would be that of the *Hashisheen*. They were a sect of Shia Islam known as the Ismailis—believers in the restoration of Ismail as the Mahdi of Islam. The founder of the order, Hasan bin Sabah, held ultraconservative interpretations of Islamic philosophy and felt that anyone who did not believe as he did became a legitimate target for death. Sabah's philosophy also espoused total obedience to the founder.

In point of fact, Sabah had established rules for entry into his order that rather parallel many of the attributes of modern cults:

> The First Rule was that the Missionary must know human psychology in such a way as to be able to select suitable people for admission to the cult....The second rule of procedure was the application of flattery and gaining the confidence of the prospective member. Third came the casting of doubt into the mind, by superior knowledge. Fourthly, the teacher must apply an oath to student never to betray and of the "truths" which were to be revealed to him. Now he was told, as the fifth stage, that Ismailism was a powerful secret organization, supported by some of the most important figures of the time.
>
> Darual, 1989, p. 29

Hasan bin Sabah was born in what is now Iran and spent his formative years as a Shia "Twelver" as his father had been before him. However, as Hasan grew, he ultimately embraced the Ismaili tenets of faith and was mentored by some of the powerful Ismailis of that time. He traveled to the court of the Fatamid Caliph in Cairo and remained there for several years until he returned to his homeland, always spreading the word of the Ismaili faith and garnering many converts to his philosophy.

Hasan became a thorn in the side of the ruling Seljuk Sultans as well as other Sunni and Shia fiefdoms who sought his arrest and execution. This compelled Hasan to establish a location for his own sanctuary. Ultimately, he and his followers conquered a fortress at Alamut, Iran, where he remained until his death 35 years later.

Alamut became his base of operations and he continued to send missionaries throughout the regions spreading his "faith." His enemies continued to harass his followers and he became a target of the Sultan's vizier (prime minister) Nizam al-Mulk. It was at this time that Hasan began the effort for which his group became best known—assassination. His first target, and his first success, was Nizam al-Mulk. The assassin took the command of his leader and went in disguise to approach Nizam al-Mulk, whereupon the assassin killed al-Mulk with a dagger. Although the assassin was killed almost instantly, this act established Hasan as a major player in the region.

For the next decade, Sabah's minions obtained additional fortresses in the region extending to Isfahan in modern day Iran. Additionally, his "emissaries" covertly conducted missionary work, spreading the Ismaili vision of Islam and obtaining additional converts. During the remainder of his life, Sabah commissioned at least 50 assassinations. His son, Hasan, succeeded Sabah upon his death in 1142 CE and continued his father's legacy of assassinations, some of them worthy of note.

Assassination of Conrad, Marquis de Montferrat (April 28, 1192)

Conrad, who ruled Tyre during the Third Crusade, was not well liked by Saladin and the Muslim population. Exactly who commissioned the assassination through the Ismaili sect was not exactly known and has been attributed to both Saladin, a military enemy of Conrad, and Richard, King of England, for whom Conrad was a political rival. Chronicled by the contemporary historian Imad ad-Din, the event was described as follows:

> Meanwhile he lounged carelessly on his couch eating his food. He ate and made his collation, unaware of the precipice ahead of him; he ate and drank, sated and solaced himself, and went out and rode his horse. Suddenly, two men fell on him like two mangy wolves and with their daggers stopped his movement and struck him down near those shops. Then one of them fled and entered a church, having put out that vile soul. The Marquis, at death's door, but still with a flicker of life in him, said, "Take me into the church," and they took him in thinking that he was safe there. But when that one of the two murderers saw him, he fell on him to finish him off and struck him again, blow on blow. The Franks seized the two companions, and found that they were two apostates of the Brotherhood of Isma'ilites. They asked them who had commanded them to commit this murder, and the assassins said it was the King of England. They also said that they had been Christians for six months and had begun a life of asceticism and purification, frequenting churches and living lives of rigorous piety. One was in service with Ibn Barzan and one with the Prince of Sidon so they could both be close to the Marquis, ensuring his confidence in them by their constant presence.
>
> Gabrieli, 1993, p. 238

The famed Muslim general Saladin himself was not entirely safe from the reach of the Assassins. By 1181–1182, a man named Sinan had been promoted to chief of the assassins in Syria. In letters to the Caliph in Baghdad, Saladin accused the rulers of Mosul of being in league with the Assassins and using them as a mediation tool with the Franks (the common name given for the Crusaders of the time). This raised the ire of Sinan, who proclaimed Saladin as the chief enemy of his sect. But attempts on Saladin's life began 10 years earlier, when Assassins were commissioned by the Vezir of Aleppo through Sinan to kill Saladin, who had besieged the city. The first attempt occurred in 1174–1175, during the siege of Aleppo (Lewis, 1967). According to Saladin's biographers, the regent of Aleppo, Gumushtigin, engaged Sinan to kill the great general:

> The appointed emissaries (assassins) penetrated the camp on a cold winter's day, but were recognized by the emir of Abu Qubais, a neighbor of theirs. He questioned them, and was at once killed. In the ensuing fracas many people were killed, but Saladin himself was unscathed.
>
> Lewis, 1967, p. 133

Yet Sinan was not done and had a second attempt made on Saladin. Again, Lewis describes the event:

In the following year, Sinan decided to make another attempt, and on 22 May 1176, Assassins, disguised as soldiers in his army, attacked him with knives while he was besieging Azaz. Thanks to his armour, Saladin received only superficial wounds, and the assailants were dealt with by his emirs, several of whom perished in the struggle.

Lewis, 1967, p. 133

Saladin did not sit idly after these attempts. The power of the Assassins in the Holy Land had expanded to the point where Saladin felt that they needed to be dealt with as any other armed enemy. Accordingly, Saladin took his army to the Syrian headquarters of the Assassins and laid siege to the fortress at Masyaf. The story is as follows and is based on an account by the Ismaili chronicler Abu Firas (Lane-Poole, 2002):

When Saladin laid siege to Masyaf, Sinan was absent, and the king's summons to surrender reached him at a village near Radamus. He told the messenger that he must have a personal interview with Saladin; and then, since access to Masyaf was blocked by the leaguer, he retired with only two companions to the top of a neighbouring mountain, whence he looked down upon the siege and awaited the event. Saladin, believing that he had the arch-enemy in his power, sent a body of troops to surround him; but hostile soldiers and peaceful messengers were alike held back by a mysterious force which numbed their limbs. Such was the miraculous power of the holy Master, in whom his followers were taught to recognize a veritable incarnation of Divine Reason. The awed reports of his baffled and perplexed envoys worked upon Saladin's fears. He remembered the two former attempts upon his life, and began to doubt whether anything human could save him from the supernatural agencies of this devil or saint. He had chalk and cinders strewed around his tent, to detect secret footsteps; his guards were supplied with linklights, and the night watches were frequently relieved. But unearthly terrors surrounded him, and his sleep was troubled. One night the watchers on the battlements of Masyaf perceived a spark like a glow-worm slowly gliding down the hill where the Master sat. It vanished among the tents of the Saracens. Presently Saladin awoke from his uneasy dreams to see a figure gliding out at the tent door. Looking round he noticed that the lamps had been displaced, and beside his bed lay some hot scones of the shape peculiar to the Assassins, with a leaf of paper on the top, pinned by a poisoned dagger. There were verses on the paper:

By the Majesty of the Kingdom! What you possess will escape you, in spite of all, but victory remains to us;

We acquaint you that we *hold you*, and that we reserve you
till your reckoning be paid

Saladin gave a great and terrible cry, and the guard and the officers
rushed in. He showed them the scones, the dagger, the verses. The
dread Master had been actually at his pillow: it was nothing short
of a miracle. (p. 119)

It was shortly thereafter that Saladin ended his siege and departed from
the Assassins' territory. While this account was that of one of Sinan's fans,
sorcery aside, such accounts did much for the fearsome reputation established
by the Assassins for 3 centuries.

It also pointed out some interesting methodologies that bear a likeness
to those of our modern age. The Assassins were a classic cult and as such,
displayed certain characteristics. First, the Assassins were ruled by a charis-
matic leader who demanded total authority (one story has it that while being
visited by a vizier [a close political advisor] from the Sultan's court, Sabah
commanded a guard to throw himself from a tower to his death on the rocks
below to demonstrate his complete control of his core followers).

Second, Sabah and his successors used a variety of controlling techniques
over their followers to maintain dominance. One could allow that the Ismailis
were operating on two levels: the public and the private, or more correctly, the
overt and the covert. The Old Man of the Mountain, as the leader was called,
would send out his "emissaries" to preach the Ismaili faith to the general public. From those public efforts, recruits who demonstrated "special" qualities
(i.e., fully committed, easily manipulated, and disaffected from their families)
were sent to the fortresses for in-depth indoctrination into the Ismaili faith and
training in the art of assassination.

Third, these recruits were the victims of total isolation—social and
physical—while in training. They were subsequently sent out either as "emissaries" or as killers and deemed necessary by the leadership.

Fourth, because of their training, these converts would exhibit fanatical
behavior that would be regularly reinforced by additional training and tasking
by the leadership.

Finally, cults would deeply enmesh themselves in secrecy and deception.
This was especially true of the Assassins, who would enter into treaties and relationships with anyone they felt would benefit from such an effort. They would
routinely abrogate such agreements or treaties as it suited them to do so.

Their training techniques included how to kill at close quarters (Close
Quarters Battle or CQB in our modern terminology), reconnaissance and
surveillance, disguise, deception, and undercover operations. Training was a
continuing aspect that allowed the leadership to continue its control of the
recruits who believed they were being called by God to do that work. The
story regarding martyrdom and being rewarded in the afterlife with 72 virgins
was originated by the Assassins as an additional incentive for their sacrifice.

Sabah went so far as to take a portion of the fortress at Alamut and convert it into "heaven." Recruits who were preparing for an assassination mission were allowed to celebrate before their mission. This included the use of hashish that caused severe intoxication of the recruits to the point of partial or full loss of consciousness. Once unconscious, the recruits were taken from the party room to the "heaven" created by Sabah, which included soft grass, wines, hashish, and young women. Aroused into consciousness, they would continue their partying until unconsciousness befell them again, whereupon they were removed to the original celebration room. Once the recruits recovered from their partying, Sabah would ask them how their trip to heaven was—God had given him charge over angels who had transported the recruits to heaven as a demonstration of what the afterlife would be like. Needless to say, the recruits were even more impressed by Sabah's power and eager to complete their assassinations.

Once dispatched, the assailants would, for all practical purposes, stalk their target. Often, they would obtain jobs or positions that would allow them access to the target on a recurring basis. They would learn his habits and routines, allowing them to select the most auspicious moment to attack and kill. This methodology would be repeated throughout the centuries by many stalkers and political/terrorist assassins.

Contemporary Assassins as Terrorists

Assassination of President William McKinley

On September 6, 1901, President William McKinley attended the Pan American Exposition in Buffalo, New York. A receiving line had been set up at the Temple of Music pavilion, where President McKinley was meeting members of the public and shaking hands with well-wishers. As the line progressed, the President was approached by a young man whose right hand appeared to be heavily bandaged. As the young man got close to President McKinley, it became apparent that the bandage concealed a firearm and two shots rang out. McKinley was struck by both bullets, one in the chest and one in the abdomen. Secret Service agents, who had been standing nearby, jumped on the assailant, aided by a civilian who had just shaken the President's hand. McKinley slumped to the ground and was taken to a nearby hospital. Although initial reports from medical personnel indicated that the President's injuries were not severe and that he was expected to recover, McKinley died from his wounds in 8 days, due principally to infection and the inability at the time to detect the damage caused by the bullets (McClure & Morris, 2004).

The assailant, Leon Czolgosz, an avowed anarchist, was tried, convicted, and executed in the electric chair 45 days after the attack. Czolgosz (pronounced Tsōlgōsh) told investigators at the time that he had been inspired to kill McKinley by the writings and speeches of Emma Goldman. "I am an anarchist—a disciple of Emma Goldman. Her words set me on fire" (Leon

Czolgosz, testimony to the District Attorney, September 7, 1901, reported by the *Buffalo Evening News*, p. 9).

Czolgosz had actually met Goldman on two occasions before the assassination, both in public forums. Based on Czolgosz' statements, Goldman and several other notable anarchists of the time were arrested and held while the investigation was conducted. However, the investigation indicated that no conspiracy existed, and that Czolgosz had acted alone. Not that Czolgosz was idolized by the anarchists themselves. In point of fact, several anarchists had written in their publications that Czolgosz was actually a government spy and not to be trusted (National Archives, article by Abraham Isaak in the anarchist journal *Free Society*, 1901). Yet, Czolgosz attributed his efforts to the anarchist philosophy and felt that he had "done his duty," as he was reported to have written after the attack (*Buffalo Evening News*, September 7, 1901, p. 9).

Between 1894 and 1900, anarchists murdered the President of France, the Premier of Spain, the Empress of Austria, and the King of Italy (Warren et al., 1964). The Secret Service felt that action taken against the anarchist movement in Europe in the wake of these assassinations was compelling them to leave Europe and come to the United States. Unfortunately, U.S. presidents continued to move about with minimal protection, and no substantive changes to presidential protection occurred until after McKinley's death.

In his confession, Czolgosz stated that he had no personal enmity toward the President, but that he did not believe in rulers of governments of any kind. He stated, "I don't believe that one man should have so much service and another man should have none." At his execution, Czolgosz referred to the President as an "enemy of the good people—the good working people." He expressed no remorse for his crime (Warren et al., 1964, p. 510).

Although Czolgosz was deemed sane at the time of the assassination, there are some who contend that he suffered from some mental problems, possibly paranoid schizophrenia. In 1898, Czolgosz had suffered a "mental breakdown," but there was no additional information regarding the nature of this incident. Inquiries made about a year after Czolgosz's execution by two "alienists" revealed their opinion that he had been delusional (Warren et al., 1964). An article in the *American Journal of Insanity* reviewed the psychiatric evaluation of Czolgosz before his trial:

> If Czolgosz was a victim of mental disease the question would
> [381][382] naturally arise as to what form of that disorder he
> was suffering from. If, in answer to this question, we undertake
> to make a diagnosis by exclusion, we find the following results:
> There was absolutely no evidence of insane delusion, hallucination
> or illusion. There was none of the morbid mental exaltation or
> expansiveness of ideas that would suggest mania in any form, none
> of the morbid mental gloom and despondency of melancholia,
> none of the mental weakness of dementia, none of the conjoined
> mental or motor symptoms that are characteristic of paresis, nor

was there anything in his manner, conduct or declarations that would suggest the morbid vanity and egotism, the persecutory ideas or the transformation of personality which usually characterize paranoia or systematized delusional insanity. In fact, at no time during the period from his arrest to the time of his execution, did he exhibit any of the mannerisms, boastful display, etc., or claim to have a "divine inspiration" or "a mission," or make any complaint or suggestion of personal wrongs and persecutions which are so characteristic of paranoiacs; nor did he, during his trial, or subsequently, evince any indication of satisfaction or delight at being the central figure of the occasion and the observed of all the observed which he was; nor was there any attempt on Czolgosz' part to simulate mental diseases. The refusal to talk with his counsel was perfectly consistent with the views which he expressed to the District Attorney soon after his arrest, namely, that he did not believe in law and that he wanted no counsel. He did however, converse with others, namely, the District Attorney from time to time before his trial, also with his guards at the Buffalo jail, with whom he frequently walked in the corridor fronting his cell for an hour or two at a time, conversing with them intelligently the while and making his wants as to bathing, toilet, tobacco, etc., known in a natural manner. He also conversed freely with the people's experts in their earlier examinations of him, and talked, though not so freely, with Dr. Hurd and myself, and when on arraignment for trial and formally asked to plead he promptly arose from his chair and answered in a clear voice, "guilty." He also responded promptly when directed by the clerk of the court to "stand up and look upon the juror" as each of the jurors was sworn, and resumed his seat in each instance [382][383] at the proper time. Beyond this he remained mute while in the court room, and yet to any one who observed him closely it was apparent that he was fully aware of, and attentive to the proceedings.

MacDonald, 1902, pp. 369–386

Before the assassination, Czolgosz was obsessed with Gaetano Bresci, assassin of the King of Italy several years before (Fischer, 2001). It was even said that Czolgosz had a clipping of this event that he kept in his wallet and would reread from time to time. Perhaps his admiration of Bresci's attack provided the impetus for Czolgosz to commit his act:

During the last five years I have had as friends anarchists in Chicago, Cleveland, Detroit and other Western cities, and I suppose I became more or less bitter. Yes, I know I was bitter. I never had much luck at anything, and this preyed upon me. It made me morose and envious, but what started the craze to kill [439][440] was a lecture I heard some little time ago by Emma Goldman.

She was in Cleveland, and I and other anarchists went to hear
her. She set me on fire. Her doctrine that all rulers should be
exterminated was what set me to thinking, so that my head nearly
split with the pain.... And when I left the lecture, I had made up
my mind that I would do something heroic for the cause I loved.

> Leon Czolgosz, testimony to District Attorney, reported
> in the *Buffalo Evening News*, September 7, 1901, p. 9

As with any act of terrorism, this public figure attack involved some
degree of planning and methodology. From his testimony, Czolgosz was in
Chicago on or about August 29, 1901, and read a newspaper that stated that
President McKinley would be at the Pan American Exposition in Buffalo,
New York. Czolgosz traveled to Buffalo that day by train. His statement indi-
cated that he intended to shoot the President, but had not yet formed a plan
(MacDonald, 1902).

Once in Buffalo, Czolgosz rented a room at a local bar and hotel owned
by a Polish American. He stated that he went to the Exposition a couple of times a day. Czolgosz stated that it was not until September 3 that
he firmly decided to make the attempt on the President. It was on this day
that Czolgosz purchased a .32 caliber revolver and ammunition. That evening, Czolgosz went to the Exposition grounds near the railroad gate,
where McKinley was due to arrive that day. McKinley exited his train
and entered the grounds, but Czolgosz stated that, although he was close
to the President, he was afraid to attempt the assassination because of
the number of bodyguards that were present, and he feared that he would
be discovered and fail in his attempt. Czolgosz stated that he returned to the
Exposition on September 4 and was able to stand near McKinley during a
Presidential speech. He decided not to make the attempt because the crowd
was large and he was being jostled frequently, which could have thrown off
his aim. Czolgosz waited until Thursday, September 5, but could not get close
enough for a clear shot. So he returned on the morning of September 6 to the
Exposition grounds. "Emma Goldman's speech was still burning me up. I
waited near the central entrance for the President, who was to board his special train from that gate....I stayed on the grounds all day waiting" (*Buffalo
Evening News*, September 7, 1901, p. 9). Czolgosz then got the idea of wrap-
ping his handkerchief around his revolver in his hand so that he could bring
the weapon to bear quickly. He went to the Temple of Music, where a final
reception for McKinley was to be held before his departure. Czolgosz got into
line and waited his turn.

> I got in line and trembled and trembled, until I got right up to him,
> and then I shot him twice through my white handkerchief. I would
> have fired more, but I was stunned by a blow in the face, a frightful
> blow that knocked me down.

> *Buffalo Evening News*, September 7, 1901, p. 9

Czolgosz stated that he had committed himself to his act, conducted research on the whereabouts of his target, selected the location of the attack, and conducted reconnaissance of the location preparatory to the attack itself. Although his entire operation took only about 8 days to design and implement, his methodology has been used by assassins throughout history.

Clarke (1982) identified four types of U.S. Presidential assassins:

- *Type I* assassins view their act as a probable sacrifice of self for a political ideal.
- *Type II* assassins are persons with overwhelming and aggressive egocentric needs for acceptance, recognition, and status.
- *Type III* assassins are psychopaths who believe that the condition of their lives is so intolerably meaningless and without purpose that destruction of society and themselves is desirable for its own sake.
- *Type IV* assassins are characterized by severe emotional and cognitive distortions that are expressed in hallucinations and delusions of persecutions and/or grandeur. As a rule, their acts are mystically "divinely" inspired—in a word, irrational or insane.

Clarke's work, and the typologies and motivations of other research groups that followed (see Chapter 1 for a review), have consistently identified a small portion of stalkers, attackers, and assassins of public figures who are motivated to advance a political, social, or religious agenda. Although a minority in relation to all others who pursue public figures, their acts of violence are often rational and effective in the context of their belief system, although the wishful outcome is often a grandiose elaboration of what actually occurs.

In the first part of this chapter, a 12th century organization was examined that had a hierarchy, a membership of committed individuals, a radical ideology that promoted the assassination of opponents, and a methodology that resulted in a high percentage of success. Our second example, Leon Czolgosz 700 years later, was not under the influence of a command and control hierarchy, nor was he a member of an autonomous cell; in fact, he was mistrusted by other anarchists and remained an associate of this extremist political philosophy not on the basis of peer influence or pressure, but his own internal commitment. He was a solo operator, radicalized over a period of a few years, and developed a methodology while "on the fly." Nevertheless, he targeted a public figure and successfully carried out his attack, although a retrospective opinion exists that he might have also been mentally ill.

Our next case is also contemporary, yet combines the command and control of the Assassins with a desire to advance the establishment of the Caliphate—a pure Islamist state ruled by the law of Sharia as opposed to the politico-religious caliphate from the 8th to the 20th centuries—through the killing of a political leader, a terrorist act that deviates from the popular notion that terrorism requires the targeting of a civilian population.

Anwar Sadat and the Egyptian Islamic Jihad

Anwar Sadat was President of Egypt during a volatile period of modern history. Once considered a radical terrorist himself, Sadat eventually worked his way through the nationalistic regime of Gamal Abdul Nasser until he became Interim President upon Nasser's sudden death on September 28, 1970. Sadat was elected as President on October 5, 1970, as Nasser's government cronies felt that Sadat could be easily manipulated. Sadat surprised them all, however, when—6 months into his presidency—he effectively fired all of Nasser's former associates and became his own man. His presidency was a roller coaster of public support and animosity. He became a hero of the Arab (Muslim) world when he orchestrated the 1973 surprise attack against Israel in association with Assad of Syria. This popularity was somewhat short lived as Sadat did two things that effectively caused his assassination: he fully participated in the 1978 Camp David Accords at the behest of President Jimmy Carter, which effectively made peace between Egypt and Israel, and he began a crackdown on dissent of all kinds in 1981, in particular the radical Islamists (Weaver, 1999)—typically members of the Muslim Brotherhood.

These events caused outrage across the Arab (Muslim) world. A feeling of betrayal permeated Egypt's more fervent Muslims, and action was forthcoming. Egyptian Islamic Jihad, a splinter group from the Muslim Brotherhood, began to plan Sadat's assassination in 1981. Allegedly, a radical cleric, Omar Abdel-Rahman, known as the "Blind Sheik," issued a fatwa (religious edict) approving the assassination of Sadat for his "crimes" against Islam. Members of the Egyptian Islamic Jihad had infiltrated the Egyptian military and it was these assets that were called upon to commit the killing. Information regarding the specific planning of the operation is a bit sparse; however, it is known that Lt. Khalid Islambouli appeared to be the commander of the assault team that carried out the assassination. A total of six attackers appeared to have been involved in the assault.

On October 6, 1981, Sadat was in the reviewing stand at the annual Victory Day parade. Being an annual event, the attackers were well aware of where their target was going to be. Additionally, Sadat's security apparatus was also well known. According to various press accounts, and as the news video shows, while the parade moved along, a troop truck containing the attackers stopped directly in front of the reviewing stand. Lieutenant Islambouli dismounted the vehicle and approached it. President Sadat stood to receive what he thought would be the officer's salute. Other soldiers rose up from the back of the vehicle and began to throw hand grenades and open fire with assault rifles. Islambouli then ran to the reviewing stand and shot Sadat point-blank in the head, shouting, "I have killed pharaoh!"

The entire assassination took about 2 minutes, resulting in 8 dead and 27 wounded. Video of the assassination shows a confused and ineffective security detail, which allowed the assassins to complete their effort. In what appeared to be a coordinated effort immediately following the assassination, rebel elements took control of the town of Asyut in Upper Egypt, and held the town until Egyptian paratroopers arrived several days later and recaptured it.

Two of the attackers were killed during the assassination and the rest were subsequently arrested. Islambouli and two others were executed for their role in the assassination while the rest were imprisoned for different periods of time (Farrell, 1981). The four key defendants reflected an alliance of Egypt's military, civilian, and religious life. They referred to themselves as "the Commanders of the Caliph." They testified at trial that Sadat's assassination was justified under Shariah law because he had deviated from Islam (Weaver, 1999). This assassination again involved an organized group with committed members, but not an autonomous cell, dedicated to a radicalized philosophy (a politico-religious belief system) that had developed intelligence on their target and implemented a simple but effective attack plan.

Robert F. Kennedy and Sirhan Sirhan

There is probably no other assassination in history that has more information available than the assassination of Robert Kennedy—with the possible exception of the assassination of his brother, President John F. Kennedy (Bugliosi, 2007). Both attacks were broadcast live on television (although Robert's assassination was captured only in audio), but in the case of Robert Kennedy, the attack took place in close proximity to witnesses, and the assassin was captured immediately and survives to the current day. However, consistent with our modern society, conspiracy theories surrounding the assassination abound.

The facts are these: On the evening of June 4, 1968, presidential candidate Robert Kennedy gave a victory speech to supporters at the Ambassador Hotel in Los Angeles, California, after winning the California Democratic Primary. At approximately 12:15 a.m. on June 5, Kennedy had completed his speech and had left the podium to depart the venue. He walked from the stage area through a kitchen pantry, accompanied by 77 supporters, aids, and celebrities. At this time, Sirhan Sirhan fired seven to eight rounds from a .22 caliber Iver Johnson "Cadet" revolver. According to the Los Angeles Medical Examiner, Kennedy was hit three times, twice in the back and once behind the right ear. Kennedy died of his wounds 25 hours later, the fatal round penetrating his cerebellum. Sirhan Sirhan was arrested at the scene of the shooting, tried in Los Angeles, and sentenced to death. This sentence was commuted to life in prison when California's death penalty was overturned in 1976. He has been in jail for the past 35 years. Subsequent to this assassination, the U.S. Secret Service began providing protection to presidential candidates, rather than just presidential nominees. It is notable that a Democratic presidential candidate named Barack Obama began receiving Secret Service protection *one and a half years* before the presidential election of 2008.

Sirhan Bishara Sirhan was born March 19, 1944, in Jerusalem, Palestine, to Christian (Eastern Orthodox) parents. Sirhan was 12 years old when his family immigrated to the United States. There was some speculation that

Sirhan may have suffered some physical abuse by his father during those years (Moldea, 1995); there is no doubt that he was exposed to cumulative trauma before the age of five in his surrounding neighborhood, and witnessed the killing of his older brother. Sirhan's father abandoned them and returned to the Middle East after only a year in the United States, when his boy was 13. Sirhan was described as a quiet and polite young man while attending John Muir High School, where he studied German and Russian and was a member of the California Cadets, where he received firearms training. Although he attended college in 1963, he was not a dedicated student and dropped out of school 2 years later. Sirhan worked often, but typically at low-wage jobs. He did develop an abiding love for horse racing, even working at a ranch in Corona, California. He frequently attended race tracks and gambled on the races. He apparently harbored a desire to become a jockey and given his small stature, he might have been ideal. However, he had a number of accidents while learning to ride and eventually abandoned the idea. He was generally impoverished, or close to it, and owned a 1956 DeSoto as his sole means of transportation.

Sirhan was not a very religious man and changed his doctrines often, ranging from his own Eastern Orthodox upbringing to the Baptists, Seventh Day Adventists, and he even demonstrated an interest in the occult after the death of his sister from leukemia when he was 20, which appeared to be a critical turning point in his life.

He kept journals that figured prominently in his trial, in which it appeared that he felt disenfranchised from what he perceived as the "American Dream."

His identity, however, was fostered as an Arab through his hatred of the Zionists, whom he equated with Nazis. Following the Six Day War in 1967, he often stated that he believed the wealthy American Jews controlled the politicians and media. He wanted to kill Kennedy on the anniversary of the Arab humiliation as a result of the Six Day War. He did.

Meloy (1992) completed a Rorschach study to suggestively determine Sirhan's mental state throughout the planning, preparation, and execution of the assassination. Although defense psychiatrists at the trial opined that Sirhan was paranoid schizophrenic and had killed Kennedy in a dissociative state brought on by the lights and mirrors in the Ambassador Hotel lobby, the prosecution doctors opined that he was a developing paranoid personality (Chapter 8). Meloy found that the testing indicated Sirhan was a depressed and suicidal individual, whose personality was organized at a borderline level. His Rorschach presented a mixed characterological picture with hysterical, paranoid, and dependent features. One of the defense psychiatrists later found his own testimony to be an "absurd and preposterous story, unlikely and incredible" (Meloy, 2006b, p. 39).

In reviewing Sirhan's activities leading up to the assassination, some of the motivations among assassins and attackers investigated by both Fein and Vossekuil (1999; "to avenge a perceived wrong") and Phillips (2006;

"resentful") can be identified as applicable to Sirhan. Based on Sirhan's diary, it is likely that he made the decision to kill Kennedy in early 1968, when he wrote, on January 31, "RFK must die" (Kaiser, 1970). This exclamation was in response to Kennedy's support for a proposed sale of 50 U.S.-made Phantom jet fighters to Israel. "When Kennedy announced his candidacy...Sirhan began practice shooting" (Moldea, 1995, p. 322). Psychological evidence suggests that Sirhan had idealized Kennedy as a father transference figure before this time (Meloy, 1992).

Sirhan denied that he had ever stalked Kennedy before the assassination and continues to assert that he has no recollection of the assault. There were indications that there were four probable stalking efforts against Kennedy before the June 5 killing (Meloy, 1992):

- May 20, 1968, in Robbie's Restaurant in Pomona, California: Sirhan was seen with an unidentified woman while Kennedy was dining in the restaurant.
- May 24: Sirhan was observed at a Kennedy rally at the Los Angeles Sports Arena.
- June 2: Sirhan practiced shooting (after purchasing two boxes of .22 caliber ammunition on June 1) and later was observed at a Kennedy campaign rally at the Ambassador Hotel.
- June 3: Sirhan apparently traveled to San Diego, California, to attend a Kennedy appearance at the El Cortez Hotel.

One must realize that in any political assassination, it is the tactical application that provides any level of success to the assassins. Whatever their motivation—political, religious, or purely narcissistic—it is the tactics that are employed that will allow assassins to observe the target, assess the situation, plan the attack, and close on the target with any hope of success. On the day of the assassination, Sirhan went to a range and practiced with his revolver. After finishing his practice on the pistol range at about 5:00 p.m., he had a meal at Bob's Big Boy, went to the Ambassador Hotel,[1] and had four alcoholic drinks over several hours. He then asked two people if Kennedy's bodyguards were with him all the time and if he would be coming through the kitchen pantry. Just before he shot Kennedy, he was heard to say, "Kennedy, you son of a bitch" (Clarke, 1982; Kaiser, 1970).[2]

Discussion

It has often been asserted that assassins are loners who operate on their own without direct affiliation to any particular group. Historically, this has been the case in many assassinations, with the earliest notable exception being the Hashisheen of the Middle East, the origin of the English word, "assassin." In many cases, some type of mental health issue may also be involved to varying degrees. Like the Hashisheen of old and many present-day extremist groups, certain types of persons—ranging from habitual criminals to clinically depressed social outcasts—are sought for recruitment for the express purpose of violence. *There is no profile of the terrorist as assassin*, just as there is no profile of an individual who will stalk, threaten, or attack a public figure (Fein & Vossekuil, 1999), yet general themes do emerge.

The Hashisheen, as al Qaeda and other extremist Islamic groups do today, tried to find, recruit, and train for martyrdom relatively young, disaffected, disenfranchised, and easily manipulated people for the purposes of violence.[3] Mid-level cell leaders, however, are usually drawn from more educated and affluent backgrounds (Meloy, 2004). Eric Rudolph and Paul Hill, both "lone terrorists" who targeted public venues and a public figure respectively (Puckitt, 2001), had conversions that were preceded by sociodevelopmental periods in which they became increasingly adrift from their historical family and community roots, often behaviorally evident in increased social isolation and intolerance of beliefs different from their own. Both Rudolph's and Hill's philosophical trajectories were increasingly vigilant and paranoid, but their belief content differed.

Eric Rudolph spent 6 months with his mother and brother[4] in Schell City, Missouri, being schooled in the teachings of the Church of Israel, an anti-Semitic and white supremacist organization. He had always wanted to become a paratrooper, but in the U.S. Army, he tested positive for marijuana, and was court-martialed, punished, and discharged from the service. In his late 20s, he withdrew into the woods in rural North Carolina, and in July, 1996, he detonated his first of four bombs at the summer Olympics in Atlanta, Georgia.[5] His letters sent to authorities attributed the acts to "The Army of God." He was on the lam for nearly 7 years before his capture on May 31, 2003, and eventual federal prosecution for the bombings and deaths of three individuals.

Paul Hill converted to Christianity at age 18, fathered three children, and pastored two Presbyterian congregations in South Carolina, until his extreme fundamentalism and intolerance of others' perspectives alienated his parishioners. He was excommunicated in 1991, began an auto-detailing business in Pensacola, Florida, and allied himself with another antiabortionist, Rev. Michael Bray, who had served time for fire-bombing an abortion clinic. He began to isolate in his attic, writing sermons and speeches to further his religious extremism. In March 1993, he appeared on the "Phil Donahue Show" after another man named Michael Griffin killed an abortion doctor, David Gunn, in Pensacola, and vehemently justified Griffin's actions. Other national media appearances followed—of course—and in May 1994, he decided to kill a doctor himself: "My eyes were opened to the enormous impact another such shooting in Pensacola would have.... Having spoken the truth I needed to exemplify it.... God had opened a window of opportunity before me, it appeared I had been appointed to step through it" (Puckitt, 2001, p. 37). Eight days later, he shotgunned to death Dr. John Britton and his escort, and wounded his wife. He concealed the shotgun in a tube normally used for antiabortion posters and hid it in the grass. Right after his arrest, he yelled, "Now is the time to defend the unborn!" (Puckitt, 2001, p. 37). Hill was tried, sentenced to death, and executed in Florida in 2003. His last words were, "May God help you protect the unborn as you would want to be protected" (www.armyofgod. com/philllinks.html).

Assassins who target a public figure to advance a political or religious agenda are terrorists, whether attached to an organized group with a command and control hierarchy, an autonomous cell, or acting alone. If there is active recruitment, the tactical element commands all of the subsequent activities leading up to the assassination. This is one area that is often overlooked until after the assassination has taken place. It has been a confusing area for law enforcement and a source of distress for intelligence agencies because the former are, by design, reactive in nature. The overt act often *initiates* law enforcement activity, although in retrospect, agencies often minimize their knowledge of the threat, or exaggerate their response to the threat, both attempts to revise history in the face of an utter failure: there is no more potent example than the positioning of various principals to justify their inaction, or inflate their action, through numerous books and interviews following the 9/11 attacks. Notably, agencies like the U.S. Secret Service and the U.S. Capitol Police have a much more proactive approach to the potential of direct attack against public figures. Unfortunately, traditional law enforcement has been slower to develop more pronounced proactive aspects.

One city-based exception is the extraordinary work of the New York Police Department in counterterrorism, most recently underscored by their publication of an analysis of the functional pathway of autonomous cells committed to a Jihadi-Salafi ideology of violence toward the unbelievers to advance the establishment of a Caliphate. The New York Police Department has identified four stages that appear to shed light on the development of such autonomous cells and, in some cases, their eventual terrorist acts. The four stages are (1) preradicalization, (2) self-identification, (3) indoctrination, and (4) jihadization (New York Police Department, 2007). Their work complements other functional-behavioral pathway analyses such as those developed by Calhoun and Weston (2003) and Borum, Fein, Vossekuil, and Berglund (1999). In their detailed report, they empirically support their theory with a close look at both domestic and foreign acts of terrorism that have been interdicted (e.g., Lackawana, New York; New York City-Herald Square Subway) or completed (2004 attack in Madrid; 2005 attack in London).

Most germaine to our chapter is the finding that a few autonomous cells have specifically targeted a public figure for assassination, and we believe this pattern is likely to continue.[6] The Toronto 18 case, which was thwarted in Canada in June 2006, was intended to behead the Canadian Prime Minister Stephen Harper, an aspect of their plot suggested by a young Canadian male named Steven Chand, who was raised a Hindu, had served in the Canadian military, and had converted to Islam (New York Police Department, 2007).

Another case involving a homegrown, autonomous cell that targeted a public figure was the Hofstad Group in Amsterdam. Composed of young

Dutch Muslims from North Africa, the group considered targeting members of the Parliament as well as the national airport and a nuclear reactor. For unknown reasons, a group member named Mohammed Bouyeri, the son of Moroccan immigrants, who was born and raised in West Amsterdam, decided to kill Theo Van Gogh, a provocative Dutch filmmaker who was railing against fundamentalist Islamists, and did so on November 2, 2004. Bouyeri seemed to have been radicalized during 7 months in prison for assault, and subsequently became more conservative and strident in his religious and political views.[7]

Bouyeri acquired his own gun and began practice shooting in October, and as the rest of his group planned their more elaborate operations, he rode up to Van Gogh on his bicycle, shot him with his pistol, nearly decapitated him, and plunged a note into his chest with the knife. He intended to die in a confrontation with police, but much to his dismay, was captured instead (Buruma, 2006). Other members of the Hofstad Group were arrested, and no subsequent terrorist acts were carried out.

Studies by the U.S. Department of Justice have revealed that terrorist organizations will surveil a potential target as many as 14 times in a 22-month period. (California Department of Justice, Protection of Critical Infrastructure Report, 2005). We have given two examples—Czolgosz and Sirhan—of lone assassins who stalked or surveilled their target before their killings, if even for a few days or weeks, the *target's behavior* shaping the eventual plan of attack. In some cases, rehearsals may be conducted. In the build up of U.S. forces in Saudi Arabia before Operation Desert Storm, surveillance by unidentified individuals against a high-ranking U.S. military officer was detected by the protection detail. Intelligence assets were brought in to investigate and conduct a surveillance detection operation. The operatives were in position and observed an actual rehearsal—vehicles casually and discreetly blocked the target's car in front and rear, and down the street, other "bandits" were positioned to block an intersection to aid the getaway. "Bandit" observers with communications equipment were also spotted on nearby roof-tops. This rehearsal was quick and discrete, but because of the presence of intelligence agents, people and vehicles were identified and the information passed along to host nation police agencies that effected arrests of the soon-to-be-attackers, thereby disrupting the attack and avoiding any injuries.

Other lone attackers have demonstrated tactical planning in their efforts. Charles Guiteau, who assassinated President James A. Garfield in 1881, and Arthur Bremer, who attempted to assassinate George Wallace in 1972—but had preferred Richard Nixon as a target—are two additional examples. Guiteau wrote the following letter in the morning hours before his assassination:

> I have just shot the President. I shot him several times, as I wished
> him to go as easily as possible. His death was a political necessity.
> I am a lawyer, theologian, and politician. I am a Stalwart of the
> Stalwarts. I was with General Grant and the rest of our men, in

New York during the canvass. I am going to the jail. Please order
out your troops, and take possession of the jail at once.

Rosenberg, 1968, p. 5

In summary, we emphasize the following findings and opinions from our
review of the data on public figure assassins as terrorists, and our illustration
of these events with two examples of "command and control" organizations
that led to public figure assassination, two examples of "lone terrorists" who
also assassinated, and several contemporary case vignettes of "homegrown"
autonomous cells who targeted public figures as part of their terrorist plans.

First, among the many motivations for public figure stalking and attacking,
one is to intentionally kill a public figure to advance a particular political,
religious, or social belief.

Second, such events are often quite rational and tactically effective within
the context of the belief system, but fall short of the grandiose fantasy of the
attacker(s) to strategically alter history, impose an absolutist belief system, or
change the course of world events.

Third, the public attacker as terrorist is either actively embedded in an
organization that helps carry out the killing—a hierarchical organization
exercising some command and control or an autonomous cell—or is an isolate
or loner who has adopted a conscious belief system that justifies his actions.
Paradoxically, he may be viewed with suspicion or ostracized by his adopted
ideological peers because of his behavioral oddities or extremism.

Fourth, public figure attacks as terrorist acts are invariably predatory—
planned, purposeful, and emotionless—rather than affective—emotional,
reactive, and impulsive (Meloy, 2006a). They typically involve days, weeks,
or months of research, planning, and preparation.

Fifth, the presence of diagnosable psychiatric disorder(s) in the attacker or
assassin does not necessarily mitigate the influence of his political or religious
belief system as conscious motivation for the crime. In fact, delusion may bring
a resolve to the ideology that would not exist otherwise.[8]

And sixth, regardless of group association and specific motivation, the
focus of intelligence and law enforcement efforts must be to gain knowledge of
the research, preparation, and planning on the "pathway to violence" (Calhoun &
Weston, 2003) *before* there is a breach and attack. This necessitates a vast formal and informal intelligence network and raises important balancing issues
concerning the assumed privacy of citizens who live in a free and open democratic society—fundamental social structures that the terrorist often hopes to
alter and law enforcement is committed to protect.

Notes

1. The Ambassador Hotel in Los Angeles has since been destroyed, but did serve
   as the location for the filming of "Bobby," an ode to Robert Kennedy by Emilio
   Estevez, just before it was leveled.

2. The Sirhan assassination is closely paralleled by the assassination of Itzhak Rabin, the Prime Minister of Israel, on November 4, 1995. Rabin was killed by 25-year-old Jewish law student Yigal Amir, who fired two shots from close range as Rabin entered his car following a public gathering. Amir felt betrayed because Rabin was giving land to the Palestinians. Although he stated that he acted alone, others were arrested and implicated in the assassination, including the leader of the extreme right wing Eyal (Jewish Militant Organization).

3. The "muscle" recruited for the 9/11 attacks on New York and Washington were typically young, unemployed males from southwestern Saudi Arabia who could obtain valid passports and had no official criminal records. These men were a striking contrast to the professional, well-educated, middle-class backgrounds of the pilots, particularly Atta, al-Shehi, and Jarrah. Atta had a masters degree from Hamburg, al-Shehi had been a soldier in the UAE military, and Jarrah had been a Lebanese playboy.

4. The familial devotion among the Rudolph family was extraordinarily evident when his brother, who was never implicated in Eric's crimes, videotaped the severing of his hand with an electric table saw and sent the tape to the FBI to underscore his commitment to Eric and his beliefs.

5. Richard Jewell, a private security guard who was investigated as a potential suspect by the FBI, was actually a hero who moved crowds away from the suspicious backpack just before it exploded. He died in August, 2007, at the age of 44.

6. We are particularly concerned about well-known CEOs in the West who personify much of what the Islamists hate and are potent symbols of secularism, technology, and free market capitalism (see Chapter 9).

7. The "spiritual sanctioner" of the Hofstad Group was Ridwan Al-Issar, who likely fled to Syria the day Van Gogh was killed (New York Police Department, 2007).

8. Theodore Kaczynski was diagnosed as paranoid schizophrenic by a Federal Bureau of Prisons psychiatrist, but appeared to be motivated as a serial bomber because of his hatred of technological society and philosophy similar to the Luddites, a social movement in the early 19th century of British textile workers who protested the Industrial Revolution.

References

Borum, R., Fein, R., Vossekuil, B., & Berglund, J. (1999). Threat assessment: Defining an approach for evaluating risk of targeted violence. *Behavioral Sciences and the Law, 17*, 323–337.

Bugliosi, V. (2007). *Reclaiming history.* New York: Norton.

Buruma, I. (2006). *Murder in Amsterdam.* New York: Penguin.

Calhoun, F., & Weston, S. (2003). *Contemporary threat management.* San Diego: Specialized Training Services.

California Department of Justice (2005). *Protection of critical infrastructure.* Sacramento, CA: Author.

Clarke, J. W. (1982). *American assassins: The darker side of politics.* Princeton: Princeton University Press.

Darual, A. (1989). *A history of secret societies.* New York: Citadel.

Farrell, W. E. (1981, October). *New York Times,* p. A1.

Federal Bureau of Investigation, 28 C.F.R., § 0.85 (1996).

Fein, R., & Vossekuil, B. (1999). Assassination in the United States: An operational study of recent assassins, attackers, and near-lethal approachers. *Journal of Forensic Sciences, 44,* 321–333.

Fischer, J. (2001). *Stolen glory: The McKinley assassination.* La Jolla, CA: Alamar Books.

Gabrieli, F. (1993). *Arab historians of the crusades.* New York: Barnes & Noble Books.

Kaiser, R. (1970). *R.F.K. must die!* New York: Dutton.

Lane-Poole, S. (2002). *Saladin and the fall of Jerusalem.* London: Greenhill. Original publication, 1898.

Lewis, B. (1967). *The assassins.* New York: Basic Books.

MacDonald, C. F. (1902). The trial, execution, and autopsy and mental status of Leon F. Czolgosz, the assassin of President McKinley. *American Journal of Insanity, 1,* 369–396.

McClure, A. K., & Morris, C. (2004). *Authentic life of William McKinley.* Whitefish, MT: Kessinger. Original publication, 1901.

Meloy, J. R. (1992). Revisiting the Rorschach of Sirhan Sirhan. *Journal of Personality Assessment, 58,* 548–570.

Meloy, J. R. (2004). Indirect personality assessment of the violent true believer. *Journal of Personality Assessment, 82,* 138–146.

Meloy, J. R. (2006a). The empirical basis and forensic application of affective and predatory violence. *Australian and New Zealand Journal of Psychiatry, 40,* 539–547.

Meloy, J. R. (2006b). *The scientific pursuit of stalking.* San Diego: Specialized Training Services.

Moldea, D. (1995). *The killing of Robert Kennedy.* New York: Norton.

New York Police Department. (2007). *Radicalization in the West: The homegrown threat.* New York: Author.

Phillips, R. (2006). Assessing Presidential stalkers and assassins. *Journal of the American Academy of Psychiatry and the Law, 34,* 154–164.

Puckitt, K. (2001). *The lone terrorist: the search for connection and its relationship to societal-level violence.* Washington, DC: Counterterrorism Division, Federal Bureau of Investigation.

Rosenberg, C. (1968). *The trial of the assassin Guiteau.* Chicago: University of Chicago Press.

Warren, E., Russell, R. B., Cooper, J. S., Boggs, H., Ford, G. R., Dulles, A. W., et al. (1964). *Report of the President's Commission on the Assassination of President Kennedy, Appendix 7: A brief history of presidential protection.* College Park, MD: The National Archives and Records Administration.

Weaver, M. (1999). *A portrait of Egypt.* New York: Farrar, Straus and Giroux.

Section II

Explaining the Risk

8

Contributions From Attachment Theory and Psychoanalysis to Advance Understanding of Public Figure Stalking and Attacking

Jens Hoffmann and J. Reid Meloy

There is endless love in my heart. It hurts so much to lose.
It hurts so much to love and it hurts so much to live on.

I was happy to see that you were wearing a yellow tie and talked
about US President Clinton in the last newscast. I see this as a
signal that you want to make contact with me.

Public figures are not able to understand that the subconscious
cannot make a distinction between appearance and reality.

Excerpts from stalkers' letters to public figures

Pathological fixation on public figures is an old phenomenon in human societies. Although the instantaneous worldwide saturation of the mass media has contributed to a burgeoning public interest in celebrities—who did not know (whether they wanted to or not) that Anna Nicole Smith was found dead in her Caribbean hotel room within moments of the event?—we find hints of obsession with famous people in rather old reports and publications (see, for example, www.tmz.com). In the 19th century, psychiatric writers began to describe clinical conditions and behaviors that today we would closely relate to stalking. For example, in 1838, the French psychiatrist Esquirol coined the term "erotomania." He saw it as an insanity characterized by an exaggeration of nonsexual love toward another person, which in reality did not exist.

In one of his case studies, Esquirol described a man who was following an actor throughout Paris. Notwithstanding her repeated rebuffs, he remained convinced that the actor was in love with him. Dr. Esquirol confronted his delusion by unempathically inquiring, "How could you believe she loves you? You are not handsome. You possess neither rank or fortune." The stalker answered him poetically, hinting that his erotomanic delusions of a mutual relationship may have served to overcome his solitude: "All that is true, but love does not reason, and I have seen too much to leave me in doubt that I am loved" (cited in Mullen, Pathé, & Purcell, 2000, p. 132).

Around 50 years later, von Krafft-Ebing, arguably the father of forensic psychiatry, described obsessions with celebrities in the past. In his classical textbook *Psychopathia Sexualis* (Krafft-Ebing, 1912), he noted that women of all ages can be fascinated by successful actors, singers, or athletes in such a manner that they overwhelm them with love letters. A more sinister form of pathological fixation on public figures was reported in cases of paranoia. Eugen Bleuler, one of the most influential psychiatrists in the beginning of the 20th century, found mental illness to be a possible trigger for violent attacks against public figures. "If the mentally ill thinks that he cannot help himself anymore with legal means, he acts in self-defense, shooting his enemy or attempting a nonserious attack on a high-ranking figure because he wants to enforce an 'unprejudiced' investigation" (Bleuler, 1943, p. 501).

On the heels of these clinical assertions, criminologists and psychiatrists who were concerned with questions of security started researching assassins and people who were fixated on political leaders. In the first of these studies, criminologist Arthur MacDonald (1911) examined cases of six men who attacked American politicians. Studying their state of mind and life histories, he characterized the assassins as unstable and continuously changing their occupation and habitation. Later research came to similar conclusions (Clarke, 1982, 1990; Fein & Vossekuil, 1998, 1999). Threateners and persons who want to come close to the U.S. president or other politicians in an unusual way have also been the object of interest. Most of them were found to be loners, with few of them married or intimately involved with someone (Dietz & Martell, 1989; Hoffman, 1943; Logan, Reuterfors, Bohn, & Clark, 1984). A description of this group more than half a century ago remains quite accurate. One finds

> The story of frustration, unsatisfied ambition, the wish for security and freedom from want, the desire for love and affection. Over a period of years these unsatisfied needs exist, and remain unsatisfied.... One may search the stories of their lives without finding much cause for happiness or satisfaction. The recurring theme in their life histories is that of frustration, loneliness, failure.

> Hoffman, 1943, p. 575

Most stalkers of celebrities seem to be equally socially isolated. In a sample of 214 persons who contacted Hollywood stars in an inappropriate way, the majority lived on their own or with their parents, only 4% cohabited with a partner, and 3% with children of their own (Dietz & Martell, 1989). In a mixed Dutch sample of celebrity and political cases, 78% of the stalkers lived alone (Malsch, Visscher, & Blaauw, 2002). A recent study examining 271 cases of U.S. celebrity stalkers found that the majority were single or divorced, and often were unemployed or underemployed (Chapter 2). Their obviously unhappy lives are also captured in another distinctive feature: public figure stalkers and attackers threaten, attempt, or complete suicide more often than the population on average (Fein & Vossekuil, 1999) (Chapters 2 and 4).

This outer instability has an equivalency in the inner world. Many of those who are fixated on public figures show signs of mental illness. Dietz and Martell (1989) found suggestive evidence of psychiatric disorder in 95% of all inappropriate or otherwise threatening letters sent to celebrities or politicians. In the largest published archival study of stalkers of celebrities—data were not gathered from clinical settings—several types of mental illness appeared in 52% of the cases (Mohandie, Meloy, McGowan, & Williams, 2006) (Chapter 2). In the U.S. Secret Service Study of 83 attackers or near lethal-approachers of public figures, 43% were delusional before their offence and 44% had a history of serious depression or despair (Fein & Vossekuil, 1999). An historical analysis of attacks on the British Royal Family showed that 65% of the attackers suffered from mental disorder; studies of attacks on politicians in western Europe since 1990 found severe mental abnormalities in 54% of the cases (Chapter 3) (James et al., 2007, in press).

If we summarize more than one and a half centuries of clinical experience, case reports, and research, a robust picture emerges of persons who stalk, threaten, and assault public figures:

1. The majority live a socially isolated life with few, if any, attachments to others. They seldom have a stable sexual pair bond.
2. Frequently, their employment and social history in their community are unstable.
3. They are often unhappy people, marked by dysphoria and despair.
4. Many show signs of severe mental illness, including psychotic symptoms.
5. By inference, their ability to "test reality," or demarcate between internal and external stimuli, is grossly impaired.
6. They generally want to be connected with, and reap the benefits of, an extraordinary and well-known person, and they feel entitled to such a bond. This aspect shows a clear pathological narcissism. Much less often, they feel persecuted or personally betrayed by the public figure, suggesting a clinical degree of paranoia.

Pathological fixations on public figures have a compensatory function. Things often went deeply wrong in the life of the stalker or attacker, and the force of grandiose fantasy has been continuously utilized as a balm. The compensation is also emotional, characterized by a yearning, an anger, and a fear. It is no coincidence that celebrities and other public figures become transference objects—a lover, a parent, a teacher, a beneficiary—at least initially imbued with perfection and larger than life. Psychodynamic and attachment theories help us to understand the psychological "deep structure" that has been shaped, if not crystallized, by those early experiences (Kienlen, 1998; Kienlen, Birmingham, Solberg, O'Regan, & Meloy, 1997; Meloy, 1992, 2002b).

Attachment Theory

Attachment theory states that a safe and sustainable psychological bond to a parental figure in early life, usually the mother, is fundamental for personality development (Bowlby, 1969). The capacity to form such a basic relationship is deeply rooted in biology in most members of our species. Survival is dependent on support, protection, and feeding from an adult, and within moments of birth, an infant will crawl to its mother's nipple if placed on her naked belly. Crawling will then not return for months, and the infant will depend on crying to bring the mother to her for feeding and caretaking. Bowlby wrote,

> Since the goal of attachment behaviour is to maintain an affective bond, any situation that seems to be endangering the bond elicits action designed to preserve it; and the greater the danger of loss appears to be, the more intensive and varied are the actions elicited to prevent it. In such circumstances all the most powerful forms of attachment behaviour become activated—clinging, crying and perhaps angry coercion.
>
> Bowlby, 1980, p. 42

Attachment theory originated during World War II (Bowlby, 1944) and has been empirically studied and validated over the past 70 years (Fonagy & Target, 2007). There are a number of salient findings from this research, which are relevant to our topic of public figure stalking:

1. Attachment is a biobehavioral system, which when activated, is accompanied by strong emotion and a compelling motivation to seek proximity to another, usually the caretaker, and in adulthood, a sexually intimate partner.
2. Attachment is deeply conditioned, and secure attachment in childhood will predict secure attachments in adulthood. Likewise, attachment marked by abuse, neglect, or loss in childhood will predict difficulties in the formation of stable and secure attachments in adulthood (Waters, Merrick, Treboux, Crowell, & Albersheim, 2000).
3. Insecure attachments are variously categorized as preoccupied, dismissive, fearful, and disorganized.
4. The clinical corollary of preoccupied attachment is borderline psychopathology.

5. The clinical corollary of fearful attachment is avoidant, phobic, or paranoid psychopathology.
6. The clinical corollary of dismissive attachment is psychopathy.
7. The clinical corollary of disorganized attachment is traumatic psychopathology, such as posttraumatic stress disorder and dissociative disorders.
8. The neuropeptides, oxytocin and vasopressin, are biologically implicated in the formation and maintenance of attachments. Increases in the neurotransmitter dopamine and decreases in the neurotransmitter serotonin have been theoretically implicated in the behavioral pathology of attachment called stalking (Meloy & Fisher, 2005).
9. There is cumulative data from a number of studies that stalking is associated with a pathology of attachment, usually preoccupied (Meloy, 2006a; Meloy & Gothard, 1995).
10. Although there are few studies of the attachment histories of public figure stalkers and attackers, the chronic instability in their capacity to work and to love as adults, their histories of loss, and their psychiatric disabilities all suggest psychopathologies of attachment, which are likely to be chronic, and may be partially causative of their stalking behavior.
11. The evident cognitive aspect of public figure stalkers and attackers is their pathological fixation on the object, a pattern of thinking found in preoccupied attachments.
12. Pathological attachment activation toward a public figure—often the result of media reports of the figure's activities—will be accompanied by an upsurge in a variety of emotion, including yearning for contact, dysphoria concerning one's present state of noncontact, and the potential for intense anger if that contact is rejected.
13. Public figure stalking has a large fantasy component (Isaacs, 1952), and implicates an impairment in reality testing, two psychological operations that are informed by psychoanalytic object relations theory.

In attachment theory, there is also explanatory power for the considerable perseverance often seen in public stalking behavior, and the typical alternating phases of inactivity and action.

> When, however, the effort to restore the bond is not successful, sooner or later the effort wanes. But usually it does not cease. On the contrary, evidence shows that, at perhaps increasingly long intervals, the effort to restore the bond is renewed: the pangs of grief and perhaps an urge to search are then experienced afresh. This means that the person's attachment behavior is remaining constantly primed and that, in conditions still to be defined, it becomes activated anew.
>
> Bowlby, 1980, p. 42

Object Relations Theory

Object relations theory is a psychoanalytic school of thought that places internal representations of self and others and the emotions that surround them in a position of centrality in the mind of the individual. These "internalized objects" are theorized to form very early in the life of the child, are both conscious and unconscious, and endure throughout life, both influencing subsequent actual relationships and being influenced by them. There is an extensive body of clinical and theoretical research concerning object relations (Fairbairn, 1952; Freud, 1961; Jacobson, 1964; Kernberg, 1976; Klein, 1948; Mahler, 1968; Winnicott, 1955). Kernberg defined the theory as a

> Metapsychology stressing the buildup of dyadic or bipolar intrapsychic representations (self and object images) as reflections of the original infant-mother relationship and its later development into dyadic, triangular, and multiple internal and external interpersonal relationships.... Each unit of self and object image is established in a particular affective context.
>
> Kernberg, 1975, p. 57

The relevance of object relations theory to the stalking, threatening, and attacking of public figures is the establishment in these individuals of a "narcissistic linking fantasy," a belief that there exists a special and idealized relationship to another (Meloy, 1998, 1999b; see also Freud, 1953, on *Bindung* [linking]). This fantasy, which has both conscious and unconscious elements, initially includes an image of self, an image of the public figure, and certain feelings that connect them for a variety of purposes, such as beneficence, romance, sexuality, or power; but the specialness and idealization in fantasy are what distinguish this object relationship from all others (specialness could even be in the guise of the victim of a paranoid conspiracy). Here is an example of a narcissistic linking fantasy in a letter sent by the man who stalked the actor Gwyneth Paltrow in 1999–2000:

> I shall be a big motivational speaker; I shall run for President Of the United States; I shall be a Minister; I shall be an Actor; I shall be a Writer of Stories and Writer of Lovers; and most Important of all, I shall make Gwyneth Paltrow a Queen, A Queen of My Heart's Desire, and the Lover of My Own.
>
> Author's files

Object relations theory and the existence of such enduring fantasies in public figure stalkers is critical to comprehending the inevitable deterioration in the relationship between the pursuer and his object, and the potential for violence.

Borderline Personality Organization

Threat managers who protect public figures carefully attend to communication in which their famous clients are idealized in a distinctive way. They know that exuberant love can turn into unflinching hate. The reason for such polarized emotions and sudden oscillations in the perception of self and others is often the presence of a borderline personality organization, first enunciated by the psychoanalyst Otto Kernberg (1975). Such organization of personality, posited to exist on the "border" between neurosis and psychosis, is characterized by primitive defenses, weakened reality testing, and the *absence* of whole object relations. The latter characteristic refers to the inability of the individual to conceive of others as whole, real, and meaningful individuals separate from himself or herself.

Psychological defenses—the immune system of the mind—come in a variety of forms and developmentally mature over time in most individuals, but all derive from a generic defense called *splitting* (Kernberg, 1995). Splitting is normally used during the first several years of life and then is replaced by higher-level operations like repression.

> Probably the best known manifestation of splitting is the division of external objects into "all good" ones and "all bad" ones, with the concomitant possibility of complete, abrupt shifts of an object from one extreme compartment to the other, that is, sudden and complete reversals of all feelings and conceptualizations about a particular person.
>
> Kernberg, 1975, p. 29

A classical case example of this psychological defense was utilized by Roberto Bardo, whose murderous attack on the actor Rebecca Schaeffer led to the passage of the first antistalking law in California in 1990. In the beginning, the young man adored Schaeffer and wrote her letters of admiration to which she responded—but only once—with a postcard. After Bardo saw a movie in which the actor was in bed with a male character and sexual activity was inferred, but not shown, his communication took on a more threatening tone and he began preparing his attack. This sudden shift from idealization to devaluation is a hallmark of splitting, and found its literal equivalent when Bardo called his sister immediately before the attack. He told her he was going to fulfill his mission to "stop Schaeffer from forsaking her innocent childlike image for that of an adult fornicating screen whore" (Saunders, 1998, p. 27).

Primitive idealization, another borderline defense derived from splitting, is the tendency to see others through the distorting lens of internalized objects as "all good." Such perceptions not only psychologically protect the borderline personality from threats and dangers, but also help manage his or her own aggression toward the object. Another function of primitive idealization is the narcissistic gratification that accompanies his or her fantasized participation in the fame and fortune of the idealized person. The inherent difficulty with any idealizing defense, however, is the predictable disappointment that the idealized object will bring to the individual, since no one, including public figures, is perfect. Perfection resides only in fantasy.

Omnipotence and *devaluation* are other defenses derived from splitting. Public figure stalkers utilizing these two mechanisms of defense, "may shift between the need to establish a demanding, clinging relationship to an idealized 'magic' object at some times, and fantasies and behavior betraying a deep feeling of magical omnipotence of their own at other times" (Kernberg, 1975, p. 33). Omnipotence implies the domination, and often devaluation, of another. Some celebrity stalkers at first glance appear insecure and full of self-doubt, while on closer inspection they evidence both entitlement ("she owes me") and grandiosity ("she needs me") in their narcissistic linking fantasies of connection to a famous person. This shy or hypervigilant narcissistic type will be discussed later. The shift from idealization to devaluation is usually prompted by a disappointment or humiliation that is attributed to the object of pursuit.

Most salient to borderline personality organization are the defenses of *projection* and *projective identification*. Projection is the attribution of characteristics within the self to another. Projective identification is an incomplete projection: characteristics, often aggressive impulses, are attributed to another, but continue to be a part of the subject's own psychology, and therefore threaten him. The subject must then attempt to control what he perceives as a threat outside himself. Sometimes public figure stalkers are compelled to act violently because they believe the public figure poses a threat toward them, and in cases of political figures, oftentimes the projective fantasy becomes intermingled with an actual threat that the state, represented by the political figure, may pose to the subject. As Lee Harvey Oswald, the assassin of John F. Kennedy, said, "there is no borderline between one's personal world and the world in general" (Meloy, 1992, p. 127). Oswald fit Clarke's (1982) Type II assassins: "Persons with overwhelming and aggressive egocentric needs for acceptance, recognition, and status" (p. 24). Oswald's assassination appears to have been a displacement of hatred toward those who narcissistically wounded him, and a rageful seeking of attention that was politically rationalized (Meloy, 1992).

Reality testing is the ability to distinguish between internal and external stimuli. The *weakening of reality testing*—a characteristic of borderline personality organization—is often evident in the misperception of the origin of emotional stimuli: "For example, rage may be sensed as coming from the object of pursuit, when in fact she is feeling and communicating intense fear. Instead of accurately perceiving the fear in her, and the rage in himself, and thus restraining his behavior, the stalker suddenly feels threatened and escalates his attack" (Meloy, 2002a, p. 114). Weakened reality testing is perpetuated by primitive defenses, as the subject's thoughts and feelings are projected onto the object of pursuit one moment, and then taken back, or *re-introjected*, the next moment. Most law enforcement personnel who have ever worked on a spousal homicide have witnessed the perpetrator professing his love for the victim in the moments after he has killed her: an Othellian commentary that captures the dangers of this borderline psychopathology.

Weakening of reality testing is illustrated by a public figure stalking case from the file of one of the authors. An adult female repetitively approached an actor at his public appearances. She asked him for a photographic opportunity, to which he agreed. One night, as he left an opening night party, she was waiting outside, but he politely declined her request to photograph him. She insulted him and subsequently began to approach his private home. One evening, she was waiting for him and threatened him with a knife. He managed to escape and called the police with his cell phone. He directed them to his home, keeping a safe distance from the woman. Before she was arrested, she told the actor that she would kill him after being released. She also injured herself slightly by wounding her abdomen with the knife.

The stalker had a different perspective on the incident, which she subsequently related to a psychiatrist. She was hanging around in the streets when suddenly a motorcyclist stopped next to her and started insulting her. It was the actor who then started punching her in the face. She ran, but he followed her. She pulled a knife in desperation when she saw that the actor also had a knife, but he still was able to cut her. The stalker lived a life of isolation, and had a long history of depression and suicide attempts, but no history of psychosis.

Where is the actual aggression? It originates in the stalker, and is projectively identified in the actor, who then becomes a threat. A cutting injury is sustained, which in fact is self-inflicted, but in fantasy is caused by the aggressive object. Threats of homicide heard by others are transformed into defensive behaviors to ward off an imminent attack. The aggressor becomes the victim. The idealized object of yearning becomes the devalued object of derision. Although not psychotic, her narrative is plausible, but false, when measured against other evidence in the case.

The Role of Pathological Narcissism

Narcissism, a "felt quality of perfection" (Rothstein, 1980), was psychologically delineated by Freud (1975; original publication, 1914) in an early paper, which differentiated between primary and secondary forms. Primary or normal narcissism is a general developmental stage in the life of every infant. Libidinal energy is focused on the self, which serves the instinct for survival. The young child over time relinquishes his self-love to other people and objects, most importantly the mother. In most cases, her affection and caretaking compensate for this decline in self-love. Secondary narcissism may emerge later in life, and is considered psychopathological. It is a relapse to an earlier developmental stage, or a failure of maturation, a regression or a fixation, respectively (Greenacre, 1960). Libidinal energy remains withdrawn from the outside world and focuses solely on the self. Others are sources of gratification rather than empathic contemplation.

The term "narcissism" originates in an ancient Greek myth. Narcissus was a young man of remarkable beauty. He fell in love with his own image while gazing into a lake. He died alone because he could not relinquish his position of self-love, despite the best efforts of his female admirer, Echo. The gods then transformed his body into a beautiful flower, the narcissus.

In modern psychology, narcissism is at once a psychodynamic, a character trait, a personality feature, and a form of self-worth regulation. Healthy narcissism balances self-love and a concern for others. It is captured in the Biblical imperative, "Love thy neighbor as thyself." In unhealthy or pathological forms of narcissism, the individual is quite dependent on the approval of others. Popular culture refers to such people as self-centered or egoistic, which is true to a degree. What is often missed is the utter dependency of the narcissistic individual on others despite his appearances. It is a "pseudo-autonomy" (Kernberg, 1975). In the absence of a rich daily diet of narcissistic supplies, such individuals will become clinically depressed and hounded by self-doubt. They are most prone to such difficulties in mid-life when lessened proclivities and strengths (physicality, sexuality, endurance, intellect, memory) have a curious way of whispering that life does end, and all return to dust. Compulsive consumption and entitled sexuality are the hallmarks of a middle-aged narcissistic subject struggling against the march of time.

Pathological narcissism has a central role in stalking, threats, and attacks against public figures because the pursuit is largely driven by grandiose fantasy. Grandiosity is the disparity between an inflated view of oneself and the facts of one's life. Such fantasies may have enumerable motivations, but they all appear to compensate for chronic failures to love and to work. They absorb an increasingly inordinate amount of time, and ironically, the longer the preoccupation, the more the subject believes he is owed a debt by the object of his pursuit (Meloy et al., 2004; Mullen et al., in press).

The Psychogenesis of Narcissism

Psychoanalytic reasoning has historically been criticized for its often conflicting theoretical positions and less than rigorous empirical validation (Fonagy & Target, 2002). Most psychoanalytic knowledge has been constructed upon the clinical observations of psychoanalysts with their patients, who are often few in number, given the frequency and duration of psychoanalytic treatment. Hence, there is no single psychoanalytic theory concerning normal and psychopathological narcissism, which is generally accepted by psychoanalysts or psychologists. We believe, however, that the work of Heinz Kohut, a Chicago psychoanalyst and founder of the so-called Self Psychology school of psychoanalytic thought during the latter half of the 20th century, is particularly helpful in understanding the psychogenetic pathway of individuals who eventually engage in public figure stalking, threats, and attacks.

Kohut (1968, 1971) theorized that narcissism is a normal developmental process that leads to healthy self-esteem and realistic ambitions in the individual. Narcissism becomes pathological when normal development does not occur, largely because of negligent or inadequate parenting. A deficiency then resides in the self-structure of the individual's personality, which will be evident in futile attempts through the years to interact with others in ways that compensate for this lack of parental devotion—a formidable task that inevitably ends in failure since the developmental window closed long ago.

In accordance with Freud's assumption, Kohut believed that the newborn child lives in a condition of primary narcissistic equilibrium. This state of perfection and being in the center of the world is unsustainable because of the unavoidable limitations of maternal care. The child tries to recapture this lost paradise of primary narcissism through the cultivation of rudimentary fantasies that sustain beliefs in the grandiosity of himself and his parents, referred to in Self Psychology as the *grandiose self* and the *idealized parent imago.*

The fantasy of the *grandiose self*—"I am perfect"—is sustained by projecting all imperfections to the outside world (Kohut, 1968). It is most empirically evident in the toddler's constant demand for attention and admiration, which most healthy parents are more than happy to oblige. In Kohut's almost poetic words, the child longs for the gleam in the mother's eye as an affirmation of its grandiosity (Kohut, 1968). Over time, however, and usually because of necessity rather than conscious choice, the mother and father limit their gratification of the grandiose and exhibitionistic needs of the child in the form of tolerable disappointments. The child reacts by developing an internal psychological structure, which assumes the parents' function in the service of maintaining narcissistic equilibrium, such as basic calming activities, the provision of emotional warmth, and their approving gaze (Kohut, 1971). This process, referred to as "transmuting internalization," eventually regulates self-esteem, maintains a balance between self-absorption and concern for others, and develops into enduring feelings of self-worth and ambition—despite the "slings and arrows of misfortune," as Shakespeare would put it.

If attention and admiration are not provided, or are excessive, a narcissistic disorder may develop. The capacity to internally regulate self-esteem does not evolve. Mild criticism becomes devastating. Narcissistic supplies from others cannot be realistically negotiated. The grandiose self as an enduring fantasy must be constantly fed by others to compensate for such deficiencies. *Mirroring transferences* define the predictable relationships that the pathologically narcissistic individual will attempt to form with others (Kohut, 1968, 1971) to satisfy these perpetual and insatiable hungers and maintain his grandiosity.

The most archaic of these transferences is called *merger through the extension of the grandiose self.* The other person is experienced as part of the self, a selfobject in Kohutian terms, and must be controlled. Mark Chapman, the assassin of John Lennon in 1980, serves as an example. Although Chapman initially idealized Lennon and identified with him—along with the adolescent angst-filled fictional character Holden Caulfield—over time he began to see

Lennon as a phony who advocated a simple, peaceful life but lived a life of glamour and materialism. His adoration morphed into hatred, and eventually into violence. The borderline contradictions in Chapman's behavior, moreover, were striking: a few hours before he shot Lennon in the back, he asked him for an autograph, and Lennon obliged (see photo above).

This case also served as a prototype in the behavioral classification scheme for violent attacks designed by several FBI agents, the *Crime Classification Manual* (Douglas, Burgess, Burgess, & Ressler, 1992). In the category "erotomania-motivated killing," the offender has a chronic merger fantasy.

> Fusion of identity occurs when an individual identifies so completely
> with another person that his or her imitation of that person becomes
> excessive. The person emulated is endangered when the imitator
> feels his own identity threatened by the existence of the person he
> has patterned his life after, or when the offender feels the person he
> has imitated no longer lives up to the offender's ideals. The person
> this offender chooses to imitate usually is perceived as someone of
> higher status, just as with erotomania. (p. 72)

Other delusional syndromes that could manifest with such merger fantasies include delusional misidentification syndrome and delusional disorder, persecutory type. In such cases, the subject would be considered psychotic.

In the *alter-ego* or *twinship transference*, the narcissistic individual assumes that the other person is like him, or her psychological makeup is quite similar to his. For instance, an unemployed man was writing continuous letters to a nationally famous businessman. He believed that they were entrepreneurs at the same level of knowledge and success, and wanted to meet with him to discuss mutual projects. In normal development, twinship transferences are most apparent in adolescents who will closely imitate each other's behavior and appearance. Since this is a more mature narcissistic transference, it is apparent throughout the life course—note the universal appeal for young males of wanting to dress like their favorite athletes, musicians, or movie stars—and is typically not charged with the intensity of emotion that may motivate the stalking and attacking of a public figure. In the homes and offices of adults who thrive on such transference fantasies, their walls are usually covered with photos of them shaking hands with famous people—as if the momentary physical proximity endows them with the same stature as the famous person.

In the *mirror transference in the narrower sense*, the unsatisfied need for approval, praise, and admiration is aggressively sought from others. John Hinckley Jr. became notorious for stalking actor Jodie Foster and then attempting to assassinate U.S. President Ronald Reagan in 1981. He captured the mirroring dynamic when he stated, "I was desperate in some bold way to get...attention" (Clarke, 1990, p. 97). One of his sources of inspiration was the movie *Taxi Driver*, a film by Paul Schrader who based his screenplay on the real life diaries of Arthur Bremer, who attempted to assassinate, and did cripple, Governor George Wallace of Alabama a few years before. Hinckley imitated the main character Travis Bickle played by Robert De Niro. In the film, Bickle attempts to romance a young and beautiful political campaigner, is rejected by her, plans the assassination of a political candidate, fails at that, befriends a young prostitute played by Jodie Foster, eventually commits a mass murder, and is regaled as a hero. Posing in front of a mirror in one scene while displaying a gun, he angrily utters, "You talkin' to me?" Meloy (1992) responded years later, "Of course, in his heart of hearts, he hoped somebody was" (p. 142). Hinckley not only stalked Reagan, but earlier had stalked and was planning to assassinate President Jimmy Carter, who preceded Reagan. Carter was in office at the time Chapman killed Lennon in December 1980. Hinckley strongly admired Chapman's act, and also became infatuated with the character of Holden Caulfield in *Catcher in the Rye*. Most notable was the narcissistic linking fantasy of Hinckley, who clearly spelled it out during an interview with Dr. Park Dietz, a psychiatrist retained by the prosecution, on June 7, 1981:

> To impress her, almost to traumatize her. That is the best word. To link myself with her for almost the rest of history, if you want to go that far.
>
> Low, Jeffries, and Bonnie, 1986, p. 44

A striking attribute of such mirroring transferences is the absence of any moral value, which is subsumed by the drive for fame and notoriety. Such behaviors where pride is felt in acts that most people find horrible implicates psychopathy, and a character structure that is devoid of conscience or superego. This has yet to be explored in public figure stalking, but there is suggestive research that psychopaths make up a small proportion of stalkers in general, perhaps 10% to 15% (Reavis, Allen, & Meloy, in press; Sheridan & Boon, 2002) (see also Chapter 10).

The second principal narcissistic configuration described by Kohut is the enduring fantasy of the *idealized parent imago*. The damaged primary narcissism of the small child is repaired by allocating the quality of perfection to the parents—"You are perfect, but I am part of you." In a step-by-step process, the child then experiences gradual disappointment in the idealized object. The child realizes that his own parents are humans with shortcomings like all others. This process takes years, and may become dramatically, and painfully, evident when the child becomes an adolescent and his parents are defensively devalued instead of idealized. Behaviors such as these that are difficult to manage at best contribute to the acquisition of permanent psychological structures within the child, the narcissistic part of the superego (also referred to in other schools of thought as the ego ideal), which continue the functions that had previously been fulfilled by the idealized parents (Kohut, 1968). The presence of such structure is evident through the behavioral articulation of personal ideals by the child, which may be quite different from what the parents want for the child's future.

But things can go wrong. Kohut (1971) gives an example of a failed idealization: a boy attempted to view his father as an admired and idealized object to whom he could attach himself. The father, however, adamantly refused to allow the child to glorify him, probably due to his own disturbance in self-esteem. The boy remained hungry for the narcissistic gratification of a father who would be enormously grateful to be the perfect embodiment of a man for his son. In cases such as this, the needed internal structure is not acquired. The psyche remains fixated on an *archaic* idealized object imago, and the personality will search throughout life for external objects of perfection. Political leaders, especially psychopathic ones, count on this hunger. The person "will forever search for external ideal figures from whom he wants to obtain the approval and the leadership which his insufficiently idealized superego cannot provide" (Kohut, 1971, p. 49). This is an *idealizing transference* and is often found in cases where public figures are stalked. It will be described in more detail later in the case of Günter Parche, a stalker who adored tennis player Steffi Graf and violently attacked her colleague and competitor Monica Seles.

Both narcissistic dynamics—the mirroring and the idealizing transferences—are concurrent and independent paths of normal development. They are affected by one another, and in cases of narcissistic psychopathology, one will usually dominate. For instance, a public figure stalker may consistently try to capture the attention and approval of the object of his or her pursuit in the contexts of requests for love, sexual union, beneficence, or simply recognition—all components of a mirroring transference. On the other hand, a public figure stalker may consistently idealize the object of his or her pursuit and shower him or her with accolades and gifts—all components of an idealizing transference. In both dynamics, the risk is disappointment or humiliation, whether intended or not, by the object.

Narcissistic Character Types

We would like to stress the predominance of two types of narcissistic character among stalkers of public figures, the *arrogant-oblivious type* and the *shy-hypervigilant type* (Gabbard, 1989; Ronningham, 2005). The arrogant type is the prototype of the pathological narcissist, most clearly captured in the criteria for Narcissistic Personality Disorder in *DSM-IV-TR* (American Psychiatric Association, 2000; Gabbard, 2007). He or she has a boastful manner, and continuously seeks attention and admiration in order to enhance his or her self-esteem; he or she is entitled and arrogant; he or she harbors fantasies of unlimited success, beauty, or ideal love; and has little empathy for others. In the language of Self Psychology, he or she aggressively pursues mirror transferences, especially from extraordinary or important people. One psychologist, who himself met criteria for narcissistic personality disorder—although masked by an intensely anxious drive to please other people—took great pride in his psychotherapy practice that catered to "supernormal" individuals: those people who were particularly bright, creative, and economically successful. His practice was built upon mutual mirroring. Among many examples from the realm of celebrity stalking is a man who continuously harassed the Australian actor Nicole Kidman for a date—he believed she had flirted with him. In 2001 he was ordered by the court to stay away from her for 3 years. He subsequently claimed that, in effect, it was Kidman who was following him. He filed a multimillion-dollar civil suit against her and began an internet campaign to convince others to boycott her films. He characterized himself as an exceptional person who was hounded by the attentions of the rich and famous. He accused the actor Ben Affleck of following him five times, once while dressed "as a Frenchman, with a pencil or toothbrush moustache and a French shirt." In 2004, this same man established another web site to advance his plan to become the next president of the United States.

In contradistinction to the arrogant-oblivious type, the shy-hypervigilant type appears at first glance to be quite modest and humble. He carefully avoids competitive and challenging situations in the social world and is very adept at hiding his feelings of grandiosity. What is not apparent is a hypersensitivity to being easily wounded and slighted, and a hypervigilance to ward off the next attack. Although short of being clinically paranoid, such individuals are convinced in their heart of hearts that they are very special and vulnerable, and when tinged with characterological masochism, they believe they suffer the most of anyone. These narcissistic characters "tend to idealize and invest in an omnipotent other person that comes to represent their own grandiose self, while they themselves present a rather deflated and inadequate self" (Ronningham, 2005, p. 101). Both projection and projective identification are the operative defenses, and in this regard, their affinity to seek idealizing transferences should be obvious. A case example from one of our files illustrates such a figure. A celebrity stalker who specialized in cyber pursuits initially adored an actor, sending her many e-mails in which he expressed his hope that they would become a couple one day. After reading in an electronic newspaper that she was involved with another man, his tone suddenly became aggressive and sexually degrading. He stole her electronic identity by capturing the e-mail addresses from her and her managing agent. In a vicious cyber attack using the e-mail address from her agent, he fraudulently announced her death to the media. Shocked relatives and friends heard the alleged news and immediately telephoned her. When the police confronted the stalker in his flat, they found a shy man living in isolation who completely avoided eye contact with the officers. After talking to him for more than 1 hour, he revealed his belief that he was extraordinarily intelligent. He also disclosed his intense feeling of pride in his ability to manipulate the electronic mails of his victims.

Narcissistic Rage

Narcissistic rage arises when one of the two narcissistic configurations—the enduring fantasies of a grandiose self or an idealized parent imago—is threatened and portends the fragmentation of the personality. The selfobjects (internal representations of others who serve to gratify) that stabilize the psyche are challenged by the dictates of reality.

> Although everybody tends to react to narcissistic injury with embarrassment and anger, the most intense experiences of shame and the most violent forms of narcissistic rage arise in those individuals for whom an absolute sense of control over an archaic environment is indispensable because the maintenance of self-esteem—and indeed of the self—depends on the unconditional availability of the approving-mirroring functions of an admiring selfobject, or on the ever present opportunity to merger with an idealized one.
>
> Kohut, 1972, p. 386

The selfobject usually humiliates, disappoints, or is threatened by a third party *in the mind of the narcissist*. None of these events may actually occur. There arises an "unmodifiable wish to blot out the offence which was per-petrated against the grandiose self, and the unforgiving fury which arises when the control over the mirroring selfobject is lost, or when the omnipo-tent selfobject is unavailable" (Kohut, 1972, pp. 386, 387). When narcissistic rage is felt, it can eventually be expressed as either affective or predatory violence, two psychobiologically based modes of violence that have been extensively researched over the past half century (Meloy, 2006b). Affective violence is sudden, emotional, a reaction to a perceived threat—in the case of a public figure stalker, this could be perceived rejection or humiliation—and does not involve any planning. Predatory violence is planned, purposeful, and emotionless, and unfolds over an extended period of time. Narcissistic rage may motivate a predatory pathway to violence, but the rage cools when a violent outcome is decided upon, and becomes instead, ruminating revengeful fantasy; there is no intense emotion before or during the violence itself. Most assassinations are acts of predatory violence (Fein & Vossekuil, 1998; James et al., 2007; Meloy et al., 2004, in press) (Chapter 3), although public figure attacks can be affectively violent (see Chapter 2).

Paranoid Conditions

Paranoia is the irrational fear of imminent assault. It is dependent on two defenses—denial and projection—and is an element of many psychiatric diagnoses, ranging from paranoid schizophrenia to paranoid personality disorder, each with a very different treatment outcome (American Psychiatric Association, 2000; Gabbard, 2007). The psychodynamics of paranoia were originally thought to involve fears of homosexuality (Freud, 1958, 1973), but contemporary psychoanalytic thinking has embraced a much broader and more comprehensive view (Meissner, 1978).

Two aspects of paranoia that are relevant to public figure stalking and attacking are the notions of an intolerance of indifference (Auchincloss & Weiss, 1992) and fearful vulnerability. There is a grandiosity underpinning all paranoia because the individual must be important enough to warrant such persecution—it is better to be wanted by the FBI than not wanted at all. Paranoid individuals are quite intolerant of indifference, and in the absence of actual affectional bonds, they appear to construct in their mind persecutory fantasies and networks that connect them to others, albeit in a way that stimulates their fear.

Fearful vulnerability in paranoid individuals is usually masked by an overt aggression, but the layperson would never surmise that paranoids are very frightened of others. However, if the psychodynamic of paranoia is considered—the attribution of one's own aggression to others—then a natural outcome would be fear of others' aggression. So it is with the paranoid stalker, who is either frightened of the aggression of his victim, even though it exists only in his fantasies; or he displaces his aggression onto third parties, what has been referred to as *triangulation* (Meloy, 1999b), to preserve his fantasized relationship with the object of his pursuit. In this way, even if the object overtly rejects him—for example, a celebrity does not look his way on the runway, or refuses to sign an autograph—he can attribute this behavior to the obstructionist behavior of her handlers or security personnel. The danger of this psychodynamic is that the paranoid then comes to believe that he must rescue his "love" object from the nefarious behaviors of these third parties. The stalker of Gwyneth Paltrow, whose letter to her was cited earlier in this chapter, believed that Ben Affleck and her security personnel had mistreated her, and he needed to travel to Los Angeles to rescue her. He showed up twice at her parents' home in Santa Monica to do so, and was arrested and charged with stalking on his second visit. He was eventually found not guilty by reason of insanity and committed to a forensic hospital in California (*People v. Dante Soiu*, Los Angeles County Superior Court).

Paranoid stalkers and attackers of public figures are violent for one of two reasons: first, they believe that they are going to be imminently attacked, and therefore launch a preemptive strike; or second, they have incubated over the course of months or years perceived slights or emotional wounds, becoming angrier and more dysphoric as they ruminate about the unfairness of their treatment, and eventually decide to launch a predatory act of violence to avenge the wrongs inflicted upon them. Sirhan Sirhan, the assassin of Robert F. Kennedy in 1968, felt betrayed by Kennedy when he voted in the U.S. Senate to sell 50 Phantom Jet fighter bombers to Israel. Over the course of the next 5 months, he carefully planned the assassination to occur on the anniversary of the Six Day War, a major humiliation for the Palestinians and Arabs in June 1967, which resulted in the occupation of Gaza and the West Bank by Israel. Sirhan's psychological history and psychiatric status were consistent with borderline personality organization with paranoid, hysterical, and dependent features (Meloy, 1992), although it was fundamentally a politically motivated killing. Sirhan wrote in his diary on May 18, 3 weeks before the assassination, "my determination to eliminate RFK is becoming…more of an unshakeable obsession" (*People v. Sirhan Sirhan*, 1969, People's Exhibit 71). There is also evidence that he approached Kennedy on at least four different occasions before the fatal attack. Although paranoid dynamics do not dominate the clinical picture of public figure stalkers, consideration of their presence by forensic evaluators is always wise.

Psychosexual Dynamics

There is little to say about the psychosexual dynamics of public figure stalkers and attackers because little is empirically known. Their personal lives are often characterized by the chronic absence of sexual pair bonding, so it is safe to assume that the majority do not have an active sex partner and are divorced from this level of intimacy. Research on the motivations for stalking and attacking public figures likewise has not found a predominance of sexual interest, other than when the victims are celebrities (Meloy, 2007; Meloy et al., 2004). Politicians and judicial figures do not seem to erotically arouse anyone, even those whose impaired reality testing is suffused with their own masturbatory fantasies and urges.

The psychosexual dynamics—the internal relationship between sexual arousal, object relations, defenses, and emotions—are likewise not predominant in public figure stalking and attacking. However, there are exceptions. The stalker of Steven Spielberg (Chapter 11) is an extraordinary example of homosexual sadistic fantasy toward a stalking victim, and the stalker of Gwyneth Paltrow sent her many sexual paraphernalia, including dildos, engraved with affectionate messages for her. The man who unsuccessfully sent a packaged bomb to the singer Björk (Chapter 4) had strong sexual overtones in his fury that she was about to interracially marry. And an analysis of a large sample of celebrity stalkers (Chapter 2) also indicates that the most targeted individuals were females who portrayed professional women in a television series, *were romantically unattached, were sexually attractive, and were emotionally vulnerable.* Such a portrait of pursuit suggests both sexual desire and affectional yearning on the part of the men who acted against these women.

The investigation of psychodynamics in public figure cases would suggest that sexual dynamics are likely to be highly charged with aggression, sexual arousal may be masked by other emotions, and sexual activity toward the object of pursuit is likely to be limited to fantasy and masturbation, rather than an overt sexual attack (Mullen et al., 2000).

The Case of Günter Parche

The case of Günter Parche illustrates both the pathologically narcissistic dynamics and the borderline personality organization often seen in celebrity stalkers. Günter Parche became famous in 1993 at age 39 when he attacked tennis star Monica Seles with a knife while she was playing a match in Hamburg, Germany. Parche was born in 1954 in a small village in eastern Germany in which he is still living. As a child, he was a loner who seldom left his home. When he was 10 years old, his mother gave him away to his aunt because she felt ill and had to go to hospital. After she returned home, she never took him back. We can assume that the attachment from mother to son was weak, and such a poor cathexis—the traditional psychoanalytic term for an energic connection—was likely reciprocated. Asked about that in court, Parche remarked, "It just arose" (Friedrichsen, 1995).

Prepubescent maternal abandonment may have contributed to a developmental disturbance regarding Parche's idealized parent imago, an internal disruption expected given his adult stalking behavior. This kind of narcissistic disorder (Kohut, 1971) would conform with the description of Parche as being a reserved, insecure, and anxious character: a shy narcissist. He also had a rather rigid and simple value system, presenting attitudes like, "I solely eat what I know," and, "I am more a domestic type" (this and the following quotations from Parche are from court records and documented in Hoffmann, 2005).

This kind of self-deficiency is compensated by deploying an idealizing transference in which connections are sought after with persons who have a larger than life quality. Parche was an intense admirer of public figures like the Pope, the U.S. president, and the federal president of Germany, but in a childish and naïve way (e.g., "I am a big fan of the United States and of the American president"). But he worshipped Steffi Graf, saying that she was as important as the Pope and the U.S. president. After seeing her on television in 1985, he became obsessed with the successful young woman. He tried to learn the rules of tennis and started collecting all her news clips. He would adorn the walls of his room with her pictures. Living in the communist part of Germany with no valuable currency, Parche spent 10,000 marks, a huge amount of money, to buy a video recorder from western Germany ("I would have spent 20,000 mark to see her again. For any other tennis player I would have paid not even 1,000 mark.") He recorded all the matches of the tennis star and watched them over and over again. "She always played only 40 minutes," he would comment.

Parche described Steffi Graf as being "dreamlike, with eyes like diamonds and hair like splendid silk." He praised her "tidiness, fidelity and pureness." But he also commented on her "fantastic figure," proclaiming that she had "the most beautiful legs of all female tennis players." The idealizing nature of his fixation on Steffi Graf became clear in the following statement after his arrest: "Stefanie Graf is a dream, not only as sportswoman but also as a human being. She is a role model for all of us and she has a big heart."

Parche sent her birthday money, but never mentioned his name and anonymously signed the greeting cards with the line, "A fan from Eastern Germany." Once he sent money to the mother of Steffi Graf and asked her to buy a bouquet of flowers for her daughter. But he never dared to physically approach his idol. Parche believed that if he accosted her, he would have died out of fear: "I would have been awestruck and my heart would stop beating."

From a Self Psychology point of view, Graf served as an internal self-object in an idealizing transference. This selfobject in the mind of Parche completed a narcissistic deficiency that originated in his failure to sustain such a normal idealizing transference with his parents, particularly his mother, as a young child. Such a transference imbues a feeling of affiliation and shared grandiosity, which are important for psychological maturation, and if missed, are hopelessly pursued as an adult. Anonymous letters in which he advised Graf to watch out while traveling by car and not take any risks made clear how dependent Parche was on Graf as a fantasized self-object to keep his own personality intact. Such warnings also suggest his own projected aggression into third parties that might harm her. "She is as important for me as god," he once remarked, a clear-sighted comment upon his own unconscious dynamics. Even his mood was regulated by her success. The days before an important match he was very nervous, lost his appetite, and had sleep disturbances. If she won the match, he was overjoyed and cried with happiness. If Steffi Graf lost, Parche became depressed, stopped talking for days, and was hounded by suicidal thoughts. He desperately needed to idealize her, keep her safe, and maintain through a "linking fantasy" his attachment to her.

Narcissistic rage toward third parties appeared in Parche when they challenged his idealized transference to the tennis star. He would write anonymous but threatening letters to well-known athletes whom he accused of disrespecting Graf in public—often based upon media-reported criticism of her playing by another. But his narcissistic rage became interminable and unbearable when Graf lost to her competitor Monica Seles during a match in Berlin in 1990. He contemplated suicide. "Even though Steffi was still number one in the worldwide ranking, I was shocked in such a way that I meditated to take my own life. Would it have been in another place, it would not have been such a disaster. But this time it was in Germany, and even worse our Federal President was present. That all was too much for me." The shock of her fall from grace and the mocking he endured from his fellow workers because of his obsession led him to resign his job. The Berlin wall had fallen a year before, so he moved to the western part of Germany. "I wanted to leave it all behind." But after a short period of time, he returned home, did not go back to his job, and started to live off his savings—the deteriorating course had begun in earnest (Meloy et al., 2004).

His solution was to physically attack Seles in a way that she would not be able to play tennis. This would make it possible for Graf to stay number one in the worldwide rankings. Most importantly, the act of violence would eliminate a threat to his idealization of Graf and therefore stabilize his narcissistically vulnerable self. Such violence in stalkers of celebrity figures is unusual, but here, once again, is triangulation (Meloy, 1999a): the perception of a third party that is a threat to the object of pursuit, and the desire to rescue the object from the threat, in this case, someone who was actually challenging the worldwide tennis stature of Graf.

For at least a year, he ruminated about the attack. He wanted "to teach Monica Seles a lesson," as he said in his own words. Parche also began degrading Seles, saying "she is not pretty. Women should not be bony." Idealizing transferences always run the risk of devaluation, which in neurotic cases may be a more realistic perception of the object's imperfections. But in this case where borderline psychopathology is evident, the remarkable solution is not a compromise with reality—the acceptance that Seles may be a better tennis player than Graf at the moment—but a decision to damage the threatening object through the use of actual violence: so rational to Parche, so bizarre to others.

The attack was fueled by narcissistic rage, but carried out in a planned and purposeful manner, an act of predatory violence (Meloy, 2006b). Parche went through all the stages of the pathway of violence: grievance, ideation, research, preparation, breach, and attack (Calhoun & Weston, 2003). His grievance was twofold: Graf could no longer be as easily idealized, and Seles was the cause. Therefore, an act of violence was the solution. He researched the location of the attack. He chose a knife as his weapon and thought about buying flowers to conceal the knife, but abandoned this plan. Believing that he would go to jail for a long time, he took down his many pictures of Graf, stored them with her news clips in a suitcase, and buried them in his garden: so-called final act behaviors that marked his preparation phase for the offense (Calhoun & Weston). Parche traveled to Hamburg a few days before the official start of the tournament and observed the training of Seles, but he did not find a way to launch his attack. He finally managed to breach security by mingling in the audience at the matches, and attacked Seles who was pausing at the side of the court, stabbing her with a knife in the shoulder (see photos on next page).

© 2007 dpa Picture-Alliance. Reprinted with permission.

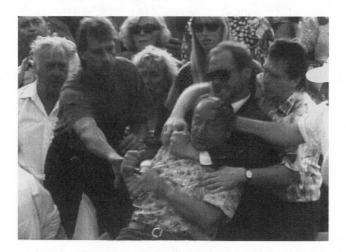

© 2007 dpa Picture-Alliance. Reprinted with permission.

During his police interrogation immediately after the attack, Parche was surprised that people insulted him. "I did it also for the audience. The reaction of the audience confused me." This disparity between his anticipation of social approval and the actuality of social condemnation is also a measure of his grossly impaired reality testing, a characteristic of borderline personality organization. Parche believed that all other people shared his feelings of hate against Seles for what she was doing to Graf. For the borderline, the world of wishful fantasy overrides the dictates of reality. In another portion of the police interview, he gave insight into his psychodynamics: "Originally I had planned to write the mother of Stefanie [Graf] a letter and telling her what I intended to do...I wanted to help Stefanie. I see the whole thing also as a warning for the parents of Monica Seles." The defense mechanism of splitting is here evident—as discussed earlier—when the child splits incompatible feelings of love and aggression against a parental figure into two separated components, the "good mother" and the "bad mother." The rage of Parche against his neglecting and abandoning mother is directed against Monica Seles and her parents. It is kept completely separate from the idealized love he feels toward Steffi Graf and her mother. In normal development, the child comes to emotionally accept that both feelings of love and aggression can be felt toward the same parent, and the parent will not leave. Such feelings do not have to be kept apart, and can be integrated into an internalized "whole object."

Parche continues to be fixated on Graf after serving less than a half-year in prison on remand. The final verdict of 2 years suspended sentence was highly criticized in the international sport and tennis communities. In 2005, a reporter of a Swiss newspaper interviewed a neighbor of Parche (Gabrysch, 2005). The man said that he had hung up the pictures of Graf again, but also added new ones: her spouse, Andre Agassi, and their two children.

But Why Violence?

Relatively few people will pathologically fixate on a public figure, even fewer will attempt an approach, and it is quite rare for a public figure to be attacked. There have been only 23 attacks on members of the British Royal Family over the past several centuries, and only 24 attacks on western European politicians during the last 15 years (James et al., 2007, in press) (Chapter 3). In the United States, assassinations and attacks against public figures have occurred 34 times in the past half century (Fein & Vossekuil, 1998, 1999), and homicidal attackers of nonpolitical U.S. celebrities number only 16 between 1949 and 2004 (Chapter 4).

Conscious motivations for violence vary considerably when public figures are attacked (Fein & Vossekuil, 1998), but a psychodynamic theory underlying the unconscious motivation for such attacks helps to explain such behavior. Meloy (1998, 1999b) proposed such a theory, marked by seven steps:

1. The individual develops a "narcissistic linking fantasy" toward the object, in this case, a public figure. The central aspect of the fantasy is a special and idealized relationship with the object, which could focus on sexual, romantic, beneficent, dominant, or even persecutory themes. The fantasy is an object relation in the sense that there are internalized representations of the self and the object, and attendant emotions or affects (Kernberg, 1975). In most cases, narcissistic linking fantasies are initially quite positive with hopeful expectations, often for a grandiose outcome or destiny.
2. There is a decision to approach the object through distal (letters, e-mails) or proximal (physical) means. Within this approach is a belief that a debt is owed by the public figure to the subject and it will be paid in full.

3. The object disappoints or humiliates. This may be an actual rebuff, although almost always magnified by the subject; or it may be personalized in fantasy, such as the fury Sirhan Sirhan felt when Robert Kennedy supported the Israelis rather than the Palestinians in January 1968.

4. The disappointment and humiliation are defended against with rage, particularly in male subjects, who have less toleration for the softer, more vulnerable feelings that may symbolize impotence or failure in the eyes of others.

5. Rage initially fuels the pursuit of the object, and if the act of violence is predatory rather than affective, a "pathway to violence" will begin to unfold (Calhoun & Weston, 2003). Predatory acts will involve little felt emotion as planning, preparation, and implementation get underway; while affective acts may be carried out in seconds following an actual rebuff, felt humiliation, and a fury to immediately strike back at the rejecting public figure (Meloy, 2006b).

6. The violence is intended to damage or destroy the object, and in some cases, the attacker himself, if planning has evolved into a homicide-suicide spectacle. Damage or destruction may be an act of revenge (Rosen, 2007), a means to reduce envy of the object, or a calculated strategy to establish a bond with the rejecting object through an attack on a third party, as seen in the triangulated attack on Reagan in 1981 to win the affection of Jodie Foster. Aggressive planning and preparation also heightens narcissism, may reduce paranoia, and can instill feelings of omnipotent control over the object, at least in fantasy. For someone whose life has been marked by loneliness and failure, and ultimately estrangement from society at large, a pathway to violence can be strangely exhilarating and inflating—the excitement of stepping onto a national or international stage for a moment, and also etching the memory of one's act into history.

7. If the violence is carried out successfully, the actual source of humiliation or disappointment is removed, and now the narcissistic linking fantasy with the idealized object can be reclaimed. This may sound bizarre and illogical, but it is the psychologic of the attacker or assassin, and such an outcome derives from the force of fantasy in these cases, and the primacy of the internalized object relation, which initiated the pathological fixation in the first place. This is the opposite phenomenon of Winnicott's (1971) healthy "object usage."

Although empirical support for this psychodynamic theory is only anecdotal at present, it is an explanatory attempt to understand the unconscious motivations of stalkers and attackers of public figures that parallels the conscious and behavioral stages of Calhoun and Weston's (2003) pathway to violence. We note that lack of a body of empirical support for a theory does not invalidate it, but invites such research in the future to prove or disprove it.

Clustering of anecdotal cases, which empirically illustrate various components of the theory, would be the next step. Psychoanalytic theory in general posits that unconscious determinants typically parallel most conscious choices, including those made by stalkers and attackers of public figures. Limiting investigations to conscious choice would make it difficult to explain the extraordinarily risky and illogical behavior of these individuals.

Research on Narcissism in Persons Who Stalk and Attack Public Figures

There is very little empirical research on pathological narcissism in people who pursue public figures. Dietz and Martell (1989) found that only 4% of subjects fulfilled the formal criteria for Narcissistic Personality Disorder in *DSM-IIIR* (American Psychiatric Association, 1987), but clinical data were virtually absent. However, 43% had an excessive sense of self-importance or uniqueness, 34% showed evidence of entitlement, 9% responded to criticism, defeat, or inattention with indifference or marked shame or rage, and 5% were preoccupied with fantasies of unlimited success, power, brilliance, beauty, or ideal love. Current criteria for Narcissistic Personality Disorder (*DSM-IV-TR*, 2000) are essentially unchanged from criteria utilized in this 20-year-old study.

In the Exceptional Case Study project of the U.S. Secret Service (Fein & Vossekuil, 1999), there is indirect evidence for pathological narcissism in many people who acted violently against U.S. public figures. Achieving notoriety or fame was found to be the second most common motive for attacks on public figures. The researchers cited a statement of a man who planned to shoot a high-ranking federal official: "Anyone who would shoot such an important and powerful person would receive a lot of attention...I would be in newspapers and on television. People would know my name. They might even write a chapter about me in a book" (Fein & Vossekuil, 1997, p. 57). The attacker hopes that his need to be someone special will be satisfied, even if the price is the life of another. This narcissistic dynamic found its clearest expression in the words of Mark Chapman, the assassin of John Lennon: "I was an acute nobody," he told authorities after his arrest. "I had to usurp someone else's importance, someone else's success. I was 'Mr. Nobody' until I killed the biggest somebody on earth" (Gallagher, 2001, p. 38). Overcoming self-doubt and self-worth regulation through an act of murder, however, does not work. Twenty years later, Chapman came to see the futility of his effort when he spoke at his first parole hearing: "Anyone could have done this. Anyone could have pulled the trigger, and I'm nobody special, and I just wish it was that way. Unfortunately it's not, but I do wish I was a big nobody again" (Court, 2000). Dietz put it well: People who pursue the famous often lack an adequate identity, and they go to people who have the most to spare, the famous (cited in Leets, de Becker, & Giles, 1995). As the fictional character Annie said in the film, *Misery*, an adaptation of the stalking, kidnap, and murder novel by Stephen King: "You'll never know the fear of losing someone like you if you're someone like me."

In psychological theories about erotomania, narcissism also plays a central role (Meloy, 1989, 1992). That was the case even for de Clérambault (1921/1999), who thought that in erotomanic delusion, pride was more important than love. "Transferred into modern terminology, one might say that the delusions provide narcissistic gratification when life cruelly fails to do so" (Segal, 1989, p. 1263). In contrast to Freud (1955) who assumed erotomania to be a defense against subconscious homosexual urges, the Austrian psychoanalyst Theodor Reik (1963) emphasized the relevance of narcissism. He saw erotomania as an attempt at self-rescue from the depths of personal contempt and perceived humiliation in the eyes of others.

In some cases, the narcissism of the erotomanic may represent masochistic subjugation to an unreachable object (Kernberg, 1988). This can find its expression in a sense of pride that one can endure the greatest rejection and still, like Sisyphus, carry on with the pursuit of one's impossible dream, the ideal love (Meloy, 1992). In pure samples of celebrity stalkers, erotomania seems to be much more common than in noncelebrity stalking studies. Dietz and Martell (1989) determined a rate of 16% among those who wrote threatening and inappropriate letters to Hollywood celebrities. Hoffmann (2005) found an almost identical number of 15% in an analysis of letters sent to television personalities. In a small group of 15 British erotomanics, 6 of them (40%) harassed a public figure (Kennedy, McDonough, Kelly, & Berrios, 2001).

Summary and Conclusions

We have attempted in this chapter to advance our belief that theories derived from psychoanalytic thinking broaden and deepen our understanding of those who threaten, stalk, and attack public figures. Without theory, research is just counting; and without research, theory is only speculation. Although psychoanalytic theory is always in need of more empirical research, it is apparent to us that individual public figure stalking cases and the few nonrandom studies of samples of public figure stalkers highlight behaviors that are usefully interpreted through the lens of psychoanalytic thinking, which may eventually have some demonstrable predictive value.

Among the wealth of psychoanalytic literature that has been published during the past century, we have chosen to focus on the work most relevant to public figure threats, stalking, and attacks: attachment theory, object relations theory, borderline personality organization, pathologies of narcissism, the psychogenesis of narcissism as understood by Self Psychology, two narcissistic character types, narcissistic rage, paranoid conditions, sexual psychodynamics, and unconscious elements of thinking and emotion that contribute to violence among these individuals. We have illustrated some of these theories through a detailed case study of Günter Parche, the man who stabbed the tennis star Monica Seles in 1993. We have concluded the chapter with a review of the very limited empirical research on pathological narcissism in such individuals.

Unrequited love—or at least disappointment or humiliation—is the very predictable outcome when a public figure is pursued. The idolized figure is now beneath contempt. Yearning becomes disgust. Love may even become hatred. Rationalizations are put into place. Delusion may bring a resolve that is immutable. Aggression intensifies. Revenge is in the air.

References

American Psychiatric Association (1987). *Diagnostic and statistical manual of mental disorders* (3rd ed., Rev.). Washington, DC: Author.

American Psychiatric Association (2000). *Diagnostic and statistical manual of mental disorders* (4th ed., Text revision). Washington, DC: Author.

Auchincloss, E., & Weiss, R. (1992). Paranoid character and the intolerance of indifference. *Journal of the American Psychoanalytic Association, 40,* 1013–1038.

Bleuler, E. (1943). *Lehrbuch der Psychiatrie.* Berlin: Springer.

Bowlby, J. (1944). Forty-four juvenile thieves. *International Journal of Psycho-analyis, 25,* 121–124.

Bowlby, J. (1969). *Attachment and loss, Vol. I: Attachment.* New York: Basic Books.

Bowlby, J. (1980). *Attachment and loss, Vol. III: Loss, sadness and depression.* London: Hogarth.

Calhoun, F., & Weston, S. (2003). *Contemporary threat management.* San Diego: Specialized Training Services.

Clarke, J. W. (1982). *American assassins: The darker side of politics.* Princeton: Princeton University Press.

Clarke, J. W. (1990). *On being mad or merely angry: John W. Hinckley, Jr. and other dangerous people.* Princeton: Princeton University Press.

Clérambault, G. G. de (1921/1999). Passionate delusions: Erotomania, claiming, jealousy. In F. R. Cousin, J. Garrabé, & D. Morozov (Eds.), *Anthology of French language psychiatric texts* (pp. 475–492). Le Plessis-Robinson: Institut Synthélabo.

Court TV (2000). Transcript of Mark Chapman's parole board hearing. Retrieved July 30, 2007, from www.courttv.com/archive/people/2000/102/chapmantranscript.html

Dietz, P. E., & Martell, D. A. (1989). *Mentally disordered offenders in pursuit of celebrities and politicians.* Washington, DC: National Institute of Justice.

Douglas, J. E., Burgess, A. W., Burgess, A. K., & Ressler, R. K. (Eds.) (1992). *Crime classification manual.* San Francisco: Jossey-Bass.

Fairbairn, W. R. D. (1952). *An object-relations theory of the personality.* New York: Basic Books.

Fein, R. A., & Vossekuil, B. (1997). *Preventing assassination: A monograph.* Washington, DC: U.S. Department of Justice.

Fein, R. A., & Vossekuil, B. (1998). Preventing attacks on public officials and public figures: A Secret Service perspective. In J. R. Meloy (Ed.), *The psychology of stalking: Clinical and forensic perspectives* (pp. 176–194). San Diego: Academic Press.

Fein, R. A., & Vossekuil, B. (1999). Assassination in the United States. An operational study of recent assassins, attackers, and near lethal approachers. *Journal of Forensic Sciences, 44*(2), 321–333.

Fonagy, P., & Target, M. (2002). *Psychoanalytic theories: Perspectives from developmental psychopathology.* London: Whurr.

Fonagy, P., & Target, M. (2007). The rooting of the mind in the body. *Journal of the American Psychoanalytic Association, 55*, 411–456.

Freud, S. (1953). *Interpretation of dreams* (Standard edition, Vols. IV and V). London: Hogarth.

Freud, S. (1955). *Some neurotic mechanisms in jealousy, paranoia and homosexuality.* (Standard edition, Vol. 18) (pp. 221–232). London: Hogarth.

Freud, S. (1958). Psycho-analytic notes on an autobiographical account of a case of paranoia (dementia paranoides) (Standard edition, Vol. XII) (pp. 3–80). London: Hogarth.

Freud, S. (1961). *The ego and the id* (Standard edition 19). London: Hogarth.

Freud, S. (1973). Bemerkungen über einen autobiographischen Fall von Paranoia. In Studienausgabe: Bd. VII, *Zwang, paranoia und perversion* (S.35–S.103). Frankfurt: Fischer.

Freud, S. (1975). Zur Einführung des Narzissmus. In Studienausgabe: Bd. III, *Psychologie des unbewussten.* (S.41–S.68). Frankfurt: Fischer.

Friedrichsen, G. (1995). Hatten Sie gerne eine Frau? *Der Spiegel*, 13.

Gabbard, G. (1989). Two subtypes of narcissistic personality disorder. *Bulletin of the Menninger Clinic, 53*, 527–532.

Gabbard, G. (Ed.) (2007). *Gabbard's treatments of psychiatric disorders* (4th ed.). Washington, DC: American Psychiatric Publishing.

Gabrysch, W. (2005). Was macht eigentlich…Gunter Parche? *NZZ Folio*, 12.

Gallagher, R. (2001). *I'll be watching you. True stories of stalkers and their victims.* London: Virgin.

Greenacre, P. (1960). Regression and fixation: Considerations concerning the development of the ego. *Journal of the American Psychoanalytic Association, 8*, 703–723.

Hoffman, J. L. (1943). Psychotic visitors to government offices in the national capital. *American Journal of Psychiatry, 99*, 571–575.

Hoffmann, J. (2005). *Stalking.* Heidelberg: Springer.

Isaacs, S. (1952). The nature and function of phantasy. In M. Klein, P. Heimann, S. Isaacs, & J. Riviere (Eds.), *Developments in psychoanalysis* (pp. 67–121). London: Hogarth.

Jacobson, E. (1964). *The self and the object world.* New York: International Universities Press.

James, D., Mullen, P., Meloy, J. R., Pathé, M., Farnham, F., Preston, L., et al. (2007). The role of mental disorder in attacks on European politicians 1990–2004. *Acta Psychiatrica Scandinavica, 116*, 334–344.

James, D., Mullen, P., Pathé, M., Meloy, J. R., Farnham, F., Preston, L., et al. (in press). Attacks on the British Royal Family: The role of psychotic illness. *Journal of the American Academy of Psychiatry and the Law.*

Kennedy, N., McDonough, M., Kelly, B., & Berrios, G. E. (2001). Erotomania revisited: Clinical course and treatment. *Comprehensive Psychiatry, 43*(1), 1–6.

Kernberg, O. F. (1975). *Borderline conditions and pathological narcissism.* Northvale: Jason Aronson.

Kernberg, O. F. (1976). *Object relations theory and clinical psychoanalysis.* New York: Jason Aronson.

Kernberg, O. F. (1988). Clinical dimensions of masochism. *Journal of the American Psychoanalytic Association, 36*, 1005–1029.

Kernberg, O. F. (1995). *Love relations. Normality and pathology.* New Haven: Yale University Press.

Kienlen, K. K. (1998). Antecedents of stalking. In J. R. Meloy (Ed.), *The psychology of stalking* (pp. 51–67). San Diego: Academic Press.

Kienlen, K. K., Birmingham, D. L., Solberg, K. B., O'Regan, J. T., & Meloy, J. R. (1997). A comparative study of psychotic and nonpsychotic stalking. *Journal of the American Academy of Psychiatry and the Law, 25*(3), 317–334.

Klein, M. (1948). *Contributions to psycho-analysis 1921–1945* (pp. 282–310). London: Hogarth.

Kohut, H. (1968). The psychoanalytic treatment of narcissistic personality disorders: Outline of a systematic approach. In P. H. Ornstein (Ed.), *The search for the self. Selected writings of Heinz Kohut: 1950–1978* (pp. 477–509). New York: International Universities Press.

Kohut, H. (1971). *The analysis of the self. A systematic approach to the psychoanalytic treatment of narcissistic personality disorders.* New York: International Universities Press. Reprinted 1977.

Kohut, H. (1972). Thoughts on narcissism and narcissistic rage. *The Psychoanalytic Study of the Child, 27,* 360–400.

Krafft-Ebing, R. von (1912). *Psychopathia sexualis.* Stuttgart: Verlag von Ferdinand Enke.

Leets, L., de Becker, G., & Giles, H. (1995). Fans: Exploring expressed motivations for contacting celebrities. *Journal of Language and Social Psychology, 14,* 102–123.

Logan, W. S., Reuterfors, D. L., Bohn, J. M., & Clark, C. L. (1984). The description and classification of presidential threateners. *Behavioral Sciences and the Law, 2*(2), 151–167.

Low, P. W., Jeffries, J., & Bonnie, R. (1986). *The trial of John W. Hinckley, Jr.: A case study of the insanity defense.* Mineola, NY: Foundation.

MacDonald, A. (1911). Assassins of rulers. *Journal of the American Institute of Criminal Law and Criminology, 2,* 505–520.

Mahler, M. (1968). *On human symbiosis and the vicissitudes of individuation, Vol. 1: Infantile psychosis.* New York: International Universities Press.

Malsch, M., Visscher, M., & Blaauw, E. (2002). *Stalking van bekende personen.* Den Haag: Boom.

Meissner, W. (1978). *The paranoid process.* New York: Jason Aronson.

Meloy, J. R. (1989). Unrequited love and the wish to kill: The diagnosis and treatment of borderline erotomania. *Bulletin of the Menninger Clinic, 53,* 477–492.

Meloy, J. R. (1992). *Violent attachments.* Northvale: Jason Aronson.

Meloy, J. R. (1998). The psychology of stalking. In J. R. Meloy (Ed.), *The psychology of stalking: Clinical and forensic perspectives* (pp. 1–23). San Diego: Academic Press.

Meloy, J. R. (1999a). Erotomania, triangulation, and homicide. *Journal of Forensic Sciences, 44,* 421–424.

Meloy, J. R. (1999b). Stalking: An old behavior, a new crime. *Psychiatric Clinics of North America, 22,* 85–99.

Meloy, J. R. (2002a). Stalking and violence. In J. Boon, & L. Sheridan (Eds.), *Stalking and psychosexual obsession* (pp. 105–124). Chichester: Wiley.

Meloy, J. R. (2002b). Pathologies of attachment, violence, and criminality. In A. Goldstein (Ed.), *Comprehensive handbook of psychology, Vol. 11: Forensic psychology* (pp. 509–526). New York: Wiley.

Meloy, J. R. (2006a). *The scientific pursuit of stalking.* San Diego: Specialized Training Services.

Meloy, J. R. (2006b). The empirical basis and forensic application of affective and predatory violence. *Australian and New Zealand Journal of Psychiatry, 40,* 539–547.

Meloy, J. R. (2007). Stalking: The state of the science. *Criminal Behaviour and Mental Health, 17*(1), 1–7.

Meloy, J. R., & Fisher, H. (2005). Some thoughts on the neurobiology of stalking. *Journal of Forensic Sciences, 50,* 1472–1480.

Meloy, J. R., & Gothard, S. (1995). A demographic and clinical comparison of obsessional followers and offenders with mental disorders. *American Journal of Psychiatry, 152,* 258–263.

Meloy, J. R., James, D., Farnham, F., Mullen, P., Pathé, M., Darnley, B., et al. (2004). A research review of public figure threats, approaches, attacks, and assassinations in the United States. *Journal of Forensic Sciences, 49,* 1086–1093.

Mohandie, K., Meloy, J. R., McGowan, M. G., & Williams, J. (2006) The RECON typology of stalking: Reliability and validity based upon a large sample of North American stalkers. *Journal of Forensic Sciences, 51*(1), 147–155

Mullen, P., James, D., Meloy, J. R., Farnham, F., Pathé, M., Darnley, B., et al. (in press). The fixated and the pursuit of public figures. *Journal of Forensic Psychiatry and Psychology.*

Mullen, P. E., Pathé, M., & Purcell, R. (2000). *Stalkers and their victims.* Cambridge: Cambridge University Press.

Reavis, J., Allen, E., & Meloy, J. R. (in press). Psychopathy in a mixed gender sample of stalkers. *Journal of Forensic Sciences.*

Reik, T. (1963). *The need to be loved.* New York: Farrar, Straus.

Ronningham, E. F. (2005). *Identifying and understanding the narcissistic personality.* Oxford: Oxford University Press.

Rosen, I. (2007). Revenge—The hate that dare not speak its name: A psychoanalytic perspective. *Journal of the American Psychoanalytic Association, 55,* 595–620.

Rothstein, A. (1980). *The narcissistic pursuit of perfection.* New York: International Universities Press.

Saunders, R. (1998). Legal perspectives on stalking. In J. R. Meloy (Ed.), *The psychology of stalking* (pp. 25–49). San Diego: Academic Press.

Segal, J. H. (1989). Erotomania revisited: From Kraepelin to DSM-III-R. *American Journal of Psychiatry, 146,* 1261–1266.

Sheridan, L., & Boon, J. (2002). Stalker typologies: Implications for law enforcement. In J. Boon, & L. Sheridan (Eds.), *Stalking and psychosexual obsession* (pp. 63–82). Chichester: Wiley.

Waters, E., Merrick, S., Treboux, D., Crowell, J., & Albersheim, L. (2000). Attachment security from infancy to early adulthood: A 20-year longitudinal study. *Child Development, 71,* 684–689.

Winnicott, D. W. (1955). The depressive position in normal emotional development. *British Journal of Medical Psychology, 28,* 89–100.

Winnicott, D. W. (1971). The use of an object and relating through identifications. In D. W. Winnicott (Ed.), *Playing and reality* (pp. 86–94). London: Tavistock.

9

Celebrities as Victims of Stalking

Jens Hoffmann and Lorraine Sheridan

There exists a widespread assumption that the celebrity experience has received the lion's share of research and other professional interest in stalking. Although it is true that legislation against and therefore early research into stalking was triggered in part by several high-profile celebrity cases, the vast majority of the literature examines general, noncelebrity victims. Although hundreds of studies and reports of stalking from a number of disciplines exist, probably less than 1% of these are devoted to celebrity victims. So, although celebrity cases inevitably receive media attention—sometimes on a global scale—little is known about the course and nature of celebrity stalking. Also, we have no reliable figures related to the extent of celebrity stalking, although anecdotal accounts and indications from relevant professionals would strongly suggest that most celebrities can expect to be the recipients of unhealthy attention at some point during their careers. In this chapter, we seek to provide an overview of the types of disturbing communication and pursuit the famous are forced to bear, and their disruptive and sometimes devastating effects.

Although systematic research documenting the experiences of stalking victims started only as recently as the last few years of the 20th century, good progress has been made. Most studies have been conducted in English-speaking countries, that is, the United States (e.g., Hall, 1998), Australia (e.g., Pathé & Mullen, 1997), and Great Britain (e.g., Sheridan, Davis, & Boon, 2001). A smaller number of works have been carried out in continental European countries, including the Netherlands (e.g., Kamphuis & Emmelkamp, 2001) and Germany (Dressing, Kuehner, & Gass, 2005), and elsewhere in non-Western countries, which include Japan (Chapman & Spitzberg, 2003), Trinidad (Jagessar & Sheridan, 2004), and Iran (Kordvani, 2000). Many of the studies have revealed similar behavioral patterns among harassers, and it is also certain that stalking often has significant negative emotional, physical, social, and economic effects on the victim (e.g., Blaauw, Winkel, Arensman, Sheridan, & Freeve, 2002; Davis, Coker, & Sanderson, 2002; Mechanic, Uhlmansiek, Weaver, & Resick, 2000; Mohandie, Meloy, McGowan, & Williams, 2006; Purcell, Pathé, & Mullen, 2002). Similar findings relating to celebrity victims are in extremely short supply.

In this chapter, we review what has been learned from the few studies that have attempted to record the experiences of celebrity victims. We will also present findings from our own research and professional intervention work. The focus will be not on public figures in general but on celebrities in a more narrow sense, meaning persons widely known for their activities in the entertainment, information, arts, and sports sectors.

Previous Findings

In the Netherlands, 105 public figures who had experienced "repeated harassment originating from an obsession with the victim as a public figure" (p. 6) took part in a study that sought to determine some characteristics of public figure stalkers and their victims (Malsch, Visscher, & Blaauw, 2002). This is the only investigation known to date where public figures themselves provided the study data by responding to questionnaires and participating in interviews. Celebrity agents and publishing house employees distributed questionnaires among clients whom they believed had been targeted by stalkers. Members of the Dutch Government were also mailed questionnaires. Thus, the sample comprised politicians, writers, performing musicians, actors, and television and radio presenters. Of the 105 public figures who responded, 35 (33%) self-reported that they had been stalked. A majority (76%) were males. The most common methods of harassment were telephone calls, letters, faxes and e-mails, the sending of flowers and gifts, physical following, surveillance of the victim's home, and harassment of family and friends. Many of the stalkers were said to be mentally disordered, with 34% of the public figures reporting that their stalker had undergone psychiatric treatment. Most of the public figures questioned took the stalking very seriously, with the majority reporting to the police.

A general finding in the Malsch et al. (2002) study was that the stalkers of politicians tended to remain distant, while the stalkers of those in the entertainment world were more likely to physically pursue their target. It was noted that those respondents who more regularly appeared on the television and radio had a greater chance of experiencing multiple stalking. Thus, the extent of media exposure may be an important risk factor. The same effect was not found, however, among politicians. Dietz et al.'s studies (1991a, 1991b) of inappropriate communications sent to politicians and Hollywood celebrities also noted distinctions between these two public figure groups. Simple presence or absence of approaches made to the two groups cannot be commented upon as pursuers were compared with nonpursuers. In the Dietz et al. studies, communications to celebrities were more intimate and informal than those to Congress members. They were more likely to contain enclosures, and these enclosures were more personal in nature. Those sending inappropriate communications to celebrities were less likely to cast themselves as enemies than were those writing to politicians. They were more likely to express idolization, and be more interested in love, marriage, and sex. The Congress communicators focused far more on perceived personal injustices and violent themes. Celebrity communicators often focused on the world of Hollywood and on the celebrity himself or herself. They expressed a wish to meet the celebrity, while those who communicated with politicians wanted their concerns and injustices to be addressed. This may all be diluted into issues of romance versus issues of power and violence (Dietz et al.). As such, within the current study, we expected that themes of yearning for intimacy and romance would feature strongly in the pursuit of celebrities.

A Study of Television Personalities as Victims of Stalking

Some research suggests that television personalities have a higher risk of stalking victimization than other subgroups of public figures. Meloy, Mohandie, and Green (Chapter 2) found that among their sample of celebrity stalkers, most of the multiple stalking cases focused upon female newscasters or television show actresses. This may be the case because television hosts and news anchorpersons can be easily incorporated into the relationship fantasy of a stalker (Hoffmann & Sheridan, 2005). By the nature of their role, they usually portray a warm, caring, and approachable demeanor, and tend to be physically attractive but not to an intimidating degree. In other words, they are more likely than the majority of public figures to be viewed as realistically attainable, and their actions carry a greater likelihood of being incorporated into a "reciprocal" fantasy. Because of their regular and predictable appearances on the television screen, they may become a pathologically fixated person's fantasy object, offering focus and interest to an otherwise lackluster life.

Method

A 55-item questionnaire was constructed specifically for this study and was distributed nationwide to well-known television personalities in Germany. The questions covered a variety of topics that included demographic details for the celebrity, the extent of the celebrity's fame and public appearances, experiences of unusual fan contacts and stalking, reactions to any harassing behavior, and the psychological impact of any stalking victimization. In the study, the term "stalking" was not utilized. Instead, the public figure was asked if he or she had experienced "a series of unusual contacts by a fan or a similar person that lasted for weeks, months, or years." The intention here was to ensure that responses were not unduly influenced by individual perceptions of what constitutes "stalking." A behaviorally oriented definition characterized by repetitive and socially inadequate contact was reasoned to make cases more comparable. The first author has good working contacts with the largest television network in Germany, allowing him to personally address invitations to participate in the study to 55 celebrities employed by the network. Fifty-three returned the questionnaire: a response rate of 96%. Further details concerning methodology may be found in Hoffmann (2005).

Demographic Characteristics of the Sample

The sex ratio between the celebrities was reasonably uniform in that 57% ($n = 30$) were female. The average age was 38.4 years (SD = 9.05) with a range of 23 to 63 years. Almost all of the public figures were working as news anchorpersons, television presenters, sportscasters, or weatherpersons. One participant was a comedian. Two thirds of the television personalities were employed in roles concerning the provision of information to the populace, and the roles of one third lay in the field of entertainment. The average duration of a respondent's celebrity status was 9.15 years (SD = 6.19) ranging from 3 months to 25 years. In addition to their primary field of repute, a majority of the television personalities also obtained media attention from other sources of activity. Half of the sample (51%) stated that they were guests on other TV shows at least once a year (talk, quiz, or game shows), and almost two thirds of respondents (62%) had been the subject of media reports at least once per year, half more than five times a year.

Unusual Contacts and Mails

In order to obtain an idea of the base rate of pathological communications received by celebrities, the television personalities were asked to estimate the proportion of unusual letters mailed to them. The vast majority of the participants stated that the "unusual" rate was 5% or less of all communications. In most cases (47%), the content of unusual communications was love related, followed by religious or political tracts (19%) and insults (9%). Overt threats were almost nonexistent.

Strange or disturbing items were sent to almost half of the participants (47%). These mailings can be grouped into the following categories: personal gifts, bizarre items, and pornographic material. Examples of personal gifts were jewelry, perfume, or home-made cookies or cakes. One well-known news presenter noted that if a fan sent home-baked treats to him, he gave them to colleagues in order to test them before eating any samples himself! Some personal gifts seemed to represent devotional objects. These included paintings or photographic compositions of the celebrity. Other items had a more bizarre quality and were difficult to encode. Examples here included very long columns of numbers, collages of seemingly random news clips, or lone slices of pizza. Without knowing more about the sender, the meaning of these items remains unclear. Pornographic material was also posted to a number of respondents, including sex toys and pornographic magazines. The most shocking items included bodily fluids such as blood, sperm, or condoms filled with urine.

These experiences of German celebrities mirrored the results of Dietz's work from 1991. Analyzing persons who sent threatening and otherwise inappropriate letters to Hollywood celebrities, Dietz et al. (1991a) found that almost the same percentage (55%) sent enclosures along with their communications, ranging from innocuous items such as poetry or business cards to the bizarre, including ammunition and a coyote head.

Stalking

Among our sample, 79% ($n = 42$) reported having been stalked at some point in their career. To our knowledge, this is the first incidence rate of stalking for a public figure sample. Although this base rate may be higher than in other public figure groups because television personalities would seem to be a particularly frequent target of stalkers, it is clear that celebrity status carries with it a heightened risk of being targeted. Although the data sets are by no means comparable, it is worth noting that when examined against a German population sample (Dressing et al., 2005), the rate for the public figure group was more than six times higher (79% vs. 12%).

There existed a marked distinction regarding the gender distribution of victimization as compared to most other stalking studies. Of the female television personalities, 83% said they had been stalked, as had a high number of their male colleagues (74%). In the Dutch study of public figure victims, the percentage of male and female respondents who reported being stalked was also similar. In many other studies of stalking, both among noncelebrity populations (Spitzberg, 2002) and within celebrity groups (Dietz & Martell, 1989), an average of 70% to 80% of all stalking victims have been women. These differing findings may be explained at least in part by the possibility that other studies focused on more severe cases of harassment than did the current survey. It is well established that the less threatening the stalking, the more likely victim gender is equally distributed (Hoffmann, 2005). Alternatively, there may be some attributes of television personalities and/or their stalkers that help equalize the incidence of inappropriate methods of communication between the sexes. Although normally stalkers and the public figures they target are of the opposite sex (Dietz & Martell, 1989), this is not always the case. Here, 79% of all celebrity victims—regardless of their own gender—reported experiences with a male stalker, compared with 50% that had been targeted at least once by a female stalker. This ratio reflects the general finding that stalkers more often are men than women (Spitzberg, 2002).

The celebrities were asked to record their longest period of harassment by one individual. The average length was 25 months (SD = 27.61 months), ranging from periods of 1 month to more than 10 years. Although these were the most extreme stalking cases the television personalities reported, this number also fits well with findings from the general research on stalking. In a meta-analysis of 175 stalking studies, Spitzberg and Cupach (2007) found that the average case of stalking lasted for 22 months, or close to 2 years. In other public figure samples that included celebrities, the mean stalking duration is reasonably diverse, ranging from 16 (Chapter 2) to 32 months (Malsch et al., 2002). The differing samples and methodologies employed by these studies do not allow for fruitful comparisons. Being harassed is a periodic experience for public figures. Only a minority (14%; or $n = 6$) of the stalked television personalities declared that they had been targeted just once. The majority had been the target of a stalker more frequently, most between two and five times in their career (62%; $n = 26$). Similarly, in Malsch et al.'s study, 59% of respondents stated that they had been targeted more than once.

Letters sent by the stalkers were clearly dominated by themes of love and adoration. Every celebrity subject who had received letters from an obsessed fan mentioned that at least one of these writings expressed feelings of affection. Delusional topics were recorded next most frequently (59% of cases), followed by religious, political, and esoteric themes (51% of cases). Both threats (26%) and insults (26%) occurred in a sizeable minority of cases. Although not matching Dietz et al.'s (1991a) percentages, these predominant themes reflect those revealed by their study of letters sent to Hollywood celebrities almost two decades earlier.

Surprisingly often (74% of cases; $n = 39$), obsessive fans tried to contact the television personalities via telephone. In the majority of cases (80%), the celebrities were contacted at their place of work, but almost half were telephoned at their home number (46%). Stopping the harassing phone calls often proved problematic, with 61% of the public figures reporting difficulties. When the content of the telephone calls was broken down, declarations of love were predominant (84%), whereas insults (19%), threats (11%), or pornographic comments (3%) occurred to a lesser extent. It is not known whether or how the content of calls evolved over time. The fact that demonstrations of love and adoration were most common, both in stalking letters and in telephone calls, corresponds with findings produced within other countries. Dietz's analyses of inappropriate letters to Hollywood stars (Dietz & Martell, 1989; Dietz et al., 1991a) as well as Malsch's survey of Dutch celebrities (2002) reached similar conclusions.

Almost half the sample (43%; $n = 23$) were physically approached by an obsessive individual. A quarter of the television personalities (25%; $n = 13$) reported that this had happened on only one occasion, but a fifth (19%; $n = 10$) had experienced multiple incidents. In virtually all cases, the celebrity's workplace was the location of encounter on at least one occasion (96%; $n = 22$). This high rate is easily attributable to the profession of the public figures, since most worked regularly at a well-known television station, the location of which could be easily traced. Still, there were many cases of approaches made elsewhere. Almost three quarters of respondents (74%; $n = 17$) stated that they experienced inappropriate approaches while making public appearances, at their own homes (40%; $n = 9$), or at the home or workplace of a relative of the public figure (14%; $n = 3$).

Participants were asked about the kind of behavior exhibited by their harassers. Only a few chose to address the television personality directly (17%; $n = 4$). In a majority of the cases the obsessed fan expressed his or her affection in a less physical manner (91%; $n = 21$). For instance, some would stand, lay, or sit wordlessly in the presence of the celebrity (57%; $n = 13$), while others inquired regularly as to the whereabouts of the television personality (74%; $n = 17$). Only a small minority displayed aggressive behaviors (13%; $n = 3$).

Just one violent attack was reported within the present study. The victim was a female television presenter. The stalker had initially sent her love letters, but after some time the emotional tone in his letters shifted from adoration to angry diatribes. Finally, the stalker drove to the television station, breached security, located the office of the news presenter, and then attempted to choke her. Fortunately, she managed to escape and therefore avoided severe physical injury. Reporting psychological trauma, she underwent psychotherapy in order to try and come to terms with the incident. Consistent with two other studies from which some kind of base rate can be derived, violence in cases of celebrity stalking occurs relatively rarely. One out of 53 television personalities in the current work produces a violence incidence rate of 2%, which is an identical percentage to that produced by Meloy et al.'s study of a much greater number of U.S.-based celebrity stalking cases (Chapter 2). In Malsch's Dutch study, none of 35 stalked public figures were attacked aggressively. Among studies of noncelebrity cases—particularly where the perpetrator is a former intimate partner of the victim—the violence rate may be more than 25 times higher (Mohandie et al., 2006).

The celebrities were asked to report in more detail the worst incident they had ever experienced with an inappropriate communicator. Next to the violent attack, reports of physical approach and pursuit were particularly unpleasant. Other distressing behavior from obsessive individuals included following the television personalities by car, breaking into their offices, seeking out the homes of the parents of the public figure, and regularly traveling hundreds of miles to see the celebrity in a public appearance. Other obsessive individuals threatened suicide, wrote about violent fantasies in which they cut off the public figure's body parts, or announced intended acts of revenge from right wing extremist groups. In another incident, a stalker wrote several times that he would pick up the celebrity and take her away to live with him; his letters also contained enthusiastic references to his armory. In several cases, phone calls to private telephone lines were felt to be alarming. In one of these cases, the stalker pretended to be a journalist and later posed as a police detective who was investigating a sexual crime, using this rather obvious ruse to ask questions about the intimate life of a female presenter.

Risk Factors

Little is known for sure about those attributes of public figures that may lead to him or her becoming a particularly attractive target to stalkers. The only empirical study that has so far addressed this issue (Chapter 2) found that female newscasters and television show actresses receive disproportionately higher levels of this form of harassment. Anecdotal reports from experts in the field of threat assessment also provide clues. Gavin de Becker, a major figure in the field of managing celebrity stalking, believes that female singers top the list of public figures at risk. "Songs go much more to visceral elements of our makeup than movies do. We've all had the experience of thinking, 'That song really says what I am feeling now.' So songs are very powerful, which is why female singers will have more problems than any other media figure" (quoted from Gross, 2000, p. 177). Forensic psychiatrist Park Dietz believes social charisma to be of particular relevance: "The nicer one appears to be, and the more approachable, the more one will attract the serious and persistent and deluded subjects. Their public personae foster an illusion of intimacy and receptivity and a willingness to come close in a nonthreatening manner to subjects who generally have difficulty with social relationships" (quoted from Gross, 2000, pp. 177–178). This would support our earlier view that television hosts and news anchorpersons who make regular and predictable appearances are particularly vulnerable.

Although the current work only examined television personalities, we nevertheless attempted to further investigate some relevant dimensions. For the purpose of statistical analyses, a variable labeled "extent of stalking victimization" was aggregated from the following individual variables: "longest experience of stalking," "number of stalkers," and "aggressive stalking." Analyses of variance were conducted to explore which factors appeared to increase the risk of a celebrity becoming a victim of serious stalking. The level of familiarity of the television personality as measured by his or her viewing rates was statistically controlled, but it appeared that this variable had no influence on the results.

Two factors were found to influence the extent of stalking as experienced by our television celebrities. The most powerful predictor was wider media coverage. That is, the extent to which the public figure had been the subject of coverage in other media was related to a greater risk of them becoming the victim of more serious stalking ($F = 4{,}602$, df $= 2$, $p < .05$). In Malsch et al.'s (2002) study, media exposure was positively related to more severe and frequent stalking among television and radio celebrities. Being regularly seen in the media, particularly in entertainment formats, would imply that celebrities more often reveal details of their private life and present a more immediate and personal identity to the public. One central quality of celebrity stalkers is that they confound fantasy and reality aspects in their perceptions of their relationships with others. As such, it is not surprising that they may connect easier to celebrities with a more private appeal. This result supports Dietz's already introduced argument that a presentation of both private details and frankness can encourage fantasies of mutual attachments. Advice to public figures to hide their private persona (for example by avoiding taking part in photo shoots in their own homes) clearly makes sense (de Becker, 1997).

The second factor significantly related to extent of stalking victimization in the current study was the time of the celebrity's television appearances. Those who worked mostly in the late evening and night-time were more seriously stalked. It may be that night-time provides a better setting for fantasy development and elaboration (Dietz & Martell, 1989). This idea was further supported when audience figures were checked, as no correlation between later appearances and higher viewing figures was observed.

An interesting and somewhat surprising aspect of the present work concerned those factors that did *not* influence the extent of stalking victimization. Contrary to the results of Meloy, Mohandie, and Green (Chapter 2), it was not the younger and/or the female celebrities that were most often targeted. In fact, age and gender did not have any significant impact. This contradicts the general impression that young females are very often exposed to both wanted and unwanted communications of love and sexual content. Also, media products and the entertainment industry perpetuate the notion that being a beautiful young woman is the best way to attract attention. Explanations as to why this important cultural and evolutionary factor did not play such a central role in fixations on public figures in this study may be grounded in the argument that common approach behavior may differ markedly from pathological attachments (Roberts, 2007).

In accordance with such thoughts, further analysis of the data revealed that the more pathological the communication became, the less relevant target gender appeared to be. Different levels of unusual contact behavior were analyzed with a focus on the amount of love-related communication received by the celebrities. The mildest form of pathological contact was unusual letters that were not classified as "stalking" by the television personalities. These represented a border region of unusual communication that had already left the realm of regular fan contacts. Here a clear gender effect was observable. The rate of love-related content in the letters to females was much higher than that contained within the mail sent to their male colleagues ($t = -2.67$, df $= 51$, $p < .01$). The next pathological stage was "stalking behavior" in the form of series of unusual letters that lasted for weeks, months, or years. In this rather mild category of stalking, the same form of gender difference was found, although not as distinctly as before ($t = -2.39$, df $= 39$, $p < .05$). Finally, a more intrusive kind of stalking communication was analyzed by examining the content of repeated phone calls. At this point, significant differences in the proportion of love-related messages to our male and female television personalities disappeared. In sum, it may be preliminarily stated that the more pathological, obsessive, and harassing the stalking behavior becomes, the less the gender of the celebrity would seem to play a role.

Effects of Stalking Victimization

As noted at the beginning of this chapter, it is well known that stalking can lead to significant mentally, physically, and socially deleterious effects in its victims. Physical and emotional effects that have been recorded include distrust of others, persistent nausea and/or headaches, exacerbation of existing medical conditions, substance use and abuse, confusion, nervousness, anxiety, stomach problems, chronic sleep disturbances, persistent weakness or tiredness, and appetite disruption (see e.g., Bjerregaard, 2000; Brewster, 1999; Dressing, Kuehner, & Gass, 2005; Nicastro, Cousins, & Spitzberg, 2000; Sheridan, Davies, & Boon, 2001; Westrup, Fremouw, Thompson, & Lewis, 1999). Actual percentages reported by individual studies vary, mainly because of differences in definitions and sampling, but are usually very high. Furthermore, symptoms are usually found regardless of whether the victim was physically attacked. At least one symptom of posttraumatic stress disorder was reported by a majority of Pathé and Mullen's (1997) victims, and Kamphuis and Emmelkamp (2001) noted that 59% of their victim sample reported symptoms comparable to those exhibited by victims of more generally recognized trauma. Social and economic losses arising from being stalked have also been observed and these include taking security measures, losing or changing jobs, moving homes, changing telephone numbers, repairing or replacing property damaged by the stalker, paying legal and medical fees, changing routines or staying indoors, and avoiding social activities (see e.g., Bjerregaard, 2000; Blaauw et al., 2002; Brewster, 1999; Dressing et al., 2005; Kamphuis & Emmelkamp, 2001; Mohandie, Meloy, McGowan, & Williams, 2006; Pathé & Mullen, 1997; Purcell, Pathé, & Mullen, 2002; Sheridan, 2001; Tjaden & Thoennes, 1998; Westrup et al., 1999). In the current work, the celebrities were asked about specific effects of being stalked; Table 9.1 summarizes the findings.

Figures produced by Dressing et al.'s (2005) German population study are also included in Table 9.1. Although it must again be noted that the two data sets are not comparable, the figures are not entirely different. The largest difference in Table 9.1 concerns moving homes, with celebrity victims being

Table 9.1. Celebrity victims' ($n = 42$) reactions to stalking compared with victims in the general population ($n = 78$) (Dressing et al., 2005)

Reaction to stalking	Celebrity (%)	General population (%)
Agitation	74	57
Fear	59	44
Changing lifestyle	63	72
Changing residence	6	17
Additional security measures	9	17
Report to the police	9	20

less likely to do so than nonpublic figure victims. Perhaps it is the case that celebrity victims feel that it is rather pointless to go to the trouble of relocating when the stalker may easily locate them at their workplace or when making public appearances. It may be concluded that celebrity victims are not immune to the well-documented negative effects of being targeted by a stalker. In the current work, female television personalities ($F = 5,363$, df $= 1$, $p < .05$) and those who were physically approached ($F = 4,104$, df $= 3$, $p < .05$) by a stalker reported higher levels of psychological stress.

Case Example 1

The following case study illustrates the negative effects that stalking can have on its celebrity victims.

An attractive 32-year-old female local news presenter received a letter from a 30-year-old man. In this letter, he stated his name and warned, "Remember that name, you'll be hearing from me." The news presenter received a total of 80 letters from this individual over a 6-month period. Over time, the letters became more and more overtly sexual. They contained constant references to stalking, such as, "Every celebrity needs a stalker." When the news presenter became engaged to be married, and wore her engagement ring on air, the stalker's letters intensified and he made repeated references to sexual and violent scenarios. The stalker talked about the murder of BBC presenter Jill Dando, writing: "I think the whole Jill Dando thing was great. I was hoping a celebrity would get killed by a stalker or someone. It's made it even better that she read the news." The news presenter was terrified. She was unable to sleep at night, and would check all the rooms in her house to ensure he was not there because she knew he was trying to discover her home address. It became difficult for her to work, partly because she was conscious that the stalker would react to what she wore and said on air. The stalker visited his victim at the television studios where she worked. He watched her and other staff members and would then write to tell her what he had seen. As time went on, the stalker's letters detailed his fantasies about becoming a serial killer and he explained that he had a psychotic disorder. He moved houses, living too far away to see his victim's regional news bulletins. Instead he paid to have videotapes posted to his new address. He made threats against the newsreader's fiancé. Each of his letters now ran to 30 to 40 pages. The newsreader reported her stalker to the police. When they searched his home, police found a textbook for law students on harassment, and a handbook on how to be a stalker that the accused was writing. The stalker was jailed for 2½ years and banned for life from having any contact with his victim. In court he said he would have gone to her home had he been able to discover her address. Following the sentence, the victim said: "The death of Jill Dando brought it home that TV presenters, however well-loved and with a good-natured image, are a target for people out there that can do something like that and find out where you live. Even now I still look behind me."

Intervention Strategies

In accordance with advice given in guidebooks written for victims of general stalking (Spence-Diehl, 1999; Pathé, 2002) and in line with recommendations offered for celebrity victims (de Becker, 1997), the television personalities reported that ignoring an obsessive fan was the best strategy for bringing stalking to an end. None of the public figures thought this intervention to be unsuccessful. In contrast, strategies that may feed the stalker's fantasy of a reciprocal relationship appeared to have unsatisfactory effects. For example, personal appeals to an obsessive fan to stop his harassing behavior have the result that the stalker receives direct attention from the celebrity. Being recognized is one of the core motives for stalking. Recognition provided by a famous person may elevate feelings of self-importance and entitlement, further encouraging the stalker to seek to establish a special relationship with the public figure. Therefore, every direct contact has the potential to escalate the stalking. We also asked those television personalities who had responded to an obsessive fan by letter or telephone if their reaction had made things worse. One third agreed. Likewise, the interference of a third party does not always bring positive results. The stalker can view the third party as a messenger from the celebrity and therefore his expectations of being recognized are fulfilled. Also, a rejection from a third party often allows the stalker to retain his fantasy that one day there will be a relationship with the public figure. He may, for example, believe that if he and the celebrity were to meet then the latter would realize their inevitable joint fate. Alternatively, third parties can be blamed for keeping the stalker and his target apart.

Case Example 2

A presenter at the beginning of her career received letters from a young man who seemed very desperate. He declared that he had fallen deeply in love with her after seeing her on his television screen. He begged for a reply, supplying his address and telephone number in the letters. Being a friendly and compassionate person and having had no previous experience of unusual contact by viewers, the presenter decided to telephone him and explain that she was married and therefore it would be more fruitful for him to focus his love interest on other, more available, young women. This call lasted no longer than 1 hour but a decade and a half later, the man is still obsessively fixated on the presenter and claims that this personal conversation forever changed his life. Directly after the phone call, his contact behavior escalated. Along with numerous letters and calls to the workplace of the television personality, he managed to find out her private address and started loitering in front of her house. His letters indicated that over the years he was increasingly suffering from a psychotic illness. Unfortunately at one point, a well-meant intervention by male friends of the presenter worsened the situation. The friends warned the stalker in a threatening manner that he should stop his harassing behavior. From this moment onward, the adoring tone in the stalker's communications changed to expressions of hate and revenge, and he began a long lasting campaign of psychological terror against the presenter.

It is instructive that a strict rebuff by the celebrity is generally far more effective than a friendly appeal to an obsessive fan. There exists a general dynamic in stalking that when a rejection is formulated by the victim in a manner that is not completely clear and unambiguous, the stalker often finds another argument to support his idea of a special union (de Becker, 1997). This is the consequence of the typical cognitive distortions and psychological defenses of stalkers. These distortions center on issues of close relationships and rejection and can be the result of early attachment pathology (see Meloy, 2007) (Chapter 8). Therefore, a strict rebuff provides the stalker with less opportunity to construct a scenario where the public figure is still interested in him than does a polite and more defensive reaction. At first glance, this advice would appear inconsistent: on the one hand any kind of reaction from a celebrity can enhance the stalker's feeling of entitlement, but on the other hand a strict rebuff may succeed. A possible explanation for this ostensible contradiction is that not all offensive and unusual approaches and contacts a public figure experiences are from fixated persons for whom fantasy and reality are blurred.

Research demonstrates that more people than are generally believed have an extraordinary interest in celebrities and sometimes strive for contact with a public figure. First referred to as the "parasocial relationship" and later conceptualized under the term of "celebrity worship," this phenomenon has gained increasing scientific interest (Sheridan, Maltby, & Gillett, 2006) (Chapters 12 and 13). The approach behavior of fans has also been examined, showing that "active fans" may go to great lengths to physically encounter a celebrity or to find out details about them such as a home address (Emerson, Ferris, & Brooks Gardner, 1998; Ferris, 2001). Unlike stalkers, these people would in most cases accept a clear line drawn by the public figure they are interested in. A similar type of individual is described by de Becker (1994) as the "naïve pursuer." Often unsophisticated, this character simply does not realize or appreciate the social inappropriateness of his approach behavior. He keeps on harassing until someone makes it unequivocally clear to him that his approach is unacceptable and counterproductive. According to de Becker, direct communication is most fruitful in such cases, invariably causing the naïve pursuer to halt his quest (see Table 9.2).

In the current study, after ignoring the obsessive fan, calling in the police appeared to be the next fruitful intervention strategy. Only 7% of the television personalities reported that this strategy had no success at all. These data confirm the results of a 1996 study conducted by the Threat Management Unit of the Los Angeles Police Department. One of the key aspects of activity of this police unit is to manage cases of celebrity stalking (see Chapter 14). Evaluating their interventions in cases of both celebrity and noncelebrity stalking, Williams, Lane, and Zona (1996) found that for most incidents, an

Table 9.2. Success rate of interventions by celebrities against obsessive fans

Intervention strategy	No success (%)	Partial success (%)	Full success (%)
Ignoring obsessive fan	0	42	58
Call in police	7	77	26
Strict rebuff	13	59	28
Interfering third party	20	40	40
Direct appeal to obsessive fan	26	39	35

offensive policy stopped the harassment. Still, anecdotal wisdom suggests that sometimes police intervention can escalate a stalking incident, particularly in cases where the law is not consequently enforced (for instance when the breaking of restraining orders goes unpunished). The key factors for an effective and successful approach seem to be determination and fast action of the responsible police unit (Chapter 14). So why does professional police intervention often curtail or at least contain the activities of the celebrity stalker? It is likely that in some cases it destroys the stalker's fantasy of a special relationship with the public figure. That is, the fixated person is forced to realize that they are not half of a "private" affair between the celebrity and themselves, but now are in conflict with a third party—the police (Hoffmann & Sheridan, 2005).

Special Aspects of the Stalking Victimization of Celebrities

It is clear that celebrities are a favored target of stalkers, probably more than any other group within Western societies. Although the rate of physical violence is much lower than that seen among the high-risk group of ex-partner stalking victims, the psychological impact on celebrities can still can be dramatic. An internationally well-known celebrity reported to one of the authors that owing to the experience of being pursued by an extremely obsessive and cunning stalker for over 4 years, she seriously considered ending her career. She said she loved her professional life, but worrying about the stalker's next steps had negative effects on all aspects of her life. Thus, she hoped that removing herself from public attention would cause the stalker to lose interest. This feeling of helplessness and entrapment is typical among stalking victims, but we must be aware of some special distinctions that apply only to celebrity cases.

In the first detailed case example presented above, a news presenter reported having difficulties at work, because she was worried how the stalker would react to her on-air appearance and behavior. This is not an isolated experience among celebrity stalking cases. Sometimes public figures are fundamentally shaken when they receive knowledge of how an obsessive fan perceives or interprets their public persona. Celebrities may feel very uncomfortable because they realize that they ultimately have limited control over their public image. One television personality admitted to one of the authors that because of a very aggressive delusional stalker he almost had to give up his own talk show. He was preoccupied with how his stalker perceived his behavior and as a result the quality of his interviews noticeably depreciated.

Unlike most victims who will have had some sort of prior social relationship with their harasser (Spitzberg & Cupach, 2007), celebrities are often unable to recognize their stalker. Having read his letters or having heard his voice on CDs or answering services, the stalker may feel psychologically close but physically invisible. Occasionally, public figures are worried because they will know from a stalker's communicated facts that he has been close by at a public appearance or even in a private context but they were unable to detect him. Having no clue as to the appearance of the stalker, they feel unsafe being out in public, which can lead, in turn, to social withdrawal. In some cases known to the authors, celebrities have engaged security services to make secret footage of the stalker in an attempt to assuage such fears. In one case known to us, the detectives were not too skilled such that the stalker came to notice their activities in front of his house. He interpreted the photographing as an indicator that the celebrity was positively interested in him and immediately intensified his contact behavior.

Contrary to public belief, in the experience of the authors, celebrities do not usually receive special attention or priority handling from authorities. Depending on legislation within the celebrity's country of residence, even when harassed or threatened to an alarming extent, police can sometimes only explain that they are powerless. For example, a male actor was attacked with a knife by a mentally ill stalker. He managed to escape uninjured and the stalker was sent to a mental institution. Before she was apprehended, the stalker told the actor that she would kill him upon being released. Because of legal complications, she was set free a few weeks later, although psychiatrists still believed her to be dangerous. The actor called the police and asked for help. A policewoman informed him that he should not worry, saying that the stalker was "only a female."

Reactions to media stories concerning the stalking of public figures often fail to elicit much sympathy from the general public. This lack of sympathy is supported by arguments such as "stalking is the price of fame," "you are not famous until you have your first stalker," or "well what do they expect after prostituting themselves in the media?" Celebrities are faced with a dilemma when it comes to media exposure. Particularly during early career stages, media appearances enhance market value, but they also heighten the risk of becoming a victim of stalking. As has been learnt by practical experience, and also suggested by the current study, intimate disclosures by public figures attract obsessive fans. At the same time, this is the material craved by the media, and therefore personal revelations guarantee the celebrity wide coverage (e.g., see tmz.com). It is especially so that statements on romantic issues can trigger stalking activities. One case illustrates this. A female public figure was harassed by an erotomanic individual who turned up at almost all her public appearances. Fortunately, his activities gradually decreased until he was not seen for 6 months. Then, in a media interview, the public figure talked about her loneliness and how she wished that the right man would step into her life. A few days later the stalker suddenly reappeared. He also began writing letters in which he referred to this statement made by the public figure.

A recent legal ruling may help protect celebrities in England and Wales. In December 2006, the British Court of Appeal upheld an earlier High Court judgment that had found that Canadian singer-composer Loreena McKennitt's privacy had been intruded upon when a former friend and employee self-published a book about her. McKennitt commented, "I am very grateful to the courts...who have recognized that every person has an equal right to a private life. If an aspect of career places one directly in the public eye or if extraordinary events make an ordinary person newsworthy for a time, we all still should have the basic human dignity of privacy for our home and family life." This case generated great interest among media and law professionals because it clarified the implications of the Human Rights Act 1998 on English law, and made clear that public figures will be protected when they have a "reasonable expectation of privacy," unless there is a serious public interest in the material in question. Of course, the level of protection awarded to celebrities who purposefully court the media to raise their professional profile is likely to be much reduced or even nonexistent.

Another important distinction between famous and nonfamous victims is that the former tend to underestimate the degree of pathological fixation and the persistence of and dangers presented by stalkers. Talking about the smallest details in public can lead to the detection of their private whereabouts. In one case, a television personality discussed his favorite place to go on holiday. An obsessed fan spent three summers at this location looking for the presenter in every hotel before she found him. This direct contact was the beginning of a stalking campaign that lasted for years. It must be made clear that stalkers can put inordinate amounts of time and effort into stalking activity. This is best conceptualized by considering one's own life. For many people, life is made up of work, family, hobbies, socializing, taking care of the home and pets, and so on. When we think about our achievements, we can appreciate all the time and effort we have put into realizing them. Stalkers can put the same amount of time and effort into little else but the stalking.

A somewhat tricky dynamic in celebrity stalking is that media reports about an incident may themselves represent one of the stalker's goals. There are two primary underlying reasons for this. First, public attention has the potential to feed the pathologically narcissistic needs of many public figure stalkers (Chapter 8), and second, the stalker will be connected with the celebrity through media coverage. Another problem is that the judicial system sometimes forces a direct encounter between the public figure and the fixated person (Chapter 18). This became apparent in the case of pop star Madonna, who was forced against her will to stand in court in the same room as her aggressive stalker. Madonna was fully aware of the psychological dynamics in the stalker, declaring, "I feel incredibly disturbed that the man who has repeatedly threatened my life is sitting across from me and we have somehow made his fantasies come true (in that) I am sitting in front of him and that is what he wants" (Saunders, 1998, pp. 40–41).

Conclusions

This chapter has provided details of the stalking experiences of a sample of German television personalities. Despite differences in sampling, methodology, and country of origin, important similarities have been found between this and several earlier works. For instance, television presenters may be at particular risk, expressions of romantic love are dominant, many celebrities are sent strange items along with missives from the stalker, celebrities are negatively affected by being stalked, celebrities are likely to be stalked more than once, and many celebrity stalkers will be delusional. Important distinctions have been seen between celebrity victims and general population victims. For example, celebrity victims have among their number a higher proportion of males than do general population victims, and stalkers of celebrities are much more likely to be delusional. These findings underline the dangers of assuming that findings and advice from the general stalking literature will apply in public figure cases. The current findings make clear the need to take celebrity stalking seriously, particularly given the grave emotional, social, and professional effects on victims. The stalking of celebrities is too often trivialized and seen as an inevitable side effect of fame. Increasing our knowledge of the dynamics of celebrity stalking cases and the motivations and characteristics of offenders can only serve to increase the efficacy of intervention strategies.

References

Bjerregaard, B. (2000). An empirical study of stalking victimization. *Violence and Victims*, *15*, 389–406.

Blaauw, E., Winkel, F. W., Arensman, E., Sheridan, L., & Freeve, A. (2002). The toll of stalking: The relationship between features of stalking and psychopathology of victims. *Journal of Interpersonal Violence*, *17*, 50–63.

Brewster, M. P. (1999). *An exploration of the experiences and needs of former intimate stalking victims: Final report submitted to the National Institute of Justice*. West Chester, PA: West Chester University.

Chapman, D. E., & Spitzberg, B. H. (2003). Are you following me? A study of unwanted relationship pursuit and stalking in Japan: What behaviors are prevalent? *Bulletin of Hijiyama University*, *10*, 89–138.

Davis, K. E., Coker, A. L., & Sanderson, M. (2002). Physical and mental health effects of being stalked for men and women. *Violence and Victims*, *17*, 429–443.

de Becker, G. (1994). *Intervention decisions: The value of flexibility*. White paper report prepared for the 1994 CIA Threat Management Conference.

de Becker, G. (1997). *The gift of fear*. Boston: Little, Brown.

Dietz, P. E., & Martell, D. A. (1989). *Mentally disordered offenders in pursuit of celebrities and politicians*. Washington, DC: National Institute of Justice.

Dietz, P. E., Matthews, D. B., Van Duyne, C., Martell, D. A., Parry, C. D. H., Stewart, T., et al. (1991a). Threatening and otherwise inappropriate letters to Hollywood celebrities. *Journal of Forensic Sciences, 36*, 185–209.

Dietz, P. E., Matthews, D. B., Van Duyne, C., Martell, D. A., Parry, C. D. H., Stewart, T., et al. (1991b). Threatening and otherwise inappropriate letters to members of the United States Congress. *Journal of Forensic Sciences, 36*, 1445–1468.

Dressing, H., Kuehner, C., & Gass, P. (2005). Lifetime relevance and impact of stalking in a European population. Epidemiological data from a middle-sized German city. *British Journal of Psychiatry, 187*, 168–172.

Emerson, R. M., Ferris, K. O., & Brooks Gardner, C. (1998). On being stalked. *Social Problems, 45*(3), 289–314

Ferris, K. O. (2001). Through a glass, darkly: The dynamics of fan-celebrity encounters. *Symbolic Interaction, 24*, 25–47.

Gross, L. (2000). *Surviving a stalker.* New York: Marlowe.

Hall, D. M. (1998). The victims of stalking. In J. R. Meloy (Ed.), *The psychology of stalking.* (pp. 113–137). San Diego: Academic Press.

Hoffmann, J. (2005). *Stalking.* Heidelberg: Springer.

Hoffmann, J., & Sheridan, L. (2005). The stalking of public figures: Management and intervention. *Journal of Forensic Sciences, 6*, 1459–1465.

Jagessar, J., & Sheridan, L. (2004). Stalking: Perceptions and experiences across two cultures. *Criminal Justice and Behavior, 31*, 97–117.

Kamphuis, J. H., & Emmelkamp, P. M. G. (2001). Traumatic distress among support-seeking female victims of stalking. *American Journal of Psychiatry, 158*, 795–798.

Kordvani, A. H. (2000). *Women stalking in Iran.* Paper presented (by proxy) to the Criminal Justice Responses to Stalking Conference, Australian Institute of Criminology, Sydney, Australia.

Malsch, M., Visscher, M., & Blaauw, E. (2002). *Stalking van bekende personen* [Stalking of celebrities]. Den Haag: Boom.

Mechanic, M. B., Uhlmansiek, M. H., Weaver, T. L., & Resick, P. A. (2000). The impact of severe stalking experienced by acutely battered women. *Violence and Victims, 15*, 443–458.

Meloy, J. R. (2007). Stalking: The state of the science. *Criminal Behaviour and Mental Health, 17*, 1–7.

Mohandie, K., Meloy, J. R., McGowan, M. G., & Williams, J. (2006). The RECON typology of stalking: Reliability and validity based upon a large sample of North American stalkers. *Journal of Forensic Sciences, 51*, 147–155.

Nicastro, A. M., Cousins, A. V., & Spitzberg, B. H. (2000). The tactical face of stalking. *Journal of Criminal Justice, 28*, 69–82.

Pathé, M. (2002). *Surviving stalking.* Cambridge: Cambridge University Press.

Pathé, M., & Mullen, P. E. (1997). The impact of stalkers on their victims. *British Journal of Psychiatry, 170*, 12–17.

Purcell, R., Pathé, M., & Mullen, P. E. (2002). The incidence and nature of stalking in the Australian community. *Australian and New Zealand Journal of Psychiatry, 36*, 114–120.

Roberts, K. A. (2007). Relationship attachment and the behaviour of fans towards celebrities. *Applied Psychology in Criminal Justice, 3*, 54–74.

Saunders, R. (1998). The legal perspective on stalking. In J.R.Meloy, (Ed.), *The psychology of stalking: clinical and forensic perspectives.* (pp. 28–59). San Diego, CA: Academic Press.

Sheridan, L. (2001). The course and nature of stalking: An in-depth victim survey. *Journal of Threat Assessment, 1*, 61–79.

Sheridan, L., Davis, G. M., & Boon, J. C. W. (2001). The course and nature of stalking: A victim perspective. *The Howard Journal of Criminal Justice, 40*, 215–234.

Sheridan, L. Maltby, J., & Gillett, R. (2006). Pathological public figure preoccupation: Its relationship with dissociation and absorption. *Personality and Individual Differences, 41*, 525–535.

Spence-Diehl, E. (1999). *Stalking—A handbook for victims*. Holmes Beach: Learning Publications.

Spitzberg, B. H. (2002). The tactical topography of stalking victimization and management. *Trauma, Violence & Abuse, 3*, 261–288.

Spitzberg, B. H., & Cupach, W. R. (2007). The state of the art of stalking: Taking stock of the emerging literature. *Aggression and Violent Behavior, 12*, 64–86.

Tjaden, P., & Thoennes, N. (1998). *Stalking in America: Findings from the National Violence Against Women survey* (NIJ report no. 169592). Washington, DC: United States Department of Justice.

Westrup, D., Fremouw, W. J., Thompson, R. N., & Lewis, S. F. (1999). The psychological impact of stalking on female undergraduates. *Journal of Forensic Sciences, 44*, 554–557.

Williams, W. L., Lane, J., & Zona, M. A. (1996). Stalking—Successful intervention strategies. *The Police Chief, 2*, 24–26.

10

Psychopathy and Predatory Stalking of Public Figures

*Mary Ellen O'Toole, Sharon S. Smith,
and Robert D. Hare*

Samuel Brown was a top executive of a Fortune 500 company. Although he had a net worth of nearly 10 million dollars, he was a family man with simple tastes that eschewed the trappings of power and wealth. Brown was a low risk victim for violence. He resided with his wife in an affluent neighborhood where violent crime was nonexistent, and people who did not live there or have a legitimate reason to be there would stand out.

One morning, as was his custom, Brown dressed, left his home, tossed his briefcase into his car, and started the engine. As he walked to the end of his driveway to retrieve the morning paper, Anthony Lake jumped out of a nearby van and drew his gun. In the ensuing struggle, Lake fired his gun, wounding Brown. Lake then shoved Brown into his van and drove away. Lake's female accomplice, tasked by him to drive a second getaway car, left the scene at the same time. Brown died a painful death, just days after he was kidnapped. Yet, over the next several weeks, Lake and his accomplice continued their elaborate extortion scheme and the victimization of the Brown family. They made numerous phone calls and sent a number of detailed ransom notes to the victim's family and employer, demanding $12 million dollars for Brown's safe release. Nearly 3 months following his abduction, Samuel Brown's decomposed body was found in a shallow grave.

> Violent crime scenes always tell a story—a story written by the offender, the victim, and the unique circumstances of their interaction. That story makes crimes dynamic events that will vary in complexity, and, like any narrative, will have a beginning, middle

and end. Of the many possible criminal narratives, those that involve psychopaths have a distinct tone and intent, set apart the way science fiction stands out from other literature.

O'Toole, 2007, p. 302

Psychopathology and Risk for Violence

Mental disorders have a long history of perceived association with violent and threatening behavior. Although the general public still embraces the misconception that anyone who commits a brutal, senseless crime must be mentally ill or "crazy" (Perlin, 2000; Stefan, 2001), the rate of violence by the mentally disordered is generally not high, except in conjunction with various aggravating factors, such as psychopathy and substance abuse. For example, the presence of psychopathic traits greatly increases the risk for violence, not only among criminals (Hare, 2003; Hemphill, 2007; Porter & Woodworth, 2006) but also among psychiatric patients, both civil (Monahan et al., 2001; Steadman et al., 1999) and forensic (Rice & Harris, 1992; Tengström, Grann, Långström, & Kullgren, 2000; Tengström, Hodgins, Grann, Långström, & Kullgren, 2004; Tengström et al., 2006). Harris, Rice, and Camilleri (2004) commented that even if the base rate of psychopathy or psychopathic features in a population is relatively low, "The personality traits associated with psychopathy are among the most important causes of aggression" (p. 1070). Several personality disorders, particularly those in the dramatic or cluster B group (antisocial, borderline, histrionic, and narcissistic) listed in *DSM-IV* (American Psychiatric Association, 1994) and *DSM-IV-TR* (American Psychiatric Association, 2000), are associated with aggressive behavior, with the most important being antisocial personality disorder (Berman, Fallon, & Coccaro, 1998). The latter is related to, but not identical with, psychopathy, the major difference being that antisocial personality disorder is defined primarily by antisocial behaviors and does not include some of the key personality traits that define psychopathy (Hare, 2006; Ogloff, 2006; Rogers, Salekin, Sewell, & Cruise, 2000; Warren & South, 2006; Widiger et al., 1996).

Criminal investigations are dynamic events during which investigators must make quick, critical, and often life-and-death decisions, on the basis of incomplete and limited information about the offender. Analyzing crime scenes for the presence of serious and debilitating mental disorders, such as schizophrenia, is a natural part of this inferential and assumptive process. However, psychopathy is less understood by law enforcement, and its crime scene indicators are often misinterpreted, or worse, ignored. We find this curious, given that psychopathy may be the overarching explanatory construct for understanding criminal behavior. Indeed, it has been described as the single most important *clinical* construct in the criminal justice system (Hare, 1996), and perhaps the most important *forensic* concept of the early 21st century (Monahan, 2006).

Analyzing crimes for psychopathic traits should become an integral part of crime scene analysis because individuals with these traits have greater potential for violence than do most other offenders. Additionally, law enforcement's ability to accomplish a beneficial resolution for the victim can be greatly diminished if investigative strategies are designed without knowledge or consideration of the traits and behaviors of offenders with this personality disorder.

Psychopathic traits also play an important role in crime scene analysis of stalking, attacking, and threatening—crimes that have distinctive features. This chapter will examine the implications of psychopathy in crime scene analyses of stalking, threatening, and attendant assaultive behaviors. Case studies are used to illustrate the operationalization of the psychopathic personality construct in terms of specific behaviors. To protect the identities of all parties in these examples, pseudonyms have been used and all potentially identifying information has been deleted or changed, while the important facts of the cases have been faithfully portrayed.

Psychopathy

In the 1996 movie, *Last Man Standing*, Bruce Willis plays John Smith, a more or less psychopathic killer-for-hire. In one scene, Felina, played by Karina Lombard, says to him, "My fear is my curse. What's yours'?" He replies, "I was born without a conscience." While we do not know whether real world psychopaths would view such a genetic endowment as a curse or a blessing, or even as a matter of complete indifference, there is no doubt that it allows them to contemplate and do things, including stalking, which most people would find difficult or impossible. Further, Smith's awareness of the importance of genetic factors in accounting for his behavior is consistent with recent research on psychopathy (e.g., Viding, Blair, Moffitt, & Plomin, 2005; Waldman & Rhee, 2006). Whatever their origins, the features that define psychopathy can be problematic for society, constituting what might be viewed as a prescription for the commission of antisocial and criminal acts. As Silver, Mulvey, and Monahan (1999) put it, "Psychopathy's defining characteristics, such as impulsivity, criminal versatility, callousness, and lack of empathy or remorse make the conceptual link between violence and psychopathy straightforward" (p. 244).

There is an extensive literature on psychopathy, its origins, nature, assessment, and implications for society in general and for the criminal justice system in particular (e.g., Cleckley, 1976; Hare, 1998, in press; Hervé & Yuille, 2006/2007; Meloy, 1988, 2000; Patrick, 2006). Briefly, psychopathy is a clinical construct used to describe individuals who are grandiose, arrogant, callous, dominant, superficial, manipulative, sensation seeking, short tempered, unable to form strong emotional bonds with others, and lacking in empathy, guilt, or remorse. They engage in a socially deviant (not necessarily criminal) lifestyle that includes irresponsible and impulsive behavior, and a tendency to ignore or violate social conventions and rules. These are individuals whose egocentricity, grandiosity, sense of entitlement, impulsivity, and general lack of behavioral inhibitions make it easy to victimize the vulnerable and to use intimidation and violence as tools to achieve power and control over others. They are capable of "reactive" forms of aggression and, more ominously, aggression and violence that are predatory, premeditated, instrumental, or "cold blooded" in nature (Hare, 2003; Meloy, 2002; Porter & Woodworth, 2006). Interestingly, Meloy and Meloy (2003) reported that the majority of clinicians surveyed felt uneasy or threatened while in the presence of a psychopath, feelings the authors suggest are part of an evolutionary-based autonomic reaction to an "intraspecies predator" (p. 21).

Given their defining characteristics we might expect that the stalking behaviors of psychopaths would tend to be predatory or instrumental in nature, with the victim being viewed more as a possession or as a target for control, retribution, or revenge than as the object of a pathologically based fantasy, obsession, or infatuation (c.f., Meloy, 2000; Reavis, Allen, & Meloy, 2008). Further, psychopaths tend to become bored rather quickly and we might speculate that most would be unlikely to engage in anything but relatively short term, instrumental stalking, with goals that primarily are financial or related to power and control.

PCL-R Assessment of Psychopathy

The international standard for the assessment of psychopathy is the *Hare Psychopathy Checklist-Revised* (PCL-R; Hare, 1991, 2003), described as "state of the art...both clinically and in research use" (Fulero, 1995, pp. 453–454). Following publication of the second edition of the PCL-R (Hare, 2003), the *16th Mental Measurements Yearbook* referred to it as "the gold standard for the assessment of psychopathy" (Acheson, 2005, pp. 429–431). The PCL-R is a reliable and valid clinical construct rating in which a *qualified examiner* uses a semistructured interview, case history information, and specific scoring criteria to rate each of 20 items on a 3-point scale (0, 1, 2), according to the extent to which it applies to a given individual. Total scores can range from 0 to 40 and typically are seen as a reflection of the degree to which an individual matches the clinical conception of a prototypical psychopath (c.f., Guay, Ruscio, Knight, & Hare, in press). The PCL-R items can be grouped into four correlated factors or domains (Hare & Neumann, 2005, 2006; Neumann, Hare, & Newman, in press). These domains are described as *Interpersonal* (e.g., grandiose, conning, manipulative, deceptive), *Affective* (e.g., shallow emotions, lack of empathy, guilt, or remorse), *Lifestyle* (stimulation seeking, irresponsible, impulsive and nomadic), and *Antisocial* (e.g., poor behavioral controls, early behavior problems, criminal versatility).

Two direct derivatives of the PCL-R are the *Psychopathy Checklist: Screening Version* (PCL: SV) (Hart, Cox, & Hare, 1995) and the *Psychopathy Checklist: Youth Version* (PCL: YV) (Forth, Kosson, & Hare, 2003). The PCL: SV is a 12-item scale that frequently is used as a screening tool for psychopathy or as a stand-alone instrument, particularly with community and psychiatric populations (e.g., Guy & Douglas, 2006; Steadman et al., 1999). The PCL: YV is a 20-item scale used with adolescents. The PCL: SV and the PCL: YV have the same psychometric properties and 4-factor structure as the PCL-R (Neumann, Kosson, Forth, & Hare, 2006; Vitacco, Neumann, & Jackson, 2005). Like the parent PCL-R, they are good predictors of criminal and violent behaviors.

Although the PCL-R and its derivatives were designed to measure the construct of psychopathy for research purposes, they are widely used as key factors in assessing treatment options and risk for recidivism and violence. The PCL-R is also used in American proceedings for civil commitment of sexually violent predators, Canadian applications to have an offender declared a dangerous offender or long-term offender, and in U.K. designations of dangerous and severe personality disorder. The past decade has seen a sharp rise in its use by forensic clinicians (Archer, Buffingtom-Vollum, Stredny, & Handel, 2006; Lally, 2003) and in its acceptance by the courts (Walsh & Walsh, 2006). Applications of the PCL-R and the construct it measures to law enforcement are outlined by O'Toole (2007) and by Logan and Hare (in press).

When using psychological instruments, it is important to keep in mind the potential influence of cultural, ethnic, and racial factors. The available evidence is that the PCL-R and its derivatives have much the same structural properties and implications for crime and violence in various racial, cultural, and ethnic groups (Bolt, Hare, & Neumann, in press; Bolt, Hare, Vitale, & Newman, 2004; Cooke, Kosson, & Michie, 2001; Skeem, Edens, Camp, & Colwell, 2004). In particular, they do not appear to be biased for or against Caucasian or African American offenders.

It is important to note that the PCL-R and its derivatives are controlled instruments. For clinical and forensic purposes, this means that the user must have the academic training, practical experience, and professional qualifications required for the administration and interpretation of psychological tests. Moreover, PCL-R items cannot be scored without reference to the specific scoring criteria listed in the Manual (Hare, 2003). However, law enforcement investigators familiar with the clinical and empirical work on psychopathy (e.g., Babiak & Hare, 2006; Hare, 1998, 2006; Meloy, 1988, 2000) can use the information to speculate about the potential role of psychopathy, and to discuss its implications in a particular case. These discussions may suggest lines of enquiry or lead to a request for more formal hypotheses concerning psychopathy from a qualified clinician. The work of investigators may be facilitated by use of the Hare P-SCAN (Hare & Hervé, 2002), an instrument designed to provide nonclinical indications of psychopathic traits and behaviors.

The P-SCAN

In most law enforcement and security cases, the information needed to conduct a formal assessment of psychopathy is lacking. Further, even if such information was available, few investigators have the professional qualifications required to use the PCL-R or its derivatives. The P-SCAN was designed to provide investigators and other professionals (e.g., probation and parole officers) with the means to form impressions, develop hypotheses, and draw tentative conclusions on the basis of their knowledge and experience with a given individual. It is not a psychological test, nor does it provide a clinical assessment diagnosis. It is a rough screening device that, when properly used, may provide important clues or working hypotheses about the nature of an individual of interest. The way information is used will depend on the context in which it was obtained. In some cases, the results and context will suggest that a formal evaluation is required by a clinician qualified to conduct psychological assessments and to use the PCL-R or PCL: SV. In other cases, the assessor may decide that interactions with the individual require an unusual degree of caution, suspicion, or even cynicism, as well as extra efforts to cross-check and corroborate information obtained from interviews and other sources.

The P-SCAN consists of a list of items depicting relatively specific behaviors and low-level inferences about an individual. They are rated on the basis of the information the investigator has about the individual at the time of the assessment. In some cases, this sort of information will be sufficient for an investigator familiar with the literature on psychopathy to work out a course of action. The protocol is computer scored or scored online (www.mhs.com), and results in a report concerning hypotheses about the overall level of psychopathy and about the four domains of psychopathy. The Appendix contains brief descriptions of the traits and behaviors reflected in Total and Domain P-SCAN scores. Also included are examples of the 30 items that make up each domain. Stein (2007) has provided an example of how the P-SCAN might work in the investigation of terrorists.

Subtypes of Criminal Psychopathy

The 4-factor structure of psychopathy, as measured by the PCL-R and the P-SCAN, is of more than academic interest, for it allows clinicians and other users to identify several "variations on a theme." For example, Hervé (2007) used the four factors or domains to construct profiles for offenders with high (>27) PCL-R scores. When subjected to cluster analysis, four types of profile emerged. The first three are labeled as follows: *Classic* (high scores on all four factors), *Manipulative* (high score on Interpersonal and Affective, and low scores on Lifestyle and Antisocial dimensions), and *Macho* or *Explosive* (high score on Affective, Lifestyle, Antisocial, and low scores on Interpersonal dimensions). The most dramatic finding is that each of these "subtypes" is high on the Affective dimension. That is, all lack empathy, have shallow emotions, and have little concern for the welfare of others. Their differences lie in their relative scores on the other three dimensions. Thus, the *Classic Psychopath* is high on all dimensions, a sort of all-rounder. The *Manipulative Psychopath* is more likely to smooth-talk his way into and out of situations than to engage in overt aggression and violence, whereas the *Macho* or *Explosive Psychopath* is more prone to direct aggression than to manipulation.

These three criminal subtypes share a very high score on the Affective dimension. A fourth group emerged from these analyses of offenders with high PCL-R total scores. It differed from the other groups primarily in its low score on the Affective dimension. The terms "pseudo-psychopathic" or perhaps "sociopathic" come to mind. Unlike the other groups, this group appeared to engage in antisocial and criminal behavior in spite of having some capacity for empathy, remorse, and concern for others. Presumably, they are primarily products of their environment, individuals whose attitudes, values, and behaviors are in tune with those of a particular subgroup but at odds with those of the larger society in which they live.

We might speculate that it is the classic or manipulative criminal psychopaths who are most likely to stalk public figures.

"Community" Psychopathy

Many psychopathic individuals manage to function in the community without being convicted of a criminal offense (Babiak & Hare, 2006; Hall & Benning, 2006; Hare, 1998). Some investigators have referred to such individuals as "successful psychopaths." However, it seems incongruous to refer to psychopaths as successful merely because they manage to avoid prison, perhaps through luck, loopholes in the law, machination and manipulation, the intervention of tolerant and supportive family members, and so forth. Although they may typically "get away with it," many of these individuals presumably engage in a variety of parasitic, predatory, and socially deviant activities—flagrant traffic violations, sexual misconduct, spousal and child abuse, bullying, dishonest business practices, and other behaviors that result in serious psychological, physical, and financial harm to others, including family and friends (Paulhus & Williams, 2002). For many of these individuals success often is ephemeral and defined without recognition of the negative impact on others. We might refer to them as *community psychopaths*, individuals with many of the attributes of psychopathy but without overt criminal acts. They would generally "fly under the radar screen," duping friends, family, and the community along the way. As such, they would pose an interesting problem for law enforcement and the investigation of stalking behavior, for it often would be difficult to "get a handle" on them.

It is possible that research will uncover subtypes of community psychopathy similar to those obtained with offenders. Meanwhile, the experiences of the first two authors suggest that many of the individuals with whom they deal appear to exhibit the interpersonal, affective, and lifestyle features of psychopathy, without evidence of its antisocial features. Such individuals seem like *chameleons* (Meloy, 2001), easily able to adapt to new situations and to present a different and convincing persona to different groups.

Psychopathy and Violent Crime-Scene Classification

The clinical and empirical literature on psychopathy is extensive (e.g., see Hare, 2003, and edited volumes by Gacono, 2000; Hervé & Yuille, 2006/2007; Patrick, 2006) and provides a useful framework for the interpretation of criminal behavior, particularly with respect to crime scene analysis and interviewing (Logan & Hare, in press; O'Toole, 2007). The literature suggests several summary statements relevant to psychopathy, stalking behavior, and the propensity for violence:

- Psychopathy is strongly associated with persistent and serious violent offending (Hare, 2003; Hemphill, 2007; Porter & Porter, 2007).
- The inhibitory mechanisms (e.g., empathy, fear of punishment) that keep most individuals from engaging in threats, intimidation, and violence are relatively weak in psychopaths (Hare, 2003).
- Psychopathic violence frequently is instrumental, premeditated, and cold blooded (e.g., an unprovoked assault or homicide, settling a score). Although psychopaths also engage in reactive violence (e.g., in self-defense or in the face of extreme provocation) their actions lack the intense affective quality that accompanies the reactive violence of other individuals (Cornell et al., 1996; Meloy, 2000; Porter & Woodworth, 2006; Woodworth & Porter, 2002). In the classification scheme described by Meloy (1988, 2000, pp. 87–98, 2006), the violence of the psychopath is more likely to be predatory than affective. In this scheme, *predatory* violence is characterized by, among other things, a lack of emotion or autonomic arousal, planned or purposeful actions, absence of an imminent threat, and heightened and focused awareness. *Affective* violence, on the other hand, involves intense emotional and autonomic arousal, reactive and immediate violence to a perceived threat, and heightened diffuse awareness.
- Acts of violence may be both instrumental and reactive at the same time, but psychopathic violence is more likely to involve instrumental elements than is the violence of other individuals (Cornell et al., 1996; Woodworth & Porter, 2002).
- Psychopathic offenders are likely to downplay the instrumentality of their violence, blaming the victim for instigating the incident (Porter & Woodworth, in press).
- Most offenders who engage in reactive violence have a preexisting relationship with the victim, whereas the victims of psychopaths are as likely to be strangers as acquaintances (Williamson, Hare, & Wong, 1987).
- Clinical, empirical, and anecdotal research has identified a connection between sadism, sexual sadism, and psychopathy, particularly in serial killers (Dietz, Hazelwood, & Warren, 1990; Hare, Cooke, & Hart, 1999; Stone, 2001).

- Psychopathic offenders are more likely to commit a *sexually* motivated homicide and to engage in significantly more gratuitous or excessive violence, including sadistic violence, than are nonpsychopathic offenders (Porter, Woodworth, Earle, Drugge, & Boer, 2003).
- Sadistic violence in psychopaths appears to be related to thrill seeking in the absence of empathy and other inhibitory mechanisms, whereas in other offenders, sadistic violence may be more related to anger and rage (Woodworth & Porter, 2002).
- Sex offenders whose victims includes both children and adults are likely to be psychopaths, dangerous, and at high risk for sexual reoffending (Porter et al., 2000; Rice & Harris, 1997).
- The combination of psychopathy and deviant sexual arousal is predictive of violent offending (Gretton, McBride, O'Shaughnessy, Kumka, & Hare, 2001; Harris, Rice, Quinsey, Lalumière, & Boer, 2003).
- Male psychopaths are more geographically mobile than are non-psychopaths (Hunter, Hemphill, Anderson, & Hare, 2003).
- Research on unlawful confinements (kidnappings) has found a high proportion of these offenders are psychopaths, and that most of these cases involved instrumental violence (Hervé, Mitchell, Cooper, Spidel, & Hare, 2004).
- Psychopathic offenders who act impulsively may do so because they make a conscious decision to act out after only a very quick consideration of the consequences (Woodworth & Porter, 2002).

Given the distinctive nature of psychopathic criminal behavior and the link between psychopathy and instrumental violence (and more specifically, predatory violence), we suggest that predation and instrumental violence should be considered strong indicators of psychopathic traits in offenders who engage in public figure stalking, threats, and attacks. Fein and Vossekuil's (1999) study supports this linkage. Although Fein and Vossekuil dispelled the myth that one set of descriptors fits all, they did find one consistent set of behaviors in assassins, attackers, and near-lethal approachers who choose public figure targets: nearly all of the attackers spent weeks, months, or years in planning. In their review of research on public figures threats, approaches, attacks, and assassinations in the United States, Meloy et al. (2004) concurred, "Subjects ruminate about assassination, they read about it.... They choose a target, they carefully plan, they engage in approach behavior and surveillance, they consider whether to escape, and they choose the moment and the weapon for the attack.... Attacks and assassinations of public figures are not impulsive, emotionally laden, sudden, or spontaneous acts, as the public often believes. They are acts of predatory violence: planned, purposeful, and emotionless" (p. 1088).

Additionally, threatening communications targeting public figures may contain indicators of predatory thinking, even though there is no physical crime scene (Chapter 20). Consistent findings across studies indicate that threats typically do not presage an approach or attack; however, when attacks do occur, they are often predatory in nature (Meloy et al., 2004; Chapter 1, Chapter 2). Therefore, law enforcement analyses of these cases should also include evaluations for psychopathic and/or predatory characteristics.

Crime Scene Analysis

The Federal Bureau of Investigation's (FBI) Behavioral Analysis Unit (BAU) is part of the FBI's National Center for the Analysis of Violent Crime located at the FBI Academy in Quantico, Virginia. Since the mid-1970s, the BAU, which evolved out of the Behavioral Sciences Unit and is commonly referred to as the Profiling Unit, has studied some of the most significant and bizarre crimes in the world, and the types of people who commit these crimes.

The FBI uses a unique two-part process to analyze violent crime scenes. This process, known as Criminal Investigative Analysis, involves identifying every behavioral and forensic variable at a violent crime scene, and then behaviorally interpreting these variables. Some of these variables include

- Victimology
- The victim selection process
- Method of victim access
- Offender risk level
- Offender-victim relationship
- Offender-victim verbal, physical, and sexual interaction, including threatening communications and the style and content of those communications
- The degree of control exercised by the offender
- The amount of planning involved in the crime
- The degree of criminal sophistication
- Forensic evidence recovered from the scene (Douglas, Burgess, Burgess, & Ressler, 1992; O'Toole, 2007; Ressler, Burgess, & Douglas, 1988)

Singular crime scene behaviors are not isolated, nor are they ascribed disproportional significance over clusters of crime scene behaviors. Violent crime scene behaviors must be analyzed as an aggregate—the totality of the circumstances—in order to construct a behavioral blueprint of the crime and the personality of the offender (O'Toole, 1999, 2007; Ressler et al., 1988).

Once crime scene behaviors have been inferred and identified, their meaning must be interpreted. The ability to interpret crime scene behavior is the cumulative result of education, specialized training in a wide range of disciplines, and experience in reviewing and analyzing many cases. This cumulative experience, as well as knowledge of current empirical research in multiple disciplines, provides a strong foundation for a sound and reliable interpretation of a violent crime scene. However, the most important component for crime scene assessment, underpinning all the other qualifications, is the analyst's strong investigative background. This experience is absolutely essential in order to reliably interpret a crime scene. Without real experience, the analysis becomes primarily an academic effort (O'Toole, 2007).

Importance of Victimology in Stalking Cases

Victimology is the complete study of the victim of a violent crime. The choice of victim and how and where the victim was accessed can provide a great deal of insight into the offender and his/her personality. Victimology involves an in-depth review and assessment of every aspect of victims and their lives— both past and present. It extends far beyond traditional demographic information, such as height, weight, eye color, and names of friends and associates. Victimology includes determining such things as the victim's risk level at the time the crime occurred; the risk level of the environment where the crime occurred; the victim's lifestyle, patterns of behaviors and habits; recent changes in his/her behavior; mental and medical conditions (both treated and untreated); physician-prescribed and over-the-counter medications and use of these drugs; the victim's personality and degree of compliance or defiance he/she will demonstrate under stressful conditions; and the victim's security practices. A complete victimology can provide the basis for developing possible motives for the crime and determining the relationship—if any— between the offender(s) and the victim. In a crime of violence, the absence of any relationship between offender and victim can provide information about the offender's personality and may be indicative of instrumental (predatory) violence.

Psychopathy and Crime Scene Analysis

Members of BAU currently use the theory and research on psychopathy, including the 4-factor model, to assist them in crime scene analysis. Certain inferences about crime scene behaviors may lead to speculations about the role of psychopathy in the crime, hypotheses that may facilitate the criminal investigation. Of course, most investigators are not qualified to conduct a formal clinical evaluation, and if they did have the necessary qualification, the information available from the crime scene would fall far short of that required for a clinical assessment. However, even a few traits and behaviors inferred from the crime scene analysis may be sufficient for the investigator to generate a working hypothesis that the perpetrator of the crime is psychopathic, or at least that psychopathic features are evident in the crime scene.

The possibility that psychopathy has played a role in the crime allows the investigator to speculate that, in addition to the few traits and behaviors inferred from the crime scene, the perpetrator has *additional* traits and behaviors typically associated with psychopathy (see Appendix). False positives concerning the potential presence of psychopathy during stalking or threat investigations are unlikely to adversely affect the outcome of investigations. However, failure to correctly interpret signs of psychopathic traits could significantly and negatively impact the outcome of cases—even to the extent of compromising the well-being of victims.

Brown/Lake Case, Continued

Lake spent a great deal of time, effort, and personal resources in planning his crime. He could be described as "mission oriented." He had spent months watching Brown's house, recording Brown's routine, and carefully planning the kidnapping down to the smallest detail. Once he had snatched Brown, Lake put him in a coffin-like box he had already constructed. Bound with ropes, blindfolded, his mouth covered with tape, Brown was entombed in an unventilated room that, at times, reached 100°F. Brown's only sustenance was water and his only pain relief from his gunshot wound was over-the-counter medication. Although Lake later insisted that he always intended to release Brown once the ransom was paid, Brown died a few days after his abduction.

Brown's death did not deter Lake from his plan. He buried Brown in the box in a remote location and continued sending ransom notes and making phone calls over the next few months, always implying that Brown was alive and would be released if his demands were met. An emotional appeal by Brown's wife made through the press went unheeded.

In the end, Lake's own elaborate plan for authorities to deliver the ransom money defeated him. The authorities set up surveillance on him after a call he made from a pay phone. When he was arrested, incriminating evidence in his car included Brown's home address and bags in which Lake planned to stuff the extortion money. Although Lake refused to cooperate with authorities, his female companion eventually led them to Brown's body. Despite his callous treatment of Brown and Brown's family, Lake portrayed himself to the authorities as a normal person who had been driven to desperate measures because of circumstances beyond his control. However, he appeared to revel in the subsequent media attention. Lake was convicted of extortion, kidnapping, and murder.

Analysis

The brief analysis of Lake's criminal behavior includes crime scene behaviors initially gleaned directly from the abduction crime scene, and crime scene and offender behaviors identified following Lake's arrest, when more detailed information became available to investigators. We do not make a formal clinical diagnosis of Lake. Instead, specific crime scene and offender behaviors consistent with psychopathy are identified and discussed in terms of how these behaviors are interpreted as possible manifestations of traits and characteristics reflected in the 4-factor model of psychopathy (see preceding text and Appendix).

We suggest that there are four aspects of the Brown stalking and abduction case, the presence of any of which could have alerted the investigators to the possibility that psychopathy was relevant to the case:

Planning and preparation

Evidence from the crime indicated that the offender (subsequently identified as Anthony Lake) had surveilled Brown over a period of time in order to obtain information about his habits, lifestyle, and neighborhood in order to effect the abduction.

Predatory violence

There was no indication from the victimology that Lake's abduction of Brown was reactive violence, that is, an immediate reaction to some real or perceived threat he might have felt. Instead, the primary mode of violence in this crime appeared to be thoughtful, premeditated, goal directed, and therefore instrumental or predatory. Lake's goal was to kidnap Brown because he was a high-value target and to extort his family and company for money. However, during the abduction Brown was shot in the arm during a struggle, a violent "sub-act" by Lake that appeared to have elements of both reactive and instrumental violence.

Abduction

Brown was kidnapped, suggesting that there was a good chance that Brown's kidnapper was psychopathic.

Selection of high-value, high-risk target

The selection of Brown as a high-value target offered the possibility of large financial payoff and media attention. It also was high risk, fraught with inherent difficulties in execution of the abduction, maintenance of the victim, and high risk of detection.

Indications of the presence of these four aspects are embedded in the following descriptions of the case. The facet of psychopathy considered most relevant to the described behaviors is listed at the end of each paragraph.

The abduction of Brown occurred in daylight in front of the victim's residence, located in an exclusive neighborhood where the violent crime rate was very low. Lake could not have controlled for all possible variables and scenarios that might have occurred to interrupt his plan that morning, despite his prior surveillances. By selecting the place and time of the abduction, he exposed himself to considerable risk of identification and apprehension: *Lifestyle*.

Before the abduction that morning, Lake had the time to reevaluate his decision and the consequences of such an act. Even if he did momentarily reconsider the consequences of committing this crime, he decided to proceed with his plan. Subsequent information obtained after Lake's arrest indicated that he planned the kidnapping for other mornings but, for a variety of reasons, he chose not to go through with it on those occasions. The abduction itself appeared to be of high risk and to have impulsive aspects; the latter was later supported by the fact that Brown was shot during the course of the initial struggle, presumably because Lake had not carefully worked out the details of the abduction: *Lifestyle*.

Kidnapping a high-value target (i.e., people, places, or objects associated with extensive wealth or value, extensive media coverage, and/or prominence in corporate, government, or entertainment industries) was of high risk for Lake despite the anticipated financial gains. This act was certain to trigger a quick and visible response from the media and the law enforcement community, including the FBI. Being the focus of this type of attention was probably thrilling to Lake. At the same time, both the law enforcement and media attention and the concomitant notoriety he received for such a singular type of crime increased. Targeting a lesser known individual would not have generated this type of response and, as a result, it probably would have been less exciting for him: *Interpersonal*.

Lake's plans to extort millions of dollars and move out of the country undetected were not realistic. For weeks he played a cat and mouse game with numerous law enforcement personnel who had unlimited resources and, more importantly, significant experience in working these cases. By inserting himself into the case and continuing the extortion, rather than abandoning the plan and leaving the area, Lake increased his chances of ultimately being caught: *Lifestyle*.

Lake continued to submit directives to law enforcement and the victim's family, telling them what to do and when they should do it. He attempted to control everything that was taking place in the case—but from a distance—like a puppet master. The extortion notes contained language that was controlling and devoid of emotion. Lake appeared to take particular pleasure in his ability to control the FBI: *Interpersonal*.

During this investigation, the victim's wife made several emotional appeals through the media for her husband's safe release. Despite these appeals and Brown's death just days after his abduction, Lake continued the extortion for weeks. However, the tone and content of his demands changed subtly after Brown's death. He no longer provided current information, such as having Brown audiotape the headlines of the daily paper, which would serve as a proof of life. Nonetheless, Lake continued his demands for money using the dead Sam Brown as a pawn. In his demands, Lake continued to say he would safely release Brown once the money was paid. This callous and deceptive behavior showed little, if any, regard for the victim, the impact this crime was having on the victim's family, or Brown's community, which was following the case closely: *Affective*.

Brown was entombed for several days in a wooden, coffin-like box left in a storage area where temperatures were estimated to exceed 100°F. He lay in his own waste, tied inside the box, and was given little, if any, sustenance and no treatment for his gun shot injury other than over-the-counter medication. News reports mentioned that Brown was a heart patient and that he relied on regular prescription medication, which he did not have; yet his kidnapper made no effort to obtain this medication. Brown's treatment was indicative of a significant lack of empathy for the victim and the physical and emotional pain he experienced: *Affective*.

Once Lake realized the impact of the abduction on Brown's family and the community, he had several choices he could have made to minimize the damage and accept the responsibility for what occurred up to that point. He could have discontinued the extortion and released the victim. He could have made an anonymous call to advise authorities where Brown was being held or where the body disposal site was located after Brown had died. Brown died only days after his abduction as a result of Lake's mistreatment and neglect. Nonetheless, Lake continued for weeks with his extortion plan, implying to both the victim's family and his employer that the victim was still alive and would be released safely if his demands were met: *Affective*.

Lake could have contacted an attorney to negotiate his surrender to authorities. He could have become a fugitive by leaving the country. Yet, he chose not to take any responsibility for his actions and to continue the crime until his arrest. Additionally, Lake chose to dispose of Brown's body in a remote location. By doing this, he prevented the body from being discovered and identified for a period of time, enabling him to continue the extortion using the lie that Brown was still alive. In addition, this manner of body disposal would result in the loss of critical forensic evidence that might incriminate Lake. This behavior suggests that Lake was not concerned about the Brown family having a proper burial for their husband and father, nor was he concerned about ending this sadistic crime. Rather, he was concerned about himself and the perpetuation of the extortion in order to get the money: *Affective*.

This is not a single offense that took place at a single point in time. This crime involved stalking, abduction, assault, murder (special circumstances), and extortion—crimes that occurred over an extended period of time. Lake demonstrated an ability to manage and sustain complex-layered criminal behaviors over a period of weeks. This offender behavior is significant and could be indicative of any or all of several factors: planning, prior criminal experience, and criminal versatility. At the very least, however, these sustained, layered, and complex-criminal behaviors suggest an offender who is adaptable and criminally versatile. His behavior indicated a clear disregard for the rules of society and the rights of others: *Antisocial*.

Finally, the manner in which he was caught suggests that he had an unrealistically high opinion of his abilities to outwit the police (*Interpersonal*) and that he had not planned the final part of the plot very well (*Lifestyle*).

Comments on the Brown/Lake Case

Although the analyses of Lake's behavior were based on the case as a whole, there was enough crime scene information to speculate that he had several psychopathic features, and to suggest investigative strategies. For example, it is unlikely that such an offender would respond to emotional appeals made by Brown's family for his safe release. Appeals that recognize and concede that the offender is in control and that meeting his demands is a priority for law enforcement will likely be more fruitful. Additionally, direct or implied challenges or offensive remarks could result in an escalation of the crime. A psychopathic offender cannot be relied on to follow through on any agreement he might make with law enforcement. He likely will not emotionally bond with the victim (Meloy, 1988, 2000, 2001), even over a period of time, and therefore the possibility of harm to the victim will not diminish with time. This offender is mission oriented, and it is not likely that he will abandon his crime, at least in the short run. Any suggestion by him regarding additional future acts he is prepared to take in order to continue the crime should be taken seriously.

Once Lake was apprehended, there was additional information available to support a hypothesis of psychopathy (most likely of the manipulative "sub-type"), with implications for interview strategies. The interviewers could assume that he would attempt to manipulate and control the interview, with a demeanor of arrogance and superiority. This would antagonize some interviewers, and selection of the right interviewer is an important consideration. Open-ended questions might encourage the offender to do most of the talking. It is likely he will brag and berate the interviewer and the competence of the police investigation. However, his arrogance and sense of superiority may compel him to inadvertently provide information helpful to the investigation. Comments or remarks about the fate of the victim or the impact of his death on the family likely would not be productive. The focus should be on complimenting the offender and his superior abilities to manipulate law enforcement, particularly the FBI, for such a long period of time, and on devising strategies that appear to minimize the consequences of his actions.

Jones/Piaget Case

Adrian Piaget had been involved in a variety of Internet-related, get-rich-quick schemes before deciding to extort money from Thomas Jones, a successful, high profile, and wealthy businessman. After researching Jones and his family on the Internet, Piaget sent a letter to Jones, claiming to be an experienced assassin with prior military experience. He threatened to kill Jones if Jones did not send him six million dollars. Piaget directed Jones to respond via message postings on a personals bulletin board on a computer service. When Jones did not reply, Piaget sent a second threat. When investigators were notified, they initially had little to work with other than the extortion letters. After they became involved, they decided to answer for Jones, with the hope that they could trace the origin of the internet communications. Pleased that Jones appeared to be willing to pay the extortion money, Piaget sent two subsequent communications. He also obtained a gun and a passport, and opened bank accounts, which gave him the ability to transfer money.

Piaget was arrested as he was traveling to intercept Jones, and his gun was located in the search of his car. Subsequent investigation determined that his claims of having military training and being an assassin were false. Additionally, he was in his mid-20s, not 34 as he had claimed. Piaget was convicted of extortion.

Excerpts From Piaget's Letter 1 to Jones

Dear Mr. Jones:

Let me first introduce myself to you. My name is not important, but the business transaction that I propose is of the utmost importance. What I am offering you is simple: Your life for six million even. At this point, you are probably wondering who the hell this is and where I may get off making you this offer. Let me tell you a little bit about myself.

I am a thirty-four year old ex-Army Ranger. My chosen profession now can only be accurately described as what it really is, and that is an assassin. I have been contracted for various hits by many private and professional sources, including our very own government as well as the Chicago Mafia. If it makes any difference, I have not enjoyed my work. But hey, ninety five percent of the working people in America are not satisfied with their current employment. I can also tell you that I have a hundred percent record on contract kills. This is good news for my employers but not of course, for my marks.

Now that I have your attention I will explain what all of this has to do with you. I want out of business. As I stated before, I do not enjoy my work. However, like a prostitute, the money is there, so it is very difficult to just walk away. This is where you come in. You see, I believe that the dozens of people who met an untimely death at my hands would have likely come up with the same (or greater) amount of money contracted, just to live.

It is with that belief that I decided to hire myself to contract someone who would be willing to pay that contracted amount, NOT to be killed. I am sorry to say that you were my obvious choice as the person to take this contract on. With that said, here is what needs to take place, to have you avoid being contract number thirty-nine completed, in my resume.... Here is where you, Thomas Jones, can help me and live to enjoy your vast financial empire as well. I would like to give you some proof as to my abilities as an assassin, but the only way to do that would be to kill either you, or your wife. I think we would both prefer that never happens.... You can pay this small price and enjoy a normal life, or you can refuse, and die with the knowledge that your selfishness and stubbornness will cost the lives of you and your wife, as well as other people you never knew...

Now we must begin the process of handling the transfer of payment to the proper offshore account. Before this happens though, I need to be made aware that you are accepting my offer to close this contract out on you.

This will be accomplished by a simple personal ad [Piaget proceeded to give step-by-step directions for placing a sexually oriented ad on an internet site, which was to be signed "Your fantasy, Mindy."] I expect to see this message posted on November 5th. If I fail to see this posted there at the end of this day, I will assume that you have mistakenly chosen to rely on the authorities or in your own pitiful security. With this in mind, I will begin the steps to fulfilling my contract. You won't know when, you won't know where, but it will come. I would probably visit your wife first so that you can fully realize the folly of your ways. It is my hope that you will not make this mistake.

After Piaget sent Letter 2, the authorities decided to respond to Piaget's request as part of their efforts to identify and apprehend him. Piaget then sent a third letter.

Excerpts From Piaget's Letter 3 to Jones

I want to sincerely thank-you for taking the needed time to let me know of your acceptance of my offer. Now comes the very interesting and very dangerous part for us both.... You must admit, that this entire "cloak and dagger" situation is quite exciting. Two individuals locked in life or death negotiations, where the slightest slip-up could have fatal results. For a multi-millionaire such as yourself, this six million dollar pay-off is probably worth the change of pace, excitement you have been lacking in your life. So pay up and live to enjoy the experience. You refuse payment, and die with that knowledge.

Analysis

A formal clinical diagnosis is not made in this case. We suggest that there are three aspects of the Jones extortion case, the presence of any of which could have alerted the investigators to the possibility that psychopathy was relevant to the case:

Planning and preparation

Evidence from Piaget's letters and arrest indicate that he researched Jones over a period of time in order to obtain information about his location, net worth, lifestyle, and family.

Predatory violence

There was no indication from the victimology that Piaget was reacting to some real or perceived threat. Although no violence occurred because Piaget was arrested before he was able to get close to Jones, his crime was researched, thought out, premeditated, and goal directed, therefore the primary intended mode of potential violence in this crime appeared to be instrumental or predatory.

Selection of a high-value, high-risk target

The selection of Jones as a high-value target offered the possibility of a large financial payoff and media attention, yet such a selection was of high risk, fraught with inherent difficulties in penetrating the target security, and had huge potential legal and criminal consequences.

Indications of the presence of these three aspects are embedded in the following descriptions of the case. The facet of psychopathy that is generally most relevant to the described behaviors is listed at the end of each paragraph.

The tone of Piaget's letter was chatty, facile, at times flippant, and contained a transparent effort to impress the target by bragging about alleged accomplishments. Piaget described himself as an ex-ranger and an assassin, implying that he is so good—100% accurate—that he has even been hired by the U.S. Government. His claim to be an assassin was a callous example of impression management designed to emphasize his superiority over the victim, to portray himself as "larger than life," and to intimidate the victim. Piaget's fabricated and elaborate accounts of his profession and accomplishments were grandiose and pompous, and suggest a ready ability to lie and deceive, perhaps a characteristic part of his normal interactions with others: *Interpersonal.*

Piaget's extortion attempt was motivated by a desire to enrich himself, with no apparent concern for the anguish and fear that his threats would have on the target and his family members. He argued that Jones' "selfishness and stubbornness" would result in death for him, his wife, and others. He continued his unrealistic attempts to extort money over a period of weeks, despite getting no response from the target after his first extortion letter and despite the potential consequences of his behavior: *Affective, Lifestyle.*

As in the Brown kidnapping, Piaget selected a high-value, high-risk target to extort. The selection posed a real challenge to Piaget, given the slim chance of successfully penetrating all of the levels of security protecting Jones and his family. The details of his plan were like bad fiction or television. Piaget's final paragraph in Letter 3 suggests that he has a chronic and excessive need for novel and exciting stimulation, and for doing things that are exciting, risky, or challenging. ("Now comes the very interesting and very dangerous part for us both.... You must admit, that this entire 'cloak and dagger' situation is quite exciting. Two individuals locked in life or death negotiations, where the slightest slip-up could have fatal results. For a multi-millionaire such as yourself, this six million dollar pay-off is probably worth the change of pace, excitement you have been lacking in your life. So pay up and live to enjoy the experience. You refuse payment, and die with that knowledge.") Being able to manipulate, control, and intimidate someone of Jones's status, as well as those around him, including law enforcement, would likely add to Piaget's thrill and excitement: *Lifestyle*.

Piaget engaged in a fairly elaborate scheme to take someone else's money for his own personal gain. This suggests that he is someone who feels comfortable in parasitically using other people to support him. His behavior put others at risk and clearly was inconsistent with the rules and norms of society: *Lifestyle, Antisocial*.

Comments on the Jones/Piaget Case

This is a less complex stalking case than the Brown/Lake case. However, of the four indicators that suggest further examination for psychopathy (abduction, planning and preparation, predatory violence, and a high-value, high-risk target), all but abduction were present. Piaget's crime also suggested the presence of interpersonal and affective traits and behaviors consistent with the manipulative subtype of psychopathy. In general, he seemed more grandiose and manipulative, and less affectively cold, than did Lake. Although he seemed to be more of a talker than a doer, he was prepared to commit a violent act if his demands were not met. In fact, he had acquired a gun and was en route to the victim when law enforcement intervened, suggesting that he was prepared to intimidate or even kill Jones.

Piaget's behavior at the crime scene and its putative association with some of the features of psychopathy have implications for investigative strategies. Challenges or insults to the offender through the media or other forms of communication could escalate the situation. This offender seemed to be a risk-taker and to enjoy the "cloak and dagger" nature of this crime. Investigators needed to be mindful of the possibility that he would engage in further dangerous and challenging behaviors, such as an attempt to make personal contact with the victim. Such behavior would certainly increase the level of threat he posed to the victim and his family.

Piaget's personality may be disarming to the interviewer. If the impressions gained from his letters are borne out during interviews, he will present as grandiose, perhaps even charming, and would attempt to control the interview and the interviewer. He might also be able to respond effectively and persuasively to questions by minimizing his intent and motivation for this crime. During the interview, the focus should be on giving this offender the opportunity to talk and brag about his abilities to design and execute the crime. Emotional themes regarding the impact of the crime on the victim or the victim's family will likely be less effective. Open-ended questions likely would encourage the offender to do most of the talking. He may brag about his abilities and describe the police work as incompetent. However, his arrogance and sense of superiority inadvertently may compel him to provide information helpful to the investigation.

Conclusions

Psychopathy is a personality disorder defined by a cluster of interpersonal, affective, lifestyle, and antisocial traits and behaviors that poses a serious problem for society. The behavioral repertoire of psychopathic individuals includes charm, manipulation, intimidation, and violence, each a tool to be used as the occasion demands. The result is a callous disregard for the rights of others and a high risk for a variety of predatory and aggressive behaviors. Clearly, these characteristics have strong implications for the strategies used by law enforcement and security professionals when they are forced to deal with stalking, threats, and attacks directed at public figures.

The high profile status of the victim alone can grab media headlines and present law enforcement investigators and security consultants with unique challenges that increase risks for both the victim and the offender. Professionals involved in assessing the potential of violence toward public figures should at least consider the possibility that the offender is psychopathic, and the implications that this may have for their investigations. Unfortunately, the initial phases of an investigation or security situation typically offers limited information, and the identity of the offender may not be known. Nonetheless, it is from limited, piece-meal information that investigators and security experts typically begin to put together a strategy. The consequences of their decisions may involve injury or even death and may require extensive personnel resources and large expenditures of money; therefore it is critical that assessments and predictions be as accurate as possible (Chapters 15, 16, 17, 19, 20). Not only can assessing for psychopathic traits assist professionals in making better decisions for the safety of the victim and the public, but this can also facilitate their conducting more successful interviews and doing more accurate risk assessment for violence and evaluations for the potential for premise liability issues.

Overlooking psychopathic indicators could lead to underestimating the potential of violence. Emotional appeals will likely be wasted on the offender because of his lack of empathy. In an abduction, the offender and victim are not likely to *mutually* bond, as, for example, with the so-called "Stockholm Syndrome"—although victims may "bond" with a psychopathic offender. Instead, the victim will continue to be an object to the offender—potentially, a disposable means to an end. Because of his need for thrill seeking, this type of offender will take greater risks, and the threats he makes should be taken seriously. If the offender demonstrates a great need to control and is committed to the crime even when it appears to be unraveling, he is likely to remain mission oriented. He may not abandon his plan but instead may see it through to a finale, which may involve escalating violence or even the abduction of more victims. The result could endanger the welfare of the victim and possibly compromise successful resolution and prosecution of the case. It can even affect the length of the sentence given the offender. If the victim is an executive in a company, as was Sam Brown, the results of overlooking psychopathic traits could have a chilling affect on the reputation and financial stability of a company.

We recognize that most crime scenes that involve stalking, threats, or attacks on public figures can suggest *some* traits of psychopathy, which, in isolation, may not be significant or even serve to mislead the investigator. However, the inferred presence of a cluster of traits and behaviors consistent with psychopathy should impel investigators and security professionals to consider the implications for planning their investigative and security strategies. Careful use of the P-SCAN may facilitate this work.

References

Acheson, S. K. (2005). Review of the Hare Psychopathy Checklist—Revised 2nd edition. In R. A. Spies, & B. S. Plake (Eds.), *The sixteenth mental measurements yearbook* (pp. 429–431). Lincoln, NE: Buros Institute of Mental Measurements.

American Psychiatric Association. (1994). *Diagnostic and statistical manual of mental disorders* (4th ed.). Washington, DC: Author.

American Psychiatric Association. (2000). *Diagnostic and statistical manual of mental disorders* (4th ed., text revision). Washington, DC: Author.

Archer, R. P., Buffingtom-Vollum, J. K., Stredny, R. V., & Handel, R. W. (2006). A survey of psychological test use patterns among forensic psychologists. *Journal of Personality Assessment, 87*, 84–94.

Babiak, P., & Hare, R. D. (2006). *Snakes in suits: When psychopaths go to work.* New York: Harper/Collins.

Berman, M. E., Fallon, A. E., & Cocarro, E. F. (1998). The relationship between personality psychopathology and aggressive behavior in research volunteers. *Journal of Abnormal Psychology, 107*, 651–658.

Bolt, D. M., Hare, R. D., & Neumann, C. S. (in press). Score metric equivalence of the PCL-R across North American and UK criminal offenders. *Assessment.*

Bolt, D., Hare, R. D., Vitale, J., & Newman, J. P. (2004). Multigroup IRT analyses of the Hare Psychopathy Checklist-Revised (PCL-R). *Psychological Assessment, 16*, 155–168.

Cleckley, H. (1976). *The mask of sanity* (5th ed.). St. Louis, MO: Mosby.

Cooke, D. J., Kosson, D. S., & Michie, C. (2001). Psychopathy and ethnicity: Structural, item, and test generalizability of the Psychopathy Checklist-Revised (PCL-R) in Caucasian and African American participants. *Psychological Assessment, 13*, 531–542.

Cornell, D. G., Warren, J., Hawk, G., Stafford, E., Oram, G., & Pine, D. (1996). Psychopathy in instrumental and reactive violent offenders. *Journal of Consulting and Clinical Psychology, 64*, 783–790.

Dietz, P. E., Hazelwood, R. R., & Warren, J. L. (1990). The sexually sadistic criminal and his offenses. *Bulletin of the American Academy of Psychiatry and Law, 18*, 163–178.

Douglas, J., Burgess, A., Burgess, A., & Ressler, R. (1992). *Crime classification manual.* New York: Lexington.

Fein, R. A., & Vossekuil, B. (1999). Assassination in the United States: An operational study of recent assassins, attackers, and near-lethal approachers. *Journal of Forensic Sciences, 44,* 321–333.

Forth, A. E., Kosson, D., & Hare, R. D. (2003). *The Hare Psychopathy Checklist: Youth Version.* Toronto, ON: Multi-Health Systems (www.mhs.com).

Fulero, S. (1995). Review of the Hare Psychopathy Checklist-Revised. In J. C. Conoley, & J. C. Impara (Eds.), *Twelfth mental measurements yearbook* (pp. 453–454). Lincoln, NE: Buros Institute of Mental Measurements.

Gacono, C. B. (Ed.). (2000). *The clinical and forensic assessment of psychopathy: A practitioner's guide.* Mahwah, NJ: Lawrence Erlbaum.

Gretton, H. M., McBride, M., O'Shaughnessy, R., Kumka, G., & Hare, R. D. (2001). Psychopathy and recidivism in adolescent sex offenders. *Criminal Justice and Behavior, 28,* 427–449.

Guay, J. P., Ruscio, J., Knight, R. A., & Hare, R. D. (in press). A taxometric analysis of the latent structure of psychopathy: Evidence for dimensionality. *Journal of Abnormal Psychology.*

Guy, L. S., & Douglas, K. S. (2006). Examining the utility of the PCL: SV as a screening measure using competing factor models of psychopathy. *Psychological Assessment, 18,* 225–230.

Hall, J. R., & Benning, S. D. (2006). The "successful" psychopath: Adaptive and subclinical manifestations of psychopathy in the general population. In C. Patrick (Ed.) (pp. 459–480). *Handbook of psychopathy.* New York: Guilford.

Hare, R. D. (1991). *The Hare Psychopathy Checklist-Revised.* Toronto, ON: Multi-Health Systems (www.mhs.com).

Hare, R. D. (1996). Psychopathy: A construct whose time has come. *Criminal Justice and Behavior, 23,* 25–54.

Hare, R. D. (1998). *Without conscience: The disturbing world of the psychopath among us.* New York: Guilford.

Hare, R. D. (2003). *The Hare Psychopathy Checklist-Revised* (2nd ed.). Toronto, ON: Multi-Health Systems (www.mhs.com).

Hare, R. D. (2006). Psychopathy: A clinical and forensic overview. *Psychiatric Clinics of North America, 29,* 709–724.

Hare, R. D. (in press). Psychological instruments in the assessment of psychopathy. In R. Felthous, & H. Sass (Eds.). *International handbook on psychopathic disorders and the Law.* New York: John Wiley.

Hare, R. D., Cooke, D. J., & Hart, S. D. (1999). Psychopathy and sadistic personality disorder. In T. Millon, P. Blaney, & R. Davis (Eds.), *Oxford textbook of psychopathology* (pp. 555–584). Oxford: Oxford University Press.

Hare, R. D., & Hervé, H. F. (2002). *The Hare P-SCAN* (Research version 2). Toronto, ON: Multi-Health Systems (www.mhs.com).

Hare, R. D., & Neumann, C. S. (2005). Structural models of psychopathy. *Current Psychiatry Reports, 7,* 57–64.

Hare, R. D., & Neumann, C. S. (2006). The PCL-R assessment of psychopathy: Development, structural properties, and new directions. In C. Patrick (Ed.), *Handbook of psychopathy* (pp. 58–88). New York: Guilford.

Harris, G. T., Rice, M. E., & Camilleri, J. A. (2004). Applying a forensic actuarial instrument (the Violence Risk Appraisal Guide) to nonforensic patients. *The Journal of Interpersonal Violence, 19,* 1063–1074.

Harris, G. T., Rice, M. E., Quinsey, V. L., Lalumière, M. L., & Boer, D. (2003). A multi-site comparison of actuarial risk instruments for sex offenders. *Psychological Assessment, 15*, 413–425.

Hart, S. D., Cox, D. N., & Hare, R. D. (1995). *The Hare Psychopathy Checklist: Screening Version*. Toronto, ON: Multi-Health Systems (www.mhs.com).

Hemphill, J. F. (2007). The Hare Psychopathy Checklist and recidivism: Methodological issues and critical evaluation of empirical evidence. In H. Hervé, & J. C. Yuille (Eds.), *The psychopath: Theory, research, and practice* (pp. 141–170). Mahwah, NJ: Lawrence Erlbaum.

Hervé, H. (2007). Psychopathic subtypes: Historical and contemporary perspectives. In H. Hervé, & J. C. Yuille (Eds.), *The psychopath: Theory, research, and practice* (pp. 431–460). Mahwah, NJ: Lawrence Erlbaum.

Hervé, H. F., Mitchell, D., Cooper, B. S., Spidel, A., & Hare, R. D. (2004). Psychopath and unlawful confinement: An examination of perpetrator and event characteristics. *Canadian Journal of Behavioural Science, 36*, 127–135.

Hervé, H., & Yuille, J. C. (Eds.) (2006/2007). *The psychopath: Theory, research, and practice*. Mahwah, NJ: Lawrence Erlbaum.

Hunter, S. M., Hemphill, J. F., Anderson, G., & Hare, R. D. (2003). *Psychopathy and geographic mobility*. Paper presented at the Annual Conference of the Western Society of Criminology, Vancouver, BC, February 20–23, 2003.

Lally, S. J. (2003). What tests are acceptable for use in forensic evaluations? A survey of experts. *Professional Psychology: Research and Practice, 34*, 491–498.

Logan, M., & Hare, R. D. (in press). Criminal psychopathy: An introduction for police. In M. St-Yves, & M. Tanguay (Eds.), *Psychology of Criminal Investigation*. Cowansville, QC: Editionsyvonblais.

Meloy, J. R. (1988). *The psychopathic mind: Origins, dynamics, and treatment*. Northvale, NJ: Aronson.

Meloy, J. R. (2000). *Violence risk and threat assessment*. San Diego, CA: Specialized Training Services.

Meloy, J. R., ed. (2001). *The mark of cain: Psychoanaytic insight and the psychopath*. Hillsdale, NJ: The Analytic Press.

Meloy, J. R. (2002). The "polymorphously perverse" psychopath: Understanding a strong empirical relationship. *Bulletin of the Menninger Clinic, 66*, 273–290.

Meloy, J. R. (2006). The empirical basis and forensic application of affective and predatory violence. *Australian and New Zealand Journal of Psychiatry*. 40, 539–547.

Meloy, J. R., James, D. V., Farnham, F. R., Mullen, P. E., Pathé, M., Darnley, B., et al. (2004). A research review of public figure threats, approaches, attacks, and assassinations in the United States. *Journal of Forensic Sciences, 49*, 1086–1093.

Meloy, J. R., & Meloy, M. J. (2003). Autonomic arousal in the presence of psychopathy: A survey of mental health and criminal justice professionals. *Journal of Threat Assessment, 2*, 21–34.

Monahan, J. (2006). Comments on cover jacket. In C. J. Patrick (Ed.) *Handbook of psychopathy*. New York: Guilford.

Monahan, J., Steadman, H. J., Silver, E., Appelbaum, P. S., Robins, P. C., Mulvey, E. P., et al. (2001). *Rethinking risk assessment: The McArthur study of mental disorder and violence*. New York: Oxford University Press.

Neumann, C. S., Kosson, D. S., Forth, A. E., & Hare, R. D. (2006). Factor structure of the Hare Psychopathy Checklist: Youth Version in incarcerated adolescents. *Psychological Assessment, 18*, 142–154.

Neumann, C. S., Hare, R. D., & Newman, J. P. (in press). The superordinate nature of psychopathy. *Journal of Personality Disorders.*

Ogloff, J. R. P. (2006). Psychopathy/antisocial personality disorder continuum. *Australian and New Zealand Journal of Psychiatry, 40,* 519–528.

O'Toole, M. E. (1999). Criminal profiling: The FBI uses criminal investigative analysis to solve crimes. *Corrections Magazine, 61,* 44–46.

O'Toole, M. E. (2007). Psychopathy as a behavior classification system for violent and serial crime scenes. In H. Hervé, & J. Yuille (Eds.), *The psychopath: Theory, research, and practice* (pp. 301–326). Mahwah, NJ: Lawrence Erlbaum and Associates.

Patrick, C. J. (Ed.). (2006). *Handbook of psychopathy.* New York: Guilford.

Paulhus, D. L., & Williams, K. M. (2002). The Dark Triad of personality: Narcissism, Machiavellianism, and psychopathy. *Journal of Research in Personality, 36,* 556–563.

Perlin, M. L. (2000). *The hidden prejudice: Mental disability on trial.* Washington, DC: American Psychological Association.

Porter, S., Fairweather, D., Drugge, J., Hervé, H., Birt, A., & Boer, D. P. (2000). Profiles of psychopathy in incarcerated sexual offenders. *Criminal Justice and Behavior, 27,* 216–233.

Porter, S., & Porter, S. (2007). Psychopathy and violent crime. In H. Hervé, & J. C. Yuille (Eds.), *The psychopath: Theory, research, and practice* (pp. 287–300). Mahwah, NJ: Lawrence Erlbaum.

Porter, S., & Woodworth, M. (2006). Psychopathy and aggression. In C. J. Patrick (Ed.), *Handbook of psychopathy* (pp. 481–494). New York: Guilford.

Porter, S., & Woodworth, M. (in press). "I'm sorry I did it...but he started it": A comparison of the official and self-reported homicide descriptions of psychopaths and non-psychopaths. *Law and Human Behavior.*

Porter, S., Woodworth, M., Earle, J., Drugge, J., & Boer, D. (2003). Characteristics of sexual homicides committed by psychopathic and nonpsychopathic offenders. *Law and Human Behavior, 27,* 459–470.

Reavis, J. A., Allen, E., & Meloy, J. R. (in press). Psychopathy in a Mixed Gender Sample of Adult Stalkers. *Journal of Forensic Sciences.*

Ressler, R. K., Burgess, A., & Douglas, J. (1988). *Sexual homicide: Patterns and motives.* Lexington, MA: The Free Press.

Rice, M. E., & Harris, G. T. (1992). A comparison of criminal recidivism among schizophrenic and nonschizophrenic offenders. *International Journal of Law and Psychiatry, 15,* 397–408.

Rice, M. E., & Harris, G. T. (1997). Cross-validation and extension of the Violence Risk Appraisal Guide for child molesters and rapists. *Law and Human Behavior, 21,* 231–241.

Rogers, R., Salekin, R. T., Sewell, K. W., & Cruise, K. R. (2000). Prototypical analysis of antisocial personality disorder: A study of inmate samples. *Criminal Justice and Behavior, 27,* 234–255.

Silver, E., Mulvey, E. P., & Monahan, J. (1999). Assessing violence risk among discharged psychiatric patients: Toward an ecological approach. *Law and Human Behavior, 23,* 237–255.

Skeem, J. L., Edens, J. F., Camp, J., & Colwell, L. H. (2004). Are there ethnic differences in levels of psychopathy? A meta-analysis. *Law and Human Behavior, 28,* 505–527.

Steadman, H. J., Silver, E., Monahan, J., Appelbaum, P. S., Robbins, P. M., Mulvey, E. P., et al. (1999). A classification tree approach to the development of actuarial violence risk assessment tools. *Law and Human Behavior, 24,* 83–100.

Stefan, S. (2001). *Unequal rights: Discrimination against people with mental disability and the Americans with Disabilities Act.* Washington, DC: American Psychological Association.

Stein, S. J. (2007). *Religious terrorism: What we don't know can kill us.* Paper presented at the Canada-NATO and Global Terrorism Winter Conference, The Atlantic Council of Canada, Toronto, Canada, January 24, 2007.

Stone, M. H. (2001). Serial sexual homicide: Biological, psychological, and sociological aspects. *Journal of Personality Disorders, 15,* 1–18

Tengström, A., Grann, M., Långström, N., & Kullgren, G. (2000). Psychopathy (PCL-R) as a predictor of violent recidivism among criminal offenders with schizophrenia. *Law and Human Behavior, 24,* 45–58.

Tengström, A., Hodgins, S., Grann, M., Långström, N., & Kullgren, G. (2004). Schizophrenia and criminal offending: The role of psychopathy and substance use disorders. *Criminal Justice and Behavior, 31,* 367–391.

Tengström, A., Hodgins, S., Müller-Isberner, R., Jöckel, D., Freese, R., & Özokyay, K. (2006). Predicting violent and antisocial behavior in hospital using the HCR-20: The effect of diagnoses on predictive accuracy. *International Journal of Forensic Mental Health, 5,* 39–53.

Viding, E., Blair, R. J. R., Moffitt, T. E., & Plomin, R. (2005). Evidence for substantial genetic risk for psychopathy in 7-year-olds. *Journal of Child Psychology and Psychiatry, 46,* 592–597.

Vitacco, M. J., Neumann, C. S., & Jackson, R. L. (2005). Testing a four-factor model of psychopathy and its association with ethnicity, gender, intelligence, and violence. *Journal of Consulting and Clinical Psychology, 73,* 466–476.

Waldman, I. D., & Rhee, S. H. (2006). Genetic and environmental influences on psychopathy and antisocial behavior. In C. J. Patrick (Ed.), *Handbook of psychopathy* (pp. 205–228). New York: Guilford.

Walsh, T., & Walsh, Z. (2006). The evidentiary introduction of Psychopathy Checklist-Revised assessed psychopathy in U.S. courts: Extent and appropriateness. *Law and Human Behavior, 30,* 493–507.

Warren. J. I., & South, S. C. (2006). Comparing the constructs of antisocial personality disorder and psychopathy in a sample of incarcerated women. *Behavioral Sciences and the Law, 24,* 1–20.

Widiger, T. A., Cadoret, R., Hare, R. D., Robins, L., Rutherford, M., Zanarini, M., et al. (1996). DSM-IV Antisocial Personality Disorder Field Trial. *Journal of Abnormal Psychology, 105,* 3–16.

Williamson, S. E., Hare, R. D., & Wong, S. (1987). Violence: Criminal psychopaths and their victims. *Canadian Journal of Behavioral Science, 19,* 454–462.

Woodworth, M., & Porter, S. (2002). In cold blood: Characteristics of criminal homicides as a function of psychopathy. *Journal of Abnormal Psychology, 111,* 436–445.

Appendix: The Hare P-SCAN©

The following material is based on the *Hare P-SCAN Research Version 2, User's Guide* (Hare & Hervé, 2002). We provide a brief description of the meaning of a high overall score on the P-SCAN and on its four factors or domains, as well as several examples from the list of the 30 items in each domain. Each item is scored by the investigator as 0 = Item does not apply; 1 = Item applies somewhat; 2 = Item definitely applies; U = Unavailable/ insufficient information. The protocol is analyzed either online with MHS or with a computer program produced by MHS. The resulting report provides the investigator with hypotheses about the extent to which the personality and behavior of the individual being assessed are consistent with the clinical construct of psychopathy and its domains. Also provided are descriptions of the traits and behaviors that a person with such a protocol likely would exhibit.

Investigators who wish to use the P-SCAN should contact the publisher, Multi-Health Systems (www.mhs.com).

Total Score

A high total score suggests that the individual of interest may have many or most of the features that define psychopathy. Such an individual is likely to be egocentric, callous, cold blooded, predatory, impulsive, irresponsible, dominant, deceptive, manipulative, and lacking in empathy, guilt, or genuine remorse for socially deviant and criminal acts. People of this sort do not share the attitudes, thoughts, and feelings that motivate and guide the behaviors of most people. Their main concerns are for themselves and for exerting power and control over others. They are quite capable of using intimidation and violence to attain their needs and wants, but their actions are "a matter of process," without the emotional coloring that characterizes the violent acts of others.

Interpersonal Domain

A high score on the Interpersonal domain or factor suggests that the individual takes a dominant, controlling, and aggressive stance during interactions with others. He or she is likely to be grandiose, egocentric, manipulative, deceptive, conning, and perhaps charming in a superficial way. Such an individual views himself or herself as the center of the universe, with a well-established sense of entitlement. This individual may be a smooth-talking con artist or a controlling, belligerent, or condescending adversary given to playing "head games." In any case, what is said should not be taken at face value without considerable corroborating evidence. Indeed, it is likely that an individual who scores high on this factor is deceptive and manipulative and has conned and deceived many people, with the result that opinions and accounts of the individual may vary greatly from one another (e.g., some highly positive and others not).

Example items

- Plays "head" games
- Dominates/controls interactions with others

- Uses threats and fear as tools for control
- Easily changes stories when challenged
- Has a strong sense of entitlement

Affective Domain

A high score on the Affective domain suggests that the individual's emotional life is shallow and relatively barren of normal deep-level feelings, and that there is little or no concern for the feelings and welfare of others, except in an abstract, intellectual sense. Emotions tend to be primitive and short lived ("proto-emotions," such as frustration and anger) and typically occur in response to specific events, such as an argument, a challenge, or defiance by others. There is little capacity for, or convincing expressions of, empathy, guilt, or remorse. The individual's social and emotional connections with others are weak and self serving. A high score suggests that the individual is relatively free from the subjective distress, worry, and apprehensions experienced by others. In short, he or she neither appreciates nor cares about what others think or feel.

Example items

- No concern for impact of actions on others
- Discusses emotions in concrete terms (e.g., love is sex)
- Displays of emotion do not seem genuine (i.e., like play-acting)
- Seems unusually cool under pressure
- Easily turns to violence to achieve goals

Lifestyle Domain

A high score on the Lifestyle factor suggests that the individual leads an impulsive, nomadic lifestyle with a tendency to live for the moment. The individual is likely to be relatively unconcerned about what has happened or might happen, probably gets bored easily, is unlikely to remain in relationships or jobs for long, and is continually searching for new experiences and sensations. People, ideas, and causes are important only as long as they can provide the individual with some benefit, and then are casually and quickly abandoned when they are no longer needed. Social and legal norms and expectations are irrelevant to the individual, and are readily violated.

Example items

- Has far-fetched plans and schemes
- Lives by own rules (i.e., no sense of duty or responsibility)
- Likes to do things that are exciting or risky
- Does not think things through before acting
- Frequently changes, schools, jobs, groups, friends, relationships

Antisocial Domain

A high score on the Antisocial facet suggests that the individual has many or most of the antisocial features of psychopathy, particularly if the score is at the upper end of the range. Individuals of this sort tend to have a varied and persistent antisocial lifestyle, with frequent and serious violations of social and legal expectations and standards from an early age. They may be easily offended, short tempered, and aggressive, and prone to engage in a wide variety of antisocial and illegal activities, exhibiting considerable antisocial or criminal versatility.

Example items

- Verbal or physical aggression with little provocation
- Frequent and varied criminal behavior
- Had conduct problems at home and school as a youth
- General disregard for court-imposed conditions and restrictions
- Offends against various types/ages of victims (known, unknown; male female)

11

Two Case Studies of Corporate-Celebrity Male Victims: The Stalking of Steven Spielberg and Stephen Wynn

J. Reid Meloy and Kris Mohandie

Stalking is largely perpetrated by men against women, even if the woman happens to be a celebrity (Mohandie, Meloy, & McGowan, 2006) (Chapter 2). There are, however, some exceptions. When the particular public figure domain, such as legislators, corporate executives, judicial officials, and presidents, is mostly populated by men, the victims of threats, stalking, and attacks are, not surprisingly, mostly males. This pattern of same gender stalking reflects the fact that most violent crime is done by males to males, but is unusual when stalking is studied alone (Pathé, Mullen, & Purcell, 2000). Spitzberg (2007) has recently reported in the largest meta-analysis of stalking studies to date that 60% to 80% of victims are women.

Violence by individuals who inappropriately communicate with, approach, stalk, or breach the security of a public figure is also quite rare (Calhoun, 1998; Fixated Research Group, 2006; Meloy et al., 2004; Scalora et al., 2002). Nonetheless, rare lethally violent events yield a highly emotional and very public impact which is driven by the media. In the blinding spotlight of a star-obsessed public, the murder of a celebrity by a stalker virtually guarantees notoriety to the offender, and elevates public perceptions of risk. Mohandie et al. (2006), however, found a 74% frequency of personal violence among prior sexually intimate stalkers but only a 2% frequency of personal violence among celebrity stalkers in a large sample ($N = 1,005$) of North American stalkers. Moreover, when age is considered, a not surprising but disturbing finding is apparent: stalkers of both public figures and private individuals are typically males or females in their fourth decade of life, but when a public figure is homicidally attacked, the pursuer is often a late adolescent or young adult male. John Hinckley, Jr. was 25 when he attempted to assassinate President Ronald Reagan. Mark David Chapman was 25 when he killed John Lennon. John Bardo was 19 when he killed the actress Rebecca Schaeffer. Arthur Bremer was 22 when he crippled presidential aspirant George Wallace. Sirhan Sirhan was 24 when he assassinated Senator Robert Kennedy. Lee Harvey Oswald was 24 when he assassinated President John F. Kennedy. Mijailo Mijailovic was 25 when he stabbed to death Anna Lindh, the Swedish Foreign Minister. And James Hadfield was 29 when he attempted to assassinate King George III on May 15, 1800. Although such anecdotal data can be dangerously misconstrued by threat assessors if they assume that *only* the young are violent, the hormonally based aggressive drives of the young male may more easily metastasize fantasies of approach and acceptance into desires to kill and become famous.

With these thoughts in mind, we offer our experience and analysis of two cases of same gender stalking in which two males, both enormously successful in the entertainment business—Steven Spielberg, the film director, and Stephen Wynn, the Las Vegas casino developer—were pursued by two men considered quite dangerous. Fortunately, in both cases, the subjects were arrested before they brought harm to their intended victims. Both Spielberg and Wynn also inhabit the rarefied world of corporate celebrities, where wealth and power are superseded only by the constant need for personal security of self and family—and the paradox of being physically imprisoned by their own fame.

The Stalking of Stephen Wynn

The Offenses

The way Mr. P tells it, he suddenly woke up in a Texas prison in 1999, hit his head on the bunk bed above him, and remembered that he was the half-brother of Stephen Wynn, a well-known Las Vegas businessman and casino developer, who amassed a fortune through the acquisition, expansion, and creation of such entertainment facilities as the Golden Nugget, the Mirage, the Bellagio, and most recently, the Wynn Las Vegas. Stephen Wynn's net worth is estimated to exceed 1 billion dollars, and he is considered the central figure in the development and revitalization of Las Vegas over the past 40 years. He was recently appointed to the Board of Directors of the Kennedy Center for the Performing Arts. Mr. P believed, however, that Stephen Wynn owed him $50 million—half the amount that he had accumulated from his initial business transactions as a casino developer. In his words, "I've got enough on my shoulder already, dude, and I respect you, Steve, but I'm not going to stop or be stopped til I get my money and reach my God planned destiny."[1]

Mr. P was 46 years old when paroled from prison in January, 2000, and within 5 days, traveled to Las Vegas and appeared at both the Golden Nugget and Bellagio, identifying himself to security as Stephen Wynn's half-brother and demanding his money. Following these unsuccessful attempts to claim his fortune, he next surfaced in Vancouver, Washington, where he found a sympathetic social worker, low income housing, and government subsidies that would sustain him over the next 6 months. He was considered polite and cooperative, although quite anxious, paranoid, and obsessed with his relationship with Stephen Wynn.

The letters began arriving in September, 2000. Within them he demanded payment of the $50 million, attempted to persuade and coerce Mr. Wynn, but made no explicit threats. As is often the case, private security chose not to involve the police, and they ignored the missives for the first 3 months until they wrote to Mr. P and told him to stop it. He did not.

Over the next 3 months, Mr. P's behavior escalated. He sent his birth certificate, nail clippings, and hair clippings to prove his identity and invited DNA testing. He sent Elaine Wynn, Mr. Wynn's spouse, flowers in a vase. He sent at least 15 letters. He began to travel down the western coast of the United States, and once again, arrived in Las Vegas in February 2001. Two events precipitated police involvement: Mr. P hand delivered a letter to the home of Stephen Wynn and his family; and Mr. P threatened his life through voice mail: "I just lost my ass tonight and I'm sick, I'm dying, and I ain't gonna f...ing die alone, I'm gonna kill him with me" (voice mail to head of Wynn's security, March 31, 2001, at 0226). Mr. P was subsequently arrested in Florida 2 months later, and extradited back to Nevada to stand trial for aggravated stalking,[2] multiple counts of extortion, and dissuading a witness from testifying. Because Mr. P was a "habitual criminal," given his felony history, he faced life in prison. Mr. P pled not guilty by reason of insanity, and was committed for a period of time as incompetent to stand trial.

A decade earlier, the adolescent daughter of Stephen Wynn was kidnapped from her home. A ransom of $1.45 million was paid within hours, and his daughter was found in a parked car at McCarren International Airport, physically unharmed. The three perpetrators—a former carnival worker and two gang members—were all arrested within 2 months and convicted of extortion, money laundering, conspiracy, and use of a firearm in a crime of violence.

During the present case grand jury indictment, Stephen Wynn testified that Mr. P placed him in fear of his life or substantial injury. He went on to say, "Until Mr. Werwinski (head of security) acquainted me with this list of letters to me and the phone messages, I didn't know that he existed. I have no knowledge whatsoever of the existence of this man or any of the things that I come to understand were in those letters and voice mails. I have no known relationship or connection to this human being in my entire life" (Grand Jury testimony, p. 16).

The History

Mr. P's mother gave birth to multiple children through impregnation by multiple men—the exact number of both is unclear. Mr. P never knew his biological father, who died before his birth, although he was named after him. Virtually nothing verifiable is known of his childhood years other than he was raised in Georgia; he reports that he dropped out of school at age 10, was often truant, left home at 12, and has never had a job that lasted longer than 6 months. He was an "undesirable discharge" from the U.S. military after going AWOL, and was married once to a prostitute for a little over a year. He has no children—or perhaps several. He has been an itinerant most of his adult life, unless imprisoned, which has been more often than not. He has a 25-year history of felony arrests and convictions in six states for theft, property damage, armed robbery, burglary, aggravated assault, possession of a concealed weapon, bank robbery, federal escape, auto theft, and the current felony charges.

His drug and alcohol experience is extensive and varied. Mr. P reports use of alcohol, cocaine, marijuana, heroin, amphetamine, and hallucinogens throughout the years. His drugs of choice are alcohol and cannabis. He also tests positive for HIV and has positive serologies for hepatitis A, B, and C. He reports that these diseases were contracted through the sharing of contaminated needles, but also has a history of bisexuality and was charged with sodomy in Georgia.

Mr. P also has an extensive mental health history, including treatment for bipolar disorder, depression, and anxiety over the decade before his arrest. Although actively treated with various psychiatric medications, including antidepressants and mood stabilizers, compliance was always an issue and the drugs did not seem to make much difference in his behavior. "I'm usually in a good mood when I'm not on the run." He had previously been diagnosed with Antisocial Personality Disorder (*DSM-IV*).

The Examination

Mr. P was evaluated to determine his sanity at the time of the crimes 2 years after he was arrested. The clinical interview lasted 5 hours, and he was administered the following tests: Rorschach, MMPI-2, Paulhus Deception Scales, Psychopathy Checklist-Revised, and the Neurobehavioral Cognitive Status Exam. He had previously been tested by other doctors on several occasions to determine his intelligence, which was reliably in the low normal range (FSIQ 90).

The clinical interview to determine Mr. P's sanity at the time of the crimes focused upon his present mental state, his inferred mental state during the stalking, his understanding of the nature of his acts, and his appreciation of the wrongfulness of his acts at the time of the stalking.[3] A psychosocial history was also taken, and a careful review of his drug history and his medical conditions as potential contributory factors to his mental state at the time was done.[4] Mr. P was verbal, cooperative, engaging, somewhat distractible, had a slight pressure of speech, was mildly circumstantial, and evidenced a euthymic mood. There were no signs or symptoms of psychosis. Mr. P refused to discuss his criminal history, but gave a detailed account of his encounters with Stephen Wynn through the years, and insisted that the examiner believe his story. He clearly understood that he was asking Mr. Wynn for his share of the inheritance: "I wouldn't have asked him if I didn't deserve it." He denied threatening him in any way, but stated, "In my letters I'd play with Steve, spook him cause he'd give me a hard time. I'd try to intimidate him. I was always drunk when I wrote the letters."

Mr. P was being actively medically treated with efavirenz, lamivudine, and zidovudine for HIV, and his CD4 cell count was 800 per L. His viral load was undetectable. He was exercising regularly and stated he felt quite healthy. His only psychiatric medication was buspirone, an antianxiety agent.

The Neurobehavioral Cognitive Status Exam showed no evidence of cognitive impairment that would indicate a need for further neuropsychological testing.

The Rorschach showed no evidence of psychosis (WSum6 = 7, X–% = 12, XA% = 82, M– = 0), although it suggested low self-esteem (EgoC = 0.18, MOR = 2), affectional hunger (T = 2), a possible affective disorder (DEPI = 5), general coping deficits (CDI = 4), and aspirational failures ($W:M$ = 13:3). He evidenced a simplistic problem-solving style (Lambda = 1.13), and intellectualized (Intel Index = 8) to defend against his own affect.

The MMPI-2 indicated a valid, clinically elevated 6–4 profile, suggesting anger, distrust, sullenness, hypersensitivity to criticism, and projection of blame onto others. Notable were clinical elevations on Pa1 (T = 82), Pa2 (T = 75), and Sc5 (T = 68), suggesting overt paranoid delusions, a hardened stance as an aggrieved person, and a moderate potential for dangerous emotional outbursts, respectively (Caldwell, 1988).

The Paulhus Deception Scales indicated some propensity for self-deceptive enhancement, but no deliberate impression management.

The Psychopathy Checklist-Revised Score was 35.8, indicating that Mr. P was a primary, or severe psychopath, which would place him at the 99th percentile when compared to 5,408 North American male offenders (Hare, 2003).

The Trial

The central issue in this case was whether or not Mr. P's belief that he was the half-brother of Stephen Wynn was a delusion or an intentional statement to persuade and deceive others. If his belief was not a delusion, there would be no affirmative insanity defense. If it was a delusion, the second prong of the test would need to be considered (nature and capacity or legal wrongfulness).

After careful consideration of all data on the case, the opinion of the forensic psychologist was that Mr. P, despite a 10-year history of diagnosed mental disorders, including bipolar disorder, anxiety disorder, depression, and polysubstance dependence, was purposefully fabricating his belief that he was the half-brother of Mr. Wynn to further a criminal enterprise. His beliefs concerning his relationship to Mr. Wynn were not delusions, but were, instead, intentional statements to persuade and deceive others, a central component of his *imposturing*.

The foundations for this opinion were numerous:

a. The sudden onset while in a cell in a Texas prison was not consistent with the development of a chronic delusion.

b. There was a rational alternative motivation for his criminal enterprise: to obtain a very large sum of money through the use of coercion and threat due to his envy of Stephen Wynn.

c. The criminal enterprise toward Mr. Wynn repeated a prior criminal attempt to coerce and threaten his brother into giving him money in early 1999.

d. His eagerness to call attention to his half-brother story was not consistent with an actual delusional individual.

e. The absence of measurable formal thought disorder on the Rorschach, which typically accompanies delusional thinking in the context of bipolar disorder, was a sign that there was no delusion.

f. The absence of any mania or hypomania during clinical interview, which is typically present when there is a grandiose delusion as a symptom of bipolar disorder, indicated that there was no delusion.

g. The MMPI-2 testing indicated no mania or ego inflation, which typically would be present if there was a grandiose delusion due to bipolar disorder.

h. The fantastic and far-fetched nature of his half-brother story indicated no actual delusion.

i. The half-brother story was asserted with the social worker over the course of 6 months in Washington in the absence of any symptoms of mania or intoxication, inconsistent with a delusion due to bipolar disorder or drug abuse.

j. The claim to be the half brother ("Don Vici") is asserted in his letters to Mr. Wynn, but Mr. P used his actual name during the same period of time when applying for a housing application, a driver's license, banking accounts, a post office box, and for complimentary tickets at various casinos.

k. He asserted that he was "delusional, insane" to his attorney, which is not something a delusional person does.

Although the nature and capacity of his acts, and his knowledge of legal wrongfulness, were therefore irrelevant because of the absence of delusion, there was also abundant evidence that did not support these prongs. For example, he knew what he wanted ($50 million) and from whom (Stephen Wynn), and this did not change over the course of 9 months (nature and capacity). He also made explicit reference to his knowledge of wrongfulness in several messages, for example, "P.S. Let's talk. Steve, okay, please call me ASAP. I don't talk nothing incriminating on the phone. Okay?" (letter to Mr. Wynn, October 31, 2000).

Other supporting evidence of these opinions included the examiner's diagnosis of Antisocial Personality Disorder; Mr. P's behavior consonant with the four suspicion indices for malingering in *DSM-IV*; his severe psychopathy that suggested an ability to manipulate and deceive others, and a strong sense of entitlement; and the ruling out of a medical cause for any delusion, based upon clinical interview and review of his medical records.

The psychodynamics for Mr. P's imposturing were both his character-ological propensity to manipulate others and his sense of entitlement, as well as his particular envy toward Mr. Wynn. Despite his extensive criminal history, psychological testing strongly suggested an individual with very low self-esteem, a deep sense of being mistreated and persecuted by others, a sense of aspirational failure, feeling socially alienated and singled out by others, and a chronic depression. His imposturing was a sustained criminal attempt to compensate for his actual feelings about himself and his chronic failures in life. He was angry and envious, and felt entitled to the wealth and fame of another. He conveyed this state of mind most succinctly in a letter he wrote to Mr. Wynn in the early phase of his stalking:

> While I sit here and watch the Country Music Awards here in my little f...ing dump, I think of your rich f...ing ass sitting there in your f...ing palace and I envy the hell out of your blood. You just don't know, man
>
> letter dated October 5, 2000

During the trial itself, Mr. P also wrote a letter to the forensic psychologist threatening him:

> I think that your ability to sit down and look an honest man in the face and lie to the maximum to gain his trust reflexs the 'psycho' as well as the 'impostor' description...it certainly fits your traits...I will ruin you when I obtain or retain these true lawyers that I am about to hire before this case is resolved
>
> letter written May 6, 2003

The Verdict

The jury found Mr. P guilty of all charges and legally sane. He was sentenced to life in prison.

The Aftermath

Three years later, Mr. P wrote to the forensic psychologist, again from prison:

> How are you? Man, you surely have a lot of titles, I just notice on page 7 of this fraudulent opinion psychological report that's dated 4-28-03 and address to coconspirator district attorney that you are a professor of psychiatry too! Out of all that schooling you surely didn't really learn much did you!? I bet you had rich parents and bought your way through school and the titles huh? Hee, hee. I just thought I'd let you know that I'm going to be suing your socks off in

the very near future! I've proved Steve is my blood brother, and that all of y'all, done what y'all did to me out of malice and malpractice, and a lot of legal jargon titles that I can define you by! Be cool now, sincerely, Mr. Donald E. J. Vici Jr. PS. One last thing! If you wish, I think it may be best for your reputation to have your attorney to contact me before I talk to the news media. Be cool. ASAP.

The Stalking of Steven Spielberg

The Behavior and Offenses

Mr. V initially tried to gain access to the Spielberg property on June 29, 1997, at about 6 p.m. At the time of this approach, he was driving a white Jeep Cherokee. He activated the security intercom, identified himself by his proper name, and indicated he was there to see Mr. Spielberg. He was asked by security if he had an appointment—which he denied—and then identified himself as a Geffen employee. He was turned away after asking if he could please "knock on his door and ask to speak to him."

On July 11, 1997, around 1 a.m.—2 weeks later—Mr. V was observed by security at another entrance to the property, this time in a dark-colored Land Rover. When questioned and released by security, he indicated that he was having "car trouble." This same security officer recalled seeing the Land Rover some time later, parked nearby. At that time, he noted that the logo of the *Jurassic Park* movies, the red dinosaur figure, was cut out and affixed to the rear window of the car. Two Spielberg movies, including *ET*, were in plain view on the front seat of the car.

Approximately 6 hours later, at about 7 a.m., Mr. V was reported and detained after running through neighboring backyards approximately a block away. He was observed by one neighbor, "on top of a lattice walking back and forth flapping his arms." Confronted by another neighbor, Mr. V stated "get out of here" while holding what appeared to be a drapery rod over his head like a javelin. Security responded and observed him coming out of some bushes with a large stick in his right hand. He was asked what he was doing and fled without answering. Ultimately, he was located again in some other bushes and complied with directions to exit and place his hands on his head, submitting to search. He had a black day planner, which contained pictures of Mr. Spielberg, as well as information about other entertainment figures.

Mr. V claimed he was being chased by Mr. Spielberg's "jackals" and that he was the adopted son of Mr. Spielberg. Law enforcement and outreach psychiatric emergency team workers responded and Mr. V agreed to a voluntary psychiatric admission. Before his admission, he was assessed by a police drug recognition expert as not under the influence at the time. He was released from the psychiatric facility later that day.

Finally, on the same day, Mr. V was seen at about 5 p.m. by the same security officer who had encountered him 2 weeks earlier. While retrieving his car at the end of his shift from its location 100 yards from the residence, this officer noticed that Mr. V had parked his Land Rover directly and extremely close behind his car, to the extent he became concerned about possible damage. Mr. V was observed to be sitting inside, "bending back toward the back seat trying to hide himself." The officer noted that "when I got off work, there was ample parking for anyone, and he had chosen to park behind my car instead of parking closer to the residence." Mr. V was spotted at yet another property access gate later that evening. The security officer called his partner in the security office and had him initiate a call to the police, then retreated with his car back to Mr. Spielberg's residence to observe Mr. V from the security office using their security cameras. They monitored his activities for approximately 30 to 40 minutes awaiting police arrival.

During this time, they noted that every time a car drove by, "he would pick up his papers or something and try to cover himself." Eventually, Mr. V moved his SUV, and then backed it onto the driveway. In reverse, Mr. V backed into the gate in a manner that led the security officer to perceive he was "trying to see how much force was needed to open those gates." Mr. V then left.

Before his departure, it appeared to the security officers that Mr. V might be masturbating. His car was eventually located nearby. It was unoccupied. He was detained and arrested by police when he returned a short while later. When asked if he had any sharp objects, he indicated he did. A consent search of his person found him to be in possession of duct tape, one pair of handcuffs, and box cutters. The duct tape and handcuffs were attached and located in his waistband. The keys to the handcuffs were on his key ring. A search of his SUV turned up two more pairs of handcuffs, as well as some assorted paperwork. The SUV was determined to be rented in his name.

When asked why he was there, Mr. V claimed that he had an appointment with Mr. Spielberg and that he wanted to demonstrate a screenplay he had prepared about a man raping another man. When asked why he had handcuffs and duct tape, Mr. V indicated that they were props. He was described as coherent, yet would mumble and ramble on.

Mr. V was again taken into custody and this time involuntarily admitted to a psychiatric hospital, where he would remain until July 17, 1997. He was later arrested for stalking, and before his release from the psychiatric hospital, he was served with a restraining order on behalf of Mr. Spielberg by Los Angeles Police Department's Threat Management Unit (TMU) detectives (see figure on next page).

In a follow-up interview conducted by Mr. Spielberg's head of security on July 23rd, Mr. V admitted that had he gained entry and Mr. Spielberg's wife was present, he planned "to tie her up and make her watch" while he raped the victim.

Police Interviews and Investigative Findings

Mr. V consented to police interviews with TMU detectives July 21 and August 4, 1997 while being held at LA County Jail. During his first interview, he

ATTORNEY OR PARTY WITHOUT ATTORNEY (Name and address):	TELEPHONE NO.	FOR COURT USE ONLY
Alschuler Grossman & Pines LLP 2049 Century Park East Thirty-Ninth Floor Los Angeles, CA 90067-3213	(310)277-1226	**FILED** LOS ANGELES SUPERIOR COURT AUG 26 1997 JOHN A. CLARKE, CLERK BY D. GETER, DEPUTY

ATTORNEY FOR (Name):

SUPERIOR COURT OF CALIFORNIA, COUNTY OF
STREET ADDRESS: 1725 Main Street
MAILING ADDRESS: Same
CITY AND ZIP CODE: Santa Monica, CA 90401
BRANCH NAME: West District

PLAINTIFF: Steven Spielberg

DEFENDANT: Jonathan Frances Norman

	CASE NUMBER:
PROOF OF PERSONAL SERVICE (Harassment)	SS007415

PERSONAL SERVICE

Instructions: After having the other party served with any of the documents identified in item 1, have the person who served the documents complete this Proof of Personal Service. Give the completed Proof of Personal Service to the clerk for filing. Neither the plaintiff nor the defendant can serve these papers.

1. I served a copy of the following documents (check the box before the title of each document you served):

   a. ☐ Order to Show Cause (Harassment)
      ☐ and Temporary Restraining Order

   b. ☐ Petition for Injunction Prohibiting Harassment
      ☐ Application for Temporary Restraining Order

   c. ☐ blank Response to Petition for Injunction Prohibiting Harassment

   d. ☒ Order After Hearing on Petition for Injunction Prohibiting Harassment

   e. ☐ completed Response to Petition for Injunction Prohibiting Harassment

   f. ☐ other (specify):

2. Person served (name): Jonathan Frances Norman

3. By personally delivering copies to the person served, as follows:
   (1) Date: 8/18/97   (2) Time: 1400 hrs
   (3) Address: Los Angeles County Jail

4. At the time of service I was at least 18 years of age and not a party to this cause.

I declare under penalty of perjury under the laws of the State of California that the foregoing is true and correct.

Date: 8/18/97

..... Paul A. Wright ....   ▶ [signature: Paul A. Wright]
      (TYPE OR PRINT NAME)   (SIGNATURE)

(See reverse for proof of service by mail)

| Form Approved by the
Judicial Council of California
CH-130 (Rev. January 1, 1987)
174 | PROOF OF PERSONAL SERVICE
(Harassment) | 76P778D-1/87 | CCP 527.6 |

admitted that he had been obsessed with Mr. Spielberg for approximately 1 month before his approaches (this is inconsistent with his roommate's report of a much lengthier obsession) and described himself as "obsessed." When he was asked to clarify what he meant by obsession, Mr. V responded "jack off," underscoring that he had a sexual obsession where he just had to be with the victim and "thought of nothing else." He stated:

> I work for David Geffen. He and Steven Spielberg are physically passionate. Steven told me to come over and act the persona of a

rapist. My lovers and I take turns wearing handcuffs.... Steven and David want me to be personified in Judaism and have adopted me as their godson. I find them highly attractive.

He said that he believed that the victim wanted to be raped by him, which is why he brought the duct tape, handcuffs, and box cutters. He also admitted that he had been walking outside the fence of the victim's compound, pacing off distances to determine how best to gain access so that he could perpetrate the rape. Mr. V admitted the prior attempt to access the property on June 29th, and intimated that he may have been there on one other occasion. He also stated he had consumed a large quantity of methamphetamine 3 days before the incident and had been awake the entire time. He also claimed to have been using cocaine. He did in fact test positive for methamphetamine on July 18th during his involuntary psychiatric hospitalization.

Mr. V stated that he researched the victim by reading various popular culture magazines, including *People, US,* and *The Hollywood Reporter.* He stated that he was pursuing conversion to Judaism and had an interest in becoming a production assistant for Warner Brothers studios. The interview concluded with Mr. V blaming his pursuit on drug use and saying that he would no longer continue to pursue Mr. Spielberg.

An examination of the day planner found in Mr. V's possession revealed a variety of articles on Mr. Spielberg and his partners in Dreamworks, including Mr. Katzenberg and Mr. Geffen. The names of the victim's children and his address were also noted. An apparent shopping list (see figure on next page) noted, among other items, three eye masks, four pairs of nipple clippers, three dog collars, nipple shockers, three locks with the same key, a bb gun at Sport's Mart, chloroform, and a shocker.

During his second interview with TMU detectives, Mr. V reaffirmed his earlier statement that he had become infatuated with Mr. Spielberg sometime in June. He also admitted buying the handcuffs at an adult book store near the end of June. Follow-up investigation revealed that he initially rented the Jeep Cherokee on June 25th, but switched cars to the Land Rover on July 8th. Warrant searches led to the discovery of important written evidence. An overview and excerpts are described in the next section.

Diary, Journal Entries, and Other Written Materials

The contents of Mr. V's journal, day planner, and other printed materials further documented his obsession with Mr. Spielberg and other celebrities, the content and nature of his thought processes and violent fantasies, and the operational steps he took to achieve his apparent objectives.

It is apparent that Mr. V researched Mr. Spielberg. He had several downloaded articles that outlined the victim's career achievements, movie productions, and business affiliations. It appeared that he paid particular attention to Mr. Spielberg's religious affiliations and charity activities, including

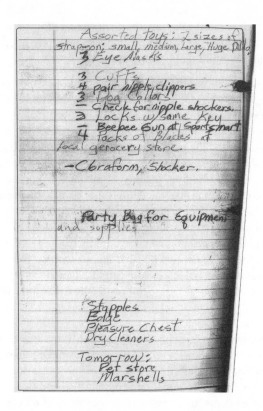

foundations that the victim belonged to that were open to membership and attendance based upon donation. Further Mr. V occasionally made notes in his journal during the time period surrounding his approaches.

Apparently delusional, conspiracy-themed content was present within these writings and materials. For example, several typewritten documents referenced the "gay mafia" and the "Black gay mafia," listing multiple high visibility public figures such as Spielberg, David Geffen, Charlton Heston, Robert DeNiro, and Elton John.

Grandiose, religious-themed material is also present in his writings. Mr. V wrote out religious prayers in his journal:

Please dear Jewish God bless me with the attainment of being
hired by the US Air Force in the officer's program before I turn
35 years old.

That (*sic*) you dear Jewish God for the direction, resources,
and continued development of gay sex, gay social life, and gay peer
direction.

Please dear Jewish God bless me with the directions, resources,
and obtainment of a pardon from all my criminal charges.

> Please dear Jewish God bless me with perfection from catching
> aids or other sexually or socially transmitted diseases.

Fantasies with violent, sexual, and paranoid themes were present in the written material (see figure on next page).

He writes:

> Today is Sunday. I am still pursuing to become one of Steven
> Speilberg's gay lovers. With him being married to Kate Capshaw
> I feel there has been a major misrepresentation.
>
> My current suggest (*sic*) is to write horror stories about a gay
> boy that is obsessed with an older man and like to cause social
> disfunction...the boy happens to be an AD to director.
>
> It is early Wednesday morning and I am getting in my Tuesday
> writing. My parole agent called me in for a second drug test within
> ten days. If I don't pass this test he will probably send me back to
> jail. He said he would not be in their Wednesday morning. So
> I may have another three days before he would issue a warrant for
> my arrest. I look at it that I have three more days to pursue Steven
> Speilberg my gay Jewish boy.

Mr. V also had in his possession a *Time* magazine article titled "The Last Day in the Life of John Lennon." This article outlined the Beatle's last day, including a section on his murderer, Mark David Chapman.

Roommate Interviews and Testimony

His roommate—with whom he had a reported "on again, off again" relationship of 6 years—was interviewed several times by investigators. He also testified to the Grand Jury. His roommate stated that he accompanied Mr. V on a "drive by" of the Spielberg compound about a week before Mr. V's July 9th approach, and that Mr. V told him of driving by the residence multiple times. Mr. V told his roommate he had obtained a star map (see figure on p. 259), which listed the victim's home address. On July 9th, Mr. V commented about the best part of the victim's wall to jump over, and indicated he wanted to rape the victim. Mr. V showed him a picture of naked men from adult magazines—their heads cut out and Mr. Spielberg's head pasted on. His roommate reportedly talked him out of an approach that evening, stating it was ridiculous and that he would be deterred by security.

When the roommate visited Mr. V at the psychiatric hospital, he noted his attire. Mr. V stated he was trying to go for the "Rambo look." On July 17th, the night of his release from the psychiatric hospital, Mr. V chose the movie he and his roommate went to see: *The Lost World*. Mr. V commented to his roommate that there was a mother and father T-Rex and a baby, and stated that Mr. Spielberg was the father, David (Geffen) was the mother, and Mr. V was the baby.

a raging hardon
with desire.
  Saturday ~~the~~ afternoon
at 1:40 PM Today is the
~~28~~ of June. ~~last night~~
~~it~~ Last night I should of
scoped out some of
the people living in
Brentwood that rely
on Tall security fenses
to protect them. This
way I could wait for
a man ~~or a woman~~ to
come home late at
night buy himself.
  I would come up
behined him and put

a gun to his head
and dress, ~~and~~ sound
and act very ~~nasty~~.
  I would ~~force~~ him to
put on a screaming
muz~~zz~~le have give
me his keys then put
~~a~~ handcuffs on him with
his hands infront of him.
  I would then have
him direct me to his
apartment. I would cuff
and gag any roommates
he might have. then
I would un cuff him but
leave the muezle on
his face

Mr. V's roommate described Mr. V as "paranoid of everything" and testified that he put sheets up over the windows, and always thought that someone was after him or watching him. He testified that the doctors told him Mr. V was "paranoia schizophrenic." During December 1994, Mr. V believed that his father was monitoring him and went to the hospital to have a CAT scan and get the monitor removed. He was then put into restraints and held overnight for drug intoxication. He also had the belief that one of his brothers was tapping his phones and was behind the conspiracy to monitor him. Mr. V, who was left-handed, would sometimes write with his right hand because the "left-handed voices" would command him to do so.

Mr. V may have worked as a male prostitute in the past. Mr. V told him that he accepted money on a weekly basis from an older man for about 10 years. He reportedly had a lot of sexual partners—male and female—but apparently was ambivalent about getting close, fearing abandonment. His roommate said he spent hours masturbating, and that he covered the windows, placed nickels over the door peephole, and was afraid he was being monitored while masturbating. Mr. V reportedly masturbated to both straight and gay porn.

Mr. V's roommate reported that Mr. V would often buy eight balls of methamphetamine via cash advances on his Visa card. At one point, he apparently had a balance of $19,000 and sent the bill to his stepmother who refused to pay it. In the past, his stepmother and mother would pay for some of his living expenses; just before his arrest, his mother had started paying the landlord directly. He added that Mr. V's father left him when he was 6 years old, was a fugitive, and that he had always wanted a father. He apparently looked to Mr. Spielberg as a father figure. Mr. V's roommate indicated that Mr. V's obsession and attraction to the victim began while he was in prison (March 1995 to November 1996). He also noted that Mr. V was very Christian while in prison and sought to convert to Judaism as he was being released. After Mr. V's father left (6–10 years old), he would occasionally sneak off to visit with his fugitive father but would have to travel under an assumed name in order to do so.

Before his arrest for the Spielberg stalking charges, Mr. V's roommate said Mr. V had been writing letters to actress Courtney Cox (which may not have been sent) and was convinced that he was going to be moving in with her. He also applied for a job with Dreamworks, a Spielberg company. During the first week of July, Mr. V watched the movie *Scream* (which has a scene involving a person being duct-taped in a closet), and *Lost World* (which has a scene with an electric zapper used on smaller dinosaurs). Mr. V's roommate commented, "This is all a big movie to him. He sees it all as a script." He indicated that Mr. V preferred jail to the hospital because he reportedly hates medication.

Criminal History and Related Behavior

Mr. V was on parole for a prior assault charge at the time of his stalking arrest. According to police reports, in March 1995, Mr. V assaulted a group of six victims (primarily Russian immigrants with limited English language capability), who were walking down an alley. Mr. V reportedly drove by, cursed, and yelled for them to get out of the way. Members of this group yelled something to the effect that they could not understand what he was saying. He suddenly stopped and drove rapidly in reverse directly at the victims. He jumped out of the Jeep, and immediately approached the first victim, punching her in the face repeatedly. Another victim attempted to intervene, at which point Mr. V began kicking him and the first victim repeatedly. As other members of the group attempted to provide help, Mr. V attacked all of them before he was finally subdued and taken into custody by a Guardian Angel citizen's patrol. The victims adamantly denied saying anything provocative to Mr. V. In July 1995, he was convicted of assault with great bodily injury and sentenced to prison for 3 years. He was released from state prison 17 months later, in November 1996.

Mr. V allegedly stalked another victim, his prior employer in a location scout business. This victim declared in his application for a restraining order filed in February 1995 that, "beginning about December 30, 1994, the defendant has followed me to restaurants, phoned me at all hours of the day and night and threatened to 'get me' by destroying my business relationships by making false and defamatory publications, both written and verbal, to my clients.... I am informed and believe that the defendant is acting under the influence of drugs, specifically methamphetamine." The victim reported that Mr. V delivered a flyer to Archdiocese contacts, which alleged that the victim was arranging sexual services with male prostitutes for a Catholic Church executive, and that he was fraudulently billing for services related to location scouting. This victim did in fact obtain a restraining order. Later, this victim was murdered in an unrelated incident.

Mr. V's roommate filed a police report in December 1994 against Mr. V for battery and stated that he had been hit by Mr. V "on more than one occasion. But because his punishment was so degrading to me and although officers were called to the scene, I never reported the others." His roommate later stated he had exaggerated some of his allegations, but confirmed he had been seriously assaulted by Mr. V on at least one prior occasion.

Family and Educational Background

Mr. V was born in 1966, the youngest of four sons, and grew up in Salt Lake County, Utah. Mr. V's father indeed was a fugitive from justice for 23 years after being convicted for a felony involving a loan scam. He was described by some as a "con artist" but was able to build a significant financial empire before his arrest; Mr. V grew up to a large extent in a world of comfort and wealth. His older brother apparently served prison time for killing a drug dealer and at the time of Mr. V's arrest was working as a minister.

After his father's disappearance, Mr. V, a latency age child, was apparently expelled from elementary school for attacking other children. Friends commented that as a teen he was known for assaulting people for "kicks," including kicking his way into an apartment to rip off a drug dealer. Mr. V graduated high school, attended UCLA, and reportedly earned a degree in international economics. It was apparently in 1985 while attending college that he began to use methamphetamine. Just before Mr. V's 1995 assault arrest, Mr. V's father finally turned himself in to authorities.

Jail Behavior

On January 8, 1998, while at county jail awaiting trial, a police report was generated regarding "special circumstances, possible stalking." Mr. V reportedly wrote out several names on his Styrofoam coffee cup, including "Geffen Varden." He drew a map of the Los Angeles area and labeled various locations, including the residence of the Spielbergs, which he marked with a heart symbol and the initials "SS." Other celebrity residences were noted, and the map was observed to be a generally accurate representation of geographical locations.

Mr. V. formally requested to be moved to a gay dorm, using his true name:

> "Dear Deputy, will you please reclassify me as gay and transfer me to a gay dorm? Robert Varden. Thank you and God bless you."

In his possession were additional writings that referenced Spielberg, David Geffen, Bill Gates, Calvin Klein, Al Gore, Michael Jackson, Tom Hanks, Barbara Streisand, and Stephen Wynn—the victim in the first case study of this chapter.

Psychological Analysis and Threat Issues

Mr. V evidenced a cognitive-perceptual disorder, substance use or dependence, and antisocial and borderline personality disorder characteristics. His thinking and perceptual abnormalities, most likely due to chronic paranoid schizophrenia, manifested in grandiose, religious, persecutory, and erotomanic delusions, as well as auditory hallucinations. He was also quite paranoid. Adding to the clinical picture of an Axis I major mental disorder was his heavy ingestion of methamphetamine, a substance that can precipitate and exacerbate paranoid, grandiose, and delusional thought processes, and known for its association with elevated violence risk. Mr. V's Axis I conditions were complicated by his likely coexisting mixed personality disorder, which appeared to have components of borderline traits (ambivalence and abandonment issues), combined with prominent antisocial personality traits (rule breaking, impulsivity, lying, aggression, lack of remorse). He may have met full criteria for both borderline and antisocial personality disorders.

Despite Mr. V's chronic psychosis, he was capable of engaging in a predatory rather than affective violence trajectory (Meloy, 2006), as is apparent in most public figure stalkers and attackers (Chapters 1, 3, 4, and 10). His violent impulses, while driven by delusional thoughts, were also fueled by violent sexual fantasies, a cognitive as opposed to affective process. His stated intent, as evidenced by his word choice, was "rape" rather than a consensual relationship. Mr. V acquired and sought to acquire the necessary implements to perpetrate such acts: securing a star map to locate the victim's residence, researching charitable functions that might be attended to access entertainment figures including the victim, accessing a large SUV that could be used for a potential abduction, changing the SUV to deter detection, possessing a rape kit that included weapons and bindings to facilitate and maintain control, testing boundaries and surveilling the target's home to determine security weaknesses, and using a ruse to seek access. He was resourceful and contemplated acquiring a bb gun, which could be used to bluff a threat, would be easy to access, relatively inexpensive, and involved no mandatory waiting period or Department of Justice checks to determine eligibility given his parole status. These steps are consistent with those used by other offenders to capture and maintain an unwilling captive (Mohandie, 2002). His changing into "Rambo" clothing is consistent with the private narcissistic ritual described by Meloy (1988) among those perpetrating predatory violent acts. At the time of his arrest, Mr. V had substantially progressed down a pathway toward violence (Fein & Vossekuil, 1998), and was approaching the final markers—breach and attack—defined by Calhoun and Weston (Chapter 5).

Mr. V was assessed at the time as being a significant and imminent threat to the victim because of his prior violence history, psychotic disorder, Cluster B personality traits, methamphetamine use, stated intentions, weapon and rape kit possession, resourcefulness, and approach attempts. He was assessed as unlikely to discontinue his pursuit behavior and that there was a high likelihood he could approach and pose a threat to other individuals of interest affiliated with Mr. Spielberg, including his business partners and family members.

While Mr. V apparently qualified for various mental illnesses at the time of his offenses, under the legal definition of insanity used in many jurisdictions, Mr. V faced an uphill battle, underscoring the important distinction between mental illness and the legal definition of insanity. Had Mr. V attempted an insanity defense—which he did not—the above identified factors would have posed a significant challenge to such a defense, given the apparent *criminal presence of mind* (mens rea) inferred by his behavior, which often negates a lack of understanding of the nature and consequences of one's acts, and a lack of knowledge of wrongfulness (Chapter 18).

Sentencing

After a jury trial, Mr. V was convicted of stalking and sentenced to 25 years to life because of his prior criminal convictions. The jury rejected Mr. V's defense that his heavy drug use precluded a finding that he had the requisite intent. Mr. V appealed the case contending, among other issues (e.g., he was required to wear a "stun belt" during the trial), that the stalking must contemporaneously create fear in the victim. This issue was based on the delay (several days) in notifying Mr. Spielberg about Mr. V's stalking and threats as the victim was out of the country filming a movie. The appeals court rejected his appeal, opining that:

> Spielberg's serendipitous absence on the days of Mr. V's efforts
> to gain access to Spielberg's residence cannot diminish Mr. V's
> criminal responsibility for his course of conduct. What matters
> is that, when he did learn of Mr. V's acts and threats, Spielberg
> suffered the requisite fear for his own safety and the safety of his
> family.

People v. Jonathan Norman, 1999

Discussion

Both of these cases illustrate the difficulties and complexities of ensuring the safety of public figures, and professional management of the clinical-forensic issues that may arise before, during, and after the stalking events.

Psychodiagnostic Issues

Although antisocial personality disorder in general, and psychopathy in particular, are unusual in stalking cases (Reavis, Allen, & Meloy, in press), both are strongly inferred in the data generated concerning these two perpetrators. Such personality abnormalities, which can be assessed indirectly through criminal history and directly through the use of observational instruments (P-SCAN, PCL-R; see Chapter 10), have important implications for public figure stalking and threat cases: such cases statistically pose a greater risk of violence, particularly targeted violence (Fein & Vossekuil, 1998); fantasized or actual behaviors that evoke suffering in the victim and are enjoyed by the perpetrator—what is clinically referred to as sadism—are likely to be more apparent (Holt, Meloy, & Strack, 1999), as they are in these cases; and manipulation and deception will pervade the cases before, during, and after the crimes (Bursten, 1972). The unusual presence of imposturing in the Wynn case has received extensive attention in the psychoanalytic literature and has been historically linked to psychopathy (Deutsch, 1955; Meloy, 2001).

Major mental disorder is also apparent in both of these cases, as it is in many public figure stalking, threat, and attack cases (see Chapter 3 and 19). Such diagnoses, however, should not infer a reduced risk of violence despite the replicated large group finding that psychosis reduces risk among stalkers (Meloy, 1998). A recent regression tree model for prediction of violence among stalkers indicates that psychosis may increase or decrease risk of violence *depending upon its interaction with other violence risk variables* (Rosenfeld & Lewis, 2005). And any one case may prove the exception to the rule. In fact, we have found that the delusions of public figure stalkers may bring a resolve to the pursuit that would otherwise be filled with ambivalence. It is critical to understand the content and nature of deviant thought processes, in light of how such patterns may enhance or reduce risk in the individual case.

The third component of psychodiagnosis in these cases often includes drug abuse or dependence, which may cloud the diagnostic picture and exacerbate the preexisting mental and personality disorders. In both of these cases, drug abuse was chronic and varied, and particularly in the context of paranoid schizophrenia, will exacerbate symptoms and may confuse forensic evaluators. The clinical rule of thumb is that an amphetamine delusional disorder will remit over time, often several months, if the subject is deprived of the drug, whereas the paranoid schizophrenic subject, even if abusing amphetamine or other stimulants, will not get better without medical intervention even if deprived of his drug of abuse once in custody.

Neuropsychological and neurological evaluations, including neuroimaging, were considered in the Wynn stalking case because of the presence of both hepatitis and HIV. Such diagnostic procedures were not deemed necessary once the subject was clinically screened for such cognitive impairments, and they were not found. Consideration of medical conditions that may contribute to the stalking of a public figure should always be done by the evaluating professional, and appropriate referrals made. Stalking likely has an underlying neurobiology (Meloy & Fisher, 2005).

Psychodiagnostic accuracy in these cases is critical for both preventive efforts—which were anemic in the Spielberg case—and criminal prosecution after arrest, particularly if the defendant raises issues concerning incompetency, insanity, or mens rea at trial. All clinical and forensic evaluations must include a thorough review of evidence generated in the case, particularly if sanity at the time of the crime is being asserted by the defense.

The psychodynamics of these cases—that is, what motivates the stalking of a public figure, both consciously and unconsciously—are as varied as the psychodiagnoses, *but unlike the diagnoses, may change over the course of the pursuit.* In the Wynn case, the conscious motivation was to get the money Mr. P said he deserved, the notion of just rewards; the unconscious motivation was his envy of Mr. Wynn and all that he had accomplished. Envy is the wish to destroy goodness (Klein, 1975), and Mr. P expressed this most readily in his written letters. Over time, his aggressive devaluation of Wynn increased, likely due to his perceived rejection by Mr. Wynn, culminating in a physical approach and homicidal threats. If the object of envy is damaged or destroyed, it was not worth having in the first place, and envy subsides. In the Spielberg case, the motivation is psychotically based and suffused with extreme sexual aggression, sadism, and control. Again, envy may be a basic underlying emotion for Mr. V, but it is more speculative. Envy in both these cases is tied to larger-than-life figures who are benignly admired or idealized objects in the world of entertainment and gambling, the personal interests of Mr. V and Mr. P, respectively. But in their minds, idealization and admiration take an insidious and aggressive turn.

General Threat Management Issues

Pubic figure stalking cases have an overall low incidence of violence, a fact that may appear to contraindicate the security efforts of potential celebrity victims (Chapter 2) (Mohandie et al., 2006). However, these cases underscore the critical value of physical and behavioral security perimeters to prevent access by the rare offender who will approach with malevolent intentions. The ready availability of information about public figures from various sources—including the Internet—likely enables would-be offenders to track their victims at public appearances, target family members, or access business and home addresses. It is apparent that security—both proactive intelligence gathering and reactive protection—serves to deter potential offenders, detect their intrusions, and interrupt offending. They create a much-needed buffer between the offender and his potential victim, and provide defensible alternative targets than just the celebrity figure. Arrest, prosecution, treatment, and confinement may continue this important control.

The limits of civil mental health commitment, particularly in the United States, may pose challenges that lessen their effectiveness as a tool with certain stalkers. The term itself, civil commitment, creates an illusion of control that is not supported in the event of an unforeseen release. In the Spielberg case example, Mr. V's rapid discharge from the psychiatric hospital and immediate return to pursue his victim could have had catastrophic results. Certainly, such "revolving door" releases can occur in ordinary arrest situations; however, there is more ability to communicate with those impacted by such early release events in law enforcement settings than in mental health commitment and release circumstances because of patient privacy issues in the latter situations. If the mental health commitment tool is exclusively relied upon, it may allow the potential stalker to go free before any change in his psychopathology or motivation—in fact, a "catch and release" pattern may fuel his anger. Active cooperation between mental health and law enforcement is critical to the management of public figure stalking cases. These subjects are *both* mad and bad (Meloy, 1997).

Underreporting of pursuit events is normative in stalking cases. Stalkers pursue more frequently than is captured in official reports (Tjaden & Thoennes, 1997). Further assessment and inquiry during interviews of the subject and those close to him, as well as other investigative techniques (surveillance, phone records, document review), may be helpful to gain this information. A clearer understanding of actual pursuit behavior and any undocumented "close calls" during approaches facilitates more accurate threat assessment and management activity.

It is common for subjects to target other victims—both public and private figures—either consecutively or concurrently with the identified victim (see Chapter 1). In these two case studies, we were not surprised that the stalker of Steven Spielberg mentioned Stephen Wynn in his writings as another potential target. Assessing other targets of interest may be helpful to threat management efforts, reduce risk to other potential victims by making them aware that they may be pursued, and provide information sharing opportunities between security operations that may enhance the accuracy of threat assessment activity.

Conclusions

We have examined in detail the stalking of two male corporate-celebrity figures by two stalkers: both males with criminal and drug abuse histories, major psychiatric disorders, likely personality disorders, and histories of chronic failures in their ability to sustain work and form stable sexual pair bonds with another person. Despite these multiple psychological, social, and perhaps even biological impairments, they pursued their targets with tenacity, cleverness, and increasing hostility and aggression as their grossly unrealistic, and outrageous goals—$50 million and sadistic rape—receded from their grasp. Fortunately, no one was hurt. The *London Times* captured our closing sentiments in an editorial written almost 170 years ago, on May 31, 1842: "The ill-mannered curiosity of the public, where propriety should teach them to abstain—the absurd, but not therefore less provoking, intrusions to which the palace itself has been subject—these are evils to which royalty must submit as a necessary consequence of the very interest which it attracts to itself, galling as they must often be to one who feels acutely the pleasures of a more easy privacy."

Notes

1. None of the facts in this case, including specific quotes from letters, physical evidence, behavioral evidence, and interview and testing data, have been changed or altered due to the introduction of all this material, both facts and expert opinions, through testimony at the public criminal trial of the defendant (*State of Nevada v. Donald Eugene Phillips*, Case No. 177173, District Court, Clark County, Nevada).
2. In Nevada, aggravated stalking relates to "any person who without lawful authority willfully or maliciously engages in a course of conduct that would cause a reasonable person to feel terrorized, frightened, intimidated or harassed, and actually causes the victim to feel terrorized, frightened, intimidated or harassed, and therein threatens the person with the intent to cause him to be placed in reasonable fear of death or substantial bodily harm" (NRC 200.575).
3. In 1995, Nevada abolished the plea of not guilty by reason of insanity and created a new plea of "guilty but mentally ill." The Supreme Court of the State of Nevada reintroduced the insanity plea as a fundamental principle of law protected by due process in *Finger v. State of Nevada* on July 24, 2001. It is essentially a McNaghten standard, wherein the defendant must be in a delusional state such that he cannot know or understand the nature and capacity of his act, or he cannot appreciate the legal wrongfulness of his act. The facts as he believed them to be must justify his actions.
4. HIV infection can cause dementia, and the use of interferon alpha to treat hepatitis can cause severe neuropsychiatric syndromes such as depression and paranoid psychosis (Avison, Nath, & Berger, 2002; Ricart et al., 2002; Schaefer et al., 2002).

References

Avison, M., Nath, A., & Berger, J. (2002). Understanding pathogenesis and treatment of HIV dementia: A role for magnetic resonance? *Trends in Neuroscience, 25,* 468–472.

Bursten, B. (1972). *The manipulator.* New Haven: Yale University Press.

Caldwell, A. (1988). *MMPI Supplemental Scale Manual.* Los Angeles: Caldwell Report.

Calhoun, F., & Weston, S. (2003). *Contemporary threat management.* San Diego, CA: Specialized Training Services.

Deutsch, H. (1955). The impostor: Contributions to ego psychology of a type of psychopath. *Psychoanalytic Quarterly, 24,* 483–505.

Fein, R., & Vossekuil, B. (1998). Preventing attacks on public officials and public figures: A Secret Service perspective. In J. R. Meloy (Ed.), *The psychology of stalking: Clinical and forensic perspectives* (pp. 176–191). San Diego, CA: Academic Press.

Fixated Research Group (2006). *Inappropriate communications, approaches, and attacks on the British Royal Family.* London: The Home Office.

Hare, R. D. (2003). *The Psychopathy Checklist-Revised (PCL-R) technical manual* (2nd ed.), Toronto: Multi-Health Systems.

Holt, S., Meloy, J. R., & Strack, S. (1999). Sadism and psychopathy in violent and sexually violent offenders. *Journal of the American Academy of Psychiatry and the Law, 27,* 23–32.

Klein, M. (1975). *Envy and gratitude and other works, 1946–1963* (pp. 176–238). New York: The Free Press.

Meloy, J. R. (1988). *The psychopathic mind.* Northvale, NJ: Aronson.

Meloy, J. R. (1997). The clinical risk management of stalking: "Someone is watching over me..." *American Journal of Psychotherapy, 51,* 174–184.

Meloy, J. R. (Ed.) (1998). *The psychology of stalking: Clinical and forensic perspectives.* San Diego, CA: Academic Press.

Meloy, J. R. (2001). *The mark of Cain.* Hillsdale, NJ: The Analytic Press.

Meloy, J. R. (2004). The empirical basis and forensic application of affective and predatory violence. *Australian and New Zealand Journal of Psychiatry, 40,* 539–547.

Meloy, J. R., & Fisher, H. (2005). Some thoughts on the neurobiology of stalking. *Journal of Forensic Sciences, 50,* 1472–1480.

Meloy, J. R., James, D., Farnham, F., Darnley, B., Pathé, M., Mullen, P., et al. (2004). A research review of public figure threats, approaches, attacks, and assassinations in the United States. *Journal of Forensic Sciences, 49,* 1086–1093.

Mohandie, K. (2002). Human captivity experiences. *Journal of Threat Assessment, 2,* 3–41.

Mohandie, K., Meloy, J. R., & McGowan, M. (2006). The RECON typology of stalking: Reliability and validity based upon a large sample of North American stalkers. *Journal of Forensic Sciences, 51,* 147–155.

Pathé, M., Mullen, P., & Purcell, R. (2000). Same-gender stalking. *Journal of the American Academy of Psychiatry and the Law, 28,* 191–197.

People v. Jonathan Norman. 75 Cal. App. 4th at 1234 (1999). Reporter's redacted transcript of Grand Jury Proceedings, dated October 8 and 9, 1997.

Reavis, J., Allen, E., & Meloy, J. R. (in press). Psychopathy in a mixed gender sample of adult stalkers. *Journal of Forensic Sciences.*

Ricart, F., Cohen, M., Alfonso, C., Hoffman, R., Quinones, N., Cohen, A., et al. (2002). Understanding the psychodynamics of non-adherence to medical treatment in persons with HIV infection. *General Hospital Psychiatry, 24,* 176–180.

Rosenfeld, B., & Lewis, C. (2005). Assessing violence risk in stalking cases: A regression tree approach. *Law and Human Behavior, 29,* 343–357.

Scalora, M., Baumgartner, J., Zimmerman, W., Callaway, D., Mailette, M., Covell, C., et al. (2002). An epidemiological assessment of problematic contacts to members of Congress. *Journal of Forensic Sciences, 47,* 1–5.

Schaefer, M., Engelbrecht, M., Gut, O., Fiebich, B., Bauer, J., Schmidt, F., et al. (2002). Interferon alpha and psychiatric syndromes: A review. *Progress in Neuro-Psychopharmacology and Biological Psychiatry, 26,* 731–746.

Spitzberg, B. (2007). The state of the art of stalking: Taking stock of the emerging literature. *Aggression and Violent Behavior, 12,* 64–86.

Tjaden, P., & Thoennes, N. (1997). *Stalking in America: Findings from the National Violence Against Women Survey.* Denver, CO: Center for Policy Research.

12

Toward the Measurement and Profiling of Celebrity Worship

John Maltby and David Giles

In the week between 15th and 19th January 2007, most of the U.K. news channels were running a story on arguments occurring between four female celebrities living in the "Celebrity Big Brother" house, a television program shown by Channel 4, in which celebrities of various renown live together for a relatively short period of time under the gaze of cameras and the general public. Some of these arguments within the house led to accusations of bullying and racism within and outside the Big Brother house, both in the United Kingdom and abroad (particularly in India where one of the housemates resides). On the aforementioned new programs, experts—people working in the media, celebrities, psychologists, people who had taken part in previous series of the program—were brought in to comment on the situation. Moreover, the Prime Minster and Chancellor of the U.K. Government were asked to comment and did indeed make statements on the situation.

Although we are tempted to question to what extent this is a news story, deserving of headlines across the news channels (after all 5 million viewers tuned into the most explosive episode doubling the average viewing figures for the series: a reflection of a "slow news day," or rival broadcasters taking delight?), the influence of and interest in celebrities, or our perceived interest, is capable of capturing the imagination and discussion of the public, the interest of the news media, and the comment of politicians.

Psychological investigation of "celebrity worship" began in the United States and United Kingdom at the turn of the last century. The corpus of relevant studies is still relatively small, but steadily increasing. The background for this work was to investigate the attention and adulation heaped upon people whom we term "celebrities." Though not the first or only research, psychological work in the area was limited and was generally confined to an observation that Celebrity Worship is potentially problematic. In this chapter, we will look at research work that has concentrated on how Celebrity Worship has been measured, how theoretical areas of psychology have informed our understanding of the construct, examine its relationship to mental health and health variables by way of establishing some applied value, and look at overlapping considerations. We also make some theoretical and practical suggestions for further research directions.

The Measurement of Celebrity Worship

We begin with the measurement of Celebrity Worship. Until the late 1990s, few psychologists had been interested in the role of celebrities. Those that had, had looked at specific aspects of celebrity following. Media psychologists often define the relationships that fans develop with celebrities as a "para-social" relationship, that is, a one-sided relationship in which one party knows a great deal about the other, but the relationship is not reciprocal (e.g., the fan knows a lot about the celebrity but not vice versa).

In an early study, Rubin, Perse, and Powell (1985) looked at one-way friendships between entertainers and their audience by studying the connections that people made with presenters who read the news. Try to imagine your local news presenter; their style of presentation is often very personal and welcoming, and they often talk about issues that are relevant and important to you and the area you live in. Rubin et al. wanted to examine how people responded to such programs, and looked at the friendships that people established with newscasters. Participants responded to questions such as "When I'm watching a newscast, I feel as if I am part of their group" and "I see my favorite newscaster as an old friend." As we can see, this research did not extend to other celebrities, but importantly showed that people do make connections with people on television, even news presenters. Meanwhile, Stever (1991) became very interested in celebrities, and concentrated on the qualities of celebrities that we usually know them best for, that is, their ability to entertain and to be possible role models. In her work, Stever found that people described celebrities in four ways:

- As a sex symbol: Attractive, good-looking and sexy
- As a talented entertainer: Talented, artistic and creative
- As a hero/role model: Helpful, honest and generous
- As emanating mystique: Lonely, shy and mysterious

However, U.S.-based sports psychologist Wann (1995) began to emphasize certain social roles of celebrities, particularly sports celebrities. Wann devised the Sport Fan Motivation Scale, which identifies eight reasons why people follow sports and sports celebrities:

- *Entertainment*: Watching sports or sports celebrities provides entertainment.
- *Group affiliation*: Following a sports team or player allows the person to join a group of fans who share the same interest.
- *Self-esteem*: Being part of a group of people who follow the same team can help someone feel as if they belong, and raise their self-esteem, particularly if their favorite team wins.
- *Escape*: Watching sports or sports celebrities allows the person to escape mundane and everyday life.
- *Family*: There are family reasons behind sports. Often young children will follow the football team that their parents support.
- *Aesthetic*: People view sports as an artistic beauty or a reflection of good taste. Soccer is often referred to as "the beautiful game."
- *Excitement*: Sport and sports celebrities provide excitement.
- *Economic*: Betting on sporting occasions can provide excitement, as well as possible fortune.

Wann's work certainly suggests that there are many psychological and social reasons for following sport and sports celebrities.

Celebrity Attitude Scale

Using all the elements mentioned above (e.g., connecting with the celebrity, seeing the celebrity as an entertainer and hero, psychological and social aspects of following sports celebrities), U.S. psychologists McCutcheon, Lange, and Houran (2002) introduced the Celebrity Attitude Scale (CAS). This 34-item scale was first administered to 262 persons living in central Florida. McCutcheon et al. suggested that Celebrity Worship comprised a single dimension in which lower scores on the scale involved individualistic behavior such as watching, listening to, and reading and learning about celebrities while the higher levels of worship are characterized by empathy, overidentification, and obsession with the celebrity.

However, later research among larger U.K. samples have suggested there are three different aspects to Celebrity Worship; Maltby and the aforementioned psychologists distributed the CAS among 1,732 U.K. respondents (781 males, 942 females) who were aged between 14 and 62 years and identified the following three dimensions of Celebrity Worship:

- *Entertainment-social dimension*. This dimension comprises attitudes that fans are attracted to a favorite celebrity because of their perceived ability to entertain and become a social focus, such as "I love to talk with others who admire my favorite celebrity," and "I like watching and hearing about my favorite celebrity when I am with a large group of people."

- *Intense-personal dimension.* The intense-personal aspect of Celebrity Worship reflects intensive and compulsive feelings about the celebrity, akin to the obsessional tendencies of fans often referred to in the literature; for example, "I share with my favorite celebrity a special bond that cannot be described in words," and "When something bad happens to my favorite celebrity I feel like it happened to me."
- *Borderline-pathological dimension.* This dimension is typified by uncontrollable behaviors and fantasies regarding scenarios involving an individual's favorite celebrities, such as "I have frequent thoughts about my favorite celebrity, even when I don't want to," and "my favorite celebrity would immediately come to my rescue if I needed help."

What is crucial is the role of interaction with the celebrity, particularly when comparing intense-personal and borderline-pathological dimensions of Celebrity Worship. Within intense-personal aspects of Celebrity Worship, the para-social relationships are passive and receptive on the part of the Celebrity Worshipper (e.g., "When something bad happens to my favorite celebrity I feel like it happened to me"), while within borderline-pathological aspects of Celebrity Worship, the para-social relationships involve individuals imagining themselves in a special relationship with the celebrity (e.g., "my favorite celebrity would immediately come to my rescue if I needed help").

Public Figure Preoccupation Index

This concentration on the more pathological aspects of Celebrity Worship has been recently extended by Sheridan, Maltby, and Gillett (2006). Their work drew on the stalking literature that originally was heavily influenced by cases of celebrity harassment but now largely pertains to noncelebrity cases. Nonetheless, there is some influential work in this field that elucidates concepts around celebrity stalking and therefore possibly extreme forms of Celebrity Worship. In the United States, Dietz, Matthews, Martell, et al. (1991) and Dietz, Matthews, Van Duyne, et al. (1991) identified that Hollywood celebrities and U.S. Congress politicians received high volumes of unsolicited, inappropriate, and threatening postal communications, as well as a large number of inappropriate visits, mainly from persons displaying signs of psychiatric disorder. In Europe, Malsch, Visscher, and Blaauw (2002) analyzed data from public figures who had experienced harassment. Just over a third of the sample of public figures were found to have been stalked. These Dutch researchers determined that common harassment methods were telephone calls, letters, faxes and e-mails, the sending of flowers and gifts, physical following, surveillance of the victim's home, and harassment of family and friends. Within these findings, the stalkers of politicians tended to remain distant, while the stalkers of those in the entertainment world were more likely to physically pursue their target. Not all

Celebrity Worship is negative. Leets, de Becker, and Giles (1995) categorized letter writers into three groups: the curious who sought specific information, those who wished to express adulation, and persons who wanted to request autographs or items for fund-raising purposes. Furthermore, Ferris (2001) observed and interviewed "active fans" who formed social networks with other fans. These fans did seek to make physical contact with a celebrity but sought to make a distinction between themselves and "stalkers."

Using such themes alongside media reports of court cases that have noted the behavior of those preoccupied with public figures, Sheridan et al. (2006) devised the 50-item Public Figure Preoccupation Inventory. Analyzing data from 1,162 participants to look for underlying factor structures to responses to these 50 items, Sheridan et al. found four factors. The first factor to emerge was an "establishing contact" factor, comprising items such as "I must have sent over a hundred letters/e-mails to my favorite celebrity" and "I have tried to phone my favorite celebrity." The second factor was a "collecting" factor, be it material related to the celebrity or experiences, for example, "I have a huge amount of material relating to my favorite celebrity" and "I have a shrine dedicated to my favorite celebrity." The third factor focused on "sexual" thoughts and feelings toward a favorite celebrity, "If I met my favorite celebrity we would flirt with each other" and "If it were not for other people, my favorite celebrity and I could have a closer relationship." The final interpretable factor is a "stalking" factor. This factor contained items such as "No amount of security could keep me away from my favorite celebrity if I decided to visit him/her" and "I would stalk my favorite celebrity if I had the means to do so."

Understanding the Psychological Construct of Celebrity Worship

So why is the psychology of Celebrity Worship necessary? It seems that all may not be well among Celebrity Worshippers.

Consequences of Celebrity Worship

There is some evidence that there may be mental health consequences of Celebrity Worship. Researchers have examined the relationship between Celebrity Worship and mental health in U.K. adult samples. Maltby, Houran, Ashe, and McCutcheon (2001) found evidence to suggest that the intense-personal Celebrity Worship dimension was related to higher levels of depression and anxiety. Similarly, Maltby, Day, McCutcheon, Gillett, et al. in 2004 found that the intense-personal Celebrity Worship dimension was not only related to higher levels of depression and anxiety, but also to higher levels of stress, negative affect, and reports of illness. Both of these studies showed no evidence for a significant relationship between either the entertainment-social or the borderline-pathological dimensions of Celebrity Worship and mental health.

Another consequence was recently reported by Maltby, Giles, Barber, and McCutcheon (2005), who examined the role of celebrity interest in shaping body image cognitions. Among three separate U.K. samples (adolescents, students and older adults), individuals selected a celebrity of their own sex, whose body/figure they liked and admired, and then completed the CAS along with two measures of body image. Significant relationships were found between attitudes toward celebrities and body image among female adolescents only. The findings suggested that, in female adolescents, there exists an interaction between intense-personal Celebrity Worship and body image between the ages of 14 and 16 years, and some tentative evidence is available to suggest that this relationship disappears at the onset of adulthood (17–20 years). These results are consistent with those of authors who stress the importance of the formation of relationships with media figures, and suggest that relationships with celebrities perceived as having a good body shape may lead to a poor body image in female adolescents.

Within a clinical context, the effect of Celebrity Worship might be more extreme, particularly when considering more pathological aspects of Celebrity Worship. Maltby, Day, McCutcheon, Houran, and Ashe (2006) examined the relationship between entertainment-social, intense-personal, and borderline-pathological Celebrity Worship and obsessiveness, ego-identity, fantasy proneness, and dissociation. Two of these variables drew particular attention: fantasy proneness (time spent fantasizing, reporting hallucinatory intensities as real, reporting vivid childhood memories, having intense religious and paranormal experiences) and dissociation (the lack of a normal integration of experiences, feelings, and thoughts in everyday consciousness and memory, related to a number of psychiatric problems).

Though low levels of Celebrity Worship (entertainment-social) are not associated with any of the clinical measures, medium levels of Celebrity Worship (intense-personal) are related to fantasy proneness (around 10% of the shared variance), while high levels of Celebrity Worship (borderline-pathological) share a greater association with fantasy proneness (around 14% of the shared variance) and dissociation (around 3% of the shared variance, though the effect size of this is small and most probably due to the large sample size). This finding suggests that as Celebrity Worship becomes more intense, and the individual perceives an extant relationship with the celebrity, the more the individual is prone to fantasies (see Chapter 1).

Sheridan et al. (2006) repeated a similar examination using the Public Figure Preoccupation Index (PFPI) and measured dissociation and absorption (a tendency to fully engage with an interest, and demonstrate imagination, focus, and order to thoughts and feelings associated with the object of attention). This research sought to capitalize on a theoretical split within extreme Celebrity Worship: between a lay view of the extreme Celebrity Worshipper as psychologically disordered and being detached from reality and a lay view of this group as focused, imaginative, and ordered in their thoughts and feelings. From this study, the authors determined that the "establishing contact" subscale of the PFPI was related to dissociative experiences and the "sexuality" and "stalking" subscales were related to absorption scores.

So what psychological variables are related to Celebrity Worship to help us understand these effects of Celebrity Worship? We will break this down into areas of personality, cognitive, social, and developmental schools of psychology.

Celebrity Worship and Personality

There has been little research on personality correlates of Celebrity Worship; however, Maltby, Houran, and McCutcheon (2003) suggested that the three dimensions of Celebrity Worship may parallel the three dimensions of Eysenckian personality theory, of psychoticism (a social pathology comprising solitary, troublesome, cruel, and inhumane traits, arguably similar to modern day interpretations of psychopathy), neuroticism (anxious, worrying, and moody traits), and extraversion (sociable, sensation seeking, carefree, and optimistic traits). In other words, the entertainment-social type of Celebrity Worship, with its emphasis on talking about and doing things regarding one's favorite celebrity, would be related to extraversion. In a similar vein, intense-personal Celebrity Worship, with its emphasis on obsessing about one's favorite celebrity, would be related to neuroticism. And finally, borderline-pathological Celebrity Worship, with its emphasis on doing things impulsively (like buying a small object once used by a favored celebrity for a thousand dollars, and showing a preference for doing something against the law for one's favorite celebrity), would be related to psychoticism. These authors found significant correlations between each aspect of Celebrity Worship and each dimension of Eysenck's personality dimensions. They found that the entertainment-social factor of the CAS reflects some of the extraversion personality traits (sociable, lively, active, venturesome), that the intense personal factor of the CAS reflects some of the neuroticism traits (tense, emotional, moody), and that some of the acts described in the borderline-pathological subscale of the CAS seem to reflect some of the psychoticism traits (impulsive, antisocial, egocentric).

Maltby et al. (2004) used an adaptational-continuum model of personality, which combines measures of personality and coping, and discovered three personality-coping factors. The first was a neuroticism component, with measures of denial and mental and behavioral disengagement loading positively on this component. A second component was a psychoticism-coping factor, with psychoticism loading on a component alongside measures of religious coping, alcohol and drug use, and humor. Religious coping loads positively on this component whereas psychoticism, humor, and use of alcohol/drugs as a coping strategy all load negatively. The final component was an extraversion-coping scale, with extraversion dominating a component on which seeking social support (for both instrumental and emotional reasons) and focusing on and venting of emotions also loaded positively. In other words, as predicted, and consistent with previous findings regarding Celebrity Worship and personality, Celebrity Worship for entertainment-social reasons is positively related to *extraversion*-coping, Celebrity Worship for intense-personal reasons is positively related to *neurotic*-coping, and borderline-pathological Celebrity Worship is positively related to *psychoticism*-coping. These findings suggest that (i) Celebrity Worshippers who do so for entertainment-social reasons are extraverted, seek information and support, and are able to display emotions, (ii) Celebrity Worshippers who do so for intense-personal reasons are neurotic, use denial, and mental and behavioral disengagement, and (iii) Celebrity Worshippers who are borderline-pathological demonstrate socio-pathological traits, use a sense of humor to cope, use drink and drugs, and are not religious.

In terms of mental health consequences of these behaviors, Maltby et al. (2004) found that only one aspect of the Celebrity Worship dimensions was significantly related to mental health. On both health dimensions identified in this study, Celebrity Worship for intense-personal reasons was associated with poorer general health (depression, anxiety, somatic symptoms, social dysfunction) and negative affect (negative affect, stress, and low positive affect and life satisfaction). Further, path analysis suggested that the relationship between Celebrity Worship for intense-personal reasons and poorer mental health was mediated by the N-COPE dimension of the adaptational-continuum model of personality and coping, which comprises the personality variable neuroticism, and the coping mechanisms, mental disengagement and denial and behavioral disengagement. This suggests that the relationship between Celebrity Worship and poorer mental health is the result of neuroticism personality traits, and coping behaviors and attitudes that reflect a tendency to fail to acknowledge or disengage with stressful events. This relationship, with these aspects of coping style, suggests that those individuals who engage in intense-personal Celebrity Worship do not deal effectively with everyday stressful events. Accordingly, Maltby et al. speculate that those who intensely worship celebrities may actually spend time worshipping celebrities at the expense of dealing with everyday events.

Other research into personality variables may hold clues to personality processes underlying Celebrity Worship. Research has looked at the relationship between Celebrity Worship and different aspects of narcissism (denoting vanity, conceit, egotism, or simple selfishness) among U.K. and U.S. samples. Among the U.K. sample, intense-personal Celebrity Worship was related to exploitativeness narcissism (example item, "I find it easy to manipulate people"), while borderline-pathological Celebrity Worship was related to both exhibition (example item, "I like to be the center of attention") and self-sufficiency narcissism (example item "I always know what I am doing"). In the U.S. sample, intense-personal Celebrity Worship was again related to exploitativeness narcissism, while borderline-pathological Celebrity Worship was related to both vanity (example item, "I like to look at my body") and self-sufficiency narcissism (example item "I always know what I am doing").

Celebrity Worship and Cognitive Variables

There exists research that has concentrated on other cognitive aspects that may be associated with Celebrity Worship. McCutcheon, Ashe, Houran, and Maltby (2003) examined the relationship between the CAS and six cognitive measures comprising creativity, verbal intelligence, crystallized intelligence, critical thinking, spatial ability, and need for cognition. High scores on the CAS across the three dimensions of Celebrity Worship consistently showed negative correlations with these measures of cognitive ability. The best predictors of Celebrity Worship concerned the tendency for an individual to be dependent, conforming, and with average or below average intelligence, as well as limited fluid intelligence leading to critical thinking errors such as the ad hominem fallacy (to address an argument by attacking or appealing to the person making the argument, rather than by addressing the substance of the argument), appeal to authority, generalization from small sample size, and circular reasoning. These findings indicate that people with higher cognitive functioning are protected from becoming involved in Celebrity Worship for various reasons: perhaps these individuals can understand that the celebrity system is in essence designed to sell a product; maybe these individuals are more interested in ideas than in people and their personalities; or maybe these individuals feel they are as talented or bright as the celebrities being promoted by the media and entertainment industry.

Two studies have looked at Celebrity Worship and cognitive flexibility. Martin, Cayanus, McCutcheon, and Maltby (2003) and Maltby, Day, McCutcheon, Martin et al. (2004) examined the relationship between Celebrity Worship and cognitive flexibility among U.S. and U.K. samples respectively. Cognitive flexibility refers to a person's (a) awareness that in any given situation, there are options and alternatives available, (b) willingness to be flexible and adapt to the situation, and (c) self-efficacy in being flexible. Both studies found acceptable effect-sized negative associations between intense-personal Celebrity Worship and cognitive flexibility, suggesting that individuals who engage in Celebrity Worship for intense-personal reasons are unable to consider options and implement alternatives to problems and are unwilling to be flexible. Therefore, when it comes to stressful situations or daily life, those who are intense-personal in their Celebrity Worship are "locked" into a way of viewing the world, and therefore, are unable to deal with novel or unusual situations. Such conclusions are consistent with descriptions of the obsessive or intense-personal Celebrity Worshipper as someone who is unable to deal with the real world, or only see singular value in their celebrity and very little else.

Houran, Navik, and Zerrusen (2005) looked at Celebrity Worship and boundary functioning. Boundary functioning refers to an individual being able to alternate between connecting and separating with the world, between being in contact with the current environment and withdrawal of attention from the environment within a broad range of mental functions and processes. Houran et al. found entertainment-social dimensions of Celebrity Worship to be related to sensation seeking, openness to experience, and cognitive rigidity, while intense-personal Celebrity Worship was related to these traits, as well as elements of identity diffusion. Borderline-pathological Celebrity Worship showed trends similar to those of intense-personal Celebrity Worship, with the addition of poor interpersonal boundaries. This suggests that people who show borderline-pathological Celebrity Worship want to socialize and interact with other people but feel disconnected from the social world to which they belong.

Social and Developmental Aspects of Celebrity Worship

Finally, the extent to which Celebrity Worship is related to a connectedness to the real world has been explored among U.K. samples, and in particular children and adolescents. In a first study, psychologists Giles and Maltby (2004) looked at the relationships that adolescents form with favorite celebrities as secondary attachments. It was hypothesized that celebrity attachments would reflect the transition from parental attachment to peer attachments and would also be related to increasing emotional autonomy. It was found that, after controlling for age-related effects, high emotional autonomy was a significant predictor of celebrity interest, as well as high attachment to peers and low attachment to parents. Different patterns were observed in accordance with the different dimensions of celebrity attachment. The entertainment-social factor was best predicted by high levels of attachment to peers, suggesting that peer interaction is an important feature of such celebrity attachments. It was also predicted by low attachment to parents, and by low levels of closeness. These findings indicate that the main function of celebrity attachments in adolescence may be seen as an extended social network—a group of "pseudo-friends" who form the subject of peer gossip and discussion. An intense-personal interest in celebrities was best predicted by low levels of security and closeness; this function of celebrity attachment seems to reflect a more problematic aspect of the transition toward emotional autonomy. These findings, then, suggest that celebrities provide adolescents with a secondary group of pseudo-friends during a time of increasing autonomy from parents, but an intense focus on a single celebrity may result from difficulties in making normal or sufficient attachments with family and friends.

Ways Forward

We would like to finish this review by summarizing the main findings in the literature and look to ways of moving the research forward.

Profiling Celebrity Worship

The first way to summarize the relevant research is to list what has been found to relate to the seven dimensions of Celebrity Worship as identified by the two main measurement tools. It must be noted, however, that the amount of research surrounding the PFPI is much smaller than that surrounding the CAS. Still, the following is what we can say about the different dimensions of Celebrity Worship that have emerged from the literature to date:

- *Entertainment-social dimension (CAS)*: Extraversion, seeking social support for both instrumental and emotional reasons, and focusing on and venting of emotions, lower cognitive functioning, sensation seeking, openness to experience, cognitive rigidity, high attachment to peers, low attachment to parents, high levels of closeness
- *Intense-personal dimension (CAS)*: Neuroticism, fantasy proneness, denial and mental and behavioral disengagement coping, depression, anxiety, exploitativeness narcissism, lower cognitive functioning, lower cognitive flexibility, sensation seeking, openness to experience, cognitive rigidity, identity diffusion, low levels of security and closeness
- *Borderline-pathological dimension (CAS)*: Fantasy proneness, dissociative experiences, uses a sense of humor to cope, uses drink and drugs to cope, exhibitionism, self-sufficiency and vanity narcissism, lower cognitive functioning, lower cognitive flexibility, openness to experience, cognitive rigidity, identity diffusion, poor interpersonal boundaries
- *Establishing contact (PFPI)*: Dissociative experiences
- *Collecting*: No data reported
- *Sexual (PFPI)*: Absorption
- *Stalking (PFPI)*: Absorption

Clearly, a first suggestion is that a lot more work should be completed in relation to both these scales, particularly with regard to the PFPI.

Measuring the Seven Dimensions of Celebrity Worship

A second suggestion is to consolidate measurement issues by combining the two measures currently available. At present, we would say that there are three ways to measure Celebrity Worship:

- To use the CAS or PFPI to obtain an overall score of Celebrity Worship, with higher scores on the PFPI reflecting more extreme aspects of Celebrity Worship
- To utilize the three factors that can be derived from the CAS to measure entertainment-social, intense-personal, and borderline-pathological Celebrity Worship
- To measure pathological Celebrity Worship by way of the four factors that can be derived from the PFPI: establishing contact, collecting, sexual, and stalking

Ultimately, new researchers are faced with a dilemma of which measure of Celebrity Worship to use, or to use a total of 84 items to measure levels of Celebrity Worship. For some this may be too many items, particularly where research time is short and may present a barrier to a growth in research. We would suggest a new measure that combines both scales, but contains fewer items. To this end, we are going to suggest a 42-item scale that utilizes items from both scales and is based on the analysis presented in two large-scale surveys (Maltby et al., 2005; Sheridan et al., 2006):

- For the CAS, the analysis is from data collected among 1,723 U.K. respondents (781 males, 942 females) aged between 14 and 62 years (mean age = 28.50 years, SD = 10.0). Among this sample, the most often reported demographic was white ($n = 1,187$); single ($n = 881$); employed ($n = 773$); most respondents reporting their education level to be leaving school with the equivalent of an education with at least one "0" level/GCSE (high school equivalency, $n = 445$).
- For the PFPI, the analysis is from data from 1,162 participants (384 males, 778 females) aged between 13 and 72 years (mean age = 29.62 years, SD = 11.5), with the majority of respondents residing in the United Kingdom (55.9%), the United States (24.4%), Canada, and Australia (both 4.3%). The majority of respondents were single (69.5%), white (78.2%), and students (51.9%).

Both these studies used factor analysis to look for underlying factors among the items. For the purposes of the current exercise, we selected the six top loading items[1] for each of the seven subscales from the two analyses:

1. **Entertainment-social[2]**

   - I love to talk with others who admire my favorite celebrity.
   - Keeping up with news about my favorite celebrity is an entertaining pastime.
   - It is enjoyable just to be with others who like my favorite celebrity.
   - I enjoy watching, reading, or listening to my favorite celebrity because it means a good time.
   - Learning the life story of my favorite celebrity is a lot of fun.
   - I like watching and hearing about my favorite celebrity when I am with a large group of people.

2. **Intense-personal**

   - If I were to meet my favorite celebrity in person, he/she would already somehow know that I am his/her biggest fan.
   - One of the main reasons I maintain an interest in my favorite celebrity is that doing so gives me a temporary escape from life's problems.
   - My favorite celebrity is practically perfect in every way.
   - I share with my favorite celebrity a special bond that cannot be described in words.
   - To know my favorite celebrity is to love him/her.
   - When something bad happens to my favorite celebrity I feel like it happened to me.

3. Borderline-pathological

- I would gladly die in order to save the life of my favorite celebrity.
- If I were lucky enough to meet my favorite celebrity, and he/she asked me to do something illegal as a favor, I would probably do it.
- If I walked through the door of my favorite celebrity's home without an invitation she or he would be happy to see me.
- I have frequent thoughts about my celebrity, even when I don't want to.
- I often feel compelled to learn the personal habits of my favorite celebrity.
- My favorite celebrity would immediately come to my rescue if I needed help.

4. Establishing contact

- I must have sent over a hundred letters/e-mails to my favorite celebrity.
- I have tried to phone my favorite celebrity.
- I have tried to get closer to my favorite celebrity's family.
- I have followed my favorite celebrity in a car or on foot.
- I have gone to see my favorite celebrity's home.
- I have talked to a doctor or psychologist about my feelings for my favorite celebrity.

5. Collecting

- I have a huge amount of material relating to my favorite celebrity.
- I have hundreds of hours of video tape of my favorite celebrity making appearances in the media.
- I have written letters or e-mails to my favorite celebrity.
- Sometimes I feel that no one understands my feelings for my favorite celebrity.
- I would travel thousands of miles to see my favorite celebrity.
- I have a shrine dedicated to my favorite celebrity.

6. Sexual

- If I met my favorite celebrity we would flirt with each other.
- I do not like my celebrity's romantic partner.
- My favorite celebrity is a notorious flirt.
- My favorite celebrity and I are destined to be together.
- I have fantasies of an intimate nature about my favorite celebrity.
- If it were not for other people, my favorite celebrity and I could have a closer relationship.

7. Stalking

- Every celebrity needs a stalker.
- Sometimes "stalking" is the only way to make a celebrity notice you.
- I would stalk my favorite celebrity if I had the means to do so.

- I wish my favorite celebrity was dead.
- Privately I would admit to stalking my favorite celebrity.
- If I could I would ensure that my favorite celebrity and myself would die together.

Theories of Celebrity Worship

We would like to summarize the different theoretical perspectives that may be useful to researchers in providing a context for their research and consideration.

The first context, suggested by McCutcheon et al. (2002), is an "absorption-addiction" hypothesis used to explain Celebrity Worship. According to this model, a compromised identity structure in some individuals facilitates psychological absorption with a celebrity in an attempt to establish an identity and a sense of fulfilment. The dynamics of the motivational forces driving this absorption might, in turn, take on an addictive component, leading to more extreme (and perhaps delusional) behaviors to sustain the individual's satisfaction with the para-social relationship.

A second context, outlined by Houran et al. (2005) emphasizes the role of erotomania. Erotomania is a disorder in which a person has a delusional belief that another person, usually of a higher social status (e.g., a celebrity), is secretly in love with them. Houran et al. suggest there is a resemblance between an erotomanic type of delusional disorder and the phenomenon of Celebrity Worship, bolstered by findings of an association between Celebrity Worship and a number of "cognitive deficits."

A third context is suggested by Maltby et al. (2006), which seeks to counterbalance the causal direction of "absorption-addiction," suggesting that as individuals reach higher levels of Celebrity Worship, there is a change in their clinical profile. Maltby et al. propose a "reflective" hypothesis, which uses a personality context, to suggest that Celebrity Worship originates from a disposition (i.e., intense fantasy proneness, tendency for uncontrollable thoughts) to the behavioral characteristics of Celebrity Worship.

Summary

We hope this chapter has provided a useful introduction to the measurement and theorizing that surrounds Celebrity Worship at present. We have examined the research work that has concentrated on how Celebrity Worship has been measured, how theoretical areas of personality and cognitive and developmental psychology have informed our understanding of the construct, and have shown how Celebrity Worship does have relevance in terms of mental health and health variables. We also suggest that the future of research is bound up in consolidating theoretical, empirical, and measurement approaches to move forward toward useful developments in the future.

Notes

1. Though the choice of six items is relatively arbitrary, we would argue against shortening it further because of the need to guard against the potential for limited variance in scores.
2. It is important to note that when administering the questionnaire, respondents are informed that for purposes of the survey, the term "celebrity" means a famous living person (or one who died during your lifetime) whom you greatly admire. Respondents are then asked to answer each of the items on a 5-point Likert (Strongly Agree to Strongly Disagree) format.

References

Dietz, P. E., Matthews, D. B., Martell, D. A., Stewart, T., Hrouda, D. R., Warren, J., et al. (1991). Threatening and otherwise inappropriate letters to members of the United States Congress. *Journal of Forensic Sciences, 36,* 1445–1468.

Dietz, P. E., Matthews, D. B., Van Duyne, C., Martell, D. A., Parry, C. D. H., Stewart, T., et al. (1991). Threatening and otherwise inappropriate letters to Hollywood celebrities. *Journal of Forensic Sciences, 36,* 185–209.

Ferris, K. O. (2001). Through a glass, darkly: The dynamics of fan-celebrity encounters. *Symbolic Interaction, 24,* 25–47.

Giles, D. C., & Maltby, J. (2004). The role of media in adolescent development: Relations between autonomy, attachment, and interest in celebrities. *Personality and Individual Differences, 36,* 813–822.

Houran, J., Navik, S., & Zerrusen, K. (2005). Boundary functioning in celebrity worshipers. *Personality and Individual Differences, 38,* 237–248.

Leets, L., de Becker, G., & Giles, H. (1995). Fans: Exploring expressed motivations for contacting celebrities. *Journal of Language and Social Psychology, 14,* 102–123.

Malsch, M., Visscher, M., & Blaauw, E. (2002). *Stalking van bekende personen* [Stalking of celebrities]. Den Haag: Boom.

Maltby, J., Day, L., McCutcheon, L. E., Gillett, R., Houran, J., & Ashe, D. (2004). Celebrity Worship using an adaptational-continuum model of personality and coping. *British Journal of Psychology, 95,* 411–428.

Maltby, J., Day, L., McCutcheon, L. E., Houran, J., & Ashe, D. (2006). Extreme celebrity worship, fantasy proneness and dissociation: Developing the measurement and understanding of celebrity worship within a clinical personality context. *Personality and Individual Differences, 40,* 273–283.

Maltby, J., Day, L., McCutcheon, L. E., Martin, M. M., & Cayanus, J. L. (2004). Celebrity worship, cognitive flexibility and social complexity. *Personality and Individual Differences, 37,* 1475–1482.

Maltby, J., Giles, D., Barber, L., & McCutcheon, L. E. (2005). Intense-personal celebrity worship and body image: Evidence of a link among female adolescents. *British Journal of Health Psychology, 10,* 17–32.

Maltby, J., Houran, J., Ashe, D., & McCutcheon, L. E. (2001). The self-reported psychological well-being of celebrity worshippers. *North American Journal of Psychology, 3,* 441–452.

Maltby, J., Houran, M. A., & McCutcheon, L. E. (2003). A clinical interpretation of attitudes and behaviors associated with celebrity worship. *Journal of Nervous and Mental Disease, 191*, 25–29.

Martin, M. M., Cayanus, J. L., McCutcheon, L. E., & Maltby, J. (2003). Celebrity worship and cognitive flexibility. *North American Journal of Psychology, 5*, 75–80.

McCutcheon, L. E., Ashe, D. D., Houran, J., & Maltby, J. (2003). A cognitive profile of individuals who tend to worship celebrities. *The Journal of Psychology, 137*, 309–322.

McCutcheon, L. E., Lange, R., & Houran, J. (2002). Conceptualization and measurement of Celebrity Worship. *British Journal of Psychology, 93*, 67–87.

Rubin, A. M., Perse, E. M., & Powell, R. A. (1985). Loneliness, parasocial interaction, and local television news viewing. *Human Communication Research, 12*, 155–180.

Sheridan, L., Maltby, J., & Gillett, R. (2006). Pathological public figure preoccupation: Its relationship with dissociation and absorption. *Personality and Individual Differences, 41*, 525–535.

Stever, G. S. (1991). The Celebrity Appeal Questionnaire. *Psychological Reports, 68*, 859–866.

Wann, D. L. (1995). Preliminary validation of the Sport Fan Motivation Scale. *Journal of Sport and Social Issues, 19*, 377–396.

13

Fanning the Flames of Fandom: Celebrity Worship, Parasocial Interaction, and Stalking

Brian H. Spitzberg and William R. Cupach

Celebrities are ubiquitous in the world. The mass media and the public seem to thrive on them. Entertainment shows gather over 100 million viewers a week and celebrity-oriented magazines garner over a billion dollars a year in sales (Tapper & Morris, 2005). Sales of such magazines account for close to one third of all newsstand circulation, and show strong signs of growth relative to other magazines (Fadner, 2005). It is small wonder, given that as many as 90% of people surveyed indicate they have "been attracted to a celebrity idol at some point in their lives," and as many as 75% indicate they have experienced "strong attachments to more than one celebrity" (Boon & Lomore, 2001, p. 439). Indeed, a quarter of a century ago, Caughey (1984, p. 49) claimed that "elaborate love relationships with unmet media figures...represent a significant, and pervasive, culture pattern in modern American society." Celebrities themselves tend to be higher in narcissism than the average person (Young & Pinsky, 2006) and are likely to enjoy and inculcate the adulation they receive. Given the profits to be made, celebrities reinforce the celebrity marketplace in which larger fan bases can be established and maintained. The very fans fueling the flames of celebrity, however, can burn those celebrities when fandom becomes fanaticism in the pursuit of association with the celebrity. Events such as the deaths of Princess Diana, Rebecca Schaeffer, and John Lennon, and the attacks on President Reagan, Teresa Saldana, and Monica Seles, reflect the darker sides of fandom and fame. Underlying such extreme events may be a continuum of disordered forms of fandom that deserve further exploration. This study investigates whether and to what extent celebrity worship and the desire for constructing "relationship" with public figures are related to a continuum of fan behavior, including stalking and aggression in the pursuit of celebrity association.

Celebrity and Fan Worship

The concept that consumers of mass communication might develop attachments with figures in the public eye is hardly new. In mid-20th century, when television was still getting its footing in popular culture, Horton and Wohl (1956) coined the term "parasocial interaction" to refer in part to the ways in which media consumers might experience aspects of media characters as a form of actual interaction and affiliation. Acting toward actors or newscasters *as if* they were actually in the living room instead of only in the television suggested the potential influence that mass communication could have. "People characterize unmet media figures as if they were intimately involved with them, and in a sense they are—they engage in pseudo-social interactions with them" (Caughey, 1984, p. 33). People engage in behavior that is imitative of celebrities, they discuss celebrities with others, engage in imaginative interactions with celebrities, and sometimes, attempt actual contact with celebrities (Giles, 2002).

Both utopian and dystopian scenarios soon arose from such possibilities (Caughey, 1984). On the one hand, parasocial interaction might be a salve for those who are otherwise isolated from society and human contact. On the other hand, parasocial interaction might heighten the sensed acuteness of such isolation. For others, it could become an addictive relationship that prevents the initiation and formation of "real" relationships. Many people in today's society already qualify as television addicts (Kuby & Csikszentmihalyi, 2002). Another dark side of parasocial interactions that has become a more prominent feature of fandom is the potential for media consumers to develop obsessive or pathological attachments to characters or people in the media.

There is some reason to anticipate such ambivalence in regard to parasocial interactions. For example, lonely people do seem to seek out a variety of alternatives to interaction, but their dependency on the media for parasocial interaction does not appear to be particularly pathological (Rubin, Perse, & Powell, 1985). On the other hand, to the extent that lonely persons do seek out media as a functional alternative to interaction, they apparently do not find it as gratifying as nonlonely persons (Canary & Spitzberg, 1993). Insecurely attached persons appear to more readily form parasocial relationships, most likely as a compensatory response to their relational anxiety and incompetence (Cole & Leets, 1999). Regardless, it appears reasonable to assume that despite their "imaginary" nature, such relationships can mimic many of the functions and patterns of "real" relationships (Boon & Lomore, 2001).

Other scholars point to the extent to which identity in society, and especially among developing youths, is influenced by the media. For example, a 2006 survey asked 792 parents in the United Kingdom what they thought their children would choose as a career. The most common choice (31%) was to be a famous performer, such as an actor, singer, or dancer (http://www.tes.co.uk/2302976).

Through processes of fantasized interactions and scenarios, adolescents get to imaginatively construct not only ways of behaving, but also features of identity and identification. Such processes "may later inform, at least initially, the adolescent's expectancies of, and attachment to, more proximal objects such as peers" (Greene & Adams-Price, 1990, p. 345). This socialization occasionally contains romantic affectations with relevance to the adolescent construction of adult attachment working models. In this sense, "crushes or secondary attachments to celebrity figures are an important aspect of self-concept development during adolescence" (Adams-Price & Greene, 1990, p. 187).

Children and adolescents, learning for the first time the nature of their own feelings and perceptions of romance, are likely to find many parallels between their actual relationships and the parasocial interactions and attachments to their favorite celebrities (Bachen & Illouz, 1996, p. 304). Given the potential importance of such a relatively nonthreatening environment in which to engage in romantic rehearsal, young people are likely to invest time, effort, and affect into parasocial interactions with idols. "Such investments foster a growing sense of involvement with the idol, serving to establish and—as such investments continue and (as seems likely) increase over time—intensify perceptions that a special connection or intimacy exists between admirer and idol" (Boon & Lomore, 2001, p. 437).

Dysfunctional and pathological trappings are likely to be arrayed on a continuum, from relatively benign or innocent fan activity to full-fledged obsession. Research has demonstrated that celebrities court fans through their publicized sexual iconography (Lambiase, 2003) and arrangement of celebrity-organized events (Ferris, 2001, 2004). Even when celebrities do not plan to encounter fans, fans often plan to encounter celebrities, representing one of many asymmetries of celebrity culture (Ferris, 2004; Hills, 2002). Most encounters, broadly conceived, are benign. For example, a study of fan letters to celebrities identified three common motives, including seeking nonsexual face-to-face contact (40%), some kind of response (e.g., mail, phone, 39%), or to transmit information to someone else (22%) (Dietz et al., 1991, p. 202). Yet, more personal and relational reasons often underlie attitudes toward celebrities. In one study, 30% of those describing their connection to an idol "endorsed the wish to 'be the celebrity' and 25% endorsed the wish to be the celebrity's romantic partner or spouse" (Adams-Price & Greene, 1990, p. 192). A study of threatening fan letters revealed a potentially darker side to such motives, in which many clearly expressed a belief that they had some kind of "personal relationship, often an important one.... The most prevalent of the inappropriate roles in which the subject had cast themselves were those of friend, adviser, or acquaintance (41%); spouse, would-be spouse, or suitor (30%); and lover or would-be lover (25%)" (Dietz et al., 1991, p. 199).

This is perhaps the strongest stereotype of the celebrity watcher: the obsessive fan, devoted to a fantasy of meeting and winning over the object of her adoration, out of touch with and resistant to reality, undaunted by negative information, governed by an overwhelming desire to be close to a star, willing to travel great distances and to seek out his house.

Gamson, 1994, p. 129

Such special connections are especially likely the more connected a media consumer is to particular shows, music, or media personage. "A highly connected viewer has a deeper, more intimate relationship with a show, the characters in the show, and other viewers of the show" (Russell, Norman, & Heckler, 2004b, p. 280). The effects of such identity-shaping influences can be both positive (Greene & Adams-Price, 1990) and devastating (e.g., Maltby, Giles, Barber, & McCutcheon, 2005) for the individual. When it becomes celebrity worship in particular, the fan's identity may begin to reveal distortions (Houran, Navik, & Zerrusen, 2005). Celebrity worship is a state of personal devotion to at least one personage in a position of media exposure and public status. The more extreme levels of celebrity worship reflect a person's inability to "successfully satisfy their hypothesized goal of establishing a sense of self or firm identity role via parasocial relationships" (Houran et al., p. 246).

Thus, fans' investments in celebrities, in the form of parasocial interaction, such as letter-writing, web chats, travel, and participation in fan culture, not only function as surrogate forms of socialization and relationship formation, but they also serve as markers of relational identity (Boon & Lomore, 2001). "Fans have attachments to unmet media figures that are analogous to and in many ways directly parallel to actual social relationships" (Caughey, 1984, p. 40). If parasocial relationship investment and commitment become excessive, however, more pathological forms of celebrity worship may evolve. Celebrity worship represents an attempt to conceptualize these more dystopic consequences of celebrity attachments.

Celebrity Worship

It is one thing to lionize celebrities to the point of linking to one's self-perception (Szymanski, 1977). It is another thing to worship celebrities. *Celebrity worship* is viewed as an obsession-like behavior pattern "whereby persons with assumed intact identities become virtually obsessed with one or more celebrities—similar to an erotomanic type of delusional disorder" (Maltby, Houran, & McCutcheon, 2003, p. 25). McCutcheon, Lange, and Houran (2002) conceptualize and measure this phenomenon as existing along three levels or stages: entertainment-social, intense-personal, and borderline-pathological. *Entertainment-social* celebrity worship tends to reflect relatively normal levels of identification with or attention to celebrities (e.g., "My friends and I like to discuss what my favorite celebrity has done"). *Intense-personal* celebrity worship reflects an increasing obsession with the celebrity (e.g.,

"I have frequent thoughts about my celebrity, even when I don't want to"). The *borderline-pathological* celebrity worshipper manifests some dissolution of boundaries regarding the celebrity (e.g., "If I were lucky enough to meet my favorite celebrity, and he/she asked me to do something illegal as a favor I would probably do it"). A series of studies have begun to paint a profile of people who are further along this continuum of celebrity worship.

As would be suggested by societal investments in the celebrity industry, celebrity worship is not uncommon: in research, as many as a third of sample respondents are above the scale midpoints of celebrity worship, and about a quarter of sample respondents score in the range of the intense-personal and borderline-pathological ranges (Maltby et al., 2003). In general, research indicates that as celebrity worship increases, there are increases in adherence to just world beliefs (McCutcheon, 2003), game playing and dependent love styles (McCutcheon, 2002), narcissism (Ashe, Maltby, & McCutcheon, 2005), and shyness but not loneliness (Ashe & McCutcheon, 2001). Celebrity worship is related to several measures of negative cognitive function (McCutcheon, Ashe, Houran, & Maltby, 2003). Even the relatively mild form of entertainment-social celebrity worship is positively related to neurotic coping styles (Maltby, Day, McCutcheon, Martin, & Cayanus, 2004). Celebrity worshippers are more likely to reveal a preoccupied attachment style (Cole & Leets, 1999; Engle & Kasser, 2005) and less likely to have a secure attachment style (Giles & Maltby, 2004).

Intense-personal and borderline-pathological worshippers appear to lack empathy (Houran et al., 2005) and are more psychotic and neurotic (Maltby et al., 2003, 2004). Intense-personal celebrity worship is negatively correlated with cognitive flexibility and social complexity (Maltby et al., 2004; Martin, Cayanus, McCutcheon, & Maltby, 2003) and positively related to anxiety and depressive symptoms (Maltby, McCutcheon, Ashe, & Houran, 2001). Borderline-pathological celebrity worship in particular is correlated to "thinner" boundaries in terms of roles. "That is, these celebrity worshippers would seem to pervasively blur the roles that society places on age groups and individuals within relationships" (Houran et al., 2005, p. 244).

Collectively, the celebrity worshipper appears to be a person who is insecure yet desperate for attachment, and is relatively incapable of reasonably maintaining normative boundaries between the "real" and the "mediated" world. Such a person may be at substantially higher risk of developing more pathological attachments to celebrities, persons of high status and attractiveness, who by nature of their mediated and nonproximate position, are capable of sustaining a rewarding relationship through the fan-celebrity relationship. Such attachments, in turn, run the risk of becoming one of obsessive pursuit or stalking. Along this line of reasoning, in a study of 299 college students, McCutcheon, Scott, Aruguete, and Parker (2006) found that obsessive relational intrusion and celebrity stalking types of activities were related negatively (albeit marginally) to secure childhood attachment with parents ($r = -.20$, $p < .01$) and to secure adult attachment ($r = -.16$, $p < .01$). In addition, the entertainment-social ($r = .25, p < .01$), intense-personal ($r = .35$, $p < .001$), and borderline-pathological ($r = .25, p < .01$) scales revealed small to moderate effects in predicting celebrity pursuit activities. Thus, the profile of celebrity worshippers is of people who tend to have permeable boundaries between fantasy and reality, who become easily obsessed, and who are capable of fixating on a particular person as an important goal to pursue. All these characteristics portray people prone to stalking a target of their obsessions.

Stalking

Stalking is a pattern of unwanted pursuit, harassment, or intrusion that threatens or intimidates a person, or would be so perceived by a "reasonable person" (Cupach & Spitzberg, 2004; Spitzberg, 2002; Spitzberg & Cupach, 2007). The first stalking law was enacted in California in 1990, in part as a reaction to highly publicized celebrity murders at the hands of fans. Consequently, a common public image of stalking is that of a crazed fan pursuing love and/or hate with a celebrity (Spitzberg & Cadiz, 2002). The vast majority of stalking in society is most certainly not fans pursuing celebrities (Cupach & Spitzberg, 2004; Tjaden & Thoennes, 1998). However, just as certainly, some people who are particularly in the public eye, and who receive high levels of media attention, are at higher proportional risk than most of being the object of someone's obsession, if nothing else, merely as a result of their greater public status, access, and exposure. There are likely to be both similarities and differences between stalkers of ordinary persons and stalkers of celebrities (Schlesinger, 2006), just as there are likely to be similarities and differences between normal fan activities and stalking (Ferris, 2001).

In many ways, "fan activities...do indeed bear a striking resemblance to the activities of stalkers. The asymmetrical awareness context, the unilateral pursuit, the lack of reciprocity, and the search for and use of access information are all characteristics of 'relational stalking'" (Ferris, 2001, pp. 40–41). The culture of celebrity engenders a reciprocal, generally complementary, and often strategically reinforced culture of fandom. Consequently, many fans seek some form of identification and connection with celebrities. From the multitude of celebrities who are always available for consumption, fans are able to seek out one or more who represent idealized targets of attraction. "From out of thousands of glamorous alternatives, why does the fan seize on one particular figure rather than another?...The admired figure represents an ideal self-image" (Caughey, 1984, p. 54). Fans are able thereby to link a celebrity to their needs to achieve a fulfilled life and identity. Such a process of linking, in turn, is likely to result in proactive fan activities devoted to following and contacting these celebrities.

Ferris's (2001) ethnographic study of television fan culture and fan efforts to contact celebrities revealed a subtle yet highly organized choreography of interaction. In the process, he found that many fans are acutely aware that they may be viewed as "stalkers," an attribution they explicitly attempt to avoid despite the admitted parallels. Although such attributions are not preferred, they generally will not deter fans from pursuing their connections with celebrities, as evidenced by the great lengths to which fans go to know more and be closer to the objects of their interest.

Fans who do engage in campaigns of pursuit risk crossing the (rope) line, and the "specter of stalking arises," as fans

> Make the same creative use of access information that celebrity stalkers do as they seek some way of having independent, regular access to the actors they love, and they may seek a relationship or type of relationship that the actor either does not desire or of which she is unaware.
>
> Ferris, 2001, p. 40

This crossing-over may occur in escalating stages, moving from relatively benign or healthy fan appreciation of celebrities, to the personalization of identification and the intensification of feelings, and ultimately to a pathological and maladaptive level (Maltby et al., 2001).

In a study of 1,800 fan letters to celebrities by 214 writers, 56% "were rated as having 'idolized or worshipped' the celebrity to whom they wrote" (Dietz et al., 1991, p. 200). The most consistent desires evidenced in these letters were for face-to-face contact (40%), and when coded for what emotional reaction the letter writer was attempting to evoke from the celebrity, 40% sought in some way "to instill feelings of love" (p. 202), with another 32% giving "evidence of sexual arousal or responsiveness" (p. 203). Although love and sexual interest may be the most common desires, it is also a foregone conclusion that many fan letters are ignored or rebuffed, and in reaction, fans can become agitated. Thus, it is not surprising that 23% of letter writers included some form of threat (p. 203).

Research on fan motivations reveals that only a relatively small minority could be considered "inappropriate," and these typically reveal bizarre requests or expectations, but even "normal fans may exhibit inappropriate behavior that varies in degree from those who might pursue unwanted encounters with the famous" (Leets, Becker, & Giles, 1995, p. 117). In the Dietz et al. study (1991), 10% of the sample of letter writers displayed "maximal patronage," in which the subject "has devoted a room or shrine to the public figure; takes multiple trips of extraordinary distances to attend public appearances of the public figure; [and] devotes a significant amount of time on a daily basis to behavior directly related to obsession with the public figure" (Dietz et al., p. 200). Although a minority of fans, this is still a sizeable number given the magnitude of audience exposure that celebrities routinely experience.

In studies of sports fans, to the extent that fans feel particularly identified with a particular group or person, they are likely to feel less in control of their behavior (Dimmock & Grove, 2005) and more aggressive toward rivals (Wann, Peterson, Cothran, & Dykes, 1999). Such inappropriate and disinhibited fans may pose risks not only to the celebrities they idolize, but to third parties viewed as rivals to the fan's affections or obstacles to the fan's pursuits. To the extent that "fans temper reality and fantasy together in the crucible of their interactions with celebrities" (Ferris, 2001, p. 44), celebrities may be at particular risk.

This study investigates predictors of celebrity harassment and pursuit. Celebrity harassment and pursuit is expected to display similar ambivalent characteristics to a phenomenon referred to as *obsessive relational intrusion* (ORI), which is a pattern of pursuit of intimacy with a person who does not want the level of intimacy being pursued (Cupach & Spitzberg, 1998, 2000a, 2000b; Spitzberg & Cupach, 2001, 2003; Spitzberg, Marshall, & Cupach, 2001; Spitzberg, Nicastro, & Cousins, 1998; Spitzberg & Rhea, 1999). When this pattern of behavior becomes threatening or fear inducing, it becomes stalking (Cupach & Spitzberg, 2004; Dutton & Spitzberg, 2007; Spitzberg, 2002; Spitzberg & Cupach, 2007). Like ORI, celebrity pursuit activities are often like flirtation and courtship: precisely what the object of pursuit finds flattering and desirable (Dunn, 2002). However, beyond some reasonable threshold, such activities become harassing, and sometimes even threatening. Precisely where this reasonable threshold between appropriate and inappropriate pursuit lies cannot be easily determined in advance (Kinkade, Burns & Fuentes, 2005; cf., Purcell, Pathé, & Mullen, 2004). Therefore, in the early stages of study, it is necessary to provide a continuum of such activities, investigate the perceived structure of such activities, and identify the predictors of the continuum of behavior.

This study is a preliminary exploration of celebrity pursuit activities among a relatively "media-savvy" population: college students. The intent is to examine the interrelationships among celebrity worship, parasocial interaction needs and tendencies, and obsessive celebrity pursuit activities. The rationale predicts that people with higher personal needs for media contact and connection, and higher levels of celebrity worship and idolization, will be more likely to indicate that they have engaged in celebrity pursuit activities, from relatively benign to more threatening forms of pursuit.

Methods

An online survey approach is described in the following text, in which college students were asked to report on a person or character in their past who would be considered a celebrity or idol and their activities in reference to the celebrity. The study is now described in detail.

Participants

Students at a large Southwestern public urban university were solicited from a general education freshman course required of virtually all students in the university, as well as upper-division communications classes. There were 474 respondents, 60% of whom were female and 56% Caucasian/White (with 13% Asian, 12% Hispanic/Mexican American, 4% Black/African American, 1% Native American, with the balance unspecified). The average respondent claimed to read 1.81 (SD = 1.85) newspapers and 1.10 (SD = 1.23) "popular culture" magazines per week.

Procedures

An online survey was developed on SurveyMonkey.com and made available to students in return for nominal extra credit. The survey was announced via an oral announcement read from a script provided to instructors of the various classes in which the study was made available. To assure complete anonymity of respondents, a secondary SurveyMonkey "extra credit" survey URL was announced on the last page of the survey, which linked the respondent to a 1-page survey in which they provided their name and instructor. Thus, the only personal identification information provided was in a secondary survey with a separate URL. Given the potential social undesirability of the item content of the pursuit activities, respondents were assured of their anonymity, and the importance of their honesty was emphasized in the instructions. The survey consisted of the following measures.

Measurement

Parasocial and Media Use Tendencies

The Need for Entertainment Scale (NES) (Brock & Livingston, 2004) is a 16-item scale measuring a dispositional desire for entertainment activity (e.g., "I need some entertainment time each and every day") and the view that entertainment is unnecessary (e.g., "I feel like my time spent on entertainment purposes is generally wasted").

The Audience-Persona Interaction Scale (APIS) (Auter & Palmgreen, 2000) assesses parasocial interaction with a favorite character. If adapted to suit more general celebrity targets, it identifies four dimensions: identity (e.g., "I have the same qualities as a favorite character or person from a show or movie"), interest (e.g., "I care about what happens to my favorite character or person from shows or movies"), group (e.g., "My friends are like the characters or persons from the shows or movies I just watch"), and problem modeling (e.g., "I wish I could handle problems as well as my favorite characters or persons from the shows and movies I watch").

The Connectedness Scale (CS) (Russell, Norman, & Heckler, 2004a, 2004b) is a 15-item scale assessing various facets through which a person can feel connected or identified with what is experienced in the media. The facets include escape (e.g., "If I am in a bad mood, watching _____ puts me in a better mood"), fashion (e.g., "I often buy clothing styles that I've seen in _____"), imitation (e.g., "I find myself saying phrases from _____ when I interact with other people"), modeling (e.g., "I learn how to handle real life situations by watching _____"), aspiration (e.g., "I would love to be an actor in _____"), and paraphernalia (e.g., "I read books if they are related to _____").

Celebrity Worship Measures

The Celebrity Attitude Scale (CAS) (McCutcheon et al., 2002) is a 22-item multidimensional measure of three complex tendencies to pursue celebrities: entertainment-social (e.g., "I enjoy watching, reading, or listening to my favorite celebrity because it means a good time"), intense-social (e.g., "I am obsessed by details of my favorite celebrity's life"), and borderline-pathological (e.g., "I often feel compelled to learn the personal habits of my favorite celebrity"). The Celebrity Idolization Scale (CIS) (Engle & Kasser, 2005) is a 15-item unidimensional measure of various tendencies to worship or idolize a celebrity. It includes items such as "I have lots of his/her pictures, pinups, and posters" and "I am more devoted to him than anyone else I know."

Celebrity Pursuit Activities

The Fan Activities Scale is a 60-item measure developed through item generation and adaptation of the existing Obsessive Relational Intrusion short form (Cupach & Spitzberg, 2004).[1] It includes a range of cluster items that ask the frequency with which subjects have engaged in each general behavior, followed by a set of exemplars. For example, a mild fan behavior is "Attending a Convention With Which the Person Is Associated (e.g., going to an event at which the person was to "show" as an attraction of the event)." A more moderate fan behavior would be "Going to or Waiting at the Person's Hotel." A more severe behavior would be "Invading Her/His Property" (e.g., breaking and entering the person's home, car, desk, backpack or briefcase, etc.). The scale is reported in the Appendix.

Exploratory Variables

Finally, a few exploratory questions were included, as well as some items intending to assure and identify respondent focus on a particular celebrity. At the end of the survey, so as to not overly bias expectancy while completing the other measures, respondents were asked, "Have you ever pursued anyone, in the hope of establishing or reestablishing a relationship, in a way that was personal and might have been interpreted as threatening by the person you were pursuing?"

Results

When asked, "At any point in your life, have you had or do you continue to have an attraction to or an admiration for a famous person or an 'idol' (for example, a musician, movie star, television star, athlete, model, politician, religious figure, and so on)?," 76.4% responded "yes." When asked "If 'yes,' what kind of business is this person in?," 59.1% indicated "entertainment/show business," 12.2% "music," 10.3% "sports," 9.2% "government/politics," 2.1% "news," and 7.1% "other." Of the 368 who responded to the item "If 'yes,' rate how strong your attraction was/is," they rated their attraction an average of 3.91 (SD = .99, range 1–5). Of the 474 respondents, when asked if they had ever pursued anyone for a relationship in a manner that might have been interpreted as threatening, 9.4% (*n* = 45) responded that they had. In all cases of remaining data analyses, unless otherwise noted, results are based only on those who indicated they had at one time had an attraction to a celebrity.

Respondents who indicated any lifetime celebrity attraction were asked to name their favorite celebrity. One of the most intriguing aspects of the resulting list (see Table 13.1) is the sheer breadth of celebrities. Despite a media industry geared toward particular celebrities, Table 13.1 reveals that most celebrities were only mentioned by one fan, and even some of the most famous celebrities only garnered a relatively small percentage of the overall sample in terms

Table 13.1. Celebrities, listed in descending order of frequency, alphabetized within counts

Celebrity	Frequency of nomination	
	Number	**Percentage**
None	119	25.1
Jessica Alba	15	3.2
Jessica Simpson	14	2.9
Justin Timberlake	13	2.7
Brad Pitt	12	2.3
Johnny Depp	10	2.0
Angelina Jolie	8	1.7
Paul Walker	8	1.7
Michael Jordan	6	1.3
Britney Spears	7	1.3
Adriana Lima	4	.8
Brandon Boyd	4	.8
Kobe Bryant	4	.8
Oprah Winfrey	4	.8
Brett Favre	3	.8
Chad Michael Murray	3	.6
Jake Gyllenhall	3	.6
Jennifer Aniston	3	.6
Jennifer Love Hewitt	3	.6
Keith Urban	3	.6
Matthew McConaughy	3	.6

(Continued)

Table 13.1. (Continued)

Celebrity	Frequency of nomination	
	Number	**Percentage**
Natalie Portman	3	.6
NSync	3	.6
Scarlett Johannson	3	.6
Allen Iverson	2	.4
Ashton Kutcher	2	.4
Barry Bonds	2	.4
Beyoncé	2	.4
Carmen Electra	2	.4
Catherine Zeta Jones	2	.4
Colin Farrell	2	.2
David Beckham	2	.4
Eva Longoria	2	.4
Ewan McGregor	2	.4
Freddie Prince Jr.	2	.4
Gwen Stefani	2	.4
Halle Berry	2	.4
JC Chasez	2	.4
John Travolta	2	.4
Josh Hartnett	2	.4
Kate Hudson	2	.4
Keira Knightly	2	.4
Ken Griffey Jr.	2	.4
Kurt Cobain	2	.4
Madonna	2	.2
Michael Vick	2	.4
Morris Chestnut	2	.4
Nick Carter	2	.4
Nick Lachey	2	.4
Orlando Bloom	2	.4
Owen Wilson	2	.4
Ricky Martin	2	.4
Ryan Reynolds	2	.4
Sandra Bullock	2	.4
Sean Diddy Combs	2	.4

(*Continued*)

Table 13.1. (Continued)

Celebrity	Frequency of nomination	
	Number	Percentage
Shakira	2	.4
Shaq	2	.4
There are many	2	.4
Tiger Woods	2	.4
Tyler Burkum	2	.4
Usher	2	.4
Aaliyah	1	.2
Adam Kennedy	1	.2
Adam Lazzara	1	.2
Alex Rodriguez	1	.2
Andy Irons	1	.2
Andy Roddick	1	.2
Anna Kournakova	1	.2
Antonio Sabato Jr.	1	.2
Ashley Olsen	1	.2
Ben Affleck	1	.2
Bert McCrackin	1	.2
Beth Gibbons	1	.2
Betty Page	1	.2
Big Tits McGee	1	.2
Billy Idol	1	.2
Briana Hicks	1	.2
Brianna Banks	1	.2
Brook Burke	1	.2
Captain Jack Sparrow	1	.2
Cat Schwartz	1	.2
Celine Dion	1	.2
Chad Micheal Murray	1	.2
Charlize Theron	1	.2
Chris Brown	1	.2
Chris Tucker	1	.2
Chris Webber	1	.2
Christina Aguilera	1	.2
Dale Earnhardt	1	.2

(Continued)

Table 13.1. (Continued)

Celebrity	Frequency of nomination	
	Number	**Percentage**
Daniel Wu	1	.2
Danny Harf	1	.2
Dwight Yoakam	1	.2
Eliza Dushku	1	.2
Ellen Degenerous	1	.2
Emmitt Smith	1	.2
Ernesto 'Che' Guevara	1	.2
Fernando Gonzalez	1	.2
Freddy Mercury	1	.2
Gabrielle Union	1	.2
Gavin Degraw	1	.2
Gavin Rossdale	1	.2
George Cloony	1	.2
Gisele Bundchen	1	.2
Harry Houdini	1	.2
Heath Ledger	1	.2
Hilary Duff	1	.2
Hunter S. Thompson	1	.2
Indi	1	.2
Jack Bauer	1	.2
Jack Johnson	1	.2
James Franco	1	.2
Jamie Pressley	1	.2
Jared	1	.2
Jay CHou	1	.2
Jenifer Lopez	1	.2
Jennifer Garner	1	.2
Jenny McCarthy	1	.2
Jesus	1	.2
Jim Brower	1	.2
Jimmy Fallon	1	.2
Joaquin Phoenix	1	.2
Joe Montana	1	.2
John Adams	1	.2

(*Continued*)

Table 13.1. (Continued)

Celebrity	Frequency of nomination	
	Number	**Percentage**
John F. Kennedy	1	.2
John Mayer	1	.2
Jon Miller	1	.2
Jonathan Taylor Thomas	1	.2
Johnny Depp	1	.2
Jude Law	1	.2
Julia Roberts	1	.2
Karen Carpenter	1	.2
Kate Beckingsale	1	.2
Katie Holmes	1	.2
Kelly Clarkson	1	.2
Ken Griffey Junior	1	.2
Kevin Garnett	1	.2
Kristen Kreuk	1	.2
LaDanian Tomlinson	1	.2
Lance Armstrong	1	.2
Landon	1	.2
Lawrence Fishburn	1	.2
LeBron James	1	.2
Leonardo DiCaprio	1	.2
Lil Wayne	1	.2
Luis Miguel	1	.2
Mandy Moore	1	.2
Mariah Carey	1	.2
Mark Hoppus	1	.2
Mark Mulder	1	.2
Mary Kate	1	.2
Matt Damon	1	.2
Matt Dillon	1	.2
Matt Leinart	1	.2
Matt Cristiano	1	.2
Meagan Hartung	1	.2
Meg Ryan	1	.2

(*Continued*)

Table 13.1. (Continued)

Celebrity	Frequency of nomination	
	Number	Percentage
Method Man	1	.2
Mia Hamm	1	.2
Mike Alstott	1	.2
Mila Jovovich	1	.2
Natalie Gulbis	1	.2
Nelly 'Cornell Haynes Jr.'	1	.2
Nicole Kidman	1	.2
Nicole Richie	1	.2
Patricia Cornwell	1	.2
Patrick Stewart	1	.2
Pharell Williams	1	.2
Prince William	1	.2
Rachel McAdams	1	.2
Ranie Yang	1	.2
RBD	1	.2
Rosalyn Sanchez	1	.2
Ryan Gosling	1	.2
Samuel L. Jackson	1	.2
Scott Weiland	1	.2
Sean Burroughs	1	.2
Sean William Scott	1	.2
Stephan Jenkins	1	.2
Stephen Colbert	1	.2
Stephen King	1	.2
Steve-o	1	.2
Tara Reid	1	.2
Teddy Geiger	1	.2
Teppei Teranishi	1	.2
Terrel Owens	1	.2
The Rock	1	.2
Tim Armstrong (Rancid)	1	.2
Tim McGraw	1	.2
Tito Ortiz	1	.2

(Continued)

Table 13.1. (Continued)

Celebrity	Frequency of nomination	
	Number	Percentage
Tom Brady	1	.2
Tony Gywnn	1	.2
Tori Amos	1	.2
Travis Barker	1	.2
Trent Reznor	1	.2
Troy Glaus	1	.2
Tupac Amura Shakur	1	.2
Ty Pennington	1	.2
Tyson Bedford	1	.2
Uma Thurman	1	.2
Val Kilmer	1	.2
Vanessa Millano	1	.2
Vince Vaughn	1	.2
Vuida Guerra	1	.2
Whitney Houston	1	.2
Will Smith	1	.2
Winston Churchill	1	.2
Total	474	100.0

of nominations. One potential implication is that virtually any person of any public celebrity or notoriety may be the source of a fan's attractions.

The various scales and subscales employed demonstrated acceptable reliability (Cronbach's alpha, α, which is a measure of average item consistency). The CAS subscales, measuring celebrity worship, produced only one marginally unreliable scale: Entertainment-Social subscale ($\alpha = .89$), Intense-Personal subscale ($\alpha = .91$), and Borderline-Pathological ($\alpha = .63$). The CIS was highly reliable ($\alpha = .97$). The NES subscales were acceptably reliable: drive for entertainment ($\alpha = .88$), utility of entertainment ($\alpha = .82$). The APIS also produced good reliabilities for its subscales: identity ($\alpha = .92$), interest ($\alpha = .87$), group ($\alpha = .89$), and problem ($\alpha = .89$). Despite its composition of very small subscales, the Connectedness subscales were all acceptably reliable: escape ($\alpha = .76$), fashion ($\alpha = .81$), imitation ($\alpha = .88$), modeling ($\alpha = .88$), aspiration ($\alpha = .78$), and paraphernalia ($\alpha = .84$).

Because the Fan Activities Scale was developed for this study, it was submitted to exploratory principal components factor analysis with oblique rotation. Factor analysis is a technique designed to identify subsets of items that respondents respond to more similarly than other subsets. When factors are identified statistically, they tend to represent a more coherent underlying concept, *as perceived by respondents*, than the a priori concepts anticipated by the original measures. Despite the 60-item length of the Fan Activities Scale, there was strong indication of acceptable intercorrelations among the items to support factor analysis (Kaiser-Meyer-Olkin measure of sampling adequacy = .95; Bartlett's test of sphericity, $p < .001$). Determining the number of factors is traditionally based on two criteria: eigenvalues larger than one (a measure of the strength of a factor's correlation with the items that define it) and the curvature of a plot of the eigenvalues (i.e., scree plot). Four components produced eigenvalues greater than one, accounting for 82.09% of the common variance in the items. The scree plot revealed precipitous leveling after the second factor, and indeed, the two-factor solution was by far the most interpretable based on the requirement of a minimum of at least three items defined by simple structure. The first factor primary loadings ranged from .47 to .99, and consisted of the more intense forms of celebrity pursuit (e.g., physically threatening, had a restraining order taken out, stalking, showing up in places where the celebrity will be, invading property, sending threatening objects, stealing possessions, etc.), though even in these 46 items, there were several relatively prototypical fan behaviors (e.g., sending unwanted gifts, following around, following in public, approaching, expressing attraction, etc.). This factor was labeled *stalking-related* activity ($\alpha = .99$). The second factor was defined by 14 items reflecting relatively benign types of pursuit (e.g., seeking autographs, purchasing items related to celebrity, sitting vigil for celebrity appearance, attending media event, etc.), and this factor was labeled *fandom* activity ($\alpha = 95$).

Table 13.2 reports the Pearson correlations (i.e., measures of association) between the celebrity worship, parasocial tendencies, and the celebrity pursuit activity factors. Using convention, correlations of .1 are considered "small," .3 are considered "medium," and .5 are considered "large" effects (Cohen, 1992). All correlations were statistically significant, although there are obviously some relationships that are more substantial than others. Ordinary fan behaviors are strongly correlated to the more intense forms of celebrity pursuit ($r = .66$), suggesting that the path of pursuit may be a slippery slope. Not surprisingly, of the celebrity worship variables, the Borderline-Pathological subscale revealed the strongest correlation with the stalking factor ($r = .48$), but contrary to expectation, the Intense-Personal subscale revealed a smaller correlation ($r = .15$) than the Entertainment-Social subscale ($r = .39$). The CIS was virtually identical to the Borderline-Pathological subscale in predicting stalking-related activity ($r = .45$).

In order to explore the most important predictors, and to reduce the potential shared variance of the predictors, a multiple regression was performed for each of the celebrity pursuit factors as dependent variables. Multiple regression is a correlation analysis that assesses the extent to which several variables are capable in combination of predicting changes in another variable. Multiple R is evaluated similarly in effect sizes as Pearson correlations, with correlations

Table 13.2. Intercorrelations among the celebrity worship and parasocial interaction tendencies, and the dependent variables of celebrity pursuit activities ($N = 362$, all correlations: $p < .01$)

Celebrity worship variables	Fandom	Stalking
Fan activities: Fandom		
Fan activities: Stalking		.66
CAS: Entertainment-Social subscale	.53	.39
CAS: Intense-Personal subscale	.42	.15
CAS: Borderline-Pathological subscale	.60	.48
NES: Utility of Entertainment subscale	.18	.40
NES: Drive for Entertainment subscale	.42	.29
Audience-Persona Inventory: Problem subscale	.41	.32
Audience-Persona Inventory: Identity subscale	.39	.29
Audience-Persona Inventory: Interest subscale	.39	.25
CS: Imitation subscale	.41	.32
CS: Fashion subscale	.33	.22
CS: Escape subscale	.34	.18
CIS	.53	.45

Note. CAS, Celebrity Attitude Scale; NES, Need for Entertainment Scale; CS, Connectedness Scale; CIS, Celebrity Idolization Scale.

of .1 considered "small," .3 considered "medium," and .5 considered "large" effects (Cohen, 1992). In both cases, all but three variables dropped out of the analysis, indicating substantially redundant variance among the predictor variables. In predicting the more mundane types of celebrity pursuit, three variables entered the model: CAS, Borderline-Pathological; CIS, Celebrity Idolization; CAS, Intense-Personal, accounting for 46% of the variance (see Table 13.3). This indicates that even relatively benign and ordinary fan behaviors are predicted by celebrity worship predispositions, and are not very predictable from the more ordinary types of parasocial and media utilization processes represented by the other variables.

In predicting the more intense or stalking-related types of fan pursuit, as with the fandom activities, celebrity worship variables (CAS: Borderline-Pathological, CIS: Celebrity Idolization) entered, but instead of the Intense-Personal subscale of the celebrity worship measure, the Need for Entertainment subscale assessing the view that entertainment is utilitarian (reverse scored in this study) entered (see Table 13.4). The entire model accounted for 36% of

Table 13.3. Multiple regression of celebrity worship and parasocial tendency variables onto fandom celebrity pursuit activities (trimmed model)

Independent variables	R	R^2	Adj. R^2	B	ΔR^2	ΔF	df	p
CAS: Borderline-Pathological	.60	.36	.36	.38	.36	206.18	1,360	.001
CIS: Celebrity Idolization	.66	.44	.43	.29	.07	45.18	1,359	.001
CAS: Intense-Personal	.68	.46	.46	.18	.03	18.53	1,358	.001

Note. CAS, Celebrity Attitude Scale; CIS, Celebrity Idolization Scale.

Table 13.4. Multiple regression of celebrity worship and parasocial tendency variables onto stalking-related celebrity pursuit activities (trimmed model)

Independent variables	R	R^2	Adj. R^2	B	ΔR^2	ΔF	df	p
CAS: Borderline-Pathological	.476	.227	.225	.31	.227	105.69	1,360	.001
NES: Utility of Entertainment	.569	.324	.320	.28	.097	51.58	1,359	.001
CIS: Celebrity Idolization	.601	.361	.356	.23	.037	20.71	1,358	.001

Note. CAS, Celebrity Attitude Scale; NES, Need for Entertainment Scale; CIS, Celebrity Idolization Scale.

the variance in stalking-related activities, less than the more benign activities, but still a strong effect.

The fact that substantial proportions of variance were accounted for in a set of activities that might well be viewed as socially undesirable, which usually would be restricted in range, suggested another exploratory analytic strategy. Specifically, it may be that measures such as celebrity worship and parasocial tendencies may not reflect cognitive predispositions, but instead may be relatively indistinguishable from the patterns of celebrity pursuit behaviors assessed by the obsessive celebrity pursuit items. To investigate this, a second-order principal components factor analysis of all the constructed variables was undertaken, with oblique rotation.

The variables appeared suitable for factor analysis (KMO = .88; Bartlett's sphericity test, $p < .001$). Three components produced eigenvalues greater than unity, accounting for 66% of the common variance. The scree plot revealed leveling after the second factor, and indeed, the three-factor solution produced several cross-loadings. The two-factor structure, however, produced a very well-defined solution (see Table 13.5). The fan activities load strongly on the same factor as two subscales of the celebrity worship construct (Borderline-Pathological, and Entertainment-Social) and the CIS, suggesting that these measures may be indexing behavioral activities more than cognitive-affective aspects of worship. The other factor is represented by the more parasocial

Table 13.5. Second-order factor analysis of the constructed variables

Constructed variables	Component	
	1	2
Audience-Persona Interaction: Interest	.843	–
CS: Escape	.799	–
Audience-Persona Interaction: Identity	.779	–
Audience-Persona Interaction: Problem	.751	–
CAS: Intense-Personal	.710	–
CS: Fashion	.681	–
NES: Drive for Entertainment	.650	–
CS: Imitation	.616	–
Fan activities: Stalking	–	.901
Fan activities: Fandom	–	.725
CAS: Borderline-Pathological	–	.687
NES: Utility of Entertainment	–	.603
CAS: Entertainment-Social	–	.568
CIS	–	.535

Note. CS, Connectedness Scale; CAS, Celebrity Attitude Scale; NES, Need for Entertainment Scale; CIS, Celebrity Idolization Scale.

interaction types of measures, as well as the celebrity worship subscale of Intense-Personal. These two factors were correlated .42, indicating that they may indeed reflect a continuum of investment in celebrity pursuit activities.

Finally, the possibility of sex differences was investigated. In the general adult population, females are far more likely to be stalked and males are far more likely to be the stalkers. Approximately 75% to 80% of stalking victims are female, and 75% to 80% of stalkers are males (Basile, Swahn, Chen, & Saltzman, 2006; Cupach & Spitzberg, 2004; Spitzberg & Cupach, 2007; Tjaden & Thoennes, 1998). Relatively little is known of differences in celebrity pursuits. Differences were tested using independent sample t-tests, which simply assess whether differences between means between two groups exceed what would be expected by chance. The strength of the difference is summarized by the η^2 statistic, which represents the percentage of variance in the difference between means that is predictable based on the group membership—in this case, sex of respondent. Conventional interpretation assigns an η of .1 as "small," .2 as "medium," and .5 as "large" (Cohen, 1992). In this sample, evidence of systematic sex difference among the variables under study was minimal. Although there were several statistically significant differences between men and women, in only one instance did a sex

Table 13.6. Mean comparisons of constructed variables by sex of respondent

Constructed variables	M_F	M_M	η	η^2
CAS: Entertainment-Social	2.19	2.30	.04	<.01
CAS: Intense-Personal	4.37	3.87	.17	.03
CAS: Borderline-Pathological	1.97	2.22	.10	.01
NES: Utility of Entertainment	3.25	3.40	.07	.01
NES: Drive for Entertainment	3.75	3.95	.09	.01
APIS: Problem	3.81	3.90	.03	<.01
APIS: Identity	3.83	3.64	.07	.01
APIS: Interest	4.58	4.24	.13	.02
CS: Imitation	2.78	3.05	.11	.01
CS: Fashion	3.86	3.25	.26	.07
CS: Escape	3.87	3.79	.04	<.01
CIS	2.13	2.49	.13	.02
Fan activities: Fandom	1.74	0.56	.06	<.01
Fan activities: Stalking	1.15	1.40	.18	.03

Note. CAS, Celebrity Attitude Scale; NES, Need for Entertainment Scale; APIS, Audience-Persona Interaction Scale; CS, Connectedness Scale; CIS, Celebrity Idolization Scale.

difference emerge that accounted for more than 3% of the variance; females are higher in attending to the media for the sake of watching fashion trends (see Table 13.6). Otherwise, the sex differences are inconsistent and account for miniscule amounts of variance.

Discussion

Celebrities and fans constitute an uneasy relationship. On the one hand, fans are ultimately and precisely what makes and keeps celebrities what they are—persons attended to by the public at large. On the other hand, celebrities often suffer the consequences of living beneath the microscope of public attention. This study sought to investigate the extent to which a relatively normal yet media-savvy population of respondents might engage in celebrity pursuit activities, and to what extent these activities might be associated with a variety of celebrity worship and media consumption tendencies. At least three general findings warrant consideration.

First, despite the occasionally apparent tendency for the media to favor a relatively small number of celebrities in any given episode of contemporary life, in this sample of college students, it is clear that there is considerable diversity and breadth of celebrities. They span a variety of fields, and by far the modal celebrity in this sample had only one fan each. This suggests that even "minor" celebrities may elicit attention from someone. This breadth is especially important, given that over three quarters of respondents indicated that at some point in their lifetimes they found themselves attracted to a celebrity idol.

Second, gender seems to make relatively little difference in pursuit activities or parasocial media proclivities. Except for the unsurprising finding that females report using media more for the purpose of attending to fashion, there were no systematic patterns of difference in the ways in which men and women utilized media or pursued celebrities.

Third, the Celebrity Worship constructs successfully predict both relatively mundane and more intense forms of fan activities. Whether this relationship is due to the predictability of celebrity pursuit, or whether it is because these constructs are actually overlapping processes remains to be confirmed. There is some evidence that celebrity pursuit may exist along a continuum, ranging from various motivations and activities surrounding increasing media consumption, to more addictive or obsessive tendencies. The second-order factor analysis indicated that media consumption tendencies differ from more explicit celebrity worship and celebrity pursuit. The correlation between the factors evidences the possibility that media consumption anchors one end of a continuum and celebrity stalking anchors the other end. The continuum itself may represent a tendency toward media obsession.

Relative to the loading of the celebrity worship and idolization measures along with the fan activities factors, it is possible these constructs are isomorphic. There is a relatively small difference between statements such as "I enjoy watching, reading, or listening to my favorite celebrity because it means a good time," "I am obsessed by details of my favorite celebrity's life," or "I have lots of his/her pictures, pinups, and posters," and the celebrity pursuit activities assessed by the fan activities scale. What is needed to perform a more definitive test, and in order for theory-testing to advance, is to separate out cognitive and affective proclivities from the behavioral. The Fan Activities Scale was developed to be explicitly behavioral in content, but the celebrity worship and idolization measures include items that span across these three domains.

As for future research, in addition to better separation among the cognitive, affective, and behavioral domains of celebrity pursuit, it will become important to establish a more theoretical perspective to celebrity stalking. One perspective we believe will have promise is relational goal pursuit theory. Relational goal pursuit theory (Cupach & Spitzberg, 2004; Cupach, Spitzberg, & Carson, 2000; Spitzberg & Cupach, 2001, 2002, 2007) is designed to explain how ordinary relationship pursuit turns into obsessive relational intrusion and stalking for some pursuers. The theory begins with the premise that desired relationships represent goals for which individuals strive. The persistence with which one pursues any particular goal depends upon the extent to which the goal is seen as desirable and feasible (DiPaula & Campbell, 2002; Locke & Latham, 1990). When a goal is valued and its attainment seems likely, then the goal is pursued vigorously. When goal attainment is thwarted, goal pursuit activity is intensified until the value of a goal is exceeded by the costs of pursuing it, or when goal achievement is deemed impossible. Under these circumstances of diminished perceived desirability or feasibility, the goal is abandoned in favor of pursuing an alternative goal. Relational goal pursuit theory proposes that an individual who obsessively and irrationally pursues a nonreciprocated relationship with another person exaggerates the importance and feasibility of the relational goal. The obsessive relationship pursuer experiences a constellation of thoughts and emotions that drive persistent and intensified relationship goal pursuit. It is reasonable to extend this framework to the obsessed fan who unrealistically and persistently pursues connection with an idolized celebrity.

One factor contributing to the obsessive relational goal pursuit is *linking*, which occurs when an individual views the attainment of higher-order goals to be contingent on the attainment of specific lower-order goals (McIntosh, 1996; McIntosh, Harlow, & Martin, 1995; McIntosh & Martin, 1992). In the case of relational goal pursuit, persistent pursuers link the lower-order goal of having a relationship with a particular person with higher-order goals such as self-worth (Carson & Cupach, 2000; Cupach & Spitzberg, 2004; Cupach et al., 2000). Because attaining the desired relationship is essential to self-worth, the importance of the relational goal is exaggerated. Higher-order goals are less substitutable and unlikely to be abandoned in the face of obstacles. Relational goal pursuit theory, therefore, suggests that fans who obsessively and excessively pursue connection with particular celebrities link the goal of establishing a relationship with the celebrity to higher-order goals, particularly under circumstances where the celebrity represents an ideal self-image for the fan (Caughey, 1984). The inflated desirability of the fan's goal of connecting with the celebrity stimulates the fan's persistent and inappropriate pursuit activity.

When progress toward achieving a goal is impeded, linking fosters rumination (McIntosh & Martin, 1992; McIntosh et al., 1995;). Thus, an obsessed fan whose attempts to connect with a celebrity are frustrated would experience repeated, intrusive, self-perpetuating, and unpleasant thoughts about the unmet relational goal (Martin & Tesser, 1989, 1996). The obsessed fan imagines the intense sadness and distress that would attend a lack of fulfillment of the relational goal. Because failure to connect with the celebrity undermines the fan's perceived self-worth, the fan makes drastic predictions about the consequences of goal failure (e.g., Pomerantz, Saxon, & Oishi, 2000). These negative thoughts are accompanied by negative affect, which in turn, fuel rumination by serving as a constant reminder of the unmet relational goal (Martin & Tesser, 1996). The perceived pathway to relief from these aversive thoughts and feelings is fulfilment of the relational goal. The obsessed fan's rumination about connecting with the celebrity, along with escalating negative affect, fosters persistence in attempting to establish a relationship with the celebrity.

Relational goal pursuit theory contends that persistent pursuers rationalize their excessive pursuit behaviors. Thus, highly obsessive fans not only idolize and idealize their desired celebrity, but they also fail to recognize the adverse consequences of their actions for the pursued celebrity. Celebrity attempts to avoid or restrain the fan's pursuit may be seen by the fan as signs of encouragement. Most importantly, persistent pursuers exaggerate their ability to attain an unrealistic and unreciprocated relationship goal (Bagozzi, 1992; Cupach & Spitzberg, 2004). Obsessed fans likely rationalize that the desired connection with an idolized celebrity is attainable with persistent effort. Admiring fans who are not so obsessive would realize the folly of trying to obtain a relationship with the celebrity, even if they strongly desire such a relationship.

Collectively, linking, rumination, negative affect, and rationalization reinforce the desirability and feasibility of the relational goal. They disinhibit the pursuer's normal conception of the appropriate effort in striving to attain a desired relationship. These processes explain obsessive relational pursuit and stalking in general, and it seems plausible that they may distinguish between the merely adoring and admiring fan who cultivates a significant *parasocial* relationship with a celebrity, from the obsessed fan whose desire for a real personal relationship with a celebrity drives the fan to harass and stalk the celebrity. To verify these speculations, measures of linking, rumination, negative affect, and rationalization that are particular to the fan-celebrity context need to be developed and tested.

Finally, given the consistent findings that associate relationship breakup as a stimulus to obsessive relational intrusion (e.g., see Cupach & Spitzberg, 2004), an important avenue for future research on the relational goal pursuit theory and celebrity stalking will be to investigate the relationship between parasocial breakups (Cohen, 2003), parasocial interaction, and ORI. The more distressed a person is in regard to the cancellation of celebrity's shows, or announcements of a celebrity's commitment to a rival paramour, combined with the person's investment in parasocial interaction with that celebrity, could be precisely the type of trigger that could account for the beginning of the ruminative and obsessive processes that engender a campaign of intrusive pursuit.

Meloy's psychodynamic theory of stalking also comfortably explains the obsessional pursuit of celebrities, particularly instances that are extreme and threatening. Meloy (1989, 1998, 2002, 2006) proposes that obsessional pursuit represents a pathology of attachment. This is consistent with a number of investigations showing that individuals with a preoccupied or anxious ambivalent attachment style (i.e., one characterized by a strong desire for connection coupled with an intense fear of rejection and abandonment) exhibit the propensity to engage in excessive pursuit and stalking-like behaviors (e.g., Davis, Ace, & Andra, 2000; Dye & Davis, 2003; Langhinrichsen-Rohling, Palarea, Cohen, & Rohling, 2000; Langhinrichsen-Rohling & Rohling, 2000; Lewis, Fremouw, Del Ben, & Farr, 2001; Tonin, 2004). Central to Meloy's psychodynamic approach is the idea that stalkers develop a *narcissistic linking fantasy* with respect to an object of pursuit. "Such fantasies are characterized by conscious thoughts of being loved by or loving, admired by or admiring (idealizing), being exactly like (mirroring) or complementing (twinship), or sharing a destiny with a particular object or person (merger)" (Meloy, 1998,

p. 18). These thoughts are accompanied by reinforcing emotions of excitement and contentment.

Linking fantasies occur to some degree in the pursuit of ordinary personal and parasocial relationships, in much the same way that goals, ruminations, and rationalizations motivate normal relationship pursuit. As Meloy (1998, p. 19) remarks, "these narcissistic fantasies serve reality in actual relationships, and may facilitate ambition, rather than envy, when they are linked to public or celebrity figures." Under normal circumstances, for example, a linking fantasy might lead an individual to seek a desired celebrity's autograph. If the celebrity reciprocates contact with a letter or photograph, this "may instill in the [fan] a feeling of reciprocal closeness, even though...it remains mostly fantasy based and prone to emotional and cognitive distortion" (p. 19).

Repeated and firm rejection by the object normally leads to the pursuer's withdrawal. It is when the narcissistic element of the linking fantasy becomes pathological that pursuit becomes obsessive. Pathological narcissism renders the pursuer extremely "sensitive to rejection and feelings of shame or humiliation that accompany it" (Meloy, 1998, p. 19). The resulting defensive rage, perhaps along with feelings of jealousy and envy, motivate pursuit designed to "dominate, devalue, and in some cases, destroy" the pursued partner or celebrity (Meloy, p. 20). A novel and ironic proposition of his psychodynamic theory is that actual devaluation of the object of pursuit who has rejected the pursuer permits restoration of the narcissistic linking fantasy.

The psychodynamic approach resonates in some ways with relational goal pursuit theory, though there are some subtle differences. First, at an abstract level, the concept of *linking* pertains to a pursuer's conception of relational connection with a desired object. In relational goal pursuit theory, the pursuer's goal of attaining a relationship with the object is linked to but not fused with other important goals (e.g., self-worth), whereas in psychodynamic theory, the pursuer believes that the object and pursuer are inherently linked, as if by destiny. Thus, the term "linking" exhibits overlapping but distinct meaning in the two theories. Second, the content of a linking fantasy includes elements of rationalization, such as idealization of the object, similar to relational goal pursuit. Third, similar to emotional flooding in relational goal pursuit, felt emotions in psychodynamic theory contribute to the perpetuation of thoughts about the desired partner in the linking fantasy. These emotions can be positive in the earlier stages of pursuit, but may become completely negative in the face of persistent rejection—manifesting primarily as rage. Fourth, the psychodynamic theory of stalking uniquely incorporates the psychopathological notion of narcissism as the engine of unwanted pursuit, especially pursuit designed to control, diminish, and devalue the object. The extent to which processes such as goal linking and rumination either mediate or moderate the distal influences of attachment disorders and narcissism on persistent pursuit of celebrities (and other desired close relationships) represents an important agenda for empirical inquiry. That is, relational goal pursuit theory accepts that narcissism or attachment disorders are reasonable sources for the goals that become superordinate in the pursuer perceptions, but there may be many other sources of these goals (e.g., culturally internalized dispositions toward proprietary beliefs or sense of relational entitlement, evolved tendencies toward jealousy, etc.). Furthermore, neither theory at this point has much to say about the actual "trigger" that links a particular object of pursuit with the narcissistic self or a superordinate goal. Why one celebrity but not another? Why a particular celebrity at a particular time or in a particular place? Pursuing answers to these tantalizing questions will yield a more complete understanding of persistent celebrity harassment and stalking in general.

Note

1. At the time this study was conducted, the authors were not aware of the Obsessive Relational Intrusion and Celebrity Stalking Scale developed by McCutcheon, Aruguete, Scott, Parker, and Calicchia (2006). Future research may need to ascertain the relationships between these two perpetration measures.

References

Adams-Price, C., & Greene, A. L. (1990). Secondary attachments and adolescent self concept. *Sex Roles, 22*, 187–198.

Ashe, D. D., Maltby, J., & McCutcheon, L. E. (2005). Are celebrity worshippers more prone to narcissism? A brief report. *North American Journal of Psychology, 7*, 239–246.

Ashe, D. D., & McCutcheon, L. E. (2001). Shyness, loneliness, and attitude toward celebrities. *Current Research in Social Psychology, 6*, 124–132.

Auter, P. J., & Palmgreen, P. (2000). Development and validation of a parasocial interaction measure: The audience-persona interaction scale. *Communication Research Reports, 17*, 79–89.

Bachen, C. M., & Illouz, E. (1996). Imagining romance: Young people's cultural models of romance and love. *Critical Studies in Mass Communication, 13*, 279–308.

Bagozzi, R. P. (1992). The self-regulation of attitudes, intentions, and behavior. *Social Psychology Quarterly, 55*, 178–204.

Basile, K. C., Swahn, M. H., Chen, J., & Saltzman, L. E. (2006). Stalking in the United States: Recent national prevalence estimates. *American Journal of Preventative Medicine, 31*, 172–175.

Boon, S. D., & Lomore, C. D. (2001). Admirer-celebrity relationships among young adults. *Human Communication Research, 27*, 432–465.

Brock, T. C., & Livingston, S. D. (2004). The need for entertainment scale. In L. J. Shum (Ed.), *The psychology of entertainment media* (pp. 255–275). Mahwah, NJ: Lawrence Erlbaum.

Canary, D. J., & Spitzberg, B. H. (1993). Loneliness and media gratifications. *Communication Research, 20*, 800–821.

Carson, C. L., & Cupach, W. R. (2000). Fueling the flames of the green-eyed monster: The role of ruminative thought in reaction to romantic jealousy. *Western Journal of Communication, 64*, 308–329.

Caughey, J. L. (1984). *Imaginary social worlds: A cultural approach*. Lincoln, NE: University of Nebraska Press.

Cohen, J. (1992). A power primer. *Psychological Bulletin, 112*, 155–159.

Cohen, J. (2003). Parasocial breakups: Measuring individual differences in responses to the dissolution of parasocial relationships. *Mass Communication and Society, 6*, 191–202.

Cole, T., & Leets, L. (1999). Attachment styles and intimate television viewing: Insecurely forming relationships in a parasocial way. *Journal of Social and Personal Relationships, 16*, 495–511.

Cupach, W. R., & Spitzberg, B. H. (1998). Obsessive relational intrusion and stalking. In B. H. Spitzberg, & W. R. Cupach (Eds.), *The dark side of close relationships* (pp. 233–263). Mahwah, NJ: Lawrence Erlbaum.

Cupach, W. R., & Spitzberg, B. H. (2000a). Obsessive relational intrusion: Incidence, perceived severity, and coping. *Violence and Victims, 15*, 1–16.

Cupach, W. R., & Spitzberg, B. H. (2000b). When a relationship won't end: Stalking after relational termination. In D. O. Braithwaite, & J. T. Wood (Eds.). *Case studies in interpersonal communication: Process and problems* (pp. 199–206). Belmont, CA: Wadsworth.

Cupach, W. R., & Spitzberg, B. H. (2004). *The dark side of relationship pursuit: From attraction to obsession and stalking*. Mahwah, NJ: Lawrence Erlbaum.

Cupach, W. R., Spitzberg, B. H., & Carson, C. L. (2000). Toward a theory of stalking and obsessive relational intrusion. In K. Dindia, & S. Duck (Eds.), *Communication and personal relationships* (pp. 131–146). New York: John Wiley.

Davis, K. E., Ace, A., & Andra, M. (2000). Stalking perpetrators and psychological maltreatment of partners: Anger-jealousy, attachment insecurity, need for control, and break-up context. *Violence and Victims, 15*, 407–425.

Dietz, P. E., Matthews, D. B., VanDyne, C., Martell, D. A., Parry, D. H., Stewart, T., et al. (1991). Threatening and otherwise inappropriate letters to Hollywood celebrities. *Journal of Forensic Sciences, 36*, 185–209.

Dimmock, J. A., & Grove, J. R. (2005). Relationship of fan identification to determinants of aggression. *Journal of Applied Sport Psychology, 17*, 37–47.

DiPaula, A., & Campbell, J. D. (2002). Self-esteem and persistence in the face of failure. *Journal of Personality and Social Psychology, 83*, 711–724.

Dunn, J. L. (2002). *Courting disaster: Intimate stalking, culture, and criminal justice*. New York: Aldine de Gruyter.

Dutton, L. B., & Spitzberg, B. H. (2007). Stalking: Its nature and dynamics. In S. M. Giacomoni, & K. Kendall-Tackett (Eds.), *Intimate partner violence* (pp. 4-1–4-20). Kingston, NJ: CRI.

Dye, M. L., & Davis, K. E. (2003). Stalking and psychological abuse: Common factors and relationship-specific characteristics. *Violence and Victims, 18*, 163–180.

Engle, Y., & Kasser, T. (2005). Why do adolescent girls idolize male celebrities? *Journal of Adolescent Research, 20*, 263–283.

Fadner, R. (2005, November 15). Newstand sales soar for celebrity magazines. *MediaPost Publications*. Retrieved October 15, 2006, from http://publications.mediapost.com/index.cfm?fuseaction=Articles. showArticleHomePage&art_aid=36309

Ferris, K. O. (2001). Through a glass, darkly: The dynamics of fan-celebrity encounters. *Symbolic Interaction, 24*, 25–47.

Ferris, K. O. (2004). Seeing and being seen: The moral order of celebrity sightings. *Journal of Contemporary Ethnography, 33*, 236–264.

Gamson, J. (1994). *Claims to fame: Celebrity in contemporary America*. Berkeley: University of California.

Giles, D. C. (2002). Parasocial interaction: A review of the literature and a model for future research. *Media Psychology, 4,* 279–305.

Giles, D. C., & Maltby, J. (2004). The role of media figures in adolescent development: Relations between autonomy, attachment, and interest in celebrities. *Personality and Individual Differences, 36*, 813–822.

Greene, A. L., & Adams-Price, C. (1990). Adolescents' secondary attachments to celebrity figures. *Sex Roles, 23*, 335–347.

Hills, M. (2002). *Fan cultures*. London: Routledge.

Horton, D., & Wohl, R. (1956). Mass communication and parasocial interaction. *Psychiatry, 19*, 215–229.

Houran, J., Navik, S., & Zerrusen, K. (2005). Bodily functioning in celebrity worshippers. *Personality and Individual Differences, 38*, 237–248.

Kinkade, P., Burns, R., & Fuentes, A. I. (2005). Criminalizing attractions: Perceptions of stalking and the stalker. *Crime and Delinquency, 51*, 3–25.

Kuby, R., & Csikszentmihalyi, M. (2002). Television addiction is no mere metaphor. *Scientific American, 286*(2), 74–81.

Lambiase, J. (2003). Codes of online sexuality: Celebrity, gender and marketing on the web. *Seuxality and Culture, 7*, 57–78.

Langhinrichsen-Rohling, J., Palarea, R. E., Cohen, J., & Rohling, M. L. (2000). Breaking up is hard to do: Unwanted pursuit behaviors following the dissolution of a romantic relationship. *Violence and Victims, 15*, 73–90.

Langhinrichsen-Rohling, J., & Rohling, M. (2000). Negative family-of-origin experiences: Are they associated with perpetrating unwanted pursuit behaviors? *Violence and Victims, 15*, 459–471.

Leets, L., Becker, G., & Giles, H. (1995). FANS: Exploring expressed motivations for contacting celebrities. *Journal of Language and Social Psychology, 14*, 102–123.

Lewis, S. F., Fremouw, W. J., Del Ben, K., & Farr, C. (2001). An investigation of the psychological characteristics of stalkers: Empathy, problem-solving, attachment and borderline personality features. *Journal of Forensic Sciences, 46*, 80–84.

Locke, E. A., & Latham, G. P. (1990). *A theory of goal setting and task performance*. Englewood Cliffs, NJ: Prentice-Hall.

Maltby, J., Day, L., McCutcheon, L. E., Martin, M. M., & Cayanus, J. L. (2004). Celebrity worship, cognitive flexibility, and social complexity. *Personality and Individual Differences, 37*, 1475–1482.

Maltby, J., Giles, D. C., Barber, L., & McCutcheon, L. E. (2005). Intense-personal celebrity worship and body image. Evidence of a link among female adolescents. *British Journal of Health Psychology, 10*, 17–32.

Maltby, J., Houran, J., & McCutcheon, L. E. (2003). A clinical interpretation of attitudes and behaviors associated with celebrity worship. *Journal of Nervous and Mental Disease, 191*, 25–29.

Maltby, J., McCutcheon, L. E., Ashe, D. D., & Houran, J. (2001). The self-reported psychological well-being of celebrity worshippers. *North American Journal of Psychology, 3*, 441–452.

Martin, M. M., Cayanus, J. L., McCutcheon, L. E., & Maltby, J. (2003). Celebrity
worship and cognitive flexibility. *North American Journal of Psychology, 5,*
75–80.

Martin, L. L., & Tesser, A. (1989). Toward a motivational and structural theory of
ruminative thought. In J. S. Uleman, & J. A. Bargh (Eds.), *Unintended thought*
(pp. 306–326). New York: Guilford.

Martin, L. L., & Tesser, A. (1996). Some ruminative thoughts. In R. S. Wyer (Ed.),
Ruminative thoughts (pp. 1–47). Mahwah, NJ: Lawrence Erlbaum.

McCutcheon, L. E. (2002). Are parasocial relationship styles reflected in love styles.
Current Research in Social Psychology, 7(6), 82–93.

McCutcheon, L. E. (2003). Machiavellianism, belief in a just world, and the tendency
to worship celebrities. *Current Research in Social Psychology, 8*(9), 131–138.

McCutcheon, L. E., Aruguete, M., Scott, V. B., Jr., Parker, J. S., & Calicchia, J.
(2006). The development and validation of an indirect measure of celebrity
stalking. *North American Journal of Psychology, 8,* 503–516.

McCutcheon, L. E., Ashe, D. D., Houran, J., & Maltby, J. (2003). A cognitive profile
of individuals who tend to worship celebrities. *The Journal of Psychology, 137,*
309–322.

McCutcheon, L. E., Lange, R., & Houran, J. (2002). Conceptualization and measurement of celebrity worship. *British Journal of Psychology, 93,* 67–87.

McCutcheon, L. E., Scott, V. B., Jr., Aruguete, M. S., & Parker, J. (2006). Exploring
the link between attachment and the inclination to obsess about or stalk celebrities. *North American Journal of Psychology, 8,* 289–300.

McIntosh, W. D. (1996). When does goal nonattainment lead to negative emotional
reactions, and when doesn't it? The role of linking and rumination.
In L. L. Martin, & A. Tesser (Eds.), *Striving and feeling: Interactions among
goals, affect, and self-regulation* (pp. 53–77). Mahwah, NJ: Lawrence Erlbaum.

McIntosh, W. D., Harlow, T. F., & Martin, L. L. (1995). Linkers and nonlinkers:
Goal beliefs as a moderator of the effects of everyday hassles on rumination,
depression, and physical complaints. *Journal of Applied Social Psychology,
25*(14), 1231–1244.

McIntosh, W. D., & Martin, L. L. (1992). The cybernetics of happiness: The relation
of goal attainment, rumination, and affect. In M. S. Clark (Ed.), *Emotion and
social behavior* (pp. 222–246). Newbury Park, CA: Sage.

Meloy, J. R. (1989). Unrequited love and the wish to kill: The diagnosis and
treatment of borderline erotomania. *Bulletin of the Menninger Clinic, 53,*
477–492.

Meloy, J. R. (1998). The psychology of stalking. In J. R. Meloy (Ed.), *The psychology of stalking* (pp. 2–24). San Diego, CA: Academic Press.

Meloy, J. R. (2002). Pathologies of attachment, violence, and criminality.
In A. M. Goldstein, & I. B. Weiner (Eds.), *Handbook of psychology, Vol. 11:
Forensic psychology* (pp. 509–526). Hoboken, NJ: John Wiley.

Meloy, J. R. (2006). *The scientific pursuit of stalking.* San Diego, CA: Specialized
Training Services.

Pomerantz, E. M., Saxon, J. L., & Oishi, S. (2000). The psychological trade-
offs of goal investment. *Journal of Personality and Social Psychology, 79,*
617–630.

Purcell, R., Pathé, M., & Mullen, P. E. (2004). When do repeated intrusions become
stalking? *Journal of Forensic Psychiatry and Psychology, 15,* 571–583.

Rubin, A. M., Perse, E. M., & Powell, R. A. (1985). Loneliness, parasocial interaction, and local television news viewing. *Human Communication Research, 12,* 155–180.

Russell, C. A., Norman, A. T., & Heckler, S. E. (2004a). The consumption of television programming: Development and validation of the connectedness scale. *Journal of Consumer Research, 31,* 150–161.

Russell, C. A., Norman, A. T., & Heckler, S. E. (2004b). People and "their" television shows: An overview of television connectedness. In L. J. Shrum (Ed.), *The psychology of entertainment media* (pp. 275–291). Mahwah, NJ: Lawrence Erlbaum.

Schlesinger, L. B. (2006). Celebrity stalking, homicide, and suicide: A psychological autopsy. *International Journal of Offender Therapy and Comparative Criminology, 50,* 39–46.

Spitzberg, B. H. (2002). The tactical topography of stalking victimization and management. *Trauma, Violence, and Abuse, 3,* 261–288.

Spitzberg, B. H., & Cadiz, M. (2002). The media construction of stalking stereotypes. *Journal of Criminal Justice and Popular Culture, 9*(3), 128–149. www.albany.edu/scj/jcjpc/vol9is3/spitzberg.pdf

Spitzberg, B. H., & Cupach, W. R. (2001). Paradoxes of pursuit: Toward a relational model of stalking-related phenomena. In J. Davis (Ed.), *Stalking crimes and victim protection: Prevention, intervention, threat assessment, and case management* (pp. 97–136). Boca Raton, FL: CRC.

Spitzberg, B. H., & Cupach, W. R. (2002). The inappropriateness of relational intrusion. In R. Goodwin & D. Cramer (Eds.), *Inappropriate relationships: The unconventional, the disapproved, and the forbidden* (pp. 191–219). Mahwah, NJ: Lawrence Erlbaum.

Spitzberg, B. H., & Cupach, W. R. (2003). What mad pursuit? Conceptualization and assessment of obsessive relational intrusion and stalking-related phenomena. *Aggression and Violent Behavior: A Review Journal, 8,* 345–375.

Spitzberg, B. H., & Cupach, W. R. (2007). The state of the art of stalking: Taking stock of the emerging literature. *Aggression and Violent Behavior, 12,* 64–86.

Spitzberg, B. H., Marshall, L., & Cupach, W. R. (2001). Obsessive relational intrusion, coping, and sexual coercion victimization. *Communication Reports, 14,* 19–30.

Spitzberg, B. H., Nicastro, A. M., & Cousins, A. V. (1998). Exploring the interactional phenomenon of stalking and obsessive relational intrusion. *Communication Reports, 11,* 33–48.

Spitzberg, B. H., & Rhea, J. (1999). Obsessive relational intrusion and sexual coercion victimization. *Journal of Interpersonal Violence, 14,* 3–20.

Szymanski, G. G. (1977). Celebrities and heroes as models of self-perception. *Journal of the Association for the Study of Perception, 12,* 8–11.

Tapper, J., & Morris, D. (2005, February 25). Celebrity media spinning out of control? Retrieved October 15, 2006, form http://abcnews.go.com/Nightline/print?id=28898

Tjaden, P., & Thoennes, N. (1998). *Stalking in America: Findings from the National Violence Against Women Survey.* Washington, DC: National Institute of Justice and Centers for Disease Control and Prevention.

Tonin, E. (2004). The attachment styles of stalkers. *Journal of Forensic Psychiatry and Psychology, 15,* 584–590.

Wann, D. L., Peterson, R. R., Cothran, C., & Dykes, M. (1999). Sport fan aggression and anonymity: The importance of team identification. *Social Behavior and Personality, 27,* 597–602.

Young, S. M., & Pinsky, D. (2006). Narcissism and celebrity. *Journal of Research in Personality, 40,* 463–471.

Appendix: The Fan Activities Scale

We live in an age of mass media and celebrity, in which we are daily exposed to persons who show up in the media. Such popularity and celebrity, both good and bad, clearly are supported by people "following" the lives and exploits of such public persons. We would like to know if you have engaged in activities that single out such a person for your attention, and if so, to what extent. This person might be someone (or more than one person) who you would consider famous, a celebrity, a public hero or villain, a figure in the mass media, a politician, community leader, or some other "person of note" who is in the public eye.

Since the age of 16, how often, if at all, have you ever engaged in any of the following activities?

1 = NEVER
2 = SELDOM
3 = OCCASIONALLY
4 = OFTEN
5 = FREQUENTLY

1. WATCHING FOR THE PERSON IN THE MEDIA (e.g., watching for them on TV, in fan magazines, tabloids, listening for news on the radio, etc.)
2. LOGGING INTO THE PERSON'S WEB SITE (e.g., joined an online fan club, engaged in blogs or online chats about the person, etc.)
3. ATTENDING A CONVENTION WITH WHICH THE PERSON IS ASSOCIATED (e.g., going to an event at which the person was to "show" as an attraction of the event)
4. ATTENDING A MEDIA EVENT AT WHICH YOU HOPE THE PERSON WILL ATTEND (e.g., going to an event at which the person may show up)
5. GOING TO EVENTS AT WHICH THE PERSON WILL APPEAR (e.g., shows, performances, awards events, etc., at which the person is featured)
6. PURCHASING ITEMS ASSOCIATED WITH THE PERSON (e.g., imprinted clothing, cologne or perfume, music, magazines, etc.)
7. SEEKING AUTOGRAPH(S) (e.g., going to signing events, etc.)
8. WRITING TO THE PERSON (e.g., e-mails, letters, etc.)
9. SENDING THE PERSON PERSONAL ITEMS (e.g., photos of you, trinkets or gifts, etc.)
10. TRYING TO MEET THE PERSON FACE-TO-FACE (e.g., going to places you know the person frequents, stand outside their home or workplace, etc.)

11. SITTING VIGIL FOR EVENTS OR OPPORTUNITIES TO BE NEAR THE PERSON (e.g., waiting in lines for long periods of time, camping overnight for an event, traveling long distances to see the person, etc.)

12. EVENT-HOPPING (e.g., going from event to event during a tour, season, or campaign, etc.)

13. OBTAINING MEMORABILIA (e.g., getting trinkets, cards, bobble-heads, or other items associated with the person or with the person's likeness or image)

14. TRYING TO GET THE PERSON'S AUTOGRAPH AND/OR PUBLICITY PHOTO

15. JOIN OR ATTEND A FAN CLUB OR OTHER GROUP ASSOCIATED WITH THIS PERSON

16. OBTAINING PERSONAL ITEMS FROM THE PERSON OR PERSON'S AGENTS (e.g., a handkerchief, pen, cap, etc.)

17. OBTAINING PERSONAL ITEMS FROM THE PERSON WITHOUT THEIR PERMISSION (e.g., sneaking an item or property from the person)

18. FOLLOWING THE PERSON WHILE OUT IN PUBLIC (e.g., by car, in a store, restaurant, etc.)

19. GOING TO OR WAITING AT THE PERSON'S HOTEL

20. TAKING ITEMS FROM THE PERSON (e.g., picking up leftover napkins, doodles, etc.)

21. TRESPASSING ON THE PERSON'S PROPERTY

22. SENDING PERSONAL DECLARATIONS OR INVITATIONS (e.g., statements of desire to meet, date, continue correspondence, etc.)

23. EXPRESS ATTRACTION OR SEXUAL INTEREST IN (e.g., statements or offers to engage in romantic or sexual interaction)

24. ATTEMPTING TO HACK INTO THE PERSON'S PERSONAL OR WORK COMPUTER

25. SENDING HATE MAIL OR MESSAGES (e.g., sending notes, instant messages, e-mails, or faxes that imply something bad may happen to the person)

26. SENDING THREAT(S) OR THREATENING OBJECT(S) (e.g., leaving images or objects where the person can find them that imply something bad may happen)

27. FANTASIZE ABOUT HAVING ROMANTIC OR SEXUAL RELATIONS WITH THE PERSON

28. TRY TO LOCATE PORNOGRAPHIC IMAGES OF THIS PERSON ON THE WEB

29. BRAGGING TO OTHERS ABOUT YOUR CONNECTION WITH THIS PERSON

30. LEAVING OR SENDING UNWANTED GIFTS (e.g., flowers, stuffed animals, photographs, jewelry, etc.)

31. LEAVING OR SENDING UNWANTED MESSAGES OF AFFECTION (e.g., romantically oriented notes, cards, letters, voice mail, e-mail, messages with friends, etc.)

32. MAKING EXAGGERATED EXPRESSIONS OF AFFECTION (e.g., saying "I love you" after limited interaction, doing large and unsolicited favors for her/him, etc.)

33. FOLLOWING HER/HIM AROUND (e.g., following the person to or from work, school, home, gym, daily activities, etc.)

34. WATCHING HER/HIM (e.g., driving by home or work, watching the person from a distance, gazing at her/him in public places, etc.)

35. INTRUDING UNINVITED INTO HER/HIS INTERACTIONS (e.g., "hovers" around conversations, offers unsolicited advice, initiates conversations when she or he are clearly busy, etc.)

36. INVADING HER/HIS PERSONAL SPACE (e.g., getting too close to her/him in conversation, touching her/him, etc.)

37. INVOLVING HER/HIM IN UNWANTED ACTIVITIES (e.g., enrolling her/him in programs, putting her/him on mailing lists, using her/his name as a reference, etc.)

38. INVADING HER/HIS PERSONAL PROPERTY (e.g., handling her/his possessions, breaking and entering into her/his home, showing up at his/her door or car, etc.)

39. INTRUDING UPON HER/HIS FRIENDS, FAMILY OR COWORKERS (e.g., trying to befriend the person's friends, family or coworkers; seeking to be invited to social events, seeking employment at their work, etc.)

40. MONITORING HER/HIM OR HER/HIS BEHAVIOR (e.g., calling at all hours to check on the person's whereabouts, checking up on the person through mutual friends, etc.)

41. APPROACHING OR SURPRISING HER/HIM IN PUBLIC PLACES (e.g., showing up at places such as stores, work, gym; lying in wait around corners, etc.)

42. COVERTLY OBTAINING PRIVATE INFORMATION (e.g., listening to the person's message machine, taking photos of her/him without their knowledge, stealing their mail or e-mail, etc.)

43. INVADING HER/HIS PROPERTY (e.g., breaking and entering the person's home, car, desk, backpack or briefcase, etc.)

44. LEAVING UNWANTED THREATENING MESSAGES (e.g., hang-up calls, notes, cards, letters, voice mail, e-mail, messages with friends, implying harm or potential harm, etc.)

45. PHYSICALLY RESTRAINING HER/HIM (e.g., grabbing the person's arm, blocking her/his progress, holding the car door while the person is in the car, etc.)

46. ENGAGING IN REGULATORY HARASSMENT (e.g., filing official complaints, spreading false rumors to officials—boss, publicists, tabloids, etc., obtaining a restraining order on her/him, etc.)

47. STEALING OR DAMAGING VALUED POSSESSIONS (e.g., vandalized the person's property; things, taken, damaged or hurt that only this person had access to, such as prior gifts, pets, etc.)

48. THREATENING TO HURT YOURSELF (e.g., vague threats that something bad will happen to you, threatening to commit suicide, etc.)

49. THREATENING OTHERS SHE/HE CARES ABOUT (e.g., threatening harm to or making vague warnings about romantic partners, friends, family, pets, etc.)

50. VERBALLY THREATENING HER/HIM PERSONALLY (e.g., threats or vague warnings that something bad will happen to the person, threatening personally to hurt the person, etc.)

51. LEAVING OR SENDING HER/HIM THREATENING OBJECTS (e.g., marked-up photographs, photographs taken of the person without her/his knowledge, pornography, weapons, etc.)

52. SHOWING UP AT PLACES IN THREATENING WAYS (e.g., showing up at gym, office or work, from behind a corner, staring from across a street, being inside her/his home, etc.)

53. GETTING IN TROUBLE OVER ATTEMPTS TO CONTACT THE PERSON (e.g., getting thrown out of an event, being blocked by security persons, etc.)

54. HAVING A RESTRAINING ORDER TAKEN OUT ON YOU BY THE PERSON

55. SEXUALLY COERCING HER/HIM (e.g., forcefully attempted/succeeded in kissing, feeling, or disrobing the person, exposed yourself, forced sexual behavior, etc.)

56. PHYSICALLY THREATENING HER/HIM (e.g., throwing something at the person, acting as if you will hit the person, running finger across neck implying throat slitting, etc.)

57. PHYSICALLY HURTING HER/HIM (e.g., pushing or shoving the person, slapping, hitting with fist, hitting with an object, etc.)

58. KIDNAPPING OR PHYSICALLY CONSTRAINING HER/HIM (e.g., by force or threat of force, trapped the person in a car or room, bound the person, took the person places against their will; etc.)

59. PHYSICALLY ENDANGERING HER/HIS LIFE (e.g., strangled the person, trying to run them off the road, displaying a weapon, using a weapon to subdue the person, etc.).

60. STALKING THE PERSON

Section III

Managing the Risk

14

Operations of the LAPD Threat Management Unit

Jeff Dunn

The 1989 murder of actress Rebecca Schaeffer was the catalyst for the first antistalking law in the United States (California Penal Code Section 646.9). The law was adopted in 1990 and has since been duplicated in various forms by all 50 States. The key elements of the California antistalking statute are:

A course of conduct (two or more acts) that involves harassing and threatening behavior

A credible threat, implicit or explicit, toward the victim or the victim's immediate family

The intent to place the victim in reasonable fear for his or her safety or that of his or her immediate family[1]

Actual emotional distress experienced by the victim from the fear created by a suspect's threats or course of conduct

In California, stalking as defined above constitutes a "wobbler" offense. The crime may be prosecuted as either a misdemeanor or felony depending upon the dynamics of the case, violation of a court protective order, and the criminal history or background of the suspect.

Rebecca Schaeffer

The murder of actress Rebecca Schaeffer has been detailed and documented in various media since her death in 1989. Schaeffer's murder has had a profound and positive impact on law enforcement nationwide. Laws have been adopted and improved, victim advocacy groups have been empowered, and the manner in which law enforcement evaluates, assesses, and manages incidents involving threatening behavior has improved dramatically. The Schaeffer case clearly demonstrated the need for early detection, assessment, and proactive case management to derail the forward momentum of individuals taking a path toward violence.

Before 1990, there were no antistalking laws. Obsessive behavior was largely viewed as a mental health issue, and there was little or no communication between law enforcement entities and private security professionals tasked with the personal protection of highly visible individuals. Schaeffer's killer, Robert Bardo, was a mentally ill young man who made no secret of his obsessive attraction to her. Bardo wrote several letters to Schaeffer's managers and promoters, expressing his love and admiration for the young star. On at least two occasions, Bardo was detained by Warner Brothers Studio security while attempting to access the sound stage where Schaeffer was filming. Each time, Bardo had gifts and flowers intended for Schaeffer, as well as a large folding knife concealed on his person. Unfortunately, nobody was comparing notes. Bardo was simply shooed away, to return another day. Rebecca Schaeffer's murder changed that. Building upon information that he had obtained through a private investigator, Bardo made contact with Schaeffer at her Los Angeles area residence. On his second visit to her apartment, Bardo became furious because Schaeffer looked irritated by his return. Bardo responded by fatally shooting Schaeffer once in the chest at close range.

The Los Angeles Police Department Threat Management Unit

Following Schaeffer's murder and the subsequent creation of the California antistalking law, representatives from the Los Angeles Police Department (LAPD) met with representatives from the entertainment industry to address the issue of networking and the need for a proactive, multidisciplinary approach to the management of threat and stalking cases. These meetings resulted in a commitment by the LAPD to establish a unit dedicated to responding to threats and threatening behavior. The Threat Management Unit (TMU) was developed in 1990, to provide a new approach to the old problem of how to handle cases involving obsessive behavior that may be harassing or threatening in nature without necessarily crossing the threshold of a criminal offense. The Threat Management Unit Guidelines note:

> Unless a specific crime has been committed, police agencies have
> historically remained uninvolved in such cases, leaving the victim
> to deal with his or her problem. However, by the time such cases
> escalate, some victims have experienced tragic consequences before
> police intervention could be initiated.
>
> Lane and Boles, 2000

The above quote contains two key points when considering stalking investigations: the long-term and continuing nature of such cases, and the need and role of a specialized unit for proactive intervention to prevent homicides or serious risk of injury to victims and their loved ones.

TMU Responsibilities

With the passage of time, events and trends have required that the TMU evolve and expand its expertise and investigative responsibilities. Presently, the TMU is responsible for investigating serious threat cases within the City of Los Angeles, which include:

Aggravated stalking and criminal threats

Threats to Los Angeles' elected public officials

Workplace violence cases involving Los Angeles city employees

Ancillary responsibilities include:

Maintaining liaison relationships with the Los Angeles' entertainment studios, United States Secret Service, FBI, and the California Highway Patrol (CHP) Dignitary Protection Unit

Staffing the Los Angeles City Threat Assessment Team (CTAT)

Staffing the Los Angeles Police Department Threat Assessment Team (LAPD-TAT)

The most significant responsibility of the TMU is the process of threat assessment, and implementing that threat assessment into a case management strategy. However, before any threat assessment of value may be done, detectives must obtain as much applicable information on the suspect and victim as available.

The Preliminary Investigation

In most large police departments, the most important part of any investigation is generally conducted by well-intended patrol officers who usually have the lowest amount of job experience. At the time that most of us attended our respective police academies, we were taught the "Dragnet" method of crime reporting: "just the facts, ma'am." Had we just deviated from the boxes on the report form, and asked a few probing questions, those victims may have told us about the ex-boyfriend or coworker that they suspected was responsible for their vehicle vandalism or late night hang-up calls. The problem has typically been that victims are not trained witnesses and do not know what information to volunteer to officers. Conversely, officers typically are not trained interviewers and only ask the questions that police report forms require. Consequently, detectives often receive crime reports with minimal information that would link what appears to be a random minor offense to a much broader stalking scenario. Responding officers should be mindful that what appears to be simple harassment may in fact be symptomatic of a developing stalking case. Some of the crimes most commonly reported by stalking victims include:

Threatening or harassing phone calls

Threatening or harassing e-mails

Trespass

Vandalism of victim's property, particularly his or her vehicle

Thefts or burglaries

Physical assaults

Identity theft and Internet postings

Regarding public figures, often the management office or security agent will be the first point of contact, and may in fact be witness to much of the suspect's activity. Officers recognizing a developing stalking trend should expand their interviews to address the following concerns:

Who is the suspect?

How are the suspect and victim known to each other?

What other activity is occurring?

When did the activity begin?

Have other police reports been filed? Where and when?

Has the victim obtained a restraining order on the suspect?

If so, have there been any violations?

Has the suspect made threats? If so, what exactly was said?

Is the victim afraid?

What has the victim done as a result of his or her fear? (Has the victim altered his or her daily regimen, changed phone numbers, obtained a restraining order, moved, etc.)

Are there any witnesses or evidence to corroborate the suspect's activities?

The above information should be documented at the time of the preliminary investigation in order to provide detectives with enough information to prioritize the case, while at the same time providing a usable worksheet to initiate a threat assessment and to formulate a game plan for the follow-up investigation. Since stalking and threat cases by their very nature are long-term, protracted problems, victims and witnesses should be advised about handling and preserving future evidence; for example, being mindful of possible fingerprints while saving written communications, e-mails, phone messages, telephone records, and gifts. Perishable gifts such as flowers should be photographed with any delivery paperwork and cards saved. Vandalisms should be reported and photographed as well, with a particular emphasis on the wording of any graffiti.

The Follow-up Investigation

Every case is different. The follow-up investigation will largely be dictated by information gleaned from the preliminary investigation and the follow-up interview of the victim and witnesses. All TMU follow-up investigations have four basic components:

Reinterviewing the victim and witnesses

Gathering evidence and corroborating statements

Assessing the threat

Case management and intervention strategizing

Reinterviewing the Victim

Keeping in mind the previously discussed elements of a stalking crime, it is vital that detectives have a complete understanding of the history of the victim-and-suspect relationship. Particularly important for domestic violence type cases, the same is true for the high profile or VIP cases, where there may have been a previous professional, business, or personal relationship. What constitutes a credible threat may vary from one case to the next, depending upon the nature of the relationship between the victim and suspect.

Several years ago, a colleague of mine investigated a domestic violence case where the suspect had battered his wife while inside their home. The police were summoned and the suspect was arrested because of the victim's visible injuries. As the officers were leading the suspect to the police vehicle, he turned to his wife and said, "Don't worry honey, I'll be out in a few days. We'll go back to Las Vegas to celebrate." This appears to be an innocuous statement, certainly not threatening in content. But what if the victim advised the police officer that the last time she and her husband went to Las Vegas, she had been beaten so severely that she was hospitalized for 3 days? That victim could have certainly interpreted that as a threat by relating that comment to her previous experience with the suspect. In taking the time to do an in-depth reinterview of the victim, the officer has now proved the credible threat element of the criminal statute.

Even the relationship of an unknown fan to a celebrity must be considered. Is the celebrity victim a sports figure, an elected official, a child actor, or an adult porn actress? What information has recently been in the news, tabloids, or Internet? How does the fan perceive this public information? In the context of these individualized dynamics, what constitutes a credible threat will vary from person to person and case to case. Knowing the nature of the victim's celebrity may also give us some insight into the personal dynamics—the thoughts, emotions, and behavior—of the suspect.

When we conduct a TMU investigation, we ask our victims to start from the beginning of their relationship or initial contact with the suspect, and end at the point that law enforcement became involved. It is not uncommon for TMU detectives to spend 3 or more hours reinterviewing the victim to get a complete understanding of the issues. This time is well spent and will pay dividends when deciding upon a case management and intervention strategy. A byproduct of this interview is the establishment of rapport with the victim. Open communication and detective availability instills comfort and confidence. Oftentimes, we will enlist victims as participants in their own investigations; asking them to obtain phone traps, restraining orders, and retain voice mail messages and e-mails. A confident and involved victim is more apt to follow through with recommended security measures, evidence gathering, and prosecution, if needed.

Another byproduct of the interview is the opportunity to educate the victim on the nature of threat investigations and law enforcement's limitations in protecting them. Simply stated, law enforcement cannot provide protection 24 hours a day, 7 days a week. In a perfect world, which unfortunately does not exist, a victim should not have to make changes in his or her lifestyle because of a suspect's actions. The victim, moreover, must be responsible for his or her own safety. To that end, officers must use caution when recommending security measures and be mindful of potential civil liability should the victim be subsequently harmed. We should identify the risks and hazards and present the victim with options and suggestions, not guarantees. Ultimately, decisions about personal safety and security rest with the victim.

Guarantees of safety aside, the following recommendations should be utilized in all stalking or threat related cases:

Cease all contact with the suspect, including all personal, telephonic, or e-mail communications

Contact law enforcement to report all incidents, and press for assurance that the assigned detective is notified as well

Keep a detailed log of all incidents to include dates, times, locations, and witnesses to what occurred

Save all evidence: gifts, letters, notes, photos, voice mail, and e-mail messages

Allow the police to conduct the investigation without third party interference. Security agents or personal attorneys should first consult with the investigating detective to avoid impacting the criminal investigation.

Evidence Gathering

This is the meat and potatoes of the follow-up investigation. Obtaining corroborating evidence will often be a deciding factor when formulating a case management plan. Do we arrest and prosecute or utilize other means of intervention? Without corroboration and/or evidence, arrest and prosecution are not even an option.

Once we have reinterviewed the victim and have identified the pertinent issues of the case, identifying and gathering evidence is nothing more than an exercise in common sense:

If the suspect is calling the victim, we need the voice mail messages and/or telephone company records (refer to section on search warrants and subpoenas).

If the suspect is e-mailing the victim, we need to retain the original e-mail and obtain identifying information from the Internet service provider (refer to search warrants and subpoenas).

If the suspect is e-mailing the victim, we also want to seize the suspect's computer for forensic testing with a search warrant or subpoena.

If the suspect has stolen property from the victim, we need to search his residence and vehicle for the victim's belongings (search warrant or parole/probation search, if applicable).

If you're in the house, take the computer. Justify it in a search warrant. Suspects often research their intended victims on the Internet, maintain notes and diaries, and post blogs with incriminating content. This information is stored on the computer hard drive and is powerful evidence for law enforcement.

If the suspect has assaulted the victim, obtain photographs of injuries as soon as possible and all subsequent medical records.

Photograph property damage, vandalism and graffiti, and obtain copies of repair estimates.

Reinterview witnesses and corroborate their statements utilizing the same techniques as previously discussed.

Search Warrants and Subpoenas

Search warrants are a fundamental tool in the investigation of stalking and threat related cases. Telephone companies, Internet service providers, and financial institutions all require a search warrant or subpoena before releasing the records we seek. Unfortunately, search warrants do not write themselves and detectives are apt to avoid using them owing to the writing time required. As a result, good evidence is often unnecessarily missed.

Detectives should maintain templates of the various search warrant formats they will need for their assignment on a word processor or computer media.

This will streamline the writing process and, to an extent, allow detectives to fill in the blanks with the information specific to the case at hand. The affidavit or support declaration will read differently depending on the location to be served and the evidence sought. A search warrant to an Internet service provider for subscriber information will be dramatically different from one for a residential search for recovery of stolen items. The most important thing to remember about search warrants is the fact that *if you don't ask for it, you don't get it.* Think about what evidence is being sought and be sure to give a foundation for the items or information in the narrative of the affidavit.

Subpoenas are generally issued by a court or prosecutor (Subpoena Duces Tecum or SDT) *after* the filing of criminal charges. This can be a much faster option for investigators once the case is in the hands of the prosecutor and should be discussed with the district attorney or other prosecutor at the time of filing.

Assessing the Threat

Once we have reinterviewed the victim, verified evidence, and identified the suspect and his or her activities relative to the case, we can now begin the process of a worthwhile threat assessment. Threat assessment is an evolving process. New and pertinent information should be continually added and considered as it becomes available. Oftentimes, an initial assessment will differ greatly after the addition of a few pieces of critical information.

Threat Assessment Versus Risk Assessment

In our operations, a risk assessment evaluates the vulnerability of potential *victims*, their positions or opinions that place them at risk, as well as the environment in which they live and work. In this context, a risk assessment is a very general, superficial process that means little unless incorporated into a much broader threat assessment with an identified threat and source.

While speaking at a domestic violence conference in New Mexico several years ago, I had the pleasure of sitting in on a presentation by now retired FBI Special Agent Eugene Rugala. At the time, SSA Rugala was the Supervisory Special Agent for the FBI's National Center for the Analysis of Violent Crime. One of his Power-Point slides struck me as being most poignant—a formulation originally made by Fein, Vossekuil, and Holden (1995):

> *Many persons who make threats do not pose threats,*
>
> *Some persons who pose threats never make threats,*
>
> *Some persons who make threats ultimately pose threats.*

This may sound like a word puzzle, but the message here is to not get caught up in focusing on the threat itself, but rather the person, behavior, and circumstances behind the threat. In fact, research reviewed by Dr. Reid Meloy, and documented in his book, *Violence Risk and Threat Assessment* (Meloy,

2000), indicated that the communication of a threat in a public stalking case may actually be a risk-*reducing* factor, as evidenced by large group statistical data. However, keep in mind that *every case is different* and the relationship between threat and risk will vary from case to case.

The threat assessment process is a multifaceted approach to evaluating the person(s) responsible for the threat being investigated. It involves the evaluation of the threat itself, the content, and the context in which it was made. In addition to evaluating the vulnerability of the victim (risk assessment), in-depth background research is conducted on the person or group responsible for the threat to determine prior criminal activity, history of previous violent acts, familiarity with the victim, access to weapons, mental health concerns, mobility, and other pertinent facts. Past behavior is the best predictor for future actions. If a person has engaged in violent activity in the past, he or she is much more likely to act out violently in the future given the right motivations or stimulus.

Stabilizing and destabilizing factors need also be weighed. Issues such as the suspect's physical health, living environment, existence of a family or friend support system, financial stability, and any significant upcoming anniversary dates need to be identified and considered. These are very critical components of the threat assessment process. The accuracy and reliability of any assessment is diminished in the absence of these pertinent data. An old rule of thumb that we learned as patrol officers is that a person who is suicidal is also homicidal. A person who feels that he or she has nothing left to live for because of health, financial, or relationship reasons can be a very dangerous person indeed. Conversely, a person who is gainfully employed and involved in a nurturing relationship with good health and future goals has a great deal to lose if his or her threat is exposed or acted upon.

We need to finally look at the suspect's behavior and actions. It is relatively easy to threaten someone from the comfort and anonymity of a computer keyboard or pay telephone. Even if the suspect identifies himself, he is doing so within the relative safety and comfort of his own environment. It requires a much greater investment by the suspect to confront his victim face to face, outside of his comfort zone.

Consequently, threats tend to become more elevated as they progress from less personal modes of contact (voice mail, e-mail, *mailed* letters) to more personal modes of contact, such as directed travel to the victim's office, home, or family member locations. When a detective observes this progression, it is time to amplify involvement in the case management strategy and to consider intervention options to slow the building momentum.

Case Management Strategies

Every case is different. There is no one-size-fits-all response to threat cases. If there were, the threat assessment process would not be necessary. Because each case is truly different, the following options are considerations that can be integrated into a case management strategy, based upon the dynamics/specifics of the particular case at hand. There are dozens of things to consider when developing a case management strategy. In all considerations, the victim's safety should be the paramount and overriding issue. The manner in which we intervene should be driven by the immediacy of the threat posed by the suspect.

Intervention Versus No Intervention

When is it best to wait and see as opposed to confronting the offender and risking exacerbation of his or her behavior? This can be a very difficult decision and should be based on consideration of a number of variables.

The Proximity of the Suspect to the Victim

We often get celebrity cases where an obsessed fan from other parts of the United States or abroad is writing or e-mailing our victims living in the Los Angeles area. In those cases, arrest and extradition are extremely unlikely unless there are some serious felony allegations. We have no quality control over any "knock and talk" intervention that may be done by local law enforcement on our behalf. Restraining orders are enforceable from state to state but would require the victim to travel to the suspect's jurisdiction to testify on any subsequent prosecution, which in turn is likely to result in minimal jail time. Keeping in mind that anything we do has a cause and effect, we may consider monitoring the suspect's communications rather than risk losing good intelligence on his thoughts and activities. We may be able to stop the communication, but we cannot stop the obsession. The last thing we want is for the suspect to go underground and then suddenly appear when the police and the victim are unprepared.

How and Where the Suspect Contacts the Victim

With public figure cases, very often the suspect's only point of contact is via the victim's management or administrative offices. Typically, these office environments have protocols in place for the review and screening of mail, phone calls, and so forth, without direct contact with the victim. As long as they are devoid of serious criminal elements, we may want to keep those calls and letters coming if the suspect's communication is providing us with useful information or insight about his activities or intentions. One should designate an office contact person to field the suspect's calls, letters, or e-mails and maintain a log of the activity. By keeping the contact limited to one or two individuals within the office, escalation in the suspect's rhetoric or frequency of calls can be better detected.

Seriousness of the Crime

Just because an act may constitute a crime does not necessarily mean that we should always arrest and prosecute. Low-grade misdemeanors such as trespass or annoying phone calls may be symptomatic of a developing stalking scenario, but alone will not result in significant jail time. Here is where we need to evaluate our suspect—does he or she have multiple prior arrests with a lengthy history of violent acts? If so, arresting and releasing a few hours later may have little deterrent effect and could exacerbate the problem. Conversely, an otherwise law-abiding person with few police contacts may respond favorably to *any* police intervention, and the few hours spent in lock-up may be all that is needed to alter his behavior. Every suspect is different. Detectives must talk to their victim and do their homework.

Evidence

Having a reported crime is one thing, proving it is something else. The follow-up investigation will determine whether sufficient evidence exists to support a criminal filing. Losing a case at filing or in trial can empower and embolden a suspect. One should know what can and cannot be proven before committing to an arrest.

Knock and Talk

If a verbal warning is to be used as a deterrent in your case management strategy, there is no substitute for a face-to-face interview with the suspect. Fundamentally, a knock-and-talk intervention is a form of intimidation. That is not to say that we bully, badger, or threaten the suspect. In fact, being professional but firm is often the best course of action. The intimidation aspect comes from the simple presence of law enforcement within the suspect's comfort zone. With that in mind, where we choose to conduct the intervention should be determined by what gives us the most leverage or psychological advantage.

The Suspect's Home

Does the suspect live alone or with family members? In many celebrity stalking cases, we deal with delusional individuals who live with family members because of mental illness. Typically, these suspects have a great deal of time on their hands to watch television, write letters and e-mails, and make annoying phone calls to our victims. By interviewing them at home, we can often elicit the assistance of family members to monitor and control the suspect's actions. Additionally, getting inside someone's home gives us tremendous insight into his or her lifestyle and environment, as well as possible clues to the level of his or her obsession with the victim (posters, magazines, notes, videos, etc.). A disordered individual can sometimes come across as organized and functional during a telephone conversation. Seeing how they live is much more telling. If the suspect is married and is concealing activity from his or her spouse, we may choose *not* to interview them at home, saving that as leverage to help manage the case. Again, *every case is different*; the more background information that is obtained on the suspect, the better one can judge what location gives the best opportunity for a successful intervention.

The Suspect's Job

This warrants great care. Embarrassing an individual in front of peers and coworkers can inflame a situation rather than resolve it. Additionally, if the subject were to lose employment as a result of our intervention, we have just added a destabilizing factor to an already potentially volatile situation. I recommend this as a last resort, when attempts to locate the suspect elsewhere have met with negative results.

The Police Station

This is the intimidation factor once again. It can be very sobering for an individual who has had few prior contacts with the police to deal with the cold environment of a police station. Conversely, this may have little effect on a career criminal, who has a lengthy arrest history. We must know the suspect.

Restraining/Protective Orders

The use of restraining orders to manage suspect behavior is often a controversial issue. Many noted security professionals advise against the use of restraining orders regardless of the case dynamics. To fortify their argument, they often cite statistical data on suspect recidivism. To be certain, restraining orders are not appropriate or effective in every case. In fact, there have been incidents when the service of a protective order has exacerbated the suspect's activities. Obviously, some suspects are not suitable candidates for a restraining order because of past violent history with the victim or severe mental health issues. However, it is our experience that the failure of a restraining order as a management tool is generally the result of either (or both) of the following factors:

Failure to report violations

Many times victims will not report what they consider to be minor infractions of the restraining order because of the "trivial" nature of the offense. In reality, what they may have experienced was actually boundary probing by the suspect to test the victim's tolerance and the police response. If not reported appropriately, the lack of response can embolden a suspect. In those instances, we can expect the behavior to escalate in subsequent violations.

Police complacency

When violations are reported and not quickly acted upon by the police, the same lack of response issues apply. Advising a victim to obtain a restraining order without being prepared to act upon the first violation is counterproductive to the case and could increase the risk to the victim.

Detectives should view restraining orders as tools rather than deterrents. We are seeking to place legal parameters around behavior that would otherwise not be criminal. We expect the suspect to violate the order, with the knowledge that we can now justify an arrest where none was possible before. Restraining orders fill a huge void in the State of California where no anti-harassment statutes exist. When used in this capacity, restraining orders can be a vital component of a case management strategy.

Mental Health Intervention

Perhaps the most useful but least utilized tool as it applies to public figure threat investigations is a mental health intervention. Most jurisdictions in the United States have statutes in place that allow sworn police officers to involuntarily detain individuals who have demonstrated that because of mental health issues, they are a threat to themselves or others, or gravely disabled to the point that they cannot care for themselves. The subjects are generally admitted into a secure mental health care facility for a 72-hour psychiatric evaluation and risk assessment. On the basis of the findings, the treating physician may extend this hold for a period of up to 14 days and beyond, depending on the level of impairment and danger to self, others, or grave disability. Now, consider the minimal detention time that same subject would have received on a low-grade misdemeanor arrest, without even addressing the overriding mental health concerns. Nothing about this process precludes investigators from later seeking criminal charges upon the subject's release from the hospital.

There are many benefits afforded with this type of intervention:

The subject has been detained, thereby providing the victim short-term relief and the opportunity to implement security measures or obtain a restraining order.

The subject has been evaluated, diagnosed, and treated for the same mental health issues that may contribute to the threatening behavior that is being investigated.

Detectives have been afforded time to prepare search warrants, arrest warrants, or interview witnesses.

The subject is exposed to ongoing treatment, monitoring, and periodic welfare checks through county mental health resources and social agencies.

In California, subjects who have been placed on *involuntary* psychiatric holds for danger to self and/or others may not own or possess a firearm for a period of 5 years from the date of hospitalization.

The TMU recently investigated a case in which the suspect, a German citizen, had been corresponding with a highly recognizable local actress. While on vacation in the Los Angeles area during the summer of 2006, the suspect approached our victim outside of her gated home and convinced her that he was an avid fan. He further explained that he was stricken with cancer and that it was his dying wish to meet her. Our victim invited him into her home and spoke to him briefly before sending him on his way. Unfortunately for the victim, but fortunately for us, he had obtained her telephone number once inside the house. Upon his return to Germany, the suspect began calling and text messaging the victim with daily delusional references to her being his lover, girlfriend, and future wife. In April 2007, the suspect phoned the victim and advised her that he was en route to Los Angeles so that they may be together forever. When told that she would not see him, the suspect replied that he was coming anyway and would kill himself on the victim's front lawn to demonstrate his love.

At the time that TMU became involved in the case, the suspect had already been admitted into the country, having cleared U.S. Customs in Washington, and was airborne on a connecting flight to Los Angeles. We met him at the airport with an LAPD SMART unit (System-wide Mental Assessment Response Team). Based upon their interview, it was determined that the suspect was so fixed in his delusion that he was a danger to himself and was placed on an involuntary psychiatric hold in a secured mental health facility. Now, with the luxury of time, we were able to coordinate with U.S. Customs, Immigration, the German Embassy, and the psychiatric facility to develop a plan of action. A week later, the suspect was discharged from the psychiatric hospital to the German Embassy security staff. Security officers escorted him to the airport and placed him on a nonstop flight back to Germany. The German Embassy then coordinated psychiatric evaluation for the suspect upon his arrival home. The individual is presently on a no-fly list and is barred from reentering the United States.

This investigation illustrates several important points, not the least of which is that "delusional" and "disordered" do not necessarily mean "incapacitated." This particular individual was quite resourceful and capable of putting a plan into action. Had the police, security, or victim's legal counsel previously intervened to prevent this suspect's phone calls, we never would have known that he was coming. We may be able to stop the calls, but we cannot stop the obsession. This could have had a very tragic outcome had the suspect "popped up" when no one expected him. Fortunately, this matter was resolved entirely because of a timely mental health intervention. Aside from his annoying phone calls, a very low-grade misdemeanor offense, there were no crimes to justify a lengthy detention or expulsion from the country once he cleared U.S. Immigration and Customs. The mental health hold provided the detention time needed to formulate a plan of action, the justification to remove the problem, and the leverage to prevent the problem from returning: a lot of "bang for the buck" considering the absence of a serious criminal offense.

Additionally, this individual received the care and attention that was badly needed both in the United States and in his country of origin.

An important aside is that because of privacy laws, hospitals may not be able to share treatment information or diagnosis with investigating officers. That does not prevent us from sharing information with the hospital. The more information that we can provide the attending staff, the better equipped they are to properly evaluate and treat our subject.

Arrest and Prosecution

In aggravated threat and stalking cases where sufficient evidence exists to support a felony criminal filing, there can be no better long-term intervention than arrest, incarceration, and probation. Many useful management tools can be brought to bear as a result of a felony conviction.

While in custody, a suspect may receive diagnostic testing and treatment. Once released, the suspect's terms of probation or parole can require drug testing, anger management or psychological counseling, outpatient treatment, and periodic reports to the court to verify compliance. Additionally, the court can issue protective orders on behalf of the victim to further restrict the suspect's activity. In extreme cases, the suspect may be required to wear electronic monitoring devices to prohibit movement beyond prescribed areas. In California, when some suspects are eventually found not guilty by reason of insanity—a rare occurrence—they must be committed to an *involuntary* outpatient treatment program once released from a forensic hospital (Meloy, Haroun, & Schiller, 1992). California law also mandates a psychiatric evaluation for individuals convicted of felony stalking and sentenced to prison. Occasionally, an individual convicted of felony stalking who has served his prison sentence will then be committed as a *mentally disordered offender* and transferred to a forensic hospital for at least a year. Perhaps the greatest benefit of these various containment strategies is the empowerment of the victim to regain control of his or her life. The luxury of time affords the opportunity for the victim to alter a lifestyle and become less accessible to the suspect.

No discussion regarding prosecution would be complete without addressing the relationship between the victim, detective, and prosecutor. In Los Angeles, the District Attorney's Office has established a specialized unit to vertically prosecute aggravated stalking and threat cases. Simply put, "vertical" prosecution allows for the same district attorney who files the case to follow through with all aspects of the prosecution: bail and discovery hearings, preliminary hearings, and trial. The ability to interact with the same prosecutor throughout the court process is a great benefit to a detective. Similarly, a public or private victim experiencing the ordeal of testifying and the unfamiliarity of the legal process is often more confident when dealing with a consistent team of investigators and a prosecutor who they can contact with any questions or concerns. Many jurisdictions offer vertical prosecution for domestic violence cases. Stalking and threat cases can be equally problematic and should be given the same emphasis.

The Future of Stalking

The future is now. With the widespread availability of computers and the expansion of the World Wide Web in recent years, almost every case handled by the TMU has a cyber element. Either the suspect has researched the victim on the Internet, has sent e-mails, or posted blogs in furtherance of the threats or harassment. With anonymizers, hot-mail accounts, and overseas service providers, the investigation of these cases can prove problematic and time consuming unless we have an identified suspect. Further complicating these investigations are publicly accessed computer systems at places such as cyber cafes and public libraries. For a computer layman, this can all seem daunting. However, it is important to remember that we are still investigating a stalking case. The computer is simply a tool used by a human suspect to further his or her criminal enterprise. With that in mind, we should approach this investigation as we would any other. We build our case and gather evidence as we would with any investigation. With computers, that often translates to the writing of search warrants for service provider records or the seizure and scanning of hard drives and other storage media.

Cops tend to resist change, particularly those of us with some gray in our hair. The fact is that computers and the Internet are here to stay. As investigators, we need to continually expand our expertise in this area if we are to remain efficient and effective. I routinely receive calls from other agencies seeking guidance in establishing their own TMU-type units. In addition to protocols, I always advise to seek out investigators with expertise in computer forensics, familiarity with the drafting of search warrants, and a background in domestic violence investigations. I have found that these talents translate well in the law enforcement-threat management world of today.

Conclusion

The few pages of this chapter cannot cover all the nuances or issues that may be encountered during a stalking or threat investigation. I have attempted to provide a template for investigations that will facilitate the identification of key issues with options for case management. I have not included many references to statistical research that has been done on stalking and threat assessment because they are derived from large group data. From a law enforcement perspective, statistics are valuable building blocks in the understanding of stalking behavior and the development of threat assessment models. But statistics alone should not dictate a case management strategy. For that same reason, I shy away from computer-based threat assessment tools. As a training aid, less experienced investigators may be able to glean key interview points by reviewing these programs, but any assessment provided would be based on large samples, and does not account for the unique facts within any one case. What appears familiar may turn out to be quite foreign.

The Los Angeles TMU maintains files of each case handled since our inception. From 1990 through April 2007, the TMU has investigated 3,098 cases involving stalking, threats, and other obsessive behavior. Although the ratios have shifted throughout the years because of added responsibilities, over 55% of the total cases handled have involved celebrities, sports personalities, elected officials, or other public figures as victims. Our files indicate that persons suffering from severe mental disorders are far *less* likely as a group to approach or confront the objects of their fixation. That particular statistic, however, would offer no comfort to the family, friends, and fans who mourn the loss of Rebecca Schaeffer. Every case needs to be evaluated independently and on its own merit. Each victim, each subject, and each case is different.

Note

1. The law does not require that the suspect intended to carry out the threat. Simple communication of a threat with the intent to place the victim in fear satisfies this element of the statute.

References

Fein, R., Vossekuil, B., & Holden, G. (1995). Threat assessment: An approach to prevent targeted violence. Washington, DC: U.S. Dept of Justice, Office of Justice Programs, National Institute of Justice, Publication NCJ 155000.

Lane, J., & Boles, G. (2000). Threat management unit guidelines. Unpublished document.

Meloy, J. R., Haroun, A., & Schiller, E. (1992). *Clinical guidelines for involuntary outpatient treatment*. Odessa, FL: Professional Resource Exchange.

Meloy, J. R. (2000). *Violence risk and threat assessment*. San Diego, CA: Specialized Training Services.

15

Risk Assessment of Public Figure Stalkers

P. Randall Kropp, Stephen D. Hart,
and David R. Lyon

A celebrity is someone who is "famous for being famous," to paraphrase Boorstin (1961). Although celebrities do not represent a new phenomenon, the rise of mass media in the 1980s gave the general public access to the intimate facts of the lives of public figures, and even allowed them to see or hear public figures on a regular basis (Turner, 2004). We are exposed to so much information about celebrities that we develop images of them that are complex and life-like, internal representations that in some respects can be as detailed and vivid as those of our own families, friends, or personal acquaintances (Boorstin, 1961; Turner, 2004).

The phenomenon of stalking has interesting ties to the concept of celebrity. Some of the earliest case descriptions of what we would now refer to as stalking involved people who became obsessed with political public figures (e.g., regents, elected officials), sometimes even attempting to assassinate them for nonpolitical motives. It was the mass media that introduced these stalkers to their victims and that fueled their obsessions. More recently, clinical interest in stalking and the development of antistalking laws were sparked to a great extent by events surrounding the stalking of celebrities—some of whom were actors, others of whom were high profile politicians, and at least one of whom was both actor and politician.

Although it is generally recognized that most stalking arises in the context of close personal relationships (e.g., following dissolution of intimate relationships), stalking cases that involve public figures are among the most complex, fascinating, and difficult to assess and manage. This chapter addresses primarily the initial task of appraising risk in public figure stalking cases and leaves discussion of stalking risk management to other chapters. It begins by highlighting the difficulties inherent in the assessment of stalking risk, especially in cases involving public figures. Next, the main approaches to risk assessment are reviewed, focusing on structured professional judgment (SPJ) as a suitable procedure for cases involving public figure targets. The chapter concludes by applying a specific SPJ instrument, the guidelines for Stalking Assessment and Management (SAM) (Kropp, Hart, & Lyon, 2007), to a case of public figure stalking.

Stalking Risk Assessment: General Challenges

Risk assessment refers to the process of evaluating individuals to (a) characterize the risk that they will act violently; and (b) develop strategies to ameliorate that risk (e.g., Hart, 1998; Heilbrun, 1997). Thus, threat assessment professionals who conduct risk assessments bear at least two responsibilities. First, they must gather relevant case information in an effort to identify and appraise factors that may increase (i.e., risk factors) or decrease (i.e., protective factors) the likelihood that a person will engage in acts of violence. Second, threat assessment professionals should seek to reduce that person's prospect of future violence by incorporating the assessment information into a management plan that takes advantage of existing protective factors and manages the identified risk factors.

We define stalking as unwanted and repeated communication, contact, or other conduct that deliberately or recklessly causes people to experience reasonable fear or concern for their safety or the safety of others known to them (see Kropp, Hart, & Lyon, 2002; Kropp, Hart, Lyon, & LePard, 2002). Stalking cases pose numerous challenges to risk assessment. Some of these problems relate to the unique nature of stalking behavior and the manner in which it varies from violence occurring in other contexts. For example, stalking is distinguishable from other forms of violence in the following ways: it typically *targets* specific individuals or organizations; although it often includes explicit threats and violence, it might also involve more *implicit* threats; and it often *persists* for extremely long periods. These qualitative differences place important limits on the lessons that the broader literature on violence risk assessment has to offer cases of stalking. This section describes these three distinctive behavioral qualities and the problem that each presents for the risk assessment of stalking.

The Targeted Nature of Stalking

The victim-perpetrator relationship is a distinctive feature of stalking that has important implications for risk assessment. Stalking is targeted violence. It is directed at a specific person who is significant in the eyes of the perpetrator. What makes the victim important is the relationship, real or otherwise, that the perpetrator sees as existing between them. For the perpetrator, no other victim will do. So while the behavioral expression of stalking at any particular time may be influenced by contextual factors, the victim is not. That is, the victim remains constant across different situations. In this respect, stalking is unique. For most other forms of violence, the person victimized is highly dependent upon contextual factors (e.g., perpetrator motive, immediate antecedent events, availability of other victims) and therefore it is extremely difficult to determine with any degree of precision who will be the next likely victim of possible future violence. The absence of specifically identifiable victims has meant, with few exceptions, that past research on violence risk assessment has been unable to examine factors concerning aspects of the perpetrator's relationship to the victim (e.g., attachment to the victim) and victim vulnerability (e.g., living situation). Yet, factors such as these may be particularly important considerations in stalking cases given the targeted nature of the violence involved (e.g., Cornish, Murray, & Collins, 1999; Fein & Vossekuil, 1998).

Stalking and Implicit Threats

Stalking constitutes a pattern of fear-inducing behavior. It encompasses individual acts which, in isolation, might be viewed as nonviolent and are often lawful, but which collectively form a pattern of implicitly threatening behavior. Indeed, implicit threats lie at the core of stalking and it is one of the qualities that separate stalking from other forms of violence. The fact that implicitly threatening conduct is an integral element of stalking is troublesome because it is not a factor considered in most research on violence. Nearly all existing research defines violence in a way that encompasses actual and attempted physical harm, but there is much less agreement on how to treat threats of harm. Some research on violence includes threats of harm only if the threatener also brandishes a weapon (e.g., Monahan et al., 2001; Quinsey, Harris, Rice, & Cormier, 1998); other research includes only explicit threats of harm, and yet other research excludes threats of harm altogether. Unfortunately, studies rarely define violence in a manner that captures the vague threats and fear-inducing behavior involved in stalking. Herein lies the problem. If research does not construe implicitly threatening behavior (i.e., stalking-like behavior) as violence, then the risk factors for violence identified by that research will not necessarily correspond to risk factors for stalking.

The Persistent Nature of Stalking

The final complicating aspect of stalking is the duration of the behavior. Stalking constitutes a course of conduct that may last for many months or even years. Perhaps 30% or more of all cases continue for a year or longer and there are cases known to persist for decades (e.g., Budd & Mattison, 2000; Canadian Centre for Justice Statistics, 2005; Mullen, Pathé, Purcell, & Stuart, 1999; Purcell, Pathé, & Mullen, 2002; Tjaden & Thoennes, 1998). Whereas most acts of violence are discrete incidents or occurrences that happen over the course of a few minutes or a few hours, stalking is better conceptualized as a process. This may be especially true of public figure stalking (Mullen, Pathé, & Purcell, 2000; Mullen et al., 1999).

Special Challenges to Risk Assessment in Public Figure Stalking

Public figure stalking is a relatively rare and, in many respects, an unusual form of stalking. It poses a number of special challenges. First, the victim-perpetrator relationship is almost always unidirectional in nature. The victim and perpetrator are wholly unconnected with one another except for the perpetrator's familiarity with the victim's public persona. Second, the perpetrators are heterogeneous with respect to their motivations and other psychological characteristics. Third, the identity of the perpetrator may be unknown and risk assessment therefore must be conducted on the basis of incomplete information. Each of these problems is discussed in the following text.

The Risk of a Public Persona

One complicating feature of these cases is their public nature. Success for many public figures depends on their popularity. It generates the votes, media ratings, or marketing power they need to sustain their careers and livelihood. In contemporary society, popularity is propelled to a large extent by publicity. This is the reason why some public figures go to such lengths to cultivate their public profile and stay in the media spotlight. A public profile, though, does not come without risks. Some people cognitively distort and personalize media messages to such a degree that they begin to feel that a special bond or relationship exists between them and the public figure. These distorted thinking patterns can lead to stalking behavior when perpetrators try to convert their emotional bond into a physical one. In other instances, public figures are seen to represent ideas, policies, or institutions that are objectionable to some people who may subsequently stalk the public figure as a way of expressing their frustration or to bring about change. Thus, public figures are caught between their need to stay in the public eye and their desire to avoid the risks that come with it. On one hand, the publicity they seek to maintain their public profile puts them at risk of becoming a stalking target. On the other hand, they are often reluctant to relinquish their position in the public spotlight because it means sacrificing their public profile and future success.

Diversity of Motivations

Public figure stalking can have diverse motivations (e.g., Meloy et al., 2004). One common motivational theme is *amorous*. It is typically found in cases where perpetrators are romantically or sexually attracted to victims, or where perpetrators suffer from erotomanic delusions and believe victims are romantically or sexually attracted to them. A second common motivational theme is *angry*. It is found in cases where perpetrators perceive that victims are responsible, at least in part, for committing some injustice. A third common motivational theme is *publicity-seeking*. It is found in cases where perpetrators want to draw attention to a cause or gain personal notoriety through their harassment of victims. This may be conceptualized as an attempt by perpetrators to "steal" celebrity from their victims. There are also other, less common motivational themes (e.g., suicidality). To make matters even more complex, multiple motivational themes may be present in a given case. The importance of these themes for risk assessment is that they may be associated with very different patterns of stalking behavior, and therefore very different strategies for managing stalkers. For example, amorous motivations are often associated with the desire of perpetrators to "move toward" the victim, seeking proximity or even direct contact, whereas angry motivations are often associated with the desire of perpetrators to "move against" victims, expressing unhappiness through threats or violence.

Unknown Perpetrators and Incomplete Assessment Information

Public figure cases are often viewed under the rubric of stranger stalking because there is no history of any meaningful contact or interaction on a private level between the perpetrator and victim. The perpetrator knows the victim only indirectly, as a result of his or her public profile. As for victims, it is quite likely they will have no knowledge of the perpetrator whatsoever before being stalked. Even after victims become the target of stalking behavior, they may not be aware of the stalker's identity if the perpetrator has taken steps to remain anonymous. The extent to which unknown perpetrators are a manifest problem in public figure stalking cases is uncertain. The only relevant data emanate from a handful of studies examining inappropriate communications and behavior, though not necessarily stalking behavior, directed toward various groups of public figures in the United States (e.g., Hollywood celebrities, politicians, judicial officials). These studies found that the proportion of unknown perpetrators ranged between 5% and 25% (e.g., Calhoun, 1998; Dietz, Matthews, Martell, et al., 1991; Dietz, Matthews, Van Duyne, et al., 1991; Scalora et al., 2002).

Unknown perpetrators complicate matters enormously. It means that the assessment information will be largely confined to the victim and the nature of the stalking behavior. Although it is oftentimes possible to gain some information about the perpetrator from his or her stalking behavior (e.g., nature of their attachment), it will be impossible to acquire a full picture of the perpetrator's history (e.g., previous stalking behavior, response to legal interventions) and current psychosocial functioning (e.g., relationship stability, acute mental illness). The absence of complete information runs contrary to the basic principle of case assessment that data need to be gathered from multiple sources and in all risk-relevant domains (Cornish et al., 1999; Fein & Vossekuil,

1998). More importantly, the missing information is critical for understanding the behavioral boundaries the perpetrator has respected (or transgressed) in the past, the motivation for the perpetrator's current stalking behavior, and the various factors that might be expected to influence the perpetrator's choices to abate, continue, or escalate the stalking in the future. Without this information, evaluators run the risk of implementing an ill-suited management plan, which could have the paradoxical effect of increasing, rather than ameliorating, the likelihood of further harm to the victim.

The solution to the problem of unknown perpetrators and incomplete case information is clear. The perpetrator needs to be identified as early on in the case as possible. Unfortunately, realizing this solution is far more complex when a public figure is involved. A corollary of being a public figure is that the target is well known and very recognizable among the general population. For this reason, the potential pool of people who might stalk a public figure is enormous, unconstrained by the need for a prior relationship or any other contact with the victim, which typically must exist when ordinary citizens are stalked. Moreover, the absence of any previous history means that victims usually have very few ideas to offer that might be useful for generating a list of possible perpetrators. In some cases, identification only comes about after further incidents of stalking when the perpetrator inadvertently or intentionally reveals more clues as to his or her identity.

Models of Risk Assessment: Implications for Public Figure Stalkers

Very little has been published on possible models of risk assessment of stalking, although there has been much debate about models of violence risk assessment in general. The main area of controversy concerns the degree of discretion that should enter the decision-making process, and most approaches can be described generally as either *nondiscretionary* or *discretionary* in nature. The lack of consensus over *how to* conduct violence risk assessments means that the issue of an appropriate model for assessing and managing stalking violence needs careful consideration. It is appropriate therefore to review the relative strengths and weaknesses of these two broad approaches for assessing the risk of violence in stalking cases.

The nondiscretionary approach to risk assessment is most commonly associated with the actuarial or statistical approach to predict violent behavior. Typically, actuarial instruments are developed in order to optimally predict a specific outcome, such as violence, in a specific population over a specific period of time (Grove & Meehl, 1996; Hart, 1998; Litwack, 2001). The items in the scales are typically selected using empirical methods, but can also be chosen on the basis of theory or experience (i.e., the rational approach), but all share the common feature that decisions about risk are the result of an algorithm that weights and totals risk factors to arrive at an estimate of likelihood of recidivism. Examples of the nondiscretionary approach include the Violence

Risk Appraisal Guide (VRAG) (Quinsey et al., 1998), which is used to predict general violence, and the Static-99 (Hanson & Thornton, 1999), used to predict sex offenses. Such methods are not well suited to assessing risk in stalkers in general, and pubic figure stalkers in particular, for a number of reasons. First, such instruments require considerable effort, time, and large samples (which are difficult to find with this form of stalking) to construct and validate. In public figure stalking cases, true cross-validation may require decades because of the lengthy period of risk many stalkers present. Second, the heterogeneity of stalking cases creates problems with respect to creating an actuarial scale. If precise actuarial instruments are to exist, they will need to be tailored to the various subtypes of stalkers. For example, a test optimized for psychotic stalkers would likely be vastly different from one optimized for stalkers who are not mentally ill. Not only would the content likely differ for such instruments, but also different management settings would need to be taken into account (e.g., mental health system versus correctional system). Third, the nature of stalking is diverse. Actuarial tests narrowly define outcome, typically in terms of the likelihood of violence over a predetermined period of time. With stalkers, evaluators are typically concerned about a range of possible behaviors (e.g., harassment through homicide) with potentially multiple victims. Finally, there is a tendency for actuarial approaches to focus on *static* risk factors, thereby assuming that risk for future violence is fixed. In reality, stalking cases are typically very complex and dynamic; risk can and usually does change across time. Regardless, even if actuarial methods were better suited to this problem, we are unaware of any such instruments in existence that can be used to assess risk in public figure stalkers.

Discretionary approaches are those that allow the evaluator some flexibility with respect to (a) the information that is gathered and considered in the risk assessment; (b) the emphasis placed upon certain risk factors in certain contexts; and (c) the decisions made regarding case prioritization and risk management strategies. Discretionary approaches can range in the degree of structure imposed on the assessment. Some approaches, which have been referred to as "unstructured professional judgment," completely lack decision-making guidelines. The absence of structure provides the advantage of being ultimately adaptable and person centered, allowing an analysis of unique aspects and context of the case at hand. In many ways, the approach is well suited for assessing and managing risk in stalkers, whose presentations are diverse and often idiosyncratic. Unfortunately, highly unstructured approaches to risk assessment rely heavily on the individual intuition and experience of the assessor, which has led to criticism that they are unreliable and unaccountable; that is, it is often impossible to trace how decisions regarding risk are made (Melton, Petrila, Poythress, & Slobogin, 1997; Monahan, 1981; Quinsey et al., 1998). This method has also been much maligned for its inability to predict future behavior (Grove & Meehl, 1996; Litwack, 2001). We do not therefore recommend approaches to risk assessment that use no structure whatsoever.

Another example of the discretionary approach to violence risk assessment has been labeled *structured professional judgment*. This approach has gained considerable credibility in the violence risk assessment literature (Litwack, 2001) and is well suited for assessing risk in the complex circumstances that most public figure stalkers present. Here, decision making is aided by the use of "best practice" guidelines that have been developed to reflect empirical and professional literatures (Borum, 1996). Such guidelines attempt to define the risk being considered, which typically includes the likelihood, severity, frequency, nature, and imminence of possible outcomes; discuss minimal qualifications for performing and evaluating risk; recommend what information should be considered as part of the evaluation and how it should be gathered; and identify a set of core risk factors that should be considered as part of any reasonably comprehensive assessment. Structuring the risk assessment process in this manner has the potential to increase the consistency, usefulness, and transparency of decisions. Examples of this approach include the HCR-20 (Webster, Douglas, Eaves, & Hart, 1997), the Spousal Assault Risk Assessment Guide (SARA) (Kropp & Hart, 2000), and the Sexual Violence Risk-20 (SVR-20) (Boer, Hart, Kropp, & Webster, 1997). Practitioners often appreciate the attempt of such guidelines to find a balance between completely unstructured methods of assessing risk and the rigid, inflexible approach of actuarial methods.

Structured Professional Guidelines for Assessing Stalkers

There are now a number of schemes published in the literature that describe approaches to risk assessment and management with stalkers. All of these methods impose some degree of structure on the process without prescribing actuarial algorithms, and therefore they all can be considered forms of structured professional judgment. Although much of this work remains unpublished in the professional literature, it has been discussed and widely disseminated at professional conferences (De Becker, 1994; Hart, 2006; Kropp, 2006; White & Meloy, 2006), published as government reports (Fein, Vossekuil, & Holden, 1995), and distributed on the Internet. These approaches typically focus on targeted threat assessment, identification of risk factors and approach behaviors, and the development of a management plan that directly addresses relevant risk factors (Fein et al., 1995; White & Cawood, 1998). Most emphasize the importance of assessing and managing approach behavior in the offender, and working with the victim to ensure that appropriate security measures are in place.

There appear to be two main streams in the published literature on risk assessment in stalkers, *clinical* and *operational*. The clinical literature focuses primarily on cases where there is a known perpetrator, and evaluations are primarily the responsibility of mental health professionals. Probably the first published attempt to outline guidelines for the *clinical* risk management of stalkers was by Meloy (1997), who offered "ten guidelines for the clinical risk management of stalking" (p. 184). He emphasized the importance of a team approach, which can include the victim, mental health professionals, police, and prosecutors. He also put forth recommendations regarding the documentation and recording of evidence of stalking behavior; management strategies including the importance of no-contact and protective orders; treatment recommendations corresponding to specific diagnostic considerations; recommendations for criminal justice intervention; and a discussion of the role of violence risk assessment. Others such as Rosenfeld (2000) have contributed papers that have added significantly to our knowledge regarding the clinical assessment and management of stalkers. Probably the most comprehensive clinical strategy to date, moreover, is that presented by Mullen et al. (2006). These authors have devised the Stalking Risk Profile, which systematically addresses five risk domains: "The nature of the relationship between the stalker and the victim; the stalker's motivations; the psychological, psychopathological, and social realities of the stalker; the psychological and social vulnerabilities of the victim; and the legal and mental health context in which the stalking is occurring" (p. 442). Mullen et al. provide specific management possibilities corresponding to various risk factors and hazards. The authors note that their approach, consistent with SPJ principles, is intended to be used on a case-by-case basis, not as a way to categorize offenders or apportion a numerical risk rating. This approach seems to hold promise for mental health professionals involved in the evaluation and treatment of stalkers in clinical and psycholegal settings.

The *operational* approach, typically referred to as "threat assessment," has been well documented, and there are several good commentaries on sound professional practice in this area (see, e.g., Calhoun & Weston, 2003; Turner & Gelles, 2003; White & Cawood, 1998). This literature addresses situations where the perpetrator is known or, as is often the case, unknown. The assessments are typically conducted by law enforcement or security personnel. One of the earliest comprehensive approaches was presented by Borum, Fein, Vossekuil, and Berglund (1999). The authors provided three fundamental threat assessment principles and proceeded to offer specific recommendations for conducting a risk assessment in targeted violence cases. Consistent with most SPJ approaches, Borum et al. emphasized the importance of multiple sources of information, properly corroborated whenever possible, which include identifying information, background information, and current life information. They then outlined common "attack-related behaviors" (p. 330), which should be addressed at a minimum, including an unusual interest in instances of targeted violence, evidence of ideas or plans of attack, inappropriate communications, following a target or visiting a possible location of an attack, and approaching a target or protected setting. They proceeded to list several useful questions to ask in a threat assessment and, in a related document (Fein & Vossekuil, 1998), offered suggestions for monitoring, controlling, and redirecting the potential perpetrator. Finally, Hoffmann and Sheridan (2005) presented a comprehensive five-stage framework for screening contacts with public figures, analyzing communications, researching and obtaining information about the stalker, and devising management strategies. All of these guidelines have brought the field forward considerably and we now understand much more about the process of risk assessment within the legal- and security-oriented professions.

Integrating the Clinical and Operational Approaches: The SAM

Our own work with public figure stalkers has taken place in diverse situations, such as court-ordered forensic psychological evaluations, police investigations, and workplace violence consultations. As a result, we have approached risk assessment from a multiagency, multiprofessional perspective, and have attempted to recommend strategies that can assist mental health professionals, police, victim service workers, corrections employees, and so forth to manage their stalking cases better. Our early attempts to address this problem (Kropp, Hart, Lyon, 2002; Kropp, Hart, Lyon, & LePard, 2002) focused on general guiding principles to risk assessment. More recently, we have attempted to organize the converging of empirical, clinical, threat assessment, and victimology literatures into a set of structured professional guidelines for assessing and managing risk in stalkers. The result, the SAM (Kropp et al., 2007), can be used by the full range of professionals who face stalking cases in general, and public figure stalkers in particular.

The content of the SAM is based on a systematic review of the existing scientific research on stalking and related forms of violence, as well as on existing standards of practice, ethical codes, and legal principles. The SAM helps users to exercise their best judgment; it is not a replacement for professional discretion. Its purpose is to introduce a systematic, standardized, and practical framework for gathering and considering information when making decisions about stalking risk. In light of the way it was developed and is intended to be used, the SAM may be considered evidence-based or "best practice" guidelines.

The factors considered in the SAM are divided into three domains (see Table 15.1). *Nature of stalking* includes 10 factors related to the pattern of behavior that comprises the current offence. These risk factors are drawn primarily from the operational threat assessment literature that focuses on the approach behaviors, threats, and communications between the perpetrator and the victim (Borum, et al., 1999; Calhoun, 2001; Calhoun & Weston, 2003; Fein & Vossekuil, 1998; Jenkins, 2001; Meloy et al., 2004; Scalora et al., 2002; Weiner & Hardenbergh, 2001; White & Cawood, 1998). *Perpetrator risk factors* are 10 factors reflecting the psychosocial adjustment and background of the perpetrator. These factors, though largely drawn from the clinical and empirical literatures on stalkers and general violence (see Boon & Sheridan, 2002; Dressing, Kuehner, & Gass, 2006; Hart, 1998; Hoffman & Sheridan, 2005; Meloy, 1998; Mullen, Pathé, & Purcell, 2000; Mullen et al., 2007; Quinsey et al.,

Table 15.1. The Stalking Assessment and Management (SAM) risk factors

Domains of risk		
Nature of stalking	**Perpetrator risk factors**	**Victim vulnerability factors**
Communicates about victim	Angry	Inconsistent behavior toward perpetrator
Communicates with victim	Obsessed	Inconsistent attitude toward perpetrator
Approaches victim	Irrational	Unsafe living situation
Direct contact with victim	Unrepentant	Inadequate access to resources
Intimidates victim	Distressed	Distressed
Threatens victim	Intimate relationship problems	Intimate relationship problems
Violent toward victim	Nonintimate relationship problems	Nonintimate relationship problems
Stalking is persistent	Substance use problems	Substance use problems
Stalking involves supervision violations	Employment and financial problems	Employment and financial problems
Stalking is escalating	Criminality	Concerns related to dependents
Other considerations	Other considerations	Other considerations

1998; Rosenfeld, 2004), are presented in plain language (avoiding professional jargon) to allow non–mental health professionals to assess them. *Victim vulnerability factors* are 10 factors reflecting the psychosocial adjustment and background of the victim. These factors were selected from the empirical and professional literatures on victims of domestic violence (that indirectly has much to offer on the subject of victim vulnerabilities) and stalking (see Barnett, 2001; Boon & Sheridan, 2002; Hall, 1998; Mullen et al., 2000). In general, factors in the first domain help the user characterize the seriousness of the perpetrator's stalking behavior, those in the second domain describe characteristics of the perpetrator that may be associated with decisions to engage in stalking, and those in the third domain describe characteristics of the victim that may be associated with decisions to engage in self-protective behavior. (As stalking is a form of targeted violence, it is impossible to get a full picture of the risks posed by the perpetrator without considering the victim's unique circumstances and vulnerabilities.) Users also have the ability to document "other considerations," which can take into account rare or unusual risk factors that are relevant to the case at hand.

Following a consideration of all three risk domains, the SAM then encourages evaluators to consider various risk scenarios with respect to the nature, severity, imminence, and frequency/duration of future stalking and violent behaviors. At this point, the SAM requires assessors to identify risk management strategies in four categories: (1) Monitoring: "What is the best way to monitor warning signs that the risks posed by the perpetrator may be increasing?" (2) Treatment: "What treatment or rehabilitation strategies could be implemented to manage the risks posed by the perpetrator?" (3) Supervision: "What supervision or surveillance strategies could be implemented to manage the risks posed by the perpetrator?" and (4) Victim safety planning: "What steps could be taken to enhance the security of the victim?" Finally, the SAM allows evaluators to offer summary risk judgments regarding case prioritization, risk for continued stalking, risk for serious physical harm, the reasonableness of the victim's fear, and whether or not immediate action is required.

The SAM was developed over a period of about 6 years, starting in 2001 and ending in 2007. The development process included three activities. First, we conducted a comprehensive review of the literatures regarding stalking, threat assessment, general violence risk assessment, and domestic violence. We also updated this review continuously during the project to keep abreast of new developments in the field. Second, we pilot-tested the SAM for use by mental health professionals in two samples, one comprising cases referred to a specialized antistalking unit of a metropolitan police service and the other comprising cases referred to an outpatient forensic psychiatric clinic. Third, we pilot-tested the SAM for use by police in Canada and Sweden. Earlier drafts of the SAM were revised in light of the findings of the various activities, and the content of the SAM was finalized in early 2007. Preliminary research is promising, showing moderate-to-high interrater reliability on the risk factors, risk domains, and summary risk judgments, and good concurrent validity with respect to other violence risk measures (Hart, 2006; Kropp, 2006).

Case Study

The following case study illustrates the application of principles discussed in the preceding text. The details are factual, with the exception that names, dates, places, and certain identifying details have been disguised.

Initial Complaint

Jennifer McVee, age 43 and single, has been an elected member of a provincial legislative assembly in Canada since July 2001. She resides in a large city and commutes by plane to the provincial capital for her parliamentary duties. Ms. McVee has a high profile position in Government as the Minister of Education. Her position has recently required her to conduct frequent televised media interviews and "town hall" style meetings across the province to promote the Government's controversial new education initiatives. Ms. McVee is an attractive and dynamic individual, often described as the government "golden girl" of politics. She is an ambitious politician and has begun a campaign to become the next party leader and premier of the province.

On June 11, 2005, Ms. McVee provided the city police with two letters received at her constituency office. The letters were written by Mr. Don Weeks, who declared that he is a long-standing "fan" of Ms. McVee and a staunch supporter of her political views. He states in the letters that he enjoyed meeting Ms. McVee at a political rally (though Ms. McVee had no recollection of such a meeting), but was disappointed that she did not return his telephone calls to her constituency office. He indicated in the letters that he expected "better treatment," and noted that there would be "consequences" should she continue to ignore his communications. While accustomed to receiving correspondence from the public, the tone of these letters was worrisome to Ms. McVee. The police agreed to investigate, which was facilitated by the fact that Mr. Weeks provided a return address on the letters.

Investigation and Follow-up

The identity of Mr. Weeks was confirmed. The police learned that he was a divorced father with custody of two young boys. He resided in a low-income neighborhood in the suburbs bordering the city. Initial record checks indicated that he did not have a documented history of contacts with the mental health system. However, it was discovered that he had been previously investigated for the criminal harassment (stalking) of a former dating partner. No other criminal record was evident. The police attended Mr. Weeks' residence to discuss the matter with him but he was not at home. However, the police were informed by a neighbor that he was employed by a publicly owned utility company and were provided a picture of Mr. Weeks by his employer.

The next day, Ms. McVee reported to the police that she spotted a "strange individual" when she was leaving the parking garage at her office. The police returned to Mr. Weeks' residence and warned him to cease all contact with Ms. McVee. This knock-and-talk strategy, as it is referred to by the police, appeared to work, as Ms. McVee did not hear anything from Mr. Weeks for approximately 2 months.

On August 25, 2005, Ms. McVee again contacted the police to indicate that Mr. Weeks had now contacted her office by telephone, threatening to harm her because he suspected she was having a relationship with a coworker (he did not provide a specific plan as to how he would harm her). The next day, the security guard at Ms. McVee's office identified Mr. Weeks when he approached the office and requested an appointment with her to discuss a business venture. The police then escorted Mr. Weeks to the station to interview him. During the taped interview, Mr. Weeks was casually dressed, well groomed, and initially appeared quite composed. During the lengthy interview, there were no obvious signs of major mental illness until the police broached the topic of his relationship to Ms. McVee. At that point, Mr. Weeks discussed at length his distress regarding the situation. He indicated that Ms. McVee has been keeping him awake at night by throwing rocks at his windows. Mr. Weeks also believed that Ms. McVee had been sneaking into his house and urinating around his toilet bowl. He then went on to blame Ms. McVee for his emotional problems, and wondered aloud why she would not return his affection. It was later confirmed that Mr. Weeks had recently taken stress leave from work because of the depression that he had been experiencing. It was also determined by the police that 2 weeks earlier, the province's child protective services apprehended Mr. Weeks' children because of allegations of neglect. Mr. Weeks was arrested and charged with criminal harassment. He was found in court to be Not Criminally Responsible on account of Mental Disorder (NCRMD) and placed in a secure forensic mental health facility for evaluation and treatment. Subsequent psychological and psychiatric assessments determined that Mr. Weeks met the criteria for delusional disorder, erotomanic type. He also displayed moderate symptoms of depression (e.g., sleep disturbances, hopelessness), but he did not appear to be suicidal.

Risk Assessment

A risk assessment was subsequently ordered to determine the appropriate steps for releasing Mr. Weeks to the community. The evaluator used the SAM as a way to guide her professional opinion about risk and risk management. After gathering and considering all available information from police reports, mental health assessments, collateral informants, and so forth, the first step for the evaluation was to consider the ten risk factors comprising Nature of Stalking section of the SAM. Here it was clear to the evaluator that Mr. Weeks had Communicated about the victim (e.g., he had complained to coworkers about her urinating around his toilet and rock-throwing), Communicated with the victim (written letters), and Approached the victim (possibly at a political rally, definitely at her office). Although there was no indication of direct contact with the victim, he did Threaten to harm her because of her "infidelity." There was also clear evidence that Mr. Weeks' stalking was Persistent, Involved supervision violations (e.g., he had violated police ordered no-contact conditions), and the behavior had Escalated from communication to approach behavior. By reviewing this section of the SAM, the evaluator was able to establish a clear pattern of stalking behavior that was persistent, threatening, and escalating.

The evaluator then considered the second section of the SAM entitled Perpetrator Risk Factors. She determined that the Mr. Weeks was clearly Angry, Obsessed, Irrational, Unrepentant (i.e., he did not appreciate that his behavior was wrong, persisting even after a police warning), and Distressed. He also had Intimate and Non-intimate relationship problems (e.g., divorce, separation from children), and Employment problems (e.g., stress leave from work).

Although the victim in this case was a reasonably well-adjusted individual, a number of issues emerged when the evaluator considered the Victim Vulnerability section of the SAM. It became clear that the victim's own self-image as a politician "of the people" required her to keep a high media profile. She was not prepared to change her approach to politics, and thereby accepted the associated risk of unwanted contact with individuals like Mr. Weeks. Moreover, she expressed compassion for Mr. Weeks and wanted the police to take a sympathetic approach to an obviously troubled individual. These issues were among the Inconsistent behaviors and Inconsistent attitudes displayed by Ms. McVee toward the perpetrator. Other victim vulnerabilities included a relatively Unsafe living situation, as Ms. McVee was living in a relatively isolated suburban neighborhood, her house surrounded by trees. Further, she did not want to move away because of Concerns related to dependents, namely, her elderly mother who lived in what was the family home for close to 60 years.

The evaluator then proceeded to identify three plausible future stalking scenarios that would influence her risk management recommendations. The first was a *repeat* scenario forecasting that Mr. Weeks would continue to communicate in affectionate and angry ways without actually contacting the victim. The *worst case* scenario involved the further deterioration of Mr. Weeks's mental state and the escalation of his behavior to involve approaching Ms. McVee's residence and workplace, and direct confrontation with her. Finally, a *best case* scenario envisioned Mr. Weeks obtaining much needed social and mental health support, thereby ceasing contact with the victim.

A risk management plan was then formulated based on the identification of the risk factors and these risk scenarios. It was determined that upon release to the community, Mr. McVee would represent a moderate priority case. The evaluator indicated that monitoring strategies would include frequent contact by a probation officer and mental health professionals to observe any changes in the psychosocial adjustment of Mr. Weeks. Monthly contacts with Ms. McVee were also recommended. Recommended supervision strategies included no contact and "no go" conditions with respect to Ms. McVee, her office, and her residence. Treatment recommendations included psychotropic medications to manage his delusional and obsessional symptoms, and individual psychotherapy (using cognitive behavioral techniques) to address his depression, loss of custody of his children, loneliness, and his distorted thinking with respect to Ms. McVee. Further, contact was made with counselors at the utility company to help facilitate his reintegration into the workplace. Finally, a safety plan was established by consulting with Ms. McVee about the static security of her home and workplace, as well as discussing a strategy for balancing her high-profile political needs with her security needs. With this management plan in place, Mr. Weeks was eventually released into the community. In the 12 months since his release in February 2006, he has made no further attempts to contact or approach Ms. McVee.

Concluding Comments

We attempted in this chapter to illustrate some of the challenges in assessing risk for violence in public figure stalkers. This field is rapidly advancing, and a glance at the literature reveals many excellent efforts to develop standards and guidelines for assessing and managing risk in these difficult cases. Efforts to develop these procedures have come from a wide range of professionals with diverse backgrounds and training. Despite the diversity, it is encouraging that the various approaches to risk assessment that have emerged are more similar to each other than they are different. For example, all existing procedures can be described as structured professional judgment, and there is considerable consensus among professionals regarding the risk assessment process and the individual risk factors that must be considered. In this chapter, we hoped to illustrate how this consensus can be reflected in a single risk assessment approach that we have labeled the SAM. However, the SAM is simply one of many viable procedures in existence, and we are optimistic that the field of risk assessment in stalkers will continue to evolve as research on risk factors and effective management strategies accrues.

References

Barnett, O. (2001). Why battered women do not leave, Part 2: External inhibiting factors—Social support and internal inhibiting factors. *Trauma, Violence & Abuse, 2*(1), 3–35.

Boer, D. P., Hart, S. D., Kropp, P. R., & Webster, C. D. (1997). *Manual for the sexual violence risk-20: Professional guidelines for assessing risk of sexual violence.* Vancouver, BC: British Columbia Institute Against Family Violence.

Boon, J., & Sheridan, L. (Eds.) (2002). *Stalking and psychosexual obsession: Psychological perspectives for prevention, policing and treatment.* Chichester, UK: John Wiley.

Boorstin, D. J. (1961). *The image: A guide to pseudo-events.* New York: Atheneum.

Borum, R. (1996). Improving the clinical practice of violence risk assessment: Technology, guidelines, and training. *American Psychologist, 51*, 945–956.

Borum, R., Fein, R., Vossekuil, B., & Berglund, J. (1999). Threat assessment: Defining an approach for evaluating risk of targeted violence. *Behavioral Sciences and the Law, 17*, 323–337.

Budd, T., & Mattinson, J. (2000). *The extent and nature of stalking: Findings from the 1998 British Crime Survey.* London: Home Office Research, Development and Statistics Directorate.

Calhoun, F. (1998). *Hunters and howlers: Threats and violence against federal judicial officials in the United States, 1789–1993.* Arlington, VA: United States Marshals Service.

Calhoun, F. (2001). Violence toward judicial officials. *Annals of the American Academy of Political and Social Science, 576*, 54–68.

Calhoun, F., & Weston, S. (2003). *Contemporary threat management: A practical guide for identifying, assessing and managing individuals of violent intent.* San Diego: Specialized Training Services.

Canadian Centre for Justice Statistics. (2005). *Family violence in Canada: A statistical profile*. Ottawa: Author.

Cornish, J. L., Murray, K. A., & Collins, P. I. (1999). *The criminal lawyers' guide to the law of criminal harassment and stalking*. Aurora, ON: Canada Law Book.

De Becker (1994, June). *A white paper report—Intervention decisions—The value of flexibility*. Draft prepared for the attendees of the Threat Management Conference, Anaheim, CA.

Dietz, P. E., Matthews, D. B., Martell, D. A., Stewart, T. M., Hrouda, D. R., & Warren, J. (1991a). Threatening and otherwise inappropriate letters to Members of the United States Congress. *Journal of Forensic Sciences*, *36*, 1445–1468.

Dietz, P. E., Matthews, D., Van Duyne, C, D., Martell, D., Perry, C., Stewart, T., et al. (1991b). Threatening and otherwise inappropriate letters to Hollywood celebrities. *Journal of Forensic Sciences*, *36*, 185–209.

Dressing, H., Kuehner, C., & Gass, P. (2006). The epidemiology and characteristics of stalking. *Current Opinions in Psychiatry*, 19, 395–399.

Fein, R. A., & Vossekuil, B. (1998). *Protective intelligence and threat assessment investigations: A guide for state and local law enforcement officials*. Washington, DC: National Institute of Justice.

Fein, R. A., Vossekuil, B., & Holden, G. A. (1995). *Threat assessment: An approach to prevent targeted violence*. Washington, DC: United States Department of Justice.

Grove, W. M., & Meehl, P. E. (1996). Comparative efficiency of informal (subjective, impressionistic) and formal (mechanical, algorithmic) prediction procedures: The clinical-statistical controversy. *Psychology, Public Policy, and Law*, *2*, 293–323.

Hall, D. M. (1998). The victims of stalking. In J. R. Meloy (Ed.), *The psychology of stalking: Clinical and forensic perspectives* (pp. 115–137). San Diego, CA: Academic Press.

Hanson, R. K., & Thornton, D. M. (1999). *Static-99: Improving actuarial risk assessment for sexual offenders*. Ottawa: Solicitor General of Canada (Corrections Research User Report 199–02).

Hart, S. D. (1998). The role of psychopathy in assessing risk for violence: Conceptual and methodological issues. *Legal and Criminological Psychology*, *3*, 121–137.

Hart, S. D. (2006). *The SAM: Stalking Assessment and Management*. Paper presented at the 2006 Annual Threat Management Conference, Anaheim, CA.

Heilbrun, K. (1997). Prediction versus management models relevant to risk assessment: The importance of legal decision-making context. *Law and Human Behavior*, *21*, 347–359.

Hoffmann, J. M., & Sheridan, L. P. (2005). The stalking of public figures: Management and intervention. *Journal of Forensic Sciences, 50*(6), 1–7.

Jenkins, D. M. (2001). The US Marshals Service's threat analysis program for the protection of the federal judiciary. *Annals of the American Academy of Political and Social Science*, *576*, 69–77.

Kropp, P. R. (2006, November). *Stalking assessment and management (SAM)*. Invited address at the 6th Annual Diverse Voices Family Violence Conference, Edmonton, Alberta, Canada.

Kropp, P. R., & Hart, S. D. (2000). The Spousal Assault Risk Assessment (SARA) Guide: Reliability and validity in adult male offenders. *Law and Human Behavior*, *24*, 101–118.

Kropp, P. R., Hart, S. D., & Lyon, D. R. (2002). Risk assessment of stalkers: Some problems and possible solutions. *Criminal Justice and Behavior, 29*(5), 590–616.

Kropp, P. R., Hart, S. D., & Lyon, D. R. (2007). *Stalking assessment and management.* Vancouver, BC: Proactive Resolutions.

Kropp, P. R., Hart, S. D., Lyon, D. R., & LePard, D. (2002). Managing stalkers: Coordinating treatment and supervision. In L. Sheridan, & J. Boon (Eds.), *Stalking and psychosexual obsession: Psychological perspectives for prevention, policing and treatment* (pp. 141–164). New York: John Wiley.

Litwack, T. R. (2001). Actuarial versus clinical assessments of dangerousness. *Psychology, Public Policy, and Law, 7,* 409–443.

Meloy, J. R. (1997). The clinical risk management of stalking: "Someone is watching over me..." *The American Journal of Psychotherapy, 51,* 174–184.

Meloy, J. R. (1998). *The psychology of stalking: Clinical and forensic perspectives.* New York: Academic Press.

Meloy, J. R., James, D. V., Farnham, F. R., Mullen, P. E., Pathé, M., Darnley, B., et al. (2004). A research review of public figure threats, approaches, attacks, and assassinations in the United States. *Journal of Forensic Sciences, 49*(5), 1–8.

Melton, G. B., Petrila, J., Poythress, N. G., & Slobogin, C. (1997). *Psychological evaluations for the courts: A handbook for mental health professionals and lawyers* (2nd ed.). New York: Guilford.

Monahan, J. (1981). *Predicting violent behavior: An assessment of clinical techniques.* Beverly Hills, CA: Sage.

Monahan, J., Steadman, H. J., Silver, E., Applebaum, P. S., Robbins, P. C., Mulvey, E. P., et al. (2001). *Rethinking risk assessment: The MacArthur study of mental disorder and violence.* New York: Oxford University Press.

Mullen, P. E., Pathé, M., & Purcell, R. (2000). *Stalkers and their victims.* Cambridge: Cambridge University Press.

Mullen, P. E., Mackenzie, R., Ogloff, J. R. P., Pathé, M., McEwan, T., & Purcell, R. (2006). Assessing and managing risks in the stalking situation. *Journal of the American Academy of Psychiatry and Law, 34,* 439–450.

Mullen, P. E., Pathé, M., Purcell, R., & Stuart, G. W. (1999). Study of stalkers. *American Journal of Psychiatry, 156,* 1244–1249.

Purcell, R., Pathé, M., & Mullen, P. E. (2002). The prevalence and nature of stalking in the Australian community. *Australian and New Zealand Journal of Psychiatry, 36,* 114–120.

Quinsey, V. L., Harris, G. T., Rice, M. E., & Cormier, C. A. (1998). *Violent offenders: Appraising and managing risk.* Washington, DC: American Psychological Association.

Rosenfeld, B. (2000). Assessment and treatment of obsessional harassment. *Aggression and Violent Behaviour, 5,* 529–549.

Rosenfeld, B. (2004). Violence risk factors in stalking and obsessional harassment. *Criminal Justice and Behaviour, 31,* 9–36.

Scalora, M. J., Baumgartner, J. V., Zimmerman, W., Callaway, D., Maillette, M. A., Covell, C. N., et al. (2002). An epidemiological assessment of problematic contacts to Members of Congress. *Journal of Forensic Sciences, 47,* 1360–1364.

Tjaden, P., & Thoennes, N. (1998). *Stalking in America: Findings from the National Violence Against Women Survey.* Washington, DC: National Institute of Justice.

Turner, G. (2004). *Understanding celebrity.* Thousand Oaks, CA: Sage.

Turner, J. T., & Gelles, M. G. (2003). *Threat assessment: A risk management approach.* Binghamton, NY: Haworth.

Webster, C. D., Douglas, K. S., Eaves, D., & Hart, S. D. (1997). *HCR-20: Assessing risk for violence* (Version 2). Burnaby, Canada: Mental Health, Law, and Policy Institute, Simon Fraser University.

Weiner, N. A., & Hardenbergh, D. (2001). Understanding and controlling violence against the judiciary and judicial officials. *Annals of the American Academy of Political and Social Science, 576,* 23–37.

White, S. G., & Cawood, J. S. (1998). Threat management of stalking cases. In J. R. Meloy (Ed.), *The psychology of stalking: Clinical and forensic perspectives* (pp. 295–315). San Diego: Academic Press.

White, S. G., & Meloy, J. R. (2006). *The WAVR-21: A new instrument for assessing workplace violence risk.* Paper presented at the 2006 Annual Threat Management Conference, Anaheim, CA. Instrument available at www.wavr21.com

16

Preventing Assassination: Psychiatric Consultation to the United States Secret Service

Robert T. M. Phillips

While most people associate the United States Secret Service with presidential protection, its original mandate was to investigate the counterfeiting of U.S. currency, a mission the Secret Service is still mandated to carry out. The United States Secret Service was formed as a bureau of the Treasury Department in 1865 following the Civil War to suppress the serious problem of rampant counterfeiting of U.S. currency during the time. At that time, it was estimated that one third to one half of the currency in circulation was counterfeit. In 1901, following the assassination of President William McKinley by Leon Czolgosz, the U.S. Congress tasked the Secret Service with its second mission: the protection of the President of the United States. Today, the Secret Service's mission remains twofold: protection of our nation's leaders, visiting world leaders, and others and investigations into crimes against the financial infrastructure of the United States.

Investigative Mission

The primary investigative mission of the Secret Service is to safeguard the payment and financial systems of the United States. This has been historically accomplished through the enforcement of counterfeiting statutes to preserve

The views and opinions expressed in this chapter are those of the author and do not necessarily reflect the official position or policies of the United States Secret Service or the Department of Homeland Security.

the integrity of U.S. currency, coin, and financial obligations. Since 1984, the Secret Service's investigative responsibilities have expanded to include crimes that involve financial institution fraud, computer and telecommunications fraud, false identification documents, access device fraud, advance fee fraud, electronic funds transfers, and money laundering as it relates to the agency's core violations. In 2002, the Department of Homeland Security was established with the passage of Public Law 107-296 which, in part, transferred the United States Secret Service from the Department of the Treasury to the new department effective March 1, 2003.

Protective Mission

The protective responsibilities of the Secret Service have expanded considerably in the modern era. Today, the Secret Service is authorized by law to protect

- The President, the Vice President, (or other individuals next in order of succession to the Office of the President), the President-elect and Vice President-elect and their immediate families of the above individuals
- Former Presidents and their spouses for their lifetimes, except when the spouse remarries. In 1997, Congressional legislation became effective limiting Secret Service protection to former Presidents for a period of not more than 10 years from the date the former President leaves office
- Children of former Presidents until age 16
- Visiting heads of foreign states or governments and their spouses traveling with them, other distinguished foreign visitors to the United States, and official representatives of the United States performing special missions abroad
- Major presidential and vice presidential candidates, and their spouses within 120 days of a general presidential election and other individuals as designated per Executive Order of the President
- National Special Security Events, when designated as such by the Secretary of the Department of Homeland Security

The protection of the President and other designees is a daunting task. The Secret Service is recognized internationally for its unparalleled security operations. The agency does not disclose the types or specific methodologies it employs to safeguard its protectees. In general, when circumstances dictate, the Secret Service regularly calls upon other federal, state, and local agencies to assist in maintaining a safe environment for the President and other protectees. When the President travels, an advance team of Secret Service agents works with host city, state, and local law enforcement, as well as public safety officials, to jointly implement the necessary security measures.

Protective Intelligence and Threat Assessment

Title 18 of the United States Code (USC) Sections 871 and 879 make it a felony violation to threaten the life of the President, successors to the presidency, and other persons protected by the Secret Service. The protection of an individual is comprehensive and goes well beyond surrounding the individual with well-armed agents. As part of the Secret Service's mission of preventing an incident before it occurs, the agency relies on meticulous advance work and threat assessments developed by its Intelligence Division to identify potential risks to protectees (United States Secret Service, 2007).

Arising from that responsibility, the Secret Service has developed comprehensive protective programs to safeguard the lives of those it is entrusted to protect. A key component of those protection activities are threat assessment and protective intelligence efforts.

Threat assessment or protective intelligence is the process of gathering and assessing information about persons or groups who may have the interest, motive, intention, and capability of mounting attacks against public officials and figures. Gauging the potential threat to and vulnerability of a targeted individual is key to preventing violence (Fein & Vossekuil, 2000).

The primary goal of Secret Service threat assessment and protective intelligence operations is to prevent assassination attempts. To do so, the Secret Service identifies, investigates, assesses, and manages persons brought to their attention who might pose a threat to protected officials. Once an assessment is made, a plan can be developed and implemented to monitor the suspected individual and to intervene, as appropriate, to prevent an attack. Attention to the individual's motives and attack-related behaviors and to the systems (family, work, community, criminal justice, mental health, and social services) that the individual is involved with are key to assessing and managing a potential threat (Fein & Vossekuil, 2000).

Protective research is an integral component of all security operations. Agents and specialists assigned to conduct protective research evaluate information received from law enforcement, intelligence agencies, and a variety of other sources regarding individuals or groups who may pose a threat to Secret Service protectees (United States Secret Service, 2007). When indicated, Special Agents in the field conduct thorough investigations on cases referred, collecting additional information to evaluate potential dangerousness posed to Secret Service protectees. The agency's Intelligence Division provides oversight and guidance to protective intelligence research, investigations and evaluations including review of reports, consultation with field agents on evaluation decisions, and provision of specialized resources such as psychiatric consultants for the management and assessment of complex cases when necessary.

Mental Health Liaison Program

Since its inception, the Mental Health Liaison Program has supported the intelligence efforts of the Secret Service in determining whether individuals do pose a threat to protectees (Luczko, 2005). The history, development, and utilization of the Mental Health Liaison Program has been well detailed by Coggins and Pynchon (1998). Today, five psychiatrists serve the program's activity nationwide.

The evolution of the program as discussed in the following text must be understood in its historical context. Over the years, the program has evolved considerably in scope, moving away from a strictly clinical/mental illness model to reflect a more risk assessment/case management model (Coggins & Pynchon, 1998). This evolution may be understood as a response to advances in the science of violence, risk assessment, and its relationship to mental illness. Coggins and Pynchon (1998) suggested that it may also reflect more thoughtful awareness about what types of mental health and law enforcement systems interactions are mutually beneficial.

Changes in the world in the wake of September 11, 2001, and other global events have given greater transparency to the multidimensional threats that confront protective responsibilities and also changed some of the demands placed upon the Secret Service. As such, the Mental Health Liaison Program may further evolve to better support the needs of the Secret Service.

In the early 1980s, after the attempt on President Reagan's life by John Hinckley, Jr., the Secret Service made an operational decision to approach the mental health community seeking assistance. The desire was to develop a broad framework upon which mental health and law enforcement professionals could collaborate.

In September 1981, under the joint sponsorship of the National Academy of Sciences Institute of Medicine and the United States Secret Service, the Committee on Research and Training Issues Related to the Mission of the Secret Service was formed (Coggins & Pynchon, 1998). Subsequently, two invitational symposia, the Institute of Medicine Workshops on Behavioral Research and the Secret Service, were convened. Chaired by W. Walter Menninger, M.D., and comprised of distinguished clinical, administrative, research, and legal leaders in the fields of psychiatry, psychology, sociology, and mental health law, the participants were tasked to examine the usefulness of behavioral science research and mental health knowledge and skills to Secret Service information collection, analysis, evaluations of dangerousness, and management of protective intelligence cases (Coggins & Pynchon, 1998; IOM, 1984).

In the spring of 1984, the Institute of Medicine released its report, Institute of Medicine Workshop on Behavioral Research and the Secret Service: Problems in Assessing and Managing Dangerous Behavior, on the topic of Behavioral Science and the Secret Service, which most notably encouraged the Service to establish consistent relationships with mental health professionals nationwide

(IOM, 1984). The report also encouraged the Service to strengthen the loosely established existing relationships that it had with the mental health community (some field offices more than others had very good relationships with local mental health professionals).

The response of the Secret Service to the Hinckley case highlights how law enforcement professionals greatly benefit by an increased understanding of, and appreciation for, the implications of mental illness to protective responsibilities. The Secret Service initiated an active and working relationship with the mental health community. The agency also undertook an aggressive program to train agents to better understand, deal with, and assess mentally ill persons and, at the same time, develop a cadre of contracted mental health professionals in various regions of the country to assist them in their protective intelligence mission.

Through the cultivation of relationships with distinguished practitioners based at institutions, universities, and in private practice, clinical expertise was made readily available to the Service and the Mental Health Liaison Program was born. It has been the genesis of the clinical threat assessment process for identifying, confronting, and managing potential assassins (Saleeba, 2000). The purpose of the Mental Health Liaison Program has been patterned after the IOM recommendations: to provide case consultation, agent training related to issues of mental illness, and consultation on broader matters spanning both mental health organizations and the Secret Service (Coggins & Pynchon, 1998).

Case Consultation

When necessary, the Secret Service looks to the Mental Health Liaison Program Consultants to assist agents in their evaluation and case management responsibilities (Luczko, 2005). Through a comprehensive review of case materials, including investigative reports, psychological, psychiatric, forensic evaluations, raw psychometric data, mental health history, and criminal history, Mental Health Liaison Program Consultants may assist the case agent in formulating a comprehensive assessment of a subject's potential risk to protectees.

Consultants may also assist in or conduct subject interviews in an attempt to provide a psychiatric evaluation of the subject from the perspective of United States Secret Service interest. It is important to note that when participating in the risk assessment process, consultants provide clinical opinions to assist the agent in assessing risk. The consultant's role is supportive to the agent's risk assessment and is circumscribed by case-specific objectives. Whether performing a record review, participating in a subject interview, or providing consultation to local mental health providers responsible for the subject's care, the consultant's opinions are summarized in an evaluation report, which is submitted to the Secret Service for inclusion in the case file (Coggins & Pynchon, 1998). The ultimate determination of whether an individual poses a risk to a protectee rests with the agent and his superiors, and not the Mental Health Liaison Program consultant.

Training

Mental Health Liaison consultants provide both orientation and advanced level training to agents and other United States Secret Service personnel regarding medical, psychiatric, pharmacological, and mental health law concepts relevant to the investigative interests and practices of the Secret Service.

Over the many years of my providing services to the United States Secret Service, considerable time and energy was spent in developing field-based training opportunities for Protective Intelligence agents. Training programs were tailored to the specific needs of agents at the Washington Field Office, and Intelligence Division, in addition to specific programs that were presented at the James J. Rowley Training Center outside Washington, DC.

Training modules addressing such topics as concepts of mental illness, understanding violent behavior, assessing dangerousness, mental health evaluation and diagnosis, psychopharmacologic treatment of behavioral disorders, effective interviewing strategies for mentally ill subjects, understanding the local/mental health care system, and the interpretation and use of the mental health resources were a part of the core presentation seminars. Additional focus was also directed to understanding the mental health law nuances of confidentiality, duty to warn, and civil commitment.

Considerable time and attention were paid to issues surrounding ethical and legal constructs that prohibited or compromised the professional relationship between mental health providers and law enforcement. These topical areas often served as the foundation for liaison-driven activities, which will be addressed subsequently in this chapter.

Most unique to my Washington Field Office experience was the conceptualization that consultation and training were seen as a continuum, and training was not limited to didactic classroom or seminar events. The relationship between the consultant and the field office was the foundation for one-, two-, or three-day training seminars in which less formal, small group case study presentations and case review sessions were regularly scheduled events.

For example, at its peak of operation, in addition to a regular monthly case conference, the Washington Field Office sponsored monthly didactic presentations that provided a more in-depth opportunity to explore the issues that had been presented in the large seminar programs. In addition to these formally scheduled activities, the availability of the Mental Health Liaison Program Consultant through weekly scheduled office hours provided the field agents an opportunity to discuss specific case concerns with the consultant and the supervisor in a more informal manner. The comprehensive nature of this training activity coupled with the regular availability of the Mental Health Liaison Program Consultant provided a highly integrated and extremely user-friendly mechanism to support the field office's needs in this area.

Professional Liaison

When necessary, consultants are called upon to establish liaison with local mental health facilities, practitioners, and professional organizations to encourage mutually cooperative relationships with the United States Secret Service and access to pertinent case information. The authors' experiences with local and regional liaison activities have largely been needs driven, as one might expect.

For example, my liaison assistance was sought during a time when agents were experiencing considerable difficulty having subjects evaluated in a timely manner and/or admitted to psychiatric hospitals in Washington, DC. I identified key mental health professionals and target institutions, such as the District of Columbia Department of Mental Health Emergency Services, St. Elizabeths Hospital, and some of the private psychiatric emergency rooms, and recommended that leadership of the Washington Field Office meet with them to open a dialogue to address specific mutual concerns. These meetings continued with regularity on a quarterly basis. They also evolved to facilitate a number of mutually beneficial professional educational opportunities, such as grand rounds training at local hospitals.

Additionally, specific training presentations and "grand rounds" were organized for local law enforcement and community mental health service providers, which the Secret Service felt necessary to have a greater understanding about its protective intelligence mission, case classification system, and related issues of concern.

Providing Clinical Consultation to Secret Service Threat Assessments

Secret Service threat assessments are very similar to clinical risk and threat assessments, with one exception. They are exclusively focused on assessing the potential risk to protectees. They also benefit from an extraordinary capacity to access data that is useful in determining risk.

The identification of risk for identification's sake is a meaningless exercise. The Secret Service assesses risk on a daily basis methodically and with a singular purpose: to protect the lives of those they serve. Their mantra is clear: identify, investigate, assess, and manage. First, identify those individuals that come to attention. Then assess whether the individual poses a danger to a protectee. If so, develop and implement a management plan.

The Secret Service Exceptional Case Study Project (ECSP) provided a behavior-based case review and analysis of "the thinking and behavior of all 83 persons known to have attacked or approached to attack a prominent public official or figure in the United States from 1949–1996," thereby dispelling many myths about assassination (Fein & Vossekuil, 1998, p. 4). This project operationalized how the idea of assassination develops into lethal or near-lethal action by focusing on motive, target selection, plan of attack, communications, and whether mental illness or life circumstances contributed to the assassination interest or behavior.

Eight major motives were identified by the ECSP:

- To achieve notoriety or fame
- To bring attention to a personal or public problem

- To avenge a perceived wrong; to retaliate for a perceived injury
- To end personal pain or to be removed from society; to be killed
- To save the country or the world; to fix a world problem
- To develop a special relationship with the target
- To benefit financially
- To effect political change

While we have learned much about the thinking and behavior of presidential stalkers and assailants from the ECSP, by design it offers little understanding of these individuals comparatively or as a collective group. The ECSP offers no typology. Rather, it cautions that there is no profile of the American assassin.

Surprisingly, there is limited published scholarship on presidential stalkers and assassins. Meloy et al. (2004) provided a comprehensive review of existing research on persons who have approached, attacked, or assassinated public figures in the United States. The earliest research narrowly focused on those who threatened the President or who appeared at the White House seeking an audience; these publications do not include considerations of persons who actually made assassination attempts (Hoffman, 1943; Sebastiani & Foy, 1965; Shore et al., 1985). Thus, that work suffered from an obvious lack of information that would permit a predictive connection between the threatener's ideations and the act. Only one study offered a profile or "presidential assassination syndrome" (Rothstein, 1964, 1966, 1971), which subsequently did not withstand psychometric scrutiny (Megargee, 1986).

Clarke (1982), in his archival study of 17 American assassins and would-be assassins, described four "types" based upon a consideration of the cultural, political, and social context of their behavior, as well as the immediate situation or circumstance in which the behavior occurs.

Arising from my years of consultation to the Secret Service in an effort to better facilitate my work and to integrate what has been learned from the existing pool of research and taxonomies in this area, I have searched for a framework that would codify these actions based on motive, the presence or absence of delusions, active psychosis, and the intent to do harm. By drawing upon the ECSP (Fein & Vossekuil, 1998) and integrating the Clarke (1982) classification with modifications, I have conceptualized five descriptive categories that attempt to capture the various motivations of presidential stalkers and assassins and the clinical context in which it occurs (Table 16.1): resentful, pathologically obsessed, infamy seeking, intimacy seeking, and nuisance or attention seeking (Phillips, 2006, 2007).

The Resentful Presidential Stalker or Assassin

While resentful stalkers comprise a minority of general cases that often arise in workplace settings (Mullen, Pathé, & Purcell, 2000), they appear to account for a significant number of presidential stalkings and most of the attempted or completed assassinations. The stalking arises from a quest for retribution.

Table 16.1. Five descriptive categories of presidential stalkers or assassins

Stalker or assassin type	Motive	Delusional thinking or active psychosis	Harm intent	Animus toward POTUS*
Resentful	Retribution	None	Yes	Yes
Pathologically obsessed	Retribution or personal gain	Persecutory or grandiose	Yes	Yes (Retribution) No (Personal gain)
Infamy seeker	Political statement	None	Yes	Not necessarily
Intimacy seeker	Realization of fantasized relationship	Erotomanic	No	No
Nuisance or	To provide help to or seek help from the President	Grandiose, narcissistic, or dependent; may be actively psychotic	No	No
Attention seeker	To see or be seen with the President	None	No	No

* POTUS, President of the United States.

Resentful presidential stalkers or assassins feel justified in their actions and are driven by anger without delusions. Their targeting behavior arises from political disagreement, displaced rage, or perceived narcissistic injury. They are committed to eliminating the target to achieve retribution and not as a means of attaining a platform to make a grand statement or to attain fame. They feel justified in their actions to the point of righteous indignation. While they may have some paranoid personality traits, they do not suffer from delusional thinking.

The Pathologically Obsessed Presidential Stalker or Assassin

Pathologically obsessed presidential stalkers and assassins are characterized by a severe psychosis of a persecutory or grandiose nature that places the President in peril because of a persistent resolve to do harm. Their delusions can often be characterized as divinely inspired or of idiosyncratic importance. Most often, they incorporate the unshakeable belief that the President is responsible for their life problem and therefore they seek redress for some imagined wrongful act. In those instances, their purpose in assassination may be seen as retributive.

In others, the psychosis is without any animosity toward the President or desire for retribution. Instead, assassination services their intense narcissistic fantasies. Although they may resemble infamy seekers in their desire to attract attention, the psychosis distinguishes them.

Their focus is actually not on the President but on others for whom their actions are intended as a statement of love or disdain.

The Presidential Infamy Seeker

Presidential infamy seekers are a special class of individuals whose presidential targeting is generally for a grand political statement or for personal reasons outside of politics. Although not delusional, the intensity of their characterologic disturbance is often palpable. Their primary characterologic construct is antisocial. Political zealotry is the common thread that binds these individuals together. It is their zealotry and willingness to sacrifice themselves at any cost for the "cause" that makes them so dangerous. Their intent to do harm is clear, but it is often only a means to an end and not necessarily the primary motivation for their actions. While the act of attempted or successful assassination constitutes by definition a negative direction of interest, infamy seekers may not bear any animosity toward the target. They seek only the opportunity to act out their particular drama on a world stage.

The Presidential Intimacy Seeker

Presidential intimacy seekers manifest the same characteristics as other intimacy seekers, as described by Mullen et al. (2000). They desire to realize a relationship with a person they delusionally believe is already interested in or in love with them. Erotomanic delusions are pathognomonic of this classification. Primarily seeking fulfillment of a fantasized sexual intimacy, presidential intimacy seekers see an imagined platonic friendship or role as a special confidant also as the primary motivation. They persist with their approach and attempts at personal contact, oblivious to any attempts to deter their advances. Their pursuit of the President can, at times, be reckless and unbridled, creating a "zone of risk" extending beyond the delusional love object that places many others in jeopardy.

The Presidential Nuisance or Attention Seeker

Presidential nuisances include those who approach the President or appear at the White House gate driven by delusional thinking without having any intent to do harm. The individuals who comprise these "White House Cases" are often quite different from those reflected in the Exceptional Case Study Project. They usually experience a thought disturbance but have no nefarious intent. The nature of their delusional experience appears far less paranoid and threatening. The reasons stated by the subject for the visit appear more grandiose, narcissistic, or dependent (seeking help for a problem), rather than in response to fear or driven by anger with an intent to do harm or seek revenge (Coggins, Pynchon, & Phillips, 1998). It is the nature and character of their delusional thinking that attracts them to the President or the White House and therefore to the attention of the U.S. Secret Service.

The absence of nefarious intent separates them from resentful presidential stalkers just as the absence of a fantasized delusional relationship distinguishes them from presidential intimacy seekers. One might actually characterize these individuals as creating more of a nuisance than posing a threat of imminent danger.

Presidential attention seekers, by contrast, approach the President driven by the notice that it garners, whether in sole service to their narcissism and sense of entitlement or because the media attention provides personal financial benefit. They are not delusional. Generally, these individuals have no history of violence. They do not make threats to persons or property, nor do they attempt to gain access or close proximity to the President for nefarious purposes. At best they can be characterized as "wannabes"—people whose primary desire is to "see and be seen" with the leader of the free world in a manner that attracts attention to them.

Whether these people are seen as nuisances or as attention seekers, agents on the scene must determine if such individuals pose a threat to the President, other Secret Service protectees, and/or whether their behavior suggests the need for emergency psychiatric evaluation. Consider the following illustrations from history and case consultation.

The Resentful Presidential Stalker: Case Example—Samuel Byck/Richard Nixon

Samuel Byck was the oldest of three boys born and raised in Philadelphia by Jewish immigrant parents. Despondent over a deteriorating marriage, jealous of the success of his brothers, and frustrated by his failure in numerous business ventures, the retired tire salesman became convinced that the American political system was corrupt. The Small Business Administration had rejected a loan application intended to support the start of his own business and he held the President responsible for his failures (Clarke, 1982).

Byck became a person of interest to the United States Secret Service in 1972 for sending threatening letters to President Nixon (White House Security Review, 1995b). It is reported that on Christmas Eve in 1973, he picketed the White House dressed in a Santa suit carrying a sign which read "Santa Sez: All I want for Christmas is my constitutional right to peaceably petition my government for redress of grievances" (Clarke, 1982).

Byck developed a plan that he called "Operation Pandora's Box," a plot to hijack a commercial airliner and crash it into the White House with the intention of killing President Nixon (White House Security Review, 1995b). Troubled that his actions might be misconstrued as those of a "maniac or madman," Byck recorded an audiotape describing his planned assault and rationale and sent copies to scientist Jonas Salk, columnist Jack Anderson, Senator Abraham Ribicoff, and composer Leonard Bernstein (Clarke, 1982).

Byck traveled to the Baltimore-Washington International Airport on February 22, 1974, with a handgun and a gasoline bomb secreted in a briefcase. He shot and killed an officer who was screening passengers for a Delta Airlines flight headed for Atlanta and boarded the jet plane. Byck then stormed the cockpit and ordered the two pilots to take off. They told him that they could not depart without removing the wheel blocks (Clarke, 1982). An angry Byck shot the pilot twice and the copilot three times (White House Security Review, 1995b).

He reportedly then grabbed a terrified passenger demanding that she help him fly the plane (Clarke, 1982). Byck was shot and wounded through the cabin window by a police officer on the ground outside of the plane. Aware that his plan was in shambles, Byck killed himself with his own gun (White House Security Review, 1995b).

Byck meets the criteria for a resentful presidential stalker because the motive for his stalking was retributive. He felt justified in his actions and was driven by anger without delusions. His targeting behavior was born of political dissatisfaction and displaced rage.

The Pathologically Obsessed Presidential Stalker: Case Example—John W. Hinckley, Jr./Ronald Reagan

John W. Hinckley, Jr. shot and wounded President Ronald Reagan on March 30, 1981, at the Washington Hilton Hotel as the President headed toward his limousine. Three other individuals were inadvertently struck by gunfire, among them Press Secretary James Brady, who sustained a debilitating head injury. Hinckley's belief that his actions would lead to fulfillment of his romantic delusions was an uncanny example of life imitating art.

Hinckley had become fascinated with the 1976 movie *Taxi Driver*, in which actor Robert DeNiro played Travis Bickle, an alienated schizoid taxi driver who began stalking a young woman who works for a senator-turned-presidential-candidate. Failing to win the woman's affection, Bickle turned his anger toward the senator and began methodically plotting his assassination, only to have his scheme foiled by the heavy presence of Secret Service agents. Bickle subsequently fixated on "Iris," a young prostitute played by a young and then-little-known actress, Jodie Foster. In the film, Bickle became a hero when he rescued Iris from her pimp in a violent gun battle.

Hinckley became obsessed with Travis Bickle and began to emulate him in dress and manner. Most importantly, he became obsessed with Jodie Foster. Hinckley traveled to New Haven in August 1980 to make contact with Foster, who was then a freshman drama student at Yale University. He left poems and letters in her mailbox and spoke to her twice by telephone, recording the conversations (Bonnie, Jeffries, & Low, 2000).

Unsuccessful in his efforts to win Foster's affection, Hinckley began stalking President Jimmy Carter on the campaign trail in the belief that assassinating the President would bring Foster closer to him. Hinckley continued leaving correspondence for Foster. Concerned that he was despondent and suicidal, his parents arranged an appointment with a psychiatrist (Bonnie et al., 2000). Although Hinckley saw the psychiatrist episodically over the next 4 months, he never disclosed appearing at a presidential campaign, his plans of assassination, or his love of Foster.

In November 1980, Hinckley's interest shifted from President Carter to president-elect Reagan, as evidenced by Hinckley's traveling to Reagan's transitional residence in Washington, DC. He also made several additional trips to New Haven and left more notes for Foster. Finally, on March 30, 1981, 1 day after he checked into the Park Central Hotel in Washington, DC, Hinckley wrote a letter to Jodie Foster outlining his assassination plan (Bonnie et al., 2000). He then went to the Washington Hilton and attempted to execute it.

Hinckley's stalking behaviors began with President Carter and then shifted to President-elect Reagan. This change in target selection is not uncommon among presidential stalkers. Many attackers and near-lethal approachers consider multiple potential targets and change their primary target several times before settling on their final choice (Fein & Vossekuil, 2000).

John W. Hinckley, Jr.'s psychosis was without any animosity toward the President or desire for retribution. Instead, his planned assassination serviced his intense narcissistic fantasies. Although he may resemble an infamy seeker in his desire to attract attention, it is the psychosis that is distinguishing. His focus was actually not the President but on another for whom his actions were intended as a statement of love. As such, he too meets the criteria for pathologically obsessed presidential stalker and assassin.

Following what was arguably the most influential insanity-defense case of the 20th century, a jury acquitted John W. Hinckley, Jr. of 13 assault, murder, and weapons counts, finding him not guilty by reason of insanity. He was committed to St. Elizabeths Hospital for the criminally insane in Washington, DC.

Presidential Infamy Seeker: Case Example—Francisco Martin Duran/William Jefferson Clinton

Francisco Martin Duran was an avid supporter of anti-Government ideologies, who saw gun control as a "Big Brother" conspiracy. He was angry with the Government and the President for signing the assault weapons ban of 1994 and for failing to reconsider his court martial and dishonorable discharge from the U.S. Army. He left work on September 30, 1994, without contacting his family or employer, and began his cross-country journey to Washington, DC, with an arsenal of weapons (Locy, 1994; *United States v. Francisco Martin Duran*, 1995). Before leaving Colorado, he told several people of his intention to kill the President and gave one person a card bearing his signature, which he said would be "valuable" someday.

En route, he passed the clock tower at the University of Texas in Austin, the site where Charles Whitman killed 13 and wounded many others, and the book depository in Dallas, Texas, the site where Lee Harvey Oswald is believed to have fired upon President Kennedy. He stayed at various hotels in the Washington area between the 10th and the 29th of October, including the Washington Hilton Hotel, the site of the attempted assassination of President Ronald Reagan (Locy, 1995b; *United States v. Francisco Martin Duran,* 1996).

On October 28, 1994, Mr. Duran wrote a letter to his wife that included a will. On that same date, he was in a hotel room watching television and saw a news report that the President was arriving in Washington the next day.

On the morning of October 29, wearing a trench coat and carrying his shotgun and the SKS assault weapon, Duran headed for Pennsylvania Avenue. He walked up and down Pennsylvania Avenue in front of the White House, passing the various entrances for tourists for several hours (White House Security Review, 1995a).

While Duran was standing in front of the north side of the White House fence in the early afternoon, two eighth-grade students on a field trip ran to a nearby spot along the fence. Pointing toward a small group of men dressed in dark business suits in the vicinity of the north portico of the White House, one of the excited students remarked, "That man looks a lot like Bill Clinton," to which his friend replied, "Yeah, it does" (Locy, 1995a, p. B4; *United States v. Francisco Martin Duran*, 1996). The man they saw, Dennis Basso, was on a tour of the White House and did bear some resemblance to the President.

Hearing this, Duran fired at least 29 shots at the White House. Eleven rounds found their mark on the North Facade. Additionally, a window in the press briefing room in the West Wing was breached by a round (White House Security Review, 1995a). Remarkably, no one was injured by the storm of gunfire.

Duran began running east along the fence while continuing to fire in the direction of the White House (*United States v. Francisco Martin Duran*, 1996). When he stopped, apparently trying to reload a second 30-round clip, a passer-by tackled him (Locy, 1995a). Soon thereafter, Secret Service agents arrived to help subdue Duran and confiscate his rifle.

A search of Duran's truck after his arrest revealed a rifle, ammunition, and a nerve gas antidote (Locy, 1994, p. A1; White House Security Review, 1995a). Several documents were found, including a letter in which he had written "Can you imagine a higher moral calling than to destroy someone's dreams with one bullet?"; a road atlas on which he had written "Kill the Pres."; a cover torn from a telephone book bearing a picture of President Clinton, which Mr. Duran had defaced by drawing a circle around Clinton's head and an "X" on his face; a handwritten document with the heading "Last will and words"; an order form for the book "Hit Man"; and several books about out-of-body experiences (Locy, 1994, p. A1; White House Security Review, 1995a). When they searched his house and office, law enforcement agents found a business card, on the back of which Duran had written "Kill all government offices [*sic*] and department heads," and assorted other pieces of anti-Government literature (*United States v. Francisco Martin Duran*, 1996; White House Security Review, 1995a, pp. 32–38).

Admittedly, Duran did not exhibit typical stalking behavior in his approach to the White House. He was not of record with the Intelligence Division of the U.S. Secret Service before the attack (White House Security Review, 1995a). It could be argued that his path through the sites of previous assassinations such as the Dallas Book Depository and the Washington Hilton were vicarious stalking behaviors. He was stalking the idea if not the experience of assassinating a President. However, Duran does meet the criteria for presidential infamy seekers because his actions targeted the President in order to make a grand political statement. Notably, when examined pretrial by a government's expert, Mr. Duran's first question upon introduction was "Doc, are we going to be on Hard Copy?" (Phillips, 1995). Duran's actions emerged out of a desire to become famous. He exhibited extreme character pathology but not psychosis. His political zealotry was palpable.

Presidential Intimacy Seekers: Case Example—Jane Doe/William Jefferson Clinton

Ms. Doe first came to the attention of the United States Secret Service in the spring of 1995, when she appeared at a presidential site with flowers that she intended to give to President Clinton. When interviewed, she spoke of a great affection for the President and indicated that she had sent many small gifts and letters to him in the past. At that time, after a full factual investigation was conducted by the Secret Service, she was deemed not to present a threat or danger to any protectee of the Service or to herself.

Subsequently, she again returned to the presidential site and was again interviewed by U.S. Secret Service agents. This time she said that she loved the President and that she returned with the hope of jogging with him. Ms. Doe said that had she known she would not be allowed to jog with the President, she would not have returned. Again, following additional investigation, the Secret Service agents thought that she did not show any threatening attitudes and no further action was taken.

Upon returning to her hometown, Ms. Doe repeatedly sent the President numerous letters expressing her love and affection, in addition to sending many small gifts, some that she purchased and others that she made, as tokens of her affection for him. It is believed that Ms. Doe made repeated visits to Washington, DC, in hopes of seeing and meeting the President.

Months later, Presidential Protection Division agents observed a woman behaving strangely along a rope line as the President was shaking hands at a political fund raiser at a Washington, DC, hotel. When the woman greeted the President, she was tongue-tied and acted somewhat bizarrely. It was noted that she broke the receiving line and returned to a position that would allow her to shake the President's hand again.

Agents interviewed the woman and determined that she was Ms. Doe who apparently was a member of the sponsoring organization and had a legitimate ticket to attend the event. Her behaviors were not deemed to be threatening to the President and she returned to her hometown. Over the course of the next several years, Ms. Doe began to radically change her appearance. She continued to correspond and to legitimately gain entry to presidential functions.

Finally, during a presidential visit to her hometown, Ms. Doe carried a cell phone while breaching the secure perimeter surrounding the presidential limousine. Entering a secure site with an object in hand that could have easily been mistaken for a weapon demonstrated the greater danger she posed to herself and others when her delusional thoughts became so intense she could not control them. Ms. Doe was subsequently civilly committed.

Presidential intimacy seekers manifest the same characteristics noted to be found among other intimacy stalkers. They desire to realize a relationship with a person they believe is already interested or in love with them. They persist with their approach and attempts at personal contact oblivious to any attempts to deter their advances.

Ms. Doe meets the criteria for an intimacy seeking presidential stalker because she possessed a delusional love interest in the President. She sought fulfillment of a fantasized relationship and made repeated attempts at approach or contact. In so doing, she recklessly created a "zone of risk," placing in jeopardy herself, the target and his protectors, as well as innocent bystanders.

Presidential Nuisance or Attention Seekers: Case Example—Richard Weaver/George W. Bush

In 1991, Richard Weaver attended a prayer breakfast at the Washington Hilton Hotel. According to his web site, Weaver is the founder and President of the Spiritual Revolution Through Christ, Inc., in Sacramento, California (Spiritual

Revolution Through Christ, 2006). He mingled in the grand ballroom with senators and dignitaries, as is customary. What distinguishes Reverend Weaver is that he managed to follow a VIP into the holding room of then-President George H. W. Bush and have his picture taken shaking hands with the President.

Richard Weaver had succeeded in meeting celebrities, sports figures, presidents, and other politicians with great ease for nearly three decades. He enjoyed the media attention and often used the photographs taken with celebrities to promote his ministry. Three weeks before the 2001 inauguration of George W. Bush, Mr. Weaver reported that he felt a strong inner sense that God wanted him to deliver a message to the President: "Your miracle election is to remind you to stand for Christ daily without political compromise. Keep Christ first and God will give you another miracle election in four years" (Montgomery & Santana, 2001). Armed with the typed message on a laminated blue card and carrying a medallion bearing the image of former president George H. W. Bush, Mr. Weaver headed to Washington.

In an interview, Mr. Weaver stated that on the morning of Inauguration Day, he was given a blue standing-room ticket by a woman who had an extra one (Montgomery & Santana, 2001). As he approached the entry, he came upon a group of VIPs and overheard one of them talking about a special entrance (Montgomery & Santana, 2001). Mr. Weaver's distinguished appearance and impeccable dress allowed him to blend in with the group as they entered the Capitol grounds.

Once inside, he asked a guard for directions to the nearest restroom. He was directed through a metal detector that placed him in a VIP seating area. Reverend Weaver claims to have taken a seat only 20 rows away from the podium to hear the Inaugural Address. Following the ceremony, he walked into the Capitol and began to wander around upstairs.

When challenged by a U.S. Capitol Police officer, Reverend Weaver said he was lost and searching for an exit. The officer escorted him to an exit, which happened to be in close proximity to the President's awaiting motorcade. Mr. Weaver presented Mr. Bush with the medallion and card (Grove, 2003).

On February 6, 2003, Mr. Weaver again gained entrance without invitation to another prayer breakfast at the Washington Hilton. After clearing magnetometers, he entered the ballroom and went from table to table socializing. When he happened upon the table of a distinguished senator at prayer, he joined in and asked if he could be seated there. The senator agreed. The table was located in front of the stage where the President spoke. As the President came down a set of stairs leaving from the stage, Mr. Weaver came from behind a rope line and stanchion, shook the President's hand, and handed him an eight-page typed "Message from God" about Iraq. When questioned by authorities, Reverend Weaver stated, "I don't try to sneak in. I just go where I think God wants me to go" (Grove, 2003, p. C1).

Reverend Weaver was not so successful during George W. Bush's second inaugural on January 23, 2005. Although he had previously told journalists that

God made him "invisible and undetectable by security," he was apprehended at a checkpoint on First Street and Pennsylvania Avenue and never made it to the Capitol (Haskell, 2005, p. 1).

Reverend Weaver was the quintessential example of a presidential attention seeker. Narcissistic and entitled, he was driven by the need to be noticed. With no history of violence and having displayed no evidence of intent to do harm, he is best characterized as a "wannabe." He wanted to be seen, to be noticed, and to be in the presence of the President.

Case Example: John Doe

Occasionally, individuals come to the attention of the Secret Service who have not made threats or attempted to approach a protectee. Nonetheless, their unusual "direction of interest" raises sufficient concern that warrants careful examination and risk assessment. The case of John Doe is most illustrative.

Mr. John Doe came to the attention of the U.S. Secret Service on December 16, 2004. A county police agency in the Washington, DC, area reported that Mr. Doe went to the police station and claimed his home was broken into and a weapon was taken by FBI agents who were conducting a covert operation in his home. Mr. Doe called them later and said he found the weapon behind his sofa.

Despite his call, the police responded to Mr. Doe's home to ensure it had not been broken into. They discovered, in plain view, 90 marijuana plants, photographs of Air Force One, which appeared to be taken with a telescopic lens, and numerous weapons. A formal search of Mr. Doe's home revealed that the home was rigged with cans and other materials to alert him of any-one's entrance. Further, multiple handguns, rifles (including an M-16), and stun guns, as well as high-powered scopes, silencers, improvised explosive devices (IEDs), grenades, bomb-making materials, and other makeshift weapons were also discovered.

Six weapons were located in Mr. Doe's bed. The IEDs appeared functional, but the gunpowder or explosives were missing. Mr. Doe also had two bags, one a computer bag with a cardboard box inside and the second a tennis racket bag, which was altered to allow the firing of a concealed weapon from within. In addition, Mr. Doe's basement was equipped with a make-shift firing range, which contained a closet lined with cinder blocks and bulletproof vests.

Also found in Mr. Doe's home was literature on the John F. Kennedy assassination, bomber Eric Rudolph, the anthrax investigations, sniper train-ing, and UFOs; a life size cardboard cutout of President Kennedy wearing a sweater with bullet holes; a GI Joe doll (with a face resembling President Kennedy), which had the head blown out by gun shots; photos of Lee Harvey Oswald and Eric Rudolph; photos of himself dressed identically to Rudolph with "fake" written under Rudolph's and "real" written under his; a police SWAT jacket; military uniforms; camouflage attire; and various wigs and hair dye. A notebook with a "to do list" was also found, which contained an entry listed as "White House trip."

Local police arrested Mr. Doe on drug-related charges. All weapons, except for a stun/taser gun and small knife, were seized from his home. When interviewed by the Secret Service, Mr. Doe explained that he always wore camouflage clothing because people are "less likely to mess with you." He stated he originally obtained all of the weapons because he thought they would be outlawed. He went on to reference the writings of James Madison, the fourth President of the United States, regarding people retaining the power to overthrow the government. He stated while he would not do so, he did not know what the future held and that he may need a weapon.

When questioned further about the weapons, he claimed to use them to test his various theories on assassinations and conspiracies. He admitted to being fascinated with President Kennedy's assassination and believed it was the result of a government conspiracy, which was carried out by the CIA. He also said he had thought about how an assassination might take place, but added he would not assassinate anyone because someone else would take their place, leaving the problem unresolved. He further explained he was interested in President Kennedy's assassination because it was the only assassination that appeared set up and where questions still remained. He said he used the GI Joe figurines to reenact the assassination and that he intended to use the shirts with bullet holes to attract attention to his theory.

Mr. Doe said he did not see violence as a means to an end, but admitted it took him awhile to come to that realization; however, he said he would be violent if attacked. He claimed if he were in a room with the President, he would not harm him. He also claimed he would tell the President that he was working on the Eric Rudolph and anthrax investigations. He believed photographs of Rudolph were fake and altered in a way to work against him.

Mr. Doe also said he took the photographs of Air Force One with a new telephoto lens and was outside testing it when the aircraft flew over his home. He stated he traveled infrequently because he found driving a car too dangerous. Mr. Doe acknowledged daily use of marijuana and admitted to growing it in his home. He added that his use increased when working on a project because it helped him concentrate. He also admitted prior use of other drugs, such as LSD. Mr. Doe described his home as an inventor's paradise and said officers who conducted the search were like "kids in a candy store." He explained he worked on many projects, mostly concerning well-known events, and developed his own theories about them. He then developed ideas for publicizing his theories utilizing different propaganda.

Mr. Doe explained that the piece of paper with "White House trip" written on it was in reference to a nurse going to the White House to administer the drug Cipro to employees who were exposed to anthrax attacks. He believed this proved the Government created the anthrax scare. Further, he said he had the military officer's uniform in the event a drastic situation occurred and he needed to disguise himself to infiltrate an army base.

Mr. Doe reported that thoughts of violence had once "tickled the imagination," but he realized it was not in him to be violent. He was also asked to explain the booby traps in his home, which he dismissed as methods to rescue and feed stray cats. He admitted to hearing voices while in college but dismissed those as "the voice of an articulated thought." He said he most feared someone entering his home at night while he slept. He added numerous times that he was not a paranoid person. He described himself in a grandiose manner, stating he did well academically and was skilled at "dealing with people with emotional problems." He also said he was most proud at working to generate wholeness of thought along the lines of love and sharing.

This case received media attention. According to news articles, the subject described himself as "an inventor who wanted to use the weapons to develop tools to help US Special Forces." He also blamed the marijuana on an invasive weed that overtook his legal indoor houseplants.

The investigating agent reported that although the subject seems capable of organizing and planning, he has difficulty following through on projects. Until his arrest, Mr. Doe had no criminal or mental history. Despite the numerous assassination materials, weapons, ballistic vests, and silencer, the subject claims to abhor violence and does not see it as a means to an end. He appears to gain satisfaction and a sense of self-importance when "investigating" what he perceives as newsworthy topics such as issues surrounding the anthrax investigation, Eric Rudolph, or President Kennedy's assassination. There was no indication Mr. Doe had formulated plans to harm any United States Secret Service protectee and, although eccentric, had not shown a specific interest in protectees. Instead, his focus was on conspiracy theories. Mr. Doe did not demonstrate any identifiable attack-related behavior. He was assessed not to pose a risk to a protectee at that time.

Conclusion

Today, the Secret Service is charged with two distinct, but equally important missions: protection of our nation's leaders and visiting world leaders; and investigation of financial crimes. The Secret Service's protective mission includes the provision of physical security for protectees and sites such as the White House complex and various foreign diplomatic missions. Equally important protective responsibilities involve the assessment of those persons who, by virtue of their behavior, may pose threats to Secret Service protectees even in the absence of threatening communications. To this end, the Secret Service operates a protective intelligence program designed to identify individuals who may pose a threat to the President or other Secret Service protectees, assess the risk potential of an individual's dangerousness to the U.S. Secret Service protectee, and manage cases that have been evaluated by the Secret Service as meriting protective concern.

Unlike clinical assessments of dangerousness, the exclusive focus of a Secret Service risk assessment is to evaluate an individual's potential risk of harm to the President and other protected officials. Recognizing the importance of relationships with the mental health community, the Secret Service developed the Mental Health Liaison Program in support of its protective intelligence activities. This program has been recognized by mental health and law enforcement professionals alike as a model for achieving a multidisciplinary approach to common interests. The Mental Health Liaison Program provides a psychiatrist consultant to assist agents with the mental health aspects of their protective intelligence investigation.

This chapter also presented a framework that integrates what the author has learned from evaluating presidential stalkers and assassins with the existing pool of research and stalking taxonomies (Phillips, 2006, 2007). This framework attempts to categorize the actions of would-be and actual assassins based on motive, the presence or absence of delusions and/or active psychosis, and the intent to do harm. It has permitted the author to provide a uniquely clinical perspective to the risk assessment process when consulting on U.S. Secret Service protective intelligence cases.

The author has found this to be of great assistance to the clinical assessment of risk when consulting to the Secret Service, as well as considering treatment options, case management issues, and prevention strategies when providing opinions to the United States Attorney, the Federal Public Defender, or to private counsel. It may also be useful when developing a therapeutic plan for the treatment of such persons by forensic clinicians who are responsible for their care (Phillips, 2006, 2007).

References

Bonnie, R., Jeffries., & Low, P. (2000). *A case study in the insanity defense: The trial of John W. Hinckley, Jr.* New York: Foundation Press.

Clarke J. W. (1982). *American assassins: The darker side of politics.* Princeton: Princeton University Press.

Coggins, M., & Pynchon, M. (1998). Mental health consultation to law enforcement: Secret Service development of a Mental Health Liaison Program. *Behavioral Sciences & the Law, 16,* 407–422.

Coggins, M., Pynchon, M., & Phillips, R. T. M. (1998, May). *White House cases: Risk assessment and management.* Issue Workshop Presentation conducted at the 154th Annual Meeting and Scientific Assembly of the American Psychiatric Association, Toronto, Ontario, Canada.

Fein, R. A., & Vossekuil, B. (2000). *Protective intelligence and threat assessment investigations: A guide for state and local law enforcement officials.* Washington, DC: U.S. Department of Justice.

Fein R. A., & Vossekuil B. (1998). Preventing attacks on public officials and public figures: a Secret Service perspective. In J. R. Meloy (Ed.), *The psychology of stalking: Clinical and forensic perspectives* (pp. 175–191). San Diego: Academic Press.

Grove, L. (2003, February 7). Gate crasher hands Bush "message from God." *The Washington Post,* p. C1.

Haskell, B. (2005, January 25). *Virginia Guard soldier helps nab "handshake man."* Retrieved April 1, 2006, from News Archive Virginia National Guard, http://www.VirginiaGuard.com

Hoffman, J. L. (1943). Psychotic visitors to government offices in the national capitol. *American Journal of Psychiatry, 99,* 571–575.

Institute of Medicine (IOM). (1984). *Research and training for the Secret Service: Behavioral science and mental health perspectives.* Washington, DC: National Academy Press.

Locy, T. (1994, November 18). Duran charged with trying to assassinate the President. *The Washington Post,* p. A1.

Locy, T. (1995a, March 23). Tourist tells how shooter was tackled. *The Washington Post,* p. B4.

Locy, T. (1995b, April 5). Duran convicted of trying to kill President Clinton. *The Washington Post,* p. D1. Metro section.

Luczko, G. (2005, October). *Preventing assassination: Psychiatry and the Secret Service.* Workshop presentation conducted at the 36th Annual Meeting of the American Academy of Psychiatry and the Law, Montreal, Canada.

Megargee, E. (1986). A psychometric study of incarcerated Presidential threateners. *Criminal Justice and Behavior, 13,* 243–260.

Meloy, J. R., James, D. V., Farnham, F. R., Mullen, P., Pathé, M., Darnley, B., & Preston, L. (2004). A research review of public figure threats, approaches, attacks, and assassinations in the United States. *Journal of Forensic Sciences, 49,* 1086–1093.

Montgomery, D., & Santana, A. (2001, January 26). Inaugural intruder credits God: Minister offered president medallion, spiritual boost. *The Washington Post,* p. B1.

Mullen, P. E., Pathé, M., & Purcell, R. (2000). *Stalkers and their victims.* Cambridge, UK: Cambridge University Press.

Phillips, R. T. M. (1995). Trial testimony in *United States v. Francisco Martin Duran* (1995) No. 95-3096, 94cr00447-01 No. 95-3096 (U.S. Ct. App. D.C. 1996).

Phillips, R. T. M. (2006). Assessing presidential stalkers and assassins. *Journal of the American Academy of Psychiatry and the Law, 34,* 154–164.

Phillips, R. T. M. (2007) Celebrity and presidential targets. In D. Pinals (Ed.), *Stalking: Psychiatric perspectives and practical approaches* (pp. 227–250). New York: Oxford University Press.

Rothstein, D. A. (1964). Presidential assassination syndrome. *Archives of General Psychiatry, 11,* 245–254.

Rothstein, D. A. (1966). Presidential assassination syndrome II: Application to Lee Harvey Oswald. *Archives of General Psychiatry, 15,* 260–266.

Rothstein, D. A. (1971). Presidential assassination syndrome: A psychiatric study of the threat, the deed and the message. In W. J. Crotty (Ed.), *Assassination and the political order* (pp. 161–222). New York: Harper & Row.

Saleeba, D. (2000, May 16). Testimony of David A. Saleeba, Special Agent in Charge, Intelligence Division, United States Secret Service, before the Committee on the Judiciary, Subcommittee on Criminal Justice Oversight, Threats to Federal Law Enforcement Officers.

Sebastiani, J., & Foy, J. (1965). Psychotic visitors to the White House. *American Journal of Psychiatry, 122,* 679–686.

Shore, D., Filson, C., Davis T, Olivos, G., DeLisi, L., & Wyatt, R. J. (1985). White House cases: Psychiatric patients and the Secret Service. *American Journal of Psychiatry, 142*, 308–312.

Spiritual Revolution Thru Christ. Accessed April 1, 2006, www.richardweaver.org

United States Secret Service. Accessed September 28, 2007, www.secretservice.gov

United States v. Francisco Martin Duran, No. 95-3096, 94cr00447-01 No. 95-3096 (U.S. Ct. App. D.C. 1996).

White House Security Review. (1995a). The October 29, 1994 shooting. pp. 32–38.

White House Security Review. (1995b). Air incursions and attempted air incursions. p. 100.

17

Offender Profiling and Celebrity Stalking Cases

Karl Roberts

This chapter will look at the use of offender profiling techniques in the investigation of celebrity stalking. The chapter will identify what offender profiling is, briefly review some of the approaches to offender profiling, introduce the concept of celebrity stalking, and review some of the key considerations when attempting to produce offender profiles in cases of celebrity stalking. Some of the problems associated with the investigation of celebrity stalking cases will be highlighted and conclusions will be drawn as to the overall utility of offender profiling in celebrity stalking.

What Is Offender Profiling?

There are various terms in use to describe essentially the same concept: offender profiling, criminal profiling, behavioral profiling, and psychological profiling. In this chapter, the term offender profiling will be employed. Offender profiling can be defined as:

> An investigative technique...to identify the major personality and
> behavioural characteristics of the offender based upon an analysis of
> the crime(s) he or she has committed.

Douglas and Burgess, 1986, p. 1

Offender profiling is an attempt to describe the type of person who committed a crime, on the basis of the manner in which it was committed. Offender profiling is not an attempt to describe a specific individual or to consider the likelihood that a specific individual has committed a specific offence, and is often used when there is no specifically identified suspect.

Offender profiling rests upon two broad, psychological assumptions. First, the behavior during the commission of a crime is related to an offender's general, nonoffending behavioral and personality characteristics. Second, these characteristics do not change greatly over time. Readers schooled in personality psychology will recognize these assumptions as broadly consistent with a trait approach to personality, that is, the idea that human personality is composed of a number of identifiable traits or characteristics that are stable over time, for example, the "Big 5," which includes openness to experience, conscientiousness, agreeableness, extraversion, and neuroticism (Costa & McRae, 1992). It is beyond the scope of this chapter to evaluate in detail the validity of these assumptions; suffice to say that there exists considerable debate within psychology as to the extent to which a strong "traitist" position is a valid description of human personality (see Mischel, 1968). Alison, Bennell, Mokros, and Ormerod (2002) described these assumptions as relying upon a "naïve trait" approach, and have suggested that global offender traits are unlikely to be useful in predicting criminal behavior because they neglect situational and context-specific aspects of the offence. The extent to which these assumptions are valid clearly constrains how "accurate" an offender profile might be, and suggests that profiles are always likely to be subject to some degree of "noise."

What Is the Purpose of an Offender Profile?

The purpose of an offender profile is ultimately to aid the police in identifying an unknown offender. It may provide a behavioral and personality description that uniquely identifies a particular subject. This is rarely the case in practice, and there is often more than one individual sharing some of the characteristics described by the offender profile. Indeed, to the author's knowledge, an offender profile has never uniquely identified the perpetrator of a specific crime. For this reason, unlike DNA profiles or fingerprints, most jurisdictions do not regard offender profiles as probative evidence of fact (e.g., Ormerod, 1999).

Where the police have a large number of potential suspects, offender profiles are useful to law enforcement in narrowing down the field of potential suspects by aiding the police in prioritizing certain individuals for further investigation. Another way in which offender profiles are used by investigators is to generate new investigative leads. In these circumstances, the offender profile might suggest an idea that the investigators had not previously considered; this is especially useful in situations where there are no suspects. To illustrate this, the author provided an offender profile to a murder case in which there were several different types of injury to the victim: deep stab wounds that caused death and shallow cuts inflicted after death. It was suggested that these wounds were inconsistent with a single offender and perhaps illustrated the involvement of two people. This led the police to reexamine the offence, looking for two individuals rather than one.

What Information Does an Offender Profile Contain?

In providing a description of an unknown offender's personality and behavioral characteristics, offender profiles aim to describe the "type" of person who would be most likely to commit a particular offence. There is considerable variation in the amount of information provided by different offender profilers. This often reflects the particular background, experience, expertise, and interests of a particular profiler. It also reflects the different methodologies that may be used in generating the offender profile (Gudjonsson & Copson, 1997).

Profiles might suggest a range of offender characteristics. These may include demographic characteristics (e.g., gender, age-group, social class); psychological/personality characteristics (e.g., social skills, intelligence, level of empathy, attitude to the offence/victim); criminal history (e.g., likely previous offending); residence details (e.g., where the offender lives relative to the victim/crime scene); social and lifestyle characteristics (e.g., friends and relationships, sexual experience, nonoffending interests and hobbies); or living circumstances. Each of the points raised may be an individual lead or a suggestion for the police to consider; when taken together, the offender profile describes a type of person.

Approaches to Offender Profiling

There are several different approaches to offender profiling. Alison, West, and Goodwill (2004) classified these into two broad groups referred to respectively as *academic* and *practitioner* approaches. Academic approaches to offender profiling are described as an attempt to understand the global patterns and general trends in offending—a nomothetic model—and then deductively apply this knowledge to specific cases (Alison & Canter, 1999). The expertise here is based on a review of large numbers of cases, usually statistically, in order to identify patterns and trends that can inform decision making in a specific case. In contrast, the practitioner approach involves an individual offender profiler providing advice largely based on personal opinion and judgments gained through detective and/or clinical experience—an idiographic model (Badcock, 1997; Boon, 1997; Gudjonsson & Copson, 1997).

There has been considerable debate in the literature about these different approaches to offender profiling and as to which one is superior. Critics of the practitioner approach argue that it lacks scientific stringency and can therefore amount to little more that the unsubstantiated opinion of an individual (e.g., Alison & Canter, 1999; Canter, 1995). Defenders of this approach point out that practitioner experience is especially useful in cases that are extremely rare, such as serial homicide (precisely the types of case where offender profiles are likely to be requested by law enforcement); here practitioner experience can be of great value in interpreting motivation of offenders and assessing the meaning of the offence to the offender (Ainsworth, 2001). Investigators frequently express the value of these approaches in such cases (Pinizzotto & Finkel, 1990).

Critics of the academic approach argue that general theories about criminal behavior might be misleading when applied to specific events because averaged data tends to ignore important situational and "individualized" elements of offences (Alison et al., 2004). Defenders of this approach often focus upon the need for a good understanding of the nature of different types of offending (demographics, typical behavior, typical offender characteristics) before one can adequately consider a specific offence (Alison & Canter, 1999). More recently, there has been recognition in some quarters that the two approaches need to be reconciled—otherwise the potential for offender profiling in aiding the police is likely to be lost in debates over respective accuracy (reliability) and utility (validity) (Alison et al., 2004). Alison et al. have therefore suggested an academic-practitioner approach that seeks to link the theory-driven data collection of the academic approach to the practitioner's skill and experience. The author fully endorses this suggestion. In his work with the police, the author has endeavored to link together knowledge from research and theory on stalking behavior and the experience of working with offenders in order to understand and make speculations about the characteristics of an unknown offender.

Offender Profiling and Celebrity Stalking

As with other types of offending, it is recommended that profilers adopt an academic-practitioner approach in cases of celebrity stalking. In doing so, it is important for the profiler to have an understanding of the relevant psychological issues surrounding stalking behavior. A full review of the psychology of stalking is beyond the scope of this chapter; interested readers are referred to the excellent reviews of the literature contained in Spitzberg and Cupach (2003).

Who Is a Celebrity?

It is perhaps useful to posit a definition of "celebrity." Boorstin (1961) defined a celebrity as *someone who is known for being well known.* Celebrity status may be achieved in many different fields, including sport, entertainment, medicine, science, politics, religion, or through a close association with other celebrities (McCutcheon, Lange, & Houran, 2002). The lives and behaviors of celebrities appear to be of great interest to other members of society (Morton, 1997), and television and other media have helped to increase such interest levels (Bogart 1980; Fishwick, 1969; Horton & Wohl, 1956; Powers, 1978). Use of the mass media, particularly by adolescents and young adults, appears to be common. Figures from the United States and United Kingdom suggest that they spend on average 2.8 hours per day watching television (Larson & Verma, 1999). In addition to this, there are opportunities to engage with other media, such as the Internet, cinema, newspapers and magazines, music, and computer games (Giles & Maltby, 2003). The effect is that many individuals are likely to be exposed to a great number of potentially influential figures within these different media. Indeed, over 75% of those questioned in a survey reported a strong attraction to a celebrity at some time in their lives, and 59% claimed that a celebrity had had an influence over their attitudes or beliefs (Boon & Lomore, 2001).

Experiences of Celebrities

Fans attempting to contact and/or approach celebrities are a relatively common phenomena (Morton, 1997), and may in fact be an accepted part of the "experience" of being a celebrity. Most fan behavior toward celebrities is relatively innocuous and generally involves requests for memorabilia, attempts to meet the celebrity to get autographs, or to be seen with the celebrity. However, in a small but significant number of cases, this behavior might have a more sinister quality and may provoke fear and distress in a celebrity (Dietz et al., 1991). Fear might be provoked for a number of reasons, such as a large number of repetitive contact attempts by the same individual, unwanted visits to a celebrity's home or workplace, threats, sending unusual items to the celebrity, sending obscene or threatening material, and even violent attacks (Dietz et al., 1991; Meloy, 1998). Where an individual's attempts to contact or approach a celebrity are unwanted, repetitive, and provoke fear in the celebrity, the behavior might be labeled criminal harassment or stalking (Meloy, 1998). The use of the term "stalking" to describe unwanted attention has its origins in the late 1980s with media reports describing the persistent pursuit of celebrities (Meloy, 1998, 2006; Mullen, Pathé, & Purcell, 2000, 2008).

The exact point when legitimate behavior toward celebrities becomes stalking is not clearly defined and has been the subject of considerable debate. It appears to depend upon the reactions of the recipient of the approach and the number of approaches made (Spitzberg & Cupach, 2003). What one individual might experience as fear provoking might be regarded with humor or perhaps even as flattery (De Becker, 1997) by another. There are stories of some celebrities regarding their experiences of having being stalked as a "badge of honor," signifying that they had "made it" (Mullen et al., 2000).

Relationships With Celebrities

Some individuals appear to develop fantasy relationships with celebrities. These relationships are often experienced as if they were "real" with similar emotional reactions and responses on the part of the fan. The behavior of the celebrity and events in their life frequently provoke feelings and emotions in individuals akin to those experienced in real-life relationships (Rubin & McHugh, 1997). The reason for this appears to stem from the observation that the cognitive and emotional processes involved in the development of real-world relationships are also implicated in the development of relationships with celebrities (Planalp & Fitness, 1999). Through frequent media exposure, audiences come to feel that they truly know a celebrity from his or her appearance, gestures, conversations, and conduct, despite having usually had no direct communication with him or her (Giles & Maltby, 2003; McCutcheon et al., 2002; Rubin & McHugh, 1987). Attachments to celebrity figures that develop in this way are referred to as *parasocial* relationships. These essentially imagined relationships tend to be experienced as real.

It has been argued that parasocial relationships are a normal part of social development during childhood and adolescence and perform important emotional and social functions (Adams-Price & Greene, 1990; Greene & Adams-Price, 1990). For example, a romantic parasocial relationship with a celebrity may allow a young person to practice a relationship at a safe distance as preparation for an adult relationship (Hinerman, 1992; Steele & Brown, 1995). In most cases, the significance and influence of celebrity figures decreases with age (Raviv, Bar-Tal, Raviv, & Ben-Horin, 1996); however, for some individuals, their relationship with a celebrity may become highly significant and may come to dominate their lives (Giles & Maltby, 2003; McCutcheon et al., 2002). A subset of these individuals may initiate stalking behavior toward a celebrity.

Stalking Behavior

While there is currently little consensus as to a precise definition of stalking, most authors agree that stalking is a label for a long-term pattern of unwanted, persistent pursuit and intrusive behavior directed by one person toward another that engenders fear and distress in the victim (Meloy & Gothard, 1995; Mullen & Pathé, 1994; Mullen et al., 2000; Zona, Sharma, & Lane, 1993). The most common stalking behaviors appear to involve attempts to contact and/or approach another individual through telephone calls, visiting the victim's home or work place, letter writing, following the victim, sending unwanted gifts, and face-to-face meetings/confrontations (Cupach & Spitzberg, 2000; Emerson, Ferris, & Gardner, 1998; LeBlanc, Levesque, Richardson, & Berka, 2001; Meloy, 1996, 1997, 1998; Mullen et al., 2000; Sheridan & Davies, 2001; Sheridan, Davies, & Boon, 2001; Westrup, Fremouw, Thompson, & Lewis, 1999). Many of these behaviors are experienced by celebrities in the context of celebrity stalking.

Offender Profiling Celebrity Stalking Cases

One of the initial considerations in attempts to profile celebrity stalking cases is the reaction of the victim to the stalking. At one extreme, some celebrities are extremely fearful of the stalker and the behavior that is directed toward them. Frequently, these individuals are those who have experienced abusive and threatening contacts, have received unusual or bizarre material from their stalker, or the stalker has managed to gain access to the celebrity's home. In common with most victims of experiences of this kind, fear is an understandable reaction, and it is this fear that usually instigates contact with the police. At the other extreme, celebrities can react with a striking lack of concern about the stalking, and often remain uninvolved in the investigative process.

In the author's experience, celebrities often leave issues such as management of a stalking case to their security or publicity companies and have little personal involvement. In some cases, the publicity company may not even inform the celebrity about the stalking case. This can cause difficulties for an offender profiler because, as will be discussed in the following text, the profiling process rests upon the availability of accurate and detailed information about the behavior of the celebrity and the stalker—both of which can be withheld. Where possible, it is recommended that attempts should be made to engage a celebrity in the investigative process so that the celebrity can be questioned about his or her own behavior and experiences of the stalker.

Motives for Celebrity Stalking

Celebrity stalkers have various motives. Mullen et al. (2000) stated that celebrity stalkers are generally drawn from the *socially incompetent* (individuals who find it difficult to function socially and are socially isolated), *morbidly infatuated* (individuals who have an intense feeling of love for and focus upon a celebrity), *erotomanic* (a psychological disorder in which individuals develop a delusional belief that their target is fixated upon them, or that they have an intimate relationship with their target), and the *resentful* (individuals who develop anger and hatred for their target). While it is the general case that celebrities, because of their exposure in various media, are more likely than most people to attract the attention of strangers, this does not mean that all celebrity stalkers are strangers. Like other members of society, celebrities have a risk of attracting the attention of individuals with whom they have had previous romantic or other passing relationships, for example, as acquaintances, neighbors, and ex-school or college friends. It is therefore important for offender profilers and law enforcement officers, in investigating cases of celebrity stalking, not to overlook the possibility that a stalker could be drawn from a celebrity's previous social contacts.

Profiling Considerations

Celebrity stalking cases vary greatly in terms of the different types of material and offender behaviors that feature in the investigation. Some individuals may send repeated letters to the celebrity and never carry out any other acts. Others may never send letters, but might physically follow the celebrity. Still other offenders will send bizarre gifts and objects to the celebrity, while others will carry out a combination of acts (see Dietz et al., 1991) (Chapter 2). The key point here is that an exhaustive list of what a profiler should look at is impossible to formulate in advance, and each case should be assessed on its own merits. There are, however, various types of information that the profiler should be aware of in order to generate an offender profile; these can be subdivided into two broad categories of information, the characteristics of the victim and of the offence.

Victim Characteristics

Media Coverage

Knowledge about the victim's characteristics can help the profiler to create a context for the offence(s). As compared with other members of society, proportionately more information about a celebrity's characteristics is available to would-be stalkers. This is because of the often intense media coverage of celebrities via magazine and television articles about their personal and professional lives. Frequently, this information is of significance to a stalker, and in some cases can be used to enable him to identify methods of approaching the celebrity. Some stalkers have, for example, identified weaknesses in security around a celebrity by reviewing magazine articles with features on a celebrity's home. As part of the profiling process, it is recommended that profilers review media coverage of a celebrity victim, especially around the time when communications are received from stalkers. Here, it is useful to look at both the content of coverage, and any changes in the coverage of the celebrity, from the usual pattern. This may help in considering potential motivating factors for the stalker, especially when the contents of his communications refer to media pieces about the celebrity and he comments on them. Feelings such as anger, frustration, or love on the stalker's part may be identified in this way.

Physical Traits

Knowledge of a victim's physical traits may help to give a sense of why the victim was targeted. This includes traits such as the victim's gender, age, height, weight, hair color, eye color, etc. Characteristics such as gender, age, and race have been shown to be critical elements in victim selection for a range of offences (Holmes & Holmes, 1996). In the case of celebrity stalking, the target is certain to have received media scrutiny of his/her physical qualities, which have been disseminated to a wide audience. If a stalker indicates an interest in these characteristics, it may reflect a particular preference that is evident in the stalker's day-to-day lifestyle. It may also be possible to link the same offender to different stalking cases where victims share similar characteristics. Where the race of the victim is an issue to the stalker, even where racist comments have been made, it may be possible that the stalker has expressed such sentiments to others. Physical traits of victims may be useful in providing some investigative leads, though only in situations where it is possible to identify that these are important traits to the stalker.

Relationship Status

In the case of celebrities, their relationship status and history are often the subject of media speculation and interest. Obsessed fans and stalkers will collect this sort of material and may have strong views concerning a marriage, a new or old partner, and feelings concerning their own status relative to the celebrity. In some cases, *the apparent failure of a celebrity's relationship may act as tacit encouragement* for a stalker motivated by romantic love for the celebrity. Such reports may lead to an increase in the frequency of contact and attempts to meet the celebrity. Profilers should examine closely the type and nature of the victim's personal relationships. Questions include:

What are the characteristics of a celebrity's relationships?

Who are the relationships with?

What are the emotional characteristics of the relationships, that is, warm and loving or filled with animosity?

How stable is a celebrity's romantic relationship?

Is the celebrity currently in a romantic relationship?

How open is the celebrity about his or her personal relationships, that is, what amount of information is a celebrity happy to let into the public domain?

This latter question is particularly useful because a stalker who is aware of intimate details of a celebrity's personal life—when such details are not generally known and have not been published—may be a more sophisticated offender, devoting more investment and resources into finding out information about the celebrity than someone who is only aware of details that are in the public domain.

One difficulty in obtaining the sort of information described in the preceding text is that often a celebrity is not happy in sharing information about his or her personal life with an investigator. This is to some extent understandable; many victims are reluctant to share personal information, and this is often brought into sharp relief by celebrities who may be fearful of such information finding its way into the public domain. The solution to this is often dependent upon how much trust can be created between the celebrity, his or her management team, the police, and the profiler. Significant others who are associated with the celebrity may be able to furnish some of this information. For example, the author worked a case in which the celebrity refused to have any personal involvement in the investigation. In this case, the celebrity was reluctant to talk to the police; indeed, initially the reports about the stalking were made by the celebrity's management company. The celebrity's manager acted as a liaison between the profiler and the celebrity and provided some of the information that was asked for, though some issues were never completely resolved. Clearly, a lack of relevant information may adversely impact any police investigation and the usefulness of any offender profile.

Personal Lifestyle

The lifestyle and daily activities of the celebrity are important considerations in profiling cases of celebrity stalking. As with other victims of crime, the daily activities of a celebrity give the profiler information about the location and type of places the celebrity frequents, the type of people he or she associates with, the sorts of drink and drug consumed, and other relevant data. This information may indicate where the opportunities exist for a would-be stalker to gain access to or gain information about the celebrity. Recent changes in the social life of a celebrity may have exposed him or her to different sorts of individuals, and the profiler should make a special effort to identify any such behavioral changes.

Education

The level of education of a celebrity is relevant in several ways. A broad education, such as attending different schools, colleges, and universities in the past, exposes the celebrity to a wider network of previous social contacts. Indeed, some stalking cases start because an ex-school or college mate sees the celebrity in the media. Similarly, an individual's educational attainment may be related to the kinds of social contacts that they make; individuals will often associate with others of a similar intellectual/educational level. This knowledge may be useful in assessing likely contacts and possible situations of exposure to a potential stalker.

Victim Behavior

The behavior carried out in the commission of any offence is an interaction between the behavior of both the offender and the victim (Canter, 2000). A criminal offence may therefore be considered as a series of action and response chains—the offender acts, the victim responds, the offender responds to the victim, and so on. Examining how the offender and victim respond to each other can give an indication of the manner in which the offender and victim view the offence, its importance to them, and the way in which they perceive each other. In profiling an unknown offender, knowledge of the behavior of the offender in response to that of the victim is very useful in gaining a sense of the attitude of the offender toward the victim and the likely motivation of the offender. Of course, the responses of victims to offenders can vary widely, including ignoring the offender, resistance, compliance, or various combinations of actions. It is important that the profiler should consider in detail the way in which the victim and/or those around him/her have responded to the activities of the offender, as well as how the offender has responded to the victim's behavior.

By way of an illustration, we shall briefly consider some of the work that has looked at the behavior of rapists. In the context of a sexual assault, some offenders are very sensitive to the victim's response, whereas others are not. Hazelwood (1995) refers to these as *pseudo-unselfish* and *selfish* rapists respectively. The pseudo-unselfish rapists are interested in the victim as a person and will often want to talk to the victim about their life, are apologetic for violent acts, and often compliment the victim. For this type of rapist, the victim's responses form a crucial part of his actions; when a victim does not comply, these offenders are more likely to change their behavior, often in order to accommodate what they perceive (frequently inaccurately) the victim wants. The offender's behavior is therefore closely related to the actions of the victim. The selfish rapists, in contrast, are unconcerned by the victim's behavior and treat the victim very much as an object. Their behavior is unrelated to that of the victim and is entirely focused upon the offender's needs irrespective of the victim's. Victim resistance is therefore likely to provoke different reactions from these two types of offender. The pseudo-unselfish rapist may abandon an action in response to resistance, whereas the selfish rapist is likely to continue it. The victim may be far more significant to the pseudo-unselfish rapist than the selfish rapist.

Similar considerations are relevant to stalking cases. Some stalkers are very interested in and responsive to the behavior of their targets, whereas other stalkers carry out behaviors that are independent of and unrelated to those of the victim; these dynamics will be considered later in the chapter.

Onset of Stalking

One of the difficulties in profiling celebrity stalking cases is identifying when the stalking behavior actually began. Celebrities receive large amounts of fan mail and attempts are made to contact and meet with them every day; for this reason it is often very difficult to identify a stalker's initial communications in the context of this other material. Where a stalker is identified, often because of an escalation in their behavior or some particularly unusual communication, attempts should be made to identify as many other communications from that individual as possible. Note should be taken of the dates of contact attempts and dates of posting/receipt of the communications to enable the investigators to consider the behavior of the celebrity and media reports concerning the celebrity at relevant times. This facilitates an assessment of the extent to which the behavior of the celebrity influenced the behavior of the stalker. Inferences about the stalker's motivation, beliefs, characteristics, and mental state depend upon whether the stalker is actively monitoring and responding to the celebrity's behavior, or if the stalker's behavior is irrespective of that of the celebrity. Stalkers who respond to a celebrity's activities are likely to be closely monitoring the celebrity's behavior and may be very focused upon the media as it relates to the celebrity. This is potentially useful as a lead in the sense that such individuals are likely to have access to and use relevant media, and this may have been noticed by witnesses.

If it is possible to ascertain when the stalking began, it is recommended that the profiler should closely examine the behavior of the celebrity in the days and weeks before the onset of the stalking. For example, high levels of publicity may serve to increase the public awareness of the celebrity and provoke a would-be stalker. The nature of the publicity should also be considered: is it routine in the sense of standard publicity for a celebrity's work, or is it related to issues of scandal, relationship breakup, or a new relationship? Many stalkers become motivated by the end of a relationship, that is, they may see an opportunity for themselves or perhaps be angry that the celebrity has begun a new relationship. No recent change in the celebrity's profile is also relevant. In this case, the onset of the stalking may be related less to the current situation and more to some ongoing focus or fixation on the part of the stalker. For example, an individual began stalking a celebrity who had fallen from the media spotlight. He expressed a sense of anger that she had become neglected by the media, and he wished to support her and reassure her of her "greatness."

Attitude and Behavior of the Celebrity Toward the Public

The attitude of the celebrity toward the public should also be considered. This is strongly related to the opportunities a stalker is likely to have to contact or approach the celebrity. An individual who actively engages with fans by being available and approachable may give unintended signals of accessibility to a would-be stalker, which serves as tacit encouragement. On the other hand, a celebrity who is very distant from the public and protected by high security levels provides a much harder target to access. Some celebrity stalkers are deterred by high levels of security and move on to other targets (De Becker, 1997).

The extent to which a stalker is able to circumvent security to gain access to a celebrity is important in considering the criminal sophistication and determination of the stalker and in assessing the importance they attach to contacting the celebrity. For example, a stalker who gains access to a celebrity (breaking into their home or workplace, approaching the celebrity when they are alone) despite high levels of security is likely to be a different type of offender than a stalker who makes no such attempt or who is deterred by the security. In the author's experience, successful attempts to breach security are often associated with greater criminal experience and sophistication on the part of the stalker. Of course, one must consider how efficient the security arrangements are and how well they are implemented, especially at the time a stalker gained access to the celebrity.

Behavior of the Stalker

When profiling any offence, it is important to consider all of the known actions of the offender while committing the offence (Ressler, Douglas, & Burgess, 1995). In stalking cases, the timing, nature, and content of communications and contact attempts is highly relevant. In the author's experience, it is also important to consider offender actions that might have been expected at a particular time or in a particular situation that the offender *did not carry out*. This is best illustrated by a case example. An individual sent a number of letters to a young female celebrity. In the letters, he was very sexually explicit and stated that he was going to carry out the acts whenever he got a chance and that she would be unable to stop him. The celebrity was somewhat cavalier about personal security and was not interested in the risk management advice that she received. Not long after receiving one of the letters, she was alone in a car park when she was approached by a male. The individual stated that he knew who she was and that he was a big fan and had sent her some letters; the man then walked away from her. There were no other people around at the time. Here the threats of sexual assault could have been realized by the offender as the two of them were alone; however, when the opportunity arose, he did not take it. If one assumes the letter writer and the approacher were the same person, *not carrying out the acts* illustrates that the sexual assault threats were merely expressions of fantasy that he was unable or unwilling to consummate.

Communication

In examining a stalker's behavior, it is important to consider the nature, timing, and content of all communications and other attempts to contact the celebrity. The timing of a contact is important because it helps illustrate the extent to which a stalker's communications are related to the behavior and/or media reports of a celebrity's activities. The timing of gifts can also be significant. The sending of gifts may be related to significant dates that are external to the stalker, such as the birthday of the celebrity, Christmas, and other religious holidays. This can indicate that the stalker has at least some level of engagement with the wider world since he has identified key dates and responded accordingly.

Gifts and Other Items

The type of gifts that are sent can be important. Some stalkers, especially those professing love for a celebrity, often send appropriate gifts such as flowers or presents. Other stalkers send more "unusual" items (Dietz et al., 1991), which can indicate delusional states or other interests that are intrinsic to the stalker. Odd or unusual items that have a specific meaning for the stalker can be useful to investigators to establish leads; such items may illustrate particular preoccupations that may have been noticed by witnesses who know the stalker.

Language Use

The language used in written communications is an important consideration in profiling a celebrity stalking case, since some communications may give an insight into the underlying motivation of the stalker (see Chapter 20). However, the content of the communications may not unequivocally indicate a stalker's motivation. At times, the communications are so unambiguous and direct that it is clear what is motivating the stalker. For example, romantic messages and expressions of love often indicate such desires, while anger motivations are most likely to contain threats of various sorts. However, communications can be more subtle, esoteric, or veiled. In these circumstances, it is difficult to unequivocally attribute a motive or any personal feelings to the stalker. For example, one individual sent several letters to a celebrity, stating in one that "on the eighth day the moon and stars will be as one" and later, "our unification will be complete when the sun and stars fuse." Whether these statements indicate love, a desire to kill the victim, or some combination of both, is not clear from this communication alone.

Changes in communication over time can indicate a stalker's changing motives and attitudes toward the celebrity. For some individuals, feelings of love for the celebrity may change to feelings of anger, hatred, or betrayal. Frequently, this is indicated by changes in language use, with an increase in the level of threats and/or abuse contained in the communications. Changes in the nature of communication should be considered in the light of the timing of the communication and its possible relationship to the current publicly reported behavior of the celebrity.

In the author's experience, the content of communications can often give some sense of the stalker's feelings of entitlement (see Chapter 8). For example, one stalker wrote, "and if you will let me I would love to spend some time alone together." Another wrote, "please, please, please meet me on Thursday." These entreaties to the victim contrast greatly with the statements of another stalker: "You will not see me coming, I will be there and I will take my dues." In the first example, the stalker appears to ask permission from the victim, whereas in the second example, only the victim's feelings of fear appear relevant to the stalker, perhaps sadistically so. This contrast in communication style gives a strong indication of the attitude of the stalker toward the victim and the sense of entitlement that is implicit in his behavior. In the first case, the stalker does not appear to feel entitled to do whatever he wishes, and seems to view the victim as a person with her own desires and wishes that may contrast with his own. The stalking appears to be conceived as an interaction between himself and the victim. In contrast, the second stalker clearly feels entitled to do as he pleases, and is unconcerned and even disinterested in the wishes of the victim. Considerations of the language used in the communications may allow the profiler to make suggestions about likely levels of empathy (the extent to which an individual is able to perceive the different viewpoint of another individual and conceive of their feelings). Certainly, one might expect higher levels of empathic concern in the writer of the first example when compared to the second. It is analogous to the pseudo-unselfish and selfish rapists described earlier.

Mullen et al. (2000, 2008) stated that celebrity stalkers most often share backgrounds that feature a lack of intimacy. This is often related to an inability to function in a socially acceptable way—actively stalking a celebrity is a good example of such behavior. Frequently such individuals have difficulties in identifying socially appropriate ways of behaving and of communicating to others. The levels of these skills an individual possesses can be assessed by considering the way in which the communications relate to the victim. Language that contains various social niceties, such as asking permission, making apologies, avoidance of threats, and so forth, is often related to a sense of what is socially acceptable language use on the stalker's part, and might indicate at least some semblance of appropriate communication skills. The topics covered in communications are also important in assessing the likely levels of social skills. Some stalkers will discuss topics that are inappropriate and even bizarre, such as sexual activities described in detail, or strange and unusual associations. The extent to which communications are socially appropriate can serve as an indication of the likely social skills of the stalker in the "real world" and the degree to which they are able to deal with other individuals in a social context.

When the language use contains bizarre contexts and associations, mental health issues are likely. Such individuals may have already come to the attention of mental health professionals and may have expressed similar sentiments to them (Chapter 3). Mental health professionals can be important witnesses in such stalking cases.

Importance of the Behavior to the Stalker

The degree of importance of the stalking behavior for an individual can be gleaned from a consideration of the time and effort invested in the behavior. For some stalkers, the sheer volume of communications and the levels of information and material that are sent to the victim are indicative that the stalker has spent considerable time and resources pursuing the activity. In one case, an individual produced one 3-hour videotape per day, for 6 days, which he sent to the victim. He also produced several pieces of artwork and over 400 pages of handwritten script to the victim. In another case, a telephone engineer was able to obtain a celebrity's telephone number and set up a computerized dialing system that telephoned the victim once every 10 minutes for a 2-week period; if the telephone was answered, he would speak, indicating that he was monitoring the connection. Assessment of the relative importance of the stalking behavior to the stalker allows a consideration of the impact that this has upon the stalker's life. In the case of the telephone engineer, he lost his job because of persistent absenteeism from work—time he was spending in monitoring the telephone calls to the celebrity. Significant investment of time and resources would be expected to be noted by individuals who are familiar with the stalker, such as employers, family, and friends. Purchasing materials in support of stalking activities may also be an important consideration for a police investigation since retailers may be aware of unusual purchases. This is much more difficult, however, with the upsurge of Internet retail purchasing.

Offence Complexity and Intelligence

If intelligence is the extent to which an individual is able to process and act upon information, intelligent individuals should be more able to create complex scenarios, indulge in more complex and better-planned offences, and produce more complex content in stalking communications. Profilers should therefore assess the complexity of the communications and the stalker's behavior in order to make suggestions about the stalker's likely level of intelligence. Consideration should be made of the type of communications, the style of language used, the level of vocabulary, the extent to which vocabulary is used appropriately, and the grammatical skill present. For example, some intelligent stalkers may use complex communication methods, such as proxy Internet servers and encrypted communications, make literary or historical references, and may show knowledge of complex issues and concepts. These individuals are also most likely to use language appropriately in their selection of various words and phrases. The complexity and detail contained in fantasies is another indication of intelligence levels, since complexity of fantasy requires continuity of thought and an ability to consider several concepts simultaneously. Therefore, the more sophisticated and detailed a fantasy, the greater the likely intelligence level of the offender. By way of an example, one stalker produced a detailed description of his sexual fantasies involving the victim. This included detailed historical and literary references to the work of the Marquis de Sade, a detailed script of what he would say to the victim and how she would respond, and details of the dates and times when he would gain access to her. His account ran to 6,000 words, was grammatically correct, and illustrated an extensive vocabulary. The stalker was university educated with a degree in English literature.

Criminal Sophistication

Profilers should carefully examine the criminal sophistication of the stalker. This is related to the stalker's ability to plan, his or her level of intelligence, and his or her previous criminal history. Criminal sophistication of a stalker can be demonstrated in several ways. For example, the extent to which a stalker takes account of forensic evidence, that is, steps to avoid DNA and fingerprint evidence, the ability to circumvent efficient security, and skills such as breaking into property are good indicators of criminal sophistication. Criminal sophistication may reflect previous offending—awareness of police forensic methods and skills in breaking and entering might indicate a history of offences such as burglary.

Offender's Location

Frequently, in offender profiling, suggestions are made as to the likely location of an offender's residence relative to that of the victim. In cases of celebrity stalking, this is more difficult. This is due largely to the fact that celebrities are often well known globally, or at least nationally. As such, communications and even attempts to meet a celebrity can and are made by individuals from varying localities, some living close to the celebrity, and others from geographically remote countries. Linguistic analysis of the language used by a stalker in a communication may help indicate the nationality of the writer, but any such analysis is no guarantee of the present location of a stalker. Indeed, many stalkers will move their homes to be closer to the celebrity (Dietz et al., 1991).

Conclusions

This chapter has considered what offender profiling is, some of its limitations, and how offender profilers might produce profiles in cases of celebrity stalking. One of the crucial elements in any attempt to profile a celebrity stalking case is the availability of accurate information, and the usefulness of any profile will be limited by the amount of accurate information that can be obtained. In this regard, a detailed analysis of both the behavior and characteristics of the victim and the behavior of the stalker is very important. In cases of celebrity stalking, there is often understandable reticence on the part of the celebrity to give detailed information about his or her behavior and personal life. Obtaining the cooperation of the celebrity and/or his or her management is crucial to any profiling attempt. The stalker's behavior is also of great significance, and time needs to be spent to accurately identify as many of the stalker's communications as possible. This is not an easy process because of the high volumes of communications that celebrities receive. Overall, offender profiles are potentially useful tools for celebrity stalking investigations; in the best case, an offender profile can provide a series of hypotheses that can suggest new investigative leads, and it may ultimately help prioritize individuals from a range of suspects. However, any profile is a description of a type of individual, and it will unlikely be a completely accurate and comprehensive description of the offender whose identity is being pursued.

References

Adams-Price, C., & Greene, A. L. (1990). Secondary attachments and adolescent self- concept. *Sex Roles, 22*, 187–198.

Ainsworth, P. B. (2001). *Offender profiling and crime analysis*. Devon, UK: Willan.

Alison, L., & Canter, D. (1999). *Profiling in policy and practice: Offender profiling series* (Vol. 2) (pp. 21–54). Aldershot, UK: Ashgate.

Alison, L., Bennell, C., Mokros, A., & Ormerod, D. (2002). The personality paradox in offender profiling. *Psychology, Public Policy and Law, 8*, 115–135.

Alison, L., West, A., & Goodwill, A. (2004). The academic and the practitioner: Pragmatists' view of offender profiling. *Psychology, Public Policy and Law, 10*, 71–101.

Badcock, R. (1997). Developmental and clinical issues in relation to offending in the individual. In J. L. Jackson, & D. A. Beckerian (Eds.), *Offender profiling: Theory, research and practice* (pp. 9–41). Chichester, UK: John Wiley.

Bogart, L. (1980). Television news as entertainment. In P. H. Tannenbaum (Ed.), *The entertainment functions of television* (pp. 209–249). Hillsdale, NJ: Erlbaum.

Boon, J. (1997). Contribution of personality theories to psychological profiling. In J. L. Jackson, & D. A. Beckerian (Eds.), *Offender profiling: Theory, research and practice* (pp. 43–59). Chichester, UK: John Wiley.

Boon, S. D., & Lomore, C. D. (2001). Admirer-celebrity relationships among young adults: Explaining perceptions of celebrity influence on identity. *Human Communication Research, 27*, 432–465.

Boorstin, D. J. (1961). *The image.* New York: Atheneum.

Canter, D. (1995). Psychology of offender profiling. In R. Bull, & D. Carson (Eds.), *Handbook of psychology in legal contexts* (pp. 343–355). Chichester, UK: John Wiley.

Canter, D. (2000). Offender profiling and criminal differentiation. *Legal and Criminological Psychology, 5*, 23–46.

Costa, P. T., Jr., & McRae, R. R. (1992). *NEO PI-R professional manual.* Odessa, Fl: Psychological Assessment Resources.

Cupach, W. R., & Spitzberg, B. H. (2000). Obsessive relational intrusion. *Violence and Victims, 15,* 357–372.

De Becker, G. (1997). *The gift of fear: Survival signals that protect us from violence.* Boston: Little Brown.

Dietz, P. E., Matthews, D., Van Duyne, C, D., Martell, D., Perry, C., Stewart, T., et al. (1991). Threatening and otherwise inappropriate letters to Hollywood celebrities. *Journal of Forensic Sciences, 36*, 185–209.

Douglas, J. E., & Burgess, A. E. (1986). Criminal profiling: A viable investigative tool against violent crime. *FBI Law Enforcement Bulletin, 12*, 1–5.

Emerson, R. M., Ferris, K. O., & Gardner, C. B. (1998). On being stalked. *Social Problems, 45*, 289–314.

Fishwick, M. (1969). *The hero, American style.* New York: McKay.

Giles, D. C., & Maltby, J. (2003). The role of media figures in adolescent development: Relations between autonomy, attachment, and interest in celebrities. *Personality and Individual Differences, 36*, 813–822.

Greene, A. L., & Adams-Price, C. (1990). Adolescents' secondary attachment to celebrity figures. *Sex Roles, 22*, 335–347.

Gudjonsson, G., & Copson, G. (1997). The role of the expert in criminal investigation. In J. L. Jackson, & D. A. Beckerian (Eds.), *Offender profiling: Theory, research and practice* (pp. 61–76). Chichester, UK: John Wiley.

Hazelwood, R. R. (1995). Analyzing the rape and profiling the offender. In R. R. Hazelwood, & A. W. Burgess (Eds.), *Practical aspects of rape investigation.* Boca Raton, FL: CRC.

Hinerman, S. (1992). 'I'll be here with you': Fans, fantasy and the figure of Elvis. In L. A. Lewis (Ed.), *The adoring audience: Fan culture and popular media* (pp. 135–159). London: Routledge.

Holmes, R., & Holmes, S. (1996). *Profiling violent crime* (2nd ed). Newbury Park: Sage.

Horton, D., & Wohl, R. R. (1956). Mass communication and para-social interaction. *Psychiatry, 19*, 215–229.

Larson, R. W., & Verma, S. (1999). How children and adolescents spend time across the world: Work, play and developmental opportunities. *Psychological Bulletin, 125*, 701–736.

LeBlanc, J. J., Levesque, G. J., Richardson, J. B., & Berka, L. H. (2001). Survey of stalking at WPI. *Journal of Forensic Sciences, 46*, 367–369.

McCutcheon, L. E., Lange, R., & Houran, J. (2002). Evidence for non-pathological and pathological dimensions of celebrity worship. *British Journal of Psychology, 93*, 67–87.

Meloy, J. R. (1996). Stalking (obsessional following): A review of some preliminary studies. *Aggression and Violent Behavior, 1*, 147–162.

Meloy, J. R. (1997). The clinical risk management of stalking: 'Someone is watching over me...'. *American Journal of Psychotherapy, 51*, 174–184.

Meloy, J. R. (1998). *The psychology of stalking: Clinical and forensic perspectives.* San Diego: Academic Press.

Meloy, J. R. (2006). *The scientific pursuit of stalking.* San Diego, CA: Specialized Training Services.

Meloy, J. R., & Gothard, S. (1995). A demographic and clinical comparison of obsessional following and offenders with mental disorders. *American Journal of Psychiatry, 152*, 258–263.

Mischel, W. (1968). *Personality and assessment.* New York: John Wiley.

Morton, J. (1997). Don't worry, it will go away. *American Journalism Review, 19,* 52.

Mullen, P. A., & Pathé, M. (1994). Stalking and the pathologies of love. *Australian and New Zealand Journal of Psychiatry, 28*, 469–477.

Mullen, P. A., Pathé, M., & Purcell, R. (2000). *Stalkers and their victims.* New York: Cambridge University Press.

Mullen, P. A., Pathé, M., & Purcell, R. (2008). *Stalkers and their victims, 2nd edition.* New York: Cambridge University Press.

Ormerod, D. (1999). Criminal profiling: Trial by judge and jury, not criminal psychologist. In D. Canter, & J. Alison (Eds.), *Profiling in policy and practice: Offender profiling series* (Vol. 2) (pp. 209–250). Ashgate, UK: Aldershot.

Pinizzotto, A., & Finkel, N. (1990). Criminal personality profiling: An outcome and process study. *Police Science and Administration, 12*, 32–39.

Planalp, S., & Fitness, J. (1999). Thinking/feeling about social and personal relationships. *Journal of Social and Personal Relationships, 16,* 731–750.

Powers, R. (1978). *The newscasters: The news business as show business.* New York: St. Martin's.

Raviv, A., Bar-Tal, D., Raviv, A., & Ben-Horin, A. (1996). Adolescent idolization of pop singers: Causes, expressions, and reliance. *Journal of Youth and Adolescence, 25*, 631–650.

Ressler, R., Douglas, J., & Burgess, A. (1995). *Sexual homicide: Patterns and motives* (2nd ed.). New York: Free Press.

Rubin, R., & McHugh, M. (1987). Development of parasocial interaction relationships. *Journal of Broadcasting and Electronic Media, 31*, 279–292.

Sheridan, L., & Davies, G. M. (2001). Stalking: The elusive crime. *Legal and Criminological Psychology, 6*, 133–148.

Sheridan, L., Davies, G. M., & Boon, J. C. W. (2001). Stalking: Perceptions and prevalence. *Journal of Interpersonal Violence, 16*, 151–167.

Spitzberg B. H., & Cupach, W. R. (2003). What mad pursuit? Obsessive relational intrusion and stalking related phenomena. *Aggression and Violent Behavior, 8*, 345–375.

Steele, J. R., & Brown, J. D. (1995). Adolescent room culture: Studying media in the context of everyday life. *Journal of Youth and Adolescence, 24*, 551–576.

Westrup, D., Fremouw, W. J., Thompson, R. N., & Lewis, S. F. (1999). The psychological impact of stalking on female undergraduates. *Journal of Forensic Sciences, 44*, 554–557.

Zona, M. A., Sharma, K. K., & Lane, J. (1993). A comparative study of erotomanic and obsessional subjects in a forensic sample. *Journal of Forensic Sciences, 38*, 894–903.

18

Prosecuting Celebrity Stalkers

Rhonda Saunders and
Sean L. Wainwright

"I think he is on a mission and he won't be satisfied until he accomplishes the mission, and I think I am the subject of the mission." On February 25, 1998, Steven Spielberg, appearing nervous and shaken, testified in a jury trial against Jonathan Norman, the man who had stalked and threatened to rape him in front of his wife.

Rhonda Saunders has been a criminal prosecutor for over 23 years in Los Angeles, California. Many of her stalking prosecutions have involved high-profile celebrity figures such as Steven Spielberg, Madonna, Gwyneth Paltrow, Anna Nicole Smith, Jerri Ryan, Major League baseball player Eric Karros, and others. These types of cases raise certain trial issues and dynamics that are not present in other kinds of cases in which the victim and/or the defendant are noncelebrities. Some of these differences involve the nature of the stalker himself or herself, such as the stalker's need for attention and notoriety or specific forms of mental disorder such as erotomania. Other differences manifest themselves in the nature of celebrity stalking prosecutions versus domestic violence, workplace and campus stalking, such as excessive media attention, jurors' existing bias for and against the celebrity victim, and the celebrity's desire for anonymity.

People v. Jonathan Norman

In March 1995, Jonathan Norman was arrested in Santa Monica for attempting to run over a group of elderly strangers with his jeep. When he failed to actually hit any of them, he backed his jeep up in another attempt to run them down. That attempt also failed, so he jumped out of his jeep, ran over to one of the women in the group, pulled her to the ground and began kicking her in the head and back with his steel-toed boot. When one of the men in the group tried to intervene, the buffed-up Norman began punching the man in the face and stomach. He was captured and pled guilty to two counts of Assault to Inflict Great Bodily Injury (Cal. Penal Code § 245(a)(1) [2005]). Before his plea, Norman underwent a psychological examination. According to Norman's friend and "would-be" lover Chuck Markovich, Norman told the therapist that he was aware that he could utilize a psychiatric defense, but would prefer, if he was to be convicted, to get a specific sentence, because "then I'll know I'm getting out. If they put you in a hospital, they can lock you there forever." Markovich testified that although he often helped to financially support Norman and they had lived together, they had never engaged in sexual conduct.

While serving his sentence in state prison, Norman became fixated for some unknown reason on director/producer Steven Spielberg. Norman was released from prison in November 1996 and immediately began collecting articles, photographs, and other memorabilia relating to Spielberg, and also spoke to Chuck about converting to Judaism. He purchased a "Map to the Stars' Homes" for $7.50 on Sunset Boulevard, which revealed Spielberg's home address.

Unbeknownst to Norman, Spielberg and his family had left their home on June 23, 1997, and flew to Ireland, where Spielberg was filming the movie *Saving Private Ryan*. On June 29, Norman drove to Spielberg's house and approached the gate. He was confronted by a security guard, and Norman told him that he worked for Spielberg's partner, David Geffen, and had an important personal delivery to make. The security guard told Norman to leave, which he did—with a glare toward the guard. A couple of days later, Norman had Chuck drive him past Spielberg's house. Norman showed Markovich a day planner in which there was a photograph of Speilberg's head affixed to a naked male body. On July 9, Norman told Markovich that he was going to climb over Spielberg's wall and rape him. He told Markovich that he had found a low point in the wall surrounding Spielberg's residence that he could scale. Markovich attempted to talk Norman out of his plan, telling him that he would be caught and arrested by Spielberg's security guards. Norman agreed, but 2 days later, he attempted to carry out his plan.

At approximately 1:25 a.m. on July 11, a Westec security officer spotted a Land Rover, identical to the one driven by Spielberg's wife, parked directly across the street from Spielberg's house. Norman was behind the wheel. Norman told the guard that he was having car trouble, but when the guard checked the car, it was operable. The guard ordered Norman to leave and Norman drove away.

Norman returned to the house at 7 a.m. the same day. Westec had responded to reports from Spielberg's neighbors that a man was running through their backyards carrying a large stick. The guard saw Norman as he was jumping over a fence separating two of the homes. He gave chase and found Norman hiding under some bushes. Norman had his day planner, with the cut-up picture of Spielberg in it. He told the guard that he was "running away from some jackals" and also said he was Spielberg's newly adopted son, David Spielberg. The Los Angeles Police Department (LAPD) arrived and Norman repeated his story to them. The day planner was turned over to the police by the security guard. The LAPD had Norman evaluated by a drug recognition expert, who determined that he was not under the influence of any drugs or alcohol. They also determined that he did not qualify to be placed under a psychiatric hold. One of the officers suggested to Norman that he voluntarily place himself under psychiatric care, and Norman reassured him that he would do that. The officer returned Norman's day planner to him and released him at 10:30 a.m.

Norman returned to Spielberg's house at approximately 5 p.m. that same day. He parked the rented Land Rover approximately 100 feet from the driveway. One of the security guards who had previous contact with Norman saw him on the security camera and recognized him as the person who had made two other attempts to gain access to the home. The guard called LAPD, and as he watched on the monitor, he saw Norman back the Land Rover into the driveway and up against the gate as if trying to break the gate down. He did not succeed and drove away. The police found Norman's car parked approximately two blocks away from the house. They searched the area but could not locate Norman. The officers waited by the car and Norman finally returned to the car, where he was confronted by the police.

When he was searched, the police found that Norman had concealed a large role of duct tape, handcuffs, and a razor-blade knife under his sweat shirt. Two more sets of handcuffs and boxes of razor blades were found in his car. They also located Norman's day planner. The picture of Spielberg had been removed but it contained the names and birth dates of Spielberg's wife and children. When Norman was asked what he was doing in the area, he told one of the officers that he had an appointment with Spielberg about a screenplay in which he would play a rapist. The handcuffs and tape were "props." Spielberg's lawyer and friend, Bruce Ramer, was notified about the situation and Ramer called Spielberg, who was still in Europe. Spielberg was very frightened and concerned, not only for his safety, but for his family's safety. He immediately authorized additional security for his house, his mother's Los Angeles house, and for himself and his family in Ireland.

Norman was taken into custody and placed under a psychiatric hold. He was not arrested. He was released from the hospital 2 weeks later. The next day, he was arrested by his parole officer for having tested positive for methamphetamines on three occasions the previous month. While in jail, Norman was interviewed by one of Spielberg's security managers, Rick Vigil. Norman told him that he intended to rape Spielberg and if the director's wife had been there, he would have handcuffed her and made her watch the rape. Norman confessed to the police that he had conducted research to learn all he could about Spielberg, that he had purchased the handcuffs and duct tape to carry out his plan to rape Spielberg, and that he had tried to jump the fence at Spielberg's home but was chased away by security dogs (the jackals). In October 1997, Norman was indicted for felony stalking by a Grand Jury and held on 1 million dollars bail. Before arraignment, Norman's lawyer and Saunders both stipulated that the Grand Jury transcripts should remain sealed until trial to avoid a media frenzy similar to the one Saunders had to contend with during her prosecution of Madonna's stalker, Robert Hoskins.

Not surprisingly, the defense tried to blame Norman's conduct on drug-induced psychosis and schizophrenia. He did not plead "not guilty by reason of insanity." Instead, his attorney attempted to establish that as a result of mental illness, the defense of "diminished actuality" applied and that Norman's mental illness prohibited him from forming the specific intent necessary to convict him of stalking. One of the elements of stalking that Saunders needed to prove to a jury beyond a reasonable doubt was that Norman had the specific intent to place Spielberg in fear for his safety or the safety of his immediate family (Cal. Penal Code § 646.9 [2005]). Another issue that she had to overcome at trial was the defense argument that Norman could not be convicted of stalking because Spielberg was in Europe filming *Saving Private Ryan* during the entire period of time the stalking conduct took place. Spielberg was unaware he was being stalked by Norman. He was first told about Jonathan Norman by Spielberg's friend and lawyer, Bruce Ramer, several days after Norman was taken into custody. Ramer called Spielberg in Ireland to warn him because it appeared that Norman was about to be released, unsupervised, from the psychiatric hospital, and Ramer feared that Norman would be lying in wait for Spielberg upon his return to Los Angeles. Saunders argued to the jury that even though Spielberg was not physically present at his home during the stalking activity, Norman believed that he was there and thus the criminal intent element was satisfied.

The jury rejected Norman's defenses and convicted him of felony stalking. Because Norman had previously been convicted of two strikes, he was sentenced to 25 years to life. Saunders requested that Norman be placed in the prison's psychiatric unit. If he is ever released from prison, he will have to register as a sex offender for the rest of his life.

The Court of Appeal upheld Norman's conviction. In a published opinion, the court held that the stalking victim's awareness does not have to be contemporaneous with the course of conduct that constitutes the stalking: "Logic dictates ... that Spielberg's serendipitous absence on the days of Norman's efforts to gain access to Spielberg's residence cannot diminish Norman's criminal responsibility for his course of action" (*People v. Norman*, 1999).

People v. Dante Soiu

Gwyneth Paltrow is a well-known stage and screen actress who is best known for her performance in the movie *Shakespeare in Love*. Dante Soiu was a 51-year-old unemployed pizza deliveryman from Columbus, Ohio. In February

1999, he saw Paltrow appear on television at the Academy Awards ceremony and became obsessed with her. He located her parents' address from the Internet and sent a bizarre letter to that address in which he stated that he was "more than a fan" and ordered Paltrow not to marry her boyfriend, actor Ben Affleck. Soiu stated that God had ordained that he and Paltrow should be together. Paltrow read the letter and became uncomfortable and concerned because of the content and tone of the letter. She immediately notified her private security company, Galahad Protection. Soiu began sending numerous letters to her, in which he claimed that it was God's will that they be together and that he was acting in God's name. He threatened that if she ignored him, she and her parents would be cursed and perish. He also wrote, "I will never let this love go…nor you."

In April 1999, Soiu's letters became sexual and he began to send Paltrow pornography and sex toys, such as a vibrating penis, upon which he wrote, "Cause I love you." Enclosed with his letters and sex toys, he sent Paltrow copies of letters that he had written to then President Clinton and members of Congress, in which he gave them political advice on how to run the country.

On May 28, 1999, Soiu came to Los Angeles and went directly to Paltrow's family's house, where he confronted her mother, Blythe Danner, in the front yard. She told him he was frightening them and to please stop sending things to their house. He apologized and walked away. The next day, he returned and left a note on the gate, "I want to thank you for forgiving me for I have been a pain to you." An FBI agent and Saunders interviewed Paltrow and her parents at their home. They all expressed fear of Soiu. Paltrow was very upset because she felt it was her fault that her parents and brother were being placed in danger by her deranged "fan." Saunders requested that the FBI visit Soiu and put him on notice that his conduct was frightening the victim and had to stop. The reason that she made this request for FBI intervention was that if she did proceed with prosecution, once Soiu had been put on notice by law enforcement that he was frightening Paltrow and her family, he could not claim as a defense that he did not know he was frightening them. One of the elements that a prosecutor would have to prove was that Soiu had the specific intent to place Paltrow in fear for her safety or the safety of her immediate family.

The following month, Paltrow received numerous envelopes from Soiu containing more pornographic pictures. On several of the pictures, Soiu wrote "Gwyn" on the female figure and "Dante" on the male. Saunders spoke to the local U.S. Attorney's Office regarding the pornography that was being sent interstate through the mail by Soiu. They told her that it did not fit their criteria for filing because pornography was judged by community standards, and in Los Angeles, the type of pornography being sent by Soiu could be found at magazine shops throughout the city.

In July 1999, FBI agents went to Soiu's apartment in Ohio. He admitted sending the letters and objects and also admitted that he knew it was wrong and that he was frightening Paltrow and her family. He promised the agents that he would stop. He did not send anything more for approximately 1 month and then began bombarding Paltrow with more pornography, sexual letters, books, and sex toys. In November, he sent Paltrow a letter asking her to marry him and enclosed a fake diamond engagement ring.

In April 2000, Soiu sent Paltrow a letter stating that he had saved enough money to travel to Los Angeles and he would be arriving shortly. Soiu came back to Los Angeles on May 13, 2000, and went directly back to Paltrow's house. He was confronted by her father, who angrily told him to leave them alone. Dennis Bridwell, Paltrow's head of security, suspected that Soiu would return, so he staked out the house. Sure enough, Soiu returned to the house at around 10:00 p.m. that night. Bridwell was waiting for him. He placed Soiu under citizen's arrest and called the local police department who arrived and took him into custody.

Saunders became aware of this case in April 1999, shortly after Paltrow had received the first letter from Soiu. Bridwell called her and told her that he was gathering all the letters and packages that were sent to Paltrow and keeping them in chronological order for possible use as evidence if the case was later filed. She was asked to help monitor the case. At first, Paltrow did not want the case to become public and was hoping that the intervention of the FBI and her security people would cause Soiu to stop his activities. She was extremely fearful, not only for her safety, but the safety of her family. When it became apparent that nothing was going to stop Soiu's mission, and that he was planning to come once again to Los Angeles, it was decided that when he showed up, he would be arrested. Because of the sexual nature of the stalking, Saunders was able to file a charge of felony stalking, substituting "Jane Doe" for Gwyneth Paltrow as the named victim in the case. Because it was purposely filed and prosecuted in a remote courthouse near Los Angeles International Airport, the press did not become aware of the case until after Paltrow and her mother had testified. Following the guilt phase of the trial, Soiu was found guilty of stalking. In the bifurcated part of the trial, Soiu was declared legally insane by the judge and sentenced to a locked down psychiatric facility until he is no longer deemed a danger to himself or others. Actual custody time, if he had been found to be sane, would have been 18 months, with good-time/work-time credits. As of 2007, Soiu was still being held in a forensic psychiatric hospital in California. He was released by a jury in February, 2008, to his brother's care in Ohio, and bypassed any conditional release placement due to his time in the forensic hospital exceeding his maximum sentence for the crime. He was found to not pose "a substantial danger of physical harm to others" (Penal Code Section 1026.5b).

Psychological Issues and Defenses

Overview

Both Jonathan Norman and Dante Soiu relied upon psychiatric defenses at their trials, with differing results. Norman put on evidence of "diminished actuality" and Soiu pled not guilty by reason of insanity. Soiu was facing a maximum sentence of only 3 years in state prison if sentenced as a felon. Rather than challenge the insanity plea, Saunders submitted the issue of Soiu's legal sanity on the reports of four mental health experts, all of whom had differing opinions on Soiu's mental condition. However, all were in agreement that he was legally insane and needed long-term psychiatric care. Out of the four evaluations, Saunders gave credence to only one expert with whom she had worked in past cases, Dr. Reid Meloy, and had found him to be thorough and discerning in his psychological analysis. She therefore stipulated to the fact of Soiu's insanity. Instead of being sent to state prison, Soiu was sent to a high security psychiatric hospital, where he remained for seven years. As a prosecutor, her main concern was for the victim's safety. The outcome of this case provided that Soiu would be "off the street" for a lengthy period of time and would not be able to harm Paltrow or her family. Soiu received much needed, long-term psychiatric treatment, which he never would have voluntarily sought.

During Saunders's career as a criminal prosecutor who has handled hundreds of stalking cases, it has been her observation that stalkers seldom, if ever, take responsibility for their conduct. They do not seek out mental health care because they believe that there is nothing wrong with them. When they are arrested and confronted with their conduct, they will try to put the blame on the victim, the police, the prosecutor, or other third parties. It is always someone else's fault. Most stalkers will never be "cured" because of their state of denial.

Erotomania

Celebrity stalkers sometimes suffer from erotomania, otherwise known as de Clerambault's syndrome, in which the stalker believes he or she has a personal love relationship with a stranger, often a celebrity, who is of higher status and/or unattainable (Meloy & Gothard, 1995). The stalker believes that the object of his obsession is also in love with him or her (American Psychiatric Association, 2000). The delusion may be accompanied by auditory hallucinations in which the stalker carries out conversations with the victim, or ideas of reference in which the stalker believes the victim is sending personal messages to him. Although this condition is generally benign, it can escalate into violence when the stalker perceives that a third party, such as a bodyguard, assistant, or relative of the victim, is an obstacle to be eliminated or that the celebrity has rejected him or her (Meloy, 1999).

Singer/actress Madonna's assistant and bodyguard were both threatened by her stalker, Robert Hoskins, because he believed that they were keeping her from him. Hoskins physically attacked her bodyguard, Basil Stephens, and was shot when they wrestled over Stephens' gun. Despite professing his love for Madonna, Hoskins told Stephens that if Madonna did not marry him, he would "slice her throat from ear to ear." Following his conviction for stalking, assault, and making criminal threats against Madonna, her assistant, and Stephens,

Hoskins repeated this threat to a Los Angeles County Sheriff's deputy while he was in jail awaiting sentencing. Saunders received a call from the deputy who had the encounter with Hoskins and informed her about the threat and that Hoskins had covered his jail cell with graffiti stating, "I love Madonna," "Madonna Love Me," and "The Madonna Stalker." At Hoskins's sentencing hearing, the deputy was called as a prosecution witness to the threat and graffiti. Hoskins was sentenced to 10 years in state prison, the maximum time allowable by law.

Dante Soiu believed that Gwyneth Paltrow's ghostly spirit visited his apartment to be with him and that their union was ordained by God. Soiu testified at trial that when he went to the supermarket, Paltrow's picture on the covers of various entertainment magazines and newspapers would whisper love messages to him. Paltrow testified that she was afraid not only for her safety, but feared that if Soiu could not get to her, he would kill her parents. Upon being convicted of stalking Paltrow, Soiu shouted to the judge, "If a man gives a woman unconditional love, she is blessed."

In the early 1990s, Los Angeles television weatherman Dallas Raines was stalked by an ex-policewoman, Martha Cane, who believed that Raines was sending secret love messages from her television set. She heard Raines' voice coming from the television set telling her that if she ran in the Los Angeles Marathon, he would leave his wife and family and marry her. When the police served a search warrant on her apartment, they found a certificate that stated that she had actually participated in the marathon. She was so convinced that Raines could see her through the television set that she bought and dressed herself in a sexy negligee and would perform dances in front of the TV whenever he was on the nightly news. If she had stayed at home in front of her television set, dancing for Raines, we would not have known about this case. Unfortunately, her obsession escalated and she tracked down Raines' home address, where she showed up several times, terrorizing Raines' wife and children. She perceived them as obstacles standing between her and her destiny with Raines. At the time she committed these acts, California had just recently passed the first stalking law in the country, but it was rushed through the State Legislature and was not very effective. She was convicted by jury of stalking and served less than 6 months in the county jail.

The Defense of Diminished Actuality

Before 1982, California law recognized the defense of "diminished capacity." This defense provided that a defendant could be legally sane at the time of the crime, but

> (I)f he was suffering from a mental illness that prevented him
> from acting with malice aforethought or with premeditation and
> deliberation, he could not be convicted of murder of the first
> degree ... If there was evidence that a mental illness prevented the

defendant from maturely and meaningfully reflecting upon the gravity of his contemplated act, then the defendant would not be guilty of first degree murder despite substantial evidence supporting a finding of premeditation and deliberation.

People v. Cruz, 1980

Although it was originally invoked in homicide cases, the defense applied to other crimes that required specific intent. It was also used to negate such particular mental states as malice, deliberation, premeditation and knowledge (Witkin, Epstein, & members of the Witkin Legal Institute, 2000). The defense of diminished capacity was eliminated by the California Legislature in response to the brutal murders of San Francisco Mayor George Moscone and Supervisor Harvey Milk by ex-supervisor Daniel White and the subsequent public outcry over White's reduced sentence.

On November 27, 1978, in San Francisco, California, Dan White, an ex-policeman and ex-city supervisor, assassinated Mayor George Moscone and Supervisor Harvey Milk. White had climbed through the basement window of city hall to avoid metal detectors and confronted Moscone, demanding back his job as a city supervisor. When Moscone refused, White shot him twice at close range, then stood over the body and shot two more bullets into Moscone's brain. White reloaded his gun and went down the hall, confronting Supervisor Harvey Milk, America's first openly gay public office holder. He shot Milk five times, killing him instantly. At trial, White's attorney argued that White had been suffering from depression that caused him to commit the murders. A psychiatrist testified on White's behalf, stating that, before the shootings, the formerly health-conscious defendant had become a junk food junkie, consuming massive quantities of "Twinkies," a sugar-laden, cake-like dessert. The psychiatrist told the jury that too much sugar can affect the chemical balance in the brain and worsen depression. White was successful at his trial by asserting the diminished capacity defense (thereafter popularly referred to as the "Twinkie defense"). The jury found White guilty of a lesser charge, voluntary manslaughter, and he was sentenced to 6 years in state prison. He was released on parole in 1984. White committed suicide the next year.

Although the legislature in California attempted to do away with the diminished capacity defense, it was replaced with the diminished actuality defense, which, for a prosecutor, creates many of the same challenges as the prior defense. California Penal Code Section 28, "Evidence of mental disease, mental defect, or mental disorder," states,

(a) Evidence of mental disease, mental defect, or mental disorder shall not be admitted to show or negate the capacity to form any mental state, including, but not limited to, purpose, intent, knowledge, premeditation, deliberation, or malice aforethought, with which the accused committed the act. Evidence of mental disease, mental defect, or mental disorder is admissible *solely on*

the issue of whether or not the accused actually formed a required
specific intent, premeditated, deliberated, or harbored malice
aforethought (emphasis added), when a specific intent crime is
charged.

(b) As a matter of public policy there shall be no defense of
diminished capacity, diminished responsibility, or irresistible
impulse in a criminal action or juvenile adjudication hearing.

(c) This section shall *not* be applicable to an insanity hearing.

California Penal Code Section 29 provides:

In the guilt phase of a criminal action, any expert testifying about
a defendant's mental illness, mental disorder, or mental defect
shall not testify as to whether the defendant did or did not have
the required mental states, which include, but are not limited to,
purpose, intent, knowledge or malice aforethought, for the crimes
charged. The question as to whether the defendant had or did not
have the required mental states shall be decided by the trier of fact.

In other words, Sections 28 and 29 allow introduction of evidence of mental
illness when relevant to whether a defendant actually formed a mental state
that is an element of the charged offense, but do not permit an expert to offer
an opinion on whether the defendant had the mental capacity to form a specific
mental state or whether the defendant actually harbored such a mental state.

The defense of diminished actuality is available to any defendant, such
as Jonathan Norman, who is charged with a specific intent crime such as
stalking or making criminal threats. However, in the Norman case, Saunders
successfully countered the defense arguments of diminished actuality and
drug-induced psychosis by appealing to the jury's common sense that when
a defendant plans and premeditates a crime, there is a rational thought process that goes into the defendant's actions. The defendant takes deliberate
steps toward the commission of his or her crime, and these steps would tend
to indicate that the defendant is capable of formulating the intent to commit
this crime and knows what he/she is about to do. The insanity or diminished
mental state defense, on the other hand, defends the defendants' actions on the
basis that he or she was not capable of formulating the requisite criminal intent
and/or could not understand right from wrong and thus should not be held liable for their actions. The diminished actuality defense and Norman's planning
and premeditation involved in stalking Spielberg were polar opposites of each
other. The existence of one was a clear indicator of the absence of the other.

Jonathan Norman, at different times, described himself to the police and
Spielberg's security guards as "David" Spielberg, the illegitimate love child
of Spielberg and producer David Geffen, Spielberg's nephew, and Spielberg's
lover. On another occasion, he identified himself as a messenger from David
Geffen's office who was sent to personally deliver a package to Spielberg. The

last time, when he was captured and placed into custody by the police a block away from Spielberg's house, Norman came up with another story: that he was an actor auditioning for the part of a rapist in one of Spielberg's films and knew that he would be seen on Spielberg's closed circuit cameras, thus bringing him to the director's attention.

Norman's attorney attempted to explain Norman's stalking conduct as a result of drug-induced psychosis causing "diminished actuality." His attorney claimed and presented expert testimony that, because of his long-term use of methamphetamines, Norman could not have formed the specific intent element of stalking: to place the victim in fear for his or her safety (Cal. Penal Code § 646.9 [2005]). If successful, the jury would have had to acquit Norman because all the elements of the crime would not have been proven. In California, one of the elements necessary to convict a defendant of stalking is that the stalker had the specific intent to place the victim in fear for his or her safety or the safety of his or her immediate family. In a criminal prosecution in which the specific intent or mental state of a defendant is an element, the defendant may request a specific jury instruction on insanity or mental state where there is sufficient evidence thereon on which to base such instructions (see generally Gimeno et al., 2006).

The difference between a defense of diminished actuality and insanity is that diminished actuality is a complete defense to a specific intent crime. Norman would have been set free if the jury had accepted this defense. On the other hand, defendants who have been found not guilty by reason of insanity are not set free, but spend an undetermined time in a locked down psychiatric facility before they are even considered for mandatory supervised conditional release (Meloy, Haroun, & Schiller, 1990).

To overcome Norman's defense, Saunders put on witness testimony and documentary evidence of Norman's thorough planning to gain access to Spielberg. She did not call a mental health expert to the stand on behalf of the People because she had learned from previous experience that jurors tend to disregard a "battle of the experts." Instead, she consulted behind the scenes with Dr. Kris Mohandie as to what would be the best approach to cross examination of the defense expert's testimony.

At trial, she argued that although it was evident that Norman's conduct was bizarre, Norman had minutely and intelligently planned his assault on the victim. The evidence presented at trial showed the extent of Norman's efforts to carry out his plan. During a search of Charles Markovich's apartment, after his friend had cleaned out evidence from Jonathan Norman's home, investigators found hundreds of pages that were downloaded from the Internet about Spielberg's personal and professional life, including the names of dozens of his business associates and their work addresses, the names and birth dates of Spielberg's children, and the names and addresses of other Spielberg relatives, including those of his mother. Investigators also found a business card and receipt from a local spy shop, Probe, Inc., indicating that Norman had purchased a book titled *Laser Sights and Night Vision* and a penlight just a couple of days before he was taken into custody. When interviewed, a clerk at the store remembered that Norman had been inquiring into the purchase of night vision goggles. Receipts from a car rental company were found indicating that Norman had rented the car that was identical to the one driven by Spielberg's wife, and an employee of the car rental company testified as to having several normal conversations with Norman regarding his need to rent that specific car. It was obvious that Norman had hoped that when his rental car approached the gate leading to Spielberg's house, the guard would see the car, assume that it was Spielberg's wife driving the car, and open the gate, permitting Norman access to the compound. Investigators also found Norman's journal, in which he had written, in graphic detail, what he was going to do to Spielberg once he gained access to him. Norman's plan to gain access to Spielberg took place over the course of several weeks. Although Norman's end goal of raping Spielberg was perverted and abnormal, the sophistication of his planning indicated both extreme premeditation and deliberation. It was also apparent from his actions that he understood that what he wanted to do was wrong: he deliberately lied to Spielberg's security guards on two occasions, ran and concealed himself from pursuing police officers, parked his car several blocks from the house after his failed attempt to break down Spielberg's gate, and brought items with him to bind and silence his potential victims (Chapter 11).

In most cases such as Norman's, jurors routinely reject psychiatric defenses because it is inconsistent to find that a defendant both planned his or her crime, yet at the same time suffered a diminished mental state so that he or she could not form the requisite criminal intent or determine right from wrong. Specific intent demonstrates a thoughtful and deliberate process, and once it has been shown, the jury rejects the convoluted issue of mental defenses, which in many cases comes down to an imprecise science of a battle of experts. Often, during voir dire, jurors have stated that they do not put much faith in psychiatric evaluations (*United States v. Layton*, 1988).

The United States Congress enacted the Insanity Defense Reform Act of 1984, which some scholars say has prohibited the defenses of diminished responsibility and diminished capacity in federal cases (see generally Dietz et al., 2006a; *United States v. Moody*, 1991). This type of federal legislation and case law indicates the icy reception given to mental defenses by lawmakers and the public. In response to criticism that exclusion of mental capacity might make it easier for prosecutors to obtain convictions, it has already been decided that this fact alone does not violate the Due Process clause of the U.S. Constitution (*McMillan v. Pennsylvania*, 1986; *Montana v. Egelhoff*, 1996).

While planning and premeditation can occur in a variety of crimes, the concept is easiest to show with stalking. In order to be a "successful" stalker (i.e., the kind that comes to the attention of law enforcement), the perpetrator must not only plan his campaign of terror against the victim in minute detail, but must also be capable of repeatedly tracking and locating the object of his or her obsession. In both stalking and homicide situations, deliberation and premeditation imply the existence of a mental state capable thereof (see generally

Gimeno et al., 2006; *State v. Close*, 1930). In terms of homicide, premeditation is the conception of the design or plan to kill (*State v. Christener*, 1976). In stalking, it is the sadistic plan to place victims in abject fear for themselves or their loved ones. In some jurisdictions, in order to establish premeditation, it is incumbent on the prosecution to demonstrate reflection, which is not so much a matter of time as of logical sequence (*Commonwealth v. Otsuki*, 1991). The concepts of "conception of a design," "reflection," and "logical sequence" are in direct contradiction to any claim of insanity or diminished reality that serves to diminish criminal responsibility.

The extent of a stalker's planning and deliberation was graphically illustrated in the Norman case. Chuck Markovich argued with Norman about his immediate plans to go over the wall at Spielberg's residence and carry out a rape. Chuck told Norman that he would be stopped by Spielberg's security people and the police, and for the time being, Norman changed his plans for that evening. It was not until 2 days later that Norman attempted to carry out his assault. Norman had time to deliberate his course of action and then knowingly chose to ignore Chuck's advice.

The process of formulating a logical sequence of events and then carrying out that sequence does not comport with a mental defense at trial. Evidence demonstrating that the defendant assessed the pros and cons of the commission of a crime and then made the decision to carry out that crime is fatal to the criminal defense of diminished actuality.

The Insanity Defense

In order to accurately critique the relationship between insanity and premeditation, an understanding of the different theories of the insanity defense is necessary. The purpose of the insanity defense is to ensure that criminal responsibility is imposed only on those persons who have the mental understanding and capacity to comply with the law (Wilkinson & Roberts, 2006).

One of the more prolific tests used in the insanity defense is the M'Naghten rule, or right and wrong test (see generally Dietz et al., 2006b; *M'Naghten's Case*, 1843). The test provides two distinct and independent escape hatches for a criminally insane defendant. The accused will be deemed criminally insane and therefore not criminally responsible for a particular act if, as a result of a mental disease or defect, (1) he did not know the nature and quality of the act, or (2) did not know the act was wrong (see generally Dietz et al., 2006b). The wrongfulness prong of M'Naghten means that defendant knew his/her conduct was criminal, but because of a delusion, believed it to be morally justified. The federal version of M'Naghten is found in 18 U.S.C.A. § 17, and states that it is an affirmative defense if at the time of the commission of the acts constituting the offense, the defendant as a result of a severe mental illness, was unable to appreciate the nature and quality or wrongfulness of his acts (18 U.S.C.A. § 17, 1984).

In jurisdictions where M'Naghten has not been adopted, there has been heavy critique of the right/wrong rationale. There have been legal and psychiatric attacks on the right/wrong differential, given the restrictions on expert testimony because of the fact that the terms right and wrong have no clinical significance (Gee, 1981).

In cases where the defendant takes deliberate steps before the crime is committed to make the commission of the crime easier, or to avoid detection while the crime is being committed, there is a clear indication that the defendant knows what he is doing, and knows that it is socially unacceptable, thus negating both the first and second prong of M'Naghten.

A second popular theory of the insanity defense is the one put forth by the American Law Institute (ALI). In the ALI's Model Penal Code § 4.01, it states that "A person is not responsible for criminal conduct if at the time of such conduct as a result of mental disease or defect he lacks substantial capacity either to appreciate the criminality [wrongfulness] of his conduct or to conform his conduct to the requirements of law." (Model Penal Code § 4.01[1], 2001). This test worked two changes in the M'Naghten test. First, the ALI test speaks in terms of substantial lack of experience and capacity as opposed to an inability to know the wrongfulness of the act (Slobogin, 2003). Second, the ALI test uses the word "appreciate" as opposed to the word "know." This modification was meant to provide an excuse to those who might know their act is wrong, but are unable to internalize the wrongfulness of the act (Slobogin).

Again, even in relation to the ALI test, which is arguably broader than M'Naghten, evidence of premeditation, such as purchasing materials before hand, concealment of identity up until the final moments before the criminal act, and statements and conduct before and after the act, are all squarely opposite to the ALI's definition of insanity. Under the ALI approach, the defendant must have the capacity to appreciate the wrongfulness or criminality of the criminal act. Evidence of premeditation could demonstrate that the defendant has the ability to plan out his or her crime and appreciate at every step of the criminal plan what the purpose of each step was and how it helped further the criminal plot. While the ALI definition does not require the defendant to know his or her actions are criminal, evidence of premeditation still goes to the defendant's ability to internalize the wrongful nature of their acts.

The concept of planning and premeditation involves a defendant making multiple rational choices in furtherance of the crime, and then choosing a course of action to carry out his or her plan. Premeditation is a result of the defendant processing his or her act and going through a logical sequence (*Commonwealth v. Otsuki*, 1991). When the defendant is making these choices and planning his or her behaviors to help further the criminal act, there is ample evidence that the defendant appreciates the nature and quality of the act. The defendant is taking steps to avoid capture by running away or making false statements to the police because he or she knows what he or she is doing is wrong, or the defendant is purchasing handcuffs or masking tape because he or she know that the victim will scream and struggle. These types of deliberate decisions demonstrate a careful thought process and an appreciation of the wrongfulness of their actions. Often, defendants will readily admit that they knew their actions were wrong or unacceptable.

Robert Bardo's murder of young actress Rebecca Schaeffer led to California passing the world's first stalking law. His elaborate planning of Rebecca Schaeffer's murder included making the conscious choice to hire an investigator to locate Schaeffer's home address, traveling to Los Angeles, and bringing a gun and deadly hollow point bullets with him to her apartment. Before his departure from Arizona to Los Angeles, Bardo told his sister that he was going to California to "save" Schaeffer and the only way he could save her was by killing her.

Upon his arrival in Los Angeles, Bardo went immediately to Schaeffer's apartment and rang her doorbell. She answered the door and they had a brief conversation. Bardo had the choice to walk away and return to Arizona, but instead, he walked down the block, methodically loaded his gun, and returned to her apartment with the intent to kill her. Immediately after the murder, Bardo fled California. This type of rational decision making is completely at odds with a claim that the defendant did not have the mental capacity to form the requisite level of intent or did not know the difference between right and wrong. Bardo entered a plea of not guilty by reason of insanity, but his defense was rejected by the court and he was sentenced to life in state prison without the possibility of parole.

Before trial, Dante Soiu entered a double plea of not guilty and not guilty by reason of insanity (NGRI). That meant that the trial was bifurcated into a guilt phase and an insanity phase. In Soiu's case, there was evidence that he fully appreciated the fear that he engendered in Gwyneth Paltrow and her family, and that he understood that what he was doing was wrong. When he confronted Blythe Danner, Paltrow's mother, in front of her house, she told him that he was putting her daughter and family in fear. He apologized and promised to stop contacting them. Rather than stopping his letters and packages, he actually increased his activities. When he was later confronted by FBI agents at his apartment on two occasions, they asked him if he knew why they were there, and he admitted that he knew Paltrow and her family were frightened and wanted him to stop contacting them. He promised the FBI agents that he would no longer try to contact Paltrow. Despite this awareness and because of his narcissistic and grandiose personality, he continued his unwanted pursuit of the victim, ignoring the pleas of the victim's family and law enforcement to cease his activities. Dante Soiu admitted to the police that he had attempted to locate Paltrow's address on a library computer, and when that failed, he searched for and obtained the address of her parent's house in Santa Monica, California.

Several states through legislation and case law have taken the position that the insanity defense may be restricted or completely done away with. The Montana Supreme Court in *State v. Byers*, 261 Mont. 17, 28 (1993), found that "no constitutional right to plead insanity exists in the law." The later case of *State v. Egelhoff*, 272 Mont. 114 (1995), however, overruled *State v. Byers*, and found that in a prosecution for deliberate homicide, an instruction that prevented the jury from considering defendant's voluntary intoxication in determining whether he had the requisite mental state to knowingly cause the death of another relieved the state of its burden to prove every element beyond a reasonable doubt and thus denied the defendant his right to due process. That decision, however, was overruled by the United States Supreme Court in *Montana v. Egelhoff* 518 U.S. 37, 56 (1996), when the court held that nothing in the Due Process clause prevents a state from disallowing evidence of voluntary intoxication when a defendant's state of mind is at issue.

In addition to *Montana v. Egelhoff*, the Supreme Court has struck other blows against constitutional protection of the insanity defense. In *Fisher v. United States*, 328 U.S. 463 (1946), the Court held that the lower court's refusal of a requested instruction permitting the jury to weigh evidence of a defendant's mental deficiencies, which were short of insanity in a legal sense, in determining the defendant's capacity for premeditation and deliberation was not in error. Given that there were no federal or constitutional questions, the Court permitted the District of Columbia to administer its criminal justice system, including exclusion of evidence of insanity, as it saw fit. Other states besides the District of Columbia have made the decision to limit evidence of insanity. Idaho, Montana, Utah, and, most recently Kansas, have all passed legislation restricting the admission of psychiatric evidence to the issue of mens rea, thus abolishing insanity as a separate affirmative defense [Idaho Code § 18-207 (Michie 1948–1997); Kan. Stat. Ann. § 22-3220 (1995); Mont. Code Ann. § 46-14-1-2 (2001); Utah Code Ann. § 76-2-305 (1999)]. The idea that an individual could have the requisite mental ability to plan a logical sequence of events resulting in the criminal act and yet not have the requisite level of intent at the time the crime was committed does not comport with M'Naghten or the ALI test.

The problem with admitting copious amounts of evidence at trial pertaining to insanity is that the evidence is often unreliable or irrelevant to the elements of the offense (Huckabee, 1989). In fact, unreliability is particularly a problem in opinions of mental health professionals involving psychodynamic psychology (Huckabee). Prof. Stephen Morse, psychologist and lawyer, writes that "psychodynamic formulation[s] are…unverifiable and unreliable causal account[s]…[providing] the fact-finder with little more than a false sense of security based on the incorrect assumption that a reasonably accurate scientific explanation has been provided." He states that "[p]sychodynamic formulations are so inherently unreliable that they cannot aid decision-making in the criminal justice system. They should not be admitted at trials, at sentencing hearings, or at any other stage of the criminal process" (Huckabee, 1989; Morse, 1982).

Professor Morse goes on to say that there are three factors that are primarily responsible for the confusing and lengthy battle of the experts that occurs every time the insanity defense is raised: the softness of mental health theory, data, and collection methods; the nonscientific character of legal issues; and the inevitable bias of mental health experts as they enter the criminal justice system as advocates (Morse, 1982).

It is important for the legal system to become as efficient as possible without sacrificing the constitutional rights of the individual. Although there are certain defendants who are legally incompetent or mentally incapable of understanding the consequences of their conduct and should be treated outside of the criminal justice system, certain savvy defendants will attempt to manipulate the judicial system through the use of bogus mental defenses and are able to call at trial certain unscrupulous mental health "experts" whose opinions are severely compromised. That is not to say all mental health experts who are called as witnesses at trial are "guns for hire," as there are many honorable true experts in the field who are willing to give unbiased, professional opinions, regardless of which side has retained their services.

Several years ago, Saunders prosecuted a death penalty case in which the defendant had stalked and then brutally hacked his ex-wife to death with a fish-gutting knife. The defendant's sister, horrified at what her brother had done, came forward and testified at the trial that when she and her mother had visited him in jail before the trial, he reassured them that he was going to put on an insanity defense and would either be acquitted or, at worst, be convicted of manslaughter. Despite 4 days of testimony by the defense's psychologist about the defendant's fragile mental state and how he had a traumatic childhood and suffered from dissociative fugue when he killed his wife, the jury not only convicted him of first degree murder with the special circumstance of lying in wait, but recommended that he be given the death penalty. At sentencing, the judge rejected the defense argument that the defendant's mental illness should be considered a mitigating factor. The judge stated, on the record, that she had listened to the defense's mental health expert for 4 days and had found the psychologist's testimony to be "not credible." The defendant—now a convicted felon—is on death row in San Quentin.

Conclusion

The trials involving Soiu, Norman, Bardo, Hoskins, and other stalkers of celebrities illustrate that the insanity and diminished actuality defenses, especially when used in stalking cases, are difficult to affirmatively prove, and often ineffective because of the planning and premeditation that defines stalking conduct. Celebrity victims share the same fears and trauma as noncelebrity stalking victims. Their lives are forever changed, and their faith in humanity is diminished.

References

American Psychiatric Association (2000). *Diagnostic and statistical manual of mental disorders* (4th ed., Text Revision). Washington, DC: Author.
California Penal Code, § 245(a)(1) (2005).

California Penal Code, § 646.9 (2005).

Commonwealth v. Otsuki, 411 Mass. 218, 229 (1991).

Dietz, L., Hinshaw, T., Leming, T., Martin, L., Zakolski, L., Adams, R. W., et al. of the National Legal Research Group (2006a). Diminished capacity or responsibility. 21 Am. Jur. 2D Criminal Law § 38.

Dietz, L., Hinshaw, T., Leming, T., Martin, L., Zakolski, L., Adams, R. W., et al. of the National Legal Research Group (2006b). "Right and wrong" (M'Naghten) rule or test. 21 Am. Jur. 2D Criminal Law § 56.

Gee, M. M. (1981). Modern status of test of criminal responsibility. 9 A.L.R. 4th 526.

Gimeno, C., Kennel, J., Levin, J. K., Oakes, K., Surette, E. C., & Williams, E. (2006). Homicide § IX(b)(6)(d), Personal relations of parties.
41 C.J.S. *Homicide* § 344. C. Gimeno and J. Kennel are staff of the National Legal Research Group.

Huckabee, H. M. (1989, April). Evidence of mental disorder on mens rea: Constitutionality of drawing the line at the insanity defense. 16 *Pepp. L. Rev.* 573.

Idaho Code § 18-207 (Michie 1948–1997).

Kan. Stat. Ann. § 22-3220 (1995).

McMillan v. Pennsylvania (1986) 477 U.S. 79, 89, n. 5.

Meloy, J. R. (1999). Erotomania, triangulation, and homicide. *Journal of Forensic Sciences, 44*, 421–424.

Meloy, J. R., & Gothard, S. (1995). Demographic and clinical comparison of obsessional followers and offenders with mental disorders. *American Journal of Psychiatry, 152*, 258–263.

Meloy, J. R., Haroun, A., & Schiller, E. F. (1990). *Clinical guidelines for involuntary outpatient treatment.* Sarasota, Fla.: Professional Resource Exchange.

M'Naghten's Case (1843) 10 Clark & Fin. 200, 210, 8 Eng. Rep. 718, 722.

Model Penal Code § 4.01(1) (2001).

Montana Code Ann. § 46-14-1-2 (2001).

Montana v. Egelhoff (1996) 518 U.S. 37, 38.

Morse, S. (1982). Failed explanations and criminal responsibility: Experts and the unconscious. *Virginia Law Review, 68*, 971.

People v. Cruz (1980) 26 Cal. 3d 233.

People v. Norman (1999) 75 Cal. App. 4th 1234.

Slobogin, C. (2003). The integrationist alternative to the insanity defense: Reflections on the exculpatory scope of mental illness in the wake of the Andrea Yates trial. *American Journal of Criminal Law, 30*, 315.

State v. Christener (1976) 71 N.J. 55, 65.

State v. Close (1930, February 3) 148 A. 764.

United States v. Layton (1988) 855 F. 2d 1388.

United States v. Moody (1991) 763 F. Supp 589.

18 U.S.C.A. § 17 (1984).

Utah Code Ann. § 76-2-305 (1999).

Wilkinson, A. P., & Roberts, A. C. (2006). Insanity defense. 41 Am. Jur. 2D POF 615.

Witkin, B. E., Epstein, N. L., & members of the Witkin Legal Institute (2000). California Criminal Law, Ch. 3 §(I)(e), Diminished capacity, former law. Cal. Crim. Law 3d, Defenses, § 22.

19

Use of Threat Assessment for the Protection of the United States Congress

Mario J. Scalora, William J. Zimmerman, and David G. Wells

Members of Congress are more likely to face threatening and disruptive harassing contacts from a range of sources since the advent of 24-hour news coverage and increased legislative oversight of federal activities. This chapter will provide a glimpse of threat assessment and management activities taken by the United States Capitol Police (USCP) on behalf of its protectees.

Established in 1828, the USCP is a full-service police agency for the Legislative Branch of the U.S. Government. The USCP has nearly 2,000 sworn, civilian employees, whose responsibility includes the Capitol area and Congressional buildings within Washington, DC, and Congressional offices across all 50 states as well as U.S. territories. Complementing the efforts of the Threat Assessment Section (TAS), which will be highlighted through this chapter, the USCP houses several specialty units, including Uniform Patrol, K-9, Hazardous Devices, Chem/Bio Response Capability, Dignitary Protection, Criminal Investigations, Electronic Countermeasures, Training, CERT, and Motorcycle & Bicycle Units.

The USCP's TAS was established in 1986. Threatening and harassing contacts may reach protectees and come to the attention of the TAS in a variety of ways. In some instances, the subject makes direct contact with the protectee (e.g., through written letters, telephone calls, faxes, e-mails, sending packages, or appearing at a congressional office). This could be received in one of the state/district offices or the office on Capitol Hill. Examples of letters referred to the TAS include the following:

> An unknown subject sent a letter to a Congressman's Capitol Hill Office stating that "Satan has the government by the neck." No identifiers on the subject were on the letter. Letter was postmarked from the Congressman's home district. (This letter was retained for future reference. No subsequent communications of this nature were received.)

> A known subject sent a letter requesting help from a senator because the subject believed that the CIA and a major corporation were causing her mental/physical anguish through microchips that had been implanted in her body. The letter contained no threats.

Problematic or threatening phone contacts also are reported with regularity, such as the one following:

> A subject called a Capitol Hill office and stated "you're going to die before you leave the building."

The TAS takes all threatening communication seriously and assesses the nature of the threat posed to the protectees in question.

In order to describe the threat assessment activity in detail, we will first delineate the diverse range of motivations often underlying the contacts of concern as well as the research-supported risk factors utilized as part of the assessment process.

Motivations Underlying Threatening and Harassing Contacts

The TAS encounters a diverse range of motivations for threatening and problematic contacts toward Congressional protectees. Among the most common motivations present throughout such problematic communications include harassment, help seeking with governmental programs or personal concerns, raising awareness for domestic or international political issues, desires to initiate relationships, threat and intimidation, as well as delusion-based themes. In a smaller number of cases, the subjects engage in threatening activity with the obvious motive of inducing fear (e.g., stalking behavior) and hoax activity to inconvenience both protectees and first responders.

Regardless of motivation, an awareness of empirically supported threat assessment risk factors predictive of problematic approach behavior is critical to ascertain the level of concern posed by a particular contact (and related pattern of contacts when applicable) as well as to determine the appropriate threat management strategy.

Threat Assessment Methodology

All communications and incidents referred to the TAS are taken seriously and undergo an initial screening/triage process that assesses the presence of initial risk factors. At a minimum, all communications and incidents referred to the

TAS are documented. This screening process determines the initial extent of the investigation and threat assessment.

When assessing the nature of threat *posed* by a subject or group of subjects, the TAS not only considers threat assessment risk factors generally accepted within the profession, but also research-supported factors that have resulted from a long standing collaborative relationship between the TAS and the first author based within a university setting. The value of utilizing such internal research cannot be understated. The research allows new investigators to quickly understand TAS's methodology as well as consistently track trends concerning problematic contacts toward protectees. The predictive value of risk factors utilized is also constantly reevaluated to ensure procedural validity. Administratively, this programmatic evaluation activity helps guide supervisory and command staff with decisions regarding the dissemination of investigative personnel and resources.

The operational research further supports the tracking of emerging trends in behaviors of concern facing TAS investigators (e.g., increased e-mail and cyber threats). This continued research has allowed the TAS to constantly evaluate the predictive validity of its approach as trends in threatening and other problematic contacts emerge. For example, electronic contacts (via e-mail and Internet) have increased substantially since the terrorist attacks of September 11, 2001. Following these events, the United States witnessed several attempts at biochemical attacks via anthrax and ricin found in correspondence mailed to members of Congress. Because of this new biochemical threat and the ensuing delay of mail delivery due to security measures, members of Congress increasingly encouraged constituents to contact their offices electronically via e-mail. With an increase in e-mail correspondence emerged an increase in the number of threats received electronically. In addition to e-mail, increased comments regarding a range of public topics have also appeared on Internet websites and blogs. The Congressional Management Foundation found that "Congress received four times more communications in 2004 than 1995—all of the increase from Internet-based communications" (Fitch & Goldschmidt, 2005, p. 4). They went on to specify that Congress received 18,335,594 letters by post and 182,053,399 communications via the Internet during 2004, compared to 53,000,000 postal letters and no e-mails during 1995. Consistent with the available communications research, such electronic communications (e.g., via e-mail or Internet postings) have been found to contain a higher level of aggressive language (e.g., Kiesler & Sproull, 1986; Siegel, Dubrovsky, Kiesler, & McGuire, 1986; Wallace, 1999). It has also been the experience of the authors that in the context of electronic communications, hostile subjects can quickly develop and send their e-mails at any time of the day, compared to hostile letter writers. Other trends that have emerged include the increased threatening activity generally encountered by protectees as growing numbers of individuals have taken more threatening or intimidating stances when contacting political figures and their staffs.

On a separate note, the TAS has encountered increasing numbers of problematic contacts from individuals with obvious symptoms of severe mental illness. At present, at least one third of problematic contacts managed by the TAS involve individuals with obvious psychotic or intense emotional symptoms (e.g., suicidal ideation).

Regardless of the modality of contact, we have researched harassing and threatening contacts toward state and federal officials spanning several thousand cases (Baumgartner, Scalora, & Plank, 2001; Scalora, Baumgartner, & Plank, 2003; Scalora et al., 2002; Scalora, Baumgartner, et al., 2003). The research resulted in identifying empirically validated risk factors for problematic approaches that are also operationally relevant for TAS personnel investigating such contacts. As detailed in Figure 19.1, the research suggests a model for the interaction of a range of contextual, subject-related (when available), motivational, target, protective, and contact-related factors pertinent for threat assessment. The factors inherent within this model, to be described in the following text, are applicable for problematic contacts from both anonymous and known subjects and do not require information within each domain (Scalora, Plank, & Schoeneman, 2007). The appendix to this chapter further details factors within each domain that may inform the threat assessment process.

The following information will detail the risk factors considered as part of threat assessment activity. Consistent with the available literature, TAS investigators do not assess threats with a known "profile" of individuals who may engage in violent or other problematic approaches. The threat assessment professionals instead evaluate not only the content and nature of the contact, but also how the contact/communication fits within a pattern of related activities and other contextual factors. In the examples provided here, no information concerning the identity of the subject or protectee is provided; such references have been changed to protect the subject's identity.

Contextual factors, though not powerful predictors of problematic approach behavior by themselves, do suggest the likelihood of increased contacts (Scalora et al., 2002). Contextual factors that potentially increase problematic

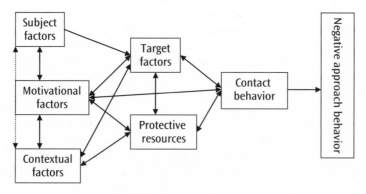

Figure 19.1. Threat assessment approach factors.

communications include recent negative attention or concern regarding the target (e.g., negative press, recent scandal) as well as a recent act of targeted violence that has garnered attention. In addition, recent media or political attention to a controversial issue also raises the likelihood of threatening contacts toward political targets (Scalora et al., 2002). Given the copy-cat nature of hoax events, it is not surprising that recent threatening, tampering, or hoax events often result in clusters of problematic threatening and hoax activity that demand substantial attention. Further, it is the experience of the authors that an anniversary significant to the subject (e.g., recent death of loved one, date of discharge from job, or military) or the target (e.g., terrorist act) also suggests the increased likelihood of problematic contacts.

Subject factors related to problematic approach are quite predictive, even in cases involving anonymous contacts. It should be noted that anonymous threats do cause a disproportionate amount of concern and are taken as seriously as any threatening communication. In addition, such anonymous communications often are found with a range of threatening communications, such as bomb threats and other hoax activity (see Logan, 1993; Tunkel, 2002 for reviews). However, some subject-related factors might be inferred in many communications in which the subjects conceal their identity, particularly in cases involving multiple contacts or single contacts with extensive detail. For example, incoherent information suggesting conspiratorial or other delusional activity may suggest the presence of serious mental illness. In the case of one individual who left the following message within a government building attached to a lengthy and disorganized treatise covering a range of disparate topics, one might assume mental health difficulties are present:

"Unless this is a training area—I don't trust any kind of one-way mine communications without any type of aware confirmation. So anyway, I have been leaving reports every couple of days and hope you are pleased with the data."

Another subject appeared at a Congressional office requesting assistance. The gentleman reported constant harassment from "black helicopters" circling his residence. He claimed that the harassment was due to his working for a "covert government agency" since the age of 4. At the age of 44, he has come to the realization that he has not received financial reimbursement for his extensive service. He is adamantly demanding assistance for his claim.

A 51-year-old woman contacted a Congressional office via phone, letter, and in person, asserting she is the "long-lost daughter" of the protectee. (It appeared that the protectee in question would have been 9 years old at the time of allegedly fathering the subject.) The subject demanded to be "brought back into the family" to receive financial assistance.

Subjects who display mental illness symptoms tied to the target or to a personal motive demonstrate a heightened risk of problematic approach behavior (Baumgartner et al., 2001; Scalora, Baumgartner, & Plank, 2003; Scalora, Baumgartner, et al., 2003). While some research has been inconsistent, the prevalence of certain mental illness symptoms, namely threat-control override symptoms, has been found by the authors to predict problematic approaches within contacts by mentally ill persons toward public officials (Scalora, Baumgartner, & Plank, 2003). Threat-control override symptoms suggest the presence of immediate harm to the individual (e.g., paranoia) as well as challenges to the ability to control one's thoughts or behavior (e.g., insertion or removal of thoughts from one's mind, control of thoughts from an outside entity such as satellites). Regardless of mental status, subjects who contact multiple targets (particularly other agencies) with their grievance were also more likely to engage in problematic approach behavior (Scalora, Baumgartner, & Plank, 2003; Scalora, Baumgartner, et al., 2003). TAS investigators also attempt to determine if subjects are describing recent life stressors that may either exacerbate or challenge coping mechanisms (e.g., recent financial or relationship difficulties). Subjects with prior arrest records, particularly those involving harassment or threat-related charges (such as violation of protection order, terrorist threat, or harassment by phone), are at heightened risk for a problematic approach.

Motivational factors are often discernible by assessing thematic information inherent within the verbal or written communication regardless of direct description by the subject. The likelihood of problematic approach is significantly heightened by the perceived level of personal relevance of the issue presented by the subject, especially if help-seeking requests or other demands are made (Baumgartner et al., 2001; Calhoun, 1998; Scalora, Baumgartner, & Plank, 2003; Scalora et al., 2002; Scalora, Baumgartner, et al., 2003). One example of a help-seeking-driven motive follows:

> The subject called Congressional office, upset with a government agency. He felt he had been "cheated" by the agency concerning a disability claim.

Sometimes, subjects present with less personal and more issue-based motivations, as in this example:

> A Congressional office forwarded to the TAS a letter advising the protectee that he "should watch himself" if he did not change his stance on a policy debated at that time.

In a similar vein, the relationship of the expressed motives or desires to the target also relates to the likelihood of approach. In other words, the more personally relevant the issue at hand is presented by the subject, the higher the likelihood of approach. For example, if the target is viewed (rationally or otherwise) as able to assist with a child custody dispute, or if the target is somehow linked to harm to the subject as noted within his delusional thoughts, a problematic approach is likely to occur. Content themes indicative of venting with regard to domestic or foreign policy by themselves were not generally related to problematic approach.

While *target* and *protective factors* are sometimes difficult to ascertain, it is clear that high profile and media-involved targets are more likely to be subjected to problematic approaches and related precursor contacts (Scalora et al., 2002). While public figures tend to encourage public contact, those who are more accessible tend to also receive more problematic contacts. In a related vein concerning protective factors, it is not surprising that targeted public figures with heightened physical or personal security tend to receive fewer problematic approaches. Contacts that make references to the nature of the target's security (or lack thereof) also raise significant concern. Correspondence addressed or packaged in such a manner to avoid security screening also raises the level of concern posed by the subject.

Concerning risk factors indicated within *contact behavior*, subjects who made multiple contacts through multiple modalities (e.g., phone, written, electronic) were more likely to engage in problematic approach behavior. Therefore, it is critical that contacts be evaluated within the context of how the communication in hand fits within a pattern of related communications (Chang, Scalora, Schoeneman, Zimmerman, & McGaffin, 2006; Scalora et al., 2002; Scalora, Baumgartner, et al., 2003). Regarding other contact behaviors, the presence of personal, racial, or sexually insulting language in themselves are not predictive of problematic approach. Further, substantial research has suggested that subjects who make direct threats are less likely to engage in problematic approach behavior (Calhoun, 1998; Dietz et al., 1991; Scalora et al., 2002; Scalora, Baumgartner, et al., 2003) (Chapters 2 and 3).

A Congressional office contacted the TAS regarding a call that was received. The staff assistant advised that the call was from a gentleman who stated that "If my employer cancels my (health) insurance, I will go after the #@#$ and I will shoot him."

However, if the threats emerged *as part of an escalating pattern of problematic contacts*, a problematic approach was likely to occur (Scalora, Baumgartner, & Plank, 2003; Scalora, Baumgartner, et al., 2003). The same research indicated that while persons with mental illness were less likely to make threatening statements, those who made threats were also more likely to engage in approach behavior. Such a finding is not surprising given that persons with mental illness are aware of the likelihood of being placed in protective custody or other legal ramifications of threatening actions. It appears that those impaired subjects who did make threatening statements were either "at the end of their rope" or sufficiently decompensated in their functioning to be unconcerned about the outcomes of their actions.

Given the recent increases in e-mail contacts toward political officials described earlier in this chapter, recent research comparing threatening/harassing letters with similar e-mail contacts have found some differences, though also some noteworthy similarities. In an initial study comparing problematic e-mails with letter correspondences, Schoeneman and colleagues found that e-mailers were more likely than letter writers to focus their correspondence on government concerns, use obscene language, display disorganized writing, and write shorter communications (Schoeneman-Morris, Scalora, Chang, Zimmerman, & Garner, 2007). In a follow-up study, Schoeneman-Morris, Scalora, Chang,

Zimmerman, and McGaffin (2006) found that the risk factors for approach found in letter writing and e-mailing subjects are consistent with those found in the previous literature that identified risk factors for approach without segregating cases by method of contact. Both letter writers and e-mailers who approached their targets were more likely than their counterparts to exhibit indicators of serious mental illness and threat-control override symptoms, to engage in prior contact with the target and to use multiple methods of contact. The authors also found that both letter writing and e-mailing approachers were also more likely to emphasize personal themes (e.g., help-seeking, entitlement claims, etc.) in their writing and to have made significantly more contacts toward their targets overall.

Conclusions

We have provided a brief overview of the range of factors considered by the TAS in managing and assessing problem contacts toward the U.S. Congressional community. Our internal data suggested that use of the procedures utilized by the TAS in assessing and managing problem contacts has substantially decreased the chances of escalation or problematic approach in an overwhelming number of cases. Because the TAS is responsible for managing problematic contacts toward its protectees throughout the United States, such success in many cases is not possible without the cooperation of numerous federal, state, and local agencies. The TAS's methodology continues to evolve, to address emerging challenges (e.g., bioterrorism, terrorism) in support of its protective mission.

References

Baumgartner, J. V., Scalora, M. J., & Plank, G. L. (2001). Case characteristics of threats toward state officials investigated by a midwestern state. *Journal of Threat Assessment, 1*(3), 41–60.

Calhoun, F. S. (1998). *Hunters and howlers: Threats and violence against federal judicial officials in the United States, 1789–1993* (USMS Publication No. 80). Washington, DC: U.S. Department of Justice.

Chang, G. H., Scalora, M. J., Schoeneman, K. A., Zimmerman, W., & McGaffin, C. (2006, March). *Factors predictive of potential threat toward political officials based on the type of approach behavior.* Poster presented at the American Psychology and Law Society Conference, St. Petersburg, FL.

Dietz, P. E., Matthews, D. B., Martell, D. A., Stewart, T. M., Hrouda, D. R., & Warren, J. (1991). Threatening and otherwise inappropriate letters to members of the United States Congress. *Journal of Forensic Sciences, 36,* 1445–1468.

Fitch, B., & Goldschmidt, K. (2005). *Communicating with Congress: How Capitol Hill is coping with the surge in citizen advocacy.* Washington, DC: Congressional Management Foundation.

Kiesler, S., & Sproull, L. S. (1986). Response effects in the electronic survey. *Public Opinion Quarterly, 50,* 402–413.

Logan, B. (1993). Product tampering crime: A review. *Journal of Forensic Sciences, 38,* 918–927.

Scalora, M. J., Baumgartner, J. V., & Plank, G. L. (2003). The relationship of mental illness to targeted contact behavior toward state government agencies and officials. *Behavioral Sciences and the Law, 21,* 239–249.

Scalora, M. J., Baumgartner, J. V., Zimmerman, W., Callaway, D., Hatch Maillette, M. A., Covell, C. N., et al. (2002). An epidemiological assessment of problematic contacts to members of Congress. *Journal of Forensic Sciences, 47,* 1360–1364.

Scalora, M. J., Baumgartner, J. V., Zimmerman, W., Callaway, D., Hatch Maillette, M. A., Covell, C. N., et al. (2003). Risk factors for approach behavior toward the U.S. Congress. *Journal of Threat Assessment, 2*(2), 35–55.

Scalora, M. J., Plank, G. L., & Shoeneman, K. A. (2007). L'évaluation des menaces anonymes. In M. St-Yves, & M. Tanguay (Eds.), *Psychologie des enquêtes criminelles: la recherche de la vérité* (Psychology of criminal investigation: The research of the truth). Cowansville, Québec: Éditions Yvon Blais.

Schoeneman-Morris, K. A., Scalora, M. J., Chang, G. H., Zimmerman, W. J., & Garner, Y. (2007). A comparison of email versus letter threat contacts toward members of the United States Congress. *Journal of Forensic Sciences, 52,* 1142–1147.

Schoeneman-Morris, K. A., Scalora, M. J., Chang, G. H., Zimmerman, W. J., & McGaffin, C. M. (2006, March). *Differential risk factors for problematic approach behavior toward legislators: Are letter writers or emailers more dangerous?* Poster session presented at the annual meeting of the American Psychology–Law Society, St. Petersburg, FL.

Siegel, J., Dubrovsky, V., Kiesler, S., & McGuire, T. (1986). Group processes in computer-mediated communications. *Organizational Behavior and Human Decision Processes, 37,* 157–187.

Tunkel, R. F. (2002). Bomb threat assessments. *FBI Law Enforcement Bulletin, 71,* 6–7.

Wallace, P. (1999). *The psychology of the internet.* New York: Cambridge University Press.

Appendix: USCP Threat Assessment Factors

Contextual Factors

Increased attention or concern regarding target or recent violence incident, topic area?

Heightened concern regarding specific protectee or issue?

Other recent threatening, tampering, or hoax events?

Anniversary of significant event to subject or protectee?

Subject Factors

Mental illness symptoms tied to target or personal motive?

Prior arrest record (particularly with prior harassment/threat-related charges)?

History of contacts with other agencies?

Access to protectee/target?

Recent life stressors implied/described?

Specific mental illness symptoms (including threat-control override symptoms) indicated?

Motivational Factors

Issue at hand personally relevant to subject?

Subject indicates relationship of motive to protectee?

Issue related to delusional activity of personal relevance to subject?

Protective Factors

Were references made to police or security involvement?

References made to protectee's security?

Contact Behavior

Multiple prior contacts/multiple methods of contact?

Nature of threatening language?

Surveillance or stalking-like behavior present, indicated or suspected?

Contact across multiple settings?

Any demands made?

Have other suspicious activities taken place relevant to protectee/target?

Escalation in rhetoric or threatening language within or across contacts?

Target Factors

Intensity of focus—subjects were focused on particular protectee or issue—but contacted multiple sites/protectees?

Target dispersion: Contacts with multiple target/protectees?

Intensity of relationship of rhetoric to target/protectee?

Potential symbolic/instrumental objectives of target?

Accessibility of protectee?

20

From Violent Words to Violent Deeds: Assessing Risk From FBI Threatening Communication Cases

Sharon S. Smith

An attractive news anchorwoman receives numerous letters professing love for her. The writer includes detailed descriptions of her attire and her travel on different days, a clear indication that he has been following her. After mailing these letters to the news station where she works, he begins leaving notes at her residence. Although initially positive and loving, the tone of his letters turns to angry rants about her "infidelity" after he observes her at a restaurant with her husband.

A company that manufactures baby food receives a letter warning that poison has been added to several jars of its product. To support this claim, the writer includes the address of a grocery store where the poisoned baby food is now on the shelf. The writer demands millions of dollars, threatening that he will not give notice the next time if the extortion money is not paid. The baby food company immediately dispatches local authorities to the store and removes all its products from the shelves. Toxicology tests reveal that several jars contain rat poison.

A wealthy businessman receives an extortion letter from someone claiming to be an assassin for hire. The writer demands millions of dollars in exchange for not killing the businessman and his family. Law enforcement eventually identifies and arrests the writer as he drives to intercept the businessman. A search of the threatener's car uncovers a recently purchased gun and maps of the target's location.

Individuals, corporations, and buildings are among the targets of written, telephone, e-mail, and personal threats every day. Threats can be a factor in many categories of crimes, such as stalking, product tampering, extortion, bombing, domestic violence, and murder. Law enforcement agencies and private security firms that investigate these cases face three major challenges: (1) assessing threatener characteristics that relate to dangerousness; (2) predicting whether or not targeted violence is likely to occur; and (3) using those reliable and valid predictors as an aid in identifying and apprehending the threatener. Once investigators make these predictions and assessments, they must decide how best to protect potential targets. The consequences of their decisions may involve injury or even death and may require extensive personnel resources and large monetary expenditures; therefore it is critical that assessments and predictions be as accurate as possible.

As assessors have become increasingly aware of and involved in threat cases, they have begun designing research for identifying salient factors for "risk of targeted violence" and "offender characteristics" (Baumgartner, Scalora, & Plank, 2001), which has approached the topic from different perspectives. Many studies have looked at stalkers because their approach behavior can pose a danger (e.g., Meloy, Davis, & Lovette, 2001; Mullen & Pathé, 1994). Some of these studies have found that mental or personality disorder diagnoses in stalkers are associated with an increased level of dangerousness (e.g., Rosenfeld & Harmon, 2002; Zona, Palarea, & Lane, 1998). Additional studies have focused on grouping threateners according to the types of targets they choose (e.g., Fein & Vossekuil, 1999). Several of these studies have examined those who approach and attack political and public officials (e.g., Calhoun, 1998; Fein & Vossekuil, 1999). Some have looked at variables in threatening communications that are associated with violence or approach behavior (e.g., Dietz et al., 1991a, 1991b). Other studies (e.g., Baumgartner et al., 2001; Scalora et al., 2002a) have examined both threatening communication and threatener/attacker variables.

Although significant differences in outcome-related variables are present among and between threatener groups, the reality for investigators is that (a) some threateners do approach or act violently, and (b) the threateners' identities often remain unknown—which means, unfortunately, that offender-related information is unavailable to investigators. *This frequently leaves the threat itself as the main source of information from which investigators must make decisions in these cases.* Analysis of verbal behavior may, therefore, illuminate certain salient factors in the threatening communication related to case outcome.

A growing body of research, much of which emanates from political psychology, indicates that the ways in which an individual uses language can be associated with psychopathological disorders and dispositional characteristics, and linked with violent behavior. One example is Hermann's (2003) methodology for measuring personality characteristics from language use, operationalized in a computer content analysis system called Profiler Plus or Profiler + (Young, 2001). The presence of certain characteristics, as measured by Profiler Plus, has enabled scientists to explain and predict some behavior of national leaders. Using text with 100 or more words to achieve reliability, Profiler Plus searches sentences "from left to right for ordered sets of tokens (words and/or punctuation) that have been identified as indicators of a concept or relationship or perhaps of a particular type of communication" (Young, p. 22). Profiler Plus measures traits of national leaders through examining leadership style, defined as the way in which leaders relate to constituents, other leaders, and their advisors. Profiler Plus uses grammatical choices to measure seven traits:

(1) The belief that one can influence or control what happens,
(2) The need for power and influence, (3) Conceptual complexity
(the ability to differentiate things and people in one's environment),
(4) Self-confidence, (5) The tendency to focus on problem solving
and accomplishing something versus maintenance of the group and
dealing with others' ideas and sensitivities, (6) General distrust or
suspiciousness of others, and (7) The intensity with which a person
holds an in-group bias.

Hermann, 2003, p. 184

Hermann hypothesized that "these seven traits provide information that is relevant to assessing how political leaders respond to the constraints in their environment, how they process information, and what motivates them to action" (Hermann, 2003, p. 186).

Another example is Gottschalk's (1995) extensive research with Gleser on measuring psychological states through content analysis of verbal behavior. This research lead Gottschalk and Bechtel (2001) to construct a software program called PCAD 2000 (Psychiatric Content Analysis and Diagnosis), which uses content analysis to identify psychological states. Searching text with 90 or more words to achieve reliability, PCAD uses the grammatical clause as the unit of analysis, rather than single words, to measure the degree or intensity of six psychobiological constructs—anxiety, hostility, social alienation-personal disorganization, cognitive impairment, depression, and hope. The theoretical framework for the Gottschalk-Gleser measurement approach includes "behavioral and conditioning theory, psychoanalytic clinical theory, and linguistic theory. In addition, the formulation of these psychological states has been deeply influenced by the position that they all have biologic roots" (Gottschalk & Bechtel, pp. 38–39). Of particular note are hostility scores that are computed in three categories of transient affect—*hostility directed outward, hostility directed inward, and ambivalent hostility* (Gottschalk, 1995). Hostility directed outward is related to the intensity of angry, assaultive, and aggressive impulses and drives toward persons or objects other than oneself. Hostility directed inward scores indicate the intensity of self-hate, criticisms of self, and feelings of anxiety-related depression and masochism. Ambivalent hostility scales reflect paranoia, which Gottschalk defined as critical, and destructive actions or thoughts of others directed toward self. Single scores on these measures, as well as on anxiety, are more indicative of a state, rather than a trait.

In summary, even though the base-rate for violence is low in threat cases, a threatener's actions can destroy or permanently alter the target's quality of life and peace of mind. Although the current state of threat research offers varying and sometimes conflicting advice, the need to identify reliable and valid predictors for targeted approach and violence remains. The goal of this research, therefore, was to identify factors that improve the accuracy of violence risk assessments that law enforcement and security consultants must increasingly make. There were three broad hypotheses: (1) There are social, demographic, and psychological characteristics of the threatener associated with the outcome of a threat case. (2) There are social and demographic characteristics of the target/victim associated with the outcome of a threat case. *Target* is defined as the person, property, or entity being threatened. *Victim* is defined as the person, property, or entity actually harmed. The victim and target may or may not be the same; for example, the threatener may have written a letter in which he threatened a target, yet he burned down the house of the target's sister. (3) There are language features, document features, and methods used to communicate threats associated with the outcome of a threat case. A *threatening communication* is defined as any written information that implies or explicitly states the potential of harm delivered to targets/victims or agents acting in their behalf. In most instances, threatening communications were letters, cards, or notes, but they included diaries or packages, which contained multiple communications. Personal visits, telephone calls, and other means of contact were measured as separate variables.

Method

Materials

This research used a correlational design that compared variables gathered through an interview questionnaire and two automated instruments (i.e., Profiler Plus and PCAD). Logistical regression was used to construct an equation to assist investigators in predicting when threateners are more likely to harm as opposed to when they would simply threaten.

The study's database consisted of 96 threatening communication cases the Federal Bureau of Investigation's (FBI) National Center for the Analysis of Violent Crime (NCAVC) analyzed and then closed during 1997 and 1998 (*closed cases* are defined as NCAVC completing its analysis). The NCAVC is a behavioral science and resource center, which offers investigative support, research, and training to United States and international law enforcement agencies confronted with bizarre, serial, violent, and complex criminal behavior. The fact that other agencies referred their cases to the NCAVC often meant that these were among the most difficult cases to solve. The NCAVC typically offers advice on investigative steps, including analyzing psychological characteristics of the threatener. The NCAVC utilizes a two-part process for reviewing and assessing threats. Threats are reviewed for content, writing style, themes, level of emotionality, grammar, packaging, enclosures, drawings, note construction, type of paper used, victimology, and the circumstances surrounding their receipt. Understanding an individual's motivation(s) for making a threat is also deemed critical in order to accurately assess its seriousness. Based on "the totality of the circumstances," a determination is made regarding the seriousness of the threat and the likelihood the offender will attempt to stalk or commit other harmful actions. Threats are then classified into one of three broad categories: high, medium, or low risk. Attendant investigative strategies and suggestions can then be provided to the investigating agency based on its threat level. Because threats vary significantly in terms of their seriousness, investigating agencies confronted with limited resources must have a method by which they can prioritize their investigations.

Although several of the cases contained multiple communications and numerous targets, the current research examined only the first written threat (determined by chronological date) sent to the first target (defined by chronological order). Had the researcher used all of the threatening communications, this would have unduly weighted some cases more than others, so the decision to use one communication weighted all cases equally. From an investigative standpoint, using the initial communication to the first target was useful because information from the first communication is often the basis for opening an investigation and handling its initial phase. Finally, since one letter is often all that assessors have for a given case, the question is, can we, from a single communication, find predictive factors that are valid indicators of whether the threatener will act or not?

Procedure

An interview protocol was developed for accessing case-related information concerning the three categories of independent variables and the dependent variable. Once each of the potential threat cases was assigned a code number, the writer conducted a detailed review of all available information in the NCAVC case files. If the case facts fell outside the predetermined parameters of this study or the communication was not a threat as defined by this research, the case was excluded. If the case review warranted continued inclusion in the database, the primary investigating officer or FBI agent was identified. The writer then contacted the investigator and, using the protocol, conducted an interview by telephone. These interviews typically took 1½ to 2½ hours each. In order to participate in the interview, investigating officers were required to sign a consent form.

All responses for threatener, target/victim, and case outcome were marked during the course of the interview. The language protocol was coded by the writer immediately after the conclusion of the interview. All harmful acts relating to each case were coded. One case that illustrates the coding process involved a threatener who sent several notes to a hospital saying that he would kill a doctor, a nurse, and a child. A few months after sending the first note, he broke into the house of one of the hospital's nurses, raped her with the barrel of a gun, and then strangled her son. Both harmful acts (the murder of the child and the sexual assault of the nurse) were coded for this case.

Once the protocol sheets were scored, they were scanned by a machine that electronically placed all scores into an SPSS spreadsheet. The threatening communications were typed, proofread, and scored using Profiler Plus and PCAD. These scores were electronically added to SPSS. Electronic, not manual, transfer of data into SPSS was used in order to reduce the possibility of human error in the coding process.

Although much of the database consisted of mailed letters, threateners employed other means of communicating, such as greeting cards, postcards, and writings on the outside of envelopes. If the threatener made multiple threats within the communication, actions were examined in descending order, from "stated action was carried out," then "some harmful action, other than what was threatened, was carried out," and so forth. Coding was done by the first appropriate category identified.

A threatener's actions were classified as Category 1 (no action) if (a) a minimum period of at least 2 years had elapsed between the receipt of the original threat and the interview of the investigating officer and (b) the threatener had not committed any harmful action during that time against the target/victim or any person or property associated with the target/victim. A threatener's actions were classified as Category 2 (approaching or stalking the target/victim) if the case facts or information in the threat itself indicated that the threatener (a) visited the residence or business address of the target/victim, (b) visited the residence or business address of any relative, friend, acquaintance, or intimate of the target/victim, (c) physically observed the movements of the target or the targets' relatives, friends, acquaintances, or intimates, (d) came within sufficient physical proximity or attempted (but was intercepted by law enforcement) to come within sufficient physical proximity that the threatener had the ability to harm the target/victim or harm something associated with the target/victim (e.g., vehicle), and/or (e) the threatener traveled to or was apprehended on the way to a drop site to obtain money or other goods in an extortion case. A threatener's actions were classified as Category 3 (some harmful action, other than what was threatened, was carried out) or Category 4 (stated action was carried out) if the threatener committed any of the following acts: burning, bombing, defacing or damaging property, disrupting events, extorting, kidnapping, murdering, physically assaulting or harming, product tampering, revealing detrimental information whether that information was true or false, sabotaging, sexually assaulting, stalking, taunting (including harassing or intimidating), using weapons of mass destruction, and "other" (e.g., poisoning).

Statistics

Pearson product-moment correlations were calculated for relationships between independent and dependent variables. Multiple regression was used to rank order predictors from each category of independent variables; then logistical regression was used to construct a predictive equation from salient independent variables.

Results

Case Outcome

Breakdown of the Action Category

Threateners committed harmful action against the target/victim (person or institution/object) in 26 of the 96 cases (27%) (see Table 20.1). "Harmful action" was broken down into three subcategories: (1) stated action carried out (3.8%), (2) some action, other than what was threatened, carried out (34.6%), and (3) threatener approached/stalked target/victim, but did not commit violent act (61.5%). The remaining 70 of the 96 cases (73%) were coded "no action" because these threateners did not harm persons or property; however, it must be noted that the number of action cases could have been higher had not law enforcement intervened in 12 of these 70 no action cases (12.5%) before harm could occur. The low numbers in the action subcategories necessitated collapsing these action subcategories so that the final analysis compared "action" to "no action" cases.

Table 20.1. Number of cases with action compared to those with no action

Case categories	n	Percentage of action cases	Percentage of total cases
Harmful action taken	26		27
Stated action carried out	1	3.8	1
Some action, other than what was threatened, carried out	9	34.6	9.4
Against persons	3	11.5	3.1
Against institutions/ objects	4	15.4	4.2
Against persons and institutions/objects	2	7.7	2.1
Threatener approached/ stalked target/victim but did not commit violent act	16	61.5	16.7
No action carried out	70		73
Intercepted by law enforcement	12		12.5

Types of Actions Threateners Committed or Attempted

Some of the 26 action cases had multiple scorings, with the number of actions per case ranging from 1 to 4. Table 20.2 displays all actions ($N = 48$) threateners committed and/or attempted. Attempted actions were defined as threateners' demonstrated behavior indicating they planned to follow through on the threat (e.g., a medical doctor ordered multiple poisons which he planned to use on his patients, but law enforcement seized the poisons en route). The most common action was stalking ($n = 17$), followed by extorting ($n = 9$), and taunting, harassing, or intimidating the victim ($n = 6$). Defacing or damaging property ($n = 3$), revealing detrimental information ($n = 3$), murder or attempted murder ($n = 3$), and physical assault ($n = 2$) were noted.

Table 20.2. Number of actions attempted or taken by threateners

Crimes	n	Percentage of all actions attempted/ taken
Burning	0	0
Bombing	1	2.08
Defacing or damaging property	3	6.25
Disrupting events	0	0
Extorting	9	18.75
Kidnapping	0	0
Murdering	3	6.25
Physically assaulting or harming	2	4.17
Product-tampering	0	0
Revealing detrimental information whether or not that information was true or false	3	6.25
Sabotaging	0	0
Sexually assaulting	1	2.08
Stalking	17	35.42
Taunting (including harassing or intimidating)	6	12.5
Using weapons of mass destruction	0	0
Other	3	6.25
Total	48	100

Threateners

Threateners were identified in only 43 of the 96 cases (44.8%). Analysis of characteristics of the 43 identified threateners was complicated by information being unavailable to answer some of the protocol questions. On the first data run, 15 threatener characteristics significantly correlated with action taken. Because Missing/Unknown and Not Applicable responses appeared to be confounding the results, a second statistical run was done with interview protocol responses broken down and reworded. On the second run, none of the social, demographic, or psychological characteristics measured by the threatener interview protocol were associated with action taken, and only marital status approached significance. Specifically, threateners who acted were somewhat more likely to be married at the time they made the threat ($r = .32203, p = .0676$).

Targets

Targets of threatening communications were divided into two categories, people (73%) and institutions/objects (27%), and their characteristics were then correlated with the outcome measure (see Table 20.3). People were significantly more likely to be harmed ($r = .21072, p = .0415$), compared to institutions/objects. Of the institutions or objects that were harmed, government or public buildings were somewhat less likely to be chosen than a business, a finding that approached significance ($r = -.18359, p = .0765$).

In cases in which the threatener identity was known (43 of 96 cases) and information was available, the relationship between the threatener and target was examined. Eighteen (42%) of the 43 targets and threateners knew each other, and were significantly more likely to be acquaintances ($r = .32733$, $p = .0282$) than family members or sexual intimates. Ten (56%) of these 18 threateners acted either by stalking or harming after sending threatening communications.

Table 20.3. Target variables associated with action taken

Target variable	Pearson correlation
Target of threat was a person	.21072*
Target was acquaintance of threatener	.32733*
Target of threat was an institution/object	−.21072*
Target was government/public building	−.18359

*$p < .05$.

Of the targets not personally known to the threatener, public figure/celebrities constituted the majority of the targets (10 cases), with 3 cases (30%) resulting in the threatener stalking or harming. Public/government officials (8 cases) were somewhat less likely to be stalked or harmed (2 cases or 25%). Business officials were targets of only two cases, with the threatener stalking in one (50%). When the target variables were analyzed using logistical regression, none had sufficient strength to be used in the predictive equation.

Language Use

It was found that several language use features, document features, and methods used to communicate threats were associated with threateners acting (see Table 20.4). Threateners were significantly more likely to approach/stalk or harm when they used the language strategy of persuasion in their threat communications ($r = .20634$, $p = .0437$), while the strategy of extorting only approached significance ($r = .17823$, $p = .0823$). Threateners were also significantly more likely to act when they asserted they would commit two types of actions: stalking ($r = .23901$, $p = .0190$) and revealing detrimental information, whether true or false ($r = .25048$, $p = .0138$). Although threateners' specific mention of time and location had no relationship with outcome in this research, threateners indicating what or who was to be targeted, either explicitly or implicitly, was associated with increased risk, but that association only approached significance ($r = .18241$, $p = .0768$). Furthermore, threateners specifying the weapons they would use only approached significance and was negative ($r = -.16458$, $p = .1110$).

Table 20.4. Language variables associated with action taken

Language variable	Pearson correlation
Threatening to reveal detrimental information (whether true or false)	.25048*
Threatening to stalk	.23901*
Using persuasion in threatening communication	.20634*
Repeatedly mentioning love, marriage, or romance	.35139***
Tone of threatening communication is polite	.26225**
Use of words indicating prejudices concerning religion	−.20234*

$*p < .05$; $**p < .01$; $***p < .001$.

This research also found that threateners were significantly more likely to act when they repeatedly mentioned love, marriage, or romance ($r = .35139$, $p = .0004$) and used a polite tone in the threatening communication ($r = .26225$, $p = .0098$); these findings support what Dietz et al. (1991a) found in their threats to members of Congress study. One correlation with action in this current research that approached significance was threateners indicating they were thinking about being with the target "forever" or "in eternity" ($r = .17290$, $p = .0921$). Conversely, threateners were significantly less likely to act if they used words indicating prejudices concerning religion ($r = -.20234$, $p = .0480$), whereas use of words indicating prejudices concerning race, gender, sexual preference, and ethnicity had no relationship to action.

This research found some document features associated with harming and approaching/stalking (see Table 20.5). Threateners were significantly more likely to act if they hand wrote the threat ($r = .21286$, $p = .0373$), but significantly less likely to act if they used inappropriate capitalization ($r = -.20447$, $p = .0469$), typed their threats on a typewriter rather than a computer ($r = -.23513$, $p = .0233$), or gave their real return address, either partial or complete ($r = -.229$, $p = .0329$); this latter finding supports the Dietz et al.'s (1991b) findings on celebrity threats.

Finally, threateners in the current study were significantly more likely to act when they communicated with targets through multiple mediums, such as telephoning or e-mailing the target, in addition to sending their threatening communication ($r = .31898$, $p = .0017$). This association was also found in studies of threats to members of Congress (Dietz et al., 1991a; Scalora et al., 2002a) and threats to celebrities (Dietz et al., 1991b).

Of the seven psychological characteristics Profiler Plus identified from language use in the threatening communications, only conceptual complexity was significantly associated with outcome. Threateners with high conceptual complexity were more likely to act ($r = .24764$, $p = .0150$). PCAD identified eight psychological characteristics from language used in the threatening

Table 20.5. Document features associated with action taken

Document features	Pearson correlation
Threat was handwritten	.21286*
Use of inappropriate capitalization	−.20447*
Threateners provided true return address (partial or complete)	−.22900*
Threat typed on typewriter, not computer	−.23513*

*$p < .05$.

communications. None was significantly associated with outcome; however, ambivalent hostility approached significance. Threateners with lower ambivalent hostility were somewhat more likely to act ($r = -.17030$, $p = .0971$).

Predictive Equation

Once the independent variables were analyzed, an attempt was made to construct a predictive equation for differentiating between action and no action cases using a two-step process. First, multiple regression was used to rank order variables within each category (threatener, target, language protocol, Profiler Plus, and PCAD) according to their association with outcome. Then logical regression analysis was used to select the best predictors from these variables for the purpose of constructing an equation that might differentiate between threateners who acted and those who did not (see Table 20.6). The variables and their designators used in the predictive equation (*patent pending*) were (1) conceptual complexity (CC), (2) ambivalent hostility (PCAD 18), (3) using words indicating prejudices concerning religion (LQ26), (4) using polite tone in the threatening communication (LQ60), (5) mentioning love, marriage, or romance (LQ62), (6) indicating the target/victim, either explicitly or implicitly, in the threatening communication (LQ17), (7) threateners giving their real return address (partial or complete) (LQ43), (8) threateners communicating

Table 20.6. Predictive equation variables and their beta weights

Variables	df	β	Wald χ^2
Intercept	1	11.2607	0.0006
Conceptual complexity (CC)	1	3.5635	2.0848
Ambivalent hostility (PCAD 18)	1	−10.5651	2.7527
Words indicating religious prejudices (LQ26)	1	−10.2594	0.0046
Polite tone (LQ60)	1	1.2062	1.6135
Mentioning love, marriage, or romance (LQ62)	1	12.7267	0.0009
Indicating target/victim, explicitly or implicitly (LQ17)	1	0.6726	0.4558
Giving their real return address (LQ43)	1	−11.8110	0.0077
Communicating through multiple mediums (LQ24)	1	1.1225	1.8577
Specifying weapons (LQ14)	1	−1.2740	2.5686

with the target/victim through multiple mediums (LQ24), and (9) threateners specifying weapons in the threatening communication (LQ14).

The first step in the predictive model (*patent pending*) is calculating y from the following equation composed of variable values and their beta weights:

$$y = 11.2607 + (3.5635 \times CC) - (10.5651 \times PCAD18) - (10.2594 \times LQ26) \\ + (1.2062 \times LQ60) + (12.7267 \times LQ62) + (0.6726 \times LQ17) \\ - (11.8110 \times LQ43) + (1.1225 \times LQ24) - (1.2740 \times LQ14)$$

The value calculated for y then becomes the exponent in the second step, which entails calculating the probability of threateners taking action from the equation:

$$P = \frac{e^y}{1 + e^y}$$

where, p is the probability of the threatener taking action and e is the base of natural logarithm. This value is a constant, always equal to approximately 2.71828.

Scores for p range from .00 to 1.00. This predictive model correctly classified 68 cases of the 96 cases (70.8%). The five incorrectly classified cases (1 false positive and 4 false negatives) constituted 5.3%, and 23 cases could not be classified (24.2%) (see Table 20.7).

Another way to look at the results is to divide cases into three groups according to their probability scores, and *this way dramatically improves the equation success rate predictions* (see Table 20.7). If cases with probability scores of .00 to .19 are predicted to be no action, the equation correctly predicted 55 of the 59 cases that fall in this range (93.2% correct prediction rate), with 4 false negatives. If cases with probability scores of .5 to 1.00 are predicted to be action cases, then the equation correctly predicted 13 of these 14 cases (92.8% correct prediction rate), with 1 false positive. The 23 cases that fell in the range of .20 to .49 could not be predicted (24.2%). Grouping cases into three broad

Table 20.7. Predictive equation success rate by probability score groups

Probability scores	Prediction	Number of cases	Number of cases correctly predicted	False positives	False negatives
.00 to .19	No action	59	55[a]	0	4
.20 to .49	Cannot be predicted	23	NA	NA	NA
.50 to 1.00	Action	14	13[b]	1	0

[a] 93.2% correctly predicted in .00 to .19 probability score range.
[b] 92.8% correctly predicted in .50 to 1.00 probability score range.
NA, not applicable.

risk categories is consistent with the classification system utilized by the FBI mentioned earlier in this chapter. It operationalizes analytical findings in terms of which threats are most serious and demand immediate attention.

Threatener Variables

While all threateners threatened violence, only 27% acted. Yet this percentage is not trivial; in fact, the percentage of "action taken" might well have been higher, since law enforcement intervention occurred in 12 cases, which likely reduced the number of action cases.

Threateners who did act rarely did exactly what they threatened. When they did act, most approached and stalked. Although a minority of the actors did use physical violence, others created considerable fear and emotional anguish in their targets. Furthermore, variance was again evident in that some threateners committed multiple acts, whereas some committed only one act. In addition, some threateners took action against persons, while others acted against property, and a few acted against both.

Although the identities of only 43 (45%) threateners in this study were known to law enforcement, initial analysis found 15 social, demographic, and psychological variables associated with threateners acting. However, the high numbers of Missing/Unknown and Not Applicable responses to threatener protocol questions appeared to weaken and perhaps confound their predictive value. For example, when questions were rewritten to elicit yes or no answers, none of the threatener variables correlated with outcome.

Why did this study find that none of the threatener variables correlated significantly with outcome, when other studies have found significant relationships between threateners' characteristics and their actions (e.g., Baumgartner et al., 2001; Scalora et al., 2002a)? One possible explanation is the heterogeneous nature of this study. Previous studies had greater homogeneity—their targets were similar (e.g., they were celebrities, members of Congress); the threateners had a common characteristic (e.g., mental disorder), or the crime was the same (e.g., stalking). In contrast, this study had greater heterogeneity; there were many types of targets (famous and not famous persons, as well as institutions/objects) and crimes (e.g., extortion, stalking, murder, sexual assault, bombing). It may be that this diversity blurred and washed out those previously identified threatener variables. Perhaps, then, in a much larger study where the sample could be broken down more finely by target and by crime, while still retaining a sufficient size to run statistical analyses, specific threatener variables might reemerge as significant in a predictive equation.

Target Variables

While none of the social, demographic, or psychological characteristics of the threateners in this research were associated with case outcome, this study did identify salient social and demographic characteristics of the target. Although institutions and objects constituted a substantial portion of the targets in this study (26 of the 96 cases, or 27%), nearly all of the action cases (22 of the 26 cases, or 84.6%) involved people, illustrating that targets were significantly more likely to be persons rather than institutions/objects. This research also found that those person-targets were significantly more likely to be acquaintances, a result that differed from studies that showed that intimates were most likely to be targets (e.g., Palarea, Zona, Lane, & Langhinrichsen-Rohling, 1999). One explanation for this could be related to the types of cases in this sample. Although the FBI was the investigating agency in some of these cases, many cases were referred from other agencies. As stated previously, this meant that these cases were often difficult to solve. Since intimates are typically the first individuals investigated as potential offenders, it may be that most of the intimate-threateners cases were resolved at the local and state level and, therefore, not included in this research sample. Finally, although two target variables independently differentiated between action and no action cases, neither reached the significance level necessary to be included in the predictive equation.

Communication Variables

Unlike other risk assessment areas (e.g., involuntary commitment, release, and parole decisions), threatening communication cases do not begin with a known person in custody. What we have is the threatening communication, and on this basis, law enforcement must make risk assessments and decisions about deploying limited manpower and resources. Thus, by necessity, communication variables are primary. While 73% of threateners in this study did not act, a finding consistent with other research (e.g., Baumgartner et al., 2001; Scalora et al., 2002b), almost one third did act, and several features related to the threat helped predict those who did, and those who might in the future. Threateners were more likely to act if they threatened to stalk and threatened to reveal detrimental information (whether true or false), though they did not necessarily do either of these. Stalking has numerous complex motives, ranging from revenge to erotomanic delusions of love relationships. In this study, stalking was most often associated with extortion cases (see Chapter 11). Similarly, threatening to reveal detrimental information was associated with extortion. One possibility for the association of these two variables with outcome relates to motive: the threateners attempting to gain something for themselves. If so, these results may be similar to those in the members of Congress studies (Dietz et al., 1991a; Scalora et al., 2002a), which found "subjects were significantly more likely to approach when articulating personal or help-seeking requests" (Scalora et al., p. 51).

Threateners providing a true return address was a risk-reducing factor, which was consistent with Dietz et al.'s (1991b) celebrities study, but not with Dietz et al.'s (1991a) or Scalora et al.'s (2002a) studies of threats to members of Congress, both of which found that furnishing identifying information was risk enhancing. The finding that threats typed on a typewriter were risk reducing could be related to the age of the threatener, in that typewriter users are more likely to be older and, therefore, less likely to carry out their threats. It is difficult to speculate about why handwriting a threat was risk enhancing, whereas using inappropriate capitalization was risk reducing. It is also unclear why, in this research, threateners were significantly less likely to act if they used words indicating prejudices concerning religion, whereas expressing prejudices concerning race, gender, sexual preference, and ethnicity had no relationship to acting. The latter findings were similar to those of Scalora et al.'s threats to members of Congress study, in which "articulating target-related themes of an insulting or degrading nature" had no relationship to approach. Perhaps the prejudicial themes are what nonactors howl about but do not then generate hunting actions (see Chapter 5).

Conceptual Complexity, Ambivalent Hostility, and Predatory Violence

When one thinks about the distinction between "howlers" and "hunters" (Calhoun, 1998), the latter group is more likely to reflect predatory violence, whereas the former is more likely to reflect affective violence. If, as Meloy (2006) suggests, determining the "mode of violence may be one of the most important criteria in assessing future violence risk" (p. 540), then scores on *ambivalent hostility* and *conceptual complexity*, when taken together, may assist threat assessors in making the distinction.

Affective violence is reactive, typically an immediate response to a perceived threat and its goal is threat reduction, which is defensive in nature (Meloy, 2006). In contrast, predatory violence is "planned, purposeful, and emotionless" (Meloy et al., 2004, p. 1088). It is a cognitively motivated attack, "primarily intended to control or influence the behavior of the target through an aversive consequence" (Meloy, 2001, p. 1211). While these dichotomies help to differentiate threats and violence in terms of the offender's motivation and intent, it is important to point out they are not mutually exclusive, and it is possible for elements of both affective and predatory behavior to be manifested by the same offender. For example, in one case, an individual began exhibiting predatory behavior by stalking a young woman after sending her a written communication professing his love for her and denigrating her current boyfriend. The woman continued her relationship with her boyfriend and the threatening letters escalated in tone and content. At one point, the threatener "keyed" or scratched the victim's car, causing significant damage to the exterior of the vehicle. The threatener took responsibility for this act during a subsequent communication. The predatory behavior included sending the threatening communications and stalking the target and her boyfriend. The damage to the victim's vehicle could be described as affective violence. The offender reacted in an emotionally violent way to her refusal to discontinue her relationship with her boyfriend.

Scores on ambivalent hostility and conceptual complexity may assist the threat assessor in detecting the presence of predatory thinking. Higher scores on ambivalent hostility would be more consistent with the thinking of paranoid threateners who respond to perceived threats to self. The act of writing the threatening communications may assist these threateners in defusing their anger. By the time their targets have received the threats, the threateners' heightened state of emotional arousal has lessened or passed. Such threateners have written, and through that process, "blown off steam," making them less likely to proceed with violence. On the other hand, lower scores on ambivalent hostility—which were associated with acting in this research—indicate lack of paranoia. "Predation as a mode of violence would be more successful, and well thought out, given the absence of such affect" (R. Meloy, personal communication, February 21, 2005).

Similarly, conceptual complexity would logically diminish before affective violence as threateners react to perceived imminent threats. Conversely, higher conceptual complexity—which was associated with threateners being more likely to act in this research—indicates deliberative thinking. The "absence of autonomic arousal and affect in predatory violence... would [allow] more room, so to speak, for cognitive deliberation... [that] is certainly greater in predatory violence as the individual plans to carry out the act and weighs various tactical maneuvers" (R. Meloy, personal communication, February 21, 2005).

Thus, it appears that *the presence of lower ambivalent hostility and higher conceptual complexity together are consistent with predatory violence.* And with "predation, we would expect the consummation of the act" (R. Meloy, personal communication, February 21, 2005).

Limitations

Some limitations in the present research should be noted. First, only cases referred to the FBI's National Center for the Analysis of Violent Crimes were included. The level of difficulty of these cases could indicate that they contain some unique elements present to a lesser degree in nonreferred cases. Second, only written threats were analyzed, and only those constituting the first written threat to the target were included in the analysis. Third, another decision made for the purpose of equally weighting all cases was the selection of only one category of action for each case (e.g., stated action carried out, some action other than what was threatened, approached/stalked but did not commit violent act, and no action carried out). Only the most harmful act attempted or committed was coded in this study, but many cases had more than one action. Fourth, the behavioral characteristics and history of the threateners were obtained from the primary investigator. Without a second independent coder, the interrater reliability cannot be determined.

Although these limitations may have had some impact on the results of this research, the size of the sample in this research is sufficiently large to allow the results to be generalized to all FBI NCAVC written threat cases (with first communications over 100 words), and possibly to other threat case samples.

Suggestions for Future Research

This study found that the presence of threatening communications was inversely related to threateners taking action, a finding consistent with previous research that "underscores the notion that articulation of threats is not necessarily predictive of higher-risk behavior" (Scalora et al., 2002a, p. 51). Despite this trend, 27% of the threateners in this study attempted or committed harmful acts, and others might have done so if law enforcement had not intervened. Threat assessment professionals should not discount the risk posed by threateners who express themselves through threatening communications, and should certainly not discount those who take the additional action step of approaching or stalking (e.g., Calhoun, 1998; Fein & Vossekuil, 1999; Meloy, 2001; Rosenfeld & Harmon, 2002; Zona et al., 1998).

Future research could examine the implications these findings have for the stalking literature. Stalking can be seen in at least two ways: first, as the outcome or dependent variable, that is, the threatener acts by stalking, and second, as an intermediate action variable, that is, stalking as a prelude to violence. This current research views stalking in both ways, and it suggests that if researchers investigate any written or verbal material stalkers direct to their targets, assessors might be able to identify variables related to action, thereby enabling them to more accurately predict those who will stop at stalking and those who will commit greater harm.

A second suggestion is to do further research on the types of predictors examined in this and previous threat assessment research, which tap into language use at the syntactic or structural level (e.g., looking for instances of *I*, *we*, or *they* to determine who threateners say will carry out their threats). The thinking behind such research is appropriately focused, in that some syntactic variables are significantly associated with action. Previous research has also tapped into semantic or content-related language by looking at information, such as thematic content and roles assumed by threateners (Dietz et al., 1991a). Further research that employs more systematic evaluation and coding of language use shown to be associated with psychological states/traits, such as cognition, emotion, and particularly predation, may provide additional information as to what the threateners' intentions truly are. Profiler Plus and PCAD are two content analysis programs that have demonstrated their usefulness in assessing psychological states associated with threateners acting. Other methods of analysis, whether they are coded manually or by computer, need to be identified and tested in future threat assessment research to determine their effectiveness.

A third suggestion for future research involves looking at other variables from the threatening communication, which appear to be consistent with higher conceptual complexity and lower ambivalent hostility. Two examples are the use of persuasion and politeness—both associated with a higher likelihood of acting in this research. Both variables suggest more deliberative and less emotional thinking. Whether or not they may be indicative of predatory thinking processes and predatory violence is a matter of speculation at this point; the question is an empirical one for future research.

A fourth suggestion is to replicate this study in the context of e-mail threats. The prevalence of e-mails as a form of communication could provide a fertile source of research material. Perhaps e-mail or text message threats will turn out to be more impulsive and affective forms of threatening rather than indicative of predation, but this needs to be empirically assessed. Since this research found that multiple ways of communicating threats were positively correlated with action, e-mailing and text-messaging, in addition to letter writing, might add to the predictive equation's accuracy.

A fifth suggestion is to consider viewing some of the variables that have been identified in studies of the mentally disordered through a predatory lens. As Monahan et al. (2001) have pointed out, mental disorder by itself has low rates of violence, but mental disorder coupled with psychopathy is related to violence. An example of a risk-enhancing variable from this research that might be viewed through a predatory lens is the threatener repeatedly mentioning love, marriage, or romance. One might initially view this variable as being affectively oriented, but that view may be ill advised and superficial. Hidden within the focus on love, marriage, or romance may be a design, purpose, and a vision of mystical union—something far more sinister and predatory than pure affect. The presence of this particular focus may reveal that the threatener has moved from surface emotion to thinking and planning—cognitive processes consistent with predation, which would significantly increase the likelihood of violence. That may explain why this variable showed such a strong beta weight in the predictive model (12.7267).

A sixth suggestion involves more traditional risk assessment areas. The results from this research may transcend threat assessment and have application in other areas of clinical and forensic decision making. Conceptual complexity and ambivalent hostility appear to reveal emotion and cognition, important for clinicians to discern when considering release or commitment decisions; thus, analyzing writings of the person under review may add critical information to the clinicians' decision-making process.

Conclusion

"Violence is a complex behavior with multiple determinants, manifestations, and outcomes" (McNiel et al., 2002, p. 153). Be that as it may, law enforcement and security agencies must assess risk of targeted violence. Simply put, they must identify the doers from the nondoers. Much of threat-related risk assessment research has focused on retrospective analysis of characteristics of known threateners and on using these characteristics as predictive tools, yet law enforcement officials often do not know the identity of the threatener/subject, making these methods useless in many ongoing investigations. This current research, in contrast, was more realistic in that it focused on the limited information available at the initial investigative stage, where the threatener's identity was not known. The question here was, "Can investigators accurately predict behavior from the limited information of the threatening communication?" The results show that a predictive model does emerge from this work, and that model has substantial accuracy. Two of these predictive model variables, specifically higher conceptual complexity and lower ambivalent hostility (paranoia), appear to signal the presence of cognition and emotion related to predatory violence. Identifying the presence of predatory thinking in threatening communications may provide investigators with an important clue for more accurately assessing when threateners are planning to move from violent words to violent deeds.

References

Baumgartner, J. V., Scalora, M. J., & Plank, G. L. (2001). Case characteristics of threats toward state government targets investigated by a midwestern state. *Journal of Threat Assessment, 1*(3), 41–60.

Calhoun, F. S. (1998). *Hunters and howlers: Threats and violence against federal judicial officials.* Arlington, VA: United States Marshals Service.

Dietz, P. E., Matthews, D. B., Martell, D. A., Stewart, T. M., Hrouda, B. A., & Warren, J. (1991a). Threatening and otherwise inappropriate letters to members of the United States Congress. *Journal of Forensic Sciences, 36*(5), 1445–1468.

Dietz, P. E., Matthews, D. B., Van Duyne, C., Martell, D. A., Parry, C. D. J., Stewart, T., et al. (1991b). Threatening and otherwise inappropriate letters to Hollywood celebrities. *Journal of Forensic Sciences, 36*(1), 185–209.

Fein, R. A., & Vossekuil, B. (1999). Assassination in the United States: An operational study of recent assassins, attackers, and near-lethal approachers. *Journal of Forensic Sciences, 44*(2), 321–333.

Gottschalk, L. A. (1995). *Content analysis of verbal behavior: New findings and clinical applications.* Hillsdale, NJ: Lawrence Erlbaum.

Gottschalk, L. A., & Bechtel, R. J. (2001). *PCAD 2000: Psychiatric content analysis and diagnosis.* Available from GB Software at http://www.gb-software.com

Hermann, M. G. (2003). Assessing leadership style: Trait analysis. In J. M. Post (Ed.), *The psychological assessment of political leaders with profiles of Saddam Hussein and Bill Clinton* (pp. 178–212). Ann Arbor, MI: The University of Michigan Press.

McNiel, D. E., Borum, R., Douglas, K. S., Hart, S. D., Lyon, D. R., Sullivan, L. E., et al. (2002). Risk assessment. In J. R. P. Ogloff (Ed.), *Taking psychology and law into the twenty-first century* (pp. 148–170). New York: Kluwer Academic.

Meloy, J. R. (2001). Communicated threats and violence toward public and private targets: Discerning differences among those who stalk and attack. *Journal of Forensic Sciences, 46*(5), 1211–1213.

Meloy, J. R. (2006). Empirical basis and forensic application of affective and predatory violence. *Australian and New Zealand Journal of Psychiatry, 40,* 539–547.

Meloy, J. R., Davis, B., & Lovette, J. (2001). Risk factors for violence among stalkers. *Journal of Threat Assessment, 1*(1), 3–16.

Meloy, J. R., James, D. V., Farnham, F. R., Mullen, P. E., Pathé, M., Darnley, B., et al. (2004). A research review of public figure threats, approaches, attacks, and assassinations in the United States. *Journal of Forensic Sciences, 49,* 1086–1093.

Monahan, J., Steadman, H., Silver, E., Appelbaum, P., Robbins, P., Mulvey, E., Roth, L., Grisso, T., & Banks, S. (2001). *Rethinking risk assessment: The MacArthur study of mental disorder and violence.* New York: Oxford University Press.

Mullen, P. E., & Pathé, M. (1994). Stalking and the pathologies of love. *Australian and New Zealand Journal of Psychiatry, 28,* 469–477.

Palarea, R. E., Zona, M. A., Lane, J. C., & Langhinrichsen-Rohling, J. (1999). The dangerous nature of intimate relationship stalking: Threats, violence, and associated risk factors. *Behavioral Sciences and the Law, 17,* 269–283.

Rosenfeld, B., & Harmon, R. (2002). Factors associated with violence in stalking and obsessional harassment cases. *Criminal Justice and Behavior, 29*(6), 671–691.

Scalora, M. J., Baumgartner, J. V., Zimmerman, W., Callaway, D., Maillette, M. A. J., Covell, C. N., et al. (2002a). Risk factors for approach behavior toward the U.S. Congress. *Journal of Threat Assessment, 2*(2), 35–55.

Scalora, M. J., Baumgartner, J. V., Zimmerman, W., Callaway, D., Maillette, M. A. J., Covell, C. N., et al. (2002b). An epidemiological assessment of problematic contacts to Members of Congress. *Journal of Forensic Sciences, 4*(6), 1360–1364.

Young, M. D. (2001). Building world view(s) with Profiler+. In M. D. West (Ed.), *Applications of computer content analysis* (pp. 17–32). Westport, CT: Ablex.

Zona, M. A., Palarea, R. E., & Lane, J. C., Jr. (1998). Psychiatric diagnosis and the offender-victim typology of stalking. In J. R. Meloy (Ed.), *The psychology of stalking: Clinical and forensic perspectives* (pp. 69–84). San Diego: Academic Press.

About the Editors

Dr. Reid Meloy is a diplomate in forensic psychology of the American Board of Professional Psychology. He was formerly Chief of the Forensic Mental Health Division for San Diego County, and is now a clinical professor of psychiatry at the University of California, San Diego, School of Medicine; an adjunct professor at the University of San Diego School of Law; and a faculty member of the San Diego Psychoanalytic Institute. He is a Fellow of the American Academy of Forensic Sciences, and is past President of the American Academy of Forensic Psychology. In 1992 he received the Distinguished Contribution to Psychology as a Profession Award from the California Psychological Association; in 1998 he received the first National Achievement Award from the Association of Threat Assessment Professionals; and in 2000 his first book on stalking received honorable mention, the Manfred Guttmacher Award, from the American Psychiatric Association. He is also President of Forensis, Inc., a nonprofit, public benefit corporation devoted to forensic psychiatric and psychological research (www.forensis.org). Dr. Meloy has published over one hundred and seventy papers and ten books, and is the co-developer with Dr. Steve White of the WAVR-21, a structured professional judgment instrument for the assessment of workplace violence risk. He is also a member of the Fixated Research Group for the United Kingdom's Home Office concerning threats to the Royal Family and British political figures, and a consultant to the counterintelligence division of the FBI.

Dr. Lorraine Sheridan is a Chartered Forensic Psychologist who completed Europe's first PhD on stalking. So far she has published more than 50 papers on the subject, and co-edited one book. Her research has taken an applied, interventionist angle and she frequently trains professionals involved in the investigation of stalking crimes. She is a police accredited offender profiler and compiles psychological reports related to offenders, highlighting the risks posed by known or unknown suspects. She regularly gives case management advice to the police, security personnel, celebrities and others on stalking, harassment, violence, risk assessment, malicious communications and similar topics. After a stint as a senior academic at the University of Leicester, England, Dr. Sheridan is now a part-time Senior Research Fellow at Heriot Watt University, Edinburgh.

Dr. Jens Hoffmann is a researcher and lecturer at the Centre for Forensic Psychology at the University of Darmstadt near Frankfurt, Germany. His research interests include stalking, workplace violence, targeted violence in schools and universities, femicide, and attacks on public figures. Dr. Hoffmann has written more than 20 professional journal articles and book chapters. On behalf of the German Bureau of Criminal Investigation he has authored a textbook on offender profiling. Dr. Hoffmann has authored, co-authored or edited seven books covering topics such as stalking, domestic violence, school shootings and intimate partner homicide. He has presented talks and workshops in eight European countries and in the United States, and has trained police forces in Germany and in Austria in assessing and managing stalking cases. In addition to his scientific work, Dr. Hoffmann heads a firm with two former police psychologists called "Team Psychologie & Sicherheit." One of their main focuses is conducting threat management for national and international corporate groups and public figures.

Index